MASTERING

MODERN BRITISH HISTORY

MACMILLAN MASTER SERIES

Accounting
Advanced English Language
Arabic
Astronomy
Banking
Basic Management
Biology
British Politics
Business Communication
Business Law
Business Microcomputing
C Programming
Catering Science
Catering Theory
Chemistry
COBOL Programming
Commerce
Computer Programming
Computers
Databases
Economic and Social History
Economics
Electrical Engineering
Electronics
English as a Foreign Language
English Grammar
English Language
English Literature
English Spelling
French
French 2

German
German 2
Hairdressing
Human Biology
Italian
Italian 2
Japanese
Manufacturing
Marketing
Mathematics
Mathematics for Electrical and
    Electronic Engineering
Modern British History
Modern European History
Modern World History
Pascal Programming
Philosophy
Photography
Physics
Psychology
Pure Mathematics
Restaurant Service
Science
Secretarial Procedures
Social Welfare
Sociology
Spanish
Spanish 2
Spreadsheets
Statistics
Study Skills
Word Processing

MASTERING
MODERN BRITISH HISTORY

SECOND EDITION

NORMAN LOWE

MACMILLAN

First published 1984 by
THE MACMILLAN PRESS LTD
Houndmills, Basingstoke, Hampshire RG21 2XS
and London
Companies and representatives
throughout the world

ISBN 0–333–51030–5

A catalogue record for this book is available
from the British Library.

Printed in Malaysia

First edition reprinted four times
Second edition 1989
10
00 99 98 97 96

CONTENTS

CONTENTS

CONTENTS

CONTENTS

CONTENTS

MAPS

NOTE ABOUT MONEY VALUES

Before the change of currency in 1971, British money consisted of pounds (£), shillings (s) and pence (d). 12d = 1s (sometimes written 1/-); 20s = £1. In terms of the new decimal coinage, 6d = $2\frac{1}{2}$p. 1s = 5p, 50s = £2.50, and so on.

ILLUSTRATIONS

ACKNOWLEDGEMENTS

The author and publishers wish to acknowledge the following photograph and illustration sources:

British Museum
Communist Party of Great Britain – James Klugman Print Collection
Conservative Party
Daily Chronicle
Hulton Picture Library
Illustrated London News Picture Library
India Office Library
Labour Party
Manchester Public Libraries
Mansell Collection
National Library of Wales
Northern Examining Association

The author and publishers wish to thank the following who have kindly given permission for the use of copyright material.

Blackie and Son Ltd for a figure from *British Foreign Policy, 1870-1914* by J. Telford, 1978.

Darlington Borough Council for an extract from the Darlington Board of Health Minute Book, Da/A1/1/1, Durham Record Office, and a poster produced by the Darlington Board of Health, Durham Record Office.

John Fairfax & Sons Ltd for a cartoon from the *Sydney Morning Herald,* Nov., 1956.

Macdonald & Co. for a figure from *The Mutiny and After* by T. F. Metcalfe in *Purnell's History of the English Speaking Peoples,* No. 94, BPC Publishing, 1971.

Methuen and Co. for adapted material from *The First Industrial Nation* by P. Mathais.

Oxford University Press for a table from *The Struggle for Mastery in Europe* by A. J. P. Taylor, 1971.

Punch for six *Punch* cartoons

Times Newspapers Ltd for material from an article by Michael Jones, *Sunday Times* 28 August 1988.

Unwin Hyman Ltd for a figure from *The Great Reform Act* by M. Brock, Hutchinson, 1973.

George Weidenfeld & Nicholson Ltd for a figure from *Recent History Atlas 1860-1960* by Martin Gilbert, 1966, and a map of Europe in 1878 from *Europe Since 1870* by J. Joll.

Every effort has been made to trace all the copyright holders, but if any have been inadvertently overlooked the publishers will be pleased to make the necessary arrangement at the first opportunity.

PREFACE TO THE
SECOND EDITION

The second edition of this book brings the story of British History right up to 1988 and the third Thatcher government. The main change is that the question sections have been completely rewritten in order to prepare students to meet the new demands of GCSE.

The GCSE National Criteria for History specify four main assessment objectives which the examinations and coursework of all Boards must test. These are the ability to:

1. recall, evaluate and select relevant knowledge and to deploy it in a clear and coherent form;
2. make use of and understand the concepts of cause and consequence, continuity and change, similarity and difference;
3. look at events and issues from the perspectives of people in the past (empathy);
4. show the skills necessary to study a wide variety of historical sources such as primary and secondary written sources, statistical and visual material, artefacts, textbooks and orally transmitted information;

(a) by comprehending and extracting information from it;
(b) by interpreting and evaluating it – distinguishing between fact, opinion and judgement; pointing to deficiencies in the material as evidence; detecting bias;
(c) by comparing various types of historical sources and reaching conclusions based on this comparison.

The first requirement of a history textbook must still be to provide the student with the basic information which he or she will be required to recall about the period, and so I have left the first edition text largely unchanged except for minor corrections and updating. The analytical approach should be suitable for helping students to understand cause and consequence, continuity and change, similarity and difference, so that assessment objectives 1 and 2 are taken care of.

The question sections are much longer in the new edition; I have tried to provide a wide variety of primary and secondary sources, to give students plenty of practice for assessment objective 4; and I have included examples of 'empathy' questions for assessment objective 3. The boards define three possible levels of empathy:

1. *Everyday empathy* This is where the candidate understands that people in the past were similar in many ways to those of today in that they were motivated by recognisable human ideas. However, weaker candidates do not get far beyond this, and tend to ascribe modern ideas and motives to people in the past.
2. *Stereotype historical empathy* This is where the candidate realises that people in the past did have different ideas about their society from people today. However, these candidates tend to assume that everybody in the society under study thought in the same way.
3. *Differentiated historical empathy* The best candidates are those who have the further perception that ideas and motives differed even within a past society. For example, people's attitudes towards the 1926 General Strike would vary widely depending on whether they were right-wing or left-wing Conservatives, Liberals, socialists, trade unionists, mine owners or miners.

I have included as wide a variety of questions as possible, given the limitations of space. Some are taken or adapted from specimen papers, but most are my own. The number(s) after each question indicates which assessment objective(s) is being tested.

Marks to be awarded for parts of questions are not shown. History GCSE papers are marked on a 'levels of response' marking scheme designed to give candidates credit for showing positively what they know, understand and can do; the marking scheme might well be adjusted after the examination, depending on how the majority of candidates interpreted the question.

I must thank my colleague Kevin Bean for his unfailing help and encouragement, Peter and Denise Somerfield for so efficiently typing the new material, and Peter Maltby, the Nelson and Colne College librarian, for helping me to trace many of the sources used in the book.

NORMAN LOWE

CHAPTER 1

INTRODUCTION

1.1 PROLOGUE: WATERLOO

In the late evening of Sunday, 18 June 1815, as the smoke and rain-clouds cleared to reveal the setting sun, the Battle of Waterloo drew to an end. Napoleon's Imperial Guard and the whole French army were in full retreat. As they streamed away from the battlefield leaving behind a mass of artillery and baggage, they were harassed by British and Prussian cavalry; meanwhile the two allied generals, Wellington and Blucher, met briefly and hailed each other as the victor. In the chaos the Emperor himself was held up for over an hour only four miles from the battlefield at the village of Genappe. There was utter confusion as several thousand men struggled and fought to cross the only bridge over the River Dyle. With only minutes to spare before the Prussian cavalry caught up, Napoleon at last forced a path through and galloped away towards Charleroi and Laon. He reached Paris on 21 June and, realising the hopelessness of the situation, abdicated four days later. He was exiled to the tiny island of St Helena in the South Atlantic; the long series of wars which had lasted almost continuously since 1792 (Britain became involved in 1793) was over. Wellington had been horrified at the carnage at Waterloo: the British had lost a quarter of their army – over 15 000 dead and wounded – including nearly all his personal staff. He shrank from ever having to use force again. Wellington was to play a prominent part in public life for over 30 years after Waterloo; when he was Prime Minister (1828-30), it was this reluctance to resort to force which in 1829 was to lead him to agree to Catholic Emancipation rather than risk a civil war in Ireland (see Section 2.7(b)).

1.2 BRITAIN IN 1815: THEMES OF CHANGE

Britain in 1815 was a victorious nation, apparently at the height of her power and prestige. But there was to be no peace and tranquillity after the turmoil of the previous 22 years; the period following Waterloo turned out to be crammed with important changes and developments, some of which (Industrial and Agricultural Revolutions) were already under way before the outbreak of war with France in 1793, and some (falling prices and slumps) which came in the aftermath of the wars. These changes brought with them innumerable problems – poverty, discontent and violence; and the ruling classes, badly shocked at the fate of the aristocracy during the French revolution, were nervous in case a similar outbreak occurred in Britain.

(a) **Industrially and commercially Britain led the world for much of the nineteenth century.** In 1815 she was still in the throes of what is known as *the Industrial Revolution* which lasted from the 1740s until the 1850s. Historians still disagree about exactly when this revolution started and finished; indeed, one can argue that it has never really come to an end and is still happening today. Some historians do not like to use the word 'revolution' because they think it implies too sudden a change and they feel that in reality the process was too gradual to be called a revolution. Nevertheless 'Industrial Revolution' is still a convenient phrase to describe the introduction of the many new inventions and techniques which transformed the Midlands, North and parts of Scotland from mainly rural areas where the majority of people worked in agriculture and where such industry as existed was carried on in homes or in small factories, into a mainly industrial society of large power-driven mills and factories concentrated in sprawling industrial towns.

The cotton textile and metal industries were the centrepiece of the revolution; the main inventions included Hargreaves's spinning jenny (1764), Arkwright's water frame for spinning, first used in his big mill at Cromford in Derbyshire (1771), Crompton's spinning mule (1779), Watt's rotary steam engine (1781) and Cartwright's power loom (1785). In 1785 a steam-engine was first used to power a cotton spinning mill and by 1800 at least 500 of them were in operation. The need for armaments during the war acted as a stimulus to the metal industries and resulted in the widespread adoption of coke-fired blast furnaces for producing iron. At the same time there was an expansion in the coal-mining industry.

However, the main expansion of industry took place after 1815. For example power-loom weaving had not caught on by 1815, even though Cartwright's loom had been available for 30 years. Yet by 1835, after it had been improved by Horrocks, there were 85 000 of them in use in England and 17 500 in Scotland; whereas imported cotton for weaving amounted to a modest 82 million pounds in 1815, it had soared to 1000 million pounds by 1860. Coal production rose sharply from about 15 million tons in 1815 to 44 million tons in 1846. Together with the industrial expansion went a marked population increase from about 18 million in 1811 to over 27 million in 1851. The increase was most noticeable in the industrial towns and cities, so that by 1851 about 80 per cent of the labouring population worked in some form of industry. Another development of crucial importance was the introduction and spread of the railway, the greatest era of railway building taking place between 1830 and 1860.

This dramatic industrial and population expansion brought with it enormous problems of overcrowded towns, excessively long hours of work, child labour, and dangerous conditions in mines and factories. One of the main themes of the nineteenth century was therefore the emergence of working-class movements like the Chartists and the Trade Unions, which hoped, in their different ways, to improve social and working conditions.

(b) Agriculture had also seen the appearance of new techniques and changes, usually referred to as the Agricultural or Agrarian Revolution. Early in the eighteenth century new crops were being introduced – turnips, clover and sainfoin – which provided winter fodder for cattle. Thomas Coke of Holkham in Norfolk demonstrated how yield could be greatly increased by using marl to enrich light soils, and bones as fertiliser, and by improving land drainage. Robert Bakewell of Dishley in Leicestershire concentrated on careful and scientific breeding of animals, and showed that by allowing only the best specimens to breed, it was possible to produce far superior cattle and sheep. Another important aspect of the agricultural revolution was *the spread of enclosures.* An enclosure was the fencing or hedging-in of a large area of medieval strip and furrow land along with the common pasture land, to form large fields. Enclosures were essential if progress was to be made, because it was impossible to introduce the new scientific farming methods on the open fields strips, which survived from medieval times in the counties of eastern and southern England.

Although these improvements had been creeping in throughout the eighteenth century, making possible a marked increase in agricultural production, they were by no means in general use over the whole country; as in industry, the agricultural changes only reached their peak in the years after 1815.

On the debit side, enclosures had the unfortunate effect of depriving many of the smallest farmers of their land. For a variety of reasons British agriculture went through a serious depression in the 20 years after Waterloo. This was followed by a period of prosperity lasting until about 1875, but then a further period of depression set in. Consequently another important theme running through the century, even when the industry as a whole seemed prosperous, was *poverty among agricultural labourers*, particularly in the South and East of England.

(c) Politically Britain was a union of England, Wales, Scotland and Ireland, under the control of a monarch (George III in 1815) and a parliament of two houses (Commons and Lords) which sat at Westminster. England and Scotland had shared the same monarch since 1603, but it was only in 1707 that the Scots had reluctantly agreed to abandon their own parliament and send MPs to Westminster instead. Ireland had joined the union even more recently. The Irish had their own parliament until 1800, but Roman Catholics who formed almost 90 per cent of the population, had only enjoyed the vote since 1793, and even then Catholics were not allowed to become MPs. The Irish were only persuaded to agree to the abolition of their parliament in Dublin by the promise of full Catholic Emancipation (the granting of full political and civil rights so that Catholics could become MPs at Westminster). However, for a number of reasons the British government had failed to keep its promise about emancipation. Irish Catholics, poverty-stricken and frustrated, were highly indignant, and throughout the nineteenth century the country was usually in some sort of turmoil. They campaigned first for *Catholic Emancipation* (achieved 1829) and then for repeal (cancellation) of the 1800 Act of Union so that they could have their own parliament in Dublin and exercise control over their own internal affairs. This long and bitter struggle ended temporarily in 1922 with the setting up of the Irish Free State; however, this did not include the six counties of Ulster (Northern Ireland) which still remain part of the United Kingdom.

Parliament, which contained elected representatives of the people (in the House of Commons), played an important part in governing the country. In comparison with other European rulers, the powers of the British monarch were somewhat restricted, and for this reason the British system is sometimes described as a *limited monarchy*. On the other hand Russia, for example, was ruled by the Tsar (Emperor) Alexander I who was an autocratic or absolute monarch. This means that he had complete power, was unrestricted by a parliament and could do exactly as he wished. The British system was therefore the envy of *liberals* all over Europe. Nineteenth-century European liberals (not to be confused with the modern British Liberal party) were people who wanted to limit the power of autocratic monarchs and replace autocracy with a system in which the middle classes had some say in the government.

Although the British parliament had a great deal of power, *the system was not democratic; a democracy* is where most of the people have a say in the government through their elected representatives. However, only the House of Commons was elected; the franchise (right to vote) was restricted to men, and only the wealthiest ones at that. Both parliament and local government were controlled by wealthy aristocratic landowners who dominated the two main political parties, Whigs and Tories. It was one of the ironies of the early nineteenth century that Britain, the world's greatest industrial power, should be governed by a group of wealthy agriculturalists, who on the whole knew little about industry; there was constant pressure for this state of affairs to be remedied. The most striking aspect of the campaign was *the struggle for parliamentary reform*: the extension of the vote to all adult males, and a fairer distribution of seats and constituencies. It was thought in many circles that to get a parliament which was genuinely representative of all the people was the best way of bringing about an improvement in the miserable conditions of the working classes.

(d) Britain's prestige abroad stood high thanks to the crucial role she had played in the defeat of France and to her developing industrial strength. Her attitude to Europe and the world was complex:

(i) Traditionally Britain was reluctant to get mixed up with European affairs; she had only become involved in the wars against France for reasons of self-defence. After 1815 her instinct was the same, and towards the end of the nineteenth century this policy became known as one of *'splendid isolation'*. In practice, however, she was not genuinely isolated:

(ii) Britain found herself drawn into European affairs because of disagreements with autocratic governments, especially those of Austria and Russia, who were determined to destroy *liberalism and nationalism*. (Nationalism was the desire of certain peoples to rid themselves of foreign rulers and have governments of their own nationality; for example Greeks wanted to break away from Turkey, Poles from Russia, and Italians from Austria. Nationalism could also be the desire to unite all people of the same nationality into one powerful state; this was important in Germany and Italy which in 1815 were still divided up into lots of separate states). Britain tended to sympathise with both liberalism and nationalism, especially when it suited her interests.

(iii) Britain was also drawn into Europe, whether she liked it or not, by trading interests, since Europe was her most important market for exports until the turn of the century. Consequently she was always on the alert in case another power seemed about to dominate Europe. British governments always talked about *preserving the balance of power*, by which they seem to have meant taking steps to make sure that no single country controlled the rest, as Napoleon and the French had done before 1815. If that happened, British profits and political influence might be ruined. It was partly trading interests which led Britain to join other European powers in taking over large sections of Africa. This operation, which took place mainly between 1880 and 1912, became known as *the Scramble for Africa*.

Given these conflicting themes, it is not surprising that British policy during the nineteenth century is sometimes difficult to understand; certainly foreign governments often found it exasperating. However, Britain managed to avoid major foreign entanglements (apart from the Crimean War of 1854-56 and the Boer War of 1899-1902) until the outbreak of the First World War in 1914.

CHAPTER 2

BRITAIN UNDER THE TORIES 1815–30

SUMMARY OF EVENTS

In 1815 *King George III* was still on the throne. Now aged 77, he had been King since 1760; since 1811 he had been insane and his eldest son George had been acting as Regent. The period from 1811 until 1820 when the unfortunate Geoge III died is known as *the Regency*. In 1820, the Prince Regent became *George IV*; he reigned until 1830, but was extremely unpopular, having a bad reputation on account of his extravagance, immorality, laziness and selfishness.

Politically, the *Tories* were in power; they had been in government more or less since 1783, though the Prime Minister, the 45-year-old *Lord Liverpool* (Robert Banks Jenkinson) had been premier only since 1812. Mild-mannered and modest, his greatest strength was his ability to manage and reconcile the ministers in his cabinet, who had a disturbing tendency to squabble among themselves. Another strength of the government was *Lord Castlereagh*, a first-rate Foreign Secretary and leader of the Tories in the Commons. Outwardly cold and imperturbable, he was nevertheless deeply sensitive and was eventually driven to suicide in 1822. The main opposition group to the Tories was known as the *Whigs*. The modern labels – Conservative and Liberal – were not yet in use.

Liverpool's government was unfortunate in having to deal with probably the most complex set of problems ever faced by any British government up to that date: economic and social distress, the demand for Catholic Emancipation in Ireland, and widespread disturbances which suggested that Britain might be on the verge of a revolution like the one which had broken out in France in 1789. Strong measures were taken to maintain law and order, but very little was done to relieve the distress. However, in 1822, Liverpool brought new blood into his government in the form of some progressive politicians – George Canning, Robert Peel and William Huskisson. As a result of this, a number of much needed reforms and improvements were introduced, which led this phase of the government to be described as *'Liberal' Toryism* (liberal meaning open-minded and favourable to reform).

Early in 1827 Lord Liverpool suffered a stroke and without his conciliatory skills, the Tories began to fall apart. In April 1827 *George Canning* became Prime Minister, but he died in August. His successor, *Frederick John Robinson, Lord Goderich*, had the greatest difficulty in persuading enough people to serve in his cabinet, and soon resigned in despair. George IV turned next to *the Duke of Wellington*, who, in January 1828, succeeded in forming a government whose most memorable act was the granting of Catholic Emancipation. The Wellington government lasted until November 1830 when *Lord Grey* became Prime Minister of a Whig government.

2.1 WHAT WERE THE BRITISH POLITICAL PARTIES IN 1815 AND WHAT DID THEY STAND FOR?

The main groups were Whigs, Tories and Radicals, though it is important to realise that they were not rigidly organised with manifestos and special policies as they are today. Leading figures had their own groups of supporters; sometimes relations between these groups were not good: among the Tories, the rival Castlereagh and Canning factions were notoriously hostile to each other. Parties therefore consisted of loosely linked factions; there was very little idea of party discipline and MPs often voted as they saw fit. For most of the time there seemed little to distinguish Whigs from Tories, since wealthy landowners formed the backbone of both groups.

(a) Whigs. The names 'Whig' and 'Tory' originated during the reign of Charles II (1660-85) at the time when there was some controversy about whether or not Charles's brother James should be allowed to succeed to the throne on Charles's death. The Whigs were the people who wanted to exclude him on the grounds that he was a Roman Catholic, whereas the Tories were those who were not prepared to exclude him. Both words – Whig and Tory – were terms of abuse flung by each side at the other: 'whig' was short for 'whiggamor', a nickname for western Scots who came to Leith for corn; 'tory' was Irish for 'robber' or 'brigand'. By 1815 the origins of the groupings had largely been forgotten. The Whigs had no particular programme or policy and were not even united. Broadly speaking they stood for a reduction in crown patronage (the power to appoint people to certain important positions and offices), sympathy towards Nonconformists (Methodists and other groups who had broken away from the Church of England), and care for the interests of merchants and bankers. Many of the Whigs were vaguely in favour of some reform of the voting system, but were unable to agree on a scheme. Whig leaders – all wealthy landowners – were Lord Grey, Lord Grenville, Lord Althorp, William Lamb (later Lord Melbourne) and Lord John Russell. Perhaps most gifted of all was Henry Brougham, a brilliant lawyer, who was rather set apart from the rest by his comparatively modest background.

(b) Tories stood, on the whole, for the preservation of the *status quo*: the powers of the monarch and the Anglican Church; they were much less tolerant of Nonconformists than the Whigs were. They also believed in the strict maintenance of law and order, having been badly frightened by the French revolution. Unlike some of the Whigs, most Tories opposed any reform of parliament, though the more progressive were in favour of some cautious humanitarian reform. Leading Tories of the more rigid type were Henry Addington (Lord Sidmouth), Lord Castlereagh, Lord Eldon and the Duke of Wellington. The 'reforming' Tories included George Canning, Robert Peel, William Huskisson and F. J. Robinson (Lord Goderich). The Tories, like the Whigs, were often deeply divided; in 1809 Castlereagh and Canning had disagreed so violently over the conduct of the war that Castlereagh had challenged his colleague to a duel with pistols. This actually took place at 6 o'clock one morning on Putney Heath, and ended with Castlereagh slightly wounding Canning in the thigh. The duel caused something of a sensation and both men had to retire from the cabinet for a time. After 1812 the Tories were more united, which says much for Liverpool's skill as a manager and conciliator.

(c) **The Radicals** had only a handful of MPs, the most influential being Sir Francis Burdett and Joseph Hume; but outside parliament Radical leaders such as Major John Cartwright, Henry 'Orator' Hunt, Francis Place, whose tailor's shop in Charing Cross Road became a famous Radical meeting-place, and William Cobbett, the journalist and publicist of the movement, were actively organising mass meetings, marches and petitions. The word radical (from the Latin 'radix' - a root) meant someone who wanted fundamental reforms which got to the root of problems. Early nineteenth-century Radicals were not an organised party, but they had one aim in common: they wanted a thorough reform of the political system and an improvement in the conditions of the working class, though they did not always agree on how these were to be achieved. They were greatly influenced by the ideas of *Jeremy Bentham* (1748-1832) which were known as Utilitarianism. A lawyer like his father, Bentham claimed that the function of governments was to promote 'the greatest happiness of the greatest number of people'; this could be achieved in two ways:

(i) The government and administration of the country must be made as efficient as possible; anything which was not efficient or useful - whether it was the education system, the penal system, the prison service or the voting system - must be modernised.

(ii) The government should interfere as little as possible with the lives and activities of individual people, since this was the best way of achieving the greatest happiness. Such a policy was known as *laissez faire* (allowing people to act as they chose, without government restrictions). Thus one of the Radicals' pet theories was *Free Trade*: the belief that import and export duties should be abolished, because they interfered with the natural flow of trade.

There was something of a contradiction in these Radical ideas since more government interference than ever before might be necessary in order to achieve efficiency in, for example, the education system. But this did not prevent Radicalism, with its clubs and debating societies, from swelling into the great protest movement of the early nineteenth century, supported by the working classes, by middle class humanitarians (people who wanted society organised in a humane fashion) and by some industrialists.

2.2 WHY WAS THERE SO MUCH DISCONTENT AND DISTRESS AMONG ORDINARY PEOPLE AFTER 1815?

The trouble was caused by a combination of many different developments which, for the sake of simplicity, can be divided into three groups:

(a) The industrial and agricultural revolutions caused widespread poverty in both town and country.

(i) *Enclosures* (see Section 1.2(b)) probably caused hardship in some areas. The movement towards enclosure had been taking place piecemeal since the fifteenth century, but it gathered pace after 1760 and there was a late surge during the war years as farmers took advantage of the high demand for wheat. There has been disagreement among economic historians about how serious and widespread the effects were. It used to be argued that enclosures ruined the yeomen (farmers of medium-sized holdings) and small peasant farmers, who were evicted from their land because they could not afford the expenses involved. Some recent historians claim that the hardship has been exaggerated; whether they are right or not, the fact is that much of the country – Kent, Essex, Sussex and the West Country – had been enclosed long before 1815; in some areas – Lancashire, Cheshire, Cumberland, Northumberland and Durham – the open-field system had never existed. There must therefore have been other reasons for the poverty in these areas in the years immediately following 1815: one obvious explanation is that *the rapid population growth* made many farm labourers redundant. Nevertheless it is likely that in areas where enclosures did take place during the war years, large numbers of smallholders lost their two or three acres together with their rights of using the common pasture for their animals, and were reduced to landless labourers. E. P. Thompson suggests that this was a deliberate policy by wealthy farmers in order to swell the reserves of cheap labour who could be called in for haymaking, harvesting, road-making, fencing and draining.

(ii) *The Speenhamland System* aggravated rural poverty. The pool of cheap labour kept farm labourers' wages so low that in 1795 the magistrates at Speenhamland in Berkshire decided to supplement wages from the poor rates either by food or money depending on the price of bread and the size of a labourer's family. This system spread rapidly, though it was never common in the North of England. Although the magistrates acted through humanity (as well as the need to calm unrest and perhaps prevent revolution), the system had two unfortunate effects: farmers reduced wages still further, or refused to employ labourers for a full week, knowing that however inadequate their earnings were, they would be topped up by the magistrates. In addition the money had to come out of the poor rate (a special rate charged by the parish for the maintenance of the poor); this meant that the rest of the ratepayers were having to subsidise the wealthy farmers, a highly unpopular state of affairs, particularly as poor rates on average doubled between 1795 and 1812.

(iii) *The new machines* in agriculture, factories and mines often reduced the demand for labour and caused hardship in certain trades. The best-known example is the case of the hand-loom weavers of Lancashire, Yorkshire and Cheshire who were gradually being forced out of business by the power-loom. They were already past their heyday in 1800 since their earlier prosperity had attracted too many extra weavers, enabling the employers to force down wages. But as the power-loom was adopted more widely after 1815 their plight became much worse. One set of statistics puts the average wage for hand-loom weavers at 21s. in 1802, 14s. in 1809, 8s.9d. in 1817, 7s.3d. in 1828 and 6s. in 1832. And there was worse still to come; according to William Cobbett after a visit to Halifax in 1832: 'It is truly lamentable to behold so many thousands of men who formerly earned 20 to 30 shillings per week, now compelled to live on 5s, 4s, or even less' (see note about money on p. xiv).

(iv) *In the industrial towns* there were unpleasant working and living conditions. It is difficult to generalise about this and in fact historians have disagreed over how objectionable working conditions were. However, there is no doubt that in many mills men had to work long hours (a 16-hour day was common); children from the age of five could be expected to work a 14-hour day; and there was resentment at the way wages were paid in some trades: there was the 'truck' system by which workers received part of their wages in goods or in vouchers which could only be spent at the 'truck' shop kept by the mill or mine-owner. What was also distressing for the industrial workers was the loss of freedom together with the regimentation of factory life, plus the fact that wages probably failed to keep pace with rising prices. Nor can there be any doubt that the growth of industrial towns was too rapid for proper planning and housing. For example Liverpool mushroomed from only 82 000 in 1801 to 202 000 in 1831, Manchester/ Salford grew from 95 000 to 238 000 over the same period, Glasgow from 77 000 to 193 000. Much of the extra population came in from the surrounding countryside, but in Lancashire there was a high influx of Irish immigrants. Cheap, jerry-built housing was thrown up close to the factories, water supplies and sanitation were primitive, and over-crowding dangerously unhealthy; in Manchester in 1820 at least 20 000 people, including many Irish, were living in cellars. This excess of cheap labour was one of the main reasons why industrial wages kept so low.

(b) The after-effects of the wars (1793–1815) aggravated these problems

(i) *The end of the war brought a sharp fall in corn prices*, causing bank-ruptcies among poorer farmers. The price reached a peak in 1812 at an average per quarter of 126s.6d; it fell dramatically to 65s.7d. in 1815, and by January 1816 it was down to 52s.6d. The fall in price was caused by the fact that farmers, having taken more land under culti-vation to meet demand during the war, were now over-producing; foreign imports were available again and in addition the harvests of 1813 and 1814 were outstandingly good. Many small owner-occupiers, already in debt because of the costs of enclosure, high war-time taxes and the increase in the poor-rate, could not stand the reduction in profits and went out of business. Wealthier farmers reduced wages and laid off some of their labourers, adding to the unemployment pool.

(ii) *There was a sudden industrial slump causing widespread unemploy-ment.* The reasons for this were several: now that the war was over, the government stopped buying armaments and uniforms, which meant the loss of orders worth around £50 million; European manu-facturers, worried by British competition, brought pressure to bear on their governments to introduce tariffs (import duties) making British goods more expensive in Europe and thus protecting the developing European industries; after a short boom (a period of increasing exports) in 1815, British exports fell away again and had dropped 30 per cent by 1818. Roughly half the blast furnaces in the country had to close down and there was a corresponding reduction in the demand for coal. On top of this there were over 200 000 demobilised soldiers and sailors flooding the labour market making a grand total of perhaps half a million unemployed by the end of 1816.

(c) Some of the government's actions made the situation even worse

(i) *The Combination Laws (1799–1800)* made combinations (trade unions) illegal, and though the laws were not effective, they aroused resentment.

(ii) *The Corn Law of 1815* forbade the import of foreign wheat until the price of home-grown wheat had risen to 80s. a quarter, which was considered to be a sufficiently profitable level for landowners and farmers to keep all their labourers in work. This increased the price of wheat which rose to 76s.2d. a quarter in 1816 and to 96s.11d. in 1817 sending the price of a four-pound loaf up from 10d. to 1s.2d. Although this pleased farmers, it was disastrous for the unemployed workers and brought a shower of accusations that the Tory land-owners were looking after themselves at the expense of the poor.

(iii) *Income tax was abolished in 1816.* It had been introduced originally in 1797 to raise extra cash for the war effort, and William Pitt, then Prime Minister, had pledged to remove it as soon as the war was over. Liverpool, under pressure from wealthy industrialists, merchants, bankers and landowners who wanted rid of income tax, kept the pledge. However, the income tax was bringing in about £15 million a year which the government could ill afford to lose, especially as the interest they had to pay on the National Debt (money borrowed by the government to finance the war and for other purposes) amounted to over £31 million a year. To make up for the loss, Liverpool's government increased the taxes on a wide range of goods, including tea, sugar, tobacco, beer, paper, soap and candles. While the rich were relieved of income tax, the poor, who had not paid it since it only applied to people earning over £60 a year, now found themselves burdened with at least some of the extra taxes on popular goods. The government's unpopularity reached a new peak.

(iv) The government reacted to protests with a lack of understanding and a policy of repression (see Section 2.4) which embittered people further.

2.3 HOW WAS THE DISCONTENT EXPRESSED?

Some people expressed their views peacefully in pamphlets and speeches and petitions, but there were also marches and demonstrations, many of which ended violently. The government was convinced that there was a widespread and centrally organised conspiracy, but in fact this was not the case.

(a) The Radicals (see Section 2.1(c)) kept up a constant stream of criticism of the government and the way society was organised. In 1816 Cobbett began a 2*d*. weekly issue of his pamphlet *'Political Register'* (known as Twopenny Trash) which was soon selling 44 000 a week. His themes were the crushing burden of taxation on ordinary people and the need to bring about a reform of parliament: 'We must have that first, or we shall have nothing good . . . Any man can draw up a petition and any man can carry it up to London.' He advocated universal male suffrage (the vote for all men) and a general election every year, thereby keeping parliament firmly in touch with the wishes of the people. This would enable a start to be made on vital social reforms. On the whole the Radicals favoured peaceful protest, realising that violence would discredit their cause, though Henry Hunt tended to become involved in agitation.

(b) The Luddite Riots (1811–17) had already begun before the wars were over. They involved workers in three trades – the croppers (woollen cloth dressers and finishers) of the West Riding of Yorkshire, the cotton weavers of Lancashire and the framework-knitters of the Midlands, particularly Nottingham. All these workers were suffering economic hardships for a variety of reasons, including the use of new labour-saving machinery; they began to relieve their feelings by smashing machinery and setting fire to factories. Beginning in Nottinghamshire, the movement took its name from Ned Ludd, a youth who was reputed to have smashed up some machinery in a fit of half-witted temper; during 1811 almost 1000 frames valued at over £6000 were destroyed and the government retaliated by making frame-breaking punishable by death. The outbreaks soon spread to Yorkshire and Lancashire; mills were attacked in Leeds, Manchester, Stockport and many other centres. At Rawfolds in the Spen Valley, a mill-owner used troops to fight off the Luddites, killing two of the attackers; at Middleton near Manchester, a power-loom mill was attacked by a crowd of several thousands, but they were driven back by musket-fire; after 10 had been killed, the crowd retaliated by burning down the mill-owner's house (April 1812). The government took a strong line, using troops to break up demonstrations and hanging 17 Luddites at York (January 1813). The main phase of Luddism was over by this time, though sporadic outbursts occurred until 1817.

(c) The Spa Fields Meetings in London (1816) caused disturbances. There were three separate meetings (15 November, 2 and 9 December), the second of which ended in a riot. The main speaker was Hunt who urged the need for a reform of parliament, universal suffrage, voting in secret (by ballot) and annual elections. However, the organisers of the meeting were more extreme than the Radical Hunt; they included Arthur Thistle-wood and Thomas Preston who wanted the eventual overthrow of the monarchy. They believed the army was on the verge of mutiny and hoped to excite the crowd into attacking prisons, the Bank of England and the Tower. Even before Hunt began to speak, a section of the crowd had rampaged through the streets and ransacked a gunsmith's shop. It was only dispersed by troops after several hours' rioting.

(d) The March of the Blanketeers (1817) set off from Manchester to present petitions to the Prince Regent in London. Manchester, full of unemployed weavers, was the centre of an impressive reform movement, and the march was well organised. About 600 men, mostly poor weavers, walked in groups of ten with blankets on their backs, each group carrying a petition (ten was the maximum number allowed by law to present a petition) asking the Prince Regent to help their unfortunate industry. About 200 were arrested at Stockport and most of the remainder were chased away by cavalry at Macclesfield. One man was allowed through to present the petition, but nothing came of this pathetic incident except that 13 of the leaders were sent to prison.

(e) The Derbyshire Rising (1817) was one of a number of similar incidents which took place in Yorkshire and the Midlands. Encouraged by a government spy known as Oliver (W. J. Richards), about 300 poor stocking-makers and quarrymen from the Derbyshire villages of Pentridge and Ripley, led by Jeremiah Brandreth, set off to seize Nottingham Castle, 14 miles away. Brandreth had assured his followers that the whole country was about to rise with them and that a provisional government would be set up which would send relief to the workers. A detachment of cavalry already alerted by Oliver was waiting at Nottingham and the rising ended ignominiously as the men ran off. Three of the leaders, including Brandreth, were executed.

(f) The Peterloo Massacre in Manchester (1819) was the most famous incident of the period. After a quiet year in 1818 thanks to an improvement in trade and the previous year's good harvest, 1819 brought a slump in exports and a return to unemployment. This led to renewed Radical demands for reform and a plan to hold a meeting of Radical leaders from all over the country in London. The Manchester Radicals organised an open-air meeting in St Peter's Fields to be addressed by Henry Hunt who was to be Manchester's representative at the London meeting. About 60 000 men, women and children turned up, and although many carried Radical banners, they were not armed and there was no disorder. The magistrates allowed the meeting to begin and had troops standing by in case there was trouble. While Hunt was speaking, the magistrates apparently lost their nerve, decided the meeting was illegal, and ordered the yeomanry (local volunteer troops) to arrest him. Unfortunately they had difficulty forcing a way through the solidly packed crowd, and regular troops were sent to help. They charged in with drawn swords, the crowd panicked and stampeded, and 11 people were killed and 400 injured; 161 of the injured had sabre wounds. Hunt was arrested but soon released on bail. There were protests from all over the country at the magistrates' handling of the situation and the incident soon became known as the 'Peterloo Massacre' – an ironic comparison with the army's activities at Waterloo. However, the government, afraid that the country was on the verge of revolution, congratulated the magistrates on their prompt action and used the incident to justify passing *the Six Acts* – a further tightening up of restrictions on Radical activities (see Section 2.4b(iv)) – which, among other things, banned any further large meetings.

(g) The Cato Street Conspiracy (1820) was the final and most extreme act in this series of protests. The leaders, who included Arthur Thistlewood and James Ings, a butcher, were apparently moved to desperation by the latest government restrictions; they conceived a half-baked plan to murder the entire cabinet at a dinner, parade the heads of the ministers on pikes, capture the Tower, Bank and Mansion House (residence of the Lord Mayor of London) and proclaim a republic. However, government spies knew all about it and the conspirators were arrested at a house in Cato Street (off the Edgware Road). Five leaders, including Thistlewood, were executed and five others transported. The incident was not particularly important except that it seemed to justify the Six Acts. Apart from an abortive attempt to start a general strike in Glasgow, the agitation died down towards the end of 1820 as the economic situation improved.

illus 2.1 *The Peterloo Massacre of August 1819*

2.4 WHAT STEPS DID LIVERPOOL'S GOVERNMENT TAKE TO COMBAT THE UNREST IN THE PERIOD BEFORE 1820?

(a) The government's attitude to the problem. Their main concern seems to have been to stem the violence and keep order rather than to remove the causes of grievance. It was because of this that they came in for so much criticism at the time from the Radicals and later from liberal historians. In fact it is easy to understand the reaction of the Tories: they had been elected by the wealthy landlords; they had seen the horrors of the French Revolution which had started with similar protests in 1789 (Lord Liverpool had actually witnessed the storming of the Bastille); and their landowning supporters had a great deal to lose if a similar revolution broke out in Britain. It is important to remember that there was no police force at that time and only a limited number of troops; consequently the government had to rely for law and order on local magistrates who had little experience of handling such situations, who had no idea of crowd control, and were liable to panic, as they did at Peterloo. The widespread nature of the disturbances after 1815 convinced the Tories that unless firm action was taken the whole country would erupt into revolution. They were probably mistaken since there is no evidence of any co-ordinated conspiracy to overthrow the government; the Radicals were not in favour of violence and extremists like Thistlewood were only a small minority. Nevertheless the Tories, ignoring the fact that some of their policies (Corn Laws and abolition of income tax) were making matters worse, embarked on *a policy of repression* (keeping the people under control, restricting liberties, quelling riots and stamping out violence), directed by Lord Sidmouth, the Home Secretary.

(b) Repressive policies

(i) *The government used spies and informers* who usually pretended that they had been sent by Radical groups in London to help organise agitation in the provinces. Having contacted local reformers, they reported full details back to Lord Sidmouth; sometimes they acted as *agents provocateurs* – that is they encouraged reformers with violent tendencies to come out into the open and take action. The most notorious of these informers, W. J. Richards (known as Oliver), while not actually planning such activities as Brandreth's Derbyshire Rising, seems to have encouraged them enthusiastically. This exaggerated the threat to law and order but enabled the government to arrest possible revolutionary leaders and appeared to justify the rest of their repressive programme. According to E. P. Thompson, 'the government wanted blood – not a holocaust, but enough to make an example'.

(ii) *The Game Law of 1816* made poaching and even the possession of a net for catching rabbits punishable by transportation to Australia for 7 years. This was designed to stamp out the sudden increase in poaching which took place after the introduction of the Corn Laws, but it was not as effective as the government hoped because juries were reluctant to convict when the penalty was so severe for such a minor offence.

(iii) *The Habeas Corpus Act was suspended in 1817.* This act (meaning literally - you must have the body) had been passed originally in 1679 and gave the right to demand a written order for a prisoner to appear in court so that he could be charged with an offence; this was to protect people from being kept in prison for long periods without being charged. If the Habeas Corpus Act was suspended, a person who had committed no offence could be arrested and held for an indefinite period without charges and without trial to prevent him from committing an offence he might have had in mind. It was the Spa Fields affair which prompted the government into the 1817 suspension; the government also banned *seditious meetings* (meetings which might have caused disobedience or violence against the government) and sent letters to magistrates urging them to be firm with agitators. Together these government actions were nicknamed the *'Gagging Acts'*; they allowed the arrest of scores of Radical leaders, though not Cobbett who had left smartly for the USA.

(iv) *The Six Acts (1819)* were the government's reply to Peterloo; these were the most drastic measures taken so far.

1 Magistrates could search houses, without warrants, for unauthorised firearms: there were severe penalties if any were found.

2 Drilling and military training by private individuals were forbidden.

3 Political meetings to present petitions must involve only people from the parish in which the meeting was taking place; this was to prevent huge gatherings like those at Spa Fields and St Peter's Fields.

4 Magistrates could search houses. without warrants, for seditious literature.

5 Magistrates could try people charged with political offences immediately without waiting for the local assizes where they would have been tried by judge and jury. This was because juries were sometimes reluctant to convict when it was obvious that evidence came from informers.

6 The stamp duty on pamphlets and periodicals was increased, making them more expensive; most of them now cost at least 6*d*. and the government hoped this would reduce the circulation of Cobbett's *Political Register* and other radical publications.

Hundreds of prosecutions followed and during 1820 the agitation and violence gradually died away.

(c) Minor reforms. The government introduced a few improvements. *The Factory Act of 1819* (the work of Sir Robert Peel senior) forbade the employment of children under 9 in the mills and limited the working hours of 9–16-year-olds to 12 hours a day. Unfortunately this was largely ineffective: it applied only to cotton mills and magistrates were expected to enforce the regulations, a task quite beyond them; what was needed was a large body of professional inspectors. Another ineffective reform was the *Truck Act of 1820* which attempted to control abuses in the system of paying wages in ways other than in money. In conclusion it has to be said that the gradual disappearance of agitation during 1820 was not caused solely by the government's repression and certainly not by their reforms; it had much more to do with the recovery in exports which helped to reduce unemployment and by a series of good harvests which brought down the price of bread. As Cobbett remarked, 'I defy you to agitate a fellow with a full stomach'.

2.5 WHO WERE THE 'LIBERAL' TORIES AND WHY DID LORD LIVERPOOL BRING THEM INTO THE GOVERNMENT IN 1822-3?

(a) **The new men** included George Canning who became Foreign Minister and Leader of the House of Commons, replacing Castlereagh who had just committed suicide; Sir Robert Peel (junior, aged only 33) became Home Secretary, replacing Sidmouth who had retired; W. J. Robinson (aged 40) became Chancellor of the Exchequer in 1823 and William Huskisson (aged 50) President of the Board of Trade in the same year. As well as being open to new ideas, they were more middle class than the majority of landowning Tories. Canning's father was a barrister and his mother an actress, a profession then considered not respectable; it was a disadvantage that took a long time to live down. Peel's father was a wealthy Lancashire cotton manufacturer.

(b) **They were brought in for a number of reasons:**

(i) Castlereagh's suicide made a major cabinet reshuffle necessary. Canning was the obvious candidate to take over as Foreign Secretary; this meant that some members of Canning's group such as Huskisson and Robinson would be brought in too.

(ii) They were all in their different ways more progressive than the men they replaced, and were prepared to introduce some reforms. By drafting them into the government, Liverpool hoped to improve social and economic conditions sufficiently to win the support of moderate reformers all over the country, as well as the support of the manufacturers. By removing some of the causes of distress, he hoped to reduce the demand for a reform of parliament, which he and his colleagues certainly did not favour.

(iii) 1822 was a suitable time to begin reforms since law and order had been restored and it would therefore not look as though the government was being swayed by violence.

(iv) Moderate reform would be a blow at the Whigs who were split between the aristocratic members who were not keen on reform and the left wing of the party who were sympathetic towards the Radicals.

(v) The Tories had been seriously embarrassed by what was known as *the Queen's Affair* (1821). On the death of George III in 1820, the Prince Regent became George IV. Already secretly married to the Roman Catholic Mrs Fitzherbert, he had, in 1795, married Princess Caroline of Brunswick. Since he and Caroline had lived apart for many years, George was determined that she should not be crowned Queen and persuaded Liverpool to introduce a Bill of Divorce into parliament on the grounds of Caroline's adultery. The King was himself highly unpopular because of his extravagance and his mistresses, and the general public, the Radicals and most of the Whigs rallied to Caroline's support, though she was certainly no saint. So great was this support that the government dropped divorce proceedings; in London huge mobs celebrated and cabinet ministers had their windows smashed. George still tried to ignore her, and the London public was treated to the spectacle of the Queen, cheered on by huge crowds, trying to force her way into Westminster Abbey to take part in the Coronation Service. She had to abandon the attempt, and fortunately for George, she died a month later. As well as bringing the popularity of the monarchy to its lowest point ever, the Affair had also shown how out of touch the government was with public opinion. This may well have reinforced Liverpool in his decision to bring in some new blood.

2.6 WHAT REFORMS DID THE 'LIBERAL' TORIES INTRODUCE BETWEEN 1822 AND 1830 TO DESERVE THIS TITLE?

Huskisson and Robinson, both able administrators and financiers, were quick to grasp the importance of overseas trade and were prepared to remove antiquated restrictions which were hampering Britain as a trading nation. Peel was ready to listen to proposals for reforming prisons and the system of maintaining law and order; he was even persuaded to support Catholic Emancipation though he had begun by being resolutely against it. Canning favoured Catholic Emancipation and supported his colleagues in their social and economic policies. They were all influenced by the ideas of Jeremy Bentham (see Section 2.1(c)), that governments should aim for greater efficiency. Two important points to remember, however, which have sometimes caused confusion, are:

1 None of the Tories was in favour of reforming parliament to make it more democratic, and therefore whatever else they did to earn the title, they were not fully 'liberal' (the word could mean 'in favour of democratic reform' as well as 'wanting a general removal of abuses').

2 The change of policy was not as sudden as some historians have made out. The beginnings of reform had already taken place before 1822. The Factory Act (1819) and the Truck Act (1820) have already been mentioned (see previous section); in addition there had been the partial abolition of the pillory (1816) and the abolition of the whipping of women (1820); a Commons Committee of Inquiry had been set up in

1819 to study the weaknesses of the legal system; the Board of Trade had already admitted the need for commercial reform before Huskisson arrived. Even Canning's foreign policy which seemed to favour liberalism overseas (see Section 3.3(a)) had its beginnings under his predecessor Castlereagh.

However, what had been a mere trickle became a flood after 1822:

(a) Huskisson and the move towards Free Trade. The problem was that British merchants were hampered by numerous *tariffs* (import duties) and other restrictions; some of these had been imposed originally to protect British industries from foreign competition by making foreign goods more expensive than similar goods produced in Britain; others had been imposed to raise cash during the wars with France. There were, for example, heavy duties on imported raw materials which were now needed on a much larger scale than ever before because of the expansion of British industry. In 1820, the merchants of London, Manchester and Glasgow had petitioned the government for *Free Trade* (the abolition of all duties), since they were convinced that British industry could beat all foreign competitors; they also argued that if Britain continued with tariffs, foreign countries would do the same in order to protect their industries from British goods. Huskisson was a follower of *Adam Smith* (1723-1790), a Scottish philosopher, who had argued (in his book *The Wealth of Nations*) that the fewer economic restrictions there were, the more successfully would a nation's economy develop.

(i) He reduced import duties by varying amounts on a wide range of raw materials and other goods: cotton, wool, silk, linen, tea, coffee, cocoa, wine, rum, spirits, books, glassware, china, porcelain, manufactured textiles, iron, copper, zinc, tin and many others. For example, the duty on imported raw silk was slashed from 5s. 7½d. to 4d. per pound and on raw wool from 6d. to 1d. per pound. The duty on imported manufactured goods not specifically mentioned in the list was reduced from 50 to 20 per cent.

(ii) He removed restrictions on the trade of Britain's colonies: they could now trade directly with foreign countries for the first time, instead of all such trade having to pass via Britain first; many goods imported from the colonies paid lower duties than similar goods from foreign countries (such as wheat and timber from Canada; wool from Australia paid no duty at all). This was known as *imperial preference* and was designed to encourage trade with the British Empire.

(iii) He modified an obsolete set of restrictions known as the Navigation Laws (introduced in the seventeenth century) which said that goods being imported into Britain and her colonies had to be carried in British ships or in ships of the country where the goods originated. This had been designed to prevent the Dutch from capturing the world's carrying trade, but by the 1820s it was quite unnecessary, and other countries were beginning to retaliate with similar policies, so that British ships were being excluded from European ports or having to pay high duties. Huskisson's *Reciprocity of Duties Act* (1823) enabled the government to sign agreements with foreign governments allowing completely free entry of each other's ships. During the next six years 15 of these agreements were signed (with, among others, Prussia, Sweden, Denmark, Brazil and Colombia).

(iv) He modified the 1815 Corn Law by introducing a sliding scale of import duties (1828): if British wheat was selling at over 73s. a quarter, there would be no duty on imported foreign wheat; as the price fell, the duty increased.

In the long term Huskisson's work bore fruit: cheaper raw materials enabled manufacturers to produce goods at lower prices so that British exports and shipping increased steadily as her industries became more competitive; smuggling began to disappear, since the reduction in duties made it unnecessary. In the short term there were a few problems: the government lost the revenue (income) which it had collected from the higher import duties, and in December 1825 there began a sudden slump in exports caused mainly by over-production. Unemployment increased again and in Lancashire there were more outbreaks of machine-breaking. Some people blamed Huskisson though this was absurd because many of his reforms only applied from the beginning of 1826. In fact he had taken Britain through the first crucially important steps towards Free Trade. Sadly his career was cut short in 1830 when he was knocked down and killed by a locomotive at the opening of the Liverpool and Manchester Railway.

(b) Repeal of the Combination Laws (1824). Since 1800 the Combination Laws had made trade unions illegal. A campaign to get these laws repealed (cancelled) was mounted by Francis Place, the famous Radical tailor of Charing Cross, whose shop was a favourite meeting place for London Radicals. He was supported in parliament by the Radical MPs Joseph Hume and Sir Francis Burdett and by many other Benthamites. *Their arguments were* that the Laws were inefficient (trade unions did in fact exist but called themselves friendly societies which workers paid into in order to get sickness and unemployment benefit); workers were dissatisfied simply because unions were illegal; once they had full rights, workers would co-operate with employers for the greater prosperity of both, and unions would no longer be necessary. In 1824 Hume succeeded in having a parliamentary committee of inquiry set up to study the situation. So well did Hume and Place train the workers who gave evidence that Huskisson was persuaded to take the extremely liberal step of repealing the Combination Laws. However, the results horrified both Radicals and industrialists. Hundreds of trade unions came out into the open and hundreds of new ones were formed. In 1825 there was a wave of strikes as workers demanded wage increases – their share of the general prosperity. Under pressure from industrialists, the government was preparing to reintroduce the Combination Laws, but Place and Hume managed to salvage something for the unions: *the Amending Act (1825)* permitted trade unions to exist for the purpose of negotiating about wages and hours of work but they were not allowed to 'molest' or 'obstruct'. Although this made it difficult to conduct strikes, it was at least an important step forward in trade union organisation.

(c) Peel and law and order. Part of Peel's talent was that he was willing to listen to and be persuaded by reasonable arguments. He studied carefully the recommendations of humanitarian reformers such as Sir Samuel Romilly, Sir James Mackintosh, John Howard and Elizabeth Fry. Bentham himself had criticised the inefficiencies of a legal system which had grown up piecemeal over 600 years. *The penal code* (the list of punishments for various crimes) was far too severe: over 200 offences, including minor ones such as stealing a loaf of bread, damaging Westminster Bridge and impersonating a Chelsea pensioner, were punishable by death; another 400 were punishable by hard labour in the convict settlements of Australia; in a notorious case in 1813 a boy had been hanged for stealing a sheep. In practice the system broke down because juries often refused to convict if it meant execution for a trivial offence, and many criminals went unpunished. *Conditions in prisons* were atrocious: they were overcrowded, filthy, insanitary and disease-ridden; child offenders were put together with hardened criminals; jailers were often brutal and there was a ludicrous system whereby they were unpaid and had to make a living from fees paid to them by the prisoners. Peel introduced a series of reforms which, between 1823 and 1830, radically changed the whole system of law and order:

(i) *Penal code reform*: the death penalty was abolished for over 180 crimes, and in the remainder (except for murder and treason) it was left for the judge to decide whether the death penalty should be imposed; punishments for other offences were made less severe. The barbaric practice of burying suicides at cross-roads with a stake through the heart was abolished. In addition the jury system was drastically reorganised and the government stopped using spies to report on possible trouble-makers. These were splendid liberal and humanitarian reforms, but there was still some way to go: people could still be sent to jail for debt and transported to Australia, while public hangings continued until 1868. Peel was unable to do much about the procedure of the law courts which remained slow and cumbersome.

(ii) *The Jails Act (1823)* removed some of the worst abuses from the prison system: magistrates were to inspect prisons at least three times a quarter; jailers were to be paid instead of having to extort cash from prisoners; women prisoners were to be looked after by women jailers; all prisoners were to have some elementary education and receive visits from doctors and chaplains. However, the act applied only to the large prisons in London and 17 other cities – smaller prisons and debtors' prisons remained as before.

(iii) *The Metropolitan Police Act (1829)* introduced the London police force. The Bow Street Runners and the army of elderly night-watch-men were not particularly efficient at keeping the peace and Peel was convinced that the law would be more effective if there was some organisation to track down and deter criminals. The Act provided for 1000 paid constables, soon to be increased to 3000, under the control of a commissioner with headquarters at Scotland Yard; the scheme was to be financed by a special rate. The new police wore top hats and blue coats with belts, but were armed only with truncheons to avoid the charge that they were a military force. Soon nicknamed Bobbies or Peelers after their founder, they reduced the crime rate spectacu-larly, and as criminals moved out of the capital, provincial city auth-orities and then country areas began to copy the London force. *It was a controversial reform*: many people felt that the police were just another form of repression and resented the police rate; even a parlia-mentary committee set up to consider the problem had announced in 1822: 'It is difficult to reconcile an effective system of police with that perfect freedom of action and exemption from interference which are the great privileges and blessings of society in this country'. However, respect for the police increased as crime and violence were reduced over the whole country.

(d) Religious reforms. Peel and Wellington (then Prime Minister) piloted two important and liberal religious reforms through parliament:

(i) *The Repeal of the Test and Corporation Acts (1828)*. These anti-quated laws dating back to the seventeenth century said that only Anglicans (members of the Church of England, the official state Church) could hold important positions in the state and on town corporations. Non-Anglicans included Dissenters or Nonconformists (such as Methodists, Unitarians, Presbyterians and Baptists) and Roman Catholics. For years the Acts had been ignored as far as Non-conformists were concerned, and their repeal was simply a recognition of what happened in practice. But the repeal was only partial: *the restrictions still applied to Roman Catholics.*

(ii) *The Catholic Emancipation Act (1829)* was passed amid tremendous controversy which ruined Peel's popularity with the Tories and finally caused the party to disintegrate (see next section).

(e) For Canning's 'liberal' foreign policies see Chapter 3.

2.7 WHY DID THE TORY PARTY DISINTEGRATE IN 1830?

Between 1827 and 1830 a series of events and problems occurred which split the Tory party and allowed the Whigs to form a government.

(a) The resignation of Lord Liverpool at the age of only 57 in March 1827 following his stroke, removed the only man among the leading Tories who had the gift of holding together the various factions in the party. The old squabbles re-emerged: George Canning became Prime Minister, but Peel, Wellington and five other ministers resigned because they disapproved of his foreign policy and his sympathy for Catholic Emancipation. Canning even had to bring some Whigs into his cabinet to make up the numbers, which shows how loose party organisation was at that time. After Canning's death in August, Goderich failed to form a cabinet, and in desperation George IV asked Wellington to form a government. He succeeded but soon fell out with Huskisson and the other 'liberal' Tories who resigned after a disagreement over parliamentary reform. Though Peel remained in the government, Wellington had lost the support of the 'liberal' Tories (now referred to as Canningites), the left-wing of the party.

(b) The crisis in Ireland culminating in Catholic Emancipation split the party further.

(i) *The problem in Ireland* arose from the fact that although almost 90 per cent of the people were Roman Catholics, the majority of landowners and all important government officials were Protestants. Catholics had the vote, but were not allowed to sit in parliament. This was a source of great bitterness particularly as the Irish had only agreed to the Act of Union (1800), giving up their own parliament, on condition that Catholics were allowed full political and civil rights, i.e. Catholic Emancipation. The British government had failed to keep its promise because George III refused to agree to emancipation on the grounds that he would be violating his Coronation Oath in which he had sworn to uphold the Protestant religion. Since George IV held the same view, no progress had been made.

(ii) *The campaign for emancipation* was led by *Daniel O'Connell*, an Irish Catholic landowner and barrister, and an exciting speaker. After emancipation had been achieved, he hoped to get the Union dissolved and the Irish parliament restored to run internal affairs, though he was quite happy that the link with England should remain as far as foreign policy was concerned. His methods were non-violent: in 1823 he founded *the Catholic Association* to which Catholics, including poor peasants, paid a penny a month (the Catholic rent). It soon became powerful, with a weekly income of £1000 and the full support of Roman Catholic priests. At elections the Association backed Protestant candidates who were pledged to vote for emancipation at Westminster, and anti-Catholic candidates were defeated in two by-elections. The repeal of the Test and Corporation Acts made O'Connell even more determined.

(iii) The crisis point was reached with *the County Clare election (1928)*. Vesey Fitzgerald, the MP for County Clare, was standing for re-election (he had just been promoted to President of the Board of Trade and a newly appointed minister had to resign his seat and submit himself for re-election). Though Fitzgerald was a Protestant landlord, he was in favour of emancipation and had been a popular MP. O'Connell decided to stand against him to show how strongly Catholics felt about the issue, though as a Catholic he would not be able to take his seat even if he won. The franchise (right to vote) was restricted: the minimum qualification was the ownership of land worth £2 a year (these voters were known as 40 shilling freeholders). However, there were enough Catholic peasants with the vote to swing the election for O'Connell who won a triumphant victory. Ireland was seething with excitement at the prospect of scores of Catholics winning seats at the next general election. There seemed every possibility of violence and even civil war if O'Connell and other future Catholic MPs were debarred from Westminster.

(iv) Faced with this prospect, *Wellington and Peel decided to give way.* Both had been bitter opponents of emancipation for years on the grounds that it would lead to the breaking of the Union between England and Ireland (which it eventually did); but both were convinced that only concessions would prevent civil war: Wellington himself said: 'I have probably passed a longer period of my life engaged in war than most men and I must say this: if I could avoid by any sacrifice whatever even one month of civil war, I would sacrifice my life in order to do it'. Peel introduced the bill for Catholic Emancipation into the Commons, Wellington bullied the Lords into passing it, and George IV accepted it after several stormy scenes (April 1829). Catholics could now sit in both houses of parliament and hold all important offices of state except monarch, regent, Lord Chancellor and Lord Lieutenant of Ireland. As a parting shot the government forced O'Connell to fight the County Clare election again and raised the property qualification to £10 so that the 40 shilling freeholders no longer had the vote (this did not prevent O'Connell from winning again). *The results of emancipation were important*: Peel and Wellington could claim to have averted civil war in Ireland, but their treatment of O'Connell and the 40 shilling freeholders lost the government most of the goodwill that emancipation should have won for them from the Irish Catholics. The Protestant Tories, especially the Irish landlords, never forgave Peel and Wellington for their 'betrayal'. Peel resigned and a bitter joke circulated that he had changed his name from Peel to Repeal; Wellington was so incensed at one of his critics, Lord Winchelsea, that he challenged him to a duel, which took place in Battersea Park (neither man was wounded). Having earlier lost his left wing, Wellington had now lost the support of right wing Tories (known as the Ultras) over Catholic Emancipation. Both groups were looking out for revenge, and it was clear that the government could not survive for long.

(c) In 1830 there were new outbreaks of violence all over England: their causes were complex: bread prices were high following the poor harvest of 1829; there was a sudden slump in exports which brought unemployment to the Midlands and North; revolutions in France and Belgium helped to fuel the unrest. All over the South of England labourers burnt ricks and smashed the threshing-machines which were throwing them out of work. Strong measures were needed, but Wellington's government seemed too weak for decisive action.

(d) The demand for reform of parliament revived after a lull during the period of calm and prosperity since 1821. Again the causes were complex (see Section 4.2); but now many of the Whigs supported the demand as the best way to prevent revolution. It was Wellington's refusal to consider even the mildest reform of parliament that brought about his downfall. At the general election in the autumn of 1830 (caused by the death of George IV and the accession of his brother William IV) candidates who favoured reform did well, and when parliament met in November, there was pressure for reform from Whigs and from 'liberal' Tories. Though he had compromised over emancipation, Wellington remained unmoved by the arguments for reform; in spite of the fact that the election system was hopelessly out of date, he announced that he thought it was the best that could be devised. Soon afterwards he was outvoted by a combination of Whigs and Tories and immediately resigned. The Whig leader Lord Grey became Prime Minister of a joint Whig, Radical and Canningite government.

2.8 VERDICT ON THE TORIES

No simple straightforward verdict is possible. Students at 'A' level and beyond who look more deeply at these Tory governments, soon realise that historians disagree about several aspects of their policies. Here there is space to refer only briefly to some of the areas of dispute as an introduction to further study. The traditional view still accepted by writers such as Derek Beales is that the Tories were reactionary (against progress, wanting to return to an earlier situation) until 1822, when they suddenly became 'liberal' reformers. More recently several new points have been suggested:

(i) There was no sudden change in 1822; the first signs were already there, and the process was simply speeded up after 1822 (see Section 2.6). J. E. Cookson suggests that the government was not reactionary before 1822: they were extremely cautious and thorough and 'were held back by their desire to present reforms which would have the widest possible acceptance'.

(ii) A clear distinction needs to be made between the Tories' political policies and their economic policies; though they may not have been progressive as far as political matters were concerned (the majority were against reform of parliament as late as 1827), they were prepared to make concessions on economic matters.

(iii) The motives of the Tories have provoked argument: the traditional view is that they followed policies (Corn Laws, abolition of income tax) favouring their own class - wealthy landowners - for purely selfish reasons. However, Boyd Hilton believes that they acted through disinterested motives: they wanted to secure food supplies and full employment and therefore supported agriculture because it seemed the most promising area of expansion. Later they realised their mistake, that industry was the major growth area, and consequently, in the 1820s, began to favour industrialists.

(iv) There is disagreement about the personal achievement of Lord Liverpool. Disraeli described him as the 'arch-mediocrity'. Others see him as the arch-reactionary responsible for repression and opposition to parliamentary reform. On the other hand he allowed important reforms to be introduced between 1822 and 1827 and showed enormous skill in holding a difficult cabinet together for 15 years. 'If Liverpool was an arch-mediocrity', writes N. H. Brasher in his defence, 'then it is a pity that Britain has had so few of the breed since'.

QUESTIONS

1. Peterloo: 16 August 1819

Study Sources **A** to **G** and then answer the questions which follow.

Source A: A letter from five Lancashire magistrates to Lord Sidmouth (the Home Secretary), 1 July 1819.

We cannot have a doubt that some alarming insurrection is being thought about. We applaud the behaviour of many of the labouring classes, which has been peaceful until now, but we do not count on this continuing. Urged on by the speeches of a few desperate rabble rousers we anticipate, at no distant period, a general rising, and possessing no power to prevent the meetings which are held weekly, we as magistrates are at a loss how to stem the influence of the dangerous and seditious doctrines which are continually spread around.

Source: quoted in R. Walmsley, *Peterloo: the Case Reopened*, Manchester University Press, 1969 (adapted extracts).

Source B: A letter from the Home Office to the Manchester magistrates, August 1819.

Careful thought convinces him (Sidmouth), the more strongly the inadvisability of attempting forcibly to prevent the meeting on Monday. Every discouragement and obstacle should be thrown in its way. He has no doubt that if anything illegal is done or said, it may be the subject of prosecution. But even if they should offer sedition . . . it will be the wisest course to abstain from any endeavour to disperse the mob unless they should proceed to acts of felony or riot.

Source: quoted in P. Revill, *The Age of Lord Liverpool*, Blackie, 1979 (adapted extracts).

Source C: Report in *The Times*, whose correspondent, John Tyas, was arrested along with Hunt, although he was well known as a strong critic of Hunt.

One banner read 'Taxation and no Representation is unjust'; on another banner 'Equal Representation or Death'; on a third 'Annual Parliaments, Universal Suffrage, and Vote by Ballot'.

A posse of 300 or 400 constables marched into the field about 12 o'clock. Not the slightest insult was offered to them.

The cavalry drew their swords and brandished them fiercely in the air: upon which they rode into the mob which gave way before them. Not a brickbat was thrown at them – not a pistol was fired during this period: all was quiet and orderly. They wheeled round the waggons until they came in front of them.

As soon as Hunt and Johnson had jumped from the waggon (to surrender) a cry was made by the cavalry, 'Have at their flags'. They immediately dashed not only at the flags which were in the waggon, but those which were posted among the crowd, cutting indiscriminately to the right and left in order to get at them. This set the people running in all directions, and it was not until this act had been committed that any brickbats were hurled at the military. From that moment the Manchester Yeomanry Cavalry lost all command of temper . . .

Of the crowd a large portion consisted of women. About 8 or 10 persons were killed, and besides those whom their own friends carried off, above 50 wounded were taken to the hospitals; but the gross number is not supposed to have fallen short of 80 or 100 grievously wounded.

Was that meeting at Manchester an 'unlawful assembly'? We believe not. Was the subject proposed for discussion (reform of the House of Commons) an unlawful object? Assuredly not. Was anything done at this meeting before the cavalry rode in upon it, contrary to the law or in breach of the peace? No such circumstances are recorded in any of the statements which have yet reached our hands.

Source: *The Times*, 19 August 1819 (adapted extracts).

Source D: A cartoon (dated September 1819) by George Cruikshank, showing the Peterloo Massacre (the head in the top left corner represents the Prince Regent).

MANCHESTER HEROES

Source: British Museum.

Source E: A letter in *The Courier*:

The meeting was then addressed by the several orators, show-ing much menacing attitude, and the shouts seemed to rend the very air and shake the foundation of the ground. The constables were tauntingly insulted wherever they were observed to stand; sticks and hats always waving on every acclamation.

About half past one the magistrates deemed it expedient to read the Riot Act, and instantly after the platform was sur-rounded in a masterly manner. The manoeuvre would have taken place without bloodshed had not the mob assailed the military and civil authorities with every resistance in their power, and particularly with missiles. Consequently the cavalry charged in their own defence; not without first being witness to a pistol shot from the multitude, against one of the gentle-men in our Yeomanry, who now lies in imminent danger.

Source: quoted in P. Sauvain, *British Economic and Social History 1700-1870*, Stanley Thornes, 1987.

NOTE: As the law stood in 1819, if a crowd did not disperse within an hour of the reading out of the Riot Act, then they were liable to be arrested.

Source F: A private letter from Lord Liverpool to George Canning, 23 September 1819.

When I say that the actions of the magistrates at Manchester were justifiable, you will understand that I do not by any means believe that the course which they pursued on that occasion was in all its parts prudent. A great deal might be said in their favour even on this head. But whatever judgement might be formed in this respect, being satisfied that they were substantially right, there remained no alternative but to support them.

Source: quoted in A. Aspinall and E. A. Smith (eds), *English Historical Documents, vol. II, 1783–1832*, Eyre & Spottiswoode, 1959 (adapted extracts).

Source G: The view of a modern historian.

My opinion is (a) that the Manchester authorities certainly intended to employ force, (b) that Sidmouth knew – and approved of – their intention to arrest Hunt in the midst of the assembly, and to disperse the crowd, but that he was unprepared for the violence with which this was carried out . . . It really was a massacre. Hunt had exerted himself in the week before the event to ensure obedience to his request for 'quietness and order'. The presence of so many women and children was overwhelming testimony to the peaceful character of the meeting.

Source: E. P. Thompson, *The Making of the English Working Class*, Penguin, 1980.

(a)   (i)   What is meant by the words 'seditious' and 'sedition' in Sources **A** and **B**?   **1, 4(a)**

    (ii)   Who was Hunt, mentioned in Sources **C** and **G**?   **1, 4(a)**

    (iii)   What important position did Lord Liverpool (Source **F**) hold?   **1, 4(a)**

    (iv)   From the evidence of Source **A**, what were the Manchester magistrates worried about?   **4(a)**

    (v)   According to Source **B**, what advice did the Home Office give the Manchester magistrates?   **4(a)**

(b)   (i)   According to the evidence in Source **C**, what policies were the 'reformers' in favour of?   **4(a)**

    (ii)   What evidence can you find in the Sources to suggest whether or not the demonstrators intended violence?   **4(a, c)**

(c)   (i)   What differences can you find between the account of events given in Source **C** and the one in Source **E**?   **4(a, c)**

    (ii)   Why do you think two such different accounts of the same events are possible?   **4(a, b, c)**

(iii)   Which of the two versions (Source **C** or Source **E**) is likely to be the more accurate? Give full reasons for your answer.

                                                          4(a, b, c)

(iv)   From the evidence in Source **E**, do you think that after the Riot Act was read, the magistrates acted as the law required? Explain your answer.   **4(a)**

(d) **(i)**   What message is the cartoonist in Source **D** trying to put across?

                                                          4(a)

(ii)   Do you think his version of Peterloo supports the account given in Source **C** or the one in Source **E**?   **4(a, c)**

(iii)   What methods does the cartoonist use to make his point? Do you think his methods have worked successfully?   **4(a, b)**

(e) **(i)**   Explain in your own words what Lord Liverpool (Source **F**) thought about the magistrates' actions.   **4(a)**

(ii)   Make lists of the evidence you can find in all the sources which supports or opposes the two opinions put forward by the writer of Source **G**.   **4(a, c)**

(iii)   What evidence is there in the Sources to support the statement in Source **G** that 'It really was a massacre'?   **4(a)**

(f) **(i)**   Why do you think these events in Manchester became known as 'Peterloo'?   **1, 2, 4(a)**

(ii)   What action did the government take later in 1819 to prevent further disturbances?   **1, 2**

2. Sir Robert Peel and Law and Order

Study Sources **A** and **B** and then answer the questions which follow:

Source A: T. F. Buxton, an Evangelical humanitarian reformer, describes the effect of imprisonment on the prisoner, in 1818.

If convicted, he may be exposed to the most intolerable hardships, and these may amount to no less than the destruction of his life now, and his soul for ever. He is instructed in no useful branch of employment by which he may earn an honest livelihood by honest labour. You have denied him every opportunity for reflection and repentance. Shutting him off from the world has only brought him a closer contact with its very worst villains. His mind has lain waste and barren for every weed to take root in. He grows used to idleness, filth and crime. You have taken no pains to turn him from the error of his ways and to save his soul. In short, you return him to the world impaired in health, debased in intellect and corrupted in principles.

Source: quoted in A. Aspinall and E. A. Smith (eds), *English Historical Documents, vol. II, 1783-1832*, Eyre & Spottiswoode, 1959 (adapted extracts).

Source B: Report of the House of Commons Committee on Prisons, 1835.

They have personally inspected the prisons in this metropolis and its neighbourhood, and have examined several of the visiting magistrates, chaplains, and officers of those and other prisons in various parts of the country. Whilst they have the satisfaction of believing that some of our prisons have of late been much improved, yet they cannot refrain from expressing their decided opinion that imprisonment in Newgate, Giltspur St. and the Borough Compter, in their present condition, must have the effect of corrupting the morals of their inmates, and clearly tend to the extension rather than to the suppression of crime.

Source: quoted in P. Revill, *The Age of Lord Liverpool*, Blackie, 1979 (adapted extracts).

(a) (i) Using your own words, make a summary of the criticisms of the prison system put forward by the writer of Source **A**. **4(a)**

    (ii) What evidence is there in Source **A** that T. F. Buxton was a man of strong religious beliefs? **4(a)**

(b) What action did Sir Robert Peel, the Home Secretary, take to try and improve conditions in prisons? **1, 2**

(c) (i) According to Source **B**, how had the Committee obtained the information for its report?

    (ii) What evidence does Source **B** provide to show how successful Peel's attempts at reform were? **4(a)**

    (iii) Why do you think that conditions in some prisons, such as the three named by the writer in Source **B**, were still bad?

        1, 2, 4(a)

(d) What other action did Peel take
    (i) to improve the penal code,
    (ii) to reduce the amount of crime? **1, 2**

(e) How successful were these attempts to improve law and order? **1, 2**

3. (a) Explain what is meant by the terms

    (i) tariffs;
    (ii) free trade;
    (iii) laissez-faire. **1**

(b) Why did many merchants want free trade in the 1820s? **1, 2**

(c) Describe the actions taken by William Huskisson after 1822 to move Britain towards free trade. **1, 2**

(d)   What were the results of Huskisson's work? Do you think it can be considered as a success?   **1, 2**

4. (a)   What was meant by the term 'Catholic emancipation'?

(b)   Why did George III, George IV, Wellington and many other leading politicians oppose Catholic emancipation in Ireland?

(c)   Describe the part played by Daniel O'Connell in the campaign for Catholic emancipation.

(d)   Why did Wellington change his mind and agree to Catholic emancipation in 1829?

(e)   What were the main terms of the Catholic Emancipation Act?

(f)   What important results did the introduction of emancipation have?   **1, 2**

5.   It is early in 1819 and you are a radical journalist. Write an article suitable for inclusion in Cobbett's *Political Register*, explaining what you think are the causes of the present widespread distress. You could mention the effects of the rapid changes in agriculture and industry, after-effects of the wars (1793–1815) and the mistakes of the government.

You could end with a brief list of your own suggestions about what ought to be done to improve the situation.   **1, 2, 3**

CHAPTER 3

FOREIGN AFFAIRS

1815–30

SUMMARY OF EVENTS

The period was dominated by two outstanding Foreign Secretaries, *Lord Castlereagh* (from 1812 until his death in 1822) and *George Canning* (1822-7). After Canning's death the dominant influence on foreign policy was Wellington, who became Prime Minister in January 1828.

The most pressing problem at the end of the Napoleonic Wars was how to deal with the defeated France and at the same time how to redraw the map of Europe whose frontiers and governments had been drastically re-organised by Napoleon. The Bourbon monarchy was restored in the person of Louis XVIII, and other details were dealt with by *the First and Second Treaties of Paris* (May 1814 and November 1815). In the intervening period Napoleon escaped from exile on the island of Elba and had to be crushed once and for all at Waterloo. The wider problems of Europe were settled at *the Congress of Vienna* (1814-15), though the arrangements, like those of most peace treaties, were controversial and were to cause problems later.

1815 saw the formation of *the Holy Alliance*, the brainchild of the Tsar Alexander I of Russia; its members were pledged to rule their countries according to Christian principles. More important was *the Quadruple Alliance* of Britain, Austria, Prussia and Russia, a continuation of the 1815 alliance which had defeated Napoleon; this became the *Quintuple Alliance* in 1818 when France was allowed to join. Its aims, broadly speaking, were to maintain the Vienna Settlement and preserve peace by holding Congresses to solve any awkward problems which arose. After the initial Congress at *Aix-la-Chapelle* (1818) it gradually became apparent that Britain was not in agreement with the other members of the alliance about how to deal with the revolutions that had broken out in Naples, Spain and Portugal, where liberals (see Section 1.2(c)) were trying to force autocratic monarchs to allow constitutions. Following the Congresses of *Troppau* (1820) and *Laibach* (1821), troops were sent in to suppress the revolutions in Spain and Naples, in spite of strong objections from Castlereagh who disapproved of interfering in the internal affairs of other states.

There were other revolutions as well, this time caused by nationalism (see Section 1.2(d) (ii)): the Spanish colonies in South America were trying to assert their independence, while the Greeks were struggling to break away from Turkish rule. These problems were considered at the Congress of *Verona* (1822). Unlike the outbreaks in Naples and Spain, these revolutions were successful, partly because of British support. In the case of the Greek revolt, Russia and France agreed with Britain; the Austrians and Prussians were so incensed at Canning's attitude that no further Congresses met and the Congress System (sometimes known as the Concert of Europe) was at an end. The general feeling in Britain was that this was no bad thing since the Austrian and Prussian idea of preserving peace and the Vienna Settlement seemed to be to keep as many autocratic governments in power as possible.

3.1 WHAT WERE THE AIMS OF THE STATESMEN WHO MET AT VIENNA IN 1814-15 AND TO WHAT EXTENT WERE THEIR AIMS FULFILLED IN THE VIENNA SETTLEMENT?

The leading personalities at Vienna were Prince Metternich (Austrian Chancellor), the Tsar Alexander I of Russia, Count Hardenberg (Prussian Minister) and Lord Castlereagh.

(a) Their aims were:

(i) To make sure that the French, who were held responsible for the wars, paid for their misdeeds.

(ii) To see that the victorious powers gained some compensation for their pains.

(iii) To prevent any further French aggression which might threaten the peace and security of Europe. This could be done by strengthening the states bordering on France and by making sure that the four leading powers remained on good terms with each other in order to maintain *a balance of power* (no single state would be powerful enough to dominate the rest). Rulers who had been expelled by Napoleon should be restored, as far as possible, as the best guarantee of peace.

There were disagreements about details: each had different ideas about what constituted a balance of power. Castlereagh was worried in case the settlement was too hard on the French so that it made them bitter and likely to go to war again to regain their losses: he argued that 'it is not our business to collect trophies, but to try, if we can, to bring the world back to peaceful habits'. There were jealousies lest one country gained more than another: Prussia wanted Alsace-Lorraine (from France) and the Kingdom of Saxony, and Alexander wanted the whole of Poland; in each case the other states were suspicious and refused to allow it.

Throughout the entire negotiations Talleyrand, the French representative, was extremely active in protecting French interests and salvaging what he could from the disaster.

(b) How successful were they?

(i) The treatment of France was finalised by the Second Treaty of Paris (November 1815); though harsher than the First Treaty, it was still reasonably lenient. France was to be reduced to her 1790 frontiers which meant losing some territory to Belgium and some to Piedmont (see Map 3.1); she had to pay an indemnity (a fine) and have an army of occupation until the fine was paid; in addition she lost many of her overseas colonies. The terms might have been much more stringent if Talleyrand had not exploited the mutual suspicions of the other powers so shrewdly: for example France kept Alsace-Lorraine though the Prussians were determined to get it. The statesmen were successful in their aim: France was penalised yet not embittered enough to want a war of revenge (note the contrast with the treatment of the defeated Germany at Versailles in 1919 – Section 21.6).

(ii) The victorious powers all gained territory mainly at the expense of countries which had been unlucky enough to end the war on the losing side. Britain gained Ceylon, Mauritius, Trinidad, Tobago, St Lucia, Malta, Heligoland, the Cape of Good Hope, and a protectorate over the Ionian Islands. After some complicated bargaining, Prussia received about two-fifths of Saxony, the Rhineland, Western Pomerania,

Map 3.1 *Europe in 1815*

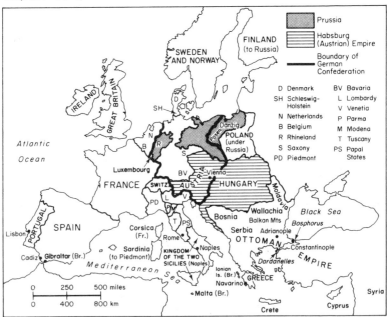

Danzig and Posen; Russia received Finland (from Sweden) and part of Poland; Austria was given Lombardy and Venetia in North Italy and a stretch of Adriatic coast. As compensation for losing Finland, Sweden was given Norway, taken from Denmark; this move was pressed by Britain so that the entrance to the Baltic would not be controlled by a single power.

(iii) Two of France's small neighbours were strengthened: the Austrian Netherlands (Belgium) were combined with Holland to make a strong barrier state to the north-east. Piedmont (also known as Sardinia) in North Italy on France's eastern frontier, regained most of Savoy and Nice, taken by France in 1796. The Bourbon family was restored to the kingdom of Naples in the person of Ferdinand I though they had a bad reputation for misgovernment. The Pope was restored to the Papal States. Also in Italy, the duchies of Parma, Modena and Tuscany were given to Austrian princes. Austria, in fact, had a firm grip on northern Italy; this was thought necessary to deter a possible French invasion of Italy. In general, therefore, the statesmen's aims seemed to have been fulfilled: a balance of power had been achieved and the Quadruple Alliance of Britain, Austria, Prussia and Russia seemed likely to preserve good relations.

There was in fact no major conflict in Europe until the Crimean War (1854-6), though of course there are many other reasons besides the Vienna Settlement for this long period of comparative peace.

On the other hand *there were criticisms of the settlement*. The main one was that it ignored the principle of nationalism: Belgians were placed under Dutch rule, Italians under Austrians; Finns, Norwegians and Poles were placed under foreign governments merely to suit the wishes of the great powers. German nationalists were disappointed: they wanted Germany united into one powerful state whereas the settlement reduced the old Germany of over 360 small states to 38 (known as the German Confederation) - an improvement, but not at all what the nationalists had hoped for. By restoring autocratic rulers such as the Pope and Ferdinand I of Naples, the congress also ignored the newly developing principle of liberalism. Although there was no major war for many years there were a number of disturbances which resulted directly from the settlement - the Belgian struggle for independence; revolutions in Naples, Piedmont and the Papal States, and the Italian fight to throw off Austrian control. The great powers were concerned in case these disturbances escalated into a major war as the French revolution had. In conclusion, it has to be said in defence of the settlement, that in 1815 nationalism was still a very new principle, produced mainly by the French Revolution. It was hardly to be expected that the statesmen of Europe would allow themselves to be influenced by such a new and, to them, suspect ideal.

3.2 WHAT WERE THE AIMS AND ACHIEVEMENTS OF LORD CASTLEREAGH IN FOREIGN AFFAIRS AFTER THE CONGRESS OF VIENNA (1815)?

Robert Stewart, Viscount Castlereagh, was an Irish Protestant aristocrat brought up in County Down. At the end of the Congress of Vienna he had enormous prestige among the statesmen of Europe and already had considerable achievements to his credit. He had played an important part in building up and maintaining the alliance which had finally brought down Napoleon. At Vienna he had successfully played the role of conciliator, persuading Prussia to tone down her demands, so that France gained a lenient peace. He had prevented both Prussia and Russia from gaining too much and had consequently preserved the balance of power. He must take much of the credit for Britain's territorial gains after the defeat of Napoleon; these confirmed British naval supremacy, providing valuable bases, sources of raw materials and markets – the basis for her future imperial and commercial expansion.

(a) **Castlereagh's aims after Vienna.** His main concern was to preserve peace and he hoped this could be achieved by continuing the co-operation between the great powers started at Vienna, thereby maintaining the balance of power. He wanted regular meetings of the powers to solve problems and quell disturbances by a *'Concert of Europe'* (states acting in concerted agreement together) instead of by confrontation. However, he did not believe it was the right of the great powers to intervene in the internal affairs of other states, and did not want Britain to become involved in any such action. Thus in 1818 when Alexander I proposed that they should sign a written guarantee to preserve all frontiers and monarchs in Europe, Castlereagh refused. His attitude was summed up perfectly by a statement he issued in December 1815: 'It is the province of Great Britain to encourage peace by exercising a conciliatory influence between the Powers, rather than put herself at the head of any combination of Courts to keep others in check. . . It is not my wish to encourage on the part of this country, an unnecessary interference in the ordinary affairs of the Continent'. As to specific details, he was keen to get the army of occupation removed from France and France herself accepted as an equal again by the other powers; this would boost Louis XVIII's popularity and help stabilise the country. Castlereagh felt it was wrong to penalise the Bourbon government too heavily for the behaviour of Napoleon.

(b) **Castlereagh's achievements.** It seemed as though his policies were beginning well; however, after 1818 his actual achievements were limited.

(i) With the help of Metternich, Castlereagh was responsible for *the Quadruple Alliance* (November 1815) of Britain, Austria, Russia and Prussia. They agreed to maintain the peace settlement and to hold regular Congresses to discuss any threats to peace and stability. The frontiers of France were guaranteed and the powers would intervene in France to prevent any attempt to restore the Bonapartes. This was an important achievement since regular conferences in peacetime were a new idea in diplomacy.

(ii) *The Congress System* got under way with *the Congress of Aix-la-Chapelle* (1818). It met to consider what to do about France which had paid off the 700 million franc indemnity and was settling down under Louis XVIII. It was decided that the army of occupation should be withdrawn and that France should take part in future Congresses, transforming the Quadruple into the Quintuple Alliance. Relatively minor problems discussed and agreed upon were the rights of Jews in Europe, Swedish payments to Denmark for the acquisition of Norway, and the treatment of Napoleon on St Helena. A discordant note was sounded when the Tsar Alexander, carried away by his Holy Alliance (which had been signed by all European rulers except George III, who was insane, the Pope, and the Sultan of Turkey), proposed that the powers should guarantee all frontiers and all monarchs; this would have meant intervening to suppress all revolutions including those provoked by bad government. Castlereagh was able to carry the Austrians and Prussians with him in rejecting this proposal. Again Castlereagh seemed to have scored a considerable success: France had been accepted again on equal terms, he had launched his new method of European diplomacy and had avoided a split in the Alliance. Unfortunately for Castlereagh the fragile harmony of the Alliance could last only so long as there were no revolutions and no divergent interests among the powers.

(iii) 1820 was a year of revolutions inspired by liberalism, in protest against autocratic government. In January, troops were gathering at Cadiz before sailing to attempt the recapture of Spain's New World colonies (Mexico, Argentina, Chile, Peru and Colombia) which had declared themselves independent during the wars. Instead the troops turned on the government and forced King Ferdinand VII to grant a democratic constitution. Similar revolutions in Portugal, Naples and Piedmont also achieved democratic constitutions. Metternich and Alexander, alarmed at the prospect of disturbances spreading from Italy into their own territories, summoned. . .

(iv) *The Congress of Troppau* (1820). Castlereagh, knowing that they intended to use the Alliance to quell the revolutions and destroy the new constitutions, refused to attend, merely sending his half-brother, Lord Stewart, as an 'observer'. He expressed his attitude in a famous State Paper (May 1820); it was not that he approved of liberal revolutions – in fact he sympathised with Metternich's fears; but he was unwilling to involve Britain in general commitments on the continent. It was not morally right for the great powers to force their wishes on smaller countries: 'the Alliance . . . was never intended as a Union for the government of the world . . . such a scheme is utterly impractical and objectionable'. In addition he knew that the Opposition in parliament would be furious if Britain supported intervention and he was extremely suspicious of Russian motives, since Alexander was itching to send an army through Europe to crush the Spanish revolution. Unimpressed by Castlereagh's objections, the other representatives issued the *Troppau Protocol* (a first draft of terms to be agreed) which asserted their right to intervene in any country where a revolution seemed in danger of infecting other countries. Castlereagh rejected the Protocol and there was clearly a serious split in the Alliance. The Congress adjourned in disarray.

(v) *The Congress of Laibach* (1821) was a continuation of the previous one. Castlereagh again sent his half-brother to show his disapproval. He did concede, however, that the Austrians should intervene in Naples, provided it was not done in the name of the Alliance. As a result Austrian troops quelled the revolts in Naples; they went on to deal with the revolt in Piedmont as well, a step Castlereagh did not approve. No action was taken against Spain or Portugal at this stage. Just before the Congress ended, the European situation was further complicated by the outbreak of the Greek revolt against Turkish rule. Relations between Britain and the rest remained tense and it was obvious that Castlereagh's idea of international co-operation was being misused by Britain's allies, though he could not quite bring himself to break away from the Alliance completely. A further Congress was planned for Verona (1822) to consider the Spanish and Greek problems, but before it met Castlereagh had committed suicide (August 1822).

His mind had broken under the strain of what R. J. White calls 'his courageous attempt to be with Europe but not of it, a diplomatic tight-rope act which must have been a nightmare to the chief performer'; he had also the difficult job of leading the unpopular Tory government in the Commons (the Prime Minister, Liverpool, sat in the Lords). In addition, though he appeared cool and arrogant, Castlereagh was a shy and sensitive man who was deeply hurt and disturbed by his unpopularity and by the abuse he had to suffer. He was already unpopular with liberals and radicals in 1815 for allowing the restoration of so many autocratic monarchs. Later he was blamed for the government's repressive policy (see Section 2.4). Not being a good speaker, he failed to explain his foreign policy clearly; consequently the parliamentary opposition and the general public believed he was committed to supporting autocracy, which seemed to be borne out by his approval of Austrian intervention in Naples. During the summer of 1821 he was convinced that sinister characters were trying to ruin his reputation by accusing him of homosexuality. He became so unbalanced that although friends removed his pistols and razors, he managed to cut his throat with a penknife. So great was his unpopularity that crowds hissed and jeered as his coffin was carried into Westminster Abbey.

Though his career was tragically cut short, Castlereagh's achievements after Vienna deserve to be remembered: he must take the credit for the introduction of the Congress System; this was a new departure in international co-operation and personal contact between the statesmen of Europe, a policy he pursued with commonsense and restraint.

3.3 WHAT WERE THE AIMS AND ACHIEVEMENTS OF CANNING IN FOREIGN AFFAIRS (1822-7) AND HOW DID HIS POLICIES DIFFER FROM CASTLEREAGH'S?

(a) Canning's aims.   Canning was not radically different from Castlereagh in his attitude, though there were differences of method and style.

  (i) He was not an enthusiastic supporter of liberalism and revolution abroad, but he did believe that whenever there was bad government, change must come.
 (ii) Like Castlereagh, Canning did not approve of great powers interfering all over the world as they saw fit - if a change was necessary, as for example in Greece, the process should be supervised by whichever of the powers was most closely concerned and not simply squashed by the whole Alliance.
(iii) Whereas Castlereagh had merely protested against the Metternich policy of intervention, Canning intended to be more decisive and actually help the revolutionaries in Greece and Portugal. Even here though, the difference was not completely clear cut, since just before his death, Castlereagh had been contemplating sending a fleet to help the Portuguese liberals.
(iv) Where he differed most from Castlereagh was that his overriding concern was to protect British interests rather than to preserve the Alliance. As Wendy Hinde puts it: 'his policy was based on a careful, even opportunist calculation of what would best preserve peace and promote England's prestige and prosperity'. Not being a founder member of the Alliance, he had no special affection for it, and did not know the European rulers and politicians personally; if it suited Britain's interests, he was quite prepared to withdraw from the Alliance. 'For *Europe*, I shall be desirous now and then to read *England*', he wrote soon after becoming Foreign Secretary.
 (v) Whereas Castlereagh's policies were misunderstood, Canning took the trouble to explain to the public what he was trying to achieve; this gained him public support and popularity, though other politicians often disapproved and thought him flashy - one critic remarked that Canning's trips round the country 'speechifying and discussing the intentions of the Gov't were ridiculous . . . quite a new system among us . . . which excites great indignation'.
(vi) Canning's specific aims were to prevent the French from interfering in Spain, preserve the new Portuguese constitution, maintain the independence of the Spanish colonies with which Britain had developed

valuable trade, and help the Greeks while at the same time making sure that the Russians did not gain too much advantage from the situation.

(b) Canning's achievements

(i) Canning failed in his first specific aim – to keep the French out of Spain. At *the Congress of Verona* (1822) it soon became clear that Britain's representative, Wellington, was isolated, since all the other powers were determined to destroy Spain's new liberal constitution. British protests were ignored and a French army was authorised to invade Spain; by April 1823 the Spanish liberals had been defeated and Ferdinand's full powers restored. It was a diplomatic failure for Britain and public opinion was outraged at the presence of French troops in Spain again only ten years after they had been driven out by Wellington. However, Canning's anti-French speeches won him popularity at home which increased as some important successes followed.

(ii) He was successful in upholding the liberal constitution in *Portugal*. Canning's fear was that unless Britain took decisive action, the French and Spanish, carried away by their crusade against liberalism, might invade Portugal and might even be tempted to regain the lost Spanish colonies in the New World. Following an appeal for help by the Portuguese Foreign Minister, a British naval squadron was sent to Lisbon (July 1823), and later, when it looked as though a Spanish army was about to enter Portugal, Canning despatched 5000 British troops to defend the Portuguese liberals. This was immensely popular with the public at home: it was felt that Canning had restored Britain's prestige after the Spanish failure and had defied Metternich and the other reactionaries in the Alliance.

(iii) Together with the USA, Britain was instrumental in preserving the independence of *Spain's former colonies*. The problem reached crisis point in the autumn of 1823 when Ferdinand VII of Spain proposed another Congress to consider action; it was obvious that Spain and France and probably the other powers as well, were in favour of a joint expedition to recapture the lost colonies. Canning was determined this should not happen, for several reasons: he felt that the people of South America and Mexico should have the right to remain free from such a reactionary tyrant as Ferdinand VII; he feared that the French might keep some of the Spanish colonies for themselves; probably most important of all, Britain stood to lose the valuable export trade which had developed with the new states, as the Spanish refused to guarantee Britain's right to trade with the colonies if they were recovered. By now Canning was convinced that the Congress System was a waste of time: 'We protested at Laibach and Verona and our protests were treated as waste paper'. Consequently he rejected the idea of a further Congress and warned Polignac, the French ambassador, that Britain would use her fleet in the Atlantic to prevent any expedition reaching South America.

Support for the British stand came from the USA which had already recognised the colonies' independence. In December 1823 President Monroe told Congress (the US parliament) that if any European power interfered in any part of America, whether it be North, Central or South, the USA would oppose it by force. This American policy became known as *the Monroe Doctrine*. The President's motive was to make Central and South America into a US sphere of influence and to warn off the Russians in case they had designs on the rest of America via Alaska, which belonged to Russia. The Monroe Doctrine was actually anti-British as well as anti-the rest of Europe: moreover Canning was disappointed that the USA had recognised the colonies as republics – he would have preferred monarchies. However, the Americans were well aware that their navy alone would be ineffectual and that only with the help of British sea-power could they enforce the Monroe Doctrine. In 1825 Canning recognised Mexico, Colombia and Argentina as independent republics and signed trade agreements with them. Metternich and the others, faced with the double threat from Britain and the USA, abandoned all hope of recovering the colonies. *Canning was triumphant*: the Alliance had been thwarted and the British defeat over Spain avenged; 'I called a New World into existence to redress the balance of the Old', he remarked. Prospects for British trade were good and Britain had shown that she could take effective action independently of the European powers. The Congress System was almost, but not quite, finished.

(iv) Canning became involved in *helping the Greeks in their fight against the Turks*, but he died (1827) before he could see it through. Though the Greeks eventually won full independence (1830), the circumstances were not particularly to Britain's advantage.

The origins of the situation lay in what was known as *the Eastern Question*: the Turkish Empire (also known as the Ottoman Empire) had once stretched far into south-eastern Europe as well as across Northern Africa. In 1683 the Turks had unsuccessfully besieged Vienna, and since that failure they had gradually been in retreat. The Turkish government usually neglected and misgoverned its outlying provinces; by 1815 it had lost its authority over North Africa and much of the Balkans, though nominally these areas were still part of the Ottoman Empire. It was because of the obvious Turkish weakness that the Greek nationalists were stirred to try and assert their independence.

In essence, the Eastern Question was the Russian attempt to take advantage of the weakening Turkish Empire, and the attempts of other powers, particularly Britain, to prevent this happening (see Section 9.2(c), and Chapter 10 for later recurrences of the Eastern Question).

Canning's motives for intervention in the Greek revolt were:

- The Greeks were not having a great deal of success since the Sultan of Turkey had received help from Mehemet Ali, the ruler of Egypt.

Ali's son Ibrahim had arrived in Greece with a large army, and by 1825 was well on the way to crushing the rebellion. There was much sympathy in Britain for the Greek cause, and many volunteers, including Lord Byron, had gone out to fight for them. The Greeks themselves sent a deputation to Britain begging help. All this put Canning under pressure to send active assistance to the Greeks.

- By the early part of 1826, it was clear that the Russians were about to intervene on the Greek side. Alexander I had been keen to help, but Metternich had dissuaded him on the grounds that revolutions, even against the Turks, must not be encouraged. However, Alexander died in December 1825, and the new Tsar Nicholas I was ready for immediate intervention. Russian policy since 1815 had been to suppress revolutions, but this one was different: Nicholas was horrified at the slaughter of Greek Christians by Egyptian and Turkish Muslims; above all though, Greek success would further weaken Turkey. Canning therefore decided that Britain must act too in order to make sure *firstly* that Turkey should not be weakened too much so that she could still serve as a buffer against Russian expansion in the Balkans, and *secondly* that Russia should not gain too much advantage, such as for example, possession of Constantinople.
- He may have intervened in order to break up the Congress System, knowing that Anglo-Russian co-operation would infuriate Metternich.

Consequently Canning, now Prime Minister, negotiated *the Treaty of London* (July 1827) by which Britain, Russia and France agreed to bring about Greek self-government, by force if necessary; a joint naval expedition set out for Greece. The Austrians and Prussians objected strenuously at this support of revolution and the Turks refused to negotiate. In August Canning died from inflammation of the liver and lungs, probably brought on by overwork. Meanwhile the joint 27 ship fleet was blockading the Turkish-Egyptian fleet of 81 ships in *Navarino Bay*. Though they were under orders to avoid hostilities, the British Admiral Codrington decided to force the issue by sailing into the bay. The Turks opened fire and a full-scale battle developed lasting four hours. It was a disaster for the Turks and their allies; 61 ships and about 4000 men were lost (October 1827). This battle was of great importance: Ibrahim was cut off from supplies and reinforcements; French troops landed and organised the evacuation of his troops. There was no prospect of the Turks recapturing Greece whose independence was recognised in 1830, although her frontiers were not decided until 1832.

After Canning's death Wellington reversed his policy and withdrew Britain from the treaty alliance, because he did not approve of aiding and abetting revolutionaries. The government apologised to the Turks and removed Codrington from his command. With no Canning to keep a watchful eye on them, the Russians declared war on the Turks and forced them to sign the Treaty of Adrianople (1829) which gave the area round the Danube delta to Russia.

In the end *Canning's work in the Near East had mixed success*. He had helped to achieve a completely independent Greece (which in 1832 was recognised as a Kingdom with Otto of Bavaria as the first King). However, his wider aim of limiting Russian gains by co-operation with her had been ruined by Wellington, who had failed to grasp Canning's intentions. Russia had substantially increased her influence in the Balkans, and Turkey had suffered military defeat.

(v) One result of the Greek revolt which, from Canning's point of view, can be seen as an achievement, was that it marked the end of the Quintuple Alliance and the Congress System as an instrument for crushing revolutions: for the first time Russia was acting *with* Britain and France in opposition to Austria, and there could be no further pretence that Europe was united. Canning had been prepared to break up the Congress System for a variety of reasons: to avoid binding commitments on the continent, to help liberals and nationalists (though this motive must not be exaggerated), but primarily to further Britain's trading and other interests. Metternich had been thwarted; no wonder he was delighted at Canning's death and thanked God for delivering Europe from 'this malevolent meteor'.

QUESTIONS

1. Castlereagh and Foreign Affairs
Study Sources **A** to **E** and then answer the questions which follow.

Source A: from the diary of Charles Greville.

August 13, 1822 . . . As a speaker he [Castlereagh] was monotonous and never eloquent . . . but he was always heard with attention . . . I believe he was considered one of the best managers of the House of Commons who ever sat in it . . . and he was possessed of good taste, good humour and agreeable manners. With these qualities, it may be asked why he was not a better Minister.

I believe that he was seduced by his vanity, that his head was turned by emperors, kings, and congresses and that he was resolved that the country which he represented should play as conspicuous a part as any other in the political dramas which were acted on the Continent. The result of his policy is this . . . that we have associated ourselves with members of the *Holy Alliance*, and gone along with the acts of ambition and despotism in such a manner as to have drawn upon us the hatred of the nations of the Continent.

Source: quoted in P. W. Wilson (ed.), *The Greville Diary*, Doubleday & Co., 1927 (adapted extracts).

Source B: from the diary of Mrs Arbuthnot, the wife of a Tory politician.

Castlereagh managed the foreign affairs of the country with a judgement and ability that will hand down his name with honour to posterity, when those of his pathetic critics will be buried in oblivion . . . When he had to make a statement or an opening speech, he was generally flat and dull and scarcely commanded the attention of the House . . . but his management was so good, and he was himself so gentlemanlike and so high minded, that he was one of the most popular leaders the Government ever had.

Source: quoted in F. Bamford and the Duke of Wellington (eds), *Mrs. Arbuthnot's Journal, vol. I*, Macmillan, 1950 (adapted extracts).

Source C: comments from a modern historian, Asa Briggs.

There was a vigorous debate in Parliament when the Whigs strongly criticised Castlereagh's surrender to European 'reaction', not knowing that Castlereagh in private was referring to the *Holy Alliance* (September 1815) between the absolute monarchs of Russia, Prussia and Austria as *'a piece of sublime mysticism and nonsense'* . . . In fact, during these years Castlereagh managed to steer clear of the Holy Alliance and refused to identify Britain too closely with the policies of the European powers . . . Before he committed suicide in 1822 Britain had begun to part company with the other great powers on the question of intervention to maintain autocratic government in Spain, Portugal and Sicily.

Source: A. Briggs, *The Age of Improvement*, Longman, 1959 (adapted extracts).

Source D: from Castlereagh's confidential State Paper, 5 May 1820.

The principle of one State interfering by force in the internal affairs of another, in order to enforce obedience to the governing authority, is always a question of the greatest moral as well as political delicacy . . . It is important to observe that to generalise such a principle and to think of reducing it to a system, or to impose it as an obligation, is a scheme utterly impracticable and objectionable . . . This principle is perfectly clear and intelligible in the case of Spain. We may all agree that nothing can be more lamentable, or of more dangerous example, than *the recent revolt of the Spanish army* . . . but it does not follow that we have therefore equal means of acting upon this opinion . . .

Besides, the people of this country would probably not recognise that our safety could be so far threatened by any state of things in Spain as to warrant their government in sending an army to that country to meddle in its internal affairs. We cannot conceal from ourselves how generally the acts of the King of Spain since his restoration have made his government unpopular, and how impossible it would be to reconcile the people of England to the use of force in order to replace power in his hands.

Source: quoted in A. Aspinall and E. A. Smith (eds), *English Historical Documents, vol. XI, 1783-1832*, Eyre & Spottiswoode, 1959 (adapted extracts).

Source E: some information provided by a modern writer, Jasper Ridley.

In 1820, the Spanish army gathering at Cadiz to embark for South America to recapture the Spanish colonies, mutinied and overthrew the *absolutist* monarch Ferdinand VII. They reintroduced the *liberal constitution* of 1812 . . . Metternich, Tsar Alexander, the King of Prussia and Louis XVIII united to suppress liberalism and Louis XVIII asked permission of the powers to invade Spain and restore Ferdinand. At the Congress of Verona in 1822 only Britain opposed the proposal and worked for a compromise. The government tried to persuade the Spanish liberals to restore some of Ferdinand's powers, hoping this would prevent a French invasion. The liberals indignantly rejected the British proposals. The French army thereupon crossed the frontier and overran Spain without much difficulty. The liberal leaders surrendered to Ferdinand on promise of their lives, but he broke his word and had them all shot. He now established an even more brutal *police state* than that which had existed before 1820 . . . The Opposition attacked the government's policy and accused Castlereagh of allowing France to 'conquer' Spain.

Source: J. Ridley, *Lord Palmerston*, Constable, 1970 (adapted extracts).

(a)   (i)   What points do Sources **A** and **B** agree about in their opinions of Castlereagh?   **4(a, c)**

(ii)   What points do they disagree about?   **4(a, c)**

(iii)   Summarise briefly in your own words the criticisms of Castlereagh's foreign policy made by Greville in Source **A**.

4(a)

(iv)   What are the advantages and disadvantages of diaries (like the ones quoted in Sources **A** and **B**) as sources of information for the historian?   **1, 4(b)**

(v)   Using evidence from Sources **A** and **B**, explain whether you think each of the writers was an admirer of Castlereagh or not.

                                                                     4(a, b)

(b)   **(i)**   What was the 'Holy Alliance' mentioned in Sources **A** and **C**?

                                                                     1, 4(a)

   ((ii)   In what way does Source **C** contradict Source **A** about Britain and the Holy Alliance?   **4(a, c)**

   (iii)   What do you think Castlereagh meant when he called the Holy Alliance 'a piece of sublime mysticism and nonsense' (Source **C**)?   **1, 2, 4(a)**

   (iv)   Which of the two Sources, **A** or **B**, do you think is right about Castlereagh and the Holy Alliance? Give reasons for your answer.   **4(a, b, c)**

(c)   **(i)**   Source **D** mentions 'the recent revolt of the Spanish army'. Using Source **E** for information, explain what had happened during the revolt.   **4(a)**

   (ii)   What evidence can you find in Source **D** to show whether Castlereagh approved or disapproved of the Spanish army revolt?   **4(a, b)**

   (iii)   According to Source **D**, what did Castlereagh think about

         A.   one state interfering in the internal affairs of another,
         B.   Britain interfering in Spain?

         In each case explain the reasons why Castlereagh held this opinion.   **4(a)**

(d)   **(i)**   In Source **E**, what is meant by the words:

         absolutist
         liberal constitution
         police state.   **1, 4(a)**

   (ii)   What impression do you get of the character of Ferdinand VII of Spain from reading Sources **D** and **E**?   **4(a, b, c)**

   (iii)   According to Source **E**, what action did the British government take to deal with the situation in Spain?   **4(a)**

   (iv)   From the evidence in Source **E**, do you think the British action was a success or a failure?   **4(a)**

(e)   **(i)**   Of the five Sources **A** to **E**, which are primary sources and which are secondary sources? Give reasons for your answer.

                                                                    1, 4(a)

   (ii)   Using the evidence in the Sources and your own knowledge, explain fully your reasons for agreeing or disagreeing with the statement about Castlereagh in the first sentence of Source **B** (in the period 1815 to 1822).   **1, 2, 4(a, b, c)**

2. The Battle of Navarino and the Greek Revolt

Read this extract written by a modern historian, and then answer the questions which follow.

> Admiral Codrington had instructions 'to prevent any Turkish or Egyptian help in men, arms, ships or ammunition arriving in Greece', but to use force only if the Turks 'insist on forcing a passage'. Realising more and more *the contradiction of two such orders*, he asked Stratford, the British ambassador at Constantinople for advice. Stratford gave the significant answer 'to avoid if possible anything that may verge on war, yet the prevention of supplies is to be enforced, if necessary, and when all other means are exhausted, by cannon shot'. This phrase was undoubtedly decisive. Codrington and de Rigny (the French admiral), obtained an interview with Ibrahim Pasha and gave him fair warning of their purpose and the consequences of resistance . . . Finally, five days after the arrival of the Russian ships, the allied fleet entered the harbour at Navarino. A dispute arose about anchorage, the boats of the *Dartmouth* were fired upon by the Turks, the infection spread, and soon a general action was in progress which ended in the complete destruction of the Turco–Egyptian fleet (20 October 1827). There will always be some controversy as to the real responsibility for the collision, but it is clear that Codrington was in some perplexity and relied upon Stratford's bold lead.

> Source: R. W. Seton-Watson, *Britain in Europe 1789-1914*, Cambridge, 1937.

(a)   (i)   Explain why Admiral Codrington's orders might be thought to be contradictory.   **1, 2, 4(a)**

    (ii)   Who was Ibrahim Pasha and what part did he play in the situation in Greece?   **1, 2, 4(a)**

    (iii)   Do you think the writer of this extract is sympathetic towards Codrington or not?   **4(a, b)**

    (iv)   From the evidence of this extract, who do you think was to blame for the start of the battle of Navarino?   **4(a, b)**

(b)   (i)   The extract mentions the arrival of Russian ships. Why were the Russians interested in the situation in Greece?   **1, 2, 4(a)**

    (ii)   Explain why Canning and the British government became involved in the Greek struggle for independence.   **1, 2**

(c)   (i)   Britain, Russia and France signed the Treaty of London (July 1827) in an attempt to deal with the situation in Greece. What did they agree to do?   **1, 2**

    (ii)   Explain why the Austrians and Prussians did not approve of this treaty.   **1, 2**

(d)   (i)   Why was the Battle of Navarino important for the situation in Greece?   **1, 2**

    (ii)   Explain why the Greek revolt was important for the future of the Congress System.   **1, 2**

    (iii)   Explain whether you think that British policy in the Near East was successful or not in the years 1827–30.   **1, 2, 4(a)**

3. (a)   What were Lord Castlereagh's aims in foreign affairs after the Congress of Vienna?

    (b)   What part did Castlereagh play at the Congress of Aix-la-Chapelle (1818)?

    (c)   Explain why Castlereagh disagreed with the other members of the Congress System from 1820 onwards.

    (d)   Make a list of Castlereagh's successes and failures as Foreign Minister from 1815 until his death in 1822.

    (e)   Why do you think Castlereagh was so unpopular at the time of his death?   **1, 2**

4.   Explain how and why Britain became involved in the following during the 1820s.

    (a)   affairs in Portugal,

    (b)   the Spanish colonies in Mexico and South America,

    (c)   the Greek revolt against Turkey.

    In each case explain whether Britain's involvement was successful or not.   **1, 2**

5.   It is 1827, shortly after the death of the Prime Minister, George Canning. You are the Member of Parliament chosen to make a speech paying tribute to Canning. Write a draft of the speech you intend to make. You can touch briefly on his faults and failures, but mainly you will be expected to concentrate on his achievements. You can refer to:

    (a)   his ways of doing things and how these were different from Castlereagh's,

    (b)   his involvement in Portugal and Spain,

    (c)   the Spanish colonies,

    (d)   the Greek revolt.

CHAPTER 4

PARLIAMENT AND THE
GREAT REFORM ACT
OF 1832

SUMMARY OF EVENTS

In 1830 the *agitation for a reform of parliament and the system of elections* burst out afresh after a lull from 1821 during a period of good trade and comparative prosperity. The demand for reform dated back into the middle of the previous century, but the new agitation seemed more widespread than before. This was shown by the general election held in the autumn of 1830, when candidates who favoured reform did well. Wellington, the Tory Prime Minister, saw no need to change the system, but the Whig government which came to power in November, decided to introduce a Reform Bill which would remedy some of the worst faults of the system.

It might be helpful here to outline briefly the *stages through which any proposed government measure has to pass before it becomes law.* The proposed changes are known as *a Bill;* this is read out in the House of Commons, printed and then given a second reading, after which the proposals are debated. A vote is taken and if a majority is in favour of the Bill, it passes to the committee stage; here a committee of between 30 and 50 MPs considers the details and if necessary, makes amendments. After this the Bill, along with the suggested changes, is read a third time and debated, and again a vote is taken. These votes are known as divisions because the members register their votes by moving into the lobbies of the House and dividing into two groups: those who approve of the Bill file back through one lobby, those against through another. A Bill which has passed all three readings in the Commons goes to the House of Lords where a similar procedure is followed. Until 1911 the Lords could reject any Bill they took exception to (except Finance Bills), even those which had passed the Commons with a comfortable majority. However, the Parliament Act of that year and a later one passed in 1949 reduced the powers of the Lords so that now they cannot interfere with Finance Bills and they can only delay other Bills for a maximum of one year (see Sections 20.3(c) and 28.1(a)). After its approval by the Lords, a Bill is sent to the monarch; if the monarch agrees to sign it, it is said to have become a law; it is now an Act of Parliament and is ready to be carried into operation.

The Whigs encountered many problems as they tried to steer their Reform Bill through these stages. It was defeated once in the Commons and twice in the Lords, but it eventually became law as the 1832 Reform Act or the Great Reform Act. After all the excitement, the reformers found that the terms of the Act were something of an anti-climax; several more Reform Acts were needed before Britain could be regarded as a genuinely democratic country.

4.1 WHAT WAS WRONG WITH THE SYSTEM BEFORE THE GREAT REFORM ACT?

Very few changes had been made since the eighteenth century, so that the system was completely out of date and took no account of the recent alterations and shifts in population caused by the Industrial Revolution. Though Britain was rapidly becoming an industrialised nation, parliament and therefore the running of the country were still dominated by land-owners.

(a) Constituencies were not organised to give fair and equal representation to all parts of the country. There were two types of constituency: *counties and boroughs*: there were 122 county MPs, 432 borough MPs, 100 from Ireland and two each from the universities of Oxford and Cambridge.

The absurdities were many:

(i) English and Irish counties were each represented by two MPs irrespective of size and population. Yorkshire, for example, had 17 000 electors while Rutland had only 609.

(ii) The Scottish and Welsh counties had only one MP each, and both Scotland (45 seats) and Wales (24 seats) were under-represented compared with England's 489 seats.

(iii) Most English borough constituencies had two MPs whereas those in Scotland, Wales and Ireland were allowed only one. Again the electorate (the group of people allowed to vote) varied widely: Westminster, Preston, Bristol, Leicester and Liverpool had over 5000 voters, while at the other end of the scale Old Sarum (Wiltshire) had seven, and Gatton (Surrey) had six. These tiny constituencies were known as *rotten boroughs*, because they had fallen into decay: Old Sarum was no more than a mound of earth, Gatton had dwindled into six houses, and Dunwich (Suffolk) which had once been a thriving community, had gradually fallen into the sea as the coast eroded away. Altogether there were 56 boroughs with fewer than 40 voters each, and each of them was represented in the House of Commons by two MPs.

(iv) Expanding industrial cities such as Birmingham, Manchester, Leeds and Sheffield had no MPs because they had not been boroughs in the late seventeenth century, when the last major redistribution of seats had taken place. Consequently the Midlands and North of England were greatly under-represented compared with the South: in 1831 Lancashire with a population of 1.3 million had only 14 MPs, while Cornwall with 300 000 people had 42 MPs.

(b) The franchise (right to vote) was restricted and haphazard. Women were not allowed to vote at all. *In county constituencies* the franchise was fairly straightforward: since 1430 men who owned freehold (land or property) worth 40 shillings had the vote; the fact that the value of money had declined meant that the county electorate was often larger than that in the boroughs. Sometimes the holders of certain church offices were considered to be freeholders – the bellringer at Westminster Abbey was allowed to vote in Middlesex. However, *borough constituencies varied widely and there were five main categories*:

(i) *Freeman boroughs* (Liverpool and Coventry) were the most common: here the vote went to all who had received the freedom of the city, usually by inheritance, by marrying the daughter or widow of a freeman, or by purchase.
(ii) *Burgage boroughs*: the vote to the owners of certain pieces of land or property; these usually had small electorates, e.g. Clitheroe (Lancashire) with fewer than 50 voters.
(iii) *Scot and lot boroughs*: the vote to all male householders who paid local rates; these varied in size from Westminster (over 5000 voters) to Gatton (six).
(iv) *Potwalloper boroughs*: the vote to all males who owned a house and fireplace to boil a pot on; some of these were large, e.g. Preston (over 5000 voters), Bedford and Northampton (over 1000 voters).
(v) *Corporation boroughs*: the vote only to members of the corporation; here the electorate was small: out of 29 such boroughs in England, 26 (including Andover, Bath, Portsmouth, Scarborough and Truro) had less than 50 voters.

What they all had in common was that the system of choosing their two MPs was not at all democratic. In the whole of England, only seven boroughs out of a total of 202 had more than 5000 voters each, while 56 had fewer than 50 voters each. In the whole of Britain, which had a population of around 24 million (1831 census) there were fewer than 500 000 voters.

(c) The way in which elections were carried out encouraged bribery and corruption.

(i) There was no secret ballot and votes were cast openly so that the candidates knew how each elector had voted. Electors often had little freedom, particularly if the candidate happened to be their landlord; there were many cases of tenants being evicted because they had dared to oppose the local squire.

(ii) In constituencies with large electorates, candidates resorted to outright bribery in the way of cash payments, jobs, government posts, contracts, and sometimes free beer. An election in Liverpool in 1830 cost the two candidates over £100 000 between them. The voting lasted the usual 15 days and the state of the contest was known from day to day. They were paying £15 a vote at the beginning, but on the last day, with the candidates neck and neck, each vote was costing £150.

(iii) In the very small borough constituencies, dealings were not quite so blatantly sordid. Usually there was no contest: the local landowner would nominate his MP and the handful of voters would approve, probably encouraged by a few gifts. *They were known as pocket boroughs* (or nomination boroughs) and were a valuable asset to their owners, who could sell the nomination to the highest bidder.

4.2 WHY DID THE DEMAND FOR REFORM REVIVE IN 1829-30?

There had always been a small group of Whig MPs in favour of moderate parliamentary reform. The Whig leader, Lord Grey, had come out in support of reform as far back as 1793; other prominent supporters included his son-in-law Lord Durham (known as 'Radical Jack'), Lord Brougham and Lord John Russell. By 1829-30 there were further pressures:

(a) The ever-increasing class of prosperous businessmen and manufacturers, though many of them were MPs, *resented the domination of parliament by landowners*. It seemed as though the latter protected their own interests with such measures as the Corn Laws, whereas the unfortunate manufacturers still had to pay duties on their raw materials; they felt that they were paying more than their fair share of taxes. Generally referred to as *the middle-class*, they wanted the system changing, not to one of complete democracy in which all adults had a vote, but just enough to give themselves a fair representation in the Commons.

(b) The passing of Catholic Emancipation in 1829 (see Section 2.7(b)) provided an added stimulus because it split and weakened the Tory party which was the chief enemy of reform. Some of the right wing Tories (Ultras) were so furious with Wellington that they came out in favour of reform just to spite him. They hoped to reduce the number of pocket boroughs, many of whose MPs had been used by Wellington to get Emancipation through.

(c) There was a sudden slump in the economy which hit both agriculture and industry. The effects were seen most dramatically in the Midlands and South of England where farm labourers' riots broke out in protest against irregular employment and low wages. In some areas disturbances were sparked off by the introduction of threshing machines which reduced the number of labourers needed; in others, workers were protesting against having to pay tithes (a tax of one-tenth of annual income, payable either in cash or produce, to the local vicar for the upkeep of the church). Beginning at Orpington (Kent) in June 1830 the outbreaks spread rapidly: burning of ricks and barns, smashing of threshing machines and attacks on parsons. There was a spate of threatening letters signed 'Swing' or 'Captain Swing' (apparently a reference to the swinging stick of the flail used in hand threshing). The new Whig government acted decisively to curb these *'Swing Riots'*; Lord Melbourne, the Home Secretary, set up special courts which tried nearly 2000 offenders. Nineteen were hanged, over 600 sent to gaol, and nearly 500 transported to Australia. By the summer of 1831 order had been restored, but the outbreaks had been alarming enough to convince many Whigs that moderate reform of parliament was the best way to avoid a revolution.

(d) In the North of England where *John Doherty* had founded a trade union for cotton spinners, strikes broke out in the Manchester area in protest at wage reductions. In October 1830 there was a coal strike at Oldham and miners began to join Doherty's union. The signs were ominous: a visitor at the opening of the Liverpool–Manchester Railway (September) noted: 'Tricolour flags (the French revolutionary standard) were displayed at some parts of the line. The spirit of the district was detestable'.

(e) Jeremy Bentham (see Section 2.1(c)) and his supporters (known as 'Philosophic Radicals') had been advocating reform of parliament for many years. In 1817 Bentham had published a pamphlet calling for annual general elections, secret ballots, and the vote for all males at 21. At first these were far too extreme for most people, but now some of them began to be taken up in unexpected quarters. *Thomas Attwood*, a Birmingham banker from a Tory background, founded *the Birmingham Political Union* (January 1830). 'The general distress which now affects the country,' he wrote, 'can only be permanently remedied by an effectual Reform in the Commons.' The Union aimed to unite middle and working classes; similar unions quickly appeared in London and other cities and later they organised themselves into a nationwide movement known as *the National Political Union*. It won the support of workers because it seemed the only peaceful way to achieve social reform.

(f) Revolutions in Europe were an important influence in Britain, particularly the one in France which overthrew King Charles X and put Louis Philippe on the throne (July 1830). Its main effect was probably to encourage the reformers and frighten many of the ruling classes (though not Wellington) into giving way.

(g) The reformers were fortunate that *George IV, who was against reform, died in June 1830*. His successor, William IV, was by no means enthusiastic but was prepared to go along with some changes. It was the practice to hold a general election on the accession of a new monarch. This took place in July–August 1830 and it was no surprise that reform candidates did well. When the Tory Prime Minister Wellington continued to hold to his view that the existing system was perfect, he was outvoted by a combination of Whigs and progressive Tories, and a Whig government was able to come into power.

4.3 WHY WAS THERE SO MUCH OPPOSITION TO REFORM?

It might appear that the case for reform was so strong that no sane-minded person could possibly oppose it. However, the system had plenty of vigorous supporters whose arguments and motives were:

(i)   It had worked well in the past and therefore there was no need to change it.

(ii)   Rotten boroughs were useful because they allowed both parties to introduce their promising up-and-coming young men into the Commons: they were also essential to provide seats for unpopular ministers.

(iii)   All the people who benefited in any way from the system were reluctant to have it changed; for example corporation members and freemen opposed an extension of the franchise because the more electors there were, the less they could expect to pick up in bribes.

(iv)   If the small boroughs were abolished, the resulting loss of the franchise would be an interference with the property rights of those people concerned; it would be like taking away someone's house or land, and once such practices were allowed, no property would be safe.

(v)   The majority of the Tories, though certainly not all of them, wanted to uphold the system because the nomination boroughs (pocket and some rotten boroughs) provided the basic core of their MPs (well over 200, whereas the Whigs had only about 70).

(vi)   Even small changes in the system must be restricted because they would encourage demands for more, and appetites would not be satisfied until full democracy had been introduced. This would upset the constitution and make the House of Commons more powerful than the Lords. This was why Peel was against reform: 'I was unwilling to open a door which I saw no prospect of being able to close'.

(vii)   Landowners were afraid that their interests would not be well served by a House of Commons dominated by the middle classes, particularly as some of the reformers were also advocating repeal of the Corn Laws.

4.4 THE PASSING OF THE BILL

Although the Whigs were well aware of the strength of Tory feelings, it is unlikely that they foresaw how bitterly they would fight the Reform Bill. Intead of taking a few weeks to pass, as they expected, it took 15 months, as well as riots, marches, and a general election before it became law. The stages were:

(i) Lord John Russell introduced the Bill (March 1831), which proposed, among other things, to abolish over a hundred rotten and pocket boroughs and to give their MPs to the industrial North and Midlands. It was greeted with jeers and howls of derision from the Tories, and though it passed its second reading in the Commons by a majority of one, the Tories were able to defeat it in the Committee stage.

(ii) The Prime Minister, Lord Grey, persuaded William IV to dissolve parliament and a general election followed (April). Naturally the Tories held on in their rotten and pocket boroughs, but in the counties, where the electorate was larger, the Whigs made sweeping gains and came back with a majority of 136.

(iii) Russell introduced a slightly different version of the Bill which passed the Commons with a comfortable majority of 109 (September). However, after a debate lasting five nights it was defeated in the Lords by a majority of 41, of whom 21 were bishops. There was an immediate outburst of public anger against the Lords, and *The Morning Chronicle* appeared with black borders as a sign of mourning for the Bill. There were riots at Derby and Nottingham, where the castle was destroyed (it was the property of the unpopular Duke of Newcastle who had expelled tenants for voting against his candidates). In Bristol rioters burned down the bishop's palace and other public buildings, and it took three troops of cavalry to restore order; at least 12 people were killed and around 400 seriously injured. Things were more orderly in Birmingham, but about 100 000 people attended Attwood's protest meeting; the Political Unions organised similar meetings all over the country. Several peers and bishops known to have voted against the Bill and even some who had not, were attacked by mobs, and the Duke of Wellington had his windows smashed (he retaliated by putting up iron shutters).

(iv) A third version of the Bill passed the Commons (March 1832) and two readings in the Lords, but in the Committee stage the Tories passed an amendment which could have weakened the Bill (May). Grey asked the King to create 50 new Whig peers, enough to give them a majority, but William refused, whereupon Grey resigned.

(v) With excitement in the country at a new climax, William invited Wellington to form a government. The Duke was prepared to do his duty and help the King: for six days he tried to form a cabinet, intending to introduce a much watered-down version of the Bill.

But most Tories regarded this as another Wellington betrayal, and when Peel refused to support him, the Duke had to admit failure.

(vi) Grey returned to office amid growing agitation. Attwood was urging non-payment of taxes and one MP wrote in his diary, 'the whole country is in a state little short of insurrection'. Now thoroughly alarmed, William agreed to create as many new peers as were necessary.

(vii) Seeing no way out, the Tory peers stayed away in large numbers, and there was no need for the King to create the peers. Consequently on 4 June 1832 the Bill passed its third reading in the Lords by 106 to 22, and on 7 June, it received the Royal Assent.

There is disagreement among historians as to how close Britain was to revolution during the Reform Bill crisis. The traditional view, which is also held by more recent writers such as E. P. Thompson, is that without the Reform Act there would almost certainly have been widespread revolution. According to Thompson, 'Britain was within an ace of revolution' and he goes on to argue that only the compromises and concessions provided by the Act averted full-scale revolt. On the other hand, the American J. Hamburger believes that the violent incidents were not as serious as historians have thought and that the danger was deliberately exaggerated by James Mill and other Radicals in order to frighten parliament into passing the Reform Bill. One of the main pieces of evidence to support his theory is that during the riots in Bristol the better-off working-class became so disgusted with the behaviour of the rioters (mostly unemployed labourers) that they ignored them and went home; if Britain had been genuinely on the verge of revolution, these riots should have acted as the starting pistol.

4.5 WHAT WERE THE TERMS OF THE ACT AND HOW FAR DID THEY PUT RIGHT THE FAULTS OF THE SYSTEM?

(a) **Terms**. The Act changed both the representation and the franchise:

(i) Boroughs with a population of less than 2000 (56 in all) lost both MPs.

(ii) Boroughs with a population of between 2000 and 4000 (31 in all) lost one MP.

(iii) This made 143 seats available for redistribution: 65 were given to the counties (e.g. Yorkshire received an extra two, giving it six in all); 65 were given to boroughs which had never had an MP (these included Leeds, Birmingham, Manchester, Sheffield, Bolton, Oldham and Bradford); eight were given to Scotland and five to Ireland. The total number of MPs in the Commons remained the same (658).

(iv) In borough constituencies the vote was given to the owners or occupiers of property rated at £10 a year or more.

(v) In county constituencies the vote was given to owners of copyhold land valued at £10 a year (copyholders were tenants whose families had held a particular piece of land for generations; the proof of their right to occupy the land was a copy of the original manorial court-roll entry which first allowed their ancestors to hold the land). The vote was also given to holders of land on long leases worth £10 a year, holders of land on short leases worth £50 year and to tenant farmers who paid £50 a year rent (40 shilling freeholders kept the vote).

(vi) Eligible voters had to register, i.e. have their names put on the electoral roll, for a fee of one shilling (5p).

(b) A few of the worst faults were remedied but many still remained:

(i) Rotten boroughs disappeared but *the constituencies* still varied enormously in size of electorate: there were 35 boroughs with less than 300 voters while Westminster now had 11 600 and Liverpool 11 300. Although the industrial towns were given MPs, the South was still over-represented: 370 MPs came from south of a line from the Wash to the Severn, whereas the area north of the line (excluding Scotland), which had a larger population, returned only 120. Scotland, Ireland and Wales continued to be under-represented compared with England.

(ii) *The electorate* increased from about 478 000 to 813 000 out of a total population of 24 million. However, this was a long way from being democratic: large sections of the population – agricultural labourers and the vast majority of industrial workers – still had no vote. Certain boroughs which already had something approaching a democratic franchise, had a smaller electorate than before; at Preston everyone who spent the night before the election in the town had been allowed to vote, but under the new system all the workers were excluded and the Radical Henry Hunt lost his seat as a result. The continuing unfairness of the new system was shown in another way: over Britain as a whole, one in seven adult males now enjoyed the vote; however, while this worked out at one in five in England, it was only one in eight in Scotland, and even worse, one in twenty in Ireland.

(iii) The Act did not introduce voting by secret ballot: consequently the corruption, bribery and 'influencing' of the voters continued unabated. John Hobhouse paid out a total of £6000 to encourage the electors of Nottingham to support him in the elections of 1834 and 1837. At Ipswich between £20 and £30 was being paid quite openly for one vote during the 1841 election (see *Pickwick Papers* for Dickens' hilarious description of a corrupt election, after 1832, in the imaginary borough of Eatanswill).

(iv) Some businessmen and industrialists came into the Commons, but the wealthy landowners still predominated. Many of the pocket boroughs had survived and there were at least 50 boroughs in England and Wales where some member of the local gentry could nominate the MP. In the counties the position of the landowners was strengthened by the fact that the tenant farmers who now had the vote felt obliged to support their candidates. Thus, as M. G. Brock remarks: 'Much the same men continued to run much the same system'. Since the position of the House of Lords remained unaffected, the Tory fears of being edged out of control were not justified, at least for the time being.

(c) Other results of the Great Reform Act were:

(i) The working classes were bitterly disappointed and began to look towards Trade Unionism and Chartism (see Sections 6 and 19).

(ii) The new registration of voters led the parties to form committees in the constituencies to keep the rolls up to date and to make sure of maximum support. In spite of some initial corruption (such as trying to remove known opponents from the list while keeping dead supporters on it), these committees were eventually to develop into the local party organisations, and so the party system was strengthened.

(iii) The disappearance of so many rotten boroughs reduced the crown's influence in politics.

(iv) The real importance of the Act turned out to be not the changes which it introduced, but the fact that it was the first breach in the system. Much to the disappointment of Grey and the Whigs who hoped it would be enough to satisfy appetites, it led to demands for further reform of parliament (satisfied in 1867 and 1884) and encouraged those who were advocating other types of reform - in factories, mines, poor law and local government.

QUESTIONS

1. The Campaign for Parliamentary Reform
Study Sources **A** to **G** and then answer the questions which follow.

Source A: A speech by Lord John Russell made in the House of Commons when he introduced his first Reform Bill, 1 March 1831:

What then would be the surprise of a stranger from afar if he were taken by his guide, whom he had asked to conduct him to one of the places of election, to a green mound, and told that this green mound sent two members to parliament. Or if he were shown a green park with many signs of flourishing vegetable life but none of human habitation, and told that this green park sent two members to parliament. But his surprise would increase to astonishment if he were carried into the North of England, where he would see large flourishing towns, full of trade and activity, and were told that these places had no representatives in the assembly which was said to represent the people. Thus the confidence which people used to have in the construction and constitution of the House of Commons is gone for ever. The whole people call loudly for reform.

Source: *Hansard*; quoted in L. Evans and P. J. Pledger, *Contemporary Sources and Opinions in Modern British History, vol I*, Warne, 1967 (adapted extracts).

Source B: From *The Extraordinary Black Book*, written to draw attention to the faults of the system; published 1831.

The great fount of evil is *the rotten boroughs*, from which has flowered national calamities, ruinous wars, lavish expenditure and enormous debt. They are the obstacle to every social improvement – civil, commercial, legal and ecclesiastical. By means of them the nobility have been able to double their private incomes and to fill every lucrative office in the army, navy and public administration with their friends and dependants . . . Because of the boroughs, all our institutions are oppressive and aristocratic . . . The aristocratic spirit pervades everything . . . all is privilege.

At Nottingham, one gentleman confessed to having paid out in the election of 1826, above £3000 in bribery in a single day . . . At Hull, one of the sitting members dared not appear before his constituents because he had not paid 'the polling money' for the last election.

Source: quoted in D. Holman (ed.), *Portraits and Documents: Earlier 19th Century*, Hutchinson 1965 (adapted extracts).

Source C: A speech by the Duke of Wellington in the House of Lords, 2 November 1830.

He was fully convinced that the country possessed at the present moment a *legislature* which answered all the good purposes of legislation, and this to a greater degree than any legislature had ever answered in any country whatever. He would go further and say that the legislature and the system of representation possessed the full and entire confidence of the country, and the discussions in the legislature had a very great influence over the opinions of the country . . . The representation of the people at present contained a large body of the property of the country and the landed interests which had a predominant place. Under these circumstances he was not prepared to bring forward any measure [of reform].

Source: *Hansard*; quoted in L. Evans and P. J. Pledger, *Contemporary Sources and Opinions in Modern British History, vol. I*, Warne, 1967 (adapted extracts).

Source D: English Boroughs in 1830.

Number of electors	Number of boroughs
Over 5000	7
1001–5000	36
601–1000	22
301–600	24
101–300	36
51–100	21
50 or fewer	56

Source: M. Brock, *The Great Reform Act*, Hutchinson, 1973.

Source E: Analysis of the House of Commons elected in 1830 – total number of MPs – 658.

Relations of peers	256
Placemen and pensioners	217
Officers in the army	89
Officers in the navy	24
Lawyers	54
East Indian Interests	62
West Indian Interests	35
Bankers	33
Agricultural interests	356
Miscellaneous	51

Source: *The Extraordinary Black Book*, 1831 (see Source **B**).

Source F: Report of a meeting held on Hunslet Moor (near Leeds), 20 September 1819.

It was resolved that a reform in the Constitution of the Commons House is an absolute necessity, the present corrupt system having nearly produced a disruption of society. Therefore in order to put an end to these great and national evils, we deem it vital that the present System of Electing Members to Parliament should be abolished and the Elective *Franchise* be extended to all persons who are called on to contribute, either by taxes or labour, to the support of the State, and that Elections be taken by the ballot annually.

Source: quoted in D. G. Wright, *Democracy and Reform 1815–1885*, Longman, 1970 (adapted extracts).

Source G: Speech by Sir Robert Peel in the House of Commons, 21 September 1831.

This bill (the Reform Bill) does not violate the forms of the *constitution* – I admit it, but I assert, that while it respects those forms, it destroys the balance of opposing powers; it is a sudden and violent transfer of an authority which has until now been shared by all orders in the state, exclusively to one.

Source: *Hansard*; quoted in D. G. Wright (see Source **F**).

(a) (i) Explain what is meant in Source **B** by the phrase 'rotten borough'.   **1, 4(a)**

(ii) Make a list of criticisms of the existing system of elections and representation in parliament put forward in Sources **A** and **B**.   **4(a)**

(b) Make a careful study of the statistics in Source **D**.

(i) Roughly what percentage of English boroughs contained fewer than 50 voters: 25 per cent, 40 per cent or 50 per cent?   **4(a)**

(ii) Roughly what percentage of English boroughs contained between 100 and 1000 voters: 25 per cent, 35 per cent or 60 per cent?   **4(a)**

(iii) What evidence is there in Source **D** which supports the criticisms made in Sources **A** and **B**?   **4(a, c)**

(c) Look carefully at the statistics in Source **E**.

(i) Which was the largest group in the House of Commons?   **4(a)**

(ii) How do you explain the fact that the list given in Source **E** adds up to 1177, yet there were only 658 MPs in the Commons?   **2, 4(a)**

(iii) Do you think the statistics in Source **E** support the criticisms of the system made in Sources **A** and **B** or not? Explain your answer fully.   **4(a, c)**

(d) (i) In Source **F**, what is meant by the word 'Franchise'?   **1, 4(a)**

(ii) What changes does the writer of Source **F** think were needed?   **4(a)**

(e) (i) In Source **C**, what is meant by the word 'legislature'?   **1, 4(a)**

(ii) What important position did the Duke of Wellington hold when he made this speech?   **1, 4(a)**

(iii) What reasons does Wellington give in Source **C** for his opposition to the reform of parliament?   **4(a)**

(iv) Do you think Source **C** contradicts Sources **A** and **B** completely or can you find any point of agreement?   **4(a, c)**

(f) (i) In Source **G**, explain what is meant by the word 'constitution'.   **1, 4(a)**

(ii) Do you think the speaker in Source **G** was a supporter or an opponent of a reform of parliament? Explain your answer fully.   **4(a, b)**

(g) (i) Make a list of the main terms of the 1832 Reform Act.   **1**

(ii) Do you think the writer of Source **F** would have been pleased with the changes brought in by the 1832 Reform Act? Give reasons for your answer.   **1, 2, 4(a, c)**

2. The Struggle to Pass the 1832 Reform Bill

Study Sources A to D and then answer the questions which follow.

Source A: A passage by a modern historian, Michael Brock.

> Grey and Brougham left for Windsor to see the king and drove so hard leaving Hounslow that they ran into another carriage and broke its pole. They presented the cabinet request for the king to create 50 or 60 new peers and were promised an answer next morning. Early next morning (9 May 1832), they learned that their request had been refused and Grey therefore resigned . . . The next three days were spent in a frantic search for a new Prime Minister . . . However, the king made it clear that he chose Wellington.

> Source: M. Brock, *The Great Reform Act*, Hutchinson, 1973 (adapted extracts).

Source B: Report of a meeting held in London on 12 May 1832.

> The persons present were all men of substance; some were very rich men. It was clearly understood that in the event of Lord Wellington forming an administration, all resistance should at once be made and in the meantime all that could be done should be done to prevent such an administration from being formed.

> Source: quoted in G. Wallas, *Place*, Allen & Unwin, 1898.

Source C: A newspaper article, 12 May 1832.

> Orders were cancelled, buyers from a distance went or were recalled home, without making their purchases; and a large number of our manufacturers and warehousemen state that, for anything they really have to do, they might just as well close their establishments.

> Source: *Manchester Guardian*, 12 May 1832 (adapted extract).

Source D: More information from Michael Brock.

> A disturbance to trade on this scale was bound to arouse fears for the stability of the banking system. By 13 May much of London was placarded with the slogan:
>
> To Stop the Duke
Go for Gold.
>
> It was feared that the banks might soon stop payment . . . *The Morning Herald* reported that some of the soldiers in Birmingham had joined the Political Union. 'The whole country', wrote Littleton in his diary, 'is in a state little short of revolution . . .'. The Duke was prompt to recognise defeat. 'The King had better send for Lord Grey at once', he said.

> Source: M. Brock, *The Great Reform Act*, Hutchinson, 1973 (adapted extracts).

(a) (i) What important position did Grey hold when he went to Windsor (Source **A**)? **4(a)**

(ii) Why did Grey and Brougham want the king to create new peers? **1, 2, 4(a)**

(iii) What evidence is there in Source **A** to suggest that the matter was very urgent? **4(a)**

(iv) Why did Grey resign? **1, 2, 4(a)**

(v) Why do you think the king wanted Wellington as Prime Minister? **1, 2**

(b) (i) Why do you think that the people at the meeting in Source **B** did not want Wellington to form a government? **1, 2**

(ii) In Source **B**, what do the words 'some were very rich men' tell you about the campaign for parliamentary reform? **1, 2, 4(a)**

(c) (i) Using the evidence in Sources **C** and **D**, describe how some people tried to stop Wellington forming a government. **4(a, c)**

(ii) Explain in your own words how these actions were expected to stop the Duke. **2, 4(a, c)**

(d) (i) Explain why the Duke of Wellington 'accepted defeat' (Source **D**). **2, 4(a, c)**

(ii) What do you think Wellington meant when he said 'the king had better send for Lord Grey' (Source **D**)? **2, 4(a)**

(e) (i) Describe in your own words what happened in parliament during the next four weeks after the king had sent for Lord Grey.

(ii) Using your own knowledge, discuss whether or not you agree with the statement in Source **D** that at this time the whole country was 'in a state little short of revolution'. **1, 2, 4(a)**

3. (a) What were the main criticisms made of the voting system and representation in parliament before 1832?

(b) Show how the following helped to revive the demand for reform of parliament in 1828–30:

(i) Catholic Emancipation (1829);

(ii) the economic slump;

(iii) Thomas Attwood;

(iv) Revolution in Europe;

(v) the death of George IV. **1, 2**

4. (a) Explain why there was a great deal of opposition to the reform of parliament before the passing of the 1832 Reform Act.

(b) Make a list of the main changes brought in by the 1832 Reform Act.

(c) How far did these changes put right the faults of the system? **1, 2**

5. It is 1830 and you are a Whig member of parliament who has made a careful study of the constituencies and the system of voting and representation. This has convinced you of the need for parliamentary reform. Write a speech in which you set out the evidence you have collected in an attempt to win the House of Commons over to your opinion.   1, 2, 3

CHAPTER 5

WHIG REFORMS AND
FAILURES 1833–41

SUMMARY OF EVENTS

Following the Great Reform Act a general election was held in which the Whigs won a large majority (December 1832). They remained in office, except for two short breaks, until the Tory victory in the general election of 1841. Grey remained Prime Minister until 1834 when, at the age of 70, he resigned, partly because he felt that his main ambition - to introduce a moderate reform of parliament - had been achieved, and partly because there was a split in the cabinet about how to deal with the continuing unrest in Ireland. The 55-year-old *William Lamb, Lord Melbourne*, took over the premiership.

Almost immediately William IV, tired of the Whig reforms, dismissed the government and invited Peel to form a ministry, even though the Tories lacked a majority in the Commons. A general election had to be held (January 1835) and although the Tories gained many seats, Peel was well short of a majority. Nevertheless he was Prime Minister from December 1834 until April 1835 (known as 'Peel's 100 days'), but was repeatedly defeated and forced to resign. William had no choice but to recall Melbourne and the government which he had sacked; this demonstrated that the traditional practice, of the Commons supporting whatever Prime Minister the King wanted, no longer applied; it was one of the by-products of the Great Reform Act and it meant that the monarch would from then on play less and less part in politics.

William IV died in 1837 and was succeeded by *Queen Victoria*, the daughter of his deceased younger brother, Edward, Duke of Kent. The usual general election took place after the death of the monarch, though this was the last time the custom was followed. The Whig majority was greatly reduced, and in May 1839 Melbourne resigned after his government had secured a majority of only five votes in an important division. This dismayed Victoria who had found Melbourne most helpful and sympathetic when she had taken over the throne at the tender and inexperienced age of 18, and who looked on the Whigs as her friends. It was assumed that Peel would form a government, but an odd incident occurred, which became known as the *Bedchamber Crisis*. Peel, cautious about taking office again without a majority, asked Victoria to remove some of the leading ladies of the Queen's household who were related to the former Whig ministers, and replace them with Tory ladies. Victoria refused, whereupon Peel abandoned the idea of forming a government, and Melbourne returned yet again, for a further two years as Prime Minister. In 1840 Victoria married her cousin, *Prince Albert of Saxe-Coburg*, and became less dependent on Melbourne.

Though Melbourne himself was not interested in change, *the Whigs were responsible for some important reforms*, particularly in the early part of the ministry before they began to run out of steam. There was the abolition of slavery, attempts to improve factory conditions, grants for education, and reforms of the Poor Law and of town government. At the same time the Whig Foreign Secretary, *Lord Palmerston*, conducted a successful and popular overseas policy (see Section 9). On the other hand, *there were problems which the Whigs seemed incapable of understanding*: unrest among the unemployed, the Chartist movement, trade depressions and a failure to balance their budgets, which all help to explain the Whig defeat in 1841.

5.1 THE WHIG ATTITUDE TO REFORM

Most of the members of the Whig government, wealthy aristocrats, seemed to think that the Great Reform Act was the one gesture towards reform that they were required to make; left to themselves, they would have been quite content to meander along without taking any further positive action. Melbourne himself, though amiable and cultured, was against nearly all the reforms being discussed. 'I am for holding the ground already taken,' he remarked, 'but not for occupying new ground rashly.' He claimed that passing new laws was only an incidental duty of governments and believed that there were no really serious problems to be solved. Two of the most progressive Whigs, Lords Brougham and Durham were dropped from the cabinet in 1835.

However, the government came under considerable pressure from several directions to keep up the flow of reforming measures:

(a) The Benthamite Radicals. The ideas of Jeremy Bentham had enormous influence (see Section 2.1(c)). Ever since the publication of his first pamphlet in 1776, Bentham had persevered with his doctrine of *Utilitarianism*: the acid test of all laws and institutions should be – are they efficient and useful? If not, they must be changed or destroyed. He must take some of the credit for the Great Reform Act; once that had been achieved, why should governments not continue to give way to pressure and concede reform in other areas of inefficiency? Although Bentham himself died in 1832 just before the Reform Bill passed, his followers kept up the pressure, publishing reports and recommendations and harassing the Whigs. The most important were *Edwin Chadwick* who produced reports on the poor law, public health and the police, and *Joseph Parkes* who investigated the defects of town government. On the other hand, many Radicals were not enthusiastic about factory reform, since they were themselves factory-owners and did not approve of government interference.

(b) The Humanitarian Movement. This was composed of people from many different spheres of life, who all had one aim in common – to improve the living and working conditions of the working classes. They were supported by *the Evangelical Movement* of the Church of England, a group which felt that the Church was not showing enough concern for the plight of ordinary people, and was consequently losing support to the Methodists. Many Humanitarians were Tories: for example William Wilberforce, leader of the anti-slavery movement; Michael Sadler and Lord Ashley (later Lord Shaftesbury), factory reform campaigners, were Tory MPs as well as Evangelicals.

(c) Some progressive factory-owners such as Robert Owen and John Fielden (see Section 12.3(g)) demonstrated that better conditions and shorter working hours increased rather than reduced output, and tried to influence other industrialists as well as governments to follow their example.

5.2 WHAT REFORMS WERE INTRODUCED BY THE WHIG GOVERN-MENTS BETWEEN 1833 AND 1841? WHY WERE THEY NECES-SARY AND HOW SUCCESSFUL DID THEY PROVE TO BE?

(a) The Abolition of Slavery in the British Empire (1833)

(i) *The problem* was that although the slave trade had been prohibited in 1807 by the British government, after a long campaign led by the humanitarian Tory MP *William Wilberforce*, slavery itself was allowed to continue. This encouraged the smuggling of slaves who continued to be shipped across the Atlantic in appalling conditions, traders cramming as many slaves as possible into their ships. There were 670 000 slaves in the West Indies alone. In 1821 Wilberforce brought out a pamphlet explaining the arguments in favour of abolition and in 1823 *T. F. Buxton*, a Tory MP, founded *the Anti-slavery Society*. In 1833, the Whig Colonial Secretary, Lord Stanley, introduced an Emancipation Bill.

(ii) There was *a good deal of opposition to the Bill*, particularly from the owners of sugar plantations in the West Indies and from merchants involved in the sugar trade: abolition would mean loss of property (a good slave might be worth around £50); there would be a labour shortage which would push up production costs to the advantage of competitors in the USA who would still have their slaves; and there was the fear of unrest and disturbances if former slaves ran riot after gaining their freedom. Many MPs had money in sugar production and trade: W. E. Gladstone's father was a sugar merchant in Liverpool, and he gave his son, newly elected to parliament in 1833, strict instructions to vote against the Bill.

(iii) *The terms of the Act*, which passed with a large majority, were:

- All slaves were to be set free within a year, and were then to serve apprenticeships of up to seven years to their former owners; this was to ease the transition from a slave economy to a wage-earner system.
- The government paid £20 million compensation to the slave-owners.

(iv) *The Act was successful* in the sense that it put right a moral wrong, though it caused problems in certain areas. Planters complained that the compensation was insufficient, and many went out of business. In Jamaica and Guiana, freed slaves preferred to settle in villages of their own instead of working on the plantations, leading to labour shortages and high wages; this contributed towards a general depression in the West Indies. In Cape Colony (South Africa) many Boers, convinced that farming would be unprofitable without slaves, decided to leave and embarked on the Great Trek (see Section 14.3(c)). Nowhere was anything done to enable the slaves to make good use of their freedom; instead Negroes remained illiterate and exploited.

(b) Althorp's Factory Act (1833) was the first effective attempt at factory regulation (for full details see Section 12.3(d)).

(c) The first government grant for education (1833)

(i) Having stipulated in Althorp's Act that children ought to receive at least two hours schooling a day, the government felt it ought to try and make this possible. There were no state schools and the only education for the masses was provided by two rival religious bodies or voluntary societies, one Anglican, one Nonconformist. In 1833 the government gave its first annual grant of £20000 to be divided between the two societies; this was increased to £30000 in 1839, and the Privy Council was to keep an eye on how the money was spent (in fact most of it went on building new schools).

(ii) The grants established an important principle: that the state should accept some responsibility for educating the poor. On the other hand, the amounts of cash involved were pitifully small and the system remained totally inadequate. Bentham's proposal that the government should set up its own system separate from the voluntary societies was ignored; consequently religious rivalry continued to be an unfortunate feature of the haphazard system.

(d) The Poor Law Amendment Act (1834)

(i) *What was wrong with the existing provision for the poor?*
- The system dated back to the late sixteenth century: each parish was expected to look after its own poor, and it became the traditional practice for paupers (people who were so poor that they were unable to support themselves) to be sent back to the parish of their birth. The cash to provide relief for the poor came from a special rate paid by the inhabitants of the parish. The 1601 Poor Law Act had classified paupers into three groups: those who could not find work (able-bodied poor), those who were too ill, too young or too old to work (impotent poor) and those who refused to work (idle poor). In practice the system varied widely throughout the 15 000 parishes: in some parishes relief payments were made to the poor at home; during the eighteenth century it became more common for relief to be given to all types of poor only inside the parish workhouse. From the late eighteenth century onwards however, the system was unable to cope with the vastly increasing numbers of poor during periods of unemployment and low wages.
- *The Speenhamland System* adopted in the South after 1795 was a well-meaning attempt to deal with the problem but it made the situation worse (see Section 2.2(a)(ii)). Depending on the size of a labourer's family and the price of bread, relief payments were made out of the parish poor rates to supplement low wages. However, this type of *outdoor relief*, as it was known (as opposed to *indoor relief* given in the workhouse) encouraged employers to lower wages still further. In addition it introduced a new principle: poor relief was originally intended for people who, whatever the reason, were out of work; now it was having to cope with people who were in jobs. This placed a tremendous burden on the parish, much to the disgust of the people who had to pay the ever-increasing rates. In 1795 the total money spent by the 15 000 parishes on poor relief was £2 million; in 1830 it was not far short of £8 million.
- *The Swing Riots* of 1830-1 (see Section 4.2(c)) highlighted the complete breakdown of the system and frightened the government into taking some action.

(ii) *A Commission was appointed* to investigate the working of poor relief (February 1832). Its main objective was to find ways of saving money on the poor rates rather than to ease the plight of the poor, which the Humanitarians wanted. The most influential member of the Commission was *Edwin Chadwick*, a Manchester lawyer and a fanatical Benthamite. He was determined that the system should be made uniform and efficient so that it gave value for money. The Commission's Report (February 1834) condemned outdoor relief: 'every penny bestowed ... is a bounty to indolence and vice'. It also disapproved of the slack way in which many workhouses were run: able-bodied poor were being kept at the parish's expense 'in sluggish sensual indolence'. Their recommendations became the 1834 Act, which, according to Chadwick himself was like 'a cold bath – unpleasant in contemplation but invigorating in its effects'.

(iii) *Terms of the Act:*

- Outdoor relief would no longer be provided for the able-bodied poor, though in some cases help would continue to be given to the sick and aged at home.
- For the able-bodied poor, and also for the impotent poor who could not be helped at home, relief would be provided in workhouses.
- In order to make larger and more efficient units, parishes were to be grouped into Unions. It was intended that each Union would contain separate workhouses for the able-bodied, impotent and idle poor.
- Conditions in workhouses were to be made as unattractive as possible, so that the poor would make every effort to find work and only come to the workhouse as a last resort. Existence in the workhouse had to be more miserable than the life of the poorest labourer outside. This would encourage 'self-help' and prevent the poor from looking on the workhouse as a haven of refuge; it was known as the *'less eligibility'* principle.
- Each Union was to have paid officials to operate the system; they were to be appointed by the unpaid Board of Commissioners and their secretary, Edwin Chadwick.

(iv) *How successful was it?* The new system was a success in the narrow sense that it helped to reduce the poor rates. Between 1830–4 the average annual expenditure on poor relief had been around £7 million; between 1835–9 it averaged only £4.5 million. Thus the Benthamites saw it as an ideal reform and it was popular with the majority of ratepayers. However, in every other respect the Act aroused the most bitter criticism, both from the working classes who suffered hardship from it, and from the Humanitarians who thought it cruel and cold-blooded. Most newspapers were severely critical, and there was a flood of pamphlets and petitions, as well as hostile demonstrations and attacks on workhouses and Guardians. *The main criticisms were:*

- The new system ignored the causes of poverty and unemployment and assumed that to be poor was always the fault of the pauper – lack of initiative, laziness or drunkeness; people would be able to find jobs if they tried hard enough. Unfortunately this theory made no allowances for the regular trade recessions and slumps which caused unemployment.
- The stoppage of outdoor relief for the able-bodied poor caused great hardship in the South. Thousands of labourers in full-time work were not receiving a living wage, and wives and children had

to take whatever work they could get in the fields to avoid starvation. The situation would have been much worse had it not been for a series of good harvests, which kept bread prices low, and railway building which provided extra jobs.

- In the industrial North it proved impossible to stop giving outdoor relief. Unfortunately for all concerned there was a trade recession during 1837-8 just when the Commissioners began applying the Act in those areas. Outdoor relief was essential as an unemployment pay if workers were not to starve in their thousands, and there were far too many to be accommodated in the workhouses. In Huddersfield a mob organised by Richard Oastler, a local Tory Evangelical, gate-crashed the first meeting of the new Board of Guardians and chased them off; it was a further two years before they were able to begin operating. At Bradford the Guardians had to be protected by cavalry, while at Todmorden on the Lancashire-Yorkshire boundary, John Fielden, a mill-owner, led a campaign to boycott the election of Guardians. Police constables were attacked and troops had to be quartered in the town to keep order. Not until 1897 was a workhouse built in Todmorden. At Colne nobody could be found to act as Guardians.

- Although by 1838 over 13 400 of the 15 000 parishes had been grouped into 573 Unions, in the majority of them it proved too expensive to provide separate workhouses; consequently all types of poor, including children, were herded together with criminals, prostitutes and lunatics. As Dickens showed in *Oliver Twist*, conditions were poor. Some historians have suggested that opponents of the new poor law deliberately exaggerated the worst features of workhouse life, and that conditions were in reality fairly tolerable. But it seems certain that during the first 15 years at least, workhouse life was harsh. Husbands and wives were separated (this was relaxed in 1842), children were separated from parents, meals had to be eaten in silence and diets were sparse; jobs provided - stone-breaking, bone-grinding and picking old rope to pieces - were either back-breaking or painful on the fingers. There was a famous scandal in Andover workhouse when the inmates, working on bone-crushing, were so hungry that they were found to be eating rotting marrow and fat from the bones. No wonder workhouses became known among the workers as Bastilles (after the notorious fortress-prison in Paris).

Thus the new poor law did not end poverty and consequently thousands of workers were driven to support Chartism (see Chapter 6). Although conditions in workhouses improved gradually during the 1850s, they were always viewed by the poor with the greatest fear and suspicion.

illus 5.1 *The women's yard of a workhouse*

(e) The Municipal Corporations Act 1835

(i) *Why was reform needed?* The government and running of towns was
confused and inefficient. There were about 250 boroughs each with its
own corporation (mayor, councillors and aldermen) which ran the
town's affairs. There were wide variations in how the corporations
were chosen and how they functioned, but the disturbing feature
was that in 186 of them, only the members of the corporation itself
were allowed to vote; they normally re-elected themselves or brought
relatives or friends on to the council. These small cliques (known as
closed corporations) fixed the local bye-laws and taxes and it was
impossible for the mass of the ratepayers to get rid of unpopular
councils by voting them out. Most of the corporations used their

privileges for personal and party advantage (the majority were Tories) and ignored matters such as water supply, drainage and street cleansing which they were supposed to look after. Even more ludicrous was the fact that most of the newly expanded industrial towns had not been recognised as boroughs and had no corporation at all. Here living conditions in overcrowded slums were a threat to public health; in 1831-2 there was a cholera epidemic which began at Sunderland and spread across the country causing thousands of deaths (see Section 12.5(c)). It was perhaps inevitable that once the Whigs had accepted the principle of parliamentary reform, local government reform would soon follow.

(ii) Following the same procedure as with the Poor Law, the Whigs appointed a Royal Commission to investigate the problem (July 1833). The Commission secretary, *Joseph Parkes*, a Radical lawyer, was determined to act quickly: 285 towns were investigated, most of which were found to be unsatisfactory. Consequently, with the help of Parkes, a Bill was drawn up and introduced into the Commons by Lord John Russell (June 1835). It became law in September 1835.

(iii) *Terms of the Act:*

- The closed corporations were abolished; borough councils were to be elected by all the male ratepayers who had lived in the town for three years.
- Councillors were elected for three years, one-third to be elected annually.
- Councillors would choose the mayor (to hold office for one year) and a group of aldermen (for six years).
- Each borough was to have a paid town clerk and treasurer and accounts were to be properly audited.
- It was compulsory for councils to form a police force; councils were allowed, if they so desired, to take over social improvements such as proper drainage and street cleansing.
- Towns and cities which had no councils could apply to become boroughs.

(iv) *There was plenty of opposition to the Bill.* It went through the Commons smoothly enough but received a rough ride in the Lords. Since most of the closed corporations were controlled by Tories, the Tory peers claimed that the Bill was an attack on personal privileges and property, in the same category as the abolition of rotten boroughs; it was a further step in the destruction of the constitution. However, although some amendments were made to the Bill, Peel and Wellington restrained the Tory peers from throwing it out altogether.

(v) *How successful was it?* There was a marked improvement over the previous haphazard and disorganised system, and the Act established the principle of elected town councils. At the same time *there were several failings*:

- By making it optional instead of compulsory for the new councils to make social improvements, the Act missed an opportunity to do something positive about the awful conditions in most towns. By 1848 only 29 boroughs had taken any action. One reason for this was that ratepayers were often interested only in keeping the rates down.
- Many towns failed to apply to become boroughs because the procedure was complicated and expensive. In 1848 there were still 62 large towns without councils.
- Although it was more democractic than before, it was mainly of benefit to the middle classes; very few working men were wealthy enough to be ratepayers.

However, although progress was slow, the Act did at least set up the machinery which would enable future social and health reforms to be carried out effectively in the towns.

(f) Other Whig reforms. There were a number of less spectacular but none the less important changes:

(i) *The compulsory registration of births, marriages and deaths (1836)*, a typical Benthamite measure, was extremely important: without it, it would have been impossible to apply the Factory Acts which sought to protect children and young people who could now rely on their birth certificates to prove their age.

(ii) Two measures did something to reduce Nonconformist resentment against the powers and privileges of the Church of England. *The Marriage Act* (1836) recognised marriages in Nonconformist chapels and Catholic churches as legal, provided that a civil registrar was there. *The Tithe Commutation Act* (1836) replaced the tithe (a tax of one-tenth of annual produce to be paid to the church) with a cash rent; though this was a move in the right direction, non-Anglicans felt it should have been abolished altogether. The Act was popular with the Irish peasants who tended to come off better with a fixed money rent, and it helped to keep Ireland fairly peaceful until 1841.

(iii) *Limited Liability Companies were permitted (1836)*. These were companies in which the shareholders did not have to pay the full losses if the company went bankrupt. This encouraged investment and proved to be an enormous boost to the spread of railways. The government sanctioned 1500 miles of new railway in 1836-7 and in 1838 the first main line was opened between London and Birmingham.

(iv) *The Penny Post* was introduced in 1840, the brainchild of Rowland Hill. He managed to convince the Whigs that the existing letter post in which charges were made according to the weight of the letter or parcel and the distance it travelled was actually losing the Post Office money; time was wasted while the postman waited at every house for payment. Hill's suggestions were adopted: the fee was to be paid in advance by means of an adhesive stamp; the charge was one penny for a half ounce letter. The Post Office objected, but Hill was proved right: business soared and so eventually did profits (though the scheme lost heavily for the first few years); the new system was swift and efficient.

5.3 WHY DID THE WHIGS LOSE THE 1841 ELECTION?

The Whigs had a number of failures and showed a fatal lack of understanding in certain areas, all of which contributed to their defeat:

(a) They showed no real understanding of the causes of unemployment in industry and agriculture and fell back on repression. The first instance of this occurred with the Swing Riots (1830-1) and there were several more. When working people began to join Robert Owen's Grand National Consolidated Trades Union (founded 1833) in their thousands, the government decided to make an example of six farm labourers from the village of Tolpuddle (Dorset) who had started their own union. They were sentenced to seven years' transportation for having sworn an illegal oath (1834). The GNCTU soon collapsed in the face of determined government opposition (for full details see Section 19.2).

(b) Important Whig reforms slowed to a mere trickle after 1835. This was partly because of Melbourne's unprogressive attitude and partly because their Commons majority was dwindling all the time. But the unpopular fact remained that the Whigs did nothing to improve either the appalling working conditions in mines or the unhealthy social conditions in towns. Hardly anything was done to continue Huskisson's commercial reforms, yet there was still a long way to go before Free Trade was achieved. As a result trade seemed to be stagnating.

(c) Further working class hostility was aroused when the government, already unpopular because of the harshness of the new poor law, rejected the first Chartist petition in 1839 (see Chapter 6). By the middle of 1841 Britain was moving into a serious depression; Manchester cotton mills were soon to be at a standstill and in Birmingham almost 100 000 people were being given poor relief. Just before the election Feargus O'Connor, one of the Chartist leaders, instructed all Chartists who had a vote to support the Tories as a protest against the Whig poor law.

(d) Whereas the Whigs failed to produce an attractive programme, the Tories were united under the leadership of Peel. Their promising new programme had appeared in 1834 as the Tamworth Manifesto (see Section 7.1(b)). Peel's reputation had grown during his ten years in opposition, and it was known that he had plans for encouraging trade and industry and therefore employment. The Tories (now known as Conservatives) seemed more likely to be able to deal successfully with the country's emergency than the tired and jaded Whigs.

It was no surprise when the Conservatives won the general election of June 1841, emerging with a comfortable majority of over 70.

QUESTIONS

1. Poor Law Reform
Study Sources **A** to **G** and then answer the questions which follow.

Source A: A letter to a newspaper by George Nicholls, Overseer of the Poor at Southwell (Nottinghamshire) 1822.

> Instead of giving way to the impulse of our feelings, by giving relief when something like distress approaches us, the overseers must resolutely refuse all parochial aid, except relief to the aged, infirm and impotent . . .
>
> The poor house ought to be so conducted as that the labouring part of the community might not see it as being better furnished, better provided, more comfortable than their homes. They should not, in winter, see all its chimneys cheerfully smoking, when their own homes are cold . . . nor all comforts filling the abode of the pauper, when their own habitations presented scenes of want and wretchedness. The dread of a poor house has decreased in about the same ratio that pauperism has increased, owing to the humane and well-meant endeavour to improve these receptacles, which are now so generally converted into abodes of comfort and even of apparent elegance. I wish to see the poor house looked to with dread by our labouring classes and the reproach for being an inmate of it extended downwards from father to son. Let the poor see and feel that their parish, although it will not allow them to perish from absolute want, is yet the hardest taskmaster and the most harsh and unkind friend they can apply to.
>
> Source: quoted in N. Longmate, *The Workhouse*, Maurice Temple Smith, 1969 (adapted extracts).

Source B: A report by Sir Francis Head after a tour of workhouses in Kent, 1832.

> The River Workhouse, on the old Dover Road, is a splendid mansion. The dignity and elegance of its architecture, its broad double staircase, its spacious halls, the lofty bedrooms and its large windows form 'a delightful retreat', splendidly contrasted with the mean little rate-paying hovels at its feet . . .
>
> In the smaller workhouses, minute classification has been found impossible. All that can be done is to put the males of all ages into one room and all the females into another. In either case the old are teased by the children who are growled at until they become cowed into silence . . . In one workhouse I saw a room full of sturdy labourers sitting round a stove with

their faces scorched and half-roasted. As we passed them they never rose from their seats and had generally an over-fed, a mutinous and an insubordinate appearance.

Source: quoted in N. Longmate, *The Workhouse*, Maurice Temple Smith, 1969 (adapted extracts).

Source C: Recommendations of the Royal Commission on the Poor Laws, 1834.

The first and most essential of all conditions is that his situation on the whole shall not be made as eligible as the situation of the independent labourer of the lowest class. Throughout the evidence it is shown that in proportion as the pauper class is elevated above the condition of independent labourers, the condition of the independent class is depressed; their industry is impaired, their employment becomes unsteady and its recompense in wages is diminished. Such persons therefore are under the strongest inducement to quit the less eligible class of labourers and enter the more eligible class of paupers. The converse is the effect when the pauper class is placed in its proper position, below the condition of the independent labourer.

The chief measures which are recommended are:

First, that except as to medical attendance, all relief whatever to able-bodied persons or to their families, otherwise than in well-regulated workhouses, shall be declared unlawful and shall cease . . . All who receive relief from the parish should work for the parish exclusively, as hard and for less wages than independent labourers work for individual employers.

Source: quoted in L. Evans and P. J. Pledger, *Contemporary Sources and Opinions in Modern British History, vol. I*, Warne, 1967 (adapted extracts).

Source D: Table showing relief paid in the 14 parishes of Stow (Suffolk).

Parish	Outdoor relief		Population		Parish	Outdoor relief		Population	
	1833	1840	1831	1841		1833	1840	1831	1841
	£	£				£	£		
Buxhall	253	163	466	533	Stowmarket	813	439	2,672	3,043
Combs	338	229	950	1,964	Stow Upland	220	129	826	903
Creeting	115	81	166	213	Wetherden	284	208	487	515
Gt. Finborough	254	100	421	467					
Lt. Finborough	3	0	73	64	Totals	£3,177	£1,829	8,308	8,765
Gipping	140	71	87	93					
Harlston	67	35	89	90					
Hawleigh	232	121	908	916					
Old Newton	322	170	679	712					
Onehouse	84	60	358	43					
Shelland	52	23	126	109					

Source: quoted in R. Watson, *Edwin Chadwick, Poor Law and Public Health*, Longman, 1969.

Source E: Report of a meeting of Poor Law Guardians at Stow in 1837.

The Board have now been acting in the execution of the Poor Law Amendment Act more than twelve months and think themselves justified in pronouncing it sound in principle, producing practical results exceeding their expectations and requiring but little alteration in detail.

The expenditure of the several parishes in this Union has been reduced in the aggregate 44.75 per cent without diminishing the comforts of the aged and infirm. The Board attribute this reduction mainly to their having offered admission to the House instead of giving money out of doors to those whose idleness formerly made them continuous applicants for Relief.

That symptoms of returning industry are clearly visible amongst this class throughout the Union.

That in particular this Board is convinced that the present arrangements for medical relief are such as to ensure attention to the wants of the Poor.

Source: as for Source **D**.

Source F: Comments on the New Poor Law by Nassau Senior, made in 1842; he was chairman of the Royal Commission on the Poor Laws 1832–34.

A more general estimate of the improvement may be made by comparing the total amount of the poor rates in 1834 with the amount in 1840. The amount for 1834 was £7,511,218, that for 1840 was £5,110,683 – the difference being nearly one third.

We attach, however, comparatively little importance to the financial results of the Poor Law Amendment Act. We are grateful to the Commissioners not for having saved £2,400,000 a year, but for having stopped the progress of the plague and improved the morals of the people. The general result may be stated to be that the labourer, finding himself no longer entitled to a fixed income, whatever his idleness or misconduct, becomes stimulated to activity and honesty by the double motive of hope and fear.

Source: quoted in L. Evans and P. J. Pledger, *Contemporary Sources and Opinions in Modern British History, vol. I*, Warne, 1967 (adapted extracts).

Source G: Extracts from *'The Condition of the Working Classes'*, by Frederick Engels, published in 1844.

Since the rich have all the power, the working classes must submit to have the law actually declare them as not required. This has been done by the New Poor Law. The regulation of these workhouses, or as the people call them, Poor Law Bastilles, is such as to frighten away everyone who has the slightest prospect of life without this form of public charity.

The workhouse has been made the most repulsive residence which the ingenuity of a follower of Malthus can invent. In the workhouse at Greenwich in the summer of 1843, a boy five years old was punished by being shut in the dead room, where he had to sleep upon the lids of the coffins. At Bacton (Suffolk) in January 1844, patients who were often restless at night or who tried to get up, were tied fast with cords passed under the bedstead, to save the nurse the trouble of sitting up at night.

Source: as for Source **F** (adapted extracts).

(a) (i) Make a list of criticisms of the Old Poor Law system (before the 1834 Act) mentioned by the writers of Sources **A** and **C**.
4(a)

(ii) What changes did the writers of Sources **A** and **C** want to see in the workhouse system?
4(a)

(iii) Do you think the writer of Source **B** approves or disapproves of the workhouse system before 1834? Give reasons for your answer.
4(a, b)

(iv) Apart from the suggestions made in Sources **A** and **C**, what other changes were brought in by the 1834 Act?
1, 2, 4(a)

(b) The statistics in Source **D** show the populations of the 14 parishes of Stow and the money spent on outdoor relief both before and after the 1834 Poor Law Amendment Act.

(i) Which parish had the smallest population and which had the largest population in 1831?
4(a)

(ii) In which parishes had the population decreased by 1841?
4(a)

(iii) From the evidence of these statistics and the evidence in Source **E**, how successful were the Stow Poor Law Guardians in reducing outdoor relief payments.
4(a, c)

(iv) Which parish achieved the largest percentage reduction in outdoor relief payments?
4(a)

(v) Why do you think some money was still being paid out in 1841?
2, 4(a, c)

(c) (i) According to the writers of Sources **E** and **F**, how had the 1834 Act improved the situation?
4(a, c)

(ii) In what ways does Source **G** either support or contradict the claims made in Sources **E** and **F**?
4(a, c)

(iii) What reasons can you think of to explain why the writers of Sources **E** and **F** were so pleased with the 1834 Act whereas the writer of Source **G** disapproves so strongly?
4(a, b, c)

(d) Using the evidence from Sources **D**, **E**, **F** and **G** and your own knowledge, explain to what extent you think the Poor Law Amendment Act of 1834 was a success.
1, 2, 4

2. The Reform of Local Government, 1835

Study Sources **A** and **B** and then answer the questions which follow.

Source A: Report of the Royal Commission on Municipal Corporations, 1835.

> In most cases an exclusive and party spirit belongs to the whole council. Members of these councils are usually self-elected, and hold their offices for life. They are commonly of one political party and their activities are mainly directed to secure the ascendancy of the party to which they belong. Individuals of different political opinions are, in most cases, systematically excluded from the governing body . . . These councils, so far from being the representatives either of the population or of the property of the town, they do not even represent the privileged class of freemen. Being elected for life, their activities are unchecked by any feeling of responsibility . . . To this system may be traced the carelessness often observed in the execution of their duties . . . The common council of the city of London presents a striking exception to the system of self-election for life, and it provides a remarkable instance of the absence of those evils which we refer to. The councilmen of this city are annually elected by a numerous electorate, and for a long series of years have watched vigilantly over the interests of their constituents.

> Source: quoted in L. Evans and P. J. Pledger, *Contemporary Sources and Opinions in Modern British History, vol. I*, Warne, 1967 (adapted extracts).

Source B: Some comments on the Royal Commission Report by a modern historian, E. L. Woodward.

> The commission appointed a number of young barristers to investigate the facts. These assistant commissioners were whigs, with Joseph Parkes, a radical, as their secretary. One of them wrote to Francis Place: 'We shall do our duty . . . our chief is an excellent Radical'. The report of the commission was unfair. It attributed to all boroughs the gross corruption of a few and assumed that popular control was a guarantee of competence though the neglect of the London docks by a democratic corporation was in striking contrast with the efficient and undemocratic management of Liverpool. On the other hand the main case was unanswerable. Peel did not try to answer it or to oppose the dissolution of the old corporations.

> Source: E. L. Woodward, *The Age of Reform 1815-1870*, Oxford, second edn 1962 (adapted extracts).

(a) (i) Using your own words, list the criticisms of borough councils made in Source **A**. **4(a)**

    (ii) According to Source **A**, in what ways was London an exception to the rest of the country? **4(a)**

(b) **(i)** In what ways does Source **B** contradict Source **A**? **4(a, c)**

(ii) What evidence can you find in the Sources to suggest why the writer of Source **B** thought 'the report of the commission was unfair'? Explain whether you think this evidence is convincing or not. **4(a, b, c)**

(iii) Do you think the writer of Source **B** disagrees entirely with the report (Source **A**) or not? Give reasons for your answer. **4(a, b)**

(c) What changes in local government were brought in by the Municipal Corporations Act of 1835? **1**

(d) **(i)** Why was there so much opposition to the Municipal Corporations Bill in the House of Lords? **1, 2**

(ii) Who was Peel mentioned in the last sentence of Source **B**? **1, 4(a)**

(iii) Why was Peel important in the passing of the Municipal Corporations Act? **1, 2, 4(a)**

(e) In what ways was the Municipal Corporations Act of 1835
(i) a success,
(ii) a failure? **1, 2**

3. Choose any two of the following Whig reforms:

The abolition of slavery (1833); Factory Act (1833); Poor Law Amendment Act (1834); Municipal Corporations Act (1835).

For each of the two you have chosen explain:

(a) why the reform was necessary;
(b) why there was opposition to it;
(c) what changes were brought in by it;
(d) whether or not it was successful. **1, 2**

4. The year is 1838 and you have just completed a tour of Britain gathering information about the working of the 1834 Poor Law Amendment Act. Trying to be as fair and unbiased as possible, write a newspaper article in which you present your findings. Among other things, you could refer to the amounts of cash saved through reduction of outdoor relief, problems of operating the Act in the rural South, distress in the industrial North, and conditions in the workhouses you have visited. **1, 2, 3**

5 It is 1841 and you are a Tory candidate in the forthcoming general election. Write your election manifesto or address in which you try to persuade the electors in your constituency to vote for you. Remember to criticise the record and achievements of the present Whig government as well as outlining the attractions of your own party. **1, 2, 3**

CHAPTER 6

CHARTISM

SUMMARY OF EVENTS

Chartism was a movement which boiled up in the mid-1830s out of working class discontent and disillusion with the efforts of the Whig governments. It was the first working class political organisation and so, in a sense, it was the forerunner of the Labour Party. With branches all over Britain, including Ireland, it aimed to change the parliamentary system so that the working classes would be in control. The Chartists drew up their demands in a six-point list known as *the People's Charter*. Three times, in 1839, 1842 and 1848, the Charter was presented to parliament in the form of a petition containing millions of signatures; three times it was overwhelmingly rejected by the Commons. After each rejection there were outbreaks of violence organised by the more extreme Chartist leaders, but on each occasion the government took swift action to restore order.

After the failure of the third petition in 1848 the movement gradually died out; it seemed at the time to have been a rather pathetic failure. However, it did have some important effects, and in time, though not until long after the Chartists themselves were all dead, five of its six aims were actually achieved.

6.1 WHY DID THE CHARTIST MOVEMENT COME INTO EXISTENCE?

The movement was caused quite simply by an overwhelming feeling of misery among the working classes together with the conviction that they were not getting a fair deal at the hands of the wealthy and governing classes. There was a whole range of grievances, some of which had been building up and worsening over many years, others which arose more recently in the 1830s.

(a) Poor conditions in factories, workshops and mines. The Whig Factory Act of 1833 had brought in a 12 hour limit on the working day for young persons of 18 and under, but it only applied to textile factories and even this was not effective in many cases; Shaftesbury continued the campaign to get a 10 hour day introduced for women and young people. There was no limit on the working hours of men. Serious injury and death were common in many factories where dangerous machinery was not properly fenced off; the 1840 committee of enquiry mentioned one case of a girl who had been caught by the hair and scalped from the nose to the back of the head. Conditions in mines were even more horrifying (see Section 12.1).

(b) **Poor living conditions.** Industrial towns were generally overcrowded and unhealthy, with no proper sanitation and sewage disposal. Edwin Chadwick's *Report on the Sanitary Condition of the Labouring Population* which appeared in 1842 revealed some appalling details: one-fifth of the inhabitants of Liverpool were living in one-room cellars; in Leeds the streets were a foot deep in accumulated rubbish; in London workers had to drink untreated water from the Thames. No wonder there were constant epidemics of cholera, typhoid, tuberculosis and diphtheria, roughly one-third of all children died before they reached the age of five. In the decade 1831–40 the death rate over the country as a whole was 23 per 1000, which was bad enough; in industrial Lancashire it was 37 per 1000.

(c) **Disillusion with the 1832 Reform Act.** It soon became clear that the high hopes of the workers that real democracy was about to arrive had not been realised. The working classes were not given the vote, and in some boroughs such as Preston and Westminster, working men actually lost the vote as a result of the Act. Pocket boroughs, 'influence' and bribery still survived and would continue to do so as long as there was no secret ballot (see Section 4.5(b)). Even the Municipal Reform Act (1835) brought no benefit to working men; again it was only the middle classes who received the vote.

(d) **The collapse of trade unionism.** In the late 1820s a number of trade unions were formed and Owen attempted to unite them into his Grand National Consolidated Trades Union (formed 1833); but the movement was dogged by all kinds of problems, including government hostility (see Section 19.2(c)). After the affair of the Tolpuddle Martyrs (1834) and the arrest and trial of the Glasgow cotton spinners' leaders (1837), the unions collapsed, many of their members joining the Chartists.

(e) **Anger at the 1834 Poor Law.** This was particularly strong in the North where the Commissioners first attempted to apply the new system in 1837 (see Section 5.2(d) (iv)).

(f) **Trade depression, unemployment and hunger.** The immediate cause of the Chartist outbreaks was always the same. J. R. Stephens, a north-country Methodist preacher, summed it up well when he declared that the movement 'is a knife-and-fork question, a bread-and-cheese question'. Some categories of workers – the handloom weavers of Lancashire, Wales and Scotland and the Leicester stocking weavers – had been suffering falling

wages and unemployment for years; they were the most consistent supporters of Chartism. But in 1837 a general trade depression set in, which
affected workers in most industries, and which only began to ease off in
1842. By the summer of 1837 there were 50 000 out of work or on short
time in Manchester. In 1839 a Lancashire handloom weaver could expect
to earn at best five shillings a week, while a Leicester stocking knitter was
managing only four shillings and sixpence. General Napier, who was in
charge of the troops sent to keep order in the Midlands and North, noted
that 'everywhere people are starving in the manufacturing districts . . . and
the guardians of the poor are guardians of their own pockets'.

All these grievances could be, and were, blamed on the 'rotten Whigs',
as a Leicester Chartist described them in 1840. They were held directly
responsible for the Reform Acts, the new Poor Law and the treatment of
the Tolpuddle Martyrs, and indirectly for bad conditions, depression and
unemployment, which they had done next to nothing to improve.

6.2 HOW DID THE MOVEMENT BEGIN AND WHAT SORT OF PEOPLE JOINED IT?

(a) It is difficult to pin-point exactly when and where the movement began
because there were many protest groups and societies in different parts of
the country which didn't necessarily call themselves Chartists to begin
with. However, it is usual to take the founding of the *London Working
Men's Association* in 1836 as the starting point. It was formed by a number of skilled craftsmen, including *William Lovett*, a cabinet-maker, and
Francis Place, the veteran Radical tailor. In 1837, at a meeting between
the LWMA and some Radical MPs, the Charter from which the movement
took its name was drawn up. Almost immediately other protest groups
began to affiliate until by 1838 there were well over a hundred branches
all over the country.

(b) The rank and file membership was overwhelmingly working class; there
was a great deal of middle class support in the early stages, with the
involvement of men like Thomas Attwood, Robert Owen and Joseph
Sturge, a Birmingham corn-miller; but they tended to abandon the movement in the early 1840s as the more violent elements came into prominence.
The most reliable and consistent membership came from the craftsmen
who were being forced out of business by new machines (northern hand-
loom weavers and Black Country nail-makers); and from workers in areas
of declining industry (Wales, Wiltshire and the south-west where the old
textile industries were in dire straits). In other industrial areas, for example
the coalfields of Yorkshire, South Wales and the north-east, workers
became involved with Chartism during times of slump and unemployment
but drifted away when trade recovered. In agricultural areas membership
was even less consistent: in Suffolk for example, though there were
Chartist groups in Ipswich and Saxmundham, it was difficult to sustain the

involvement of agricultural labourers because of their relatively isolated situation in the countryside.

6.3 WHAT WERE THE CHARTISTS' AIMS?

(a) Basically they wanted a drastic change of the parliamentary and political system so that the working classes would be in control. As Bronterre O'Brien, one of the Chartist leaders, put it in 1833, 'they aspire to be,at the top instead of the bottom of society – or rather that there should be no bottom or top at all'. Only when this was achieved, or so they believed, would anything positive be done to improve the general plight of working people. *The Charter contained their six specific demands:*

(i) Universal male suffrage (a vote for all men at the age of 21).
(ii) Voting to be done by secret ballot.
(iii) Equal electoral districts (constituencies) so that each MP would represent roughly the same number of voters.
(iv) No property qualification for parliamentary candidates, to enable working men to stand for parliament.
(v) Payment of MPs, so that working men who had no other income except from their trades, would be provided for when they left their jobs to enter parliament.
(vi) Annual elections. In the words of a Chartist voter, this would be 'the most effectual check to bribery and intimidation . . . though a constituency may be bought once in seven years, no purse can buy a constituency in each ensuing twelvemonth'.

All the branches agreed on the six points, but at different times and in different places, Chartist groups put forward further aims. Most of them wanted the abolition of taxes on newspapers. *The London Democratic Association* (a rival group to the LWMA) mentioned 'the repeal of the infamous New Poor Law Act', an eight hour day for all workers in factories and workshops, abolition of child labour, the promotion of 'public instruction and the diffusion of sound political knowledge', the destruction of inequality and 'the establishment of general happiness'. The Birmingham group wanted the abolition of the Corn Laws.

(b) From the outset there were serious differences of opinion about how these aims were to be achieved. Like so much else to do with the Chartists, this is difficult to generalise about because many of the leaders changed their minds as the campaign developed. For the sake of simplicity though, we can divide them into the 'moral force' and the 'physical force' Chartists.

(i) *Lovett, Place and the LWMA* (together with Attwood, the Birmingham banker) were probably the most consistent leaders. They were moderate and peaceful, hoping to achieve their aims by discussion and persuasion, by means of orderly meetings and pamphlets. They accepted that this could only happen gradually, but it would be 'without commotion or violence' and without breaking the law.

(ii) *Feargus O'Connor* was impatient with the moderates. An Irish Protestant who had become MP for Cork in 1832, he wanted quick results. After founding the rival London Democratic Association (1837), he took over the Leeds Radical newspaper, the *Northern Star*, which he soon turned into the main Chartist propaganda machine, with a weekly sale of 50 000 copies. A brilliant agitator and fiery speaker, he swayed the masses into supporting the idea of a general strike and also seemed to favour armed revolution. However, he was not himself prepared to risk force, and backed out on more than one occasion. Not surprisingly, he fell out with every other important Chartist leader at one time or another, but somehow retained his popularity with the rank and file.

(iii) *Bronterre O'Brien*, an Irish lawyer, and *Julian Harnay*, who helped organise the groups in Sheffield and Newcastle, were two of the real militants, both quite prepared to use force. Harnay, who went around in a red cap and fancied himself as the British version of Marat (a French revolutionary leader murdered in 1793) wanted a full-scale revolution on the French model. However, even they cooled down after *John Frost*, another militant, had been sentenced to transportation for life for leading an uprising at Newport (Monmouthshire) in 1840.

6.4 THE THREE PHASES OF THE CHARTIST MOVEMENT

(a) 1838-9

(i) During 1838 there was a series of huge open air meetings addressed by Chartist leaders: 100 000 gathered on Glasgow Green to hear O'Connor, at least 30 000 at Manchester and a similar number at Leeds. When O'Connor tried to address a meeting at Newcastle, the crowd was dispersed by cavalry.

(ii) In February 1839 a National Chartist Convention met in London to organise a petition and its presentation to parliament. It was here that the first serious differences of opinion occurred as the leaders argued about how best to proceed. Some of the extremists wanted to proclaim a general strike immediately, while Lovett and Attwood hoped to keep within the law. Attwood and the Birmingham contingent walked out in disgust at the extremists, though for the time being the moderates just about kept control. In May the Convention moved to Birmingham where there was more support for Chartism, and the petition was completed after some vast meetings in the Bull Ring at which Lovett, O'Brien and Harnay appeared.

(iii) The first Chartist petition containing one and a quarter million signatures was brought to the Commons in a decorated cart. It was introduced by Attwood who asked that parliament should grant the six points. The Home Secretary, Lord John Russell, led the attack on the petition and it was overwhelmingly rejected by 235 votes to 46 (July 1839).

(iv) This rejection suggested that nothing could be achieved by moderation, and the physical force supporters seized the initiative, attempting to organise a general strike or 'sacred month' as the Chartists called it. There were protest meetings, riots, fights and strikes with many leaders calling for an armed uprising. The Whig government, which had reacted cautiously when Lovett and the moral force leaders were in the ascendant, now decided to act. The army was increased by 5000 and new police forces set up in Birmingham, Manchester, Bolton and other industrial centres. General Napier who was in charge of forces in the North, sympathised with the working classes and blamed the situation on 'Tory injustice and Whig imbecility'. He tried to avoid confrontation and showed local Chartist leaders how suicidal any attempt at revolution would be, given the strength of his artillery and cavalry. This, together with the arrest of many of the leaders probably prevented any serious outbreak in the Midlands and North.

(v) Wales, where conditions in the mining valleys were, if anything, the worst in Britain, saw the most serious violence, the *Newport rising* (November 1839). John Frost, a local draper and former mayor of Newport, led an attack on the town by 5000 miners, apparently aiming to release a Chartist leader from gaol. However, the authorities knew well in advance and positioned troops in the Westgate Hotel. As the Chartists approached they were met by volleys of musket fire; at least 20 were killed and the rising soon ended in confusion. Frost and two other leaders were sentenced to death but this was changed to transportation.

Although there were occasional incidents and a number of large open-air meetings, there was a lull in Chartist activities during 1840-1 partly because all the main leaders, even the peaceful ones like Lovett, were in gaol, and because there was a temporary trade revival.

(b) 1842

(i) As the most influential leaders finished their sentences and emerged from gaol, the Chartists gathered themselves together for another effort. Members were to pay a penny a week each to build up a strike fund.

(ii) Another National Convention met and a second petition was drawn up containing three and a quarter million signatures. Reputed to be six miles long, it was carried to parliament in a huge procession of over 100 000 people, with brass bands playing. It was introduced in the Commons by Thomas Duncombe supported by John Fielden, and although Peel and the Conservatives were now in power, it suffered a similar fate to that of the first petition - rejected by 287 votes to 49 (May).

illus 6.1   *The 1842 Petition carried to Parliament*

(iii) Again violence followed the rejection, though this was probably caused as much by wage reductions which took place in all industrial areas from Scotland down to the Midlands, as the depression reached its worst. At Wolverhampton strikers besieged the workhouse and had to be dispersed by dragoon guards. In the Lancashire 'Plug Riots', strikers hammered the plugs out of factory boilers, forcing them to close down. By August work in the industrial North was at a standstill: there was serious rioting in towns such as Preston, Stockport, Rochdale, Bury and Bolton, while at Manchester several policemen were killed and thousands of strikers looted food shops. The situation seemed close to a general strike and perhaps even a revolution.

(iv) O'Connor, who had so often advocated violence, was horrified at this turn of events, and condemned the strike in the *Northern Star*. Peel's government took prompt action and rushed troops to trouble spots, using the new railways. Within a week order had been restored and hundreds of Chartist leaders thrown in goal; strikers had no choice but to return to work. Again there was a lull in Chartism, and membership declined rapidly as trade revived in 1843.

(c) 1848: the Chartists' last fling

(i) In the mid-1840s O'Connor, still the most exciting and influential of the Chartist leaders, put all his energies into his *Land Plan*. The idea was to buy country estates where thousands of Chartists from industrial towns could settle, each family with its own smallholding (small farm). As well as making the settlers independent, this would also ease the unemployment problem in manufacturing areas. O'Connor founded the Chartist Co-operative Land Society in 1845, renamed the National Land Company in 1847. Chartists bought shares in the company for £1.6s. each, and eventually four Chartist colonies were started: O'Connorville near Watford, Lowbands and Snig's End near Gloucester and Charterville near Witney (Oxfordshire). Each family had a two-, three-, or four-acre plot and a cottage, and paid an annual rent of £1.5s. an acre.

(ii) Early in 1847 another trade depression set in and unemployment soared. By May there were 24 000 out of work in Manchester and 84 000 on short time. This new wave of distress brought the Chartists back to politics again and in July O'Connor was elected as MP for Nottingham. Encouraged by the news of a successful revolution in Paris (February 1848), they set about producing their third petition. It was completed early in April 1848 at another National Convention in London; this time it contained five points (secret ballot was the one omitted), and was reported to have been signed by almost six million people.

(iii) There was to be an open air rally on Kennington Common on 10 April followed by a mass procession to Westminster to present the petition. Some of the speakers at the Convention urged revolution and it was decided that if this third petition was rejected, the Chartists would call a National Assembly to force parliament to accept the Charter. It was said that O'Connor had even drawn up a new constitution with himself as president of a British republic.

(iv) In fact both O'Connor and O'Brien played down the physical force approach in their speeches, but Russell's Whig government took no chances. The march on parliament was banned and O'Connor was told that only 10 people would be allowed through to present the petition. The Duke of Wellington stationed troops at key points in the capital and signed up 150 000 special constables. The Kennington Common rally went ahead but far fewer people turned up than had been expected and heavy rain dampened the Chartists' enthusiasm. No attempt was made to storm parliament, since it would have been difficult to force a way across the bridges over the Thames; the event ended lamely with O'Connor and a handful of supporters delivering the petition to the Commons in three cabs.

(v) When it was examined closely the petition was found to contain less than two million signatures, some of which - Queen Victoria, Wellington, Mr Punch, Sir Robert Peel, Flatnose and No Cheese - made it look ridiculous; again the Commons rejected it by a huge majority.

(vi) At the same time O'Connor's Land Scheme found itself in serious difficulties: much of the land was poor, the settlers had no experience of farming, the smallholdings were not large enough to support whole families, and O'Connor himself, though certainly not dishonest, made a hopeless muddle of the finances. In August 1851 the National Land Company was wound up in complete failure.

(vii) Although there were some violent incidents in the Midlands and North following the rejection of the third petition, Chartism never again achieved the same impact. O'Connor could still draw a crowd of 20 000 at Leicester in 1850, but in general there was a slow fade-out of the movement after 1848; by 1852 the circulation of the *Northern Star* was down to only 1200 from its 1839 peak of around 50 000. O'Connor became insane and had to be confined in an asylum at Chiswick; he died in 1855.

6.5 WHY WERE THE CHARTISTS UNSUCCESSFUL IN THE 1840s AND WHAT WAS THE SIGNIFICANCE OF THE MOVEMENT?

(a) From the beginning the Chartists had no chance of having all six points accepted at that particular time; there was no way that parliament, still dominated by aristocratic landowners, was going to hand over power to the working and lower middle classes, which is what acceptance of the petition would have amounted to. In addition:

(i) There were serious divisions and disagreements among the leaders about whether to use moral persuasion (Lovett, Place and Attwood), or physical force (Frost, O'Connor and Harnay). Lovett was hopeful that the industrial society would eventually lead to prosperity for all, but O'Connor hated the new machinery and wanted a society of small landholders; his Land Scheme was condemned as impractical by the other leaders. O'Connor outshone all the rest and made much more impact nationally, but unfortunately he was reckless and unstable, apparently preaching violence one minute and drawing back the next.

(ii) There were many local differences which made unity difficult and central organisation weak.

(iii) The Chartists never won sufficient middle class support; many potential backers who sympathised with the six points were frightened off by the Chartists' violence and by their attacks on wealth and property and preferred to put their energies and cash into the more respectable Anti-Corn Law League (see Section 7.5). In 1841 when Lovett seemed to be bridging the gap between the classes by attracting the support of Joseph Sturge, a wealthy corn-miller, O'Connor attacked Lovett, accusing him of trying to 'domesticate the charter' and this New Move, as it was called, broke down.

(iv) Their aims were too complicated: as well as the six points there were numerous other social aims which meant that they were trying to achieve too much all at once, which only confused people. This was in marked contrast to the Anti-Corn Law League which knew exactly what it wanted (the abolition of the Corn Laws) and hammered away at that single aim until it was achieved. The Chartists might have done better to have concentrated on getting MPs elected so that they would have had a more effective voice in the Commons (as the League did).

(v) The authorities kept one step ahead of the Chartists and always knew of their plans; for instance police spies had informed them about the Newport Rising in 1839. Both Whig governments (in 1839 and 1848) and Peel's Conservatives (in 1842) took prompt action, arresting leaders, moving troops swiftly by train to areas of disturbances and using the new electric telegraph.

(vi) The reforms of Peel's government between 1841 and 1846 (see Sections 7.2 and 7.3) led to some improvement in trade and conditions. Britain was moving into a period of great economic prosperity which was reflected to some extent in rising wages and increased food consumption: the average price of a four pound loaf which had cost $11\frac{1}{2}$ pence in 1847 was under 7 pence in 1850. As living standards improved, support for the Chartists and their complicated programme melted away and workers preferred to join trade unions or the co-operative movement.

(b) It would be wrong to dismiss Chartism as insignificant simply because it failed to achieve its political aims in the 1840s. Its most important achievement was that it focused public attention on the appalling hardships of the workers. It was no coincidence that Peel and the Conservatives (1841-6) immediately took steps (Mines Act, Factory Act, Commission on Public Health in Towns leading to the 1848 Public Health Act) to try and remove the grievances which had given rise to Chartism in the first place.

6.6 WHEN WAS THE CHARTISTS' POLITICAL PROGRAMME ACHIEVED?

Bit by bit over the next 80 years, five of the six points were achieved. First to come was the abolition of the property qualification for MPs in 1858, followed by the introduction of the secret ballot in elections (1872). Manhood suffrage was achieved in stages by the Reform Acts of 1867 and 1884 and by the Representation of the People Act of 1918, which went further than the Chartists had intended by giving the vote to women aged 30 and over; in 1928 women were given the vote at 21. These acts also redistributed seats so that constituencies became approximately equal (though even today there are some variations: Northern Ireland constituencies contain many more voters than the average constituency in the rest of Britain). Payment of MPs was introduced in 1911. The only one of the points not achieved is annual general elections; however, the 1911 Parliament Act did reduce the length of parliaments so that there has to be a general election every five years instead of every seven.

QUESTIONS

1. The Chartist Campaign of 1838-9
Study Sources A to F and then answer the questions which follow.

Source A: from the Chartist Petition drawn up in 1838.

> We, your petitioners, dwell in a land whose merchants are noted for their enterprise, whose manufacturers are very skilful and whose workmen are proverbial for their industry . . . Yet we find ourselves overwhelmed with public and private suffering. We are bowed down under a load of taxes, and our workmen are starving. Capital brings no profit, labour no reward; the workhouse is full and the factory deserted. We have looked on every side to find out the causes of distress, and we can discover none in nature or in Providence.
>
> It was the fond expectation of the people that a remedy for most of their grievances would be found in the Reform Act of 1832 . . . They have been bitterly deceived . . . The Reform Act has transferred power from one domineering faction to another, and left the people as helpless as before . . .
>
> We perform the duties, therefore we must have the privileges of free men. Therefore we demand universal suffrage. To be exempt from the corruption of the wealthy and the violence of the powerful, the suffrage must be secret. We demand annual parliaments and . . . for every representative chosen, a fair payment for the time which he is called upon to devote to the public service.
>
> **Source:** quoted in R. G. Gammage, *History of the Chartist Movement*, Browne & Browne, 1854 (adapted extracts).

Source B: An artist's impression of Chartists in Newport, 1839.

Source: National Library of Wales.

Source C: from the Objects of the London Working Men's Association, 1839.

2. To seek by every legal means to place all classes of society in possession of their equal political and social rights.

7. To publish our views and sentiments in such a form as shall best serve to create a moral yet energetic public opinion; so as eventually to lead to a gradual improvement in the condition of the working class, without violence or commotion.

Source: quoted in Dennis Holman (ed.), *Portraits and Documents: Earlier Nineteenth Century 1783-1867*, Hutchinson, 1965 (adapted extracts).

Source D: from a speech by William Taylor, a Lancashire Chartist leader, in 1839.

We are to be free, though we wade through streams of blood . . . Do we read in ancient or modern history of any nation in bondage becoming free without the use of physical force?

Source: quoted in Christopher Thorne, *Chartism*, Macmillan, 1966.

Source E: from a newspaper article in *The Bolton Chronicle*, Saturday 17 August 1839.

SERIOUS AND ALARMING RIOTS IN BOLTON

On Sunday last the Chartists marched to church . . . great fear was expressed by inhabitants of the town that violence would be attempted; therefore about 15,000 special constables were sworn in. It is not for us, as reporters, to express our opinion regarding the origin of such Chartist meetings . . . whether incited by the mayor or his friends, it is not for us to consider.

TUESDAY – at five o'clock [a.m.] the Chartists again assembled, numbering about 300. The police officers at first made no attempt to disperse the mob when it first collected, but later arrested the leaders. Then showers of stones were thrown in all directions and the commotion arrived at a tremendous pitch. The mayor and magistrates consulted and the riot act was read. The military was instantly called out and their prompt arrival discouraged the multitude.

Source: *The Bolton Chronicle*, 17 August 1839 (adapted extracts).

Souce F: the opinions of Sir Charles Napier, the general sent to deal with the Chartists in the north of England in 1839:

[1839] June 29th. I hate the poor law, but it is not a cause of the mischief in itself, it is only a train to fire the mine: the evils produced by the manufacturing system and the debt are attributed by the people to the new poor law . . . a population starving one week, earning forty shillings the next . . .

August 17th. Bolton is the only place where shot has been fired, but only three there, and those from the eagerness of the magistrates.

August 19th. Everywhere a sudden calm has succeeded the storm; it is unnatural, for the causes of discontent still exist. The fact is that the Chartist leaders' calculations are quite at fault; they have found the difficulty of uniting their people in simultaneous efforts. The mayor and corporation of Bolton are said to be Chartists and the constables everywhere are, more or less, and all avow that the people are oppressed. Men are restless and discontented with poverty; they have all its sufferings and have not the principal pleasures.

Source: quoted in R. Brown and C. Daniels (eds), *Nineteenth Century Britain*, Macmillan, 1980 (adapted extracts).

(a) **(i)** According to Source **A**, how long was it before people's disappointment with the Reform Act caused them to write the petition?   4(a)

    (ii) What evidence does Source **A** provide about why the Chartists were disappointed with the Reform Act?   4(a)

(iii) What other reasons does Source **A** give for the Chartists' dissatisfaction? 4(a)

(iv) Why does the writer of Souce **A** think that voting should be done in secret? 4(a)

(v) Which two points of the Charter are not mentioned in Source **A**? 1, 4(a)

(b) (i) What evidence is there in the picture (Source **B**) that the Chartist activities in Newport became violent? 4(a)

(ii) How do Sources **B, C, D, E** and **F** differ in the evidence they provide about the Chartists' methods of achieving their aims? 4(a, c)

(iii) Why do you think there is some disagreement among these sources? 4(b)

(c) (i) What evidence is there in Source **F** which supports some of the claims made in Source **A**? 4(a, c)

(ii) What differences can you find between the accounts of events in Bolton given in Sources **E** and **F**? 4(a, c)

(d) (i) Do you think the writers of Sources **E** and **F** were sympathetic to the Chartists or not? Give full reasons for your answers. 4(a, b)

(ii) What advantages and disadvantages do the following types of Source have for a historian trying to write about Chartism:
1. newspaper reports – as in Source **E**?
2. eye-witness accounts – as in Source **F**? 4(a, b)

(iii) In this case, how reliable do you think Sources **E** and **F** are likely to be? 4(a, b)

(e) Using all the Sources and any other information you have, explain why the Chartists did not achieve their aims in the immediate future. 1, 2, 4(a, c)

2. Read the extract below and then answer the questions which follow.
Speech by Mr Macauley in the House of Commons during the debate on the second Chartist petition, May 1842:

> I believe that universal suffrage would be fatal to all purposes for which government exists. I conceive that civilisation rests on the security of property and this petition contains a declaration that the remedies for the evils of which it complains are to be found in a great and sweeping confiscation of property. I am firmly convinced that the effect of any such measures would be to overthrow those institutions which now exist, ruin those that are rich, make the poor poorer and make the amount of misery in the country even greater than it is supposed to be . . .

> **Source:** *Hansard*, 1842 (adapted extracts).

(a) (i) Which one of the Chartists' six points does Mr Macauley mention in his first sentence? 1, 4(a)

   (ii) Do you think the speaker supports or opposes the Chartist petition? Give evidence to support your answer. 4(a, b)

   (iii) Write a brief summary, in your own words, of Mr Macauley's remarks about the petition. 4(a)

(b) (i) What were the other five points of the 1842 Chartist petition, not mentioned by Mr Macauley? 1, 4(a)

   (ii) How did the Chartists hope that the lives of the workers would be improved if parliament accepted their petition? 1, 2

   (iii) What happened to this petition at the end of the debate in parliament? 1

(c) (i) Why was another Chartist petition presented to parliament in 1848? 1, 2

   (ii) What steps did the government take in 1848 to prevent violence? 1, 2

   (iii) Were these steps successful? 1, 2

(d) Do you think it would be right to say that Chartism was a complete failure? Give reasons for your answer. 1, 2

3. (a) What six main points did the Chartists demand?

  (b) Why did the Chartist movement begin?

  (c) Why did the Chartists fail to get their points accepted in the 1840s?

  (d) Which of their aims had been achieved by 1914? 1, 2

4. It is early in 1842. As a well-known Chartist leader, you have been asked to produce an article for the *Northern Star*. Write a draft of your article. Among the things you could write about are:

  (a) why you think people ought to join the movement;

  (b) your part in the events of 1839;

  (c) why you think the first Chartist petition was rejected;

  (d) your hopes and intentions for the future. 1, 2, 3

CHAPTER 7

SIR ROBERT PEEL, THE CONSERVATIVES AND THE CORN LAWS 1830–46

SUMMARY OF EVENTS

At the end of 1830 the Tory party had disintegrated in the wake of Catholic Emancipation (see Section 2.7(b)) and was also deeply divided about what attitude to adopt towards reform of parliament. Reaching rock-bottom in 1833, the party gradually began to revive under the leadership of Sir Robert Peel. When Melbourne's Whig government began to falter, Peel and his party – now known as Conservatives – held office for a short time (December 1834 to April 1835), but lacking a majority, they soon had to resign. Peel's reputation grew steadily and in August 1841 the Conservatives won a large electoral majority. Peel was Prime Minister from 1841 until 1846.

He had to face some alarming problems: an economic slump, appalling working and living conditions in industrial areas, agitation and violence from the Chartists and pressure from *the Anti-Corn Law League*. However, Peel showed the same determination as he had earlier when he was Home Secretary (1822–30). Often facing opposition from many of his own party, he pushed through *important economic reforms* (re-introduction of income tax, further steps towards free trade, and the Bank Charter Act) and *social reforms* (Mines Act, Factory Act and an enquiry into health conditions in towns).

These were considerable achievements, and all seemed to be going well, when Peel was brought down by *the repeal of the Corn Laws*. Influenced by the Anti-Corn Law League's campaign and by a disastrous famine in Ireland, Peel decided that the Corn Laws must go. Many of the Tory land-owners, amounting to about two-thirds of the party, were bitterly opposed to the repeal, convinced that it would damage British agriculture and reduce their profits by letting in too much cheap foreign corn. Whig support enabled Peel to get the repeal act through, but the rebel section of his party soon forced him to resign and the Conservatives split into two groups. After doing so much to rebuild his party during the 1830s, it seemed as though Peel had now destroyed it again.

7.1 PEEL AND THE REVIVAL OF THE TORY/CONSERVATIVE PARTY

(a) **Peel** was the son of a wealthy Lancashire cotton manufacturer (also called Robert) who had bought a large estate at Tamworth (Staffordshire) which he represented as a Tory MP from 1790. The elder Peel had great political ambitions for his son; he sent him to Harrow and Oxford and secured him a seat in parliament in 1809 when he was only 21. The young Peel soon made a good impression with his speeches and in 1812 Lord Liverpool appointed him Chief Secretary for Ireland, a position he held until 1818. This was a difficult period in Ireland with the Irish Catholics violently opposing the Act of Union. Peel acquitted himself well, managing to contain the violence by setting up the Irish Constabulary, the first effective police force Ireland had ever had. With his reputation as an able and honest administrator standing high, Peel became Home Secretary in 1822 and was responsible for the penal code reform and the introduction of the Metropolitan Police (see Section 2.6(c)). Following the downfall of the Tory government in November 1830, the Whigs were in power for most of the next ten years; it was during this time that Peel devoted himself to building up the new Conservative party.

(b) What was Peel's contribution to the development of the Conservative party?

(i) Peel gave the party a new image, both in his speeches in parliament, and outside parliament in a document known as the *Tamworth Manifesto*. This was issued in December 1834 as an election address to the people of Tamworth which he represented in parliament after his father's death in 1830. In it he explained that although he had at first opposed parliamentary reform, he now accepted the 1832 Reform Act as 'a final and irrevocable settlement of a great constitutional question'. He and his party were in favour of 'a careful review of institutions . . . undertaken in a friendly temper, combining, with the firm maintenance of established rights, the correction of proved abuses, and the redress of real grievances'; in other words he was prepared to introduce moderate reform wherever there was a genuine need for it, while at the same time preserving all that was good about the British system. In a later speech Peel referred to these aims as 'conservative principles'. The Tamworth Manifesto was important because it was the party's new programme; it showed that the Conservatives as they were now called, stood for a safe programme of cautious reform midway between the old Tories who were against all change and the Radicals whose ideas about reform were alarming to moderates.

(ii) He gained wider support for his party from moderate people of all classes, particularly from middle class manufacturers and businessmen who had been neglected by the Whigs. The attractiveness of the Tamworth Manifesto and the party's new image were partly responsible for Peel's success, plus the fact that he came from a middle class background himself.

(iii) Under Peel, local Conservative associations and clubs were set up all over the country, so that the party was far more highly developed at constituency level than the Whigs. According to Norman Gash, however, Peel did not take the initiative here: he 'had notoriously little interest in the humdrum details of the party management'; F. R. Bonham, the Tory election manager, was responsible for this improvement.

As a result, the gap between Conservatives and Whigs gradually closed in the elections of 1835 and 1837 until in June 1841 Peel led his party to a triumphant victory. Reasons for the Conservative success are fully explained in Section 5.3. In less than ten years Peel had revived and given new direction to a party which had seemed defunct. Some historians think he deserves to be remembered as the founder of the modern Conservative party; others feel that Disraeli has a better claim to this distinction, since Peel, having revived the party, almost killed it off again with his repeal of the Corn Laws (see Section 7.6).

7.2 WHAT DID PEEL DO TO HELP THE BRITISH ECONOMY?

The country was facing serious economic problems when Peel became Prime Minister in 1841. Exports had fallen sharply bringing an industrial slump, industry seemed to be stagnating, and there had been a series of poor harvests since 1837 which kept bread prices high. As well as causing hardship and misery for the workers, the slump was accompanied by a financial crisis in which many small banks had collapsed. The Whigs had left a deficit (the amount spent over and above income) of over two million pounds. Peel aimed to encourage trade and do something to ease the problems of the workers. He acted positively:

(a) He took some important steps towards free trade. Although Huskisson had removed many tariffs (import and export duties) in the 1820s (see Section 2.6), the Whigs had taken no further action; there were still about 1200 commodities subject to tariffs. Peel, influenced by a group of northern industrialists calling themselves the *Manchester School* (they included John Bright and Richard Cobden), came to believe that tariffs were stifling British industry. *The argument was* that import duties made raw materials (such as cotton, wool and iron ore) more expensive, thereby keeping production costs too high. Foreign countries resented British tariffs and were less willing to trade than they would otherwise have been. Tariffs, including the duty on imported corn, made imported food more expensive and caused difficulty for the poor. Removal of tariffs would bring down the cost of British goods abroad, increase exports, stimulate industry and provide more jobs. In addition, the cost of living would be cheaper, to the benefit of the working classes. In Peel's own words: 'We must make this country a cheap country for living, and thus induce people to remain and settle here. Enable them to consume more by having more to spend'. In his *budgets of 1842 and 1845* he boldly swept away a large proportion of the remaining duties, so that after 1845:

(i) Duties on over 600 articles had been removed completely;
(ii) Duties on about 500 others had been greatly reduced.

To take a few examples, this meant that there were no longer any export duties at all, and there was no import duty on raw cotton, livestock, meat and potatoes. Cheese imported from British colonies paid a duty of only 1*s*.6*d*. per hundredweight instead of 10*s*.6*d*. There was even a slight reduction in the import duty on corn, though not enough to satisfy the Anti-Corn Law League.

These measures worked exactly as Peel had hoped: they helped to bring about a trade revival, exports increased, unemployment fell rapidly, and food was cheaper (though bread was more expensive than it need have been thanks to the Corn Laws). Britain began to move out of the 'hungry forties' and into a Golden Age of prosperity which lasted until around 1875 (see Section 15.1).

(b) Income tax was re-introduced at the rate of seven pence in the £ on incomes over £150 a year (1842). This controversial tax had been abolished by the Tories in 1816 (see Section 2.2(c)), but Peel brought it back as a temporary measure for three years to make up for the losses in revenue (annual income) which the government would suffer with the abolition of so many duties. It turned out to be so profitable that Peel persuaded parliament to renew it for a further three years; since then no government has been able to afford to abandon it.

Between them the trade revival and the income tax were strikingly successful: Peel had soon turned the Whig deficit of two million pounds into a healthy surplus.

(c) The Bank Charter Act (1844) was an important financial measure made necessary because many banks were unreliable. The problem was that all banks, no matter how small, could issue banknotes, with no limit on the amount. When demand for currency was high among businessmen (for example to finance railway building), there was a tendency for banks to issue too much paper money which they lent out for investment in new companies. If any companies got into difficulties (as many railway companies did), investors often lost their money and could not repay the bank. Some banks, having over-issued notes, lacked sufficient gold reserves to see them through, and always, during a slump, some small banks would collapse. This gave the impression that the currency was unsound, and Peel realised that trade could only expand if the currency were stable. The 1844 Act aimed to bring about 'by gradual means the establishment of a safe system of currency'.

(i) No new banks were allowed to issue notes.

(ii) Existing banks were restricted to their average issue during the three months preceding the passing of the Act; if any existing banks amalgamated they lost the right to issue notes.

(iii) The Bank of England could issue notes worth up to £14 million, but any paper money issued beyond that had to be covered by gold reserves in the Bank's vaults.

The Act was generally successful: it had the effect of gradually phasing out the note-issuing function of ordinary banks, so that the Bank of England came to control the amount of currency in circulation; there was less danger of over-issuing notes. English currency became extremely stable and London was regarded as the world's leading monetary centre.

(d) The Companies Act (1844) dealt with another finance and business problem: the fact that there were no controls on the formation of companies. Anybody could start a company simply by publishing an advertisement, and could then begin receiving money from foolish investors. During the 1830s many such dubious companies went bankrupt or dishonest directors absconded with the capital; either way the investors suffered. The Act aimed to prevent 'reckless speculation' (investing money when there is a risk that it might be lost): all companies now had to be officially registered and were to issue prospectuses and regular accounts. The Act had some success but its weakness was that it did not apply to companies which had to get special approval from parliament; these included railway companies where some of the worst racketeers operated.

7.3 WHAT DID PEEL DO ABOUT THE SOCIAL PROBLEMS?

Peel was well aware of the disgraceful conditions in some factories, mines and industrial towns; on the other hand he knew that not all manufacturers were bad: his own father had been a humane and enlightened employer. His instinct told him that the best way of dealing with these problems was not to pass laws, but to wait until his economic policies bore fruit; then all the workers would have jobs and would be able 'to consume more by having more to spend'; hardships would gradually disappear. Another reason for not taking direct action was that he might lose the support of middle-class businessmen if he tried to regulate working hours and conditions. However, when unemployment reached a new peak in 1842, and troops had to be despatched to deal with Chartist violence (see Section 6.4(b)), a new urgency came into the situation. Peel was also under constant pressure from Shaftesbury and the Ten Hour Movement (which wanted a ten-hour working day for women and children). Eventually *the Mines Act (1842)* and a *Factory Act (1844)* did something to improve conditions (for full details see Section 12.3(e–f)). Most of the credit for these Acts belongs to Shaftesbury, rather than to Peel; in fact, Peel himself was responsible for defeating Shaftesbury's proposal of a ten-hour maximum working day, and both Acts had serious weaknesses. Again under pressure, this time from Edwin Chadwick, the government appointed a Royal Commission to enquire into the 'state of Large Towns and Populous Districts', which produced alarming findings in 1844 and 1845. Peel, now hampered by the Corn Law crisis, took no further action and it was left to Russell's government to introduce the first Public Health Act in 1848. Social reform therefore was not Peel's most successful area.

7.4 PEEL, O'CONNELL AND IRELAND

(a) **Following the 1800 Act of Union** (see Section 1.2(c)), nearly every government in the nineteenth century had to deal with problems of one sort or another in Ireland. We have already seen (Section 2.7(b)) how the Tory party split over Catholic Emancipation in 1829. The Irish were not satisfied with Emancipation, partly because success had been soured when at the same time the Tories took the vote away from the 40 shilling freeholders.

When the Whigs were in power (1830-41), Daniel O'Connell, the Irish leader who now sat at Westminster as MP for Clare, did not press *his next great ambition, the repeal of the Act of Union*. For most of the time he co-operated with the Whigs, hoping to win some concessions, such as the abolition of tithes, which were highly unpopular with the Catholic peasants. However, there were some outbreaks of violence and it was disagreement about how to deal with it that caused Grey to resign as Whig Prime Minister in 1834. O'Connell did secure a few concessions, including the Tithe Act (see Section 5.2(f)) and the inclusion of Irishmen in the Irish police force, but overall he was disappointed.

(b) **During Peel's ministry**, Irish affairs came to the forefront and in 1846 were instrumental in bringing Peel down and splitting the Conservative party.

(i) O'Connell's comparative lack of success after 1829 meant that he was beginning to lose his hold over the Irish; younger and more violent men, Smith O'Brien, Gavan Duffy and John Mitchel, calling themselves *'Young Ireland'*, were impatient with O'Connell's moderation. The ageing leader, now 65, decided to stage a last attempt to force the British to repeal the Act of Union by agitation and the threat of civil war, a policy which had worked with Peel and Wellington over Catholic Emancipation. Supported by the Catholic priests, O'Connell began to address large meetings, stirring up intense excitement; he told a crowd of over 100 000 at Tara (the seat of medieval Irish kings) that within a year the Act of Union would be smashed and the Irish would have a parliament of their own. The climax of the campaign was to be a vast open-air meeting at Clontarf (October 1843).

(ii) Peel was determined not to be frightened into giving way again; he believed, rightly, that this time Ireland was not on the verge of civil war as it had been in 1829. He announced that the Union would never be cancelled and that rebellion would be crushed. Troops were sent to Ireland and the Clontarf meeting banned.

(iii) This placed O'Connell in a difficult situation: if he allowed the meeting to go ahead, it would be treated as rebellion, while if he cancelled it, 'Young Ireland' could accuse him of surrendering to the British. In the event he was not prepared to risk violence; he called the meeting off, and it was clear that Peel had outmanoeuvred him in the war of nerves.

(iv) O'Connell was arrested, tried for conspiracy (remarks in his earlier speeches were said to be seditious), found guilty, sentenced to one year in gaol and fined £2000. The House of Lords reversed the verdict and O'Connell was released, but there was no disguising his defeat. His influence gradually faded as 'Young Ireland' assumed the leadership; he died in 1847.

(v) Peel combined his firm line with some mild concessions. He appointed the *Devon Commission* to investigate problems of land-holding in Ireland; this reported in 1845 but there was no time to act before the government fell. He tried to please the Catholics by increasing the annual government grant to *Maynooth College* (which trained Catholic priests) from £9000 to £26 000. This aroused hostility among his Protestant supporters, many of whom voted against it; in fact, the grant only passed the Commons because the Whigs supported it.

Irish affairs had divided the Conservatives deeply, and Peel had been unable to tackle the country's basic poverty. Unfortunately worse was soon to come both for Peel and the Irish . . .

(vi) By July 1845 it was clear that the Irish potato crop had been ruined by blight; the country was on the verge of famine, bringing new urgency to the Corn Law repeal problem.

7.5 THE STRUGGLE FOR THE REPEAL OF THE CORN LAWS 1838-46

Along with Chartism, the campaign to repeal the Corn Laws was the other great protest movement of the nineteenth century. The two movements provide a striking contrast: Chartism a failure, the Anti-Corn Law League a triumphant success in 1846.

(a) Formation of the Anti-Corn Law League

(i) Ever since the introduction of the Corn Laws (1815) banning the import of foreign corn until the price of home-grown corn reached 80 shillings a quarter (see Section 2.2(c)), critics had argued that they should be repealed, because they kept bread prices far too high. Huskisson's sliding scale of import duties (1828), did nothing to alter their general argument that the Corn Laws were in operation simply to guarantee farmers high profits by keeping out as much foreign corn as possible.

(ii) Between 1830 and 1835 harvests were good and wheat prices fairly low; in 1835, for example, wheat averaged 39s.4d. a quarter and a four pound loaf cost 7d. compared with 96s.11d. a quarter and $14\frac{1}{2}d.$ a loaf in 1817. After 1835 there was a run of poor harvests, corn was scarcer and prices rose. In 1839 wheat averaged 70s.8d. a quarter and a loaf 10d. - not as disastrous for the poor as in 1817, but bad enough, bearing in mind the serious industrial depression which began in 1837. 10d. a loaf was the average - at times in 1839 it was as high as $13\frac{1}{2}d.$ ($1s.1\frac{1}{2}d.$); this was when unemployment was rising and a Lancashire hand-loom weaver was earning no more than 5s. a week; a family of two adults and three children would need at the very minimum five loaves a week.

(iii) Agitation for repeal was strong in Manchester, the main distress centre. Here the Anti-Corn Law Association was started in 1838, followed by similar groups in other cities. In March 1839 they merged into the Anti-Corn Law League with its headquarters in Manchester. It was inspired mainly by manufacturers and businessmen; the leaders were *Richard Cobden*, a southerner who ran a calico factory in Manchester, and the Quaker *John Bright*, a Rochdale cotton manufacturer.

(b) Arguments for and against abolishing the Corn Laws. *The case for abolition* involved a lot more than merely cheaper bread, though that was an important consideration:

(i) Removal of the Corn Laws was part of the general move towards free trade already started by Huskisson. Like all other duties they were seen by Benthamites as an unnatural restraint on trade; they kept imports of foreign corn to a minimum and forced bread prices up simply to ensure good profits for landowners. According to Cobden and Bright, this was un-Christian. Abolition would bring cheaper bread, to the benefit of the poor. The League thus attracted a good deal of working-class support so that it became a powerful alliance of middle classes and workers.

(ii) Once bread prices fell, real wages would increase (workers would be able to buy more with their wages even though the actual money paid to them remained the same), enabling workers to buy not only more bread, but more of other goods as well. This would provide a much needed stimulus to British industry.

(iii) The importing of foreign corn would encourage British farmers to become more competitive so that they would have no need of protective tariffs.

(iv) Buying corn from abroad would encourage foreign countries to import more British manufactured goods. As trade between nations expanded all round, it would improve international relations and contribute towards world peace. This argument appealed particularly to the pacifist Bright and gave the campaign its moral crusade flavour.

The case for retaining the Corn Laws was put strongly by the landowners and by their ally *The Times* newspaper.

(i) Removal of the Corn Laws would allow an influx of cheap foreign wheat which would ruin British farmers and cause mass unemployment among agricultural labourers, who would migrate to the towns, adding to the existing problems of overcrowding and leaving the countryside depopulated.

(ii) Britain would become too dependent on foreign corn which might be cut off in wartime.

(iii) The whole campaign was a selfish middle-class capitalist plot: manufacturers only wanted cheaper bread so that they could reduce wages. This argument had some success among industrial workers and helps to explain why the Chartists were hostile to the League.

(c) **Methods and activities of the League.** Their simple and logical case was put over and over again by Cobden, Bright and other leaders; there was no violence and they almost always kept within the law:

(i) They used masses of paper propaganda: they published a fortnightly and later a weekly newspaper called the *Anti-Bread Tax Circular* and bombarded the public with millions of leaflets and pamphlets hammering home their arguments and ridiculing their opponents. They made excellent use of the new Penny Post (introduced 1840) and made sure that every elector received at least one batch of League literature.

(ii) They held mass meetings both in the open air and indoors. *In Manchester the Free Trade Hall* was built to hold 8000 people (1843); the same year a League headquarters was set up in London which organised no fewer than 136 meetings in that year alone. The country was divided into 12 areas each with a paid agent whose job was to arrange meetings and speakers. Cobden and Bright emerged as expert orators, though in the early days many League speakers had a rough reception from Chartists in industrial towns and from farmers in country areas. At a meeting in Manchester the audience hurled chairs at the speakers on the stage, while at Saxmundham (Suffolk) a speaker was thrown down a flight of stairs and had to be rescued by police.

(iii) Much time and effort were expended in fund-raising – the wealthy middle-class often needed persuasion to put their names on the donation lists and there were bazaars and tea-parties to organise. In 1843 over £50 000 was raised; in 1844 £100 000; a bazaar in Covent Garden Theatre (May 1845) raised £25 000.

(iv) Cobden won the support of Daniel O'Connell, who provided an enormous boost by ensuring that Irish workers co-operated with the League, rather than with the Chartists. At meetings in the north, Irish labourers often acted as bodyguards against Chartist rowdies.

(v) Like the Chartists, the Leaguers presented a number of monster petitions to parliament, but as soon as it became obvious that these were useless, they concentrated on getting as many MPs as possible elected to parliament. Their first attempt was encouraging: at a by-election in Walsall (January 1841) they put up J. B. Smith who stood as an *Abolitionist*; after a violent campaign Smith was only narrowly defeated by the Tory candidate (363 to 336). The League used its funds to enable members who had no vote to buy 40 shilling freehold property (these could usually be bought for between £30 and £60) which carried the right to vote; in the general election of 1841, eight Abolitionists were elected, including Cobden himself for Stockport. Bright won a by-election at Durham in 1843, and by 1845 there were 12 Abolitionist MPs. Now the League could bring constant pressure to bear on the government; as Cobden himself remarked, 'you speak with a loud voice when you are talking on the floor of the House, and if you have anything to say that hits hard . . . it reaches all over the kingdom'.

(d) Stages in the repeal

(i) In the first two years the League made little progress: there was violent opposition from Chartists and farmers, and Russell, the Home Secretary, refused to receive deputations and petitions.

(ii) After the 1841 election the Abolitionist MPs began to make some impact, so much so that Peel slightly reduced the corn import duties laid down in Huskisson's 1828 sliding scale. He hoped that this would be sufficient to silence the more moderate League supporters, and in fact there was something of a lull in the campaign until 1845.

(iii) At some time between 1842 and the beginning of 1845 (*before* the Irish famine) Peel himself made up his mind that the Corn Laws were not serving any useful purpose and that British farmers ought to be perfectly capable of maintaining their profits without them, provided they modernised their methods; an up-to-date farming system would make a perfect partnership with expanding industry. No doubt the League's arguments were partly responsible for Peel's change of mind: after Cobden had delivered a particularly effective attack on the Corn Laws in the Commons (March 1845), Peel screwed up his notes and whispered to the MP sitting next to him, 'You must answer this, for I cannot'. Peel's problem was that the Conservative party was pledged to keep the Corn Laws, and if he moved too quickly, he would infuriate the landowners and split the party. He hoped gradually to prepare the party for repeal and then allow the country to decide at the next general election, due in 1848.

(iv) In the summer of 1845 the Irish potato crop was ruined by blight. In a country where the peasants' basic diet consisted entirely of potatoes, this was disastrous. With the poor facing starvation, Peel arranged for £160 000 worth of maize to be imported from the USA to be sold at

1*d*. a pound to the Irish. But this was soon used up; in hundreds of villages in the west of Ireland there was no food of any sort and thousands were dying of starvation. At the same time the English and Scottish potato crop failed and the corn harvest was a poor one. In November 1845 Peel told his cabinet that the Corn Laws must go immediately; this was the only way to get cheap food into Ireland. Whether he really believed this or whether he was using the Irish famine as an emergency excuse to force repeal through is not certain. (In fact repeal made little difference to the situation in Ireland.) Either way a majority of the cabinet opposed the idea, and Peel resigned (December 1845).

(v) After Russell had failed to form a Whig government, Queen Victoria recalled Peel who had by now won over most of his cabinet, but not his party. A Repeal Bill (which would phase out the Corn Laws over the next three years) was introduced into the Commons. There was a fierce debate lasting five months during which about two-thirds of the Conservative MPs revolted against Peel. The Protectionists were led by Benjamin Disraeli and Lord George Bentinck. They made bitter personal attacks on Peel, claiming that the situation in Ireland was not serious enough to warrant such a Bill, and accusing Peel of breaking his promises and betraying his party again as he had over Catholic Emancipation.

(vi) The Repeal Bill passed the Commons (May 1846), but only with Whig support: the rebel Conservatives all voted against Peel. Thanks to Wellington's support the Bill passed the Lords without too much trouble and became law in June. But Disraeli and the Protectionists were determined on revenge. To help restore order in Ireland Peel had introduced a Coercion Bill into the Commons; on the same night as the Corn Law Repeal Bill passed the Lords, Disraeli and some of the rebel Conservatives combined with the Whigs and the Irish MPs to defeat the Coercion Bill. Peel resigned and never held office again.

(e) What were the effects of the Corn Law repeal? Oddly after the controversy and excitement, the results of the repeal were an anti-climax:

(i) There was no dramatic fall in wheat prices for the simple reason that whenever the British harvest was poor, so was the European one; there was no vast inflow of European wheat and supplies from North America were not yet available in large enough quantities. However, economists believe that repeal did at least keep British wheat prices steady at a time when world prices generally were rising.

(ii) British farmers did not suffer immediate ruin; they soon developed better methods - fertilisers, more mechanisation, drainage pipes, stronger strains of wheat - which increased yield per acre. As town populations increased steadily the demand for food grew and farmers were ensured reasonable profits. It was not until the 1870s that

British farming began to suffer competition from massive imports from America (see Section 15.4).

(iii) Repeal did not seem to help the Irish significantly; the 1846 potato crop failed as badly as the one in 1845, and 1847 saw only a slight improvement, so that the famine continued until 1848 when there was a good harvest. Since there were no large stocks of life-saving European corn available and Irish grown corn continued to be exported to England throughout the famine, the condition of the Irish peasants was pitiful. To add to their miseries a cholera epidemic broke out in December 1846; it is estimated that at least a million people died from starvation and disease and a further million emigrated to Canada and the USA.

(iv) Repeal probably encouraged other countries to reduce duties on goods from Britain although there were many other reasons for this reduction; there was much more behind the British trade expansion than the abolition of the Corn Laws.

(v) It destroyed Peel and split the party; after this the Conservatives were out of office (except for two short and ineffective periods in 1852 and 1858) until 1866.

Of course in June 1846, none of these results could be foreseen; as far as the League members were concerned, all else was forgotten as they celebrated their triumph.

(f) Why was the Anti-Corn Law League successful?

(i) The League concentrated on the one aim which was simple to understand (unlike the Chartists who tried to achieve too much all at once), and their arguments were reasonable and logical.

(ii) It was a middle-class inspired movement which provided it with sufficient funds to form a national organisation and mount an effective propaganda campaign (the Chartists - violent and threatening revolution - failed to win significant middle-class support).

(iii) They had outstanding and united leaders (especially Cobden and Bright) who were successful in winning 12 seats to put their case effectively in parliament. It was this continued pressure plus the strength of their case which convinced Peel that the Corn Laws must eventually go, though not necessarily immediately (the Chartist leaders were less able, could not agree on what tactics to follow, and failed to make an impact in parliament).

(iv) The Irish famine helped bring matters to a head, causing Peel or perhaps giving him an excuse, to abandon the Corn Laws earlier than he would otherwise have done.

7.6 WAS PEEL A GREAT STATESMAN?

Taking the *Oxford Dictionary* definition of a statesman as 'a person taking a prominent part in the management of state affairs', there can be no disputing that Peel was a statesman; but there have been widely varying views about how 'great' he was. W. Bagehot, writing in 1856, thought that though Peel was a great administrator, he was not a great statesman because he was not capable of creative thought; he merely borrowed other people's ideas. Bagehot made the point, well worth thinking about, that Peel had begun by opposing most of the measures which were later considered his greatest achievements (such as Catholic Emancipation and the Corn Law repeal); he was good at repealing things but not so impressive when it came to thinking of something new. G. Kitson Clark, writing his biography of Peel in 1936, believed that in spite of all his successes there was 'a lack of vision in Peel'.

On the other hand, Peel's was a career full of striking achievements, first as Irish Secretary (1812-18), then as Home Secretary (1822-30) and finally as Prime Minister. Norman Gash sums up his premiership clearly and simply: 'Financial stability had been achieved, trade revived, Chartism virtually extinguished, O'Connell's repeal movement checked, the great institutions of state safeguarded, and good relations with France and the USA restored [for his government's achievements in foreign affairs see Section 9.3] . . . More than any other one man he was the architect of the early Victorian age'. Yet how could he be a great statesman if he left his Conservative party in ruins? The answer is simple: Peel believed that the national interest was more important than party. When the Conservatives refused to go along with him over the Corn Laws, Peel was disgusted with them and disillusioned with party politics. Soon after the split he wrote: 'Thank God I am relieved for ever from the trammels of such a party'.

Peel died in 1850 at the early age of 62, from injuries sustained when he was thrown from his horse. Although many who knew him in politics thought him dull and cold (O'Connell said that when he smiled it was like the gleam of the silver plate on a coffin lid), the general public certainly felt that the country had lost its most brilliant politician. Among the many tributes which poured forth was this excruciating but sincere verse:

> Talk of Canning and Pitt for their talents and wit,
> And all who upheld that high station,
> Oh! there has ne'er been such a noble Premier
> As Sir Robert before in the nation,
> In every way he carried the sway,
> For the good of his country, God rest him.

QUESTIONS

1. The Abolition of the Corn Laws, 1846

Study Sources **A** to **G** and then answer the questions which follow.

Source A: A speech by Richard Cobden, 1839.

> We propose to keep people well informed as to the progress of
> our campaign by means of the penny post, by one letter a
> week . . . We intend to visit every borough in the kingdom, and
> we shall invite the electors to meet us. We shall urge them to
> have a *Free-trade* candidate to supplant every monopolist who
> still retains a seat for a borough . . .
>
> The single and undisputed object of the League is to put
> down commercial *monopoly* . . . The Corn-law is the great
> tree of monopoly, under whose evil shadow every other restric-
> tion exists. Cut it down by the roots and it will destroy the
> others in its fall. The sole object of the League is to put an end
> once and for ever to the principle of maintaining taxes for the
> benefit of a particular class.
>
> Free Trade! What is it? Why, the breaking down of barriers
> that separate nations . . . those barriers behind which nestle
> feelings of pride, revenge, hatred and jealousy, which every
> now and then burst their bounds, and deluge whole countries
> with blood . . . those feelings which assert that without con-
> quest we can have no trade . . . I see in the Free Trade principle
> that which will draw men together, thrusting aside the antag-
> onism of race, creed and language, and uniting us in the bonds
> of eternal peace.

> **Source:** J. Bright and J. E. T. Rogers (eds), *Speeches by
> Richard Cobden*, Macmillan, 1880 (adapted extracts).

Source B: An Anti-Corn Law League leaflet.

WORKING MEN!
You Pay a Tax of Tenpence
*Upon every Stone of Flour you and your wives
and little ones consume.*

If there was not the Infamous CORN LAW you and your Families
might buy THREE LOAVES for the same money that you now pay for
Two.

Upon every Shilling you spend for Bread, Meat, Bacon, Eggs,
Vegetables, &c., you pay 4d. Tax for Monopoly.

DOWN, DOWN
WITH THE
Infamous Bread Tax!

Source: N. McCord, *Free Trade*, David & Charles, 1970.

Source C: Speech by Sir Robert Peel in the House of Commons during the Corn Law Repeal Bill debate, February 1846.

This night you will select the motto which is to indicate the commercial policy of England. Shall it be 'advance' or 'recede'? Which is to be the fitter motto for this great Empire? Survey our position, consider the advantage which God and nature have given us . . . Iron and coal, the sinews of manufacture, give us advantages over every other rival in the great competition of industry. Our capital far exceeds that which they can command. Our national character, the free institutions under which we live, an unshackled press . . . all combine to place us at the head of these nations which profit by the free interchange of their products. And is this the country to shrink from competition?

Choose your motto. 'Advance' or 'Recede'. Vote for 'Advance' and it will encourage in every state the friends of a liberal commercial policy. Sardinia has taken the lead. Naples is relaxing her protective duties and favouring British produce. Can you doubt that the United States will soon relax her hostile Tariff? Act thus and you will have done whatever human wisdom can do for the promotion of commercial prosperity . . . Of course there is no guarantee that prosperity will continue without interruption – it seems to be unavoidable that the time of depression shall follow the season of excitement and success . . . may God grant that by your decision tonight you will have the consolation of knowing that such calamities have not been caused by laws of man restricting, in the hour of scarcity, the supply of food.

Source: quoted in L. Evans and P. J. Pledger, *Contemporary Sources and Opinions in Modern British History, vol. I*, Warne, 1967 (adapted extracts).

Source D: Speeches by Benjamin Disraeli in the House of Commons during the Corn Law Repeal Bill debate, February–May 1846.

When we complain of the right hon. gentleman [Peel] not treating his party fairly, we speak of the great body of the community whose views they represent . . . I say that it is the first duty of a minister to maintain a balance between the two great branches of national industry . . . and we should give a preponderance to the agricultural branch; this is not in order to pamper the luxury of the owners of land, but it is because our present system is the only security for self-government; the only barrier against that centralising system which has taken root in other countries. My constituents are not landlords; they are not aristocrats; they are not great capitalists; they are the children of industry and toil; but they believe that their social and political interests are involved in a system by which their rights and liberties have been guaranteed; and I agree with them. I have the same old-fashioned notions . . .

When I examine the career of this minister [Peel] I find that for between 30 and 40 years, he has traded on the ideas and intelligence of others. He is a burglar of others' intellect . . . there is no other statesman who has committed petty larceny on so great a scale.

Source: R. Grinter, *Disraeli and Conservatism*, Arnold, 1968; R. Brown and C. Daniels, *Nineteenth Century Britain*, Macmillan, 1980 (adapted extracts).

Source E: Some information from a modern historian.

At the end of February, 231 Conservatives voted against the second reading of the Corn Bill, while only 112 voted for it. But what surprised Peel more was the vigour of his opponents, which transformed what he imagined would be a short if bloody battle into a five months campaign. It was not until the 28 June that the bill passed its third reading in the Lords, and by that time Peel had been the recipient of more malicious criticism than he could ever have thought possible. The attacks were led by Benjamin Disraeli, who could hardly believe that fate had made so vulnerable the man who had refused to admit his suitability for office in 1841, and who had since done nothing to make good his mistake.

Source: K. H. Randell, *Politics and the People 1835-1850*, Collins, 1972.

Source F: Some comments from another modern historian.

Peel's repeal of the Corn Laws in 1846 was the decisive compromise with industry by the party of agriculture. Disraeli condemned this whole policy; the argument that he merely seized an opportunity for personal advance is very attractive, as he quickly made free trade part of Conservative policy, and found his party excluded from office for a generation by distrust of his tactics. But there was also a genuine and lasting dislike of all that the Whig/Liberal group stood for and the repeal would advance – the doctrine of the equality of man and the methods of private enterprise that drove industry forward.

Source: R. Grinter, *Disraeli and Conservatism*, Arnold, 1968.

Source G: An article in a journal, the *Fortnightly Review*, 1878.

The growing distrust felt towards the Prime Minister, Sir Robert Peel, as he pursued his liberalising course in economic policy, made a Protectionist Party possible, and to its formation Mr. Disraeli devoted himself . . . But it was not within his moral right to call disgraceful, conduct which he had earlier praised. Sir Robert Peel was the convert, the honest convert, of public opinion. The proper contrast is between the statesman who does something about delayed convictions at the right time, and the trading politician who resists measures which he knows to be just and necessary in order to humour a particular group of people or to justify personal spite or ambition.

Source: quoted in R. Grinter, *Disraeli and Conservatism*, Arnold, 1968.

(a)   Explain what Cobden meant in Source **A** by the following terms:

   (i)   monopoly,

   (ii)   Free-trade.   **1, 4(a)**

(b) (i)   According to Source **A**, what were Cobden's reasons for wanting the Corn Laws abolished?   **4(a)**

   (ii)   What other reasons, not mentioned in this speech, did the Anti-Corn Law League put forward in support of their campaign?
                                                                              1, 2, 4(a)

(c) (i)   From the evidence of Sources **A** and **B**, what methods did the League use in their campaign?   **4(a, c)**

   (ii)   What techniques did the designer of the leaflet (Source **B**) use to get his message across? Explain whether or not you think he does it successfully.   **4(a, b)**

   (iii)   What other methods, not mentioned in Sources **A** and **B**, did the League use in their campaign?   **1, 2, 4(a)**

(d) (i)   Explain in your own words the reasons put forward by Peel in Source **C** for his opposition to the Corn Laws.   **4(a)**

   (ii)   What evidence can you find in Source **C** to suggest that Peel might have been influenced by the famine in Ireland?   **4(a)**

(e) (i)   What arguments does Disraeli put forward in Source **D** in support of the Corn Laws?   **4(a)**

   (ii)   What other arguments, not mentioned in this speech, did supporters of the Corn Laws put forward?   **1, 2, 4(a)**

   (iii)   What criticisms does Disraeli make of Peel in Source **D**?   **4(a)**

   (iv)   Why did Disraeli think that Peel was 'not treating his party fairly', at the beginning of Source **D**?   **1, 2, 4(a, b)**

   (v)   What did Disraeli mean when he called Peel 'a burglar of others' intellect'?   **1, 2, 4(a, b)**

(f) (i)   According to Source **E**, roughly what proportion of Conservative MPs voted against the abolition of the Corn Laws?   **4(a)**

   (ii)   What was it that had surprised Peel more than anything during the debate?   **4(a)**

(g) (i)   How do the writers of Sources **E** and **F** differ in their views about why Disraeli attacked Peel so bitterly during the debate?
                                                                              4(a, c)

(ii) From the evidence of Sources **E**, **F** and **G**, how genuine do you think Disraeli's motives were in attacking Peel? Explain your answer fully. **4(a, b, c)**

(iii) Do you think that the writer of the article in Source **G** was an admirer of Peel or of Disraeli? Give reasons for your answer.

4(a, b)

(h) Using the Sources and your own knowledge, explain why the Anti-Corn Law League was successful. **1, 2, 4(a, c)**

2. Sir Robert Peel

Read this extract from a biography of Sir Robert Peel and then answer the questions which follow.

> Scarcely any other English statesman has achieved the enactment of so many wise measures. The resumption of cash payments, the amendment of the criminal law, the institution of the Irish constabulary and the London police, Catholic emancipation, the emancipation of trade, and a crowd of reforms only less beneficial than these, make up a record of useful labour which has seldom been surpassed . . . What matters more is that Peel spent much of his life opposing several of the reforms which he afterwards carried, and which he could not have carried without that power which he had acquired by opposing them. There seems to be little doubt that he was honest in resistance as well as in concession, that in each case he furthered what he believed to be the public good . . . A man who never modifies an opinion is simply stupid. But a man who is always shifting from one opinion to another, lacks something which a man should have . . .
>
> Party government cannot be sound unless parties represent principles, and parties cannot represent principles if the leader will not keep faith with his followers.
>
> **Source:** F. C. Montague, *Life of Sir Robert Peel*, W. H. Allen, 1888.

(a) (i) According to the writer of the extract, which were the 'wise measures' achieved by Peel? **4(a)**

(ii) Describe how Peel introduced 'the emancipation of trade' during his 1841–46 government. **1, 2**

(b) Another important reform introduced by Peel was the Bank Charter Act of 1844. Explain:

(i) why this Act was necessary;

(ii) what changes it introduced;

(iii) whether or not it was successful. **1, 2**

(c) (i) Describe the part played by Peel in the development of the Conservative party.

(ii) Do you think he deserves to be remembered as the founder of the party? **1, 2**

(d)   Do you think the writer of this extract was an admirer of Peel or not? Give full reasons for your answer.   **4(a, b)**

3.   Describe and explain the importance to Sir Robert Peel and the Conservative party of **(a)** the Tamworth Manifesto (1834) and **(b)** the Repeal of the Corn Laws (1846).

4.   Describe and explain how the policies introduced by Peel during his 1841–46 government;

(a)   helped:
- **(i)**   the working classes,
- **(ii)**   industrialists and merchants,
- **(iii)**   the Irish, but

(b)   annoyed landowners and farmers.   **1, 2**

5.   Sir Robert Peel died in 1850 from injuries sustained when he was thrown from his horse. He was 62. Write the drafts of two contrasting obituary notices such as might have been written by:

(a)   a Tory who had supported Peel over the repeal of the Corn Laws (for example, Lord Aberdeen),

(b)   a Tory who had wanted to keep the Corn Laws and felt that Peel had betrayed his party (for example, Benjamin Disraeli).   **1, 2, 3**

CHAPTER 8

DOMESTIC AFFAIRS 1846-67:
RUSSELL, GLADSTONE, DISRAELI
AND THE REFORM ACT OF 1867

SUMMARY OF EVENTS

Although this was a time of general economic prosperity, *the political scene was confused and unstable* following the Conservative split over the Corn Law repeal. Those Conservatives, including *W. E. Gladstone and Lord Aberdeen* who had voted with Peel for the abolition of the Corn Laws, were known as *Peelites*; those who had wanted to keep the Corn Laws (*Protectionists*) were led officially by *Lord Derby*, though *Disraeli* supplied the brains. The two groups would have nothing to do with each other, and the Peelites usually voted with the Whigs. This enabled *Lord John Russell*, leader of the Whigs, to form a government with Peelite support, even though the Whigs lacked an overall majority. The Whigs improved their position in the 1847 general election, winning 325 seats to the Tory Protectionists' 226. However, the Peelites with 105 seats held the balance, and the Whigs could not afford to ignore their wishes if they wanted to remain in power. In the 1852 election the Peelites dwindled to 40 (Peel himself had died in 1850), but they still held the balance, and actually formed a coalition government with the Whigs; the Peelite leader, Lord Aberdeen, was Prime Minister (1852-5). The Peelites gradually faded out as most of them joined the Whigs or Liberals, as they were now being called. But the Conservatives had still not recovered fully from the split, and were only in government for three short spells during this period. The list of governments illustrates the instability:

Party	Prime Minister	In Office
Whig	Lord John Russell	1846-52
Conservative	Lord Derby	February-December 1852
Whig/Peelite coalition	Lord Aberdeen	1852-5
Liberal	Lord Palmerston	1855-8
Conservative	Lord Derby	1858-9
Liberal	Lord Palmerston	1859-65
Liberal	Lord John Russell	1865-6
Conservative	Lord Derby	1866-8
Conservative	Benjamin Disraeli	February-December 1868
Liberal	William Ewart Gladstone	1868-74

Domestic politics were for the most part uneventful during these years, with certain exceptions, notably the final fling of *Chartism* in 1848 (see Section 6.4(c)) and *some useful social reforms* introduced by Russell's government of 1846-52. Gladstone, who was Chancellor of the Exchequer for much of the time between 1852 and 1866, continued *the move towards Free Trade*, his policies reaching a climax with a series of remarkable budgets (1860-4). The most striking feature on the domestic scene was not in politics at all: it was the great surge of industrial and agricultural prosperity sometimes referred to as *the Golden Age of Victorian Britain* (see Section 15.1).

In the middle of the period much of the public's attention was occupied with events abroad – *the Crimean War of 1854-6* (see Chapter 10) and *the Indian Mutiny of 1857* (see Chapter 11); public interest in foreign affairs was maintained during *Palmerston's* second spell as Prime Minister, from 1859-65 (see Section 9.5).

During the 1860s the question which again came to the forefront of domestic affairs was the need for a further reform of parliament. After long wrangling reminiscent of the struggle to get the 1832 Reform Bill through, Derby's Conservative government was responsible for the *Reform Act of 1867,* another major step towards a democratic system of parliamentary government. Much to the disgust of the Conservatives, the newly enlarged electorate responded at the general election of 1868 by voting in a Liberal government with a majority of over 100.

8.1 HOW SUCCESSFUL WERE THE DOMESTIC POLICIES OF RUSSELL'S GOVERNMENT OF 1846-52?

Broadly speaking the government had its main successes up to 1850, but after that it ran into trouble and achieved little of any significance.

(a) Ireland was the most pressing problem, with famine and cholera continuing until 1848. The government did its best in an impossible situation, and the country had at least settled down by the end of 1848. However, the terrible suffering and loss of life served only to fuel Irish hatred of the English (see Section 13.3(a)).

(b) The Chartist outburst of 1848, which might well have got out of hand, was decisively dealt with (see Section 6.4 (c)).

(c) Social reforms included *two Factory Acts, Fielden's in 1847 and Grey's in 1850*, both concerned with limiting the working day for women (see Section 12.3) and the *1848 Public Health Act* (see Section 12.5(a)). This was a pioneering piece of legislation which allowed Local Boards of Health to be set up to improve sanitation and water supply, but the fact that it was not compulsory robbed it of much of its effectiveness. The government grant for education was increased in 1847 (see Section 12.7(a)).

(d) After 1850 the government aroused opposition and lost support over several issues:

(i) The 1851 budget was highly unpopular among manufacturers and businessmen who had hoped to see income tax (standing at 7*d*. in the £) abolished.

(ii) Russell appeared to be against parliamentary reform when he opposed a private member's bill which would have made the voting qualification the same in both counties and boroughs. The Radicals, already disappointed over the budget, were so annoyed with Russell that they voted for the motion which was passed against Russell's wishes. At this point the Prime Minister resigned (February 1851) but the Conservatives, lacking a majority, failed to form a government, so Russell came back for another year. This was long enough to see through the Great Exhibition (see Section 15.1(a)).

But the government grew steadily weaker and was finally brought down by Palmerston in retaliation for his dismissal by Russell a few weeks earlier (see Section 9.4(e)).

8.2 WHAT CONTRIBUTION DID GLADSTONE MAKE TO THE DEVELOPMENT OF THE BRITISH ECONOMY WHILE HE WAS CHANCELLOR OF THE EXCHEQUER?

William Ewart Gladstone, the son of a wealthy Liverpool merchant, was educated at Eton and Christ Church, Oxford, and first entered parliament as a Tory in 1832. For a time he was President of the Board of Trade in Peel's 1841-6 government, helping to formulate Peel's great tariff reforms. When the Conservatives split over the repeal of the Corn Laws, Gladstone remained a Peel supporter, which kept him out of office until 1852 when he became Chancellor of the Exchequer in the Whig–Peelite coalition (until 1855). The Conservatives tried to entice him back, but he was now moving firmly towards the Liberals, and when Palmerston invited him to take up his old post, Gladstone accepted. He was Liberal Chancellor of the Exchequer from 1859 until 1865, and became Liberal leader in the House of Commons on Palmerston's death.

(a) Gladstone had strong views about economic policy:

(i) While serving with Peel, he had been converted to the idea of Free Trade. The more manufacturers and businessmen could be freed from having to pay tariffs, the more cheaply they could produce their goods; these would be all the more competitive on the world market and British exports would increase.

(ii) Full employment and low food prices would enable the working class to enjoy a share of the general prosperity.

(iii) Gladstone believed it was important to keep both government expenditure and taxation to a minimum: 'All excess in public expenditure ... is not only a pecuniary waste, but above all, a great moral evil'. He hoped to abolish the income tax and generally make government finance more efficient.

(iv) The result of all this would be to create the right environment for people to prosper, to live economically and to build up their savings; in other words, people should help themselves, rather than expect the government to spend vast amounts of cash on welfare schemes.

(b) Gladstone's aims put into practice:

(i) *The attack on tariffs* began immediately in the 1853 budget: he abolished nearly all remaining duties on partially manufactured goods and on food, including fruit and dairy produce, and halved nearly all remaining duties on fully manufactured goods; these changes affected over 250 separate articles. The 1860 budget continued this trend, import duties being abolished on a further 375 articles; this left only another 48 articles being taxed. Even this was whittled down further when Gladstone reduced the duty on sugar (1864) and later halved the duty on tea (from 1s. to 6d. a pound).

(ii) *Income tax reduction* proved more difficult to achieve; Gladstone hoped to phase it out gradually, ending it altogether in 1859. He was reluctant to abolish it at a stroke in his 1853 budget because he needed the revenue it produced to make up for that lost from the tariffs he was abolishing. His plans were thwarted by the outbreak of the Crimean War in 1854 which forced him to raise income tax to 1s. 2d. in the £. After the war he realised that it was far too valuable a tax to disappear completely, but he reduced it bit by bit until it was down to 4d. in the 1865 budget.

(iii) *The Cobden Treaty (1860)* with France sprang from a mixture of economic and political motives. The details were worked out by Richard Cobden negotiating with Napoleon III's government in Paris. Cobden was convinced that Free Trade between the great nations would remove many of the causes of international friction. Since the British were eternally suspicious of Napoleon III's intentions, Gladstone was prepared to give Cobden a free hand in the hope of reducing tension. The agreement was that France reduced import duties on British coal and manufactured goods and in return Britain reduced duties on French wines and brandy, all of which fitted in well with Gladstone's tariff policy.

(iv) Gladstone introduced a clever new practice in the way laws dealing with financial matters were passed. Instead of introducing a number of separate bills, he combined them all into one large bill for the 1861 budget. This brought greater speed and efficiency into the passing of financial legislation. However, his real motive was to manoeuvre the House of Lords into approving the abolition of duty on paper; in 1860 they had voted out the bill abolishing the duty, in case it encouraged the growth of a cheap left-wing press. The Lords could hardly throw out the entire budget just to save the paper duty; so Gladstone had his way and the combined budget has remained until the present day.

(v) *The Post Office Savings Bank (1861)* was opened, and after only a year it had attracted 180 000 investors who deposited between them almost two million pounds. This was a most important achievement not only because it encouraged ordinary people to save, but also because it provided the government with a new supply of cash which it could draw on if necessary.

(c) Gladstone's policies had far-reaching effects:

(i) Free Trade provided a great stimulus to the British economy. The 1860 Cobden Treaty alone produced a threefold increase in British trade with France by 1880. In general between 1850 and 1870, British exports increased fourfold, while the outstanding success story was provided by coal exports which increased in value fivefold during the same 20-year period. Of course all this was not due solely to Gladstone's tariff policies: there were other causes such as the improvement in communications (railways and steamships); but Gladstone certainly created the right atmosphere for the great Victorian boom to develop (see Section 15.1).

(ii) The working-classes were probably better fed, since wages rose rather more than food prices. There was, for example, a marked increase in the consumption of such commodities as tea and sugar. On the other hand, Gladstone's economy drive (he reduced national expenditure from over £70 million in 1860 to about £66 million in 1866) meant that much needed social reform in the field of public health, sanitation, housing and education could not take place.

(iii) Gladstone's reputation among fellow politicians and with the general public was much enhanced by his achievements. It was no surprise when he became leader of the Liberals in 1868, and his popularity partly explains the Liberal victory in the general election held later that year.

8.3 WHY DID THE DEMAND FOR PARLIAMENTARY REFORM REVIVE IN THE EARLY 1860s?

After the passing of the 1832 Reform Act, most people, including Lord John Russell, who had introduced the bill, believed that this was the end of the matter. But gradually the situation changed and several influences, both internal and external, combined to bring about a widespread feeling that further reform was necessary.

(a) There had been important population changes since 1832. The total

population of Britain increased from 24 million in 1831 to 29 million in 1861; by 1865 the adult male population of England and Wales had risen to over five million, and yet of those, only fractionally over a million had the vote; the vast majority of the working class was therefore still voteless. People had continued to move into the ever-expanding industrial areas, but there had been no corresponding changes in constituencies and no new ones created. Clearly some extension of the vote and some redistribution of seats was necessary.

(b) Radicals both inside and outside parliament, with *John Bright* as their acknowledged leader, kept up a constant pressure for reform. Bright was convinced that democracy as it operated in the USA, Australia and Canada, should be tried in Britain. During the winter of 1858-9 he launched himself upon a series of great speeches which brought reform more publicity than it had enjoyed for a decade; it was time, he argued, that ordinary people were given a share in controlling their own fortunes; 'palaces, baronial castles, great halls, stately mansions, do not make a nation. The nation in every country dwells in the cottage', he told a Birmingham audience in October 1858.

(c) The Trade Union movement campaigned for reform. During the 1850s, associations of skilled workers, known as Model Unions, began to spread (see Section 19.3). These new craft unions were more moderate than earlier unions, and their leaders, men like *Robert Applegarth* of the Sheffield carpenters and bricklayer George Howell, demonstrated that they were responsible people, concerned to improve standards for the workers and to reform parliament by legal means, not by revolution. They were in contact with Radical MPs, and succeeded in impressing a large section of the Liberal party, and many of the Conservatives as well, with their sense of responsibility. As early as 1861 working men in Leeds were organising reform conferences and in March 1864, *The Reform Union*, an alliance of working and middle class reformers, was set up at a meeting in the Manchester Free Trade Hall.

(d) The American Civil War (1861-5) was an important external stimulus. For most Radicals this was a simple case of freedom (the North) struggling to assert itself against tyranny and slavery (the South), and provided splendid publicity for the idea of equal rights and opportunities within a nation. The war had another effect: the northern blockade of southern ports cut off cotton supplies to the industrial towns of Lancashire, bringing serious unemployment and hardship during late 1861 and right through 1862. Yet by the end of 1862, as the cotton workers realised that the North stood for the abolition of slavery, they swung their support firmly behind the North, whose warships were the direct cause of their distress. This reaction impressed many politicians as a sign of working-class political maturity.

(e) Gladstone was converted to the idea of reform by a combination of Radical and trade union pressure. He first revealed his change of mind publicly in the Commons in 1864 when he said, 'Every man who is not

124

illus 8.1 *The cotton famine in Lancashire*

THE DISTRIBUTION

incapacitated by some consideration of personal unfitness or political danger, is morally entitled to come within the pale of the constitution'. This angered his Prime Minister, Palmerston, who was still against reform and who retorted, 'I entirely deny that every sane man has a moral right to a vote.' Gladstone's approval of the Lancashire cotton workers' political maturity led him to declare that it was 'a shame and a scandal that bodies of men such as these should be excluded from the parliamentary franchise'. The death of the anti-reform Palmerston (1865) removed the most serious obstacle to reform in the Liberal party.

(f) The visit of Giuseppe Garibaldi to London (April 1864) gave added publicity to the idea of liberal reform. In 1860 he had played a vital and heroic part in the unification of Italy and was still popular with the British public as a liberal and a democrat. A group of his admirers eventually became *the Reform League* (February 1865) which had extensive Trade Union support.

(g) The Conservatives accepted that pressure would eventually bring about further reform: Disraeli, their leader in the Commons, was even prepared to introduce limited reform of parliament himself, provided it didn't go too far. His reasoning seems to have been that if further reform really was inevitable, as Bright kept telling everybody, then the Conservatives ought to jump in and take the credit for it. In fact the Tories did bring in a very mild reform bill (March 1859) but it was thrown out, most of the Liberals voting against it because it did nothing to extend the vote in the boroughs and would have brought very few workers in.

8.4 BY WHAT STAGES WAS REFORM ACHIEVED?

(a) Russell and Gladstone introduced a moderate reform bill in March 1866, which proposed to give the vote in the boroughs to householders paying £7 a year rent (instead of £10) and in the counties to tenants paying £14 a year rent (instead of £50). This was expected to bring an extra 400 000 voters onto the lists. No mention was made of redistributing seats. There was lively opposition in the Commons from:

(i) The Conservatives, who thought the bill went too far; *Lord Cranborne* (later Lord Salisbury) compared the state to a joint-stock company, arguing that 'the wildest dreamer never suggested that all the shareholders should hold a single vote without reference to the number of shares they might hold'. Even Disraeli thought that the bill would bring into parliament 'a horde of selfish and obscure mediocrities, incapable of anything but mischief'.

(ii) A section of the Liberals led by *Robert Lowe*, who claimed that the working classes were ignorant of politics, would be incapable of deciding who to vote for and would be open to bribery. They were full of 'venality, ignorance, drunkenness and the facility for being intimidated'. Bright nicknamed Lowe and his supporters *the Adullamites* (after the Bible story about the discontented Israelites who left Saul to join David in the Cave of Adullam).

The opposition introduced an amendment to reduce the number of new voters, and when the Commons passed the amendment, Russell resigned (June). It was a sad end to Russell's career in politics, since he had hoped to bow out with reform as his crowning achievement.

(b) The incoming Conservative government hoped to move slowly and introduce some mild reform in 1868. However, public interest was now thoroughly aroused, and *pressure built up for immediate action*: Bright embarked on another speaking tour to campaign for reform; there was a short, sharp economic crisis which developed early in 1866, several companies went bankrupt and there was widespread unemployment. Bread was expensive following the poor harvest of 1865 and there was a sudden cholera epidemic which killed 8000 people in London alone. In July a demonstration was planned to take place in Hyde Park. When the Government closed the Park to the meeting there were some disturbances during which 1400 yards of railings were demolished. It was the combination of all these circumstances which convinced the Conservatives that reform could not wait. Derby and Disraeli decided to make a bid for popularity which would prolong their stay in office and 'dish the Liberals'.

(c) Both Disraeli and Derby were prepared to introduce a much more drastic bill than Gladstone's if it would bring the Tories a long period in power. Their problem was that Cranborne and his supporters in the cabinet threatened to resign if the bill went too far, so in February 1867 a measure was introduced which was so mild that it caused an uproar in the Commons when it was read out. It was obvious that the Liberals would not vote for it, and rather than be forced to resign, Disraeli decided to risk upsetting Cranborne by introducing a more radical measure. Cranborne and two other cabinet members resigned, but Disraeli pushed ahead with his bill. As it passed its various stages in the Commons the Liberals proposed several amendments, all accepted, which made the final bill even more extreme. This Conservative bill became law in August 1867, and is usually known as *The Second Reform Act*.

8.5 WHAT WERE THE TERMS AND EFFECTS OF THE 1867 REFORM ACT?

(a) Terms

(i) *In the boroughs* the vote was given to all householders (both owner-occupiers and tenants) who paid rates, provided they had lived in their house at least one year. Lodgers paying £10 a year rent also received the vote.

(ii) *In the counties* the vote was given to all ratepayers paying £12 a year

in rates, and to copyholders and leaseholders holding land valued at £5 a year.
(iii) Boroughs with a population of under 10 000 lost one MP. This released 45 seats for redistribution; 25 of them were given to the counties, 15 to boroughs which had not had an MP up till now, one was given to the University of London, and a third member was given to Liverpool, Manchester, Leeds and Birmingham.
(iv) The franchise in Scotland was brought into line with the English pattern, and seven seats were transferred from England to Scotland.
(v) In Irish boroughs the vote was given to £4 ratepayers.

(b) The effects of the Act, apart from the obvious one of increasing the size of the electorate, were something of an unknown quantity at the time. Even Derby admitted that they were 'making a great experiment and taking a leap in the dark', while the historian Thomas Carlyle said it was 'like shooting Niagara'.

(i) The size of the electorate was almost doubled from about 1.36 million to 2.46 million.
(ii) Most of the new voters were industrial workers living in the towns, so for the first time there was something approaching democracy in the boroughs.

However, there were some other results which showed that the leap in the dark fell a long way short of full democracy:

(iii) In the counties the voting qualification was high enough to keep agricultural labourers (the majority of the rural population) and people such as miners living in rural pit villages without the vote. This was totally illogical discrimination, but was designed to preserve the power of wealthy farmers and landowners. If democracy had to be conceded in the boroughs, the wealthy were determined to salvage at least something for themselves in the countryside.
(iv) Voting was still held in public; the lack of secrecy meant that working class borough voters were bound to be swayed by their employers and landlords (the 1872 Ballot Act solved this problem – see Section 13.2(f)).
(v) The distribution of seats still left a lot to be desired. Many small towns with only just over 10 000 inhabitants – such as Tiverton for example – still had two MPs like Glasgow which had over half a million. The South and East were still over-represented compared with the industrial Midlands and North; Wiltshire and Dorset between them were represented by 25 MPs for a population of 450 000, yet the West Riding of Yorkshire with over two million had only 22 MPs.

As time went on other results became apparent which had not been fore-seen in 1867:

(vi) The increased borough electorates meant that there were too many voters to bribe; politicians began to realise that they must explain and justify their policies, and gradually the whole nature of politics changed as the election campaign in the constituencies became the accepted procedure. The Liberals were the first to appreciate this, with Gladstone leading the way in the 1868 general election.

(vii) The creation of the large three-member constituencies like Birmingham and Leeds led to another development: the rule was that each elector could only vote for two candidates; this meant that, for example, one of the three Birmingham Liberal candidates might not poll enough votes to be elected, while the other two received far more than was necessary. It was, in fact, the Birmingham Liberals who first realised that this wastage of votes could be avoided by having a local organisation to direct the distribution of Liberal votes to make sure that all three candidates were elected. The Conservatives soon followed suit and before long party organisations developed both at national and constituency level to whip up support at election time and to nurse the voters between elections.

In spite of his triumph, Disraeli (who became Prime Minister on Derby's retirement) still lacked a Commons majority, and hoped that the 1868 election would bring its reward. To his intense disappointment the Liberals won with a majority of 112. *The reasons were*: Gladstone and Bright conducted a vigorous election campaign, speaking all over the country, whereas Disraeli merely sent a printed election address to his constituents, and missed a splendid opportunity of winning over the new borough voters with a programme of much-needed social reform. Gladstone won middle and working class Nonconformist support by announcing that the Liberals would disestablish the Anglican Church in Ireland.

QUESTIONS

1. The Passing of the 1867 Parliamentary Reform Act
Study Sources **A** to **F** and then answer the questions which follow.

Source A: a speech by John Bright, 1866.

We now come to the Rochdale District Co-operative Corn Mill Society, which does a large business. It has a capital of £60,000 and turns over £164,000 per annum. It has also a committee, but neither the president, nor treasurer, nor secretary, nor any one of this committee has a borough vote. Now what is taking place in Rochdale societies is occurring in greater or less degree in all the societies, of which there are five or six hundred throughout the country . . . You have one million electors now, and there are eight million of grown men in the United Kingdom; can you say that only one million shall have votes and that all the rest are to remain excluded? Is the thing possible?

Source: quoted in D. G. Wright, *Democracy and Reform 1815-1885*, Longman, 1970 (adapted extracts).

Source B: a speech by W. E. Gladstone in the House of Commons, April 1866.

An enormous benefit has been effected by the freedom of the press, when for the humble sum of a penny, or even less, newspapers are circulated by the million, carrying home to all classes of our fellow countrymen, accounts of public affairs, enabling them to feel a new interest in those affairs . . . And the working community has responded fully to all calls made upon it to improve itself. Take for example the Working Men's Free Libraries throughout the country . . . Then again, Sir, we called upon them to be thrifty, and we started for them Post Office savings banks; and what has been the result? There are now 650,000 depositors in those savings banks. Parliament has been striving to make the working class progressively fitter and fitter for the franchise; and can anything be more unwise, not to say more senseless, than to persevere from year to year in this plan, and then blindly refuse to recognise its logical upshot – namely, the increased fitness of the working class for political power.

Souce: quoted in L. Evans and P. J. Pledger, *Contemporary Sources and Opinions in Modern British History, vol. I*, Warne, 1967 (adapted extracts).

Source G: Speeches by Robert Lowe, a Liberal MP, in the House of Commons, May 1867.

The right hon. gentleman opposite [Disraeli] has adopted a course which is infinitely creditable to his dexterity as a tactician. He well knew that had he proposed the measure as it is now before us, and shown it to his party at first, they would have started back from it in horror. The right hon. gentleman has treated them as we treat a shy horse . . . take him gently up, walk him round the object, and then, when the process has been repeated often enough, we hope we shall get the creature to pass it quietly . . . clearly he was determined from the beginning that *household suffrage* was the principle he intended to introduce . . .

You are about to take away the management of affairs from the upper and middle classes, and you are about to place it in the hands of people of whose politics you know nothing, for the best of all possible reasons – because they do not know what their politics are themselves. But they will not be always without politics; and what will they be? Their politics must take one form – Socialism . . .

The first stage will be an increase of corruption, intimidation and disorder, of all the evils that happen usually in elections. The second will be that the working men of England, finding themselves in a full majority, will awake to a full sense of their power. They will say 'We can do better for ourselves; we have our trade unions; we have our leaders all ready'.

Now, I ask the House again, with the example of America before us, is it wise to push forward in this direction. We see in America, where the people have undisputed power, that they do not send honest, hard-working men to represent them in Congress, but dealers in office, bankrupts, men who have lost their character and been driven from every respectable way of life, and who take up politics as a last resource.

Source: quoted in D. G. Wright, *Democracy and Reform 1815–1885*, Longman, 1970 and in R. Grinter, *Disraeli and Conservatism*, Arnold, 1968 (adapted extracts).

Source D: some information from a modern historian, Robert Blake.

The events of the next two years (1866–7) seem to be paradoxical. The Liberals bring in a moderate Reform Bill in 1866. There is a right wing revolt against it within the party. The Conservatives in alliance with the rebels defeat the Bill. The government resigns. So far all is going according to form. But the new Conservative government does not act according to form. It brings in and carries a Reform Act which, by giving household suffrage in the towns, extends the franchise much more widely than the Liberal Bill that the Conservatives have helped to reject only twelve months earlier. To explain this paradox there have been three main theories:

ONE – the Liberal theory: that the Bill in its final form was forced on Disraeli by Gladstone, as the price paid by unscrupulous Tories for remaining in office. The true facts were recognised by the newly enfranchised town householders who showed their gratitude to Gladstone by returning the Liberals with an increased majority in the first election under the new Act.

TWO – the Tory democracy theory: that the Reform Act was not forced on a reluctant Disraeli, but fulfilled an aim which he had held for many years – to further some kind of alliance between the aristocracy and the urban working class. If the new franchise did not lead to a Conservative break through in 1868, the party certainly triumphed in 1874, when the town householder had had time to see who was his true friend. The social reforms of 1875 and 1876 lend further colour to the view that the Conservatives were appealing to the working man. Far from yielding to pressure in 1867, Disraeli was educating his party.

THREE – the Labour theory: that the politicians were subject to the pressure of mass working class agitation expressed through the activities of the Reform League. According to this theory, the really crucial event was the demonstration by the League in Hyde Park in May 1867, in defiance of the government's ban. This, it is alleged, is the direct cause of Disraeli's adding another 400,000 voters to the borough electorate.

Source: R. Blake, *The Conservative Party from Peel to Thatcher*, Collins/Fontana, 1985 (adapted extracts).

Source E: Speech by Disraeli in the House of Commons during the Reform Bill debate, July 1867.

I think that the danger would be less, that the feeling of the larger numbers would be more national, than by giving the vote just to a sort of class set aside, looking with suspicion on their superiors, and with disdain on those beneath them. I think you would have a better chance of touching the popular heart, of evoking the national sentiment, by bringing in the great body of those men who occupy houses and fulfil the duties of citizenship by the payment of rates.

Source: quoted in D. G. Wright, *Democracy and Reform 1815– 1885*, Longman, 1970 (adapted extracts).

Source F: from a biography of Gladstone, written by John Morley, a Liberal politician.

It was at Mr. Gladstone's demand that lodgers were given the vote, and that the distribution of seats was extended into an operation of enormously larger scale.

Source: J. Morley, *The Life of William Ewart Gladstone, vol. I*, Macmillan, 1903.

(a)   (i)   What methods does Bright use in Source **A** to put his view that the franchise should be extended?   **4(a)**

    (ii)   Explain why Gladstone (Source **B**) wanted to give the vote to some working people.   **4(a)**

    (iii)   What events of 1866 increased the pressure for a further reform of parliament? Read Source **D** for a clue to one of these events.   **1, 2, 4(a)**

(b)   (i)   What did Robert Lowe mean in Source **C** by the term 'household suffrage'?   **1, 4(a)**

    (ii)   What opinion did Lowe seem to have of the working classes? Quote from the speech to illustrate your answer.   **4(a, b)**

    (iii)   How does Gladstone (Source **B**) disagree with Lowe about the working classes?   **4(a, b, c)**

    (iv)   What does Lowe think of American politics and politicians?   **4(a, b)**

(v) From the evidence of this speech, would you say that Lowe had a high opinion of Disraeli or not? Give reasons for your answer. **4(a, b)**

(vi) Using your own words, make a short list of the reasons why Lowe opposed any further reform of parliament. **4(a)**

(c) What do you think Blake means in Source **D** when he writes that the events of 1866–7 'seem to be paradoxical' (i.e. contradicting themselves)? **1, 2, 4(a)**

(d) Blake (Source **D**) outlines three different theories to explain why Disraeli and the Conservatives brought in and passed the Reform Act of 1867.

(i) What evidence does he mention which backs up the first theory? **4(a)**

(ii) What evidence does he mention to back up the second theory? **4(a)**

(e) (i) What evidence can you find in Source **C** to suggest which of Blake's theories Lowe believed to be the correct one? **4(a, c)**

(ii) From the evidence of Source **F**, which theory did Morley think was the correct one? Give reasons for your answer. **4(a, c)**

(iii) Using the evidence of Sources **D** and **F**, can you suggest why Morley might have held this opinion? **4(a, b, c)**

(iv) Which of the three theories does Disraeli himself seem to be supporting in Source **E**? **4(a, c)**

(v) What reasons can you suggest to explain why Disraeli could be expected to hold this opinion? **4(a, b)**

(f) (i) Using the evidence from the Sources, make a list of the reasons why the 1867 Reform Bill was introduced and passed. **4(a, c)**

(ii) What were the main terms of the Act? **1, 2**

(iii) Explain whether or not you agree or disagree with the statement that the 1867 Reform Act 'fell far short of democracy'. **1, 2**

2. Gladstone as Chancellor of the Exchequer

Read this extract from a modern biography of Gladstone and then answer the questions which follow:

> On 18 April, 1853, Gladstone introduced his first Budget. It was based, like all his Budgets, on a foundation of ruthless economy in all departments of public expenditure . . . He asked the House to agree to a continuation of the intensely unpopular income-tax. He planned that it should stand at sevenpence in the pound for two years; at sixpence for two years after that, and at threepence for three further years. He said that by 1860 he thought it would be possible to dispense with it. He explained his view that the income-tax was, in essence, immoral.

It tempted statesmen to be extravagant and it tempted the tax-payer to carry out fraudulent evasions. He intended to continue it for seven years only, so that he could carry out another great slash at the customs duties. He proposed to remove the duty altogether on 123 articles, and to reduce it on a further 133. That would assist the nation's wealth to bear fruit in the pockets of the people.

Source: P. Magnus, *Gladstone*, John Murray, 1954 (adapted extracts).

(a) (i) Explain what Gladstone meant by 'ruthless economy in all departments of public expenditure'. **1, 2, 4(a)**

   (ii) Another of Gladstone's principles was 'Free Trade'. Explain how he thought this would help the British economy and people. **1, 2**

(b) (i) According to the extract, what were Gladstone's plans for the income-tax over the next seven years? **4(a)**

   (ii) What reasons does Gladstone give for not liking the income-tax? **4(a)**

   (iii) Why do you think Gladstone did not abolish income-tax immediately if he disliked it so much? **4(a)**

   (iv) Explain why it proved impossible for Gladstone to carry out these plans as he had intended? **1, 2**

(c) (i) Describe how Gladstone moved further towards free trade in his budgets of 1860 and 1864. **1, 2**

   (ii) What was agreed in the Cobden Treaty of 1860? **1, 2**

   (iii) Explain how this fitted in well with Gladstone's economic policies. **1, 2, 4(a)**

(d) What effects did Gladstone's policies as Chancellor of the Exchequer have on:

   (i) the British economy;
   (ii) the working classes;
   (iii) his own future career in politics? **1, 2**

3. (a) Explain what part the following played in causing the demand for more parliamentary reform in the early 1860s:

   (i) the American Civil War;
   (ii) population changes;
   (iii) the trade unions;
   (iv) John Bright and the Radicals.

(b) What were the main terms of the 1867 Reform Act?

(c) What were the results of the 1867 Reform Act:

   (i) in the counties;
   (ii) in the boroughs;
   (iii) for party organisation? **1, 2**

4.   It is 1864, shortly after the formation of the Reform Union in Manchester. As one of the leaders of a craft union, write a letter to your local MP. He is a Liberal who is well satisfied with the 1832 Reform Act and is thought to be a supporter of Robert Lowe. In your letter you try to convince him that the time has come for a further reform of parliament and that the working man is fit to receive the vote. Among other things you could mention

(a) the faults in the existing system of representation and voting,

(b) your own experiences and activities as a leader of a moderate and responsible trade union,

(c) your annoyance at Lowe's criticisms of the working classes.

1, 2, 3

CHAPTER 9

LORD PALMERSTON AND
FOREIGN AFFAIRS 1830–65

SUMMARY OF EVENTS

John Henry Temple, Viscount Palmerston, was a leading figure in British politics for much of the nineteenth century. He had a remarkable career lasting from 1807 until 1865 (when he died at the age of almost 81), all of it spent in the House of Commons. This might seem surprising since English peers sit in the House of Lords and not in the Commons; but in fact though Palmerston was born in London, the peerage had been given to the family for their estates in Ireland. Irish peers were barred from the Lords, and this meant that Palmerston, like Castlereagh, was eligible to become an MP in the Commons.

Palmerston began as a Tory MP in 1807 and was made Secretary at War in 1809 (aged only 25), a position he held until 1828. He had a reputation as an efficient administrator but was perhaps better known for his numerous love affairs. He was in sympathy with Huskisson and the 'enlightened' Tories; when Huskisson disagreed with Wellington, Palmerston also resigned and soon joined the Whigs. When the Whigs came to power in 1830, Grey appointed him Foreign Secretary. After that *his career ran as follows*:

1830–41   Foreign Secretary in the Whig governments of Grey and Melbourne.
1846–51   Foreign Secretary in Lord John Russell's Whig government.
1852–5   Home Secretary in Lord Aberdeen's coalition government.
1855–8   Liberal Prime Minister.
1859–65   Liberal Prime Minister.

During his first two periods at the Foreign Office, Palmerston became immensely popular with the general public because he was prepared to stand up to foreign countries, giving the impression that the British were far superior to all other peoples. In his relations with other politicians and ambassadors he was often arrogant and abrasive; he upset Queen Victoria who felt he should have consulted her more; in 1851 the Prime Minister, Russell, removed him from office because he had acted rashly without informing either the Queen or the rest of the cabinet. While he was away from the Foreign Office the Crimean War (1854-6) broke out; without Palmerston to look after foreign affairs, the government ran the war badly (see Section 10.2); many people felt that only Palmerston had the necessary flair to bring the war to a successful conclusion and eventually the Queen, against her will, appointed him Prime Minister. This brought new energy to the conduct of the war which soon ended with what seemed to be advantageous terms to Britain. From 1859-65 Russell was Foreign Secretary, and though he was not a man to be ignored, Palmerston usually had his own way. With the earlier rift between them now healed, the two men made a good partnership and successes in foreign affairs continued. After 1862 Palmerston encountered setbacks and suffered a decisive diplomatic defeat at the hands of the Prussian Minister-President, Bismarck. The long run of successes was over and the two veterans, Russell over 70 and Palmerston nearing 80, seemed out of step with the times.

9.1 WHAT WERE THE PRINCIPLES BEHIND PALMERSTON'S CONDUCT OF FOREIGN AFFAIRS?

(i) He was determined to defend British interests wherever they seemed threatened and to uphold Britain's prestige abroad. Whether it was a question of protecting British trade with China, maintaining the British position in India (against Russian ambitions), opposing the spread of French influence in Spain, or looking after the interests of British citizens abroad (Don Pacifico), Palmerston was prepared to take whatever action he thought necessary.

(ii) Like Canning, he wanted the public to be aware of those interests, and developed a remarkable skill in using the press to publicise the issues and enlist support from all classes in society.

(iii) He was in favour of the spread of liberalism (the introduction of constitutional governments like the one in Britain). He believed that, following the 1832 Reform Act, the British system was ideal and that similar systems should replace the autocratic monarchies of Europe, even if this had to be achieved by revolution. Thus he welcomed the revolutions in France (1830) and Greece (1843 and 1862).

(iv) He supported nationalism, sometimes actively especially if British interests were being advanced (Belgian revolt against Holland (1830-9) and Italian unification (1859-60)).

(v) He hoped to maintain world peace and wanted Britain 'to be the champion of justice and right'. Ideally this should be achieved by diplomatic means rather than by interfering militarily in the internal affairs of other states.

(vi) He wanted to preserve the balance of power, which, put at its simplest, meant making sure that no one country became strong enough to dominate the rest of Europe.

In practice none of these principles was binding, except the first: this was of paramount importance. Palmerston was a great improviser, using events and circumstances to maintain Britain's status as a great power. Although he approved of nationalism, he sent no help to the Poles or the Danes (1863 and 1864); he wanted liberalism to spread, yet he continually supported Turkey against Russia, and there could hardly have been a less liberal state than Turkey; the important consideration was that this policy protected British interests against Russia. 'We have no eternal allies and we have no perpetual enemies', he said in parliament. 'Our interests are eternal, and those interests it is our duty to follow.'

9.2 PALMERSTON AS FOREIGN MINISTER 1830-41: HOW SUCCESSFUL WAS HE?

Palmerston took over at the Foreign Office at a difficult time; he was faced almost immediately with three tricky problems: the Belgian revolt against Holland, revolutions in Spain and Portugal, and the outbreak of war between Egypt and Turkey. All three involved in some way or other, *British relations with France*.

(a) The Belgian revolt

(i) Although in 1815 it had seemed a good idea to unite Belgium with Holland (see Section 3.1(b)(iii)), the arrangement had not been a success. The Belgians felt that their interests were being ignored by the Dutch dominated government. Revolution broke out in Brussels (August 1830); by October Dutch troops had been chased out and Belgium declared an independent state. This could not be ignored by the other powers since it was a breach of the 1815 Vienna Settlement which they had all promised to uphold. The situation provided a searching test for Palmerston: if he used it well, he could turn it to advantage for Britain - an independent and friendly Belgium would be good for British trade and naval interests. The new constitutional French king, Louis Philippe, who had himself just been brought to power by the revolution of June 1830, favoured the Belgians and could be expected to support them. But though both Britain and France seemed to be working for the same end - Belgian independence - the danger for Britain was that the new Belgium might turn out to be very much under French influence, and the French were still viewed as the traditional British enemy. A further complication was that the autocratic governments of Austria, Russia and Prussia wanted to suppress the Belgians in order to discourage would-be revolutionaries in their own territories.

(ii) *Palmerston's aims* were: to co-operate with Louis Philippe so that together they would be strong enough to warn off Austria, Russia and Prussia, thus preventing a European war and ensuring Belgian independence. At the same time he wanted to make sure that if French troops entered Belgium in reply to Belgian requests for help, they would leave smartly as soon as the Dutch were defeated. Palmerston suspected that once French troops were entrenched in Belgium, Louis Philippe might be tempted to annex the country and he was determined to resist any such move.

(iii) *Palmerston took the lead* as chairman of an international conference which met in *London* in November 1830. Working closely with the French representative, *Talleyrand*, who wanted to maintain good relations with Britain, Palmerston prevailed upon both sides to accept a ceasefire. Belgian independence was recognised in principle, even, surprisingly, by Austria, Russia and Prussia, probably because their attention was occupied by other revolutions in Poland and Italy. The Dutch king William also accepted the decision, though reluctantly (January 1831).

This was by no means the end of the crisis; two questions remained to be settled: to choose a king for the new state and to fix its frontiers. A new alarm occurred for Britain when the Belgians invited Louis Philippe's second son to become their king. Palmerston, seeing this as almost a union between France and Belgium, threatened war if the French accepted, and began fleet movements; Louis Philippe, a cautious character, declined the invitation and the throne was given to the pro-British Leopold of Saxe-Coburg.

The frontier question caused further problems: Leopold demanded that Luxemburg should be included in Belgium, and when the London Conference seemed likely to support him, the Dutch king, who was also Grand Duke of Luxemburg, broke the ceasefire and sent troops to occupy Belgium (August 1831). French forces moved in and within ten days had driven the Dutch out; thus the situation which Palmerston had dreaded had come about: French troops, established deep in Belgium, were reluctant to withdraw. Again Palmerston took a firm line; 'One thing is certain', he warned, 'the French must go out of Belgium or we have a general war, and war in a given number of days'. Again Louis Philippe gave way, though French public opinion was outraged at this second climb-down. The dispute dragged on until in 1839 the Dutch at last recognised Belgian independence and neutrality, which all the great powers agreed to guarantee in the *Treaty of London*.

(iv) *Palmerston had been strikingly successful*: thanks to his efforts a new constitutional state friendly to Britain had been created in an area vitally close to the British coast. The French had been kept out of Belgium; though relations with France were strained for a time, the two governments worked well together during the later stages of the dispute, especially after Leopold married Louis Philippe's daughter. All this had been achieved without a European war. It gained Palmerston the reputation of being a champion of nationalism, but of course his primary aim had been to do what was best for Britain. Even Talleyrand was impressed: 'Palmerston', he wrote, 'is certainly one of the most able, if not the most able, man of business whom I have met in my career'.

(b) Portugal and Spain

(i) *The problem*: by a strange coincidence the rightful rulers of both Portugal and Spain were child queens – Maria of Portugal and Isabella of Spain. The supporters of both favoured constitutional (liberal) government and both were opposed by uncles (Miguel in Portugal, Carlos in Spain) who favoured autocratic government and aimed to destroy the liberal constitutions. *In Portugal* Maria had been kept in power by British troops sent by Canning (see Section 3.3(b) (ii)), but when Wellington withdrew them, Miguel seized the throne. Early in 1832 Maria's party rose in revolt against Miguel; they captured Oporto and civil war developed. Meanwhile *in Spain*, Isabella's mother, acting as Regent for the three-year-old queen, was in the process of setting up a constitutional government, when Carlos raised an army against her. As a first step he crossed into Portugal to help Miguel. The situation was similar to the one in Belgium: France strongly supported both constitutional parties, while Russia, Austria and Prussia were itching to interfere in order to maintain autocracy.

(ii) *Palmerston's aims* were clear: he intended to support the queens, working in close conjunction with the French (who were proposing joint action). As in the case of Belgium, he was determined to prevent the French from gaining more than their fair share of influence; there were important British naval and commercial interests to be safeguarded in the Mediterranean, and Gibraltar, at the southern tip of Spain, was a British colony. Finally he hoped that joint Anglo-French action would deter Russia, Austria and Prussia from intervening.

(iii) Palmerston was responsible for sending both direct and indirect help; a British fleet cruised menacingly off the Portuguese coast while British finance equipped a naval expedition commanded by British officers. In 1833 this force defeated Miguel and drove him out of Portugal. The following year Palmerston masterminded a treaty between Britain, France, Spain and Portugal in which they promised joint action against the uncles. This *Quadruple Alliance* began promisingly: Miguel was prevented from returning to Portugal and Carlos was captured and brought to Britain as a prisoner.

(iv) *British policy seemed to be successful* in the short term, 'a capital hit and all my own doing', boasted Palmerston. *In Portugal* success was lasting; Miguel never returned, constitutional government of a sort survived, and Portugal became a firm ally of Britain. However, Carlos soon escaped, made his way back to *Spain* and resumed the struggle for the throne. The civil war (known as the Carlist Wars) lasted until the defeat of Carlos in 1839, and by then Britain's relations with Isabella's government were somewhat strained because of a row over Spain's non-payment of debts to Britain. The Quadruple Alliance broke up in 1836 when the French withdrew, apparently annoyed at Britain's good relations with Spain and Portugal. Added to the disagreement over the Near East (see below) it meant that Anglo-French relations were anything but good. But at least French influence in the Iberian Peninsula had been kept to a minimum and the alliance lasted long enough to keep Austria, Russia and Prussia out.

(c) Mehemet Ali, Turkey and the Eastern Question 1831-41

(i) In 1831 a crisis occurred stemming from the Greek revolt against Turkey (see Section 3.3(b) (iv)) which was to end successfully for the Greeks in 1833. *Mehemet Ali*, nominally the Turkish governor of Egypt (though he was practically independent), had been promised a reward for helping the *Sultan Mahmud* against the Greeks, but had received nothing. He demanded Syria, and when Mahmud refused, Mehemet's son, *Ibrahim Pasha*, moved his troops into Syria. The Turks tried to drive them out but were soundly defeated at Konieh (December 1832). Ibrahim advanced towards Constantinople, the Turkish capital, whereupon Mahmud issued a general appeal for help. Since most of the powers were occupied with Belgium, the *Tsar Nicholas I* of Russia eagerly seized this opportunity for intervention in Turkey. A Russian fleet entered the Bosphorus while Russian troops moved towards Constantinople, both ostensibly to defend the capital against Ibrahim.

(ii) Palmerston was dismayed at the Russian presence in Turkey; he suspected them of wanting to annex the European part of Turkey including Constantinople, so that they could control the Dardanelles, the exit from the Black Sea. Russian warships would be able to sail through the Straits at will, posing a serious threat to Britain's interests in the eastern Mediterranean and possibly even to India. *His aim* therefore was to end the conflict between Mahmud and Mehemet as quickly as possible, and so remove the Russians' excuse for intervention.

(iii) *Palmerston sent a British fleet* into the eastern Mediterranean, and Britain, France and Austria, all worried about Russian expansion, threatened and cajoled the Sultan into giving Syria to Mehemet, Ibrahim withdrew his troops from Turkey, so that the Russians had no excuse for staying. However, Nicholas, in a strong position, could not resist demanding a high price for his help. He forced Mahmud to sign *the Treaty of Unkiar Skelessi* (July 1833) by which Russia and Turkey agreed to give each other military help whenever necessary; Turkey would allow Russian warships free passage through the Dardanelles, and would close them to ships of every other country in wartime.

(iv) *This was a setback for Palmerston* and a diplomatic triumph for the Russians who would now be extremely powerful in the eastern Mediterranean; Turkey was reduced almost to a protectorate of Russia, dependent for survival on Russian military support. Palmerston fumed and fretted and was determined to destroy Unkiar Skelessi. However, Nicholas ignored all protests, and for six years no opportunity offered itself.

(v) *Palmerston's chance came in 1839* when the Sultan, who had never intended to let Mehemet keep Syria, suddenly launched an invasion. Once again Ibrahim was called into action and yet again the Sultan found his armies decisively defeated. The earlier situation seemed about to repeat itself as Ibrahim moved towards Constantinople. *The French complicated the situation* by aiding and advising Mehemet on military matters; they were hoping to build up their influence in Egypt to add to their recent capture of Algiers (1830) at the western end of the Mediterranean. The future seemed bleak for Turkey when Mahmud died (July 1839) to be succeeded by a 16-year-old boy.

(vi) *Palmerston this time was prepared: he aimed* to preserve Turkey as a reasonably strong state capable of standing up to Russian ambitions. Help for Turkey must be provided jointly by several European powers, not just by Russia alone. Another motive for wanting to bolster up Turkey, as Jasper Ridley points out, was because Palmerston was afraid that 'the collapse of Turkey would lead to a scramble for the pieces which would trigger off a major European war'. He was also determined to frustrate the French and knew he could count on Russian support. Above all though, Palmerston hoped to use the situation to destroy Unkiar Skelessi. The first step towards all this was to curb Mehemet Ali, who according to Palmerston was 'an ignorant barbarian, a former waiter at a coffee shop', but who impressed some western ambassadors as courteous, witty and charming.

(vii) *Palmerston made most of the running*: in July 1840 he engineered an agreement in London between Britain, Russia, Austria and Prussia; France was not even consulted. The four powers offered Mehemet Ali terms: he could remain as hereditary ruler of Egypt and keep the southern half of Syria, provided he immediately made peace with Turkey. Though it was not an unreasonable offer, Mehemet rejected it, expecting French military help if the powers moved against him. A major European war seemed likely, and Franco-British relations, which had recently been harmonious over the settlement of Belgium, reached rock bottom. However, Palmerston was convinced that although the French premier, *Adolphe Thiers*, was in an aggressive mood, the cautious Louis Philippe would never risk taking on four other powers. He instructed the British ambassador in Paris to inform Thiers that 'if France begins a war, she will to a certainty lose her ships, colonies and commerce . . . and that Mehemet Ali will just be chucked into the Nile'.

(viii) *Allied action against Mehemet now went ahead*: a British and Austrian force captured his ports of Acre and Beirut, while a British fleet bombarded Alexandria (in Egypt). Louis Philippe knew that it would be madness for France to become involved, and Thiers was forced to resign. Mehemet had to accept harsher terms from the powers (this time including France). He was allowed to remain ruler of Egypt but had to return Syria to the Sultan. A further agreement known as *the Straits Convention* was signed in July 1841. By this all the powers, including Russia, agreed that the entrance to the Black Sea should be closed to the warships of *all* nations while Turkey herself was at peace. This cancelled Russia's special advantage granted by the Treaty of Unkiar Skelessi; Nicholas made this concession in the hope of gaining British friendship.

(ix) This complex problem turned out to be probably *Palmerston's greatest triumph*: he had bolstered up Turkey so that there were no disagreements among the powers over who should take what; Russian expansion had been controlled and the routes to India safeguarded; French ambitions in the eastern Mediterranean had been thwarted; and all without a war. Palmerston's actions showed clearly that his major concern was to protect British interests even if it meant abandoning co-operation with constitutional France and working with the autocratic governments of Russia and Austria which he had opposed over Belgium, Spain and Portugal.

(d) China and the Opium War

(i) *Early in 1839 a dispute arose between Britain and China* about the British import of opium from India into the Chinese port of Canton. British merchants had built up the opium trade into a highly profitable operation. The Chinese government claimed that opium smoking was ruining the health of the population, and banned the trade. They seized opium worth over a million pounds belonging to British merchants at Canton, and poured it into the sea. Tension increased when the British refused to hand over to the Chinese some British sailors who had killed a Chinaman in a drunken brawl. The reason given was that the Chinese used torture to extract confessions and therefore the British refused to accept the jurisdiction of Chinese courts.

(ii) *Palmerston demanded compensation* for the opium and guarantees that British merchants would be free from interference. The Chinese rejected both requests and Palmerston despatched a naval and military expedition to Canton. *His aim* was partly to defend British honour and win compensation, but more important, to force the Chinese to open up their vast market of 350 million people to more British trade (until now the British had only been allowed to trade at Canton). The fighting which followed is known as the *Opium War*.

(iii) The British fleet bombarded and captured Canton and had no difficulty in forcing the poorly led and equipped Chinese to sign an agreement based on Palmerston's demands. *The Treaty of Nanking* (signed in August 1842 by the Conservatives after the Whig defeat) allowed the British to trade at five treaty ports (Canton, Shanghai, Amoy,

illus 9.1   *British warships attacking Chinese junks during the Opium War*

Foochow and Ningpo), exempted British merchants from Chinese law, granted six million pounds compensation and leased the island of Hong Kong to Britain (until 1997). Other European powers were granted similar privileges.

(iv) The Opium War seemed to be a success and a whole new and vast market seemed to be assured for British exports. However, there was to be more trouble later as the Chinese tried to reduce their concessions. In addition Palmerston was severely criticised in the Commons on the grounds that it was morally wrong to force Britain's will on a weak and defenceless country.

The Whig government fell in August 1841 and Palmerston was away from the Foreign Office for over five years. His policies had been triumphantly successful, especially during his last two years in office. Even the Conservative Disraeli wrote about his 'brilliant performances'; in the words of Jasper Ridley, 'by 1841 the Palmerston legend was already firmly established'.

9.3 CONSERVATIVE INTERLUDE 1841-46

The Conservative Prime Minister, Peel, allowed his Foreign Secretary, *Lord Aberdeen*, a fairly free hand. Aberdeen was much less aggressive and bombastic than Palmerston, and favoured a policy of calmness and conciliation whenever possible. He did not like the idea of Britain interfering in the internal affairs of other countries and withdrew the troops that Palmerston had sent to Portugal. He settled peacefully a potentially dangerous dispute with the USA over the frontiers of Maine and Oregon with Canada. Much of Aberdeen's time and energy were spent trying to improve relations with France, which Palmerston had left in some disarray. He found that he could work amicably with the new French minister, *Francois Guizot*, with whom he reached compromise agreements on policing the Atlantic (in a joint attempt to stamp out the slave trade) and on the establishment of a French protectorate over the Pacific island of Tahiti. More troublesome was the affair of *the Spanish Marriages*. Louis Philippe was anxious for one of his sons to marry the young Queen Isabella of Spain. The British objected to this, suspicious that some kind of union between France and Spain might take place; this plus the French occupation of Algiers made the British nervous about the safety of Gibraltar. They suggested that Isabella (aged 11 in 1841) should marry a Saxe-Coburg prince (who would be friendly to Britain) or one of her own Spanish cousins (which would at least keep the French out). Early in 1846 an understanding was reached that Isabella should marry one of her cousins and Louis Philippe's son should marry Isabella's younger sister, but only after Isabella had had children, so that there would be little chance of the two crowns becoming united. However, nothing was put in writing and it was at this stage in the negotiations that Peel's government fell over the Corn Law crisis, and Palmerston returned to the Foreign Office (June 1846).

9.4 PALMERSTON AT THE FOREIGN MINISTRY AGAIN 1846-51

Palmerston was less successful at winning specific advantages for Britain during his second turn in office, and he was outmanoeuvred by Louis Philippe over the Spanish Marriages. However, incidents such as the Don Pacifico affair and the visit of General Haynau, though empty triumphs in themselves, greatly added to Palmerston's popularity with the public.

(a) The Spanish marriages 1846

(i) Palmerston had been thoroughly impatient with Aberdeen's delicate handling of this problem and was determined to settle quickly. The French, deeply distrustful of him and expecting him to press the claim of the Saxe-Coburg prince (a cousin of Prince Albert), saw a chance to get revenge on Palmerston for the Mehemet Ali affair. Following French bribery of the Spanish Queen Mother, two weddings took place: Isabella married her cousin, the elderly Duke of Cadiz, rumoured to be sexually impotent, while her sister Luisa married the Duke of Montpensier, Louis Philippe's younger son.

(ii) *This was a diplomatic defeat for Palmerston*: if Isabella had no children and Luisa became queen, Spanish and French interests would be closely united. Even Queen Victoria for once found herself in agreement with Palmerston and wrote to Louis Philippe accusing him of breaking the previous agreement. In the end though, the marriages did Louis Philippe no good: the recent co-operation between France and Britain was brought to an abrupt end, which gave great comfort to Russia and Austria. Isabella had children (though probably not her husband's), so that Montpensier was excluded from the Spanish throne, and in 1848 Louis Philippe himself was overthrown by a revolution.

(b) 1848: the year of revolutions

(i) During this momentous year (the year of the third Chartist petition), revolutions took place in many European countries, inspired by a mixture of liberalism and nationalism. Louis Philippe was replaced by a republican government; the Italians of Lombardy and Venetia tried to throw off Austrian rule; the people of Hungary and Bohemia fought for more national freedom from Austria, while in Vienna, Chancellor Metternich was forced to flee.

(ii) *Palmerston's attitude showed his policy in all its contradictions*. He had some sympathy with all the revolutionary movements, particularly the Italians: 'I cannot regret the expulsion of the Austrians from Italy', he wrote; 'her rule was hateful to the Italians'. With his reputation as a friend of liberals and nationalists, he might have been expected to do all in his power to help the revolutionaries. But *British interests came first*: though he liked the idea of an independent united state of Italy, he wanted the tottering Austrian empire to survive as a check to Russian expansion. He was also worried in case the new French republic sent military help to the Italians, which could give the French too much influence in northern Italy.

(iii) Britain therefore took no direct action, though as usual there was plenty of verbal activity from Palmerston. He tried to persuade the Austrians to grant independence to Lombardy and Venetia before the French intervened; nothing came of it and the French dithered so long about whether to send help, that the Austrians regained control of Italy. Eventually all the revolutions in Austria, Germany and Italy were brought under control, and all Palmerston could do was protest against the atrocities committed by the Austrians against the Hungarian rebels. He supported the Turks when they refused to hand over to the Austrians the Hungarian nationalist leader *Louis Kossuth* who had escaped to Constantinople; after British warships were despatched to the Bosphorus, the Austrians and Russians took no action.

(iv) A general war had been avoided and the balance of power preserved; but although Palmerston's support for Kossuth was popular with the British public, there can be no disguising the fact that Britain had had very little impact on the main course of events in 1848.

(c) **The Haynau Incident (1850)**. In September 1850 the Austrian General Haynau came to Britain on an official visit. He was one of the generals responsible for putting down the revolutions in Italy and Hungary, where he had ordered numerous hangings and the flogging of women. While he was visiting Barclay and Perkins' Brewery in Southwark, some of the workmen, realising who he was, set upon him and chased him through the streets. He took refuge in a public house and had to be rescued by police. Victoria demanded that an apology should be sent to the Austrians; Palmerston sent an official apology, but added that Haynau had been asking for trouble in coming to Britain, in view of his unpopularity, and that he regarded Haynau as 'a great moral criminal' because of the atrocities he had committed. Palmerston showed the Queen a copy of the apology only after it had been sent. Victoria was furious with him, particularly since he had recently promised not to send any despatches before she had first read and approved them. It was obvious that if Palmerston continued to act without consulting the Queen there would soon be a major showdown.

(d) **The Don Pacifico Affair (1850)**

(i) There was a long standing dispute between King Otto of Greece, and Britain, France and Russia, arising from the refusal of the Greeks to pay even the interest on the massive loans granted by these governments to help the newly independent Greece establish itself in 1832. The dispute came to a head when Don Pacifico, a Portuguese Jewish merchant and money-lender who lived in Athens, had his house burned down by an anti-Semitic mob. Don Pacifico had been born in Gibraltar and could therefore claim to be a British citizen; when the Greek government rejected his demand for £27,000 compensation, he wrote directly to Palmerston asking for British support.

(ii) Palmerston threatened force, but for a long time the Greeks ignored him. Early in 1850 a British fleet was in the eastern Mediterranean (protecting Kossuth); Palmerston decided to use it to frighten the Greeks into paying compensation. For a month British warships blockaded the Piraeus (the Port of Athens) and other main ports, seizing all Greek merchant ships. After a good deal of haggling it was agreed that some compensation should be paid, though not the original sum demanded which was far too high (Don Pacifico was actually paid £6550).

(iii) This was something of a success for Palmerston; British prestige abroad had been maintained, but his high-handedness and belligerence caused a first-rate political row. The French and Russians, who had agreed, with Britain, to protect the new state of Greece, protested strongly that they ought to have been consulted. Queen Victoria, Prince Albert, the Conservatives and even some of his own cabinet thought Palmerston had gone too far. When it looked as though his opponents might force him to resign he rose magnificently to the occasion with a brilliant speech lasting four and a half hours, delivered to a crowded House of Commons. He defended his entire foreign policy since 1830 and ended; 'as the Roman in days of old held himself free from indignity when he could say *Civis Romanus sum* (I am a Roman citizen), so also a British subject, in whatever land he may be, shall feel confident that the watchful eye and the strong arm of England will protect him against injustice and wrong'. The speech won Palmerston a comfortable vote of confidence (June 1850); but the blaze of popularity which followed tended to obscure the fact that Britain had gained nothing from the affair except to annoy France, Austria and Russia who claimed that Palmerston was nothing more than a bully, especially when dealing with weaker states.

The Don Pacifico affair was one of several incidents which brought relations between Palmerston and Victoria and Albert to breaking point, and culminated in Palmerston's resignation.

(e) The Affair of Louis Napoleon and the downfall of Palmerston (1851)

(i) The breaking point between Queen and Foreign Minister came in 1851, and ironically it was concerned with affairs in France. *Louis Napoleon Bonaparte*, the nephew of Napoleon I, had been elected President of the French Republic in 1848 following the overthrow of Louis Philippe. On 2 December 1851, in a cleverly organised *coup d'état*, he had himself proclaimed President for the next ten years, and became virtually a dictator.

(ii) *Palmerston approved of this*, believing that a strong government would prevent France from falling under socialist control. Queen Victoria would have preferred to see Louis Philippe restored; both she and Russell (the Prime Minister) felt that Britain should remain strictly neutral and make no comment. However, Palmerston acted carelessly: without consulting the Queen or the cabinet, he told the French ambassador that he congratulated Louis Napoleon on his success.

(iii) This was the chance the Queen had been waiting for and she demanded that Palmerston should be sacked immediately. Russell, knowing that this time Palmerston could expect very little support for his action (the British public was still suspicious of all Bonapartes and feared the worst a year later when Louis Napoleon had himself declared Emperor Napoleon III), asked for and received his resignation.

(iv) By resigning Palmerston avoided a confrontation with Victoria and Albert, but left unsettled *the question of who really controlled British foreign policy*: was it the Foreign Minister or was it the monarch, who by tradition usually had the last word in foreign affairs? Though he was furious at having to leave the Foreign Office, he agreed to go to avoid a public dispute with the Queen which might have damaged the monarchy. However, he blamed Russell for not standing by him; early in 1852 he and his supporters took great delight in voting with the Conservatives to bring down Russell's government. This brought in Lord Derby's short-lived Conservative government (February–December 1852) followed by Lord Aberdeen's coalition (a government made up of people from different political parties) which involved Britain in the Crimean War (1854–56).

9.5 THE FINAL PHASE: PALMERSTON AS PRIME MINISTER 1855-65

Palmerston became Liberal Prime Minister in February 1855 after Aberdeen's coalition had failed to bring the war to a speedy conclusion. Except for one short period (Derby's Second Conservative government, February 1858–June 1859), Palmerston remained Prime Minister until his death in October 1865. For the first year he was fully occupied with the Crimean War, which requires a chapter to itself (Chapter 10). After this came a second war with China, problems of Britain's attitude towards Italian and German unification, and a dispute with the USA which came close to involving Britain in the American Civil War (1861–5).

(a) The Second War with China 1857–60

(i) The Chinese had been reluctant to keep to the terms of the 1842 Treaty of Nanking and tried to keep out as many foreign merchants as possible; the authorities at the treaty ports regularly victimised Chinese merchants who traded with the British. To protect these friendly merchants, the British started granting British registration to Chinese vessels trading at Hong Kong, hoping that the Chinese would not dare interfere with ships flying the British flag. In 1856 the Chinese authorities at Canton seized a small ship called the *Arrow* which belonged to a Chinese pirate and had been robbing merchant ships off Canton. The *Arrow* had been registered as a British ship and was flying the British flag; consequently the British consul at Canton demanded the release of the crew and an apology for insulting the British flag. The Chinese released the crew but refused an apology, whereupon British warships from Hong Kong bombarded Canton causing considerable damage.

(ii) Palmerston was placed in an awkward situation: since the *Arrow* was a pirate ship (and its British registration had expired) the Chinese had a good case; the British governor of Hong Kong who ordered the bombardment, should have consulted Palmerston first. However, Palmerston felt obliged to support the British officials once they had taken their stand. *He had a double motive*: there was the need to uphold British prestige and avenge the insult to the flag; more important, he was determined to force the Chinese to accept full-scale trade with Britain, whether they wanted it or not.

(iii) After winning a general election (in which the Liberal majority was increased) fought on the Chinese issue (March 1857), Palmerston felt justified in sending a strong expedition to press British claims. The French supported the British and together they captured Canton (1858) and Peking (1860) after which the Chinese agreed to all demands. Several more ports including Tientsin, were opened to trade with western powers: foreign diplomatic representatives were to be allowed at Peking; the opium trade, instead of being banned, was to be regulated by the Chinese authorities.

(iv) *Palmerston had triumphed again* and his popularity rose to new heights; British merchants were delighted at the prospects of a trade expansion with the Far East; even foreign powers were, for once, happy with Palmerston, since they too hoped to take advantage of the opening-up of China. Again however, as with the Opium War and the Don Pacifico Affair, Palmerston's actions can be questioned from a moral point of view. The 1856 bombardment of Canton which started the war was a breach of international law; the war itself was another example of Palmerston bullying a much weaker power.

(b) Palmerston and Italian unification 1859–60

(i) Early in 1859 Italy was still divided into separate states. Lombardy and Venetia in the north belonged to the Austrians; three small states, Parma, Modena and Tuscany were ruled by Austrian dukes; the three largest states were independent: Piedmont (including the island of Sardinia) was ruled by King Victor Emmanuel and his Prime Minister Count Cavour; the Papal States (including Rome) belonged to the Pope; the Kingdom of Naples (including the island of Sicily) was ruled by Francis II.

(ii) Italian nationalists wanted to free the northern states from Austrian domination, and Cavour hoped to bring about a united Italy under Piedmontese leadership, with a democratic constitution similar to Britain's. In 1859 the Piedmontese, with considerable military help from Napoleon III, attacked the Austrians, defeated them twice (at Magenta and Solferino) and captured Lombardy. The French pulled out of the operation before Venetia had been captured, but Parma, Modena and Tuscany announced their intention of uniting with Piedmont. The Austrians immediately rushed more troops into Venetia with the clear intention of preventing the union.

(iii) *At this point Palmerston acted*: he announced that Britain would not allow armed intervention by the Austrians; 'the people of the Duchies have as good a right to change their rulers, as the people of England, France, Belgium and Sweden', he claimed. The Austrians decided against intervention and the Duchies remained with Piedmont.

(iv) The next step towards Italian unification began in 1860 when the nationalist leader Giuseppe Garibaldi led an armed force by sea from Genoa (in Piedmont) and captured Sicily from the unpopular king of Naples. Again the British were able to help: British warships protected Garibaldi's invasion force as it went ashore in Sicily. Later they were in the vicinity as Garibaldi's expedition crossed the Straits of Messina from Sicily to the mainland. Napoleon III had threatened to stop him but dare not make a move against the British fleet. Consequently Garibaldi captured mainland Naples which soon united with Piedmont to form the Kingdom of Italy; all these changes were recognised as legal by the British government.

(v) *Palmerston's motives were mixed*: both he and Russell, as well as British public opinion as a whole (apart from Victoria and Albert) were sympathetic towards Italian nationalism and unification. They disapproved of Austria's repressive rule in northern Italy and of the atrocious government in Naples which Gladstone had described after a visit there in 1851 as 'the negation of God'. But as usual there was more to it than that: if there was to be a new state of Italy, Palmerston wanted to make sure it would be grateful and friendly to Britain. This would be to Britain's advantage in the Mediterranean and a valuable counterbalance to French hostility in that area. Friendship might also lead to a lowering of Italian tariffs against British goods, which would be of great benefit to British merchants.

(vi) Palmerston's Italian policy turned out to be his last great success in foreign affairs. He and Russell won the reputation as friends of the new Italy, whose unification had been made possible because Britain had restrained other powers from intervening. British sea-power had enabled her to make this contribution.

(c) Britain and the American Civil War 1861-5

(i) In 1861 war broke out between the North and South of the USA, partly over the question of slavery (which existed mostly in the

South) and partly over whether states had the right to leave the Union (which the South was trying to do). *Public opinion in Britain was divided in sympathy*: middle and working classes, very much against slavery, tended to sympathise with the North especially after President Lincoln promised to abolish slavery throughout the US (1863). However, in political circles there was much support for the South (the Confederates) on the grounds that all peoples should have the right to decide by whom they wished to be ruled.

(ii) With sympathies so divided, Palmerston and Russell announced that Britain would remain strictly neutral. However, both North and South hoped to win British help. Two incidents occurred, both involving ships – the *Trent* and the *Alabama* – which caused tension between Britain and the North.

(iii) *The Trent Incident* took place in November 1861 when two Confederate agents, Mason and Slidell, were on their way to Europe on board the *Trent*, a British ship, to try and whip up support for the South. A Northern cruiser stopped the *Trent*, seized the agents and took them to Boston. This was a breach of international law and an insult to the British flag, which must be avenged. Palmerston wrote a very strongly worded protest demanding an apology and the release of Mason and Slidell; extra troops were despatched to Canada and feelings ran high on both sides. Fortunately Prince Albert persuaded Palmerston to tone down some of his more insulting phrases, and Lincoln was sensible enough to give way. The agents eventually arrived in Britain, but had no success with their mission. Prince Albert probably deserves much of the credit for keeping Britain out of the war; it was to be his last contribution to politics; he died from typhoid in December 1861 at the early age of 42.

(iv) *The Alabama Incident (1862)* could have been avoided if Palmerston or Russell had acted promptly. The South, attempting to build up a navy, had ordered a number of ships from British yards. The first one sailed from Liverpool in March 1862 disguised as a merchant ship, but eventually became the cruiser *Florida* which proceeded to attack Northern merchant ships. A second ship destined to become the *Alabama* was being built at Birkenhead; Lincoln's government protested that this was a breach of the 1819 Foreign Enlistment Act which forbade the building and equipping in Britain of military vessels meant for either side in a war in which Britain was neutral. Although the Northern protest was reasonable, Russell delayed so long before ordering the vessel to be detained, that she slipped out of the Mersey and for the next two years inflicted severe damage on Northern merchant shipping. The North blamed the British government and claimed compensation; Russell denied all responsibility and refused to pay compensation or to allow the matter to go to arbitration. However, he later had three further ships detained, so avoiding any more friction with the North. (Later, after the North had won the war, Gladstone accepted arbitration – see Section 13.4(b).)

(v) Meanwhile the Northern blockade of Confederate ports was preventing exports of raw cotton from reaching the Lancashire textile industry. During 1862 *the cotton famine* reached its worst, throwing over half a million people out of work in Britain's most important export industry. The situation only eased in the spring of 1863, as alternative supplies of cotton began to arrive from Egypt.

In the spring of 1863 the 'two dreadful old men' as Queen Victoria called Palmerston and Russell, were still handling foreign affairs with some success. They had made a contribution to Italian unification, and though they had bungled the *Alabama* incident, they had at least kept Britain out of the American Civil War. But in the last two years of his government Palmerston suffered two failures – over the Polish revolution and the affair of Schleswig-Holstein; Palmerston's inept handling of these situations was described by Lord Derby, a leading Conservative, as a policy of 'meddle and muddle'.

(d) Palmerston and Poland 1863

(i) Poland was in an unfortunate situation; it had once been an independent state, but between 1772 and 1795 it had been partitioned between Russia, Austria and Prussia who all seized large areas for themselves. Like the Italians, the Poles looked forward to the day when they could escape from foreign rule and have a united Poland; but there was little chance of this happening since the Poles, unlike the Italians, had three lots of foreigners to expel.

(ii) In 1863 the Poles in Russia broke out in revolution, and Russian troops were moved in to crush the rising. Bismarck (the Minister-President of Prussia) gave diplomatic support to the Russians, in case the outbreak should spread to the Polish areas of Prussia.

(iii) Palmerston and Napoleon III protested to the Tsar about his brutal treatment of the rebels and hinted at some action to support the Poles. However, when Napoleon III proposed a European congress, Palmerston rejected the idea because he suspected Napoleon's motives. No help of any sort arrived and the Poles were quelled with great cruelty.

(iv) *This was Palmerston's first obvious failure in foreign affairs* and was a striking contrast to his role in helping the Italian nationalists. In Italy the presence of the British Fleet was enough to warn off the Austrians; the Russians were already in Poland and only a major military effort by Britain and France could have driven them out. Palmerston and Russell knew from the beginning that such action was out of the question and should not have made threats which they could not carry out. Their actions only encouraged the Poles to resist longer than was sensible and left them feeling distinctly let down; Britain had been clearly outmanoeuvred by the Tsar, and Napoleon III who should have been treated as an ally, was mortally offended. All in all British prestige took a severe knock.

(e) Palmerston, Bismarck and Schleswig-Holstein 1863-4

(i) In 1863 a long-standing dispute came to a head over whether the Duchies of Schleswig and Holstein should belong to Denmark or remain independent. By *the Treaty of London (1852)* the great powers had decided that the Duchies should remain as independent units, but the new king of Denmark, Christian IX, who also happened to be Duke of Schleswig-Holstein, was under pressure from Danish public opinion to incorporate the Duchies into Denmark. A majority of the people of Holstein were German-speaking, and German nationalists were strongly opposed to any move which would take Germans into Denmark. In November 1863 Christian announced the incorporation of Schleswig, though this was a breach of the 1852 Treaty. *Bismarck*, who had ambitions of extending Prussian control over the whole of North Germany, saw this as an opportunity to take Schleswig-Holstein for Prussia. He threatened military action unless the Danes dropped their claim; he insisted that the 1852 agreement should be kept, but naturally made no mention of his own designs on the Duchies.

(ii) *Palmerston decided that Britain must support Denmark*; again there was the usual mixture of motives: British public opinion was strongly pro-Danish; the Prince of Wales had recently married Princess Alexandra of Denmark, which led the Danes to expect British help. Palmerston was also rightly suspicious of Bismarck: 'what is at the bottom of the German design is the dream of a German Fleet and the wish to get Kiel as a German seaport'. A strong Denmark would increase British influence in Northern Europe.

(iii) Palmerston therefore told parliament that if any state attacked Denmark, 'those who made the attempt would find that it would not be Denmark alone with which they would have to contend'. This was intended to frighten Bismarck off and encourage the Danes.

(iv) Bismarck, who had Austrian support, guessed that Palmerston was bluffing and that Britain would need French help which they were unlikely to get after Palmerston's abrupt rejection of Napoleon III's proposal for a European congress. In February 1864 a joint Prussian and Austrian force invaded the Duchies, but when the Danes appealed urgently for British help, the cabinet decided not to risk involvement in a major war against Prussia and Austria.

(v) The Danes had no alternative but to surrender (July 1864) Bismarck dropped the pretence that the Prussian action had been taken to uphold the 1852 Treaty, and the two Duchies were handed over to Prussia and Austria.

(vi) *Palmerston had failed again*: he had seriously under-estimated the astuteness of Bismarck and the growing strength of the Prussian army; this led him to make threats which Britain could not carry out with sea-power alone. At the same time he refused to consider joint military action with the French in case Napoleon seized the Rhineland.

From the beginning he had been supporting a state which was in the wrong; if Britain had insisted on a Danish withdrawal from the Duchies, there would have been no treaty violation, and Bismarck would have had no excuse for the invasion; British encouragement of the Danes had played into Bismarck's hands.

Palmerston died in October 1865 after catching a chill. On the whole he had been remarkably successful; only in the last couple of years did he seem to be getting out of touch with important developments. He failed to see that Bismarck and not Napoleon III was likely to be the main threat to the balance of power, and continued acting as though Britain was still the dominant power in Europe, as she had been immediately after 1815. But circumstances were changing: in less than six years after Palmerston's death, the Prussians defeated both the Austrians and the French, Napoleon III was a refugee in England, and Bismarck had united Germany. In all these highly important events British influence was nil. The balance of power had shifted decisively, and not in Britain's favour.

QUESTIONS

1. Palmerston and the Reactions to his Foreign Policies
Study Sources A to G and then answer the questions which follow.

Source A: speeches in the House of Commons by Lord Palmerston, 1848–49.

The principle on which I have thought the foreign affairs of this country ought to be conducted is, the principle of maintaining peace and friendly understanding with all nations, as long as it was possible to do so consistently with a due regard for the interest, the honour, and the dignity of this country. My endeavours have been to preserve peace. *All the governments of which I have had the honour to be a member, have succeeded in accomplishing that object . . .*
We have a deep interest in the preservation of peace because we are desirous to carry on with advantage those peaceful relations of trade that we know must be injured by the interruption of our friendly relations with other countries. On the other hand it is essential for the protection of that commerce to which we attach so much importance, that it should be well understood by every nation on the face of the earth that we do not intend to submit to wrong, and that the maintenance of peace on our part is subject to the indispensable condition that all countries shall respect our honour and our dignity, and shall not inflict any injury upon our interests . . . At the same time I am quite ready to admit that interference ought not to be carried to the extent of endangering our relations with other countries.

Source: D. Holman (ed.), *Earlier Nineteenth Century 1783–1867*, Hutchinson, 1965 and F. E. Huggett, *What They've Said about Nineteenth Century Statesmen*, Oxford, 1972 (adapted extracts).

Source B: a letter written by Lord Shaftesbury, the Tory humanitarian social reformer, written in 1876.

The institution of a true and vigorous foreign policy suited to the honour and position of the Kingdom of England was one of Lord Palmerston's guiding principles . . . Vigorous assertion of this principle in the face of very hostile and sensitive powers, was often misinterpreted as a readiness for war, nay even as recklessness . . . From war, I believe, he shrank with horror; but he was strongly of the opinion that the best way to avoid it was to speak out boldly, and ever be prepared to meet the emergency. Both in private and in public life he was of a very gentle and forgiving spirit. There might be, but very rarely, now and then little bursts of irritation, but they soon passed away. Of public resentments he had no memory at all. In all my experience I have not seen any man so kind to all alike, so delicate, tender and considerate . . .

Source: quoted in J. Ridley, *Lord Palmerston*, Constable, 1970 (adapted extracts).

Source C: Article in *The Times*, on the death of Palmerston, 19 October 1865.

One of the most popular statesmen, one of the kindliest gentlemen, and one of the truest Englishmen that ever filled the office of Premier, is today lost to the country. The news of Lord Palmerston's death will be received in every home throughout these islands, from the palace to the cottage, with a feeling like that of personal bereavement. The secret of his popularity was his boundless sympathy with all classes of his countrymen. Nor was his kindness and friendliness merely superficial . . .

Others may advise Her Majesty with equal wisdom and sway the House of Commons with equal or greater eloquence; but his place in the hearts of the people will not be filled so easily. His name will long be connected in the minds of Englishmen with an era of unbroken peace and unparalleled prosperity.

Source: *The Times*, 19 October 1865.

Source D: The opinion of Talleyrand, a French statesman who was ambassador to Britain from 1830–34.

Lord Palmerston is certainly one of the ablest statesmen I have ever met with in all my official career. He possesses indefatigable energy, an iron constitution, inexhaustible mental resources and great facility of speech in Parliament . . . There is one point in his character, however, which to my mind, entirely outweighs all these advantages, and would prevent his being considered in the light of a real statesman – he allows his passions to influence him in public affairs, to the extent of sometimes sacrificing the greatest interests to his personal feelings; nearly every political question resolves itself with him into a personal one; and whilst seeming to defend the interests of his country, it is nearly always those of his hatred or revenge that he is serving. He is very skilful in hiding this secret motive, under what I might call patriotic appearances.

Source: quoted in F. E. Huggett, *What they've Said about Nineteenth Century Statesmen*, Oxford 1972 (adapted extracts).

Source E: A private and confidential letter from Prince Albert to Lord John Russell, the Prime Minister, written in 1850.

The Queen has two distinct complaints to bring against Lord Palmerston . . . First, his policy has generally had the effect that England is universally detested, mistrusted and treated with insult even by the smallest powers. There is not a sovereign or a government who do not consider Lord Palmerston as a personal enemy; there is not a people who is not convinced that their internal disagreements and sufferings are stirred up by England, in order to keep them weak and unable in consequence to compete with the English manufacturers. Since 1846 England has not had a single success [in foreign affairs] . . .

Secondly, as a minister the sovereign has a right to demand from him that she be made thoroughly acquainted with the whole object and tendency of the policy to which her consent is required, and, having given that consent, that the policy is not altered from the original line, that important steps are not concealed from her and her name used without her sanction. In all these respects Lord Palmerston has failed towards her . . . Besides which, he has let it appear in public as if the sovereign's negligence in attending to papers sent to her caused delays and complications.

Source: quoted in D. Holman (ed.), *Earlier Nineteenth Century 1783–1867*, Hutchinson, 1965 (adapted extracts).

Source F: A private note written by Palmerston to Sir George Bonham, the Governor of Hong Kong, 29 September 1850.

The Time is fast coming when we shall be obliged to strike another Blow in China. These half-civilised governments such as those of China, Portugal, Spanish America, all require a dressing every eight or ten years to keep them in order. Their minds are too shallow to receive an impression that will last longer than some such period, and warning is of little use. They care little for words and they must not only see the Stick but actually feel it on their shoulders before they yield to that only argument which to them brings conviction.

Source: quoted in W. C. Costin, *Great Britain and China, 1833-1860*, Oxford, 1937.

Source G: some information from a modern historian.

Following the Opium War with China (1839) in which Britain forced the Chinese to open to her, five ports, relations between the two remained strained. In 1856 the British at Hong Kong became involved in a dispute with the Chinese at Canton over a vessel built and owned by Chinese merchants and wrongly flying the British flag as a screen for acts of piracy. The British demanded an apology from the Governor of Canton for his seizure of the pirates aboard the *Arrow*, and when this was refused, the British bombarded the city. A state of war with China resulted . . .

Lord Derby brought forward a motion in the House of Lords strongly condemning the government's Chinese policy. *On the last night of the debate Disraeli denounced the government's 'weak and shambling case'.* When the debate ended in the defeat of the government by 16 votes, Palmerston ordered Parliament to be dissolved. In the following general election Palmerston and the Liberals were returned triumphantly to power with a majority of 70. He had opened his address to his electors at Tiverton by a volley of violent phrases: the Chinese governor of Canton was 'an insolent barbarian who had violated the British flag, broke the treaty promises, and planned the destruction of British subjects by murder, assassination and poison'. This address clearly suited the electors of the day and the victor flatly refused to change his policy by one iota. The disgraceful war against the Chinese continued.

Source: R. W. Seton-Watson, *Britain in Europe 1789-1914*, Cambridge, 1955 (adapted extracts).

(a) **(i)** Explain in your own words what Palmerston though was the main principle which Britain ought to follow in foreign affairs (Source A). **4(a)**

(ii) What reasons does he give for wanting Britain to follow that principle? **4(a)**

(iii) What evidence can you find in the other Sources to support or contradict the truth of the statement made by Palmerston in the sentence in italics (Source A)? **4(a, c)**

(b) **(i)** After studying Sources **B** and **C** carefully, make a list of what the writers of these Sources thought were Palmerston's good points. **4(a, c)**

(ii) Which points about Palmerston do Sources **B** and **C** agree on? **4(a, c)**

(iii)   What evidence can you find in Source **G** which supports the statement in Source **C** that Palmerston was very popular?
          4(a, c)

(c)   (i)   In what ways does the writer of Source **D** seem to contradict Sources **B** and **C**?   **4(a, c)**

     (ii)   Do you think the writer of Source **D** is an admirer of Palmerston or not? Explain your answer.   **4(a, b)**

(d)   (i)   In Source **E**, what criticisms is Prince Albert making of Palmerston?   **4(a)**

     (ii)   Using your own knowledge, explain whether or not you think Albert is correct when he writes that 'since 1846 England has not had a single success'.   **1, 2, 4(a)**

    (iii)   What contradictions can you find between Sources **C** and **E**?
          4(a, c)

    (iv)   From the evidence provided by Sources **B**, **C**, **D**, and **E**, what possible reasons can you suggest for their differing opinions about Palmerston?   **4(a, b, c)**

(e)   (i)   In Source **F** Palmerston mentions striking 'another Blow in China'. From your own knowledge, and from the clues provided in Source **G**, explain briefly what the earlier 'Blow in China' had been.   **1, 2, 4(a)**

     (ii)   What do you think Palmerston means when he says (Source **F**) 'they must not only see the Stick but actually feel it on their shoulders'?   **2, 4(a)**

    (iii)   In what ways could this note by Palmerston (Source **F**) be taken as a contradiction of what he says in Source **A**?   **4(a, c)**

    (iv)   From the evidence provided by Sources **F** and **A**, can you suggest any explanation for this apparent contradiction?
          4(a, b, c)

(f)   (i)   What evidence can you find in Source **G** to support Disraeli's claim that the government had 'a weak and shambling case' over its conduct of the *Arrow* affair?   **4(a)**

     (ii)   Why do you think Palmerston and the Liberals won the general election mentioned in Source **G**?   **4(a)**

    (iii)   Do you think the writer of Source **G** approves or disapproves of the British action in China? Give reasons for your answer.
          4(a, b)

(g)   What do you think are the advantages and disadvantages of each of the Sources **A** to **F** for the historian trying to find reliable information about Palmerston?   **4(a, b)**

2. Palmerston, the Eastern Question and Schleswig-Holstein

Study Sources **A** and **B** and then answer the questions which follow.

Source A: a letter from Palmerston to Bulwer, a British minister in Paris, 22 September 1840.

I still believe that the French Government will be too wise and prudent to make war; bullies seldom execute the threats they deal in, and men of trick and cunning are not always men of desperate resolves. But if Thiers should again hold to you the language of menace, pray convey to him in the most friendly manner possible that if France throws down the gauntlet, we shall not refuse to pick it up; and that if she begins a war to assist Mehemet Ali, she will to a certainty lose her ships, colonies and commerce before she sees the end of it; and that Mehemet Ali will just be chucked into the Nile.

Source: quoted in J. Ridley, *Lord Palmerston*, Constable, 1970 (adapted extract).

Source B: speech by Palmerston in the House of Commons, 23 July 1863

The British government, like France and Russia, wishes that the independence, the integrity, and the rights of Denmark may be maintained. We are convinced that if any violent attempt were made to overthrow those rights and interfere with that independence, those who made the attempt would find in the result that it would not be Denmark alone with which they would have to contend. I am convinced that the German Diet will not act on the ultimatum they have sent to Denmark; I do not think there is even a remote danger of war over Schleswig-Holstein.

Sources: as for Source A (adapted extracts).

(a) (i) According to Source A, how likely did Palmerston think it was that France would make war in support of Mehemet Ali? 4(a)
   (ii) What reasons does he give for holding this view? 4(a)
   (iii) What message does he want Bulwer to give to the French?
4(a)

(b) (i) Who was Mehemet Ali mentioned in Source A? 1, 4(a)
   (ii) Explain why he had become important in international affairs in the years after 1830. 1, 2
   (iii) What offer did Britain, Russia, Prussia and Austria make to Mehemet Ali in 1840, and why did he reject it? 1, 2
   (iv) Why were the French thinking of giving military help to Mehemet Ali? 1, 2
   (v)   Why was Palmerston not in favour of France helping Mehemet Ali? 1, 2
   (vi) Describe and explain how the Mehemet Ali affair was settled in a way favourable to Britain. 1, 2
   (vii) Why is Palmerston's handling of this Near Eastern crisis often thought to be his greatest success? 1, 2

(c) (i) According to Source B, which country was threatening Denmark? 4(a)

160

(ii)   What did Palmerston mean when he said 'it would not be Denmark alone with which they would have to contend'?

4(a)

(iii)   What similarities can you find between the two views on war expressed by Palmerston in these two Sources?   4(a, c)

(iv)   Was Palmerston correct when he said that there was not even a remote danger of war? Explain your answer.   1, 2, 4(a)

(v)   Describe how the Schleswig-Holstein crisis was brought to an end.   1, 2

(vi)   Why can Palmerston's handling of this crisis be described as a failure?   1, 2

(d)   Explain why it was that Palmerston was able to handle Mehemet Ali and the Eastern Question successfully but failed over Schleswig-Holstein?   1, 2

3. Choose any 4 of the following:

The Belgian revolt (1830); revolutions in Spain and Portugal (1832); Mehemet Ali and the Eastern Question; the Opium War with China (1839); the Spanish marriages; Italian unification (1859–60); the Polish revolution (1863); the Schleswig-Holstein question.

For each of the 4 you have chosen:

(a)   explain why Britain became involved;
(b)   describe how Palmerston handled the situation;
(c)   explain whether or not the outcome was successful for Britain.

1, 2

4.   It is 1839 and you are a Belgian nationalist who has been closely involved in the struggle for independence from Holland. Write a letter to a friend describing the events of the last eight years, during which Belgium won her independence. Explain why you thought it was so important for Belgium to assert her independence, your fears about French motives for wanting to help, the importance of Britain's part in the struggle and your reasons for feeling grateful for Palmerston.

1, 2, 3

CHAPTER 10

THE CRIMEAN WAR (1854-56)

SUMMARY OF EVENTS

The Crimean War involved Britain, France, Turkey and Piedmont all fighting Russia. It was caused partly by *the Eastern Question* and partly by the ambitions of *The Emperor Napoleon III* of France which brought him into conflict with *the Tsar Nicholas I* of Russia.

A joint allied force landed in the Crimea (September 1854) with the object of capturing *Sebastopol*, the great Russian naval base. The allies, badly organised and ill-equipped, made heavy weather of the campaign, though they managed to win the three major battles that were fought: the crossing of the *River Alma* (September 1854), *Balaclava* (October) which included the notorious Charge of the Light Brigade, and *Inkerman* (November). Sebastopol eventually fell (September 1855) and the new Russian *Tsar Alexander II*, faced with pressing financial and social problems, was prepared to end hostilities. After long negotiations *the Treaty of Paris* was signed in March 1856. At the time both Britain and France were highly satisfied with the peace terms, but as it turned out, the war had not solved the Eastern Question permanently; 20 years later it was to flare up again (see Section 14.4).

Apart from its military and political importance, the Crimean War was remarkable for two other reasons. For the first time a newspaper correspondent, William Howard Russell of *The Times*, sent back detailed reports so that the British public was better informed than ever before about what was happening on the spot. Partly because of Russell's vivid descriptions of the disgraceful conditions, *Florence Nightingale* and her team of nurses went out to try and bring some order to the chaos in the base hospitals where the wounded were looked after.

10.1 WHAT CAUSED THE WAR?

There have been differing opinions over the years about exactly why the war broke out. Some historians believe that Nicholas I of Russia deliberately provoked a war with Turkey so that he could destroy the Ottoman

Empire and seize a large slice of the Balkans for Russia. Others believe that none of the countries involved really wanted a war and that they all drifted into it because of a series of misunderstandings. The second view, held by such historians as A. J. P. Taylor and M. S. Anderson, is the more widely accepted one today. Several issues and rivalries were at stake:

(a) The basic hostility lay between Russia and Turkey over the Eastern Question. As we saw earlier (Section 3.3(b) (iv)), the Turkish Empire, weak and badly governed, was in decline; regarded by other states as 'the Sick Man of Europe', it was expected to distintegrate in the near future.

Map 10.1   *The Eastern Question and the Crimean War*

The Russians wanted to profit from this situation as much as possible; they were handicapped militarily and commercially by the fact that most of their ports were ice-bound for many months of the year, while ships sailing to and from the ice-free Black Sea ports could, in war-time, be prevented by the Turks from passing through the Bosphorus and the Dardanelles, the two narrow straits which form the outlet from the Black Sea (see Map 10.1). Russian influence in the Balkans down as far as Constantinople, would enable them to control the Straits. In 1833 the Treaty of Unkiar Skelessi had given the Russians much of what they wanted, but their advantages had been cancelled out by the Straits Convention of 1841 (see Section 9.3(b)). By 1852 the Turks had had no success in reorganising and strengthening their Empire, and experienced observers were convinced that it would collapse shortly. The British ambassador at Constantinople, Stratford Canning, an admirer of the Turks, resigned in 1852, believing that 'the Turkish Empire is evidently hastening to its dissolution'. There was also the question of religion: the Russians – Greek Orthodox Christians – saw themselves as the protectors of the Christian inhabitants of Turkey (in the Balkans and Armenia) against the cruelties of the Muslim Turks.

(b) The Russians seem to have been torn between two possibilities:

(i) To divide the outlying provinces of Turkey up between themselves (taking parts of the Balkans) and Britain (taking Egypt). Nicholas had suggested this during a visit to Britain in 1844. However, the drawback was that other powers, Austria and France, might also want a share.

(ii) To try and preserve the Turkish Empire in its weak state in the hope that they, the Russians, would be able to exercise close control over the government at Constantinople; this would reduce the influence of other states to a minimum.

Russian indecision explains why there has been disagreement about their real intentions; Taylor believes that by 1852 the Russians had decided on the second policy. Either way there was bound to be friction between Russia and Turkey.

(c) Napoleon III of France started the crisis that led on to war. Having recently become Emperor, Napoleon needed a success in foreign affairs and was eager to win the support of French Roman Catholics. In the mid-eighteenth century the Sultan had granted French Roman Catholic monks the right to look after *the Holy Places* in Palestine. These included the church of the Nativity and the Grotto of the Holy Manger in Bethlehem, and two churches in Jerusalem, all of which were held sacred by Christians. The republican government which came to power in France in 1793 was hostile to Catholics and withdrew its support from the monks. Gradually Greek Orthodox monks had taken over control of the Holy Places, and it was this situation which gave Napoleon his chance to interfere. He demanded that the Sultan should grant the privilege of guarding the Holy Places solely to the French monks. After the French ambassador had sailed through the Dardanelles in a 90-gun warship on his way back to Constantinople, the Sultan gave way to the French demands (1852).

(d) Nicholas, afraid that the French might soon rival Russian influence in Turkey, sent Prince Menschikoff to Constantinople (February 1853) to demand that the rights of the Greek Orthodox monks should be maintained, and in addition, that the Tsar should be recognised as the protector of all Christians living in the Turkish Empire. If this were allowed it would give the Russians a permanent excuse to interfere in Turkish affairs. The Sultan restored the privileges to the Orthodox monks, but rejected Menschikoff's further demands (May 1853), although the Russians were threatening to invade the Turkish provinces of Moldavia and Wallachia.

(e) The British were extremely suspicious of Russian intentions; they feared, probably wrongly, that they were plotting the destruction of the Turkish Empire and hated the idea that Russian warships might be able to come and go through the Dardanelles as they pleased. It was widely believed that Russian interference in Afghanistan was the first step in an attempt to oust the British from control of India. After Russian troops had helped the Austrians to suppress the 1848 Hungarian revolution, British public opinion became violently anti-Russian. However, Lord Aberdeen's coalition government was divided about what line to take; Palmerston (who was Home Secretary) and Russell wanted to stand up to the Russians; Russell was convinced that 'the question must be decided by war, and if we do not stop the Russians on the Danube we shall have to stop them on the Indus' (a river in northern India close to the Afghan frontier). Aberdeen himself was more cautious and disliked the idea of supporting the Turks, who often persecuted Christians, against the Christian Russians. He believed the problems could be solved by negotiations; his attitude probably gave Nicholas the impression that Britain would not support Turkey if he were to step up Russian pressure. However, Aberdeen, influenced by Palmerston and Russell and by British public opinion and the press, agreed to send a naval force to Besika Bay, just outside the Dardanelles (June 1853). It was soon joined by a French force.

(f) From this point events began to escalate towards war:

(i) Nicholas was not impressed by this British and French action and thought it was all bluff. Having threatened Turkey, he now felt the threats must be carried out; confident of support from Austria and Prussia, he sent Russian troops to occupy Moldavia and Wallachia (July 1853), though they made no further moves towards Constantinople. Palmerston blamed Aberdeen for the Russian occupations, believing that if the British and French fleets had sailed into the Black Sea as he had proposed instead of remaining outside the Dardanelles, the Russians would not have dared to violate Turkish territory.

(ii) Palmerston wanted the British fleet to move into the Black Sea and arrest Russian ships which could be held hostage until Russian forces withdrew from Moldavia and Wallachia. Aberdeen rejected this idea and the British cabinet was so divided that no decisive action was taken either to warn the Russians off or to promise support to the Turks.

(iii) The Austrians, also suspicious of Russian intentions around the Danube, organised a conference in Vienna to find a solution. Attended by Prussians, French and British, the conference produced proposals known as the *Vienna Note*. It suggested that the Sultan should make a few concessions to the Tsar, and should promise to consult both the Russians and French about his policy towards the Christians. Nicholas, now realising that help from Prussia and Austria was unlikely, accepted the proposals, but the Turks rejected them, thinking that Nicholas was weakening.

(iv) Nicholas met Francis Joseph, the Austrian Emperor, and Frederick William IV of Prussia, in a final attempt to win support, but the most they would agree to was to remain neutral if war broke out. However, the British and French, who knew of the meetings but not what had been decided, thought that the three monarchs had hatched a new plot to partition the Turkish Empire. Consequently on 8 October, the British government ordered the fleet to Constantinople, where it was joined by French warships.

(v) The Sultan, feeling certain of British and French support, had already declared war on Russia on 4 October, though Stratford Canning (now Lord Stratford de Redcliffe and back as British ambassador to Turkey) persuaded the Turks to take no action for the time being.

(vi) When the British and French fleets approached Constantinople, the Turks could restrain themselves no longer; on 23 October their troops crossed the Danube and attacked the Russians in Wallachia. The Russians replied by attacking and sinking part of the Turkish fleet near Sinope on the Black Sea (30 November). Though this was a justifiable action since war had been declared, British public opinion regarded it as a 'massacre', and pressure on the government to declare war on Russia intensified.

(vii) The British government still dithered about what to do next and it was Napoleon who took the lead in sending the French fleet into the Black Sea. This forced Aberdeen to order the British fleet to follow (January 1854). Still there was no declaration of war: the allies were there to protect Turkish shipping.

(viii) Britain and France made one last effort to avoid all-out war: in February they sent Nicholas an ultimatum demanding the withdrawal of Russian troops from Moldavia and Wallachia. When this was ignored, the two western allies declared war on Russia (March).

M. S. Anderson probably sums up the causes best: the war 'was thus the outcome of a series of misjudgements, misunderstandings and blunders, of stupidity, pride and obstinacy rather than of ill will. More than any great war of modern times, it took place by accident'. A. J. P. Taylor makes the point that all the participants got themselves into situations from which they could not retreat without their prestige being seriously damaged, and that the war was caused by fear and suspicion of each other rather than by conscious aggression towards each other. The British government must take its share of the blame for not taking a tougher line against the Russians much earlier, which might have dissuaded Nicholas from sending his troops into Turkey; once committed to the occupation of Moldavia and Wallachia, the Russians could hardly withdraw without seeming to climb down. Governments are usually blamed for involving countries in war, but on this occasion Aberdeen did all he could to keep Britain out of it; it was the pressure of public opinion expressed through influential newspapers like *The Times* that pushed the British government into action.

10.2 EVENTS IN THE WAR

(a) The British military expedition commanded by the 66-year-old Lord Raglan, a veteran of the Peninsular War, arrived at Gallipoli and Scutari together with the French, in May 1854. Their objective was to protect Constantinople and to help the Turks drive the Russians from the provinces. As the allied forces moved towards Varna, the Russians surprisingly withdrew from Moldavia and Wallachia (August). This was not through fear at the allied approach but because:

(i) They were finding it difficult to maintain their position against Turkish attacks.
(ii) The Austrians, afraid that their interests would be threatened by Russian control of the Danube, threatened to declare war on the Russians unless they withdrew.

The Russian withdrawal floored the allies, since their objective had been achieved without a shot being fired. As Taylor puts it: 'they were thus faced with the problem – how to check an aggressive power when it is not being aggressive?' The governments decided that having progressed so far, a blow of some sort should be struck at the Russians. The expedition was ordered to sail from Varna to the Crimean peninsula to capture the naval base of *Sebastopol*. This, it was hoped, would destroy Russian power in the Black Sea, and make life easier for Turkish shipping.

(b) The 60 000 strong allied force (30 000 French, 26 000 British and 4000 Turks) landed at Eupatoria to the north of Sebastopol, and in spite of numerous problems, had some successes:

(i) Faced by a Russian army of around 40 000, the allies managed to force their way across the *River Alma* and advanced towards Sebastopol (20 September). Instead of attacking it immediately, they marched round Sebastopol and set up a base at Balaclava which was thought to be a good harbour; this would enable supplies to be brought in so that the allies could lay siege to Sebastopol.

(ii) *The Battle of Balaclava* was fought (25 October) when the Russians launched a surprise attack in an attempt to push the invaders into the sea. The British held off the attack and the troops distinguished themselves with great bravery, particularly the cavalry. The 'thin red line' of the Heavy Brigade delayed the Russian advance until reinforcements arrived; more famous was the Charge of the Light Brigade, led by Lord Cardigan. It was a courageous but mistaken attack on some Russian heavy artillery which achieved nothing and was extremely costly – 113 men were killed and 134 wounded out of 673.

(iii) A second Russian attack under cover of fog was driven off at *Inkerman* (5 November). Again the British and French troops acquitted themselves impressively; though they lost 775 men killed, they inflicted four times that number of deaths on the Russians and took many prisoners.

However, it was almost a year before the allied objective was achieved and Sebastopol fell (September 1855). In the meantime the troops had to endure the most appalling conditions during the severe winter of 1854-5.

(c) By the end of 1854 it was clear that *many mistakes had been made* and that there were *serious shortcomings in the British military system*, some of which were revealed by William Howard Russell, *The Times* war correspondent.

(i) There were disagreements between the British and French commanders, the most serious of which was over what to do immediately after the crossing of the Alma. Raglan wanted to advance and make a swift attack on the north side of Sebastopol, but his French counterpart, St Arnaud, refused on the grounds that they had insufficient troops for a frontal attack. While the armies were marching round to the south of the city, the Russian engineer Todleben seized the chance to strengthen its fortifications. Whereas an immediate attack would have had an excellent chance of success, the delay probably added months to the campaign. Balaclava was a bad choice for a base – its harbour was too small and it was served by primitive roads which Raglan did nothing to improve, so that they became almost impassable in the winter.

(ii) The officer class was less efficient than it might have been because of the practice of selling commissions; wealth rather than ability was what counted. A prime example of incompetence was the Charge of the Light Brigade; although the cavalry performed brilliantly, they charged up the wrong valley, thanks to a badly worded order from Raglan and a less than intelligent response from Lords Cardigan and

Lucan. Military organisation matched the poor leadership. There had been hardly any modernisation or improvement in the army since the Battle of Waterloo 40 years earlier. The troops were poorly equipped and trained and badly paid. In its desire to save money, the government refused Raglan's request for a special corps to handle food and other supplies and transport; thus the army was constantly short of food, clothing and ammunition. In the winter blizzards of 1854-5 the troops were still wearing the summer uniforms they had arrived in; they were completely unprepared for a winter campaign.

(iii) Medical arrangements were grim: the wounded and sick had to endure a nightmare journey across the Black Sea to the base hospitals at Scutari. The hospitals were badly organised and had no properly trained nursing staff; there was a chronic shortage of beds, dressings, bandages, soap, food and drugs. Many patients had to be left lying on the bare floor, and sanitation was non-existent. More people died from dysentery and cholera than from wounds sustained in battle.

(d) Public opinion became increasingly critical of the government for its incompetent handling of the war; in February 1855 Aberdeen resigned and *Palmerston became Prime Minister for the first time.* The public expected great things from the new leader, and the situation began to improve as soon as he took office. However, this was not all Palmerston's doing; *Florence Nightingale* and her team of trained nurses had already begun to reorganise the Scutari hospitals, reducing the death-rate and improving morale. Reinforcements and adequate supplies were arriving and a decent road had been built from the harbour at Balaclava to the trenches around Sebastopol. *Palmerston's contribution* was to send out a sanitary commission which greatly improved conditions both at Scutari and in the Crimea, to set up a special transport department which largely solved the problem of supply and to sack some of the more inefficient administrators in the Crimea – what he called 'that knot of Incapables who have been the direct cause of the disability and deaths of thousands of our brave men'.

(e) Militarily, as the allies brought in reinforcements, solved the supply problems, and even constructed a light railway from Balaclava harbour to the trenches, *the siege tightened around Sebastopol.* Even so, several assaults during the summer of 1855 failed and it was not until September that Sebastopol was captured. Some sections of the British public including Queen Victoria, wanted the allies to follow up their victory by forcing the Russians out of the Crimea altogether. However, both sides had had enough; Nicholas II had died from pleurisy after catching a chill while reviewing his troops (March), and the new Tsar Alexander II was anxious for peace so that he could concentrate on Russia's many internal problems. What finally convinced him was an Austrian threat to join the war (January 1856) unless he agreed to peace negotiations.

10.3 THE TREATY OF PARIS (1856) AND THE RESULTS OF THE WAR

(a) Peace talks opened in Paris in February 1856, much to the delight of Napoleon III whose prestige stood high; *the terms of the treaty (signed in March) were*:

(i) Moldavia and Wallachia were to have self-government for internal affairs, though they still had to acknowledge Turkish suzerainty (right of general supervision). The powers agreed to guarantee this new semi-independence and Russia had to give up its claim to protect the provinces.

(ii) Russia had to hand over the southern part of Bessarabia to Moldavia, which meant that the Russian frontier no longer reached up to the River Danube. In addition the Danube was to be a free waterway for all nations.

(iii) The Straits Convention of 1841 (see Section 9.2(c)(viii)) was repeated: the Black Sea was neutralised – no warships were allowed on it but it was open to merchant shipping of all nations. The treaty added that the Russians must not build any military or naval strongholds along the Black Sea coast.

(iv) Russia had to abandon its claim to protect the Christians in Turkey, and the independence of the Turkish Empire was guaranteed. In return the Sultan promised to treat his Christians fairly and to modernise and strengthen his state.

(b) How far were Britain's war aims achieved? The general idea had been to check Russian expansion in the Balkans, to keep the Russian navy out of the Mediterranean and to bolster up the Turkish Empire to act as a buffer against Russia. To some extent all three aims were achieved:

(i) Russian influence in the Balkans was checked when Moldavia and Wallachia were given semi-independence. When the provinces united to form the new state of Romania (1858) it acted as a real barrier against any further Russian attempt to annex parts of the Balkans.

(ii) Russia was not allowed to have a fleet in the Black Sea and so could not threaten British sea-power in the Mediterranean. However, this clause of the peace treaty was difficult to enforce without keeping a Franco-British fleet permanently on the Black Sea to make sure the Russians behaved themselves. In 1870 during the Franco-Prussian War the Russians announced that they no longer recognised the ban and that they would build a Black Sea Fleet and fortify the coastline. The neutralisation of the Black Sea therefore lasted only just over 14 years.

(iii) The Turkish Empire had been protected and saved from collapse, but in fact the Sultan kept neither of his promises and Turkey remained as weak as ever.

Ever since the war there has been debate about whether the results justified the cost in money and lives – Britain alone lost over 22 000 killed. Cobden and Bright thought it was a waste of time, since the threat from Russia was a 'phantom'. Recently historians have taken a different view: Asa Briggs (in *The Age of Improvement*, Longmans, 1959) believes that the war 'dealt a very real blow to Russian influence in Europe as a whole. In the aftermath of the revolutions of 1848 Russian power had reached its peak; it was never to be so strong again until the twentieth century'. On the other hand, the war had not solved the Eastern Question; but at least when another Balkans crisis arose in 1875-8 (see Section 14.4), Alexander did not push things as far as another war with Britain.

(c) Other results of the war:

(i) Some improvements were made in the British army: the system of supply was modernised, training standards raised, a modern breech-loading rifle introduced, and the price of commissions was reduced by a third. But it was not until Edward Cardwell became Secretary for War in 1868 that a really thorough reform took place.

(ii) Following Florence Nightingale's work in the Crimea, nursing was taken more seriously in Britain. Using the £50 000 presented to her by the grateful public, Miss Nightingale set up a training school for nurses at St Thomas's Hospital, London (1861). The idea soon spread over the country bringing a marked improvement in standards, as well as improvements in medicine and hospitals.

(iii) Britain's poor performance in the early stages of the war probably caused Bismarck to risk ignoring Palmerston's warning and go ahead with his invasion of Denmark in 1864 (see Section 9.5(e)). This, together with the recent check on Russian power, prepared the way for the unification of Germany by Bismarck.

QUESTIONS

1. The Outbreak of the Crimean War
Study Sources **A** to **H** and then answer the questions which follow.

Source A: The Tsar Nicholas I of Russia speaking to the British ambassador about Turkey, early in 1853.

> We have *a very sick man* on our hands, and we need a frank discussion as to the fate of Turkey. I want to speak as a friend and a gentleman, and as one keenly interested in the fate of millions of Christians . . . I cannot allow Britain to take Constantinople, but for my part, I am willing to undertake not to establish myself there as proprietor . . . Constantinople

must not belong to any Great Power; as to *the Principalities*, which are in fact an independent state under my protection, they might well remain so; I am quite ready that England should take Egypt and Crete in any partition.

Source: R. W. Seton-Watson, *Britain in Europe 1789–1914*, Cambridge, 1937 (adapted extracts).

Source B: a letter from Lord Aberdeen, the Prime Minister, to Lord John Russell, September 1854.

The assurances of prompt and effective aid, given by us to the Turks, would in all probability produce war. These barbarians hate us all and would be delighted to take their chance of some advantage by getting us mixed up with the other powers of Christendom. It may be necessary to give them moral support and to try to prolong their existence, but we ought to regard as the greatest mischief any engagement which compelled us to take up arms for the Turks . . . Britain ought to keep perfectly independent and free to act as circumstances may require.

Source: as for Source A (adapted extracts).

Source C: a letter from Lord John Russell to Lord Clarendon, the Foreign Secretary, September 1854.

The emperor of Russia is *clearly bent on accomplishing the destruction of Turkey*, and he must be resisted . . . plainly I shall stand for the Turk against the Russian.

Source: as for Source A (adapted extracts).

Source D: a letter from Lord Palmerston to Sidney Herbert, the Secretary for War, September 1854.

Turkey is not in decay, and for the last thirty years has made greater progress and improvement than any other country . . . If the Tsar wishes the Christians of Turkey to be safe from oppression, then let him relieve the Principalities of the miseries inflicted by his own armies. Beyond that, let him be satisfied, as we all are, with the progressively liberal system of Turkey. If he wants to interfere between the Sultan and his subjects, then let us manfully assist Turkey and let the fortune of war decide between the Emperor's wrong and the Sultan's rightful cause.

Sources: as for Source A (adapted extracts).

Source E: cartoon showing Lord Aberdeen and the British lion.

[Reproduced by permission of the Proprietors of 'Punch.'

WHAT IT HAS COME TO.

Aberdeen. " I MUST LET HIM GO ! ''

Source: *Punch*, October 1854.

Source F: speeches by John Bright in the House of Commons, October–
November 1854.

> War will not save Turkey if peace cannot save her; but war will
> brutalize our people, increase our taxes, destroy our industry,
> postpone the promised parliamentary reform . . .; as to the
> supposed Russian threat to India – in the light of past history,
> we are more likely to attack Russia from India than the Russians
> to attack us there, for our Asian policy, much more than
> Russia's, has been designed to increase our power . . .
>
> Is it really necessary for us to interfere in a dispute between
> Russia and Turkey? The Turks declared war on Russia against
> the advice of the British and French governments, but the
> moment war was declared by Turkey, our Government openly
> applauded it. My doctrine would have been non-intervention
> in this case. The danger of Russian power was a phantom . . .;
> our love for civilisation when we subject the Greeks and
> Christians to the Turks, is a sham.

Source: quoted in D. Read, *Cobden and Bright*, Arnold, 1967 (adapted extracts).

Source G: a poem by Tennyson, published in 1855

> So I wake to the higher aims
> Of *a land that has lost* for a little *her lust of gold*,
> And love of a peace that was full of wrongs and shames,
> Horrible, hateful, monstrous, not to be told . . .
> For the Peace, that I deem'd no peace, is over and done,
> And now *by the side of the Black and Baltic deep*,
> And deathful-grinning mouths of the fortress, flames
> The bloodred blossom of war with a heart of fire . . .
> It is better to fight for the good than to rail at the ill;
> I have felt with my native land, I am one with my kind,
> I embrace the purpose of God, and the doom assigned.

Source: Alfred, Lord Tennyson, *Maud*, in Tennyson, *Poetical Works*, Oxford, 1953.

Source H: the view of a modern historian.

It has often been agreed that British policy, or lack of it, allowed the Russo–Turkish War to occur and then failed to prevent Britain being dragged into it. On the one hand, a firmer British stand, the Palmerston–Russell policy, would have made it clear to Russia from the outset that Britain would not tolerate any interference with Turkey. On the other hand, it is claimed, if Britain had been more determined with Turkey, showing that she was not prepared to assist her against Russia, the Sultan would have been more ready for compromise. Aberdeen disliked the idea of assisting the Turks, especially when the Turks treated Christians harshly, and he tried to bring pressure on her to settle with Russia . . . However, he was not able to pursue this policy throughout, because influential *members of his cabinet* – Palmerston and Russell – *held contrary views*.

However uncertain the government was, public opinion was perfectly clear: the press lambasted the government for not standing up to the Russians. When a Turkish flotilla cruising in the Black Sea was sunk at Sinope by the Russians, public opinion became almost hysterical. So the divided Cabinet, finding it increasingly difficult to resist popular demand, issued an *ultimatum* demanding a Russian withdrawal from the Principalities. When it was not complied with, war was declared on 27 March 1854.

Source: D. R. Ward, *Foreign Affairs 1815–1865*, Collins, 1972 (adapted extracts).

(a) (i)   In Source **A**, who does Nicholas mean by the phrase 'a very sick man'?   **4(a)**

    (ii)   What does he mean by 'the Principalities'?   **1, 4(a)**

    (iii)   From the evidence of Source **A**, do you think Nicholas is friendly or hostile to Britain? Explain your answer.   **4(a, b)**

(b) (i)   In Source **B**, what does Lord Aberdeen feel about giving military help to the Turks?   **4(a)**

    (ii)   From the evidence of Source **B**, do you think Aberdeen approves of the Turks or not? Explain your answer.   **4(a, b)**

(c) (i)   Would you agree or disagree that the evidence in Source **A** supports the claim made by Russell in Source **C** that Nicholas was 'clearly bent on accomplishing the destruction of Turkey'?   **4(a, c)**

    (ii)   How does Lord Palmerston in Source **D** differ from Tsar Nicholas in Source **A** in his view of the situation in Turkey?   **4(a, c)**

    (iii)   In what ways do the writers of Sources **C** and **D** differ from Source **B** in their attitudes towards Turkey?   **4(a, c)**

(d) (i)   In the *Punch* cartoon (Source **E**) what message is the cartoonist trying to put over?   **4(a)**

    (ii)   From the style and detail of the cartoon, do you think the cartoonist is sympathetic to Aberdeen or not? Give reasons for your answer.   **4(a, b)**

(e) (i)   What reasons does Bright give in Source **F** as to why Britain ought not to go to war against Russia?   **4(a)**

    (ii)   What does he mean when he says '[Britain's] love for civilisation . . . is a sham'?   **4(a)**

    (iii)   How does Bright (Source **F**) contradict or support points made in Sources **B**, **C** and **D**?   **4(a, c)**

(f) (i)   In Source **G**, why does the poet use the phrase 'by the side of the Black and Baltic deep'?   **1, 4(a)**

    (ii)   What do you think the poet means when he mentions the land 'that has lost . . . her lust of gold'? You will find a clue in Source **F**.   **4(a, c)**

    (iii)   How does the poet show that he thinks war was justified and that Britain was in the right to go to war?   **4(a, b)**

(g) (i)   What evidence can you find in Sources **B**, **C** and **D** to support the statement in Source **H** that some members of the cabinet held views contrary to those of the Prime Minister?   **4(a, c)**

    (ii)   What is meant in Source **H** by the word 'ultimatum'?   **1, 4(a)**

(h) (i)   From the evidence of the Sources and your own knowledge, how much blame do you think each of the following should take for the outbreak of the Crimean War:

        Tsar Nicholas III; the French Emperor Napoleon III; Lord Aberdeen; Lord Palmerston and Lord John Russell; public opinion in Britain?   **1, 2, 4(a, c)**

(ii)   Do you think it is possible, from the evidence provided by these Sources, to decide which of the above was most to blame? Explain your answer fully.   **1, 2, 4(a, b, c)**

2. Problems During the Crimean War

Study Sources **A** to **C** and then answer the questions which follow.

Source A: diary of Lieutenant-General Sir C. A. Windham.

9th Dec. 1854.   Our supply of provisions is getting worse and worse, all owing to the want of transport from Balaclava. Now what can be more inexcusable than this? Here we have a fleet twice as large as the French with not half the men to feed, and yet they want for nothing. Our horses are literally starving and the Medical Department is disgracefully neglected – only one miserable carriage to transport the sick, and hundreds of poor devils dying upon the road with no means whatsoever of assistance; men rolling on the ground with cholera and not a drop of laudanum for them.

12th Dec.   All our sick are carried to Balaclava by the French mules, our own ambulance corps being perfectly useless.

Source: quoted in D. Holman, *Portraits and Documents: Earlier Nineteenth Century*, Hutchinson, 1965 (adapted extracts).

Source B: report of the Select Committee on conditions in the Army, 1855.

It appears that the sufferings of the army resulted mainly because the government were not acquainted with the strength of the fortresses to be attacked. They expected that the expedition would be immediately successful, and as they did not foresee the possibility of a long struggle, they made no provision for a winter campaign. It was all planned by the government without sufficient information or care.

Source: quoted in A. Briggs, *Victorian People*, Penguin, 1965 (adapted extracts).

Source C: information from a modern historian.

Many officers regarded the service as an amusing occupation to while away the time when they were not hunting. Only wealthy men could purchase promotion. Though the Military College had been established for some years, few officers bothered to attend it. Problems of high command and staff work were almost entirely neglected.

Source: A. Swinson, *Crimean Ordeal*, in *Purnell's History of the English Speaking Peoples*, No. 93, BPC Publishing, 1971.

(a) (i) In Source **A**, what was the main fortress being attacked in the Crimean War? **1, 4(a)**

    (ii) What are the main complaints made by the writer of Source **A** about conditions in the Crimea? **4(a)**

    (iii) What does Source **A** suggest about the French forces in the Crimea? **4(a)**

(b) (i) According to Source **B**, why did the government not plan for a winter campaign? **4(a)**

    (ii) What explanations are given in Sources **B** and **C** for the difficulties described in Source **A**? **4(a, c)**

    (iii) What explanation can you think of for the fact that 'few officers bothered to attend' the Military College (Source **C**)? **2, 4(a)**

(c) (i) Who was the leader of the government mentioned in Source **B**? **1**

    (ii) Who took over in February 1855 when that leader resigned? **1**

(d) (i) Describe how Florence Nightingale helped to solve the medical problems during the war. **1, 2**

    (ii) How were some of the other problems mentioned in Source **A** dealt with? **1, 2**

(e) Explain how and why the Crimean War was brought to an end in January 1856. **1, 2**

3. You are an officer in the British army who has survived the Crimean War and kept a diary for the years 1854–6. Give some extracts from your diary dealing with the background, events and conclusion of the war. Among other matters, you could refer to:

    (a) your views on Russia and the international situation early in 1854;

    (b) why you were irritated with the Aberdeen government for trying to remain neutral;

    (c) why you were pleased when Britain declared war on Russia;

    (d) why you became disillusioned with the conditions in the Crimea as well as your views on who was to blame;

    (e) your comments on the main battles (Alma, Balaclava, Inkerman);

    (f) your thoughts after the war about whether the results were worth all the bloodshed. **1, 2, 3**

4. (a) Explain briefly why Britain entered the Crimean War in 1854.

    (b) What were the main terms of the Treaty of Paris (February 1856) which ended the war?

    (c) Explain whether you think Britain's aims in the war were achieved. **1, 2**

CHAPTER 11

BRITAIN, INDIA AND THE

MUTINY OF 1857

SUMMARY OF EVENTS

The British had been in India since the early seventeenth century, when *the East India Company* had established trading settlements (known as factories) at Surat (1612) and Madras (1640) and later at Bombay (1661) and Calcutta (1690). In the early days the Company was there purely for trade and not to take political control of India. In the early eighteenth century the central administration of India began to break down; the Mogul Emperor found it difficult to maintain his authority against ambitious local princes. In this situation the Company trading posts were forced to defend themselves both against hostile princes and against a rival French trading company. Both sides trained and equipped Indian soldiers, known as sepoys, to help defend their settlements.

By 1764, largely thanks to the work of Robert Clive, who successfully supported friendly princes against hostile ones, the French threat had been curbed and company control was established in Bengal and Bihar and in the areas around Madras and Bombay. The job of running these areas was fast becoming too much for the East India Company, so the *1784 India Act* gave the British government overall authority; this was to be exercised through the Governor-General, based at Calcutta, who would decide the political policy to be followed in the British parts of India, while the Company continued to control trade. During the Franco-British wars (1793–1815) the Company got itself into financial difficulties and the British government gradually assumed most of its functions.

Successive Governors-General after 1800 were anxious to extend the area of British control. By 1857, partly through a series of bloody wars and partly by devious political manoeuvring, the vast majority of India and Burma was either controlled directly by the British government or had accepted British protection.

The British became careless and failed to read certain danger signals. British complacency suffered a painful jolt, when in May 1857 the Bengal sepoys suddenly mutinied and murdered all Europeans they could lay hands on. There were at least five times more Indian troops than Europeans,

Map 11.1 *India*

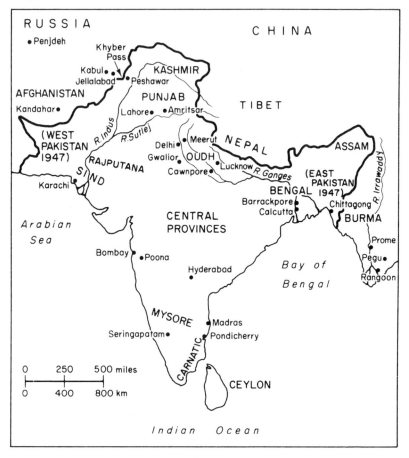

and for a time it seemed as though the British might lose control of the whole of India. Fortunately for the British, only the Bengal sepoys mutinied; those in Madras, Bombay and the Punjab remained loyal. Even so there was a bitter struggle with terrible atrocities on both sides; it took the British until the end of September to regain control, and it was another full year before all resistance ended. Relations between the British and Indians were never quite the same again.

11.1 HOW WAS BRITISH POWER IN INDIA EXTENDED BETWEEN 1800 AND 1857?

After the 1784 India Act there was a long line of Governors-General appointed by the British government. The office of Governor-General carried with it enormous personal power and prestige, and every one of them made a contribution to the extension of British power in India. It was not always a case of sheer aggression by the British; sometimes native princes were persuaded to sign alliances with them; sometimes neighbouring tribes raided British territory and had to be subdued, giving the British an excuse to annex new areas. As well as initiating military campaigns, some of the Governors-General introduced reforms to improve administrative efficiency and social conditions.

(a) **Lord Wellesley (1798-1805)** began by attacking the ruler of Mysore, Tipu Sahib, who was supporting the French and had sworn to drive the British from India. Tipu was defeated and killed (1799) and Mysore came under British control, soon to be followed by the Carnatic. Wellesley's attitude towards the remaining independent Indian princes (known by various titles meaning 'ruler', 'prince', or 'governor', such as nawab, rajah, maharajah, nizam (in Hyderabad), peshwa (in Maratha areas)) was to persuade them to sign *subsidiary alliances* with the British: the native ruler could run the domestic affairs of his state while British troops would protect him from attack. In return for protection the ruler had to pay towards the expenses of the troops who would be based in his territory, accept a British resident (an adviser representing the British government) and promise not to sign treaties with other princes. The nizam of Hyderabad was the first to accept British 'protection', followed by the nawab of Oudh and by three Maratha chiefs. In seven years Wellesley had transformed the British position in India. Less impressive, however, were his superior attitude towards the Indians, especially Hindus (Indians were not allowed in top administrative posts and could not attend social events organised by whites) and his excessive vanity which, as reliable reports had it, caused him to wear his medals and decorations even in bed.

(b) **Lord Minto (1807-13)** did not find life as quiet as might have been expected following Wellesley's exploits: some sepoys had mutinied near Madras and the Maratha chiefs resented their treatment by the British. The Sikhs of the Punjab, led by Ranjit Singh from his capital at Lahore, had already captured Kashmir from the Afghans and now had designs on neighbouring British territory across the Sutlej river. Minto, however, was soon able to restore internal order and persuaded Ranjit Singh to sign an agreement at Amritsar promising not to cross the Sutlej river.

(c) **Lord Hastings (1813-23)**, like Minto, had to face attacks from tribes outside British territory. Most troublesome were the Gurkhas of Nepal to the north of Bengal. It took a difficult 18-month campaign (1814-16) in the Nepal mountains to force the Gurkhas to abandon their claims to British territory. Most of Nepal was left as an independent state and the Gurkhas have remained friendly to Britain ever since. Meanwhile the Pindaris, robber bands of Maratha tribesmen, were causing trouble in central India. When Hastings sent troops against them, several of the Maratha chiefs including the rajah of Nagpur, rose against the British. In the large-scale campaign which followed, the British deployed over 100 000 troops against more than twice that number, and the Marathas were finally defeated at the Battle of Kirkee (1817). Feeling that subsidiary treaties with such rulers were a waste of time, Hastings decided to annex their territories; the Deccan became part of the province of Bombay and Nagpur became the Central Provinces. Hastings must take the credit for stabilising the northern frontiers of British India and after his annexations the only significant parts of India not under British control (either directly or indirectly) were the Punjab and Sind in the north-west. He even found time for internal improvements such as the introduction of irrigation schemes and the building of new roads and schools.

(d) Lord Amherst (1823-8) was hoping for a peaceful time, but like his predecessors, he found himself harassed by raids; this time they were on the eastern frontier of Bengal where the aggressive king of Ava on the Irrawaddy river, occupied British territory near Chittagong (1824). Reluctantly Amherst despatched an 11 000 strong expedition by sea, which sailed up the Irrawaddy, capturing Rangoon and Prome. As the British approached Ava itself, the king promised to abandon his claims and to hand over to the British the coast of Burma from Chittagong down to the Irrawaddy delta. However, the cost had been heavy: the British troops had inadequate supplies and were hampered by monsoons and floods. Over half the force perished, most of them from tropical diseases.

(e) Lord William Bentinck (1828-35), thanks to the energy of his predecessors, was able to enjoy a period of peace in which he put the country's finances on the road to recovery after the enormous expense of the military campaigns, and distinguished himself as a social reformer. It was during his time in India that *two conflicting British attitudes towards the Indians became apparent*:

- An increasing readiness to accept much of the Indians' own laws and customs and to respect the Indians themselves. *The India Act (1833)* stated 'that the interests of the Native subjects are to be consulted in preference to those of Europeans, whenever the two come into competition; and that therefore the Laws ought to be adapted rather to the feelings and habits of the natives than to those of Europeans'. It added that 'no native of India . . . should be disabled from holding any place, office or employment by reason of his religion, place of birth, descent or colour'. Bentinck's own motto was 'British greatness is founded on Indian happiness'.
- The belief that western culture and methods must be introduced before India could become fully developed.

In fact India was so backward that *the drive towards westernisation became dominant*:

(i) Bentinck decided that English should be the language of instruction in all state-aided schools; the government would provide money to set up more schools and colleges of higher education. Thus began the process of imposing on educated Indians a European culture which was probably not appropriate for them, though it can also be argued that the use of English as a common language helped to unite India.

(ii) He began to stamp out two ancient but barbaric customs:

suttee - the practice of burning Hindu widows on the funeral pyres along with their dead husbands.
thuggee - sacrificial murders by members of a secret society called thugs.

(iii) He deposed the unpopular rajah of Coorg for cruelty to his subjects and the maharajah of Mysore for incompetent government.

(iv) Bentinck was influenced by *a new motive - fear of Russian ambitions* in the north-west, through Afghanistan. This led him to renew the alliance with Ranjit Singh of the Punjab signed originally during Lord Minto's time, while the rulers of Sind were persuaded to sign an agreement allowing merchants to trade along the Indus river, on condition that no weapons or armaments were carried.

(f) Lord Auckland (1835-42) was the least successful of the Governors-General before the Mutiny; in fact his stay in India ended in disaster - British defeat in the *First Afghan War (1839-42)*. Auckland decided that Britain must gain control of Afghanistan in order to keep the Russians out. In 1839 he launched an invasion of Afghanistan with the intention of removing Dost Mahomed, the amir based at Kabul, and replacing him with Shah Suja, who had previously been driven out by the Afghans themselves. *Auckland's actions are difficult to defend*: he had earlier assured Dost Mahomed that he had no intention of interfering in Afghan affairs; Dost was anxious to keep on good terms with him and much preferred the British to the Russians; Shah Suja was extremely unpopular and would never be accepted back by the Afghans; and finally, the British army, which lacked sufficient transport and supplies, went into Afghanistan through Sind, thereby breaking Bentinck's agreement.

The army captured Kabul and set up Shah Suja, but the outraged Afghans rose in revolt and besieged the British forces in Kabul and Kandahar. It was decided to retreat into India, but in January 1842, 4500 British troops were caught in a narrow pass between Kabul and Jellalabad and were completely annihilated; only one survivor struggled through to Jellalabad.

(g) Lord Ellenborough (1842-4) arrived in India soon after the massacre. He sent a large relief expedition which forced its way through the Khyber Pass, recaptured Kabul (September 1842) and rescued the British prisoners still being held. However, the country was too rebellious to hold down for long, so the British withdrew to India. British prestige had been restored to some extent, but they had failed to achieve their original objective: Dost Mahomed was back in power in Kabul, Shah Suja had been murdered, and the Afghans had to be left severely alone.

Carried away by the success of his expedition, Ellenborough sent troops into Sind, defeated the rulers and annexed the territory. This was a totally unjustified and unprovoked attack which the British government strongly disapproved of. Ignoring their protests, Ellenborough next launched an invasion of the state of Gwalior, which was soon defeated and taken under British 'protection'. Peel's government felt that this was going too far, and dismissed him; he was replaced by his brother-in-law.

(h) Lord Hardinge (1844-8) had no sooner arrived in India than he had to deal with a Sikh invasion from the Punjab across the Sutlej into British territory. So long as the capable and popular Ranjit Singh had been alive, the Sikhs had been friendly, but since his death in 1839 the Sikh army had dominated the country. Deeply suspicious of the British because of the activities of Auckland and Ellenborough, the Sikhs were convinced that the Punjab was next on the list for annexation by the British, and decided to strike first. They were savage fighters, but after a series of bloody and costly engagements, the British captured Lahore, the Sikh capital (February 1846). The young maharajah Duleep Singh was placed on the throne with Sir Henry Lawrence as resident; though the Punjab was not annexed, it seemed firmly under British control. As Hardinge left India in January 1848 he pronounced that 'it will not be necessary to fire a gun in India for seven years to come'. He was wrong.

(i) Lord Dalhousie (1848-56), who had been a successful President of the Board of Trade under Peel until 1846, was still only 36 when he arrived in India. His period in power was packed with incident; he was responsible for extending British power still further (though not always by design) and for introducing important reforms.

(i) Three months after his arrival the Sikhs of the Punjab rose in revolt again, and another costly campaign was required to restore order. This time Dalhousie decided to annex the Punjab, and Duleep Singh was deposed and sent to Britain. This enabled much needed and, on the whole, popular reforms to be introduced, with such success that the Sikhs remained loyal even during the Mutiny.

(ii) More of Burma came under British control after the Burmese had broken the agreement signed with Amherst (1826) by harassing British traders on the Irrawaddy river. In 1852 the Burmese attacked some British ships; Dalhousie feld strong action was needed to discourage similar anti-British moves in India. A carefully organised expedition was sent, avoiding Amherst's mistakes; with only 377 casualties, Rangoon and Pegu were captured, bringing the Burmese coast as far south as Tenasserim under British rule.

(iii) Within India Dalhousie was responsible for bringing under British rule a number of states which had until this point been governed by native rulers. This was achieved by using what was called the *'doctrine of lapse'*: Hindu tradition allowed a childless man to adopt an heir, and this applied to native rulers as well. However, Dalhousie decided that in certain cases of political succession, this should not be allowed to happen – if a native ruler died without heir, his family's claim to the throne lapsed, and the state reverted to the British. By this method Dalhousie managed to annex seven states, of which the most important was Nagpur with a population of four million (1853). He also annexed the large northern state of Oudh after removing the nawab who had been notoriously incompetent and cruel for years.

(iv) There were important advances in administration, communications and education. Dalhousie created a central legislative council and set up a Public Works Department to carry out his ideas. Two thousand miles of road were built including the Grand Trunk Road from Calcutta to Peshawar; 18 000 miles of irrigation canal were completed, the showpiece being the spectacular Ganges Canal, opened by Dalhousie himself in 1854. He began the construction of railways to link Bombay, Calcutta and Madras and introduced the Indian telegraph service. 753 post offices were built and a uniform postal rate adopted. An engineering college which eventually became a university was founded at Roorkee; hundreds of village schools were started, and the education of women encouraged.

All this was a tremendous achievement, but Dalhousie knew that he had offended many people; at the end of his stay in India he warned the British government to remain alert: 'No prudent man would ever venture to predict a long continuance of peace in India'. The government took little notice and only just over a year had passed when the Mutiny broke out.

11.2 WHAT WERE THE CAUSES OF THE MUTINY?

In general the reforms of Bentinck and especially Dalhousie, though well-intentioned and beneficial in many ways, were too quick and far-reaching for the conservative and traditionally minded Indians. They disliked the drive towards westernisation and the attempt to impose an alien culture on them. Dalhousie left behind a number of individuals and groups nursing grievances and a sense of injustice, for political, economic and religious reasons:

(a) Dalhousie's annexations using the 'doctrine of lapse' and especially the annexation of Oudh in 1856 alarmed other Indian rulers who began to feel that it was the beginning of a British plan to expel them all. They regarded the British behaviour as dishonourable, since in some cases it broke existing treaties. The dispossessed rulers and their courtiers were left smarting and eager for revenge. Dalhousie realised how risky the annexation of Oudh would be but decided it was essential for the welfare of the population. In fact, many ordinary people were as outraged as the nawab himself. One loyal sepoy, writing about his experiences, was certain 'that this seizing of Oudh filled the minds of the sepoys with distrust, and led them to plot against the Government'. Unfortunately for the British, many of the sepoys in the Bengal army came from Oudh.

(b) There were economic grievances both in town and countryside:

(i) The British flooded India with all kinds of cheap, mass-produced goods, which were gradually putting Indian urban craftsmen out of business; one Indian complained that 'the introduction of English articles into India has thrown the weavers, spinners, cotton dressers, the carpenters, the blacksmiths and the shoemakers, etc., out of employ, so that every description of native artisan has been reduced to beggary'.

(ii) In the countryside the British tried to make the land more efficient by introducing European practices such as individual ownership of land and fixed money rents. But this caused enormous problems because both peasants and landlords, unaccustomed to making regular cash payments, got into debt and had to sell their land. According to Bernard Porter,

> the pattern of rural life was breaking up in many areas: families were forced to abandon lands they had tilled for generations; the old familiar feudal masters were replaced by new ones, sometimes unsympathetic with rural ways; and the loss of the old *élites* was regretted, apparently, by their faithful peasantry.

This was particularly true in Oudh.

(c) There were religious grievances among civilians and among sepoys in the army:

(i) The Brahmins (Hindu priests) objected to the abolition of suttee, though to Europeans it seemed a sensible and humane reform. To add insult to injury, in 1856 Dalhousie permitted Hindu widows to remarry, a further breach of Hindu custom.

(ii) Much of the resentment arose because of *the caste system*: Hindu society is divided into four castes or classes, which make up the social scale. At the top are the priests, and below them the next caste, rulers and soldiers; third in the social scale are traders and farmers, and fourth artisans (craftsmen), People outside these groups were known as 'untouchables' who were regarded as the dregs of society. Members of different castes did not mix socially. Thus innovations such as the railways on which all classes were expected to travel together, and the

British practice of everybody being equal before the law, seemed to be an insult to the higher castes and were taken to be an attack on the caste system. Similarly the spread of education and especially the education of women seemed to threaten the structure of Hindu society. The increasing numbers of Christian missionaries arriving in India confirmed suspicions that the British were trying to destroy not only Hinduism but Islam and Buddhism as well.

(iii) In the Bengal army there were discipline problems caused by the caste system. Since 1830 many high-class Hindus had been allowed to join the army as ordinary private soldiers, but they thought themselves superior to some of their officers and were unwilling to take orders from somebody of a lower caste. When the government tried to improve matters by forbidding the wearing of caste marks, this further offended Hindu principles. A rumour went round that two regiments of sepoys were about to be sent on operations to Burma, sailing across the Bay of Bengal to get there. The Hindus were afraid that they would lose caste by crossing water; in fact there had already been a mutiny for the same reason at Barrackpore (1824) which had quickly been put down by a few well-directed cannon blasts. The British had failed to learn the obvious lesson.

(d) British defeats in Afghanistan (1839–42) together with their recent undistinguished performance in the early part of the Crimean War (1854-6) showed the Indians that the British were not invincible. Also encouraging to the Indians was *the obvious unpreparedness of the British*: the arsenals at Delhi and Allahabad were inadequately guarded; some of the European troops had been withdrawn for service in the Crimea, Persia and Burma; there were scarcely 40 000 European troops in the whole of India, against 230 000 sepoys; in fact in Bengal itself, the most troubled area, there were only 5000 Europeans and nearly 55 000 sepoys. The British, far too careless and casual, seemed unaware of the growing resentment, and unconcerned at the prophecy that British rule in India would end on 23 June 1857 (exactly a hundred years after Robert Clive's famous victory at the Battle of Plassey).

(e) The affair of the greased-cartridges was the immediate cause of the outbreak. Cartridges for the recently introduced Enfield rifle had to be ripped open with the teeth before loading. A rumour spread that the grease for these cartridges was made from cow and pig fat. This caused consternation among both Hindus and Muslims, since the cow is sacred to Hindus and the pig considered unclean by Muslims. This united the two religious groups against the British; at Meerut the sepoys refused to touch the new cartridges, and 85 of them were given long prison sentences. The following day (10 May 1857) the Meerut sepoys mutinied and killed their European officers.

11.3 EVENTS IN THE MUTINY

(a) After the initial shock at Meerut, the Mutiny spread rapidly through Bengal, Oudh and the North-West Provinces. The Punjab, only recently annexed and garrisoned by regiments of Bengal sepoys, might have been a danger area; however, the Sikhs remained loyal and helped the governor, John Lawrence, to disarm the Bengal regiments. After this the Punjab remained quiet, and there was very little trouble elsewhere, as the Madras and Bombay armies remained mostly loyal. Hyderabad was a critical area with its large Muslim population, but the nizam turned out to be completely reliable, and so did the king of Nepal who allowed his Gurkha soldiers to fight for the British. The main centres of fighting were at Delhi, Cawnpore and Lucknow.

(b) Delhi was crucially important since it was regarded by northern Indians as the seat of power. The Meerut rebels quickly marched on Delhi and were joined by the Indian regiments based there; they soon captured the city, slaughtering all the British they could lay hands on. A small British force of 3500 set out to relieve Delhi and fought its way to the Long Ridge just outside the city. It could make no headway against 40 000 sepoys with 114 cannons mounted on the walls. In fact they did well to survive until August when a relief force from the Punjab under John Nicholson, arrived on the Ridge. In September the British blasted their way into Delhi with heavy artillery and after a further week's fierce fighting, the city was recaptured, though Nicholson himself was killed. The British shot three local princes as a reprisal for the slaughtering of European women and children.

(c) At Cawnpore a tiny British force of less than 700 was besieged by 3000 rebel sepoys commanded by the Nana Sahib, who had had his large pension stopped by Dalhousie (he was the adopted son of the peshwa of Poona who had been deposed by the British). After three weeks they were almost out of food and water, and since there were about 400 women and children with them, they decided to surrender and accept the Nana Sahib's offer of a safe conduct by boat down the river to Allahabad. As the crowded barges were about to push off, the Nana Sahib turned his cannons on them and sprayed them with grapeshot at point blank range. Only four soldiers and a hundred women and children survived, and they were held as prisoners. When a British relief force under Sir Henry Havelock was within two days of Cawnpore, the Nana Sahib had the prisoners hacked to death and their bodies thrown down a well. The city was taken on 17 July; the British were horrified at the remains of the massacre and took terrible revenge. Captured sepoys were made to lick up the blood from the floors of the prison huts before being hanged. The one British regret was that the Nana Sahib escaped and was never captured.

(d) At Lucknow, the capital of Oudh, there were only about 1000 European troops holding out against 60 000 rebels, though only 10 000 of these were trained sepoys. Havelock advanced from Cawnpore, but although he managed to force his way into Lucknow (25 September) there were still insufficient British to drive the rebels off. The siege lasted another two months before Lucknow was relieved by Sir Colin Campbell's force advancing from Calcutta (17 November). However, with over 100 000 rebels still in the area, there remained much fighting for Campbell to do and Lucknow was not finally secured until March 1858. At this point the Governor-General, Lord Canning, in an attempt to end resistance in Oudh, announced that all the landowners should forfeit their lands. But in an area where hatred of the British was stronger than anywhere else in India, this had the opposite effect and it was not until the end of 1858 that the Oudh rebels were finally subdued.

(e) Why did the Mutiny fail to achieve its objectives? There is some disagreement about what the objectives of the rebels were. Some Indian historians see the Mutiny as a national revolution with the ultimate aim of expelling the British from India. However, this was probably not the case. If it had been a war of independence, the whole country would have risen with the civilian population joining in as well. If this had happened, the Indians would have stood a good chance of success. British historians therefore see the Mutiny as a spontaneous response to frustrations and grievances. *The rebels' aims* were to restore their old rulers, customs and institutions; beyond that they were vague – there were certainly no plans for a united India. *The Mutiny failed because*:

(i) It was not a national rising: fewer than half the sepoys actually mutinied, and many important native rulers, for example in Hyderabad Gwalior and Rajputana, stayed loyal; some of them even supplied troops to help the British.

(ii) Except in Oudh, the civilian population was hardly involved, either because they had not been affected by British reforms, or because they had done well out of them (many upper class Indians had benefited from an English education and were playing an important part in the commercial life of the big cities). Very few Muslims took any part in the Mutiny.

(iii) No outstanding Indian leader emerged; there was no coordination between the different centres of unrest and no overall plan of campaign. Fatal mistakes were made: for example, at the beginning of the Mutiny, while the British at Delhi were still stunned with shock, the sepoys waited about for three weeks wondering what to do next.

(iv) Though individual British commanders made mistakes, the British had much better leadership than the Indians. The Governor-General, Lord Canning, was able to direct operations from Calcutta, while Havelock, Nicholson and Campbell distinguished themselves, though their forces were heavily outnumbered.

11.4 WHAT WERE THE RESULTS OF THE MUTINY?

(a) The British government was forced to admit that something must have gone sadly wrong with the way India had been ruled, to cause such a serious outbreak. In order to secure greater efficiency, Lord Derby's Conservative government (1858-9) introduced *the Government of India Act (1858)*. This abolished the East India Company which for years had been slack and easy-going, and transferred all its powers, properties and territories to the Crown. A Secretary of State and a Council of 15 members were created to look after the running of India and the Governor-General had his title changed to *Viceroy* (meaning 'in place of the king') to show that he represented the British monarch in India. The Indians were promised that there would be no further interference with their religions (a promise which was kept) and that they would have equality of opportunity with the British (which was not kept - see below (d)).

(b) **Lord Canning** (Governor-General 1856-8 and then Viceroy until 1862) followed a policy of moderation towards the Indians. He refused to carry out wholesale executions, to the annoyance of much of the British public, which nicknamed him 'Clemency Canning'. Though reforms were continued, the pace was much slower, and care was taken not to offend religious and local customs. The doctrine of lapse was abandoned and the British went to great pains not to offend native rulers and princes in other ways. This policy was successful and on the whole the Indian upper classes, realising that it was impossible to get the British out by force, remained loyal well into the twentieth century.

(c) The British abandoned their policy of expansion for the time being. In 1863 when civil war broke out in Afghanistan, they wisely refused to become involved, preferring to concentrate on improving the vast territories they already held.

(d) As a result of the atrocities committed by both sides during the Mutiny, there remained considerable ill-feeling between the British and the Indians, in spite of Canning's efforts. The British felt they could never trust the Indians again: they sent more troops to India, disarmed the civilian population, and increased the proportion of Europeans in the army; the artillery was kept wholly in British hands. Equality of opportunity was never a reality; for example, although entrance to the Indian Civil Service was thrown open to anyone who could pass an examination, this had to be taken in London, which involved the problem of a candidate losing caste if he crossed the sea. Consequently only one Indian took the examination before 1871; Indians were relegated to low-level positions. In fact a much deeper gulf than ever before had come between the British and Indians, and this gulf was never bridged.

QUESTIONS

1. The Indian Mutiny of 1857
Study the Sources **A** to **F** and then answer the questions which follow.

Source A: an article in *The Times*, 8 June 1857.

> *To bring high-caste Hindoos into contact with lard is, of course, a mistake*, but we doubt if it would in itself lead to disloyalty extending over several months. Those who know India well are not unprepared for the appearance of a restless, sullen, disorderly feeling on the part of the millions whom we rule, and especially of the troops . . . By education, by a glimpse of history and natural science, by the spectacle of railways and telegraphs, and by the great events which have lately passed in Europe, the Hindoo has been roused from his sluggishness. In the old times when the *sepoys* had no knowledge and no ambition, there was pretty nearly always something for them to do. An enemy was always on our frontier and there were tribes of robbers, murderers or fanatics to be put down. But now we have conquered all enemies within and without. There is no activity, no excitement beyond monotonous routine duties. We cannot help feeling that this dull and aimless existence is too much even for the apathy of the Hindoos.
>
> We can well imagine the effect on the quick, suspicious temper of a Hindoo of all that is passing in India. *Everything around him is in a state of change*. But the sepoy has time to brood over imaginary wrongs and to suspect that he is subjected to cunning temptations. It may be that this ill-feeling is the last stand made by the Hindoo mind against the growing influence of European culture. It is not impossible that at a time when widows are marrying and men of all castes are sitting together in a railway carriage, the last efforts of those utterly resistant to change should be made.

Source: *The Times*, 8 June 1857 (adapted extracts).

190

Source B: Map of India at the time of the Mutiny.

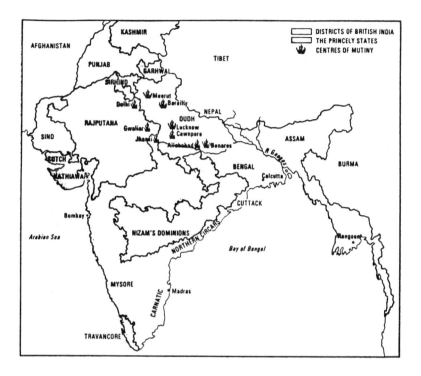

Source: T. F. Metcalfe, *The Mutiny and After*, in *Purnell's History of the English Speaking Peoples*, No. 94, BPC Publishing, 1971.

Source C: a soldier's account of the relief of Cawnpore.

When we reached the Bibigarh and saw the horror inside, none of us could speak. It looked as though cattle had been slaughtered in there. The walls were covered with bloody hand-prints and on the floor were pieces of human limbs, clothing, bibles, shoes, trinkets and lockets . . . Looking into a well I saw that the severed heads, limbs and mangled bodies had been thrown into it and it was full to within six feet of the top. I have faced death in every form, but I could not look down that well again.

Source: quoted in J. Harris, *The Indian Mutiny*, Hart-Davis MacGibbon, 1973 (adapted extracts).

Source D: letter from Lord Canning, Governor-General of India 1856–58, to Queen Victoria, written just before the end of the Mutiny.

One of the greatest difficulties which lie ahead will be the violent bitterness of a very large proportion of the English community against every native Indian of every class. There is a raging and indiscriminate vindictiveness, even amongst many who ought to set a better example, which it is impossible to contemplate without something like a feeling of shame for one's fellow-countrymen. Not one man in ten seems to think that the hanging and shooting of forty or fifty thousand mutineers can be anything else but right; nor does it occur to them that it is simply impossible for the Sovereign of England to hold and govern India without employing and trusting natives. There are some who entirely refuse to believe in the faithfulness or goodwill of any native towards any European.

Source: quoted in A. C. Benson and Viscount Esher, *The Letters of Queen Victoria*, John Murray, 1907 (adapted extracts).

Source E: The hanging of mutineers.

Source: India Office Library.

Source F: Contemporary drawing of mutineers about to be blasted from cannons.

Source: Mansell Collection.

(a) **(i)** Explain what the *Times* article (Source **A**) means when it says it was a mistake 'to bring high-caste Hindoos into contact with lard'.   **1, 2, 4(a)**

    (ii) What is meant in Source **A** by the phrase 'high-caste'?   **1, 2**

    (iii) What was a 'sepoy', mentioned in Source **A**?   **1**

(b) **(i)** Make a list of the reasons mentioned by the writer of Source **A** as possible causes of the Mutiny.   **4(a)**

    (ii) According to Source **A**, 'everything round him is in a state of change'. Give two examples of change mentioned elsewhere in Source **A** which might have upset the Hindus. Explain your answer.   **4(a)**

    (iii) From the evidence of Source **A**, what was the attitude of the British towards the Indians?   **4(a, b)**

(c) From the evidence of the Map (Source **B**)

    (i) How many main centres of Mutiny were there?

    (ii) How widespread was the Mutiny throughout India?   **4(a)**

(d) **(i)** How does Source **C** help to explain the first sentence of Source **D**?   **4(a, c)**

    (ii) From the evidence of Source **C**, what was Lord Canning's attitude towards the Indians at the end of the Mutiny?   **4(a, b)**

    (iii) Judging from Sources **A** and **C**, how typical was Canning among the British in his attitude towards the Indians?   **4(a, b, c)**

(e) (i) How do Sources **E** and **F** show that Canning's worries, mentioned in the first sentence of Source **D**, were well founded?
4(a, c)

(ii) According to Source **D**, 'it is simply impossible . . . to hold and govern India without employing and trusting natives'. How does Source **E** demonstrate the truth of this statement? 4(a, c)

2. British Rule in India

Study Sources **A** and **B** and then answer the questions which follow.

Source A: The state of Oudh.

The last major area to be brought under British control was the state of Oudh, annexed by Dalhousie the year before the Mutiny. Here, the Moghul emperor's chief minister had set himself up as an independent ruler on the collapse of the imperial authority. Oudh had been left isolated by the tide of British expansion. Indeed, its ruler was frequently squeezed to pay for British campaigns. As a reward, he had been given the title of 'king' in 1819. On occasion, over the years, the king was threatened with annexation and told to clean up his administration, but improvements were no more than superficial and temporary.

Source: M. Edwardes, *British India*, Sidgwick & Jackson, 1967.

Source B: an account of a journey through Oudh in 1849–50, by Sir William Sleeman, a British official in India.

The landholders keep the country in a perpetual state of disturbance and render life, property and industry everywhere insecure. Whenever they quarrel with each other or with the local authorities of the Government, from whatever cause, they take to indiscriminate plunder and murder over all lands not held by men of the same class; no road, town, village or hamlet is secure from their merciless attacks; robbery and murder become their diversion – their sport; and they think no more of taking the lives of men, women and children who never offended them than those of deer or wild hog. They not only rob and murder, but seize, imprison and torture all whom they suppose to have money till they ransom themselves with all they have or can beg or borrow.

Source: quoted in M. Edwardes, *British India*, Sidgwick & Jackson, 1967.

(a) From the evidence of Source **A**

(i) When was Oudh annexed by the British?
(ii) Who was the ruler of Oudh?
(iii) How had the British rewarded the ruler?
(iv) Why had the British given him this reward?
(v) Why do you think Oudh 'had been left isolated by the tide of British expansion'? 4(a)

(b) **(i)** In what ways does Source **B** support the claim in Source **A** (last sentence) that 'improvements were no more than superficial and temporary'? **4(a, c)**

(ii) What were the motives for the landholders' behaviour described in Source **B**? **4(a)**

(iii) Using the evidence of the Sources and your own knowledge, explain why you think the British government annexed Oudh. **1, 2, 4(a, c)**

(iv) What do you think are the advantages and disadvantages of Source **B** for the historian? **4(a, b)**

(c) **(i)** Lord Dalhousie, who annexed Oudh, introduced a new policy called 'the doctrine of lapse'. Explain what this policy was and how Dalhousie applied it. **1, 2**

(ii) Dalhousie also introduced important changes in communications, administration and education. Describe briefly one example of each. **1, 2**

(d) **(i)** An earlier Governor-General, Lord William Bentinck (1828–35) was responsible for stamping out the ancient Hindu customs of suttee and thuggee. Write a paragraph about each, describing the custom and explaining why the British wanted it stamping out. **1, 2**

(ii) One of Bentinck's mottos was: 'British greatness is founded on Indian happiness'. To what extent did the British look after the happiness of the Indians during the period 1828 to 1857? **1, 2**

3. (a) Explain how each of the following helped to cause the Indian Mutiny of 1857:

(i) Dalhousie's 'doctrine of lapse';
(ii) economic problems;
(iii) religious problems.

(b) Describe any other problems or events which might have helped to cause the Mutiny.

(c) What were the main results of the Mutiny? **1, 2**

4. Explain the feelings and reactions of each of the following:

(a) an Indian prince talking to his advisers about Dalhousie's 'doctrine of lapse' and the annexation of Oudh (1856);

(b) a Hindu sepoy in the Bengal army who hears the rumour that the new cartridges are to be greased with a mixture of cow and pig fat;

(c) a British soldier who has taken part in the relief of Cawnpore (July 1857). **1, 2, 3**

CHAPTER 12

SOCIAL REFORM:

FACTORIES, MINES,

EDUCATION

SUMMARY OF EVENTS

For the great mass of the people in early nineteenth-century Britain, the quality of life, the conditions in which they lived and worked and spent what little leisure time they had, left a lot to be desired. There has been some disagreement among historians about how unacceptable living and working conditions were. Arnold Toynbee and J. L. and Barbara Hammond writing before 1920, gave the left-wing view – that as a result of the industrial revolution, workers were shamefully exploited and lived in squalid slums. Sir John Clapham thought that this was a gross exaggeration and produced statistics which, he claimed, proved that the living standards of the poor were actually improving. Recently it has been shown that life for the workers *before* the industrial revolution was not the bed of roses which some writers had seemed to suggest: long working hours, slum conditions and families living on the verge of starvation were just as common in rural Britain as they were in the new industrial towns. More recently still the work of E. P. Thompson (*The Making of the English Working Classes*) has questioned Clapham's findings. In spite of the disagreements, it is probably fair to claim that in a majority of factories and mines, cripplingly long hours were worked by men, women and children, many of whom lived in disease-ridden slums and cellars. Education for the working classes was almost non-existent, apart from that provided by voluntary groups and societies.

In an age of *laissez-faire*, the instinct of governments was to ignore these problems; the development of the industrial society which had produced the situation had occurred without any interference from the state, and it was assumed that individuals would find their own solutions, also without interference from the state. *Self-help* was a virtue much prized by the Victorians.

It was only very gradually that governments began to pay attention to the mass of evidence being placed before them about the unacceptable conditions. After considerable debate some sections of the ruling class accepted that only through state intervention could the worst excesses be removed. However, even after the principle was accepted, there was determined opposition from industrialists and others who resented state interference, and effective reform was therefore slow to come.

FACTORY AND MINE REFORM

12.1 WHY WAS FACTORY AND MINE REFORM NECESSARY?

(a) The factory system particularly mills and workshops driven by steam, was still comparatively new, and there were no restrictions or controls of any kind. Fierce competition led employers to pay as little as possible for as much work as possible. With nobody to protect the interests of the workers, it was inevitable that exploitation and abuse of all kinds would creep in.

(b) Many factories were dangerous and unhealthy. Machinery was not properly fenced off and textile mill-owners often used small children to clean spinning machines and looms, while they were in motion. An adult spinner might use two or three small children working as 'piecers'; their job was to crawl under machinery no more than a foot above the floor to tie broken ends. Serious accidents were common; *the 1840 Royal Commission Report* mentioned a case at Stockport where a girl had been caught by her clothing and carried round an upright shaft; 'her thighs were broken, her ankle dislocated, and she will be a cripple for life'. The report went on to say that in the Stockport area 'fatal accidents generally happen from want of boxing-off; there has been a considerable number of accidents and loss of life within the last three months'. The long-term effect of bending and standing for long periods was that children developed weak, curved legs and arched backs. Sometimes there were respiratory diseases caused by working for so long in the hot and humid atmosphere of a textile mill, where the air was contaminated by clouds of microscopic cotton dust.

There was danger in other industries too: the Staffordshire potteries were notoriously bad for health; though some employers, like the Wedgwoods, were enlightened and caring, one Stoke-on-Trent doctor wrote: 'the potters as a class are as a rule stunted in growth and frequently deformed in the chest; they become prematurely old and are certainly short lived'. Workers in match factories often developed a disease known as 'phossy-jaw' which caused the teeth to fall out and the jaw bone to rot away.

(c) Mines had special problems. There were frequent gas explosions since the Davy safety lamp was not compulsory. Small children, both boys and girls, sometimes as young as four years old, were employed underground hauling trucks full of coal along passages which were too low for adults, or opening and closing ventilation doors, or filling coal trucks. *The Royal Commission Report which came out in 1842* revealed some appalling details: a 12-year-old girl had to carry a hundredweight of coal on her back, stooping and creeping through water in a low tunnel; children had

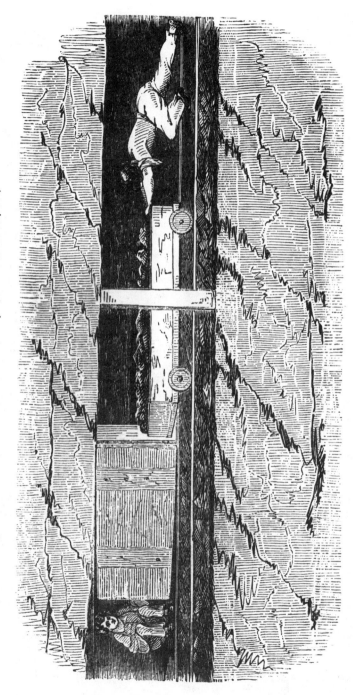

illus 12.1   Children working down a mine (sketch from the 1842 Royal Commission Report)

to climb dangerous ladders up the pit shaft with huge baskets of coal strapped to their backs. The report also expressed outrage that naked and semi-naked men, women, girls and boys all worked together, which had a demoralising effect on the women and girls.

(d) *Both adults and children had to work excessively long hours* in textile factories. A parliamentary committee of enquiry in 1832 produced evidence to show that thousands of small children, particularly girls, were working from six in the morning until half-past eight in the evening, with only half an hour allowed for eating. Towards the end of the shift they began to drop off to sleep and, depending on the foreman, had to be shaken or beaten with a strap to keep them alert. It was just as bad in other industries: Charles Shaw, a Tunstall potter who started work as a mould-runner at the age of six, recalled that 'my wage was a shilling a week. For this I had to work from between five and six o'clock in the morning and work on till six, seven or eight o'clock at night'. His job was to light the fire in the stove-room and spend the rest of the day rushing backwards and forwards bringing the raw clay to the potter and then running to take the plaster moulds (each bearing a soft plate) into the hot stove-room where the plates were hardened off.

(e) *Pressure grew steadily for some government action.* The main leader in the early days was a Leeds Tory, *Richard Oastler*, who, after the failure of his career as a merchant, became estate manager at Fixby Hall, near Huddersfield. He was shocked by the appalling conditions he saw in the Bradford woollen mills. A deeply religious man (he was an Evangelical Anglican), he was stirred to write a letter to the Leeds *Mercury* (1830) in which he claimed that child workers were being treated worse than slaves: 'Thousands of our fellow creatures, both male and female, the miserable inhabitants of a Yorkshire town, are this very moment existing in a state of slavery, more horrid than are the victims of that hellish system "colonial slavery"'. Soon famous throughout the North, Oastler found himself the leader of a huge movement, publishing pamphlets, and organising public meetings and demonstrations demanding factory reform. Typical of the campaign were the mass marches which converged on York on Easter Monday 1832; the result was a petition containing over 130 000 signatures which was handed to parliament.

Inside parliament the movement found an effective voice in another Tory Evangelical, *Michael Sadler*, who demanded a maximum working day of 10 hours for children. He was supported by other Tories and by humanitarians, who between them made up a formidable alliance. Their case was simple; as Derek Fraser puts it: 'it was a moral or religious crusade against an intolerable evil ... it simply could not be right for these things to persist'. However, there was bitter opposition to *the Ten Hour Movement*, from most factory and mine owners.

12.2 WHAT ARGUMENTS WERE USED BY THE OPPONENTS OF REFORM?

(a) Benthamite Radicals (see Section 2.1(c)), many of whom were factory owners, believed that any state intervention was bad because it tampered with the natural working of the economic system. *Laissez-faire* was all important. (There were exceptions, notably John Hobhouse who was a Radical supporter of factory reform.)

(b) A shorter working day for children would mean restricting adult working hours, therefore causing a reduction in output. This in turn would mean lower profits and lower wages. One economist, Nassau Senior, Professor of Political Economy at Oxford, argued that the entire profit of industry was made in the last hour's work each day; therefore to reduce the working day even by one hour, would destroy profits. This theory had already been shown to be nonsense by Robert Owen, a progressive manufacturer who had reduced working hours in his textile mills at New Lanark, and had continued to make a comfortable profit; but many still clung to the argument.

(c) Better working conditions would push production costs up, making British goods expensive on foreign markets. British exports would decline, causing unemployment. Apparently the British working classes had only a miserable choice available to them – to endure exhausting working hours and appalling conditions or to suffer total poverty in unemployment.

(d) Some argued that children working long hours in industry was acceptable because it had gone on for centuries in agriculture without any protest. It was even suggested that child labour was to be encouraged since it gave them something to do and kept them out of mischief; too much leisure for the poor could be dangerous.

12.3 WHAT IMPROVEMENTS WERE MADE AND WHY DID IT TAKE SO LONG FOR THE ACTS TO BECOME EFFECTIVE?

Before 1833 there were no fewer than six attempts by act of parliament to improve conditions in textile mills, but every single one was a failure; the most important were:

(a) The Health and Morals of Apprentices Act (1802) was the work of the elder Sir Robert Peel. It was designed to help young apprentices working in textile mills:

(i) Apprentices were not to work more than 12 hours a day and must not work after 9 p.m.

(ii) They should be given two suits of clothes a year and sleep no more than two to a bed, with separate sleeping quarters for boys and girls (this was to regulate those manufacturers who used workhouse children and had them sleeping at the mill).

The weakness of this act was that no inspectors were appointed to make sure that it was enforced; instead it was left to local magistrates who might be relatives or friends of the mill-owner. Even Peel himself acknowledged that it was hardly ever enforced.

(b) The Factory Act of 1819 was again the work of the elder Peel, who was influenced by discussions with Robert Owen (see Section 19.2). His cotton mills at New Lanark with their model villages and model schools for workers, had shown that reasonable profits could go hand in hand with humane living and working conditions. Peel's bill began its passage through parliament in 1815, but by this time the opponents of reform were well organised so that the Lords delayed it and watered it down. The final terms *applied only to cotton mills*:

(i) No children under the age of nine could be employed (Peel and Owen had wanted it to be under ten).

(ii) Young people aged nine to 16 must not work more than 12 hours a day (the original bill passed by the Commons said 11 hours); the work to be done between 5 a.m. and 9 p.m. with one and a half hours off for meals.

Again *the weaknesses of the act* were the same: no inspectors were appointed, and magistrates were expected to enforce the terms. Peel apparently hoped that the offer of rewards would encourage informers, but very few workers dared risk the wrath of the mill-owner by reporting him to a magistrate. On the whole the act was ignored, and in any case it did not apply to children in other industries. On the other hand, *it was an important step* because it established the principle that parliament could interfere with parents' decisions about their children: no parent could now choose to send an eight-year-old to work in a cotton factory (at least in theory).

(c) The Factory Act of 1831 was a good example of the alliance between different political groups. It was introduced by Sir John Hobhouse, a Radical, and was carried with Tory support. It extended the 12-hour limit to include 17- and 18-year-olds, but was as disappointing as previous acts because there were still no inspectors; in addition there was the problem of deciding a child's age since there was, as yet, no official registration of births.

(d) The Factory Act of 1833 was the first really effective piece of factory legislation. It was introduced by the Whig Chancellor of the Exchequer, Lord Althorp, though in fact all the credit was due to the Tory Evangelical Lord Ashley (later 7th Earl of Shaftesbury). The background was quite complicated:

Oastler and the Ten Hour Movement, bitterly disappointed by Hobhouse's Act, redoubled their efforts to achieve a statutory ten hour day, with Sadler leading the campaign in the Commons. However, in the 1832 general election (the first after the Reform Act) Sadler was defeated at Leeds and never managed to get back into parliament again. This seemed a fatal blow, but the leadership of the movement was taken over by Ashley, who turned out to be just as impressive and as dedicated as Sadler. Ashley introduced Sadler's bill proposing to limit the working day of all textile operatives aged nine to 18 to ten hours. The hope was that by restricting young people's hours in this way, the factories would have to close after ten hours, giving adult workers too the benefit of a ten-hour day. The Whig government, under pressure from the mill-owning lobby, delayed the bill until a Royal Commission had investigated the situation. Dominated by the Benthamite Edwin Chadwick, the commission was efficient, detached and unemotional. It recommended (June 1833) that although ten hours was too long for young children, by the age of 14 they were almost adults and were strong enough to work a longer day; vitally important was its suggestion that paid inspectors should be appointed to supervise the new regulations.

Impressed by Chadwick's report, the Commons immediately defeated Ashley's Ten Hour Bill (July 1833). Althorp introduced a Whig bill based on Chadwick's recommendations, which quickly became law (August 1833). In some ways the new Act fell short of what Ashley wanted, while in other ways it went far beyond what he and Sadler had in mind; it applied to all textile mills except silk and lace:

(i) No child under nine could be employed.
(ii) Children from nine to 13 were limited to an eight hour day, and were to receive at least two hours of education a day.
(iii) Young people from 14 to 18 were limited to a 12 hour day, to be worked between 5.30 a.m. and 8.30 p.m.
(iv) Four inspectors were appointed at an annual salary of £1000 each, to supervise the working of the Act; they had the power to enter any mill.

This was obviously a great advance on previous legislation, applying as it did to woollen and worsted as well as to cotton mills and at long last introducing an inspectorate; but *it was still a disappointment for the Ten Hours men*:

(i) Most mill-owners responded by using a relay system of child labour, so that factories could be kept open for the whole time between 5.30 a.m. and 8.30 p.m. and adults still had to work in excess of 12 hours.
(ii) There still remained the problem of establishing a child's age; many parents needed the extra wages and often claimed that their 10, 11 and 12-year-old children were really 13-year-olds. However, this dif-

ficulty was soon overcome by the compulsory registration of births, marriages and deaths, introduced in 1836.

(iii) The education clauses turned out to be ineffective: no money was provided for building schools, and only the most progressive factory owners complied.

(iv) Four inspectors were not enough to cover the whole country adequately. After one had died of overwork in 1836, assistants were appointed. Their reports showed that although many manufacturers complied with the regulations, it was still easy for the unscrupulous ones to evade them.

Ashley had no intention of giving up. In 1840 he persuaded parliament to appoint a committee with himself as chairman to investigate the working of Althorp's act. Its report (which included the details about Stockport mills mentioned in Section 12.1(b)) showed that factory work was still horrifyingly dangerous, and this led to:

(e) The Factory Act of 1844. In 1841 the Whig government was replaced by the Conservatives under Peel who was not in favour of a 10 hour day; 12 hours was as far as he would go. Even so, *the act was a great advance*:

(i) Children could start work at the age of eight (instead of nine) which seemed to be a backward step, but . . .

(ii) Children aged eight to 13 could only work a six and a half hour day.

(iii) Women over the age of 13 were limited to a 12-hour day.

(iv) Dangerous machinery had to be fenced and meals were to be eaten in a separate place.

(f) The Mines Act of 1842. Meanwhile Ashley had been active in other areas; he was equally concerned about conditions in mines, and he pestered parliament so much that a Royal Commission on the Employment of Women and Children in Mines was appointed. Its report (published in 1842) contained sketches showing some of the dangerous and unpleasant jobs which young children had to do. Until now mining conditions had received much less publicity than those in factories, and the public was deeply shocked by what the report revealed. Ashley's Mines Bill passed the Commons comfortably but ran into trouble in the Lords, which contained many aristocratic mine-owners. Led by Lord Londonderry, they were determined to weaken it as much as possible. *In its final form the Act*:

(i) Forbade the employment of women and girls in the mines, and of boys under the age of ten. (Ashley's original bill said no boys under 13 to be employed.)

(ii) One inspector was appointed to enforce the provisions, but this was obviously inadequate.

(g) Fielden's Factory Act (1847) (The Ten Hours Act). The Ten Hour Movement lost its leader in parliament when Ashley resigned (1846) over Peel's decision to abolish the Corn Laws (see Section 7.5). His place was taken by *John Fielden*, the Radical MP for Oldham and a progressive owner of cotton mills in Todmorden. He introduced a bill to limit the working day of all women and of young people up to the age of 18 to ten hours. At the same time Oastler made sure that there were massive supporting demonstrations and marches through the North of England, and to the intense jubilation of the movement, the bill passed without amendment, only three years after the Commons had decisively rejected similar proposals.

Reasons for the change in attitude were:

(i) Peel, who had insisted on a 12-hour day, had now fallen from power and the Conservative party was split. Many Tories who sympathised with Ashley and Fielden but had been unwilling to go against Peel's orders in 1844, were now free to vote for the Ten Hours Bill.

(ii) Some Tory landowners, infuriated by the repeal of the Corn Laws, may have voted for the bill as a way of revenging themselves on the manufacturers, who had supported the Corn Law repeal.

(iii) In 1847 there was a trade depression during which demand for British textiles was reduced. For this reason most factories were only working a ten-hour day, which seemed to upset the mill-owners' argument that they would be forced out of business if a ten-hour day was brought in.

The triumph was shortlived: as trade revived, manufacturers began to use the relay system, keeping their mills working from 5.30 a.m. until 8.30 p.m., so that adult males were still required to work over 12 hours. Ashley, back in parliament, kept up the agitation for a limit on factory opening hours, and eventually he agreed to a compromise with the mill-owning interests. This became law as –

(h) The Factory Act of 1850:

(i) Factories should only be open for 12 hours, of which an hour and a half must be for meals.

(ii) The working day for women and young people was to be ten and a half hours.

(iii) On Saturdays the factories must close at 2 p.m. and women and young people must only work seven and a half hours.

Although some of Ashley's supporters were annoyed with him for agreeing to the extra half-hour, the Act was nevertheless a great achievement. As well as a ten and a half hour day and the half-day off for women and children, it meant that in most cases the men's working day was also limited, even though this was not specifically mentioned in the Act. The shorter working day did not cause a fall in production as many manufacturers had feared. Gradually the health and efficiency of the textile workers improved and serious accidents were almost eliminated.

As yet these laws only applied to textile mills; it now remained to extend government control and regulation to those trades and industries where workers were still unprotected. Ashley (who became Earl of Shaftesbury in 1851) could not rest until all workers had been brought under some sort of protection. There were other reformers of course – he was not personally responsible for all the subsequent improvements; but it was usually Shaftesbury who stole the limelight. As late as 1884, at the age of 83, he was still making speeches in the Lords and giving evidence to Royal Commissions (he died in October 1885).

(i) **Mining Legislation**. The 1842 Mines Act had said nothing about safety in mines and there continued to be regular explosions and disasters. *The Coal Mines Inspection Act (1850)* provided more inspectors to enforce the earlier act and to produce detailed reports on conditions and safety standards. However, it was a slow and difficult job to get even these modest advances, since the coalowners in the Lords bitterly opposed all attempted legislation; Lord Londonderry thought that the 1850 Act was 'infernal'. *The Mines Regulation and Inspection Act (1860)* increased the number of inspectors and said that no boys under 12 must work underground. In 1862 it was laid down that every mine must have at least two shafts to improve the chances of escape if there was an explosion. By this time the *Royal School of Mines* (opened in 1851) was doing invaluable work training inspectors and developing new and safer techniques. *The 1872 Coal Mines Regulation Act* insisted on the introduction of some of these safer methods: fan ventilators, stronger timbering, wire ropes, improved winding machinery and better safety lamps. Finally *the 1887 Mines Act* introduced stringent regulations about blasting precautions and the provision of first-aid and ambulance facilities.

(j) **Factory and workshop legislation.** In 1862 Shaftesbury secured the appointment of the Children's Employment Commission to investigate conditions in the other industries. As a result of the Commission's Reports, *two vitally important Acts were passed in 1867* by the Conservatives: one extended the textile mill regulations to all other workshops employing more than 50 people (such as iron and steel works, potteries, glass and paper mills and printing works); the other extended the regulations to workshops and ordinary houses where fewer than 50 people were employed. This was a tremendous victory for Shaftesbury; but he had not quite finished yet – in 1871 he made a moving speech in the Lords about conditions in brickfields. 'I saw little children, three-parts naked, tottering under the weight of wet clay, some of it on their hands and some on their shoulders, and little girls with large masses of wet, cold and dripping clay pressed on their abdomens. They had to endure the heat of the kiln, and to enter places where the heat was so intense that I was not myself able to remain more than two or three minutes.' As a result brickfields were brought under the Factory Act regulations.

Disraeli's Conservative government (1874-80) introduced further improvements:

(i) *The Factory Act of 1874* actually reduced the working day to ten hours (instead of ten and a half) which Shaftesbury had hoped for all along; no child could be employed until he was ten (instead of eight); no young person could work full-time until he or she was 14 (instead of 13).

(ii) *The Factory and Workshops Act of 1878* put right a weakness of the 1867 legislation, which had placed responsibility for inspecting workshops employing under 50 people on to the shoulders of local authorities, many of which had failed to make regular inspections. The new Act brought these premises under government inspection. This was an important advance, although there were still problems in making sure that the regulations were kept in private houses.

The Factory of Act 1891, another Conservative measure, raised the minimum age at which children could be employed in factories to 11 (see Section 16.5(b)).

PUBLIC HEALTH

12.4 WHAT WERE THE MAIN PROBLEMS OF PUBLIC HEALTH IN INDUSTRIAL TOWNS?

(a) The basic problem was the rapid increase in the population of Britain, which almost doubled (to over 27 million) between 1801 and 1851. Much of the increase was concentrated in industrial towns and cities which had grown too quickly for the influx of people to be housed satisfactorily. Between 1801 and 1861 the population of Glasgow increased from 77 000 to 420 000, Liverpool from 82 000 to 444 000 and Manchester (with Salford) from 89 000 to 441 000. Even more spectacular was the case of Bradford whose population increased eightfold during the same period. In the late 1840s the cities of northern England absorbed thousands of starving Irish fleeing from the potato famine. At first empty cellars and attics were pressed into use; later cheap accommodation was built so that workers could live near the factories. Since there were few building regulations, this tended to consist of rows of cramped back-to-back houses (in northern England) or huge tenement blocks (in Scotland). Everywhere there was the problem of overcrowding – in 1847 a typical street (Church Lane) in the East End of London had 1095 people living in only 27 houses; this is an average of 40 people to a house, and probably eight to a room.

(b) There was a lack of proper amenities – street cleansing, pure water supply, drainage and sewerage disposal.

(i) In working class houses there was no such refinement as the water closet type of lavatory; usually there was an outside privy which might have to serve as many as 20 houses; these privies were not connected to sewers, but drained into cesspits which were emptied by hand. A doctor who visited a particularly bad part of Liverpool reported: 'I found the whole court inundated with fluid filth which had oozed through the walls from two adjoining ash-pits or cesspools and which had no means of escape in consequence of the court being below the level of the street, and having no drain . . . the court had remained for two or three years in the state in which I saw it'. A Manchester doctor wrote about 'streets full of pits, brimful of stagnant water, the receptacle of dead cats and dogs'. In Nottingham 'the courts have no back yards, and the privies are common to the whole court; they present scenes of surpassing filth . . . the refuse is allowed to accumulate until, by its mass and its advanced putrefaction, it shall have acquired value as manure'.

(ii) Drinking water was usually supplied by private companies, but only the wealthiest people had water piped to their houses; the rest had to use stand-pipes, taps or pumps outside in the street, which would probably only be turned on for part of the day. Many towns had to use river water which was always polluted. London's water supply came mostly from the Thames into which no fewer than 237 sewers were emptied. In 1841 a Leeds newspaper described the River Aire (which supplied much of the city's drinking water) as being 'charged with the contents of about 200 water closets and similar places, a great number of common drains, the draining from dunghills, the Infirmary (dead leeches, poultices for patients), slaughter houses, pig manure, old urine wash and all sorts of decomposed animal and vegetable substances'.

(iii) There were unsatisfactory arrangements for funerals and burials which added to the general health hazards. Corpses were often kept in the house for a week or more (to give the family time to raise cash for the funeral expenses) even when death was due to an infectious disease such as cholera or typhoid. Cemeteries and churchyards were grossly overfilled; according to Edwin Chadwick's report on burial (1834), in London, 'on spaces of ground which do not exceed 203 acres, closely surrounded by the abodes of the living, layer upon layer, each consisting of a population equivalent to a large army of 20 000 adults and nearly 30 000 youths and children is every year imperfectly interred'. Some graveyards contaminated the district's water supply.

(c) The death-rate from infectious diseases was high: the appalling fact was that in 1840, one child in three died before reaching the age of five. Cholera was perhaps the most terrible of all these diseases. It first appeared in Britain at Sunderland in 1832 and rapidly reached epidemic proportions, killing 21 000 people in England and Wales, 9000 in Scotland and 20 000 in Ireland. An even worse epidemic followed in 1848-9 which at its height was killing 2000 people a week in London alone; altogether 90 000 died in that outbreak and there were further epidemics in 1854 and 1867. It was not known at the time that the cholera bacillus is carried in water that may otherwise be pure, which is why it affected the rich with their piped water supplies as well as the poor. The stages of the disease were horrifying; beginning with vomiting, the skin then turned blue, purple and finally brown or black; eventually the patient was afflicted with severe breathlessness, followed by rigid spasms of the legs and thighs, and almost invariably by death. Much more common and everyday were diseases such as typhus (usually referred to simply as 'the fever'), typhoid and tuberculosis (consumption), scarlet fever, diphtheria, measles and even ordinary diarrhoea, all of which were caused by contaminated water and lack of proper sewage disposal. Though they were all killers, the most lethal was tuberculosis which caused between a quarter and one-third of all deaths during the first half of the century. The national death rate increased as the industrial towns mushroomed; before 1831 the figure was in the region of 19 per thousand, but during the 1830s it rose steadily to 22.4 (in 1838) and reached a peak of 25.1 in 1849. However, this was the average figure; in crowded urban areas the death rate was usually around 30 per thousand, and in Glasgow during the 1832 cholera epidemic it hit 49 per thousand.

(d) There was no organisation or body either locally or nationally with the expertise or the funds necessary to tackle such enormous problems, except of course the government.

All these problems were highlighted by Edwin Chadwick's *Report on the Sanitary Condition of the Labouring Population of Great Britain (July 1842)*. A fanatical Benthamite always striving for greater efficiency, Chadwick had already had a hand in the 1834 Poor Law Commission Report (see Section 5.2(d)(ii)). After the Poor Law Amendment Act of the same year Chadwick was the Secretary to the Poor Law Commissioners, and he became interested in the causes of disease in the hope of reducing the expense of supporting the sick. What his report did was to hammer home the point that filthy conditions were the main causes of disease. He produced some startling statistics of life expectancy which shocked the public: whereas a lawyer in a rural county such as Rutland could hope to live (on average) to be 52, a labourer in a Manchester slum would be lucky to survive until 17, while in Liverpool his average life expectancy would be only 15.

12.5 WHAT ADVANCES WERE MADE IN PUBLIC HEALTH DURING THE NINETEENTH CENTURY?

In his Report Chadwick suggested a number of measures which would improve public health. These included providing all houses with piped water, which could be used for flushing sewage away from the houses into main sewers; instead of being large square tunnels built of porous brick, sewers ought to be smaller, tube-shaped and made of non-porous (glazed) pottery. The new system should be organised and controlled centrally, like the New Poor Law. But improvements were very slow to come, mainly because of the enormous expense involved. How did one set about, for example, supplying cities the size of Glasgow and Manchester with a system of pure, piped water? When progress did take place it was due partly to government action, but more to advances in medicine and to great engineering projects.

(a) **Government action.** Before 1848, any action to improve sanitary conditions was taken on a local basis without any central direction. Liverpool had its own Sanitary Act (1846) which made the town council responsible for drainage, sewerage, cleansing and paving, and was the first city to have a permanent Medical Officer of Health. But the nature and efficiency of these local *Improvement Committees* as they were called, varied widely. Chadwick's Report had made it obvious that legislation was needed to cover the country as a whole, and after tremendous pressure and agitation Russell's government introduced:

(i) *The Public Health Act of 1848.* This gave local authorities the power to appoint Boards of Health whose work was to be supervised by the General Board of Health, headed by Chadwick himself and including Lord Shaftesbury. Unfortunately *the Act had a fatal weakness*: there was no compulsion on local authorities to set up Boards; by 1854 only 182 Boards had been appointed in England and Wales, covering only two million people out of a population of 18 million. Most of those set up were ineffective; only 13 of them had started large-scale water and sewage works. Meanwhile the government continued to pass local acts; for example:

(ii) In 1858 three million pounds was provided to prevent sewage being pumped into the Thames above London. Even this did not prevent 10 000 Londoners from dying in the 1866 cholera epidemic, and the national death-rate was still running at over 23 per thousand.

(iii) *The Sanitation Act of 1866* recognised that the 1848 Act had been a failure, and it therefore compelled local authorities to improve local conditions and remove nuisances. According to *The Times* this 1866 Act 'introduces a new sanitary era'.

(iv) *The Public Health Act of 1872* (introduced by Gladstone's Liberal government) clarified the position by dividing England and Wales into districts under specific health authorities, each of which was to have its own permanent Medical Officer and staff. Unfortunately this Act was another failure because it was not clear what the duties of the health boards were, and most of them were reluctant to spend the cash necessary for radical health reform.

(v) *The Public Health Act of 1875.* It was left to Disraeli and the Conservatives to rationalise and consolidate the complicated patchwork of health legislation. The Act was the work of Disraeli's Home

Secretary, *R. A. Cross*, and has been rated by some historians as one of the greatest pieces of legislation in the nineteenth century. It laid down in clear detail what the *compulsory duties* of local authorities were: they had to ensure that there was adequate sewage, drainage and water supply; nuisances were to be removed, offensive trades regulated and contaminated food to be sought out, confiscated and destroyed. Cases of infectious disease were to be notified to the Medical Officer, who had to take appropriate action. Other regulations dealt with markets, street lighting and burials.

(vi) *The Artisans' Dwellings Act (1875)*, also the work of Cross, attempted to deal with the problem of slum housing. Local authorities were given the power, if they wished, to buy up and demolish insanitary property and to replace it with modern, healthy accommodation. It was the violent opposition from many of his own party, who thought the bill a blatant invasion of landlords' rights, that caused Cross to abandon the idea of making slum clearance compulsory. This seriously weakened the Act, but at least a start had been made, and Birmingham under its Mayor, *Joseph Chamberlain*, was one of the first cities to initiate a massive slum clearance programme (see also Section 14.2(a)).

(vii) *The Housing of the Working Classes Acts (1890 and 1900)* were two more Conservative measures which remedied the deficiencies of the 1875 Act. Now local authorities were compelled to demolish unhealthy housing and to provide other accommodation for those made homeless. Owners of slum property could be compelled to sell it to the council for demolition. What was needed next was legislation to carry slum clearance a step further by regulating the planning of towns. Unfortunately a great opportunity to encourage careful and systematic planning of new building schemes and new towns was lost in:

(viii) *The Housing and Town Planning Act (1909)*. This allowed local authorities to introduce town planning schemes in order to avoid piecemeal building, if they wished. But there was no compulsion and the Act was so complicated that only one major scheme was started in the whole country before 1914.

(b) **Medical improvements.** Already in the late 1790s Edward Jenner had introduced his vaccination technique which controlled smallpox, though the disease was still dangerous; about the same time Humphry Davy (who was later to invent the miners' safety lamp) had used nitrous oxide (laughing gas) as a partial anaesthetic for use during operations. But it was another half a century before any further advances were made:

(i) The introduction of chloroform (late 1840s) as a general anaesthetic gave surgeons more time to perform operations, though there was still the problem of how to avoid infection in the wound.

(ii) A major breakthrough came in the early 1860s when Louis Pasteur, a French chemist, discovered the germ theory of disease, that decay and putrefaction as well as infectious diseases are caused by micro-organisms or bacteria, not just by filth and bad smells, as Chadwick thought. A Glasgow surgeon, Joseph Lister, building on Pasteur's work, developed an antiseptic technique using carbolic acid; this reduced infection after operations and helped to bring down the death rate.

(iii) Standards of nursing improved steadily thanks to the work of Elizabeth Fry who founded the Institute of Nursing Sisters, and of Florence Nightingale who developed the Nightingale School of Nursing in St Thomas's Hospital, London.

(iv) There were improvements in the education of doctors and in 1858 the Medical Act set up the General Council for Medical Education and Registration whose function was to supervise standards of efficiency among doctors.

(c) **Engineering achievements.** This might seem an odd heading to include in a chapter on public health, but in fact the provision of large-scale water, sewage and drainage schemes required some remarkable feats of civil engineering. One of the first cities to attempt such a scheme was Manchester, which in 1847 began work on its huge Longdendale waterworks which was to cost in the region of three-quarters of a million pounds. When it was completed ten years later, it could supply the city with 30 million gallons a day, whereas the previous private companies had managed no more than two million gallons. As soon as a continuous supply of water was available, work could go ahead on laying sewers. Liverpool soon followed with a massive water scheme supplied from reservoirs at Rivington Pike, which by 1857 could hold 3000 million gallons; by 1875 most of the city's housing had water closets connected to sewers. London's system of waterised sewers was completed by 1866. Most cities and towns of any size had followed suit by 1900.

In spite of the beginnings of improvement, the death rate was still hovering around 24 per thousand in 1870. Slowly but steadily over the next 30 years Britain became a healthier place to live in; the 1901 census showed that overcrowding was beginning to thin out and the death rate had dropped to just below 18 per thousand. Even so, every now and again some sort of epidemic occurred which upset the growing late-Victorian complacency - a typhoid epidemic in Blackburn in 1881, cholera in London in 1893, and in 1902, smallpox in several ports. The investigations of Charles Booth (1889-1903 in London) and Seebohm Rowntree (1901 in York) showed that there was still some way to go to the achievement of the final victory over filth and infectious diseases.

EDUCATION

12.6 WHAT KINDS OF SCHOOL WERE IN EXISTENCE BETWEEN 1815 AND 1870 AND WHY WAS THERE NO STATE SYSTEM OF ELEMENTARY EDUCATION?

(a) Before 1833 there was no government support for education, which was organised entirely by private individuals or by religious groups and sometimes by companies of the City of London. Consequently there was a hotch-potch of different sorts of school:

(i) *Public schools.* There were eight major ones (Eton, Harrow, Westminster, Rugby, St Paul's, Shrewsbury, Winchester and Merchant Taylors') and lots of minor ones. Although called 'public' schools, they were in fact only open to those members of the public who could afford the fees - wealthy aristocrats, landowners and industrialists. The education they provided was based on the classics (Latin and Greek), and in the early part of the century did not even include mathematics. It was only very gradually that the public school curriculum was modernised, thanks to the work of progressive teachers such as Thomas Arnold (Headmaster of Rugby from 1828-42) who insisted on mathematics and French being taught regularly.

(ii) *Grammar schools.* Many of these were ancient foundations going back to the sixteenth century. Unlike public schools, they did not take boarders, but the subjects taught were similar - heavily weighted towards Latin and Greek. Fees were charged, though most grammar schools provided some free places for poor children.

(iii) *Private schools.* Also fee-paying, these were newer schools started by people who were impatient with the old-fashioned curriculum of public and grammar schools. One of the earliest was the Liverpool Royal Institution School (1819) which taught mathematics, modern languages and science.

All these were completely outside the reach of the great mass of the population, who were lucky to receive a few years of elementary education - basic reading, writing and arithmetic - in what were known as *Voluntary Schools.* These included Sunday Schools (Robert Raikes had founded the Sunday School Union in 1780), dame schools run by elderly ladies and often no more than child-minding establishments, and charity schools like those set up by the Society for Promoting Christian Knowledge. After the 1833 Factory Act, a number of factory schools were set up and during the 1840s large numbers of Ragged Schools were started in very deprived areas, with Ashley as president of the Ragged Schools Union. The most widespread and best organised of the Voluntary Schools were those run by the Church of England and the Nonconformist Churches:

(i) The Church of England (Anglicans) organised their schools through *the National Society*, founded in 1811 by Andrew Bell.

(ii) The Nonconformists worked through *the British and Foreign Schools Society* (1814) whose leading light was Joseph Lancaster, a Quaker, who ran his own schools at Borough Road in London.

There was bitter rivalry and hostility between these two groups, though their teaching methods – based on *the monitorial system* – were similar. In order to save money, and because of the shortage of teachers, older pupils (known as monitors) taught small groups of children. According to Lancaster: 'the whole system of tuition is almost entirely conducted by boys; the school is divided into classes, and to each of these a lad is appointed as monitor; he is responsible for the morals, improvement, good order and cleanliness of the whole class. To be a monitor is coveted by the whole school'.

There was wide variation in the quality of elementary education provided, and in some industrial areas there were no schools at all for working class children. In 1818 only one in 17 of the population was receiving any elementary education.

(b) Why was there no state system of education? Many people felt that the only way to secure an efficient education system was for the government to organise it. Jeremy Bentham thought it would eliminate the dangerous rivalry between different religious denominations. In 1820 a Whig politician, Henry Brougham, introduced a bill which would have set up schools in parishes where there were none already in existence, but it was easily defeated.

Reasons for lack of progress:

(i) The same *laissez-faire* outlook which delayed government intervention in the other problem areas applies equally to education; if the poor wanted education, they must see to it themselves; it was no part of the government's function to provide such an expensive service.

(ii) There was a strong belief that education of the working classes was unnecessary; all they needed were the skills of the job for which they were destined, and these could be learned perfectly well by simply doing the job. And if children spent their time being educated, industrialists would lose their source of cheap labour.

(iii) An educated working class could be dangerous: one MP, Davies Giddy, told parliament in 1807 that education would teach workers 'to despise their lot in life instead of making them good servants in agriculture and other laborious employments to which their rank in society had destined them'. He added that it would enable them to read seditious pamphlets and 'render them insolent to their superiors'. In 1825 another MP, afraid of revolution, delivered himself of the view that 'whenever the lower orders of any great nation have obtained a smattering of knowledge, they have generally used it to produce national ruin'. Two years later a Tory MP argued that 'as education

has increased amidst the people, vice and crime have increased ...
the majority of criminals consist of those who have been educated'.

12.7 SHOW HOW AND WHY THE GOVERNMENT INTERVENED IN EDUCATION

(a) Gradually those who were in favour of government intervention gained the ascendancy in parliament. The Whig government which came to power in 1830 was under pressure from its Radical Benthamite wing and at last in 1833 the first breakthrough was made. However, *in the period 1833-70* the government did not provide any schools itself; it merely made cash available and attempted to make sure that the voluntary societies used it efficiently:

(i) In 1833 the government gave a total of £20 000 to the Anglican and Nonconformist societies to help them provide more school buildings. £10 000 was voted for building schools in Scotland.

(ii) In 1839 the grant was increased to £30 000, on condition that a committee of the Privy Council was set up to supervise how the money was spent. The secretary of the committee was James Kay-Shuttleworth, who had been a doctor in the slums of Manchester; later, as a poor law commissioner, he developed workhouse schools and set up his own training college for teachers. At his suggestion school inspectors were appointed; they soon began to produce disturbing reports about the inefficiency of the monitorial system.

(iii) In the 1840s teacher training colleges were established by the religious societies, following the example of Kay-Shuttleworth's Battersea College. He also introduced the *pupil-teacher scheme* by which able students were apprenticed to good voluntary schools at the age of 13 for five years, after which, with the help of government grants, they could go on to teacher training colleges. To finance this new scheme which gradually replaced the monitorial system, the government grant was increased to £100 000 (1847). Within 10 years it had topped £500 000 and in 1856 the government set up the Department of Education to look after administration.

(iv) *The Newcastle Commission* reported (1861) that although one in seven of the population was receiving some education, the majority were still unable to read a newspaper or write a letter. It recommended that grants to schools and teachers' salaries should depend on how well pupils acquitted themselves in examinations.

(v) *Robert Lowe*, head of the Education Department in Palmerston's Liberal government (1859-65) accepted this recommendation and introduced a *'payment by results' system (1862)*. School inspectors tested the pupils in reading, writing and arithmetic and the number who passed determined both grant and salaries. The system aroused tremendous criticism because although it made schools more efficient and saved money, it led to a great deal of mechanical cramming and reciting of lists of facts learned off by heart, as well as causing nervous strain among teachers. Even so the system lasted until 1897.

The year 1870 saw the beginning of a new era: Gladstone's Liberal government (1868–74) decided that it was up to the state to make sure that every child received some education; if necessary it would provide schools itself.

(b) Why did the government decide that a state system of elementary education was needed?

(i) The 1867 Reform Act which gave the vote to borough industrial workers meant that they needed some education to enable them to decide how to vote. According to Lowe himself, 'from the moment you entrust the masses with power, their education becomes an imperative necessity; you have placed the government of this country in the hands of the masses and you must therefore give them an education'.

(ii) Britain was lagging well behind Prussia and the northern states of the USA in the provision of education, and both seemed to be doing well militarily and economically. Prussia had easily defeated Austria/Hungary in 1866 and the North had turned out the eventual winner in the American Civil War (1861–5); it was already clear that both would soon be challenging Britain's industrial lead. These developments helped to swing opinion in Britain in favour of mass education.

(iii) The rapid population growth meant that the voluntary societies were unable to keep up; in fact they were losing ground – in some large industrial cities less than one in ten of the population was receiving any education.

(iv) The supporters of education for the masses were waging a more vigorous campaign than ever before; spearheading the movement was Joseph Chamberlain's National Education League, started in Birmingham in 1869.

(v) Gladstone was anxious for greater efficiency and believed in 'equality of opportunity' for everybody.

(vi) Finally Britain's economy was booming, so that the government felt able to provide the extra cash that would be needed to finance a full state system of education.

(c) Forster's Education Act (1870).

W. E. Forster, MP for Bradford and Gladstone's head of the Education Department, had a difficult problem, since he had somehow or other to include the religious voluntary schools within the new legislation; there were so many of them that they could not be ignored and certainly not abolished. Also he had to try not to seem to be favouring either Anglicans or Nonconformists. The result was bound to be a compromise.

(i) The existing Anglican and Nonconformist voluntary schools were allowed to continue with increased grants from the government.

(ii) In areas where there was no voluntary school or where the existing schools could not provide enough places, a locally elected School Board was to be set up. Its function was to organise Board Schools for children aged five to twelve. These schools were to receive government grants as well as extra finance from a special local rate to be collected by the Board.

(iii) As an attempt to sidestep the religious problem it was left to each Board to decide whether religious education was to be given in their schools; if so it should be restricted to Bible study and this should be 'undenominational' (i.e. it should not be taught with an Anglican or Nonconformist bias).

(iv) Attendance was not made compulsory (because there were as yet insufficient school places for all children) and it was not made free. However, Boards could pay the fees for poor children either in the new Board Schools or in the voluntary schools.

Forster's Act caused a great political row: the religious bodies resented the fact that their schools received no money from local rates, and that the new schools might provide no religious teaching at all. Nonconformists were particularly annoyed because they had hoped that Forster would abolish Church Schools, whereas he had actually strengthened the already strong Anglican position in many areas. To add insult to injury Nonconformists found themselves having to pay the local education rate, much of which would be used to finance 'godless' Board Schools. Equally galling was the possibility that some Boards would use their rates to pay the fees of poor children being educated in Anglican schools. This unfortunate situation led to bitter struggles in which the different religious groups fought for control of their local School Board.

The Act can also be criticised on the grounds that it resulted in a dual system of education – in which Church schools were handicapped by a shortage of money. However, it achieved what Forster and Gladstone had in mind – 'to complete the present voluntary system ... to fill up the gaps'. B. H. Abbott claims that the Act 'remains a remarkable piece of social legislation, playing a vital part in civilising the masses in the nation's vast industrial cities'. Certainly between 1870 and 1880, the number of children receiving elementary education had more than doubled to almost three million, as the new Board schools sprang up all over the country.

(d) Further developments in elementary education were:

(i) *Sandon's Education Act (1876)*. Lord Sandon, head of the Education Department in Disraeli's second government (1874–80), decided that local School Attendance Committees should be set up to encourage as many children as possible to take advantage of educational opportunities; parents were to be responsible for making sure that children received basic instruction, and the committees *could* help parents who were too poor to pay the school fees, though this was not compulsory.

(ii) *A. J. Mundella's Education Act (1881)* was a Liberal measure which made *attendance at elementary school compulsory* for all children between five and ten. There was still the problem of fees which worked out at around three pence per child per week, far too much for poor families to afford, if they had several children.

(iii) *The Fee Grant Act (1891)*, a Conservative measure, which meant that in practice *elementary education was now free*.

(iv) During the 1890s, Lowe's payment by results system was gradually phased out, thanks to recommendations made by the *Cross Commission (1888)*. Grants to schools were now based on attendance, and 'bald teaching of facts' was replaced by 'the development of interest and intelligence'.

By the end of the nineteenth century the vast majority of children were receiving some basic instruction and the quality of that education was improving.

(e) The Balfour Education Act (1902) was the next major landmark. A. J. Balfour, Conservative Prime Minister from 1902-05, decided that radical changes were needed in the way elementary education was being organised, and that some government policy was needed about secondary education. *His reasons were*:

(i) Because of a shortage of money, the voluntary schools (of which the great majority were run by Anglicans) were much inferior in every way to the Board Schools.

(ii) *The Bryce Commission reported (1895)* that there was a chronic shortage of suitable technical education, while Britain's industrial competitors – USA, Germany and Belgium – were far ahead in this field.

The details of the new Act were worked out by R. L. Morant, Balfour's educational adviser:

(i) The School Boards were abolished; county councils and county borough councils were to run both voluntary and Board schools and were made responsible for organising secondary and technical education.

(ii) For the first time, voluntary schools were to receive money from the rates to enable them to bring their standards up to those of the Board schools.

(iii) Local authorities, working through their own education committees, could help existing secondary schools (mostly old grammar schools) with money from the rates; they were also directed to set up their own fee-paying secondary schools.

The Balfour/Morant Act was vitally important: it meant a general raising of the standards of elementary education and more uniformity, though it perpetuated the dual church/state system. It also meant that the state was going to see to it that secondary education was more widely available; this caused the appearance of a new phenomenon – the state grammar school. Unfortunately these at first tended to model themselves on the old private grammar schools with their concentration on Latin and Greek and with insufficient attention to technical and scientific subjects. At the time, the Act caused another religious controversy, bitterly disappointing the Nonconformists again. They had hoped that Balfour would abolish Anglican and Roman Catholic schools, which were mostly teetering on the verge of bankruptcy. Instead they were rescued by money from the local rates (to which the Nonconformists themselves had to contribute). In some country areas, particularly in Wales, the only school available was an Anglican one, which Nonconformists had to allow their children to attend.

(f) Further steps towards secondary education for all were:

(i) In 1906 Campbell-Bannerman's Liberal government introduced what in effect became *the 11-plus system*. All secondary schools which were receiving government grants had to reserve 25 per cent of their places for children coming up from elementary schools; they would be awarded scholarships on the results of a special entrance examination.

(ii) *H. A. L. Fisher's Education Act (1918)* was passed by the Lloyd George government shortly before the end of the First World War. It raised the school-leaving age from 12 to 14 and required local authorities to provide what it called 'day continuation classes' or part-time education to the age of 18 for those children who left school at 14. Grants to secondary schools were increased so that more scholarships could be awarded and State Scholarships were introduced so that secondary school pupils could go on to University.

Education had clearly come a long way since 1833, but there was still much to be done. In fact very little was done about Fisher's day continuation classes, because after the war, governments claimed to be short of the necessary funds. Although much was made of the fact that an 'educational ladder' had been established, it was still very rare for a child from a working-class home to get to University. As J. A. Hobson (a well-known Edwardian expert on politics and economics) put it: 'What is needed is not an educational ladder, narrowing as it rises, to be climbed with difficulty by a chosen energetic few ... it is a broad, easy stair that is wanted ... one which will entice everyone to rise'.

(Later developments were the 1926 Hadow Report, see Section 22.3(b) and the 1944 Butler Act, see Section 27.7(b) (ii).)

QUESTIONS

1. The Case for Factory Reform

Study Sources **A** to **E** and then answer the questions that follow.

Source **A**: Evidence given by Samuel Coulson to the Parliamentary Commission on Factory Children's Labour, 1831–32.

At what time, in the brisk time, did those girls go to the mill? – In the brisk time, for about six weeks, they have gone at three o'clock in the morning, and ended at ten or nearly half-past at night.

What intervals for rest and refreshment were allowed during those nineteen hours of labour?

– Breakfast a quarter of an hour, dinner half an hour and drinking a quarter of an hour.

Had you not great difficulty in awakening your children to this excessive labour?

– Yes: in the early time we had to take them up asleep and shake them when we got them on the floor to dress them, before we could get them off to their work; but not so in the common hours.

What time did you get them up in the morning?

– In general at two o'clock to dress them.

So that they had not above four hours of sleep at this time?

– No, they had not.

The usual hours of work were from six in the morning till half-past eight at night?

– Yes.

Did this excessive term of labour cause much cruelty also?

– Yes, with being so much fatigued the strap was frequently used.

Source: Northern Examining Association. Specimen Question.

Source **B**: Evidence given by John Hall to the Parliamentary Commission on Factory Children's Labour, 1831–32.

Do you live at Bradford?

– Yes.

Are you the overlooker of Mr. John Wood?

– I am.

Will you have the goodness to state the present hours of working in your factory?

– Our present hours are from six until seven.

With what intervals for rest and refreshment?

– Half an hour for breakfast and forty minutes for dinner.

Do you believe that the children can endure the labour you have been describing without injury?

No, I do not.

When your hands have been employed for some time, do you
see any alteration in their appearance?
– In the course of a few weeks I see a paleness in their faces,
and they grow spiritless and tired.
Have you remarked that cases of deformity are very common
in Bradford?
– They are very common. I have the names of, I think about
200 families I have visited myself that have deformed children,
and I have taken particular care not to put down one single case
where it might have happened by accident, but only those
whom I judge to have been thrown crooked by the practice of
piecening . . .

Source: as for Source A.

Source C: Evidence of William Forster of Plomton Mill near Knares-
borough to the Parliamentary Commission on Factory
Children's Labour, 1831–32.

I often wish that Michael Sadler and Richard Oastler had my
mill hands to govern. If they had they would, I am persuaded,
soon abandon their visionary opinions. If the hours of child
labour are reduced, mills will be unable to work a full twelve-
hour day, with a consequent reduction in the earnings of the
adult workers as well as the profits of the mill-owners. The
youngest child employed by me is never exhausted by 12 hours
labour, which they clearly show by playing and romping when
the hours of labour terminate.

Source: as for Source A.

Source D: An illustration from 'The Life and Adventures of Michael Armstrong the Factory Boy' by Frances Trollope, published in 1840. Michael, who has been put to work at the 'mules' repairing broken threads, is greeting a former playmate.

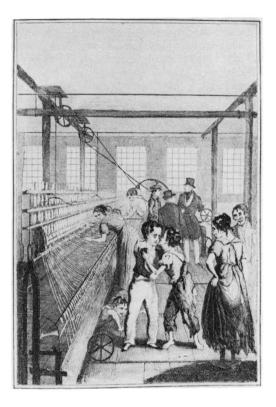

Source: as for Source **A**.

Source E: From a letter written by a Lancashire mill owner in 1845.

As to the conclusions I have come to from the working of my . . . mill . . . for 11 hours instead of 12 hours each day . . . I am quite satisfied that both as much yarn and cloth may be produced at quite as low a cost in 11 as in 12 hours . . . It is my intention to make a further reduction to $10\frac{1}{2}$ hours, without the slightest fear of suffering loss . . . I find the hands work with greater energy and spirit; they are more cheerful and happy . . .

About 20 years ago . . . we had about 30 young women in our Manchester warehouse. I requested that they would work 12 hours (a day) instead of 11. At the end of the week, I found that they had not a mere trifle more work done; but supposing there was some incidental cause of this I requested that they would work 13 hours (a day) the following week, at the end of which they had produced less instead of more work. They were exhausted and making bad work and little of it. Since then I have been an advocate of shorter hours of labour.

Source: as for Source **A**.

(a) (i)   According to Source **A**, at what time did the children usually start work?   **4(a)**

    (ii) At what time did they start work during busy periods?   **4(a)**

    (iii) Factory owners often claimed that the long hours of work in their mills did the children they employed no harm. What evidence can you find in Sources **A** and **B** to contradict this view?   **4(a, c)**

(b) (i)   In what ways does Source **C** disagree with Sources **A** and **B** about the effects of mill work on children?   **4(a, c)**

    (ii) Why do you think the witnesses giving evidence in Sources **A** to **C** disagree?   **4(a, b, c)**

(c)   Some mill owners claimed that the Parliamentary Commission of 1831–33 was *biased* and that its evidence was *misleading*. Using your own knowledge of the subject and the evidence in Sources **A**, **B** and **C**, suggest reasons why they said this.

                                      1, 2, 4(a, b, c)

(d)   Study Source **D** carefully. To which of the Sources **A** to **C** does it appear to give support? Give reasons for your answer.

                                             4(a, c)

(e)   In what ways does Source **E** suggest that William Forster (Source **C**) was wrong to be against a reduction in the hours children could work in mills?   **4(a, c)**

(f)   Sources **C** and **E** are both from mill owners, but they disagree;

    (i)   What are the main points on which they disagree?

    (ii) Do you think that these two Sources, since they contradict each other, are no use to historians? Give reasons for your answer.   **4(a, b, c)**

(g)   Sources **A** and **B** suggest that long hours of work in textile mills were bad for the workers. Source **E** suggests that long hours may even have been bad for the owners' profits. Using the Sources and your own knowledge, explain why it took so long to carry out an effective change in the laws governing hours of work in factories.   **1, 2, 4(a, c)**

Source: Northern Examining Association. Specimen question.

2. Problems of Public Health

Study Sources **A** to **E** and then answer the questions which follow.

Source A: a report on Leeds in 1842.

> Courts and cul-de-sacs exist everywhere. In one cul-de-sac in Leeds there are 34 houses, and in ordinary times there dwell in these houses 340 persons, or ten to every house. The name of this place is Boot and Shoe Yard, from whence the Commissioners removed, in the days of Cholera, 75 cartloads of manure which had been untouched for years . . . For the most part these houses are built back-to-back; a house of this description will contain a cellar, a house and chamber . . . To build the largest number of cottages on the smallest possible space seems to have been the original view of the speculators. Thus neighbourhoods have arisen in which there is neither water nor privies.
>
> Source: R. Baker, *An Enquiry into the State and Condition of the Town of Leeds*, 1842.

Source B: description of Leeds, from Edwin Chadwick's Report of 1842.

> With broken panes in every window-frame, and filth and vermin in every nook. With the walls unwhitewashed for years, without water, with floors unwashed from year to year and without privies . . . There are some streets elevated a foot, sometimes two, above the level of the causeway, by the accumulation of years, and stagnant puddles here and there, and deposits of excrement on all sides. They are undrained, unpaved, and unventilated and uncared for by any authority but the landlord, who every week collects his miserable rents from his miserable tenants.
>
> Source: E. Chadwick, *Report on the Sanitary Condition of the Labouring Population*, W. Clowes and Son, 1842 (adapted extracts).

Source C: report on conditions in Darlington, February 1850, by William Ranger.

> In one court I found 15 persons in two small rooms ill at the same time of typhus fever, lying on the floor on straw, and I had to step over from one to another to attend them . . . There is no system for collecting refuse from the streets and courts, except that once a fortnight one man and a horse, with a boy, are employed on the day following the holding of the cattle market . . . This sluggish and polluted stream [the river Skerne] ought not to be the open sewer for all the filth in Darlington.
>
> Source: quoted in R. Watson, *Edwin Chadwick, Poor Law and Public Health*, Longman, 1969 (adapted extracts).

Source D: poster advertising the first appointments to be made by the Darlington Board of Health.

DARLINGTON
LOCAL BOARD OF HEALTH.

The Board purpose at their next Meeting, to appoint the following Officers, viz:—

A COLLECTOR of Rates, a SURVEYOR, and an INSPECTOR of NUISANCES,

And will receive Written Proposals from Applicants.

The Collector will be required to find approved Security for £300.

The proposals for the Offices of Surveyor and Inspector of Nuisances, may be made to undertake them either together or separately.

Information as to the precise nature of the duties of each office may be obtained on *personal* application at my office, and sealed proposals stating the remuneration required, and indorsed " Application for the office of ————— to The Darlington Local Board of Health," (and in the case of the Collector with the names of the proposed Security) must be sent to me not later than Twelve o'clock at noon, on Thursday the 17th Instant.

The Board give no pledge to accept the lowest offers.

By order, JOHN S. PEACOCK,
CLERK TO THE BOARD.

Darlington, October 8th, 1850.

J. MANLEY, PRINTER, 41 HIGH ROW, DARLINGTON.

Source: Darlington Corporation and Durham Record Office.

Source E: extracts from the Minute Book of the Darlington Board of Health for 1854–55.

Drains of scientific construction now spread out throughout a great portion of the town, so that before the close of the present year Darlington will in all probability be thoroughly drained . . . though the dreadful pestilence [cholera] raged within a few miles it has again left us unscathed. In the low-lying district east of the Skerne, the death rate has fallen from 68 to 23 per 1000. Still there is much to do – the most difficult obstacle now is to remedy the present faulty construction of the dwellings of the working classes. It is but an act of self-defence; for the rich man who lives in a comfortable and luxurious home, must keep in mind that his mansion cannot be safe, when the dark and filthy hovel breeds pestilence beside it.

Source: Durham Record Office, Da/A1/1/1, quoted in R. Watson, *Edwin Chadwick, Poor Law and Public Health*, Longman, 1969 (adapted extracts).

(a)   (i)   Which two diseases are mentioned by name in these Sources? **4(a)**

      (ii)   What dangers to health are mentioned in both Sources **A** and **B**? **4(a, c)**

     (iii)   What danger to health is referred to in Sources **A** and **C**, but not mentioned at all in Source **B**? **4(a, c)**

     (iv)   Edwin Chadwick said that the greed of landlords and builders was one of the reasons for the lack of progress in public health. What evidence can you find in Sources **A** and **B** to support Chadwick? **4(a, c)**

(b)   (i)   How do Sources **C** and **D** show that the authorities in Darlington were trying to take advantage of the Public Health Act of 1848? **1, 2, 4(a, c)**

      (ii)   From the evidence of Source **D**, how were any interested people to go about finding out more information about the advertised jobs? **4(a)**

     (iii)   What instructions were given about applying for the jobs? **4(a)**

(c)   (i)   From the evidence of Source **E**, how successful had the Darlington Board of Health been in their attempts to deal with the problems outlined in Source **C**, by 1855? **4(a, c)**

      (ii)   What does Source **E** show about the attitude of the middle class towards the working class at this time? **4(a, b)**

     (iii)   What are the strengths and weaknesses of Sources **A, B, C** and **E** for the historian? **4(a, b)**

(d)   (i)   The 1848 Public Health Act is generally considered to have been a failure. From your own knowledge, explain why this was so. **1, 2**

      (ii)   If the Act was a failure, does this mean that some of the evidence in Source **E** is unreliable? Explain your answer. **4(a, b)**

(e)   'By 1900 Britain had become a healthier place to live in.' Describe briefly how this had been achieved by

      (i)   government action after 1850;

      (ii)   medical improvements;

     (iii)   improved engineering. **1, 2**

3. (a)   In 1825 an MP said: 'Whenever the lower orders of any great nation have obtained a smattering of knowledge, they have generally used it to produce national ruin.'

      (i)   Explain in your own words what you think he meant by this statement. **1, 2, 4(a)**

      (ii)   What other reasons can you think of to explain why there was no attempt to introduce a state system of education until 1870? **1, 2**

   (b)   Robert Lowe, a Liberal politician who was Head of the Education Department from 1859 until 1865, said in 1867: 'You have placed the government of this country in the hands of the masses and you must therefore given them an education'.

(i) Explain what you think he meant by this statement. **1, 2, 4(a)**

(ii) What other reasons did the government have for introducing Forster's Education Act in 1870? **1, 2**

(iii) What were the main changes brought in by Forster's Education Act? **1, 2**

(iv) The Act of 1870 aroused a lot of criticism. Explain briefly what the main complaints were about. Do you think the complaints were justified? Give reasons for your answer. **1, 2**

4. It is 1833 and Parliament has just passed Lord Althorp's Factory Act, which, among other things:

(i) limited children aged 9–13 to an 8 hour day;

(ii) limited young people aged 14–18 to a 12 hour day;

(iii) appointed 4 inspectors.

Describe and explain the feelings and reactions of each of the following on hearing the news:

(a) a supporter of Oastler and the 10 Hour Movement;

(b) a Lancashire cotton factory owner who is afraid of losing money;

(c) a 10 year old child who has regularly been working a 12 hour day in a textile mill. **1, 2, 3**

CHAPTER 13

GLADSTONE'S FIRST MINISTRY 1868–74

SUMMARY OF EVENTS

As we saw at the end of Chapter 8, the Liberals won the 1868 general election with a large majority of 112. W. E. Gladstone became Prime Minister for the first time (December 1868), taking over from his great Conservative rival, Benjamin Disraeli, who had been Prime Minister (also for the first time) since the previous February. During the late 1860s and the 1870s, the confusion in British politics which had lasted since the break-up of the Conservative party in 1846, suddenly cleared. Politics became a well-defined struggle between two united parties – Liberals and Conservatives – who alternated in government until the Liberals split in 1886 over the question of Irish Home Rule.

Parliament was dominated by the two party leaders, Gladstone and Disraeli. They came from vastly different backgrounds – Gladstone the son of a wealthy Liverpool merchant of Scottish ancestry, Disraeli the son of a comfortably-off Jewish writer and novelist whose family had come over from Italy. Both were brilliant speakers and debaters, and they heartily detested each other, losing no opportunity to attack each other's policies, with sometimes thrilling oratory. Disraeli once described Gladstone as 'a sophisticated rhetorician, inebriated with the exuberance of his own verbosity' and later, more directly, as 'that unprincipled maniac'. Gladstone had something to say about Disraeli's principles: 'his doctrine is false, but the man is more false than the doctrine'. It was a real 'duel of the giants' which lasted for almost 20 years. As M. R. D. Foot puts it: 'To the popular imagination, in the days before the entertainment industries had distracted so much attention from politics, Disraeli and Gladstone appeared a pair of Titans, locked in colossal combat'.

Whatever Disraeli thought about his principles, or lack of them, Gladstone now had his chance in this first ministry, to put into practice what he saw as the principles of Liberalism. There was a rush of long overdue reforms, which so dismayed Queen Victoria that she referred to Gladstone as 'that half-mad firebrand'. Much of his time was absorbed with his largely unsuccessful attempts to solve the problems of Ireland. As so often happens when a government introduces radical changes, so many different people had been offended by the reforms that the Liberals were soundly beaten at the 1874 general election, and the Conservatives were back in power with a majority for the first time in almost thirty years.

13.1 WHAT WERE GLADSTONE'S PRINCIPLES AND AIMS?

(a) He was deeply religious and for a time when he was a young man he thought of becoming an Anglican priest. Right through his career, politics and religion were closely related and his policies were dictated by what he thought was moral and righteous. Politics was the means of carrying out God's will.

(b) He believed that the government should try to make sure that everybody had 'equality of opportunity'. Consequently he aimed to abolish special privileges which he considered unjust, wherever they existed, whether in the Army, the Civil Service or the Universities.

(c) He believed in the Benthamite virtues of efficiency and economy, even though the two might be contradictory. According to Magnus 'he loathed waste because he regarded all money as a trust committed by God to man'.

(d) Oddly enough his religious beliefs did not convince him of the necessity of practical social reform to improve working and living conditions and public health. Apart from possibly proving expensive, too much government help might destroy the moral fibre of the nation. It was for the individual to make the best of his circumstances. The 1872 Public Health Act was Gladstone's only major reform to improve actual material conditions, and that was not a success.

(e) In foreign affairs his religious views led him to favour a policy of peace and tranquillity and to respect the rights of other countries. This was in great contrast to Lord Palmerston's method of conducting overseas affairs, and there was the risk that foreign governments would interpret the Gladstone approach as a sign of weakness. However, he did protect Britain's interests in Egypt and the Sudan during his second ministry (1880-5).

(f) He had a great desire, which became almost an obsession during his later ministries, to pacify Ireland.

13.2 SHOW HOW GLADSTONE'S DOMESTIC REFORMS WERE NECESSARY BUT UNPOPULAR

Every single one of the Liberal reforms succeeded in upsetting at least one influential group of people and sometimes more. But Gladstone pressed on regardless, fortified in the knowledge that he was carrying out God's will.

(a) Forster's Education Act (1870). By the late 1860s it was clear that the patchwork of elementary schools provided by the religious voluntary societies was totally unable to cope with the rapidly increasing population. The Forster Act was a creditable attempt to 'fill in the gaps' and 'cover the country with good schools'; there could never be 'equality of opportunity' unless the whole population had the benefit of elementary education. Even more important in Gladstone's eyes, education would enable the working classes to study the scriptures. However, the Act aroused tremendous opposition from Nonconformists (for full details see Section 12.7(b) and (c)).

(b) The University Tests Act (1871)

(i) This was a clear case of Gladstone removing a glaring injustice and promoting equality of opportunity in the Universities. Action was needed because there was an ancient statute still in operation which allowed only Anglicans to become teachers or members of the administration, or to hold scholarships and fellowships at Oxford and Cambridge Universities.

(ii) The new Act abolished this special privilege of the Church of England and threw these posts open to all suitable candidates, whatever their religion.

(iii) Nonconformists were pleased but not sufficiently to make them drop their opposition to the Education Act. Many Anglicans acknowledged that it was a just reform (Gladstone himself was an Anglican), but others resented their loss of privilege, and Lord Salisbury, future Conservative Prime Minister, led a bitter but unsuccessful attack on the bill in the House of Lords.

(c) Civil Service Reform (1871)

(i) The problem with the Civil Service was that appointments were still made according to recommendations from an MP or a peer. It depended on who the aspiring candidate knew and on what strings he could pull, and even sometimes on how much he could afford to pay for the post. Inevitably a large proportion of the men appointed in this way were lazy or incompetent. But as the administration of the country became more complex, a more efficient Civil Service was needed.

(ii) Gladstone, with the strong support of his Chancellor of the Exchequer, Robert Lowe, another efficiency fiend, introduced the principle that recruitment must be by examination. This was a first-rate reform which opened up the Civil Service to the best brains in the country, and its efficiency and professionalism increased accordingly.

(iii) Many of the aristocracy, who had previously dominated the Civil Service, were bitterly opposed, in fact the Foreign Office had to be excluded from the reform because Gladstone's own Foreign Minister, Lord Granville, flatly refused to agree to it for his department.

(d) Trade Union Reform (1871). The legal position, privileges and powers of Trade Unions had never been precisely defined; the Liberals came up with two measures, both in 1871, to clarify this state of affairs:

(i) *The Trade Union Act* recognised unions as legal bodies with rights to own property and funds, to protect their property and funds at law, and to strike. Trade unionists greeted this with delight which almost immediately turned to disgust at the second measure:

(ii) *The Criminal Law Amendment Act* which stated that although unions could organise strikes, picketing of all types, even peaceful, was forbidden. In practice, it would be impossible to make a strike effective.

Some historians believe that this Act was Gladstone's most serious miscalculation in home affairs, since it lost him much working class support. But again his religious views explain his attitude: he was utterly against any kind of force to sway opinion, and picketing could easily lead to violence.

(e) The Public Health Act of 1872 (see Section 12.5(a)) was a half-hearted attempt to deal with Britain's chaotic health problems. It was a great disappointment to those who were looking to the government for positive leadership and a large-scale injection of cash. Gladstone was not sufficiently interested, and the people who ran the local boards of health seemed to think that their most important function was to keep expenditure to a minimum. It was a classic example of the Benthamite contradiction — efficiency being sacrificed to economy.

(f) The Ballot Act (1872)

(i) Voting in elections was still carried out in public by a show of hands, a system which lent itself to bribery, corruption and intimidation of all kinds.

(ii) Gladstone's Act made voting secret, but although it made elections more orderly affairs it did not completely remove bribery and corruption; there were still ways of buying votes – free beer in pubs and transport for voters being the most obvious. It was not until the Corrupt Practices Act (1883) passed during Gladstone's second ministry that corruption was successfully controlled.

(iii) Although it was a just measure leading to more efficient electoral processes, the Ballot Act was highly unpopular with landlords and employers who could no longer control the way their tenants and workers voted. Lord Hartington, leader of the right-wing Liberals, was one of the severest critics of the bill.

(g) The Licensing Act (1872)

(i) Widespread drunkenness was one of the most striking features of mid-nineteenth-century Britain. Gladstone and his Home Secretary, Henry Bruce, looked on this as a moral issue; they felt that there were too many public houses and that the massive profits made by brewers ought to be controlled.

(ii) Bruce was forced to tone down the original version of his bill, so fierce was the outcry from the brewers. The final version was a very mild measure which gave magistrates the power to issue licenses for the opening of public houses, so that in areas where it was felt there were already too many, magistrates could close some pubs. It also specified that pubs must close at midnight in towns and at eleven o'clock in country areas, and it forbade the adulteration of beer (one of the commonest practices was to add salt to the beer, which increased the thirst and subsequent sales).

(iii) Though mild, the Act was highly unpopular with the working classes, and there were a number of near riots when police tried to enforce closing hours. Brewers resented what they saw as an attack on their independence and profits; others disliked the Act because it interfered with personal liberty. The Bishop of Peterborough, attacking the bill in the Lords, voiced his opinion that he would prefer to see 'England free better than England sober'. Some historians believe that the liquor trade became solidly Conservative because of the Licensing Act, which was consequently a major cause of the Liberal defeat in 1874.

(h) The Judicature Act (1873)

(i) The British legal system was in an unbelievable muddle. It had developed piecemeal from medieval times, with new courts being created to meet specific demands. By the nineteenth century there were seven major courts, including Queen's Bench, Common Pleas and Exchequer, and the legal processes were slow and inefficient.

(ii) Lord Selborne (Gladstone's Lord Chancellor) prepared the successful Act which greatly simplified the situation, uniting the seven courts into one Supreme Court of Judicature.

(iii) This was the least controversial of the Liberal reforms, though there were some objections to the clause which deprived the House of Lords of its right to act as the final court which people could appeal to if they were dissatisfied with any verdict in a lower court. In 1876 Disraeli's government restored this right.

(i) Cardwell's army reforms

(i) *The glaring faults and inefficiencies of the army* had been exposed by the Crimean War (1854-6) and the Indian Mutiny (1857). The root cause of the trouble was that the army, like the Civil Service, acquired its officers not on merit, but by the purchase of commissions. Any wealthy young man could buy himself into the officer class, whether he knew anything about military matters or not. For example, a lieutenant-colonelcy could be acquired for between £4500 and £7000; the price variations were because commissions were often auctioned to the highest bidder. An officer was free to sell his commission whenever he chose; money, not brains was what counted in the promotion stakes. The Commander-in-Chief was the Duke of Cambridge, a cousin of Queen Victoria, who often referred to him as 'poor George', on account of his unfortunate habit of making already bad situations even worse. He was slow-witted and against all changes. For the Liberals, army reform was essential as an attack both on inefficiency and on privilege (the army was considered the natural preserve of the aristocracy). It was made more urgent by the Prussian victories over Austria (1866) and France (1870-1) which revealed a new, highly professional and potentially dangerous military power.

(ii) *Edward Cardwell*, the Secretary for War, was responsible for planning the reforms which were introduced at intervals throughout the ministry:

- Troops were withdrawn from Britain's self-governing colonies, which were encouraged to raise their own forces.
- Flogging was abolished in peacetime.
- The Commander-in-Chief was made subordinate to the Secretary for War.
- The purchase of commissions was abolished – selection and promotion of officers was to be on merit.
- The different sections of the war department were all combined under one roof in the War Office.
- The regiments, which had previously been known only by numbers, were reorganised. Cardwell divided Britain into 69 districts, each with its own county regiment of two linked battalions, one on active service overseas, the other at home in Britain. The new regiments were given the names of their home county (e.g. Durhams, Gloucesters).
- The length of service was reduced from 12 years overseas followed by a period in the reserves, to six years overseas and six in the reserves. This was a more sensible arrangement since many men ended up broken in health after 12 years in India.
- The Martini-Henry breech-loading rifle was introduced as the main infantry weapon.

(iii) *The reforms inevitably aroused a lot of opposition* from the aristocracy whose privileges were being threatened and believed that the main qualification for an officer was to be a gentleman and a sportsman rather than a professional. The Duke of Cambridge was suspicious of officers who had been to Staff College; 'Brains!' he said, 'I don't believe in brains!' Faced with this sort of mentality, it was not surprising that Cardwell's bill to abolish the purchase of Commissions was defeated in the Lords. It was only when Gladstone showed that he was prepared to bypass the Lords by persuading Queen Victoria to issue a royal warrant to the same effect, that the Lords decided they had better pass the bill. This was quite an achievement by Gladstone, since Victoria herself considered the army reforms 'unwise'.

(iv) *Cardwell's work was an outstanding success.* The more humane and civilised conditions of service encouraged a better type of recruit and made possible a large and efficient reserve (increased from only 3500 to almost 36 000). The artillery received an extra 5000 men and 156 large horse-drawn guns (bringing the total to 336). In fact, thanks to Cardwell, Britain had the beginnings of an efficient modern army which made possible successful overseas campaigns like the one in Egypt in 1882 (see Section 16.2(c)).

(v) On the other hand, Cardwell would have gone much further if opposition had been less violent. He failed to create a permanent General Staff of the type already in existence in Prussia and France; this was one of the causes of the disasters in the early part of the Boer War. Incredibly, artillery officers preferred to continue using old-fashioned muzzle-loading cannon, even though recent Prussian victories had been achieved with breech-loading artillery. Nor had he managed to get rid of the Duke of Cambridge who continued with his stubborn blocking of all further change until his retirement in 1895. Though he was one of the most brilliant men in the Liberal party, Cardwell was so exhausted and disillusioned by his long struggle that he retired from active politics in 1874.

13.3 GLADSTONE AND IRELAND

(a) Ireland since 1846

(i) The plight of Ireland can probably best be illustrated by simply looking at *the population figures:* from a peak of 8.2 million in 1841 the population fell dramatically over the next decade and continued to fall, until by 1911 the figure was only 4.4 million.

The Irish peasants suffered the utmost miseries during the famines of 1846-8; at least a million people died of starvation and cholera and in desperation another million emigrated to the USA and Canada. During the 1850s and early 1860s, Ireland slipped from the forefront of the British newspapers, but that did not mean that the basic problems of Irish society had disappeared. The majority of the poverty-stricken peasants were still engaged in a grim struggle for survival. Occasionally their frustrations broke out in acts of violence against the property of wealthy landlords. The British government responded by ignoring the root causes of the problem and merely sent more troops to hold the Irish down.

(ii) A new phase in Irish affairs opened in 1867 when a society known as

illus 13.1   *The Irish famine*

the Fenians (formed in the USA in the 1850s) began operations in Britain. They were pledged to revolution and wanted an Irish republic completely separate from Britain. There were several risings in Ireland in 1867. Manchester was the scene of a violent incident in which a group of Irishmen rescued two Fenians from a prison van; a policeman was killed and three of the rescuers were later hanged. This incident aroused some excitement in Ireland which in turn stirred the Fenians to greater efforts: in December 1867 they tried to free two of their members from Clerkenwell Gaol in London by blowing a hole in the prison wall with gunpowder. Their attempt went sadly wrong - twelve people were killed and over a hundred seriously injured. The Fenians had limited support in Ireland itself, but their activities were important because they helped to convince Gladstone that something must be done to help the Irish. Apart from anything else, he was acutely conscious of the expense of holding the Irish down - there were more troops stationed in Ireland than in India.

(b) What were the grievances of the Irish in 1868? They fell into three main areas - *religious, economic and political.*

(i) *The Protestant Church of England (Anglican)* was the official or 'established' church in Ireland, but about 88 per cent of the Irish were Roman Catholic (just over 5.3 million out of a population of just under 6 million, according to the 1861 census). They had to pay tithes (a tax amounting to ten per cent of their annual income) to the Protestant church, even though they never attended its services, and since they also had to support their own churches and priests, the burden was heavy.

(ii) *There was intense poverty* because of the lack of industry and the land situation. Until the Act of Union (1800) there had been a prosperous Irish linen industry. But the Act introduced free trade between Ireland and England, and competition with the more advanced British ruined the Irish linen industry, causing widespread unemployment and forcing peasants to rely on farming for a living. The Irish economy therefore depended on agriculture being organised efficiently. However, most of the land was owned by wealthy Anglo-Irish landlords, many of whom lived in England, leaving agents to manage their property in Ireland. Irish peasants could only obtain land by renting it from the 'absentee' landlords. As the population grew rapidly during the nineteenth century, demand for land increased and original tenants sublet part of their holding; sometimes holdings were subdivided several times, so that by 1841, at least half the agricultural land of Ireland consisted of plots of less than five acres. The potato was the staple crop because it was possible to produce enough from one acre to keep a family of eight alive, whereas two acres would be needed to provide wheat for making bread. If tenants improved their holdings (by ditching, fencing or hedging) so that the value was enhanced, landlords would increase rents. The whole system was uneconomic; many landlords were only interested in profits, and being dissatisfied with their paltry income from rents, took to evicting tenants, so that small plots could be consolidated into large farms, where modern methods of agriculture could be introduced. Between 1860 and 1870 the number of people seeking poor relief almost doubled, and peasants could only retaliate against evictions by joining secret societies and indulging in acts of violence.

(iii) *There was a feeling of separateness among the Irish* who viewed the English as aliens. Many Irishmen blamed the English for the decay of their country. Such was the English lack of sympathy for the hardships of the Irish, and lack of understanding of Ireland's problems, that the feeling grew among the Irish that only when they were allowed to manage their own affairs would the country recover and prosper. *The Home Rule League*, formed in 1870 by *Isaac Butt*, a Protestant barrister, campaigned for a separate Irish parliament in Dublin to look after Irish internal affairs. At this stage the majority of the Irish were not thinking in terms of a complete break with Britain, and would have been happy for the Dublin parliament to be subordinate to Westminster for foreign affairs.

(c) What measures did Gladstone take and how successful were they?
Gladstone was the first British politician to show a real understanding of the Irish problem and a genuine desire to do something constructive about it, instead of simply holding the Irish down by force. His concern sprang from his religious conviction that all people had certain basic rights of freedom and fair treatment; it seemed to him that in both religious and economic matters, these rights were being denied to the Irish. When the news was brought to Gladstone in 1868 that he was about to be called on to form the next government, he was busy felling a tree on his Hawarden estate; the story goes that he laid down his axe and announced, 'My mission is to pacify Ireland'. *He did not have a great deal of success*, either during his first ministry or later. One of his difficulties was that Irish demands kept changing, becoming step by step more extreme, so Gladstone found that each of his concessions came too late and had already been overtaken by events. This was not necessarily the fault of the Irish: in fact the situation demanded the sort of drastic remedies which Gladstone was not prepared to take. This was not always because he was unwilling; the problem was that every time he tried to make a concession he had to face deeply entrenched opposition from groups in the British parliament – Anglican bishops and the Anglo-Irish landlords – whose interests were threatened.

(i) *The Irish Church Act (1869)* disestablished the Anglican Church in Ireland; this meant that although the Church still existed in Ireland, Anglicanism was no longer the official state religion and Roman

Catholics had no more tithes to pay to it. Much of its property and wealth was taken away and used to improve hospitals, workhouses and schools. There was strenuous opposition to it in the Lords, and the bill only passed after Queen Victoria had intervened.

The Act was the first major breach in the Union between Ireland and Britain, and was naturally well received by the Catholics. However, its effect on the general situation was slight, since the other grievances still remained. It won Gladstone some popularity with the Roman Catholic Church leaders, but this was later lost by the failure of his attempt to convert Trinity College Dublin into a University that could be attended by both Catholics and Protestants (Catholics were refusing to attend the College in its existing form because it was a Protestant institution). However, Catholic leaders wanted their own University, while Protestants objected to Catholics being admitted. In the end the bill pleased nobody and it was defeated in the Commons (1873).

(ii) *The First Irish Land Act (1870)* was an attempt to give some sort of protection to peasants. The courts were to make sure that landlords did not charge exorbitant rents; evicted tenants who had improved their holdings were to receive some compensation, even if they had been evicted for non-payment of rents. In addition a scale of damages was introduced for eviction, which varied according to the size of the holding; however, this did *not* apply if the tenant had been evicted for failure to pay rent. Unfortunately for all concerned, *the Act was an almost total failure*. It did not define how high an exorbitant rent was, and so landlords raised rents to ridiculously high levels which tenants could not possibly afford, and then evicted them for non-payment of rent. The courts which were supposed to be protecting tenants almost always supported landlord against tenant. In such cases, although he might receive a little compensation if he had improved his plot, the evicted tenant would get nothing on the scale of damages. What the Irish peasant most wanted – security of tenure (i.e. to be safe from eviction) – was therefore not provided by the Act. Why Gladstone allowed such an obviously ineffectual measure to be introduced is still a matter of some debate. Perhaps it had something to do with his respect for the view that property owners should be able to do as they wished with their estates; possibly he feared that a more radical measure specifying a fair rent and preventing evictions altogether would not pass the Lords. Whatever his reasons, the Act, far from solving the land problem, only served to arouse more ill-feeling, and peasant frustrations led to further violence and outrage in the countryside. So serious did the situation become that Gladstone introduced a *Coercion Act (1871)* giving the police extra powers of arrest and imprisonment. In spite of his good intentions, Gladstone had been forced back on the old policy of repression. This was a tragedy: if only he could have somehow produced an effective Land Act, all the bitterness might have been taken out of the situation. In that case, as

Karl Marx suggested, Ireland might have been more docile than Wales, and the demand for Home Rule would have been limited.

(iii) *The demand for Home Rule* left Gladstone unmoved during his first ministry, though he was to change his mind later (see Section 16.1(d)). There was hardly any support for it among English MPs, though nobody could have been more reasonable in his demands and his approach than Isaac Butt. When it became clear the Irish were making no progress using reasoned arguments and gentle persuasion, Butt was cast aside in favour of more extreme leaders, like *Charles Stewart Parnell*, who were prepared to use less gentlemanly tactics.

13.4 SHOW HOW GLADSTONE'S FOREIGN POLICIES CAUSED HIM TO BECOME UNPOPULAR

Gladstone was hampered in his foreign policies by his desire to protect Britain's interests while at the same time respecting the rights of other nations and avoiding foreign entanglements that might involve Britain in war; this must be avoided at all costs: Britain's army, even with Cardwell's reforms, was not in the same class as the German professional army. There were also the financial considerations: Gladstone had been very critical of Palmerston whose aggressive overseas policies had been expensive. Unfortunately for the Liberals, these considerations caused Gladstone to follow reasonable and realistic policies, which often appeared weak and spineless, in marked contrast to the recent Palmerstonian approach.

(a) Britain and the Franco-Prussian War (1870-1). The British government decided to remain neutral in this struggle which began in July 1870. There was no clear-cut reason why she should support one side or the other, and indeed there was no other realistic possibility: the Germans already had nearly half a million troops in the field whereas Britain, at a pinch, could have managed to get ten thousand across the Channel. However, British interests were involved in the war in two ways:

(i) *There was a danger that Belgium might be invaded* and it was well known that Napoleon III of France hoped to annex it sooner or later. Britain had traditionally been concerned to make sure that no major power controlled this stretch of European coastline, strategically placed as it was, so close to the British coast and the Thames estuary. In August Gladstone induced both Prussia and France to sign an agreement with Britain guaranteeing Belgian neutrality. This was seen as a triumph for Gladstone: both countries kept the agreement, Belgian neutrality was preserved and British interests safeguarded.

(ii) After France had suffered shattering defeats at Sedan (September) and Metz (October), the Russian government, with the support of Bismarck, announced that she no longer considered herself bound by the Black Sea clauses of the 1856 Treaty of Paris (see Section 10.3): she would patrol the Black Sea with her fleet, build bases and fortify the coastline. *This destroyed one of the main British advantages gained from the Crimean War* and provoked a storm of anti-Russian feeling in Britain. But the Russians had timed their announcement to perfection: with France, Britain's ally in the Crimea, on the verge of collapse, there was very little that she could do about it. After some diplomatic manoeuvring, a conference of the powers was held in London (January 1871) to review the situation. Britain suffered a clear diplomatic defeat: it was agreed that the Black Sea clauses were cancelled, though Lord Granville (the British Foreign Minister) saved face to some extent by securing a general agreement that from now on no government must break parts of a treaty unless all the other signatories agreed. The British government probably did as well as could be expected in the circumstances; A. J. P. Taylor believes (in *The Struggle for Mastery in Europe*) that the Russians signed the general agreement in all good faith and that because of it, they were prepared to agree to a re-negotiation of the Treaty of San Stefano in 1878 (see Section 14.4(e)). But the British public felt that Gladstone had acted weakly in allowing the Russians to steal a march over Britain – he had somehow let Britain down in a way which Palmerston would never have allowed.

(b) Gladstone and the Alabama case. Ever since the American Civil War (1861-5), the American government had claimed compensation from Britain for the damage caused by the *Alabama* and other ships built in Britain (see Section 9.5(c)). In 1868 Disraeli's government had expressed Britain's readiness to submit to arbitration, but it was Lord Granville, the Liberal Foreign Minister, who represented Britain at the arbitration conference held in Geneva. It was decided that Britain should pay the USA £3 250 000 in compensation, a decision which Gladstone accepted (1872). This was probably the sensible and moral thing to do, but coming after the Black Sea affair, it seemed to confirm the impression that Gladstone lacked backbone. There was a widespread feeling that the amount was unjustifiably high and that Gladstone should have said so. There is no doubt that the incident contributed towards the Liberals' growing unpopularity. One Conservative MP remarked that they showed 'a strange mania for eating dirt'. Shortly afterwards Gladstone was booed as he entered St Paul's for a thanksgiving service for the recovery of the Prince of Wales from typhoid; when Disraeli came along there was tumultuous applause.

13.5 WHY DID THE LIBERALS LOSE THE 1874 GENERAL ELECTION?

In January 1874 Gladstone decided that the time was ripe for a general election (though the Liberals had lost seven by-elections during 1873) and parliament was dissolved. His main programme was a pledge to abolish income tax, which he confidently assumed would be enough to swing the electorate. He was astonished and dismayed at the result: a decisive Conservative victory. The figures were: Conservatives 350, Liberals 245 and

Irish Home Rulers 57. The latter appeared in parliament for the first time because the 1872 Ballot Act allowed Irish tenants to vote as they wished without fear of reprisals from landlords. The Liberals were defeated partly because Gladstone's policies had offended so many influential people and because the Conservatives for the first time for many years appeared as a realistic alternative to the Liberals.

(a) Many of the Liberal reforms outraged the upper and wealthy classes, whose special privileges had been attacked, e.g. Civil Service and army reforms (especially abolition of the purchase of commissions). Many Anglicans resented the Irish Disestablishment Act and the University Test Act; some industrialists were annoyed at the legal recognition of Trade Unions. The Ballot Act was unpopular because it reduced landlords' influence at elections.

(b) The working classes were offended by Gladstone's apparently odd behaviour of offering help to the unions with one hand and taking it back with the other when he made picketing illegal. There was disappointment that the Liberals had introduced so little effective social reform and no further extension of the franchise. Gladstone himself thought that the Licensing Act was the decisive cause of his defeat: 'We have been borne down in a torrent of gin and beer', he told his brother, thought Robert Blake believes that although it may have cost him some votes, it was not the main reason for the defeat.

(c) Nonconformists were still smarting over the Forster Education Act; they vented their disapproval by abstaining rather than by voting Conservative, but it was still damaging, since traditionally Nonconformists were the mainstay of Liberal support.

(d) There was widespread dissatisfaction in all classes with Gladstone's conduct of foreign affairs.

(e) The Conservatives, ably led by Disraeli, had been mounting an effective attack on the government since April 1872 when Disraeli addressed a huge meeting in the Manchester Free Trade Hall. In a blistering speech lasting over three hours, during which he fortified himself with two bottles of white brandy, Disraeli ridiculed the Liberals as 'a range of exhausted volcanoes - not a flame flickers on a single pallid crest'. He went on to give the Conservative party a new image - a party which stood for the building up of the British Empire and which aimed to improve 'the condition of the people'. Disraeli was in fact seeking to cash in on Gladstone's weaknesses and omissions, and his popularity grew appreciably. During the election itself the party had the benefit of a highly efficient organisation built up by John Gorst and his new Conservative Central Office. Finally, Blake makes the point that many householders who had been enfranchised by the 1867 Reform Act voted for the first time in 1874, and voted Conservative – a belated thank you to Disraeli.

QUESTIONS

1. The Liberal Government and Foreign Affairs, 1868-74
Study Sources **A** to **G** and then answer the questions which follow.

Source A: the opinion of a modern historian.

> Rarely in our history has there been so complete a contrast between two famous contestants as that between Gladstone and Disraeli. Their profound difference in outlook and the questions over which they joined issue stand at the very root of foreign affairs and international relations.
>
> Source: R. Seton-Watson, *Disraeli, Gladstone and the Eastern Question*, Macmillan, 1935.

Source B: some information from another modern historian.

> The first task with which Gladstone had to deal was the seeming threat to Belgian neutrality with the outbreak of the Franco–Prussian War in 1870. It has been suggested that energetic action by Gladstone could have averted the outbreak of war between France and Prussia . . . Britain could perhaps have prevented war, but only by committing herself to intervention on one side or the other, and to this, public opinion was certainly opposed. It was also clear to Gladstone that Britain had not the military means at her disposal . . . The threat to Belgium, however, could not be ignored, and by August both belligerents had signed a treaty with Britain guaranteeing Belgian neutrality. An important British interest was successfully safeguarded.
>
> Source: B. H. Abbott, *Gladstone and Disraeli*, Collins, 1972.

Source C: Map of Europe in 1878.

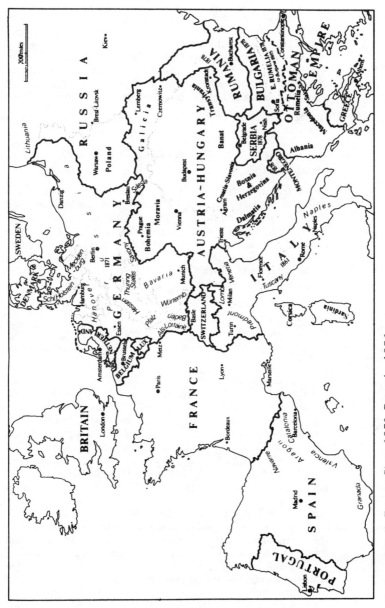

Source: J. Joll, *Europe Since 1870*, Penguin, 1976.

Source D: speech by Gladstone in the House of Commons, 10 August 1870.

What is our interest in maintaining the neutrality of Belgium? It is the same as that of every great power in Europe. It is contrary to the interests of Europe that there should be uncontrolled increase in the size of any one state. Is there any man who hears me who does not feel that if, in order to satisfy a greedy appetite for expansion, Belgium was absorbed, by no matter which power, the day that absorption took place, would hear the death knell of public right and public law in Europe?

Source: *Hansard Parliamentary Debates*, 1870 (adapted extracts).

Source E: speech by Disraeli in the House of Commons, in reply to Gladstone's speech.

I infer from the statement of the right honourable Gentleman that Her Majesty's Government have taken decided steps to maintain and defend the neutrality of Belgium. I accept this as a wise and spirited policy, in my opinion, not the less wise because it is spirited . . . Viewing it from a very limited point of view, it is of the highest importance to this country that the whole coast from Ostend to the North Sea should be in the hands of free and flourishing communities.

Source: *Hansard Parliamentary Debates*, 1870 (adapted extracts).

Source F: comments by a historian writing soon after the events took place.

The war introduced a new element of disturbance into English politics: Russia took advantage of the crippling of France to repudiate the clause of the Treaty of Paris of 1856 which neutralised the Black Sea and excluded foreign vessels from the Bosphorus. Many Englishmen were greatly worried by this unceremonious action, which they regarded as humiliating for themselves . . . The English government soon found that they would be practically alone in Europe if they were to attempt to bind Russia down to the treaty, so they invited the Powers to send representatives to a conference in London. The conference met and Russia was released from her engagement . . .

The critics of the government tried to make capital out of this, maintaining that we might have done more to keep the treaty in operation by taking up a firmer attitude to Russia. Mr. Disraeli on two occasions brought the matter before the House of Commons, saying that the conference had been called together merely to record the humiliation of this country. On many later occasions Mr. Gladstone has been blamed for his alleged lack of spirit in this business, as well as in the case of the *Alabama*. However, an impartial review of all the circumstances have led me to the conclusion that England could not help herself at that moment, and that the action of the Czar was perfectly natural.

Source: L. Apjohn, *William Ewart Gladstone: His Life and Times*, Walter Scott, 1884.

Source G: speech by Disraeli at Manchester, 3 April 1872.

As I sat opposite the Treasury Bench, the Ministers reminded me of one of those marine landscapes not very unusual on the coasts of South America. You behold a range of exhausted volcanoes. Not a single flame flickers on a single pallid crest . . . It would have been better for us all if there had been a little more energy in our foreign policy, and a little less in our domestic legislation.

Source: quoted in B. H. Abbott, *Gladstone and Disraeli*, Collins, 1972.

(a) **(i)** Explain in your own words the main point made by the writer of Source A. **4(a)**

(ii) Which war is referred to in Source **B**? **4(a)**

(iii) Using the evidence of Sources **B**, **C** and **D**, explain why there seemed to be a threat to the neutrality of Belgium. **4(a, c)**

(iv) Using the evidence of Sources **C**, **D** and **E**, explain why the British were so anxious to maintain the neutrality of Belgium. **4(a, c)**

(b) **(i)** Do you think that Disraeli (Source **E**) is supporting what Gladstone has said in Source **D** or not? Explain your answer fully. **4(a, c)**

(ii) From the evidence of Source **B**, why did Britain not interfere militarily in the war? **4(a)**

(iii) According to Source **B**, how was the problem of Belgian neutrality solved? **4(a)**

(c) **(i)** According to Source **F**, how had Russia taken advantage of the situation described in Source **B**?

(ii) Using your own knowledge and the evidence of Source **F**, why did many Englishmen feel this Russian action was humiliating for Britain? **1, 2, 4(a)**

(d) **(i)** According to Sources **F** and **G**, what criticisms were being made of Gladstone and his government? **4(a, c)**

(ii) Would you say that the writer of Source **F** was sympathetic to Gladstone or not? Give reasons for your answer. **4(a, b)**

(e) **(i)** From your own knowledge, explain briefly what the *Alabama* incident was, referred to in Source **F**. **1, 2, 4(a)**

(ii) What part did Gladstone play in the *Alabama* incident? **1, 2**

(iii) Why was Gladstone criticised for this action? **1, 2**

(f) (i)   What are the advantages and disadvantages of Sources **D, E, F** and **G** for the historian?   **4(a, b)**

(ii)   From your own knowledge and the evidence of the Sources, would you agree with the claim made by Disraeli in Source **G**, that Gladstone's conduct of foreign policy ought to have been more energetic, during the years 1868–74?   **1, 2, 4(a, c)**

(iii) Do you think that the evidence of the other Sources supports the point made in Source **A**, for the period 1868–74 (i.e. Gladstone's First Ministry)?   **4(a, c)**

2. Liberal Reforms

Study the extract and then answer the questions which follow.

> Gladstone gave his full backing to Cardwell's army reforms and played a full part in the battle to abolish the purchase of commissions in 1871. The obstruction by the Tories in the Commons and the rejection of abolition by the Lords were two of the many incidents which confirmed Gladstone's view of the upper classes as selfish and lacking in moral sense. Gladstone was much attacked by them for his *coup d'état* in which abolition of purchase was carried out by royal warrant. On this occasion Gladstone and Cardwell were backed by a united cabinet and even the Queen played her part without objection.

Source: E. J. Feuchtwanger, *Gladstone*, Allen Lane, 1975 (adapted extracts).

(a)   Using your own knowledge, explain why Gladstone and Cardwell wanted to abolish the purchase of commissions in the army.   **1, 2**

(b) (i)   According to the extract, how did the Tories try to prevent the government from abolishing the purchase of commissions?
                                                                                      4(a)

(ii)   What was Gladstone's view of the upper classes, according to this extract?   **4(a)**

(iii) How did Gladstone overcome the opposition to his policy?
                                                                                      4(a)

(iv)   Why do you think the writer of this extract uses the phrase '*coup d'état*' in connection with the abolition of the purchase of commissions?   **4(a)**

(c) (i)   What other changes did Cardwell introduce into the army?
                                                                                      1, 2

(ii)   How successful were these changes?   **1, 2**

(d)   Gladstone and the Liberals also introduced important changes in the Civil Service, the system of voting and the licensing of public houses. For each one of these:

(i) Describe the changes that were introduced;
(ii) Explain which groups of people opposed the change and the reasons for their opposition. 1, 2

3. 'My mission is to pacify Ireland', Gladstone is reported to have said in 1868.

(a) Explain why Ireland needed to be pacified in 1868.

(b) Describe how Gladstone tried to deal with Ireland's problems by introducing the Irish Church Act (1869) and the First Irish Land Act (1870).

(c) Explain why both these attempts were less successful than Gladstone hoped. 1, 2

4. It is early in 1874 and you are an Irish Roman Catholic supporter of Home Rule who is to make a speech in Dublin at a meeting of the Home Rule League. Write a draft of your speech, mentioning among other things:

(a) your feelings about Gladstone's religious policies;

(b) your disappointment with the 1870 Land Act;

(c) your opinions about Gladstone and the English;

(d) your reasons for having decided that Home Rule is the only way forward for Ireland. 1, 2, 3

CHAPTER 14

DISRAELI AND THE CONSERVATIVES IN POWER 1874–80

SUMMARY OF EVENTS

This was the first Conservative government to have real power since the collapse of Peel's ministry in 1846. The Conservatives were now more or less united under Disraeli's leadership and enjoyed a comfortable majority of nearly 50 over Liberals and Home Rulers, who usually voted with the Liberals. It was an eventful ministry: Lytton Strachey in his biography of Queen Victoria called it 'six years of excitement, of enchantment, of felicity, of glory, of romance'. Disraeli was much more to the Queen's liking than Gladstone; the Liberal leader exhausted her with complicated documents and explanations – she complained that 'he speaks to me as if I were a public meeting'. Disraeli on the other hand was careful to charm and flatter her; 'everyone likes flattery', he said, 'and when you come to royalty you should lay it on with a trowel'. In 1876 Disraeli accepted a peerage, taking the title *Earl of Beaconsfield.*

In keeping with his ideas of '*Tory Democracy*', or '*New Conservatism*' the early part of the ministry saw *important social reforms* dealing with housing, public health, factories, education and trade unions. *In overseas affairs* he was determined to restore Britain's prestige which was felt to have waned under Gladstone. When *the Eastern Question* flared up again, Disraeli took a firm stand against the Russians, culminating in *the Congress of Berlin in 1878*; this was hailed as a great triumph for Britain and a resounding diplomatic defeat for the Russians. He did all he could *to defend and strengthen the British Empire*, in Egypt, India, South Africa (Zulu War) and Afghanistan.

In the meantime *all was not well with the British economy*: in the late 1870s industry ran into a serious depression, while agriculture suffered a near-disaster because of rapidly growing foreign competition. Even so, most people were surprised when the general election of March 1880 reversed the situation in parliament, bringing Gladstone and the Liberals back again with an overall majority of around 50. Disraeli took his defeat well, but his health was deteriorating, and he died just over a year later (April 1881).

14.1 DISRAELI'S EARLY CAREER AND HIS POLITICAL OUTLOOK - TORY DEMOCRACY

(a) Benjamin Disraeli was the son of a Jewish writer and scholar whose family had come to England from Venice in the middle of the eighteenth century. The young Disraeli was educated at an obscure private school and then worked as a solicitor's clerk. He wrote several novels and tried unsuccessfully to get into parliament - as a Whig. At the fourth attempt he was elected as an MP - for Maidstone (1837), having changed his allegiance to the Tories. He already had a reputation as something of a gambler and a flashy dresser. He had appeared at one society dinner dressed in green velvet trousers, a canary coloured waistcoat, low shoes with silver buckles, lace at his wrists, and his hair in tightly curled ringlets. His maiden speech in parliament was a disaster: he used such extravagant and flowery language that he was shouted down with catcalls and shrieks of laughter. He soon improved his technique and was furious when Peel failed to offer him a place in his government in 1841. Perhaps because of this *he led the attack on Peel over the Corn Law repeal* in 1846 (see Section 7.5(d)). He was Chancellor of the Exchequer in the Conservative governments of 1852, 1858-9 and 1866-8 and was largely responsible for the 1867 Reform Act (see Section 8.4); apart from that he had achieved nothing of great significance. He was Prime Minister for a few months in 1868 after Lord Derby's retirement; this was a remarkable achievement, given his unconventional background. Although he had been baptised a Christian at the age of 13, he had to put up with a great deal of anti-Semitic feeling. It speaks volumes for his brilliance as a politician that in spite of all these disadvantages, he was able, as he put it, to 'climb to the top of the greasy pole'.

(b) By the time he became Prime Minister for the second time in 1874, Disraeli had perfected his ideas about the direction he wanted the Conservative party to take; these are sometimes referred to as *Tory Democracy* or *New Conservatism*;

(i) He believed that there was value in privilege and tradition and wanted to preserve the power of the long-established institutions - the Anglican Church, the aristocracy and above all, the monarchy. But it was essential that these institutions used their power wisely and unselfishly, for the good of the whole community.

(ii) It was vitally important for the government and the privileged classes to help working people. In his novel *Sybil* (1845) Disraeli had written about how there were really two separate nations living in Britain - the Rich and the Poor; though he had no intention of upsetting the class structure, he believed that something must be done to improve the conditions of the poor. He said so in his Manchester speech of 1872: 'Pure air, pure water, the inspection of unhealthy habitations, the adulteration of food . . . it is impossible to overrate the importance of the subjects; after all, the first consideration of a Minister should be the health of the people'. This was a paternalistic approach (treating the poor kindly as a benevolent father looks after his children).

(iii) Disraeli hoped that social reform would lead to an alliance between the privileged classes and the mass of the population, which would strengthen the monarchy and aristocracy; as he revealingly remarked: 'the Palace is unsafe if the cottage is unhappy'.

(iv) The Conservative party, in other words, must adapt itself and come to terms with the new democratic and industrial age. If it failed to win working class support, it would be condemned to remain a permanent party of opposition. He was highly critical of the Liberals because of their attack on privilege; he called them an 'anti-national party' and despised them because they seemed to look after the interests of the middle class at the expense of the workers. This, he said, made them 'odious to the English people'.

(v) He took up imperialism as a positive Conservative theme and hoped to develop the British Empire as a powerful economic and political union under the monarchy. Only in this way, he believed, could Britain continue to compete successfully with the great continental empires of the USA, Germany and Russia.

(c) Disraeli's motives have aroused some controversy. He has been accused of not genuinely caring about social problems and of taking up social reform simply to score points over Gladstone who neglected it. Political hard-headedness probably came into it: it was an obvious way to attract and hold on to working class support. On the other hand, Disraeli had talked and written sympathetically about the conditions of the poor as far back as the 1840s; it was not something that he had suddenly taken up in 1872 because of Gladstone's failings.

14.2 WHAT DID DISRAELI'S GOVERNMENT DO FOR THE WORKING MAN?

(a) Improvements in public health and living conditions

(i) *The Public Health Act* and *The Artisans' Dwellings Act*, whose details were worked out by Richard Cross, Disraeli's Home Secretary, were passed in 1875 (see Section 12.5(a)).

(ii) *The Sale of Food and Drugs Act* (also 1875) laid down stringent regulations about the preparation and adulteration of food.

(iii) *The Enclosures Act* (1876) was designed to protect the public's right to use the common pasture land; landowners were restricted from absorbing such land into their estates, so that it would be kept free from building. Thus the idea of the green belt was born.

(iv) It was made illegal to tip solid industrial waste into rivers (1876) and liquid could only be discharged if it was non-poisonous.

All these acts met with success, although the Artisans' Dwellings Act would have made more impact if it had been compulsory. Even so, as B. H. Abbott points out, 'the legislation of those years laid the foundations of modern public health so thoroughly and lastingly that no major changes were required for over 60 years'.

(b) The Factory Acts of 1874 and 1878 introduced important new limitations on working hours (see Section 12.3(j)).

(c) Labour relations and trade union legislation

(i) *The Conspiracy and Protection of Property Act (1875).* Trade unionists had been bitterly disappointed by their treatment at the hands of the Liberals in 1871: although unions had been given legal recognition, picketing, even if it was peaceful, was not allowed, so that it was more or less impossible to make a strike effective. This new measure, again introduced by Cross, made peaceful picketing legal and allowed unions to carry out as a group whatever actions an individual was permitted to take, in support of their case; unions could not now be charged with conspiracy for taking such action.

(ii) *The Employers and Workmen Act (1876),* another Cross measure, put both employer and worker on an equal footing in cases of breach of contract. Previously, if a workman broke his contract, it was treated as a criminal offence, whereas if an employer did it, it was regarded only as a civil offence, for which the penalties were much lighter. Now both were treated as civil offences.

These two acts mark a vitally important breakthrough in the development and recognition of trade unions as acceptable and respectable bodies (see Section 19.3(b)). Trade union leaders were delighted, and so was Disraeli who remarked that these laws 'will gain and retain for the Conservatives the lasting affection of the working classes'.

(d) Sandon's Education Act (1876) was less effective than it might have been because it lacked the element of compulsion (see Section 12.7(d)).

(e) The Merchant Shipping Act (1876) was passed after a vigorous campaign by its author, Samuel Plimsoll. The problem was that there were no regulations governing the loading and repair of merchant ships. It was not unknown for unscrupulous shipowners to overload decrepit and over-insured vessels so that they could make a handsome profit if the ships sank. Plimsoll's bill was designed to prevent this scandalous sacrifice of seamen's lives, but the shipowning interests in parliament delayed it as long as they could. Plimsoll became so exasperated that he caused a scene in the Commons, literally jumping up and down with rage and shaking his fist at Disraeli. This produced results and the bill passed. A line (known as the Plimsoll line) was to be painted on the side of every ship to show the maximum loading point. However, the shipowners had the last laugh, for the time being, because the act allowed *them* to paint the line where they thought fit. Only in 1890 did Board of Trade officials begin to apply the regulations as Plimsoll had intended.

Taken together, all these measures 'constitute the biggest instalment of social reform passed by any one government in the nineteenth century' (Blake); Alexander Macdonald, one of the Engineers' leaders, was so impressed that he went on record as saying that 'the Conservative Party has done more for the working class in five years than the Liberals have done in fifty'.

14.3 WHAT IS MEANT BY THE TERM 'IMPERIALISM' AND HOW SUCCESSFUL WAS DISRAELI IN PURSUING IT?

Imperialism was the belief that it was a good idea for Britain to control territory abroad (colonies, protectorates and dependencies) which would be valuable for trade (sources of raw materials and markets for British exports). The idea of Empire was not new, but Disraeli added his special twist to it: it should not simply be a case of Britain making use of her overseas possessions; she had a duty to bring the benefits of British civilisation – 'courage, discipline, patience, reverence for public law, and respect for national rights' – to primitive peoples. Kipling later described this duty as 'the white man's burden'. Disraeli also had in mind that the Empire could be called on for military help if Britain became involved in war.

Later, 'imperialism' became a term of abuse; Gladstone was one of the first critics who claimed that imperialism was bad because it interfered with the rights and freedom of overseas peoples; in addition it was expensive – a waste of British wealth and manpower; defence of the Empire would be a constant strain on British resources.

Disraeli had no specific plans for pursuing imperialism, but in the early years of his ministry he made excellent use of circumstances. This, together with his successful stand against the Russians at the Congress of Berlin in 1878 (see next section), coming after six years of Gladstonian 'weakness' in overseas affairs, dazzled the public. Towards the end of his term, however, the imperialist adventures in South Africa and Afghanistan, though they both ended successfully, were badly mishandled along the way.

(a) Disraeli and Egypt: The Suez Canal shares (1875)

(i) The Suez Canal (opened in 1869) was controlled jointly by the French and the Khedive Ismail, the ruler of Egypt. In 1875 the Khedive, who was in serious financial difficulty, decided to sell his shares which amounted to seven-sixteenths of the total. There was a strong possibility that a French company would buy them, posing the threat of complete French control of the Canal, which had already proved itself a vital link between Britain and India.

(ii) The Khedive was asking for four million pounds which the French company had difficulty in raising. Disraeli seized the opportunity: after securing the approval of the cabinet, not without difficulty, he stepped in and bought the shares for the British government, using four million pounds lent by the banking house of Rothschilds.

(iii) It is difficult to imagine any other politician of the time acting with such flair and panache, and there is no doubt that it was a splendid piece of opportunism. Although Britain had fewer than half the shares in the Canal, the important point was that France had been prevented from gaining exclusive control, which would have given them great bargaining power over the Khedive, and the shorter trade-route to India had been safeguarded. The British were soon able to get the tolls reduced, and ownership of the shares turned out to be profitable; by 1898 they were valued at over £24 million. The cost of transporting cargo to and from Australia and New Zealand was reduced by 75 per cent.

(iv) Gladstone was highly critical of the purchase, calling it 'a ruinous and mischievous misdeed'. He believed that it would result in an eventual British occupation of Egypt, and although Disraeli denied any such intention, Gladstone was later proved to be right (see Section 16.2(c)).

(b) Victoria becomes Empress of India (1876). This was not Disraeli's idea; it had been discussed on and off since the Mutiny in 1857, and the Queen herself was eager for it. Disraeli was anxious to oblige, and the Royal Titles Act duly passed through parliament, though only after surprisingly spirited resistance in both houses. Gladstone called it 'theatrical bombast'. However, there seemed good reason for Victoria to take the title:

(i) It demonstrated that the British had every intention of staying in India, and it was hoped that the new personal link with the Queen would mean more to the Indians than their relationship with an impersonal parliament.

(ii) It was a symbolic gesture warning off the Russians who were extending their influence into Persia and Afghanistan, and who, it was feared, had designs on India.

(c) South Africa: The Zulu War (1879). Again this was not part of Disraeli's intentions; it was forced upon him by the actions of the men on the spot and Disraeli was furious when the situation turned into war.

(i) *The background* was complicated: the Cape of Good Hope was originally colonised by Dutch settlers, but as a result of the Congress of Vienna (1815), ownership of the Cape passed to Britain. Many of the Dutch farmers, known as Boers (or Afrikaners), disliked British rule, and in 1836 many thousands of them left the Cape in *The Great Trek*. They founded two new states of their own, Transvaal and the Orange Free State. The British still claimed sovereignty over them, and for many years relations between the new Boer republics and the two British colonies – the Cape and Natal – remained strained. Tension eased after the British recognised the independence of the Transvaal (by the Sand River Convention, 1852) and the Free State (by the Convention of Bloemfontein, 1854).

(ii) A constant threat to both British and Boers was the presence on the Transvaal/Natal border of the large and aggressive Zulu tribe under their king, *Cetewayo*. The Boers had already had one major clash with the Zulus at Blood River (1838) in which 3000 Zulus were slaughtered. Cetewayo was eager to avenge this defeat, though he was not unfriendly to the British.

(iii) Disraeli's Colonial Secretary, *Lord Carnarvon*, who in 1867 had been responsible for uniting the four provinces of Canada into a single federation (see Section 18.1(e)), had similar plans for South Africa. He hoped to bring the Transvaal and the Orange Free State under British control in a union with the Cape and Natal. The snag was that the circumstances in South Africa were completely different from those in Canada: the Boers were hostile to the idea and the Cape and Natal, where lots of Boers had remained, were unenthusiastic.

(iv) Carnarvon decided that the Boers, who were also being harassed by another tribe, the Bapedi, as well as by the Zulus, would be glad of British protection. He sent *Sir Theophilus Shepstone*, an ex-governor of Natal, to the Transvaal to sound the Boers out. He found them extremely nervous about Cetewayo's intentions and also nearly bankrupt with only twelve shillings and sixpence in the treasury. Reluctantly the Transvaal president, Burgers, agreed to a British annexation of the republic (though he was allowed to protest in public); Shepstone promised the Boers self-government later.

(v) Carnarvon also appointed *Sir Bartle Frere* as High Commissioner for South Africa with instructions to set up a federation. Frere was a well-known supporter of expansionist policies and was indignant when he discovered that Shepstone had promised the Boers self-government. He decided that the Zulu threat would have to be destroyed before a peaceful federation of South Africa could be achieved. Disraeli and the cabinet did not want a war in South Africa at this time, as they were preoccupied with the situation in the Balkans and the British were already involved in hostilities in Afghanistan. Frere was given strict orders not to start a native war, but he deliberately disobeyed instructions and took it upon himself to launch an invasion of Zululand (January 1879).

(vi) The beginning of the war was disastrous for the British: the Commander, Lord Chelmsford and his section of the invading army, were surprised by a 20 000 strong Zulu army at *Isandhlwana*. Chelmsford had ignored advice from the Boers to *laager* his wagons (arrange them in a circle) and suffered a crushing defeat, losing over a thousand men. The same night a much smaller force which had *laagered* properly, held out against the Zulus at *Rorke's Drift* and saved Natal from invasion, though casualties were heavy. In June there was a further blow when the Prince Imperial (son of the former French emperor Napoleon III), who had volunteered to fight with the British, was killed by a Zulu raiding party. These events caused a public outcry in Britain.

(vii) Disraeli was intensely angry with Frere, but felt he had to send reinforcements to South Africa. In the end Chelmsford redeemed himself by decisively defeating the Zulus at *Ulundi*, Cetewayo's capital (July 1879). Cetewayo was captured and deported and the Zulu threat was finally removed.

(viii) However, much criticism had been aroused; the Liberals enjoyed themselves complaining about the unprovoked attack on the Zulus, the loss of life and the expense involved, and although Carnarvon and Frere were to blame, Disraeli had to take the responsibility. Even the victory left a new problem: now that the Zulu threat had disappeared, the Transvaal demanded its independence again. It was clear that a more subtle approach would have been to delay or even abandon altogether the complete destruction of Zulu power, so that the continuing menace would frighten the Transvaal into remaining under British protection. It was a problem which Gladstone inherited in his next ministry (see Section 16.2(b)).

(d) The Second and Third Afghan Wars (1878-80)

(i) The British were interested in what happened in Afghanistan because they looked on it as a buffer state to protect India from Russian attentions. Disraeli wanted to build up good relations with the Amir of Afghanistan, Sher Ali, in the hope that he would have nothing to do with the Russians, who were also hoping to bring Afghanistan within their 'sphere of influence'.

(ii) Disraeli appointed *Lord Lytton* as Viceroy of India, with instructions to persuade Sher Ali to accept a British mission at his capital, Kabul. Lytton, like Sir Bartle Frere, was a well-known advocate of expansionist or 'forward' imperialist policies, and as it turned out, he too could not be relied upon to obey orders. According to Blake, 'he was curiously unbalanced in judgement' and became dangerously impatient when he failed to make progress with Sher Ali. It was not a wise appointment.

(iii) In July 1878 a Russian military mission arrived in Kabul. Disraeli ordered Lytton to take no action until the situation had been discussed with the Russians through proper diplomatic channels. However, the Viceroy, itching to get the Russians out, ignored this and sent 35 000 troops under Sir Frederick Roberts into Afghanistan. The Russians withdrew, Sher Ali was driven out and his son Yakub Khan was placed on the throne. In May 1879 he signed a treaty of friendship with Britain; a British minister and staff took up residence in

Kabul. Although Disraeli was secretly displeased with Lytton, this Second Afghan War seemed to have been completely successful.

(iv) The achievement did not last: in September 1879 the British minister and the entire mission were murdered by rebel tribesmen and a Third Afghan War was necessary to re-establish British control. Roberts again took Kabul but it was now clear that a large section of the Afghans resented British influence and serious fighting broke out in the south of the country. Before order was restored, Disraeli's government had been defeated (April 1880), and it was left to Gladstone to preside over the final stages of the problem. Roberts carried out a brilliantly executed 300 mile march from Kabul to Kandahar, the main centre of resistance, and in August completely annihilated the rebel army. Again British control was complete.

(v) The Liberals criticised the 'wanton invasion' of an independent nation and even Lord Salisbury, the Foreign Minister, thought Disraeli should have kept tighter control over Lytton. The Gladstone government removed Lytton and withdrew British troops and the British mission from Afghanistan. It looked as though all Roberts's efforts had been a waste of time. However, the new Amir, who owed his position to Roberts, remained friendly to Britain for the next 20 years, and the Russians refrained from interfering in Afghanistan again, except for the Penjdeh incident in 1885 (see Section 16.2(e)). It is possible to argue therefore that Disraeli's policy had been a success after all – British military efficiency made a deep impression both in Afghanistan and in Russia.

(e) **Disraeli and Ireland**. In general Disraeli had no understanding of small nations, such as those in the Balkans, who were struggling for independence. He saw Ireland in the same light – a troublesome possession trying to break away from Britain as the Balkans peoples were trying to win freedom from Turkey. Given his desire to consolidate the Empire, he naturally did not see Home Rule as the solution to Ireland's problems. Towards the end of his government, the situation in Ireland deteriorated further because of a severe agricultural depression; an increasing number of peasants failed to pay their rents and landlords evicted them on a larger scale than ever before. But Disraeli was unmoved; according to Blake, 'he was at heart wholly out of sympathy with the Irish . . . and he never did or said anything helpful to them'. One of his last pronouncements before the general election of 1880 was to warn the British government of the dangers of Home Rule.

14.4 THE EASTERN QUESTION AND THE CONGRESS OF BERLIN 1875–8

(a) **Background to the Balkans crisis**. The crisis which erupted in the Balkans in 1875 was a recurrence of the Eastern Question which had plagued international relations since early in the nineteenth century. For a full explanation of its origins see Section 3.3(b) (iv). It was hoped that the Eastern Question had been solved by the Treaty of Paris (1856) which ended the Crimean War: the Russians were not allowed to have warships on the Black Sea - a severe check to their ambitions in the Balkans and Near East. The Sultan of Turkey had promised to treat his Christian subjects fairly, so that the usual Russian excuse for intervention in the Balkans - that they wanted to protect the Christians living under Turkish rule - would no longer be available. But British calculations were upset in two ways:

(i) In 1870 the Russians announced that they no longer felt bound by the Black Sea clauses (see Section 13.4(a)).

(ii) The Turks ignored their promises and continued to over-tax and generally to persecute their Balkan Christians. This led to a rebellion in Bosnia and Herzegovina, which soon spread to Serbia, Montenegro and Bulgaria.

The main European powers - Germany, Austria, Hungary, Russia, France and Italy (but excluding Britain) sent the Berlin Memorandum to the Turks, protesting about their harshness and calling on them to make peace and behave themselves.

(b) What was Disraeli's attitude?

(i) He was deeply suspicious about Russian intentions - if she intervened to help the Balkan Christians, there seemed every chance that the whole of the Balkans, perhaps even Constantinople and the Dardanelles, would fall under Russian control.

(ii) He also distrusted the motives of the Austrians and Germans and suspected them of scheming with the Russians to partition the Ottoman Empire.

(iii) He therefore wanted to preserve Turkish power as the best way of maintaining British interests in the Near East. He had no sympathy with the peoples of the Balkans in their struggle for independence.

(iv) For these reasons he refused to support the Berlin Memorandum, but this refusal encouraged the new Sultan Abdul Hamid to think that he could rely on British support no matter what happened. The Turks redoubled their efforts to crush the rebels and in Bulgaria some terrible atrocities were committed. Turkish irregular troops, known as Bashi-Bazouks, took vicious reprisals on Bulgarian peasants, slaughtering at least 12000 men, women and children. This was embarrassing for Disraeli: he felt bound to condemn the Turks though he did not change his determination to support them against Russia if necessary.

(c) Gladstone's attack on the Turks

(i) Gladstone's attitude was the direct opposite of Disraeli's. He saw it as a purely moral issue - the threat from Russia paled into insignificance beside the appalling Turkish massacres of innocent Christians. He was so incensed that he published a pamphlet, *The Bulgarian Horrors and the Question of the East* (September 1876), which rapidly became a best-seller. It contained a blistering attack on the evils of Turkish rule, their 'abominable and bestial lusts', and the foul deeds by which women and children had been violated, roasted and impaled. He hoped that the Turks 'one and all, bag and baggage, shall clear out from the province they have desolated and profaned', and he went so far as to urge the Russians to expel them from Bulgaria as soon as possible.

(ii) As a result, much of British public opinion turned against the Turks, making it more difficult for Disraeli to maintain an anti-Russian front. He retorted that Gladstone was worse than any Bulgarian Horror, and relations between the two men became irretrievably embittered. In fact many Liberals thought Gladstone had grossly over-reacted and was tempting fate by encouraging the Russians.

(d) War between Russia and Turkey

(i) The Russian Tsar Alexander II, possibly influenced by Gladstone's attitude, announced that he could no longer stand by and allow Turkish atrocities to continue (November 1876). Frantic negotiations followed during which the Russians gave assurances that they would not capture Constantinople and the Dardanelles, and that they had no intention of interfering with the Suez Canal and India; consequently Britain agreed to remain neutral.

(ii) The Russians declared war on Turkey (April 1877); their forces marched southwards into the Balkans and besieged the fortress of Plevna which held out from June to December. The Russians did not distinguish themselves and progress was painfully slow against unexpectedly strong Turkish resistance. However, by January 1878 they had reached Adrianople, not much more than 100 miles from Constantinople.

(iii) Doubts began to creep in – would the Russians keep their promises? Now that Constantinople was threatened, British public opinion veered round to become pro-Turkish; mobs hooted Gladstone in the streets and smashed his windows.

(iv) Disraeli acted promptly: he demanded an armistice and ordered British warships to Constantinople where they arrived in February 1878. By now Russian troops were in San Stefano on the outskirts of Constantinople. Disraeli warned that if they captured it, Britain would declare war; tension was high and a European war seemed imminent as the British prepared an expeditionary force.

(v) The attack on Constantinople never came. The Russian commanders realised that the Turks would throw everything into the defence of their capital; the Russian troops were nearing exhaustion and there were not enough of them to defeat 100000 Turks. Disraeli claimed, perhaps with some justification, that the British threats had also influenced the Russians. Peace negotiations opened and . . .

(e) The Treaty of San Stefano was signed between Russia and Turkey (March 1878). Naturally the terms were favourable to Russia and there was an immediate outcry from Britain and Austria when they became known:

   (i) Serbia, Montenegro and Romania were recognised as independent of Turkey.

  (ii) Russia took Bessarabia from Romania giving her control of the Danube mouth. This alarmed the Austrians who depended on the Danube as a vital trade outlet into the Black Sea; nor was there any mention of Bosnia and Herzegovina being given to Austria which the Russians had mentioned as a reward for Austria remaining neutral.

 (iii) A large independent state of Bulgaria was set up; referred to as Big Bulgaria, it stretched right across the Balkan peninsula with coastlines both on the Black Sea and the Aegean Sea. For 'an initial period'

Map 14.1 *Balkan frontiers after the Congress of Berlin 1878*

Bulgaria would be administered by Russian army officers. This was the most sensational clause of all; the British and Austrians were convinced that Big Bulgaria would be a satellite of Russia, giving her the use of a port on the Aegean, so that she would be able to by-pass the Dardanelles. The Balkan peoples had exchanged rule by Turkey for rule by Russia.

Britain and Austria protested in the strongest terms: Disraeli called up the reserves and sent 7000 Indian troops to Malta. Moderate opinion prevailed in Russia and it was decided not to risk a conflict with both Britain and Austria. Bismarck, the German Chancellor, offered to act as 'honest broker', and the Russians agreed to attend an international Congress in Berlin to renegotiate the peace terms.

(f) The Congress of Berlin (June–July 1878). Many of the issues had been settled at preliminary discussions, but there were still some important points to be decided when the representatives met. Disraeli himself led the British delegation, ably assisted by the new Foreign Secretary, Lord Salisbury. Disraeli dominated the Congress with his vitality and the force of his personality, though most of the detailed work was carried out by Salisbury. Between them they achieved nearly everything they wanted and still had time to enjoy the incessant receptions, parties and banquets. The terms of the new agreement were:

(i) The idea of a Big Bulgaria was dropped; it was divided into three: a small independent state of Bulgaria in the north (Little Bulgaria), in the centre an area known as Eastern Roumelia, belonging to Turkey but having self-government under a Christian governor; the rest – Macedonia – was to remain part of the Turkish Empire, with no Christian governor.
(ii) The Austrians were allowed to occupy and administer Bosnia and Herzegovina, though nominally it still belonged to Turkey.
(iii) The Turks allowed Britain to occupy Cyprus in return for military help if Russia should attack again; there were more Turkish promises of fair treatment for the Christians.

(g) How successful was the Congress? At the time it was thought of as a great British victory, and a personal triumph for Disraeli who drove from the station to Downing Street through cheering crowds. 'We have brought back peace with honour', he declared. It was the crowning achievement of his career: not only was he a successful Prime Minister, he was also now a highly respected international statesman who had achieved most of what he hoped for at Berlin:

(i) Russia had been checked in her advance through the Balkans towards the Dardanelles and British interests in the Near East safeguarded – and all without war.
(ii) The association of Austria, Germany and Russia (the *Dreikaiserbund* – League of Three Emperors) which Disraeli had so mistrusted, was

destroyed. Russia was now on poor terms with Austria and her relations with Germany (which had failed to support her at Berlin) were never the same again.

(iii) Turkey had been bolstered up against further Russian expansion attempts and Britain had a strong position in the eastern Mediterranean with the acquisition of Cyprus.

Blake believes that Disraeli deserves immense credit because the Congress gave Europe over 30 years of peace.

Some other historians have emphasised the drawbacks of the settlement:

(i) Bulgaria, far from becoming a Russian puppet state as expected, was determined to maintain her independence and turned out to be strongly anti-Russian. Salisbury later admitted that he and Disraeli had 'backed the wrong horse', meaning that from the British point of view it would have been better to have kept Big Bulgaria.

(ii) The Austrian occupation of Bosnia aroused resentment in Serbia which was hoping to expand in that area. In the words of A. J. P. Taylor, this 'contained the seeds of future disaster' – it was the beginning of Austro-Serbian friction which was to culminate in the outbreak of the First World War in 1914.

(iii) The Turks again failed to keep their promises and made no attempt to reform or strengthen their state. Many of the Balkans peoples remained under Turkish rule which was therefore unacceptable to them. Thus the Eastern Question was not solved permanently and there would be further disturbances and crises.

In the autumn of 1878 though, none of this was apparent, and if a general election had been held then, there is little doubt that Disraeli and the Conservatives would have won easily.

14.5 WHY DID THE CONSERVATIVES LOSE THE 1880 GENERAL ELECTION?

After a surprise by-election victory in which the Conservatives won the Liberal stronghold of Southwark, Disraeli judged that the tide was running in his favour. The general election (April) showed that he had miscalculated badly; the figures were: Liberals 353, Conservatives 238, Irish Home Rulers 61. Yet it was less than two years since his triumph at Berlin; *what had gone wrong?*

(a) There was disappointment and criticism about subsequent overseas events which spoiled the Disraeli image of the international diplomatic master. There was the mishandling of the Zulu War and the fiasco in Afghanistan which had not been resolved when the election took place.

(b) There was growing disapproval of the lack of social reform. Although the government had begun well, after 1876 no major reforming measure was introduced. This was partly because Disraeli was occupied with foreign affairs and partly because the 59 Irish MPs, having failed to secure Home Rule by reasoned argument, resorted to tactics of obstruction; more than once they kept the Commons up all night talking about Irish affairs and the government could find no way of dealing with them.

(c) 1875 saw the beginning of an industrial slump which caused unemployment to shoot up rapidly. In 1872 only about one per cent of trade union members were out of work, but by 1879 the figure was as high as 11 per cent. In some trades the situation was even worse - 22 per cent of registered engineers were without work. It was the first taste of foreign competition which was to oust Britain from her economic leadership of the world, and the beginning of what became known as *The Great Depression* (see Sections 15.2 and 15.4).

(d) There was an even more severe agricultural depression caused by a massive influx of cheap corn from North America and by a series of wet summers. Hundreds of farmers went bankrupt and thousands of farm labourers were put out of work. Most other European countries introduced tariffs, but Disraeli refused to do so, and was naturally criticised for it by the farming interests; his argument was that free trade in corn would keep down the cost of living for the workers.

(e) Gladstone, who had retired from the Liberal leadership after their defeat in 1874, re-emerged as the real Liberal leader and conducted a stunning campaign starting in his constituency of Midlothian and travelling the length of the country. He attacked Disraeli's policies as 'immoral and iniquitous': the Afghan war was 'a crime against God', and Cyprus was 'a valueless encumbrance'. Perhaps his most successful speech was the one in St Andrew's Hall, Glasgow, to a crowded audience of over 6000. For a man of over 70, *The Midlothian Campaign* (November–December 1879) followed by a repeat performance just before the election, was a remarkable achievement. Disraeli, approaching 80 and in failing health was unable to provide an effective answer.

(f) Finally the Liberal party organisation had reached peak efficiency under the guidance of Joseph Chamberlain (see Section 17.1(b)), whereas the Conservative organisation had stagnated since 1874 and was caught unprepared for an election.

14.6 VERDICT ON DISRAELI

Soon after Disraeli's defeat, Gladstone crowed: 'the downfall of Beaconsfieldism is like the vanishing of some vast magnificent castle in an Italian romance'. Did Disraeli's career have any lasting effect on British politics or was Gladstone right? Opinions are divided:

(a) Blake, among others, believes that Disraeli's great and lasting achievement was to hold the Conservative party together through a difficult period and then to demonstrate that it was still capable of forming an effective government. After all, when a political party has failed to win a general election for over 30 years, even its staunchest supporters could be forgiven for writing it off. He also made it the party of the Empire and the party with a strong foreign policy, i.e. the party of British nationalism. By showing concern for the social conditions of the poor, Disraeli enabled the Conservatives to attract a large enough slice of the working-class vote to keep them in existence as a major party.

(b) Some other historians feel that Disraeli's impact has been overestimated. Paul Smith claims that Peel had already made the Conservatives into a modern party when they won the 1841 general election, and that Disraeli actually retarded its development by leading the attack on Peel over the Corn Laws. The next leader of the party, Lord Salisbury, abandoned the social reform policy, so that aspect of Beaconsfieldism certainly did not survive long.

But whichever view one accepts, there is no escaping the fact that Disraeli was a first-rate parliamentarian; Blake calls him 'an impresario, an actor manager . . . there is a champagne-like sparkle about him which has scarcely ever been equalled and never surpassed among statesmen'.

QUESTIONS

1. Disraeli and Conservative Policies
Study Sources **A** to **F** and then answer the questions which follow.

Source A: speech by Disraeli at the Crystal Palace, 24 June 1872.

> I have always been of the opinion that the Tory Party has three great objects. The first is to maintain the institutions of the country, especially the monarchy . . . The second great object is to uphold the Empire of England. If you look at the history of this country since the arrival of Liberalism — forty years ago — you will find that there has been no effort so continuous, so subtle, and supported by so much energy, as the attempts of Liberalism to bring about the disintegration of the Empire . . .
>
> Gentlemen, another great object of the Tory Party is the improvement of the condition of the people . . . The health of the people is the most important question for a statesman . . . It involves the state of the dwellings of the people, the regulation of their industry, the inspection of their toil, the purity of their provisions, and it touches on all the means by which you may wean them from habits of excess and brutality.

A leading member denounced these policies the other day as a 'policy of sewage'. But to one of the labouring multitude of England, it is not a policy of sewage, but *a question of life and death* . . . and moreover, the Palace is unsafe if the cottage is unhappy.

Source: quoted in P. Adelman, *Gladstone, Disraeli and later Victorian Politics*, Longman, 1983 edn. (adapted extracts).

Source B: from the memoirs of R. A. Cross, Disraeli's Home Secretary from 1874–1880.

When the Cabinet came to discuss the Queen's Speech [in 1874], I was, I confess, disappointed at the lack of originality shown by the Prime Minister. From all his speeches, I had quite expected that his mind was full of legislative schemes; but this did not prove to be the case. On the contrary, he had to rely on the various suggestions of his colleagues, and as they themselves had only just come into office, there was some difficulty in framing the Queen's Speech.

Source: as for Source A (adapted extract).

Source C: speech by Gladstone at Dalkeith, 26 November 1879, during the Midlothian Campaign.

Go from South Africa into the lofty hills of Afghanistan, as they were last winter, and what do we see? I fear a yet sadder sight than was to be seen in the land of the Zulus. You have seen during last winter from time to time that from such and such a village, attacks had been made upon the British forces, and that in consequence the village had been burned. Those hill tribes had committed no real offence against us. We, in the pursuit of our political objects, chose to establish military positions in their country . . . The meaning of the burning of the village is that the women and children were driven forth to perish in the snows of winter . . . Does this not rouse in you horror and grief, to think that England should be associated with such consequences, not for any political necessity, but for a war as frivolous as any ever waged in the history of man.

Source: as for Source A (adapted extracts).

Source D: the opinion of a modern historian.

Disraeli had a flighty mind which drifted from smart triviality to adolescent day-dreaming and back again . . . He was first and last a great actor, watching his own performance and that of others with ironic detachment. He cared for causes only as a means of combat . . . His novel *Sybil* is supposed to contain a profound social analysis. In fact it says no more than that the rich are very rich and the poor very poor – by no means a new discovery. *His own policy*, when he came to power, *turned out to be nothing more startling than municipal wash-houses* . . .

His only genuine emotion in politics sprang from personal dislike – of Peel in his early career, of Gladstone even more strongly towards the end.

Source: A. J. P. Taylor, *Dizzy*, in *Essays in English History*, Penguin, 1976.

Source E: comments from another modern historian.

Disraeli lacked the administrative and legislative ability of Peel, Gladstone and Balfour. His mind was like a catherine wheel shooting out sparks – most of them fell on damp earth . . . Where he excelled was in the art of presentation. He was an impresario and an actor manager. He was a superb parliament-arian, one of the half dozen greatest in our history . . . but another side of him was a slightly mocking observer surveying with sceptical amusement the very stage on which he himself played a principal part. To him, more than to most, politics was 'the great game'.

Source: R. Blake, *Disraeli*, Eyre & Spottiswoode, 1966 (adapted extracts).

(a) (i) Explain in your own words what the three main objectives of the Tory Party ought to be, in Disraeli's opinion, according to Source **A**.   4(a)

(ii) What criticisms does Disraeli make of the Liberal Party in Source **A**?   4(a)

(iii) What evidence does Source **A** reveal about Disraeli's attitude towards the working class?   4(a)

(iv) What do you think Disraeli meant in Source **A** when he said that the condition of the people was 'a question of life and death'?   1, 2, 4(a)

(v) Does the evidence of Source **A** suggest that Disraeli was genuinely concerned about the condition of the working class or not? Explain your answer.   4(a, b)

(b) (i) Which one of the three objectives mentioned by Disraeli (Source **A**) do you think R. A. Cross, the author of Source **B**, would be most concerned about? Give reasons for your answer.   4(a, c)

(ii) Why was Cross disappointed with Disraeli, according to Source **B**?   4(a)

(c) (i) Which one of the three objectives mentioned by Disraeli (Source **A**) is Gladstone most concerned with in Source **C**?   4(a, c)

(ii) Which two wars does Gladstone refer to in his speech?   4(a)

(iii) What criticisms is Gladstone making of British policy (Source **C**)?   4(a)

(d) (i) Which of Disraeli's three objectives (Source **A**) is *not* mentioned by A. J. P. Taylor in Source **D**?   4(a, c)

(ii)   Using your own words, make a list of the criticisms of Disraeli made by Taylor in Source **D**.   **4(a)**

(iii)   Using Source **B** and your own knowledge of the period, explain whether you think Taylor's point about Disraeli's social policy (in italics in Source **D**) is a fair one.   **4(a, c)**

(e)   (i)   What points of agreement can you find between Taylor (Source **D**) and Blake (Source **E**).   **4(a, c)**

       (ii)   From the evidence of Source **E**, do you think Blake is an admirer of Disraeli or not? Give reasons for your answer.

                                                                         4(a, b)

(f)   (i)   Of the five Sources **A** to **E**, say which are primary and which are secondary sources. Give reasons for your answers.   **4(a, c)**

       (ii)   Look again at the sources which you think are primary. Which of them do you think is most helpful to the historian studying the career of Disraeli? Explain your choice fully.   **4(a, b, c)**

2.   Study the cartoon on p. 265 and then answer the questions which follow.

       The cartoon appeared in *Punch* at the time of the Balkans Crisis in 1875.

       Source: *Punch*.

(a)   (i)   Which four states do the dogs represent?   **4(a)**

       (ii)   What points is the cartoonist trying to put over?   **1, 2, 4(a)**

       (iii)   Why do you think John Bull representing Britain is shown wearing a policeman's helmet?   **1, 2, 4(a, b)**

       (iv)   What methods does the cartoonist use to show which of the three major states represented in the cartoon (Britain, Russia and Turkey) he sympathises with?   **4(a, b)**

(b)   (i)   Explain why and how Disraeli and Gladstone disagreed over their attitude towards Turkey during the Balkans Crisis of 1875–78.   **1, 2**

       (ii)   What were the main terms of the Treaty of San Stefano (March 1878) and why did Britain object to them?   **1,2**

(c)   (i)   Describe how the Treaty of San Stefano was changed at the Congress of Berlin.   **1, 2**

       (ii)   'A major victory for British diplomacy'. Explain whether or not you agree with this verdict on the Berlin settlement.   **1, 2**

3. (a)   Explain what was meant by the word *imperialism* at the time of Disraeli's second spell as Prime Minister (1874–80).

    (b)   What was Disraeli's attitude towards the British Empire?

    (c)   Describe Disraeli's overseas policies to do with:

       (i)   Egypt and the Suez Canal Shares;

       (ii)   Queen Victoria as Empress of India;

       (iii)   South Africa and the Zulu War;

       (iv)   The Afghan Wars.

[*Reproduced by permission of the Proprietors of 'Punch.'*

THE DOGS OF WAR.

BULL A 1. " TAKE CARE, MY MAN ! IT MIGHT BE AWK'ARD IF YOU WAS TO LET 'EM LOOSE ! "

(d) For each of the above, explain whether or not you think Disraeli was successful.   1, 2

4. Disraeli died in April 1881. Write two contrasting obituary notices for him:

(a) one which might have appeared in *The Times*, a newspaper sympathetic to Disraeli;

(b) one which might have appeared in the *Quarterly Review*, a Liberal magazine.   1, 2, 3

CHAPTER 15

VICTORIAN PROSPERITY

AND DEPRESSION

SUMMARY OF EVENTS

During the first few years of Queen Victoria's reign – from 1837 to about 1844 – industrial prosperity seemed variable, and there were several short trade depressions. The situation began to stabilise with a great surge of railway building from 1844 to 1847, and after that, industry moved into *a period of remarkable prosperity which lasted until 1873*. Agriculture enjoyed a similar 'Golden Age', usually known as the period of *High Farming*, which proved wrong, for the time being at any rate, the prophets of doom who had forecast that the repeal of the Corn Laws in 1846 would ruin British farming.

The period from 1873 to 1896 is usually referred to as the Great Depression. British industry went through a difficult period: although exports of most commodities continued to increase, prices and therefore profits, were falling, mainly because of overseas competition. There was something of a recovery between 1896 and 1914, but by the outbreak of the First World War in 1914, it was clear that the USA and Germany had toppled Britain from her position as the world's leading manufacturing nation. In agriculture the depression was much more severe and although there was a slight recovery around the turn of the century, it was only during the war years (1914–18) when foreign wheat was difficult to obtain, that British farming began to revive.

15.1 ILLUSTRATE AND ACCOUNT FOR BRITAIN'S INDUSTRIAL PROSPERITY IN THE MID-NINETEENTH CENTURY

(a) **The Great Exhibition of 1851** is probably the best illustration of Britain's prosperity at this time. The suggestion for it came from the Royal Society of Arts, whose president, Prince Albert, was full of enthusiasm for the idea. The exhibition was housed in *the Crystal Palace*, a vast construction of glass and cast iron, designed by Joseph Paxton and erected in Hyde Park. One-third of a mile long and over 100 feet high, it contained a display of every conceivable type of British machinery (much of it work-

illus 15.1 *The Great Exhibition*

ing) and manufactures: railway engines, steam ploughs, steamship engines, cranes, steam hammers for heavy industry, printing machines, screw-making machines, Lancashire cottons and Nottingham lace; there was even a silent piano (made out of papier maché) and an unsinkable deckchair. To demonstrate that Britain was a free trade country, exhibits were included from foreign countries – Dresden china and silks and tapestries from France. There were over six million visitors during the five months the exhibition was open, many of them from abroad, and lots of new export orders followed. Britain was regarded as 'the workshop of the world'.

(b) Over the next 20 years British industry enjoyed a striking export boom the like of which had never been experienced before. This can best be illustrated by looking at the *export figures in Table 15.1 for the main manufacturing industries*.

Table 15.1

Annual average for each five-year period

Year	Iron and steel (in thousand tons)	Coal (in million tons)
1845–9	458	2.5
1850–4	1225	3.2
1855–9	1411	5.99
1860–4	1536	7.83
1865–9	2027	9.86
1870–4	2965	12.31

Annual average per decade

Year	Cotton textiles (in million yards)	Woollen goods (including carpets) (in thousand yards)
1840–9	978	93 316
1850–9	1855	161 563
1860–9	2375	236 267
1870–9	3573	311 601

Source: P. Mathias, *The First Industrial Nation*, pp. 481–7.

The total value of exports from Britain increased:

Year	£ million
1840–9	55.4
1850–9	100.1
1860–9	159.7
1870–9	218.1

Another way in which prosperity showed itself was that the wages of the industrial working class increased, on average, by about 50 per cent in the period 1850–75. Prices also rose, but only by about 20 per cent on average; this meant that workers enjoyed a rise of around 30 per cent in *real wages* (what they could actually buy with their money).

(c) Reasons for prosperity

(i) The basis was that Britain was still enjoying the advantages of having been the first nation to industrialise. As yet there was no real competition from abroad, and the countries which were to become serious competitors later were still lagging far behind for one reason or another. The USA was having difficulty supplying its own rapidly increasing population and was held back by the Civil War (1861–5); Germany did not become a unified state until 1871. Both these countries were important buyers of British manufactures.

(ii) Further inventions were made which helped to keep Britain in the forefront; most important were the new processes in the metal industry which resulted in mild steel taking over from malleable iron as the most popular metal.

Henry Bessemer patented a converter system which could produce steel in large quantities at much lower prices (1856); this caused railways and shipping-lines to change to steel for rails and metal plating. *William Siemens*, a German engineer working in Britain, patented his open-hearth process (1867) which could produce a stronger type of steel.

(iii) The population growth increased the demand for manufactured goods at home. Between 1851 and 1871 the population of Britain rose from 27.4 million to 31.5 million, and this acted as a stimulus to industry.

(iv) Gladstone as Chancellor of the Exchequer (1853–5 and 1860–5) made an important contribution to the prosperity by removing almost all the remaining tariffs (see Section 8.2). This meant that there were no artificial restrictions on trade, Britain could obtain cheap raw materials and flood the world with cheap manufactured goods.

(v) The spread of railways contributed to the boom in many ways. In 1843 there were less than 2000 miles of track, but the rest of the decade saw an enormous investment of cash in railway building. This 'Railway Mania' as it became known, resulted in the construction of a further 5000 miles of track by 1850 and in 1875 a total of 14 510 miles of track was open. Thousands of extra jobs were provided as well as a large market for the iron industry, for rails, locomotives, coaches and wagons. Railways became an important consumer of coal, and railway towns like Crewe and Swindon mushroomed as workshop and repair centres. The cheap, fast transport provided by the railways enabled new inland coalfields to be developed, together with the iron ore mines in North Yorkshire. Most important of all, they made it possible to transport manufactured goods of all kinds to the ports much more quickly. This, together with the rapid spread of steam-power in merchant shipping after 1850, played a vital part in increasing British exports.

(vi) There was plenty of capital available for investment in industry. There were more reliable banking and credit facilities since the 1844 Bank Charter Act (see Section 7.2(c)). Once industrial progress had got under way, the vast profits which were earned from, for example, exports of cotton textiles, provided a continuous flow of capital which was used to finance further expansion. There was even some left over to be invested abroad – in 1875 at least £12 000 million of British capital was invested in railway and factory projects overseas. Much of this cash was used by foreigners to buy British goods. The discovery of gold in California (1849), Australia (1851) and New Zealand (1861) added to the capital available and further increased the demand for British manufactures.

15.2 IN WHAT WAYS AND WHY CAN BRITAIN BE SAID TO HAVE SUFFERED AN INDUSTRIAL DEPRESSION AFTER 1873?

(a) Although the last quarter of the century is often described as the time of the Great Depression, there was no serious industrial slump with sharply falling exports like the depression of the early 1930s (see Section 24.2). In most industries the general trend of production and exports was still rising. The steel industry enjoyed a massive expansion during the so-called depression; in coal and cotton textiles, output and exports continued to increase, though *the rate of growth was slowing down*; although production of iron decreased, this was only to be expected as steel became more widely adopted. One recent economic historian, S. B. Saul, even went so far as to call his book about the period, *The Myth of the Great Depression*. However, economists described it as a depression because:

(i) Prices were falling, and therefore although exports were increasing, they were worth less in cash; this is shown by the statistics for exports of cotton textiles in Table 15.2.

Table 15.2

Year	Cottons exported (in million yards)	Value (£ million)
1870–9	3573	71.5
1880–9	4675	73.0
1890–9	5057	67.2

Source: P. Mathias, *The First Industrial Nation*, pp. 468, 486.

(ii) Consequently profits were declining; as the economists put it, profit margins were being squeezed.

(iii) Employers often tried to cut down costs and maintain profit levels by laying off workers, causing periodic bursts of unemployment. In the 20 years before 1874, the average rate of unemployment among trade union members was 4.6 per cent, but from 1875–95 the average was 5.4 per cent. Some individual years were serious: the 1879 figure was 11 per cent and 1886 10 per cent. However, it was not a period of sustained unemployment: 1882–3 and 1889–90 were good years when no more than 2 per cent were out of work.

Pressure from businessmen, never slow to voice their concern when profits take a turn for the worse, caused the government to appoint *a Royal Commission in 1886* to investigate the problem; its conclusion merely stated the obvious: there was 'a diminution, and in some cases, an absence of profit, with a corresponding diminution of employment for the labouring classes'.

(b) What caused the depression? Some historians have tried to explain it in terms of a single cause: falling prices were the result of the world economy running short of gold; another favourite single explanation was that the depression was the inevitable down-turn in the economy following a boom. While there is probably some truth in both theories, the generally accepted view nowadays is that *the depression was produced by a complex combination of factors*:

(i) There was a reduction in railway building: between 1845 and 1870 an average of 2000 miles of new track were opened in each five-year period. After 1870 the figure fell by half, and between 1885 and 1900 an average of only 750 miles of track were built in each five-year period. Thus there was a gradual falling off in demand for metals and a loss of jobs.

(ii) Britain was beginning to suffer serious competition from abroad, especially from the USA and Germany. This was inevitable: once other countries learned the techniques for themselves and began to industrialise, they were bound to challenge Britain's lead. The statistics in Table 15.3 show how the USA and Germany were overtaking Britain and how Britain's growth rate was much smaller than theirs.

(iii) The British were now experiencing the disadvantages of having been the first nation to industrialise: their machinery and equipment was old and in some cases obsolete, whereas the Americans and Germans could start with the latest technology available. The Germans, for instance, were able to install the Siemens furnaces for making steel; they also took full advantage of a later invention by the cousins Percy Gilchrist (a Welsh steelworks chemist) and Sydney Gilchrist-Thomas (a clerk in a London police-court), who in 1878 discovered how to manufacture steel from iron-ore which had a high phosphorous

Table 15.3

Coal production (in million tons)

	1850	1860	1870	1880	1890	1900	1910	1914
Germany	6	12	34	59	89	149	222	277
USA	–	3.4	10	64.9	143	244	350	455
Great Britain	57	81	112	149	184	228	268	292

Pig-iron production (in million tons)

	1850	1860	1870	1880	1890	1900	1910	1914
Germany	–	–	1.3	2.5	4.1	7.5	9.5	14.7
USA	–	0.8	1.7	3.9	9.4	14	27	30
Great Britain	2.2	3.9	6	7.8	8	9	10	11

Steel production (in million tons)

	1850	1860	1870	1880	1890	1900	1910	1914
Germany	–	–	0.3	0.7	2.3	6.7	13.8	14
USA	–	–	–	1.3	4.3	10	26	32
Great Britain	–	–	0.7	1.3	3.6	5	5.9	6.5

Source: A. J. P. Taylor, *The Struggle for Mastery in Europe 1848–1918* (Oxford, 1971) pp. xxix–xxx.

content. The British were saddled with the earlier Bessemer converters. which the Germans had abandoned and which were more expensive to run than the Siemens and Gilchrist-Thomas methods. Similar advances had been made in other industries: in the American cotton industry there was the introduction of ring-spinning instead of the slower and more expensive mule-spinning still used in Lancashire; America pioneered new machines like the typewriter and the sewing-machine; the Belgians made advances in the glass industry enabling them to produce better quality glass more cheaply than the British. Over the whole range of industry the British were therefore suffering in two ways: they were being gradually pushed out of their markets in Europe and America (most states introduced tariffs to protect their developing industries); and foreign imports were making an increasing impact on the British market (the British government, still believing in *laissez-faire*, would not introduce tariffs).

(iv) There was a failure of management to respond positively to the new challenges:

- The most common unit was the family firm; top management tended to be chosen not because of ability but because of family connections; unfortunately, inspiration and interest often deteriorated by the time a firm had reached its third or fourth generation of owners. In the USA and Germany recruitment depended much more on ability.
- There was not enough effort to develop new industries, with the result that British export trade relied too heavily on a few staple products. The Germans meanwhile surged ahead in the 'new' industries such as electrical engineering, chemicals and dyestuffs.
- There was not enough effort to improve designs and reduce costs by introducing the latest machinery; this might have enabled the British to hold on to their American and European markets. However, they preferred to switch exports to India, to other parts of the Empire and to China; this was especially true of the cotton industry. Management was too complacent, preferring to repair the old machinery rather than invest profits in new premises and equipment; in fairness though, the fall in profits during the 'depression' probably goes some way towards explaining the lack of investment.
- Even when they were prepared to invest, industrialists sometimes made the wrong decisions: between 1896 and 1914 there was a boom in cotton exports, and hundreds of new mills were built in Lancashire; but instead of taking the opportunity to install the latest automatic looms already widely used in the USA and Germany, manufacturers on the whole decided to invest in the traditional type looms.
- Too little attention was paid to the importance of science, especially in chemicals and electrical engineering.

(v) Trade unions may have held up the introduction of some new machines and processes in an attempt to make sure that skilled workers were not pushed out of their jobs.

(vi) Britain's education system was not geared to producing academically trained scientists and engineers. The public schools concentrated on the classics and worked on the assumption that gentlemen did not go in for practical training. A nationally organised system of elementary and secondary education was very slow in arriving (see Section 12.6) and even when it did, the science taught was not designed to prepare students for top level technological training. In the 1870s science was scarcely taught in British universities except to medical students; yet in 1872 there were already 11 purely technical universities and 20 other universities in Germany, all organised and financed by the government.

15.3 WHAT IS MEANT BY THE TERM 'HIGH FARMING' AND WHY WAS THE PERIOD 1846-74 ONE OF PROSPERITY FOR BRITISH AGRICULTURE?

(a) **High Farming** was the title of a pamphlet written by a Wigtownshire farmer, James Caird, and published in 1849. In it he explained his ideas about how farmers should respond to the threat of foreign competition following the abolition of the Corn Laws in 1846. They should farm their land more intensively, using all the latest techniques and inventions in order to increase yield and lower costs; it would thus be possible to cope with the lowering of prices which cheap foreign imports would bring, while still maintaining profits. According to F. M. L. Thompson, the early part of this period (1846-53) was one of only faltering prosperity, and it was only in 1853 that prices of farm produce stabilised at an encouraging level. The period of 'High Farming', the real Golden Age of British agriculture, lasted only about 20 years after 1853; it was when farmers with money to spare 'opened their purses and embarked on the new course in a big way'. It was a period of prosperity for farmers, whose incomes probably doubled; even farm labourers were becoming slightly better off as far as wages, housing and food were concerned.

(b) **What were the reasons for prosperity?**

(i) The new 'High Farming' techniques resulted in much greater productivity. Widespread use of clay piping improved land drainage; there was an increase in 'mixed farming', i.e. growing wheat and root crops *and* raising cattle, sheep and pigs as well. Artificial fertilisers - nitrate of soda, superphosphates, sulphate of ammonia, Peruvian guano and German potash - came into use. Pedigree breeds of cattle - Hereford, Aberdeen Angus, Ayrshire and Channel Island - were improved; by the early 1870s the major profit for most farmers came from their livestock. There were also improvements to ploughs and hoes, and the spread of the horse-drawn reaper. More spectacular were the steam threshing-machines and steam ploughs, though these were not so important; Thompson calls them 'the white elephant of high farming, a plaything of rich landowners with money to spare for anything new in farm gadgetry'.

(ii) Scientific farming was encouraged by the Royal Agricultural Society of England (founded 1838) which published a journal and organised agricultural shows. An experimental station was set up in 1842 at Rothamsted to carry out research into soils and fertilisers.

(iii) Britain's growing population meant an ever-increasing demand for the farmers' products, and therefore higher prices and profits. Although wheat prices remained steady, the price of all types of meat, butter, cheese and wool (for clothing) rose by close on 50 per cent.

(iv) Vitally important was the fact that because of the lack of fast shipping and of refrigeration facilities, there was very little competition from foreign produce, except Russian and American wheat. Imports of wheat gradually increased during the 1860s, which explains why wheat prices were steady while prices of meat and dairy produce rose.

(v) Railways enabled livestock and perishable goods such as meat, milk and market garden produce to be transported quickly and cheaply over long distances for sale in the cities. Farmers who had previously been too far away from towns and cities now had a whole new market at their disposal. Counties such as Norfolk and Herefordshire could produce milk for London, and Aberdeenshire was supplying meat to industrial Lancashire and London.

(vi) Finally even the weather was kind to the farmers with a run of mostly good summers and good harvests between 1850 and 1873.

15.4 WHY AND WITH WHAT RESULTS WAS THERE A DEPRESSION IN AGRICULTURE AFTER 1873?

The Golden Age changed quite suddenly into a depression which was especially severe in areas which relied heavily on wheat and cereal production; prices and profits fell, harvests were smaller and many fields went out of cultivation. However, livestock and dairy farming were not so badly affected; the boom in this section lasted well into the 1880s, when foreign imports began to bring down prices.

(a) Reasons for the depression:

(i) Bad weather played an important role; the summer of 1873 was wet and the harvest poor; the autumn of 1875 was exceptionally wet, and after that came 12 years of above average rainfall and below average temperatures. Crops were ruined and harvests disappointing. Worse still, the wet weather helped to spread pneumonia and foot and mouth disease among livestock; there were also epidemics of liver-rot among sheep, and swine fever, causing heavy losses to farmers.

(ii) The most important cause of the depression was the import of cheap foreign food which was now available to make up the shortages. The building of the transcontinental railways opened up the fertile prairies of North America as vast wheat-growing areas, and the development of large merchant steamships enabled American, and later Canadian, Indian, Australian and Argentinian, wheat to be transported swiftly and cheaply to Britain. For example, in 1868 the cost of transporting a ton of wheat from Chicago to Liverpool was 65s.; in 1882 it had fallen to only 24s. Consequently the price of wheat fell, on average, by half; at one point it hit a record low level of 17s. 6d. a quarter. These trends are illustrated in Tables 15.4 and 15.5.

(iii) Disraeli's government (1874–80), despite intense pressure from farming interests, took the decision not to protect British agriculture by the reintroduction of tariffs.

Table 15.4   *Imports of wheat and
flour to the UK (average per decade)*

Year	(in thousands of cwt)
1840-9	10 667
1850-9	19 326
1860-9	33 697
1870-9	50 406
1880-9	70 282
1890-9	85 890
1900-9	102 851

Source: P. Mathias, *The First
Industrial Nation*, pp. 472-5.

Table 15.5   *Wheat prices (annual
average for 5 year periods)*

Year	(shillings per quarter)
1840-4	57.85
1845-9	54.00
1855-9	57.62
1865-9	53.62
1870-4	55.00
1875-9	47.67
1885-9	31.58
1895-9	27.82
1900-4	27.37
1910-14	32.93

Source: as Table 15.4.

In the 1880s the introduction of refrigeration ships brought frozen mutton from Australia and New Zealand and chilled beef from Argentina. At the same time, according to Thompson, 'the traditional English breakfast of Danish bacon and eggs was being established'.

(b) Results of the depression

(i) Farmers who relied heavily on wheat and cereal growing, particularly in southern and eastern counties, had a hard time; many went bankrupt, some tenant farmers fell into arrears with rents, and landowners suffered reduced profits from rents. The area of land producing cereal crops fell substantially from 9.6 million acres at the height of the Golden Age in 1872 to 6.5 million acres in 1913. On the other hand, in the Midlands, in Lancashire and Cheshire, and in Scotland, where mixed farming was common, the depression was comparatively mild.

(ii) Many farmers survived by turning arable land over to pasture, and switching to livestock, dairy and poultry farming. Others turned to orchards and market gardening, producing fruit, vegetables, flowers and bulbs; the area under pasture increased from 17.1 million acres in 1872 to 21.5 million in 1913. Although it is true that meat, butter and cheese prices fell during the late 1880s and the 1890s in the face of foreign imports, this was not as disastrous as the fall in cereal prices. There were three reasons for this: (1) the price of animal feed fell substantially; (2) British meat was of a higher quality than imported frozen and chilled meat; (3) the growing demand for milk in the industrial towns and cities could only be met by British cattle.

(iii) There were important social effects. In areas where arable farming was abandoned, many agricultural labourers were thrown out of work, and there must have been considerable hardship for a time. In 1871 there were close on one million farm labourers in Britain, but by 1901 the number had fallen to just over 600 000. Some had moved to London, others had emigrated to the USA, Canada, Australia and New Zealand.

(iv) The depression brought the benefit of cheaper food, so that people who were lucky enough to be in work could enjoy a slightly higher standard of living. For the remaining agricultural labourers, falling prices meant that although their money wages fell, their real wages probably remained steady.

(c) Agriculture seemed to have recovered slightly after 1900: by 1914 total output had increased by 5 per cent, and prices, even of wheat, were rising again. This apparent recovery took place because the blast of foreign competition had forced farmers to adapt and become more efficient, or go under. *The Eversley Commission (1893-7)* urged more people to take up dairy and poultry farming or turn to market gardening. Many took the advice, further slimming down the less profitable cereal producing sector. The government helped by forbidding the import of live cattle (1892); although the prime purpose of this move was to control cattle diseases, it removed an important element of competition. In the end, therefore, it was not so much a recovery as the fact that the survivors had learned how to live with world-wide foreign competition.

QUESTIONS

1. The Agricultural Depression
Study the Sources **A** to **E** and then answer the questions which follow.

Source **A**: statistics showing wheat and flour imports and prices in Tables 15.4 and 15.5 (on p. 276).

Source **B**: extract from an article published in 1881.

> Foreigners form their own opinions from their own observations. When they see industries dying out under *Free Trade* in England, and springing into vigorous life under *Protection* in France, Belgium, Germany and America; when they see the ruin of agriculture, the depression of all manufacturing industries; when they see that as our population increases, our means of employing and feeding them decreases, they do not look much further for arguments against Free Trade.
>
> **Source:** E. Sullivan, *Isolated Free Trade*, August 1881, quoted in L. Evans and P. J. Pledger, *Contemporary Sources and Opinions in Modern British History, vol. I*, Warne, 1967.

Source **C**: comments by a modern historian.

> There was a great depression in agriculture from 1873–96 which had profound effects on landownership. Most contemporaries saw this as a disaster caused by a run of atrocious weather and by a swiftly rising flood of imported foodstuffs, which left English agriculture prostrate. Most historians have agreed with them. First American prairie wheat in the 1870s, and then Canadian, Indian, Australian and Argentine wheat, knocked the price of English wheat down from an average of 56s. a quarter in 1867–71 to27s.3d. in 1894–98. The price of other grains did not fall by so much as wheat's 50 per cent, but still fell substantially, as did the price of wool. With the perfection of refrigerating techniques, the import of frozen and chilled meat grew quickly, from the middle of the 1880s, and meat prices also fell . . . The effects were to be seen in mounting arrears of rent, bankrupt and ruined tenants, and falling rent rolls; and they were to be seen written across the countryside in a dwindling arable acreage, in farms thrown up, and in land allowed to run to weed and waste.
>
> **Source:** F. M. L. Thompson, *English Landed Society in the Nineteenth Century*, Routledge & Kegan Paul, 1963 (adapted extracts).

Source **D**: report of the Royal Commission on Agriculture, 1897.

> It is clear that the depression has not equally affected all parts of Great Britain. In arable counties where its presence is most

manifest, it has entailed very heavy losses on occupiers and owners of land, in some districts considerable areas have ceased to be cultivated and there has been a great withdrawal of land from the plough . . . The heavier the soil, and the greater the proportion of arable land, the more severe has been the depression . . . In England the situation is undoubtedly a grave one in the eastern and in some parts of the southern counties. In the pastoral counties of Great Britain, the depression is of a milder character, but in most of them the fall in the value of livestock between 1886 and 1893, and the persistent fall in the price of wool have diminished farming profits and rents. In districts suitable for dairying, market gardening and poultry rearing, and in the neighbourhood of mines, quarries, large manufacturing centres and towns, where there has been a considerable demand for farm produce, there has been relatively less depression.

Source: quoted in N. Tongue and M. Quincey, *British Social and Economic History 1800–1900*, Macmillan, 1980 (adapted extracts).

Source E: a survey of rural England commissioned by the *Daily Express*, 1902.

Owing principally to the lowness of prices, from whatever cause arising, and the lack of labour, in the majority of districts English agriculture is a failing industry, though at present, in the absence of serious war and want, this gradual failure does not appear to affect the general prosperity of the nation. Yet I maintain that it is affecting it, not only by the lessening of a home-grown food supply, which might be vital in the case of a European struggle, but in an even more deadly fashion by the withdrawal of the best of its population from the wholesome land into cities which are not wholesome for mind or body . . . I am convinced – and this is a very important national aspect of the question – that most of our reverses during the recent [Boer] war were due to the placing of town-bred bodies and intelligences, both of officers and men, against country-bred bodies and intelligences [the Boers].

Source: Sir H. Rider Haggard, *Rural England*, quoted in P. Keating (ed.), *Into Unknown England 1866–1913*, Fontana, 1976 (adapted extracts).

(a) (i) According to Source A, during which ten year period did the greatest increase over the previous ten years take place in wheat and flour imports? **4(a)**

(ii) During which five year period did the greatest fall in wheat prices take place? **4(a)**

(iii) By approximately what percentage did wheat prices fall between 1840–4 and 1895–9? **4(a)**

(iv) To what extent do these statistics in Source **A** support the statement in Source **C** that from 1873–96 there was a great depression in agriculture? **4(a, c)**

(v) Do you think the statistics in Source **A** support the statement that 'from 1900 to 1914 British agriculture recovered slightly'? Explain your answer fully. **4(a)**

(b) **(i)** What countries are mentioned in Source **B** as having protection? **4(a)**

(ii) Explain what the writer of Source **B** means by the word 'Protection'. **1, 4(a)**

(iii) Explain what he means by the term 'Free Trade'. **1, 4(a)**

(c) **(i)** According to Source **C**, what did contemporaries think was causing the depression? **4(a)**

(ii) What evidence does Source **C** contain which suggests that contemporaries were right? **4(a)**

(d) **(i)** According to Source **C**, what were the effects of the agricultural depression? **4(a)**

(ii) On what results of the depression does Source **D** agree with Source **C**? **4(a, c)**

(iii) In what ways does Source **D** suggest an interpretation of the results of the depression different from Source **C**? **4(a, c)**

(e) **(i)** Do you think Source **E** supports Source **C** or Source **D**, or both? Explain your answer fully. **4(a, c)**

(ii) What is it that worries the writer of Source **E** about the long-term effects of the depression? **4(a)**

(iii) How does the writer of Source **E** show that he prefers the country to the town? **4(a, b)**

(f) **(i)** Which of the Sources **B** to **E** are primary and which are secondary? Give reasons for your answer. **4(a, b)**

(ii) Which one of these Sources do you think is the most reliable and which the least reliable? Explain your choices fully. **4(a, b)**

2. The Industrial Depression

Study Sources **A** to **D** carefully and then answer the questions which follow.

Source A: cartoon in Punch, 1896.

(Tenniel, 1896, reproduced by permission of the Proprietors of 'Punch'.)

CAUGHT NAPPING.

'There was an old lady as I've heard tell, she went to market her goods for to sell	She went to market on a market day and she fell asleep on the world's highway	By came a pedlar—German—and stout, and he cut her petticoats all round about.'

Source: *Punch*, 1896.

Sources **B**, **C** and **D** are all comments from modern historians.

Source B: It might be questioned whether all Britain's losses can be attributed simply to the emergence of new industrial competitors; perhaps they stemmed from internal deficiencies. A country whose industrial structure is too narrowly based on a few traditional industries is obviously going to be more restricted as regards trading opportunities.

Source: D. Aldcroft, *The Development of British Industry and Foreign Competition*, Allen & Unwin, 1968.

Source C: If Britain was behind the times in technique and methods of production, she was even further behind the times in her selling methods . . . a frequent complaint was scarcity of British trade representatives abroad . . . poor packing of goods and inadequate credit facilities.

> Source: D. H. Aldcroft and H. W. Richardson, *The British Economy 1870–1939*, Macmillan, 1969.

Source D: It is important to remember, however, that Britain retained a wide lead in many industrial sectors to 1914. Most of these had their roots in the industrial revolution; cotton textiles and textile machinery, heavy machine tools, locomotives, ships and steam-engines.

> Source: S. B. Saul, *The Myth of the Great Depression 1873–1896*, Macmillan, 1969.

(a) (i) How does the Punch cartoonist of 1899 (Source **A**) try to explain the causes of the industrial depression in Britain? **4(a)**

   (ii) Do you think the cartoonist is an admirer of German industrial development or not? Explain your answer fully. **4(a, b)**

   (iii) Which other country, not mentioned in the cartoon, was a strong competitor of Britain by 1896? **1, 4(a)**

(b) (i) How far does Source **B** agree with Source **A** in its explanations of Britain's industrial depression? **4(a, c)**

   (iii) What further reasons does Source **C** suggest for the depression? **4(a, c)**

(c) (i) Using your own knowledge, explain in what ways Britain was, as Source **C** puts it, 'behind the times in technique and methods of production' after 1873. **1, 2**

   (ii) What other reasons, not mentioned in the Sources, can you suggest for the depression? **1, 2**

(d) (i) How does Source **D** seem to disagree with Sources **A, B** and **C**? **4(a, c)**

   (ii) If S. B. Saul (Source **D**) is correct in what he says, why do you think so many historians have described the period after 1873 as one of industrial depression? Explain your answer fully. **1, 2, 4(a)**

3. British industry is usually said to have enjoyed a period of prosperity from about 1844 until 1873, and to have suffered a depression from 1873 until 1896.

   (a) Describe briefly some of the aspects of the prosperity.

   (b) Explain the reasons for this prosperity.

(c)   In what ways can the period after 1873 be described as one of industrial depression?

(d)   Explain the causes of the depression.   1, 2

4.   The year is 1900 and you are looking back after a lifetime as a Norfolk farmer. Describe:

(a)   your feelings as a young man about the Repeal of the Corn Laws (1846) and your fears for the future of farming;

(b)   how you overcame your difficulties by adopting 'High Farming' methods;

(c)   your experiences and reactions during the agricultural depression of 1873–90;

(d)   your thoughts about who or what was responsible for the depression.   1, 2, 3

CHAPTER 16

GLADSTONE AND SALISBURY 1880–95

SUMMARY OF EVENTS

The period was very much dominated by events in Ireland; governments usually tried to solve the problems by a combination of coercion and pacification, but without any lasting success. Of the six governments that held office, four were directly brought down by Irish affairs; the governments were:

Party	Prime Minister	In Office
Liberal	W. E. Gladstone (2nd ministry)	1880–June 1885
Conservative	Lord Salisbury (1st ministry)	June 1885–February 1886
Liberal	W. E. Gladstone (3rd ministry)	February–August 1886
Conservative	Lord Salisbury (2nd ministry)	1886–1892
Liberal	W. E. Gladstone (4th ministry)	1892–March 1894
Liberal	Lord Rosebery	March 1894–June 1895

Gladstone began his second ministry with a large majority, but very little went right for him. *His Second Irish Land Act (1881)* failed to satisfy Parnell and the Irish Nationalists, who would settle for nothing less than Home Rule. Disraeli had left him several problems abroad - in Afghanistan, Transvaal, Egypt and the Sudan. Gladstone's handling of these situations aroused criticism, and though his policies resulted in Egypt in effect becoming part of the British Empire, he was also held responsible for the death of General Gordon in the Sudan. Though there was time for a few domestic improvements, notably *the Parliamentary Reform Act of 1884*, the Radicals felt that there ought to have been many more.

Believing that there was more to be gained from the Conservatives, Parnell had no hesitation in using Irish Nationalist votes to turn Gladstone out and put Salisbury in (June 1885). When Gladstone announced that he had been converted to Home Rule, despite the opposition of many of his own party, Parnell switched his support back to the Liberals. However, Gladstone's *1886 Home Rule Bill* was defeated in the Commons, 93

Liberals voting against it. The Liberal party, deeply split over Ireland and other matters, was defeated in the following general election.

During the six years of Conservative rule there were several important developments: Ireland was given firm treatment along with some modest concessions; in foreign affairs Salisbury was concerned to keep Britain aloof from binding agreements with other powers – a policy which became known, misleadingly, as *'splendid isolation'*; and there were the early stages of the *Scramble for Africa*, when the powers of western Europe somehow managed to divide Africa between them without a war. This was unexciting stuff for ordinary working people who were more concerned with the unemployment situation and the cost of living; the attentions of many of them were turning towards trade unions and events such as the successful dockers' strike of 1889.

In 1892 the Liberals won just enough seats to form a government with Irish Nationalist support. The main aim of the 83-year-old Gladstone was to secure Home Rule for Ireland; soon after his *Second Home Rule Bill* was defeated by the Conservative-dominated House of Lords, Gladstone resigned. Rosebery's short government was notable mainly for the way in which the Lords continually prevented Liberal bills from becoming law; this was the beginning of the growing confrontation between the two houses, which was to reach its climax with *the Parliament Act of 1911*. With Gladstone's retirement, the Liberals lost their attraction for the electorate, and were heavily defeated in the election of 1895. Ten years of unbroken Conservative rule followed.

16.1 HOW DID GLADSTONE TRY TO PACIFY IRELAND BETWEEN 1880 AND 1886 AND WHY DID HE FAIL?

(a) The situation in Ireland had deteriorated during Disraeli's government. The agricultural depression, caused by cheap American corn, made farming in Ireland even less profitable than before; landlords reacted by evicting more peasants in order to consolidate holdings, and violent incidents – murder, rick-burning and maiming of cattle – were common as desperate peasants retaliated. *The Irish Land League* was formed in 1879 by *Michael Davitt*. He was an Irish Catholic whose family had been evicted from their land when he was a child; he had spent seven years in Dartmoor for being involved in Fenian outrages. The League soon gained massive support throughout Ireland, and it demanded three concessions for the peasants. *Known as the 'three Fs', these were*:

(i) *a fair rent*;
(ii) *fixity of tenure* (a guarantee that tenants could not be evicted provided they paid the rent);
(iii) *free sale* (the right to sell their land if they wanted to).

The League was soon working closely with the Home Rule Movement under its formidable leader Charles Stewart Parnell, a Protestant landowner with an Anglo-Irish father and an American mother. Aloof, icily disdainful and withdrawn, he detested the English. He had been MP for County Meath since 1875 and had organised the Irish Nationalist obstruction campaign in the Commons.

(b) Gladstone was hampered by opposition in the House of Lords, from the Land League, and from a section of his own party which felt he was being too lenient with the Irish.

(i) A bill was introduced (1880) to give compensation to Irish tenants who were evicted, but the Lords, many of whom owned land in Ireland, rejected it by a huge majority (282 to 51). Over 10 000 people had been evicted in that year alone and there was widespread misery and desperation. The Land League retaliated by boycotting anyone who took over a farm from which the previous tenant had been evicted; he should be 'isolated as if he were a leper'. The first person to be dealt with in this way was *Captain Boycott*, the agent of a wealthy landowner in County Mayo; after evicting a tenant for non-payment of rent, Boycott found that servants, shopkeepers, labourers, in fact everybody, would have nothing to do with him, and troops had to be sent in to protect his property. A new word was thus added to the language, and the boycott idea spread rapidly.

(ii) The government replied with *a Coercion Act (1881)* which suspended Habeas Corpus (see Section 2.4(b)).

(iii) Gladstone would not be content with repression alone and was soon responsible for *the Second Irish Land Act (1881)* which gave the Irish what the Land League wanted – the Three Fs, plus Land Courts to decide fair rents. The Act was a remarkable achievement and shows how genuinely committed Gladstone was to easing the misery of the Irish peasants; it took 58 sittings in the Commons and all Gladstone's tremendous skill and experience to pilot it through; the Lords only passed it because of Queen Victoria's influence. Unfortunately it did not solve the Irish problem, though there was very little wrong with the Act itself, except that it was ten years too late. Parnell decided that since his campaign had squeezed such a great concession out of Gladstone, then continued pressure might bring the ultimate prize – Home Rule. The Land League therefore boycotted the new Land Courts, ordered a non-payment of rent campaign, and did all it could to sabotage the working of the Act. Evictions and violence continued.

(iv) Gladstone, shocked and disgusted by the Irish tactics, had Parnell and other league leaders arrested and imprisoned in Kilmainham Gaol, Dublin. This solved nothing, violence increased and a rash of secret extremist societies broke out.

(v) After six months both Gladstone and Parnell were anxious to break the stalemate; Parnell was afraid that he might lose control of the movement while he was absent in gaol. An understanding (sometimes known as the *Kilmainham Treaty*) was reached, through intermediaries (April 1882). Parnell agreed to call off the rent strike and control the violence and in return Gladstone promised an Arrears Bill to let tenants off their rent arrears which had accumulated during the recent campaign. Parnell was released. This agreement was an admission by Gladstone that only Parnell could control the Irish; it was probably around this time that Gladstone realised that Home Rule would have to come sooner or later.

(vi) *The Phoenix Park murders* ruined chances of immediate progress. Only four days after Parnell's release, Lord Frederick Cavendish, the new Chief Secretary for Ireland, who had only been in the country a few hours, and T. E. Burke, the permanent under secretary, were attacked and stabbed to death with surgical knives, while they were walking in Phoenix Park, Dublin. The murderers were members of an extremist group known as the 'Invincibles'. Parnell was shocked and denounced the group, but more murders followed, and it seemed as though Parnell's influence was declining. The English public was now convinced that the Irish were impossible to deal with and opinion hardened against Home Rule.

(vii) Gladstone bowed to pressure and an even more severe Coercion Act was passed which enabled the government to track down and arrest the 'Invincibles', five of whom were hanged.

(viii) Gladstone and Parnell tried hard to make the Kilmainham agreement work. The Arrears Act was passed, the Second Land Act began to operate and during 1883 affairs in Ireland gradually settled into a period of comparative calm which lasted until June 1885. This must be seen as a partial success for Gladstone, but it was not a permanent solution.

(c) Parnell puts the Conservatives in. Parnell still wanted Home Rule and he controlled a powerful group of 60 Nationalist MPs. He decided that instead of obstructing parliament, there might be more to be gained by co-operation with one of the major parties. There was little prospect of the Liberals giving him what he wanted, since there was strong right wing opposition to any further concessions. However, Lord Randolph Churchill, a brilliant up-and-coming young Conservative, eager to gain Irish votes, seemed to be offering major concessions. It made no difference to Parnell which party helped him, so he decided to take a chance with the Conservatives. In June 1885 the Liberal government was defeated in a Commons vote by an alliance of Conservatives and Irish Nationalists. Gladstone resigned and a Conservative government took office with Lord Salisbury as Prime Minister. He was totally dependent on Irish votes, and consequently gave them two major concessions:

(i) The Coercion Acts were dropped.

(ii) *Lord Ashbourne's Act* introduced a scheme to give financial help to peasants to enable them to buy land.

A general election was held in November 1885, and Parnell, delighted with his gains so far, instructed all Irishmen living on the mainland to vote Conservative. The election result was a strange one: the Liberals lost 18 seats but still had a majority of 86 over the Conservatives (335 Liberals to 249 Conservatives); by an odd coincidence the Irish Nationalists had won 86 seats, which meant that if the Parnell–Salisbury alliance continued, the result was a dead heat. The Conservative government carried on with Parnell holding the balance: he could keep the Conservatives in office, or he could withdraw his support and allow the Liberals back in. By now Gladstone realised that only Home Rule would pacify the Irish, though he kept his feelings to himself. He hoped that the Conservatives would be the ones to introduce it, since they would have a better chance of getting the approval of the Lords. By early December, it was clear that Salisbury was not prepared to go so far as Home Rule; it was only a matter of time before Parnell removed him.

(d) Gladstone and the First Home Rule Bill (1886)

(i) Gladstone decided in favour of Home Rule during the summer of 1885. *There were several reasons for his change of mind.* Violence was on the increase again following the Conservatives' removal of the Coercion Acts, and Gladstone was afraid that the campaign would spread to England. Some leading British officials in Dublin, including Sir Robert Hamilton (successor to the murdered Burke), who knew the situation at first hand, believed that Home Rule was the only way to get consistent government in Ireland. Above all Gladstone realised that Irish nationalism, like Italian nationalism, was such a deeply felt desire that the only just and reasonable course was to satisfy it. Gladstone did not reveal his conversion to Home Rule because he hoped that the Conservatives would introduce it and because he was afraid of splitting the Liberals, many of whom were opposed to the idea and would require gradual persuasion. Lord Hartington, brother of Lord Frederick Cavendish and leader of the Liberal right wing (Whigs), was a bitter opponent of any further concessions to the Irish.

(ii) Sensational developments took place when, on 15 December 1885, Gladstone's son Herbert, leaked the news of his father's conversion to the press. Having the news sprung upon them so suddenly outraged Hartington and his supporters and made Gladstone's job of winning them over almost impossible. Hartington announced that he would never support Home Rule, but Gladstone was determined to go forward. The Conservative government was defeated by the combined Liberal and Irish votes, and Gladstone became Prime Minister for the third time (January 1886).

(iii) *The First Home Rule Bill* was introduced in April. It proposed that Ireland should have its own parliament in Dublin and no Irish MPs would sit at Westminster. The Dublin parliament would control all internal affairs; foreign affairs, defence and trade would remain under the direction of Westminster. The bill met bitter opposition in the Commons from the Conservatives. Lord Randolph Churchill stirred up religious prejudices with the argument that the Protestant minority in Ulster would not be well treated by a Dublin government dominated by Catholics, and that Ulster should therefore oppose Home Rule by every means possible. His slogan was 'Ulster will fight, and Ulster will be right'. There was also opposition to the Bill from the Hartington faction, and from Joseph Chamberlain, leader of the radical wing of the Liberal party. In June the Bill was defeated by 343 votes to 313; 93 Liberals voted against it.

(iv) Gladstone decided to appeal to the country, but in the following general election the Liberals lost heavily and were reduced to only 191 seats. The mainland electorate had given its verdict – decisively against Home Rule, and once again Irish affairs had brought down a British government. More than that, the Liberal party was deeply divided; the anti-Home Rule Liberals remained as a separate group, under Chamberlain, known as *the Liberal Unionists*. Many later joined the Conservatives and it was 20 years before the Liberal party recovered fully. Chamberlain is usually blamed for thwarting Gladstone and splitting the party.

(e) Why did Chamberlain oppose Home Rule? There has been disagreement about his motives:

(i) Irish historians put it down to sheer ambition; it was widely expected that Gladstone would resign the leadership if Home Rule was defeated; this would leave the way clear for Chamberlain to become Liberal leader. His English biographers feel this is unfair on Chamberlain.

(ii) Chamberlain believed that improved administration and social conditions would pacify the Irish, and felt that these could be achieved by a system of county boards, which would be a less drastic solution than complete Home Rule. Gladstone rejected this idea.

(iii) He disliked Home Rule because it meant the separation of Ireland from the rest of Britain; this might cause other British territories to demand independence, leading to the disintegration of the Empire.

(iv) He was annoyed, with some justification, that Gladstone had not consulted him at any stage during the drawing up of the bill, and he felt that the government's time would have been better spent on introducing social reform.

16.2 THE LIBERALS AND THE EMPIRE

Gladstone's views on imperialism were well known – he disapproved of it because it interfered with the rights and freedom of overseas peoples to govern themselves; also it would be expensive – the Empire would have to be defended, causing a constant drain on British resources. He had criticised Disraeli unmercifully (see Section 14.3), but once back in office, he found to his annoyance that he was saddled with several imperial problems left by Disraeli: Gladstone wanted to disentangle Britain, but it was not so easy as he had expected.

(a) In Afghanistan Gladstone reversed Disraeli's policy (see Section 14.3(d)) by withdrawing British troops. This was regarded by the Conservatives as a typical example of Liberal weakness abroad, but in fact relations with Afghanistan remained good for the next 20 years.

(b) In the Transvaal Gladstone was not so successful. Shortly before the outbreak of the Zulu War in 1879, the Transvaal, recently annexed by Britain, had been promised self-government once the Zulu threat had been removed. This having been achieved by the Zulu War, the Transvaal Boers expected immediate independence, given Gladstone's powerful condemnation of the annexation. However, nothing happened, partly because Gladstone was busy with financial affairs and because he was beginning to think about setting up a South African federation, to include the Transvaal and the Orange Free State. In January 1881 he told the Transvaal that immediate self-government was out of the question. The Boers rose in revolt and in February defeated a tiny British force of 359 men at *Majuba Hill*; a hundred of the British were killed, including the commander, Sir George Colley. Gladstone was in a dilemma, faced with two possible courses of action:

(i) Send out more troops, to avenge the defeat and crush the Boers, which public opinion, the Queen and the Conservatives demanded.
(ii) Make peace and concede independence to the Transvaal.

Showing great courage, Gladstone took the second course: *the Pretoria Convention* (August 1881) recognised the Transvaal's independence, 'subject to the suzerainty of her Majesty'. When the Boers protested at the suzerainty clause, Gladstone agreed that it should be dropped. There was an angry public outcry at this 'surrender', and Queen Victoria sent Gladstone a strongly worded letter of protest. But Gladstone was unrepentant – he had no intention of involving Britain in an expensive colonial war. It was probably the right decision in the circumstances, but he had handled the situation badly with unfortunate consequences:

(i) He had given way to force, whereas if he had allowed independence earlier, British prestige would have been preserved.
(ii) The Boers took it as a sign of British weakness, and became more arrogant in their relations with Britain. Their attitude was a contributory cause of the Boer War which broke out in 1899 (see Section 17.2).

(c) The British occupation of Egypt. Gladstone had to accept that Britain was deeply involved in Egypt because of her ownership of almost half the

Suez Canal shares (see Section 14.3(a)). He found himself compelled, much against his will, to intervene in Egypt to safeguard British interests.

(i) The Egyptian government was in worse financial difficulties than before, trying to pay the interest on massive French and British loans which had been made to finance railways, roads, docks and agricultural projects. When an epidemic of cattle plague broke out in 1878, the country was brought to the verge of bankruptcy.

(ii) Britain and France, concerned about their financial interests, tried to force the ruler, the Khedive Ismail, to allow European advisers to control his country's finances. When he refused, they prevailed upon his overlord, the Sultan of Turkey, to replace Ismail with his son Tewfik (1879).

(iii) There was widespread resentment in Egypt at this foreign interference, and a strong anti-foreign Egyptian Nationalist party emerged led by an army officer, *Arabi Pasha*, who by May 1882 seemed poised to depose Tewfik. It seemed likely that Arabi would seize the Canal and repudiate Egypt's debts.

(iv) Gladstone, acting jointly with the French, sent a fleet to Alexandria as a warning gesture, but this provoked serious anti-European rioting at Alexandria, in which about 80 Europeans were killed. Arabi, far from overawed by the presence of the foreign fleets, began to fortify Alexandria.

(v) At this point the French decided to take no further action, but Gladstone authorised the bombardment of Alexandria's defences. A 12-hour artillery battle followed which ended with British troops occupying the city (July 1882).

(vi) Gladstone asked parliament for £2.3 million for an expedition 'to substitute the rule of law for that of military violence in Egypt'. The money was granted, and 16 400 British troops under Sir Garnet Wolseley were soon *en route* for Egypt. Having landed at Alexandria, they destroyed Arabi's army at *the Battle of Tel-el-Kebir* (September) and captured Cairo. Arabi was exiled to Ceylon and Tewfik restored to the throne.

(vii) *Sir Evelyn Baring* (later made Lord Cromer) was appointed Consul-General of Egypt, and virtually ruled the country for the next 23 years. He was a highly efficient administrator: as early as 1888 he had balanced the Egyptian budget, and he went on to introduce irrigation schemes and other reforms. Egypt had all the appearance of being a British colony, though Gladstone did not annex it and claimed that the British occupation was only temporary. The British stayed in Egypt until 1954.

(viii) Gladstone's decisive action astonished the public and boosted his popularity. He might have been expected to sympathise with the Egyptian nationalists, yet it was a more 'forward' policy than anything Disraeli had initiated. It shocked the veteran pacifist John Bright who resigned from the cabinet, remarking that Gladstone's intervention was 'simply damnable – worse than anything ever perpetrated by Dizzy'. *Why did Gladstone agree to the occupation of Egypt*? The reason was simply that financial and strategic considerations outweighed sympathy for the nationalist movement. The possibility of Arabi repudiating Egypt's debts horrified Gladstone; if Arabi seized the Suez Canal, British shipping would be at a disadvantage and the route to India threatened. It was Britain's duty 'to convert the present interior state of Egypt from anarchy and conflict to peace and order'.

(ix) *The policy was viewed as an outstanding success* - British interests had been safeguarded and British prestige abroad enhanced. However, some imperialists felt that Gladstone ought to have annexed Egypt outright or at least declared it to be a British protectorate.

(d) General Gordon and the Sudan. There was soon another opportunity for Britain to seize territory, but this time Gladstone acted predictably and did not take it. The affair was so badly mishandled that it turned out to be *the most spectacular failure of the entire ministry*.

(i) The Sudan had been ruled by Egypt since 1823, and the Sudanese, especially in the north, resented Egyptian rule because it was corrupt, it had abolished the profitable slave trade, and it had close connections with Europeans who were non-Islamic. Muhammed Ahmed, a local religious leader, proclaimed that he was the *Mahdi* - the saviour of Islam from foreign influence. He roused most of the country against the occupying Egyptian troops.

(ii) Tewfik, the newly restored ruler of Egypt, sent an Egyptian army commanded by a British officer, Hicks Pasha, to subdue the rebels, but the force, Hicks Pasha included, was slaughtered by the Mahdi and his Dervishes (November 1883).

(iii) Gladstone was faced with a difficult decision: should he send a British army to conquer the Sudan or should he leave it to the Mahdi? He decided against sending a British expedition, partly because Sir Evelyn Baring advised that the only reasonable course was to withdraw, so great was the Mahdi's popular support, and because he sympathised with the Sudanese in their nationalist struggle against the Egyptians.

(iv) However, there were still a number of Egyptian garrisons in the Sudan, commanded by British officers, who could not be left at the mercy of the Mahdi; the government therefore sent out *General Charles Gordon* with orders to organise the evacuation of the garrisons as quickly as possible. This was where the first mistake lay ...

(v) Gordon was not the sort of man to be relied on to organise a retreat. He had made himself famous through military exploits in China, Africa, India and the Crimea. In the words of Magnus, 'fearless, erratic, brilliant, perverse, always notoriously undisciplined, he exercised an extraordinary fascination over his fellow-countrymen'. He had already been governor of the Sudan (1877-9) and early in

1884 he told the press that he considered it quite feasible to resist the Mahdi.

(vi) Gordon arrived in Khartoum, the Sudanese capital, in February 1884, but instead of hurrying on with the evacuation while there was still time, he decided to stay put; a fanatical Christian, he believed it his duty to save the country from the Mahdi, and asked for British troops to be sent to keep open the Nile route from the Sudan into Egypt. This request was refused. By the end of March the Mahdi's forces had closed in and Gordon was besieged in Khartoum.

(vii) Public opinion and the Queen demanded that help be sent immedititately, but Gladstone, furious with Gordon for disobeying orders, hesitated. All through the summer the cabinet argued about what action to take and it was not until October that a relief force under Wolseley left Cairo on its 1600 mile journey up the Nile. It arrived at Khartoum on 28 January 1885 only to find that the city had fallen to the Mahdi two days earlier: Gordon was dead.

(viii) The nation was stunned and Gladstone was blamed. Angry crowds hooted and jeered in Downing Street, and instead of being the GOM (Grand Old Man) he became the MOG - murderer of Gordon. In April Gladstone outraged public opinion further by withdrawing Wolseley's forces and leaving the Sudan to the Mahdi. The cabinet was certainly blameworthy for not sending help sooner, and the Liberals were deeply unpopular.

(e) The Penjdeh Incident (1885) brought a crisis in Anglo-Russian relations which was sensibly handled by Gladstone. On 30 March, encouraged by British embarrassment over the Sudan, the Russians seized the Afghan village of Penjdeh, a few miles from the Russian frontier. Gladstone responded vigorously, warned the Russians that Britain would not tolerate such aggression, and called up the reserves. The Russians withdrew and agreed to submit their claim for Penjdeh to arbitration. Gladstone had shown that he could be firm when he felt that international morality had been violated; unfortunately the effect was spoiled when the arbitrators awarded Penjdeh to the Russians, but this was after Gladstone's government had fallen.

Gladstone's record in imperial and foreign affairs during this ministry was not impressive. Contemporaries found it difficult to understand his motives, and his actions seemed contradictory: he had abandoned the Transvaal and tried to give Ireland Home Rule with one hand while occupying Egypt with the other; all these situations were to cause further trouble later. Worst of all he had allowed the national hero Gordon to get himself killed in Khartoum.

16.3 WHAT WERE THE DOMESTIC ACHIEVEMENTS OF THE LIBERAL GOVERNMENT?

There were several important domestic reforms:

(a) The repeal of the malt tax (1880) removed a long-standing grievance of farmers, who had campaigned against it more vigorously than ever as they began to feel the pinch of the agricultural depression. Disraeli had disappointed the farmers, but Gladstone obliged, even though he had to increase income tax by a penny in the pound to make up the lost revenue.

(b) The Married Women's Property Act (1882) was designed to protect the property of married women. When a woman married, her husband became the legal owner of all her worldly goods; he could spend her savings and sell her house, and the system was an open invitation for unscrupulous fortune-hunters to take advantage of innocent and unsuspecting wealthy young ladies. The new Act gave a married woman the right to continue as the separate owner of property of all kinds.

(c) The Corrupt Practices Act (1883) went a long way towards removing abuses and corruption during general elections. It specified the amount of money that a party could spend on the campaign in each constituency, the sum being based on the number of voters; it also introduced rules about the type and number of carriages that could be used to take voters to the polls.

(d) The Parliamentary Reform Act (1884) and the Redistribution of Seats Act (1885) were the major domestic achievements.

(i) *The demand for further parliamentary reform* came from Joseph Chamberlain and the Radical wing of the Liberal party who were disappointed with Gladstone's reforms to date in this ministry. Their case was unanswerable: the 1867 Reform Act had given the vote to householders in towns, but in the counties the voting qualification was still high enough to prevent agricultural labourers and other workers from voting; thus the power of wealthy farmers and landowners was preserved. This was undemocratic, and Chamberlain was bitterly critical of the landowners whom he described as a class 'who toil not, neither do they spin . . . whose fortunes have originated by grants made in times gone by . . . and have since grown and increased while they have slept'. Another anomaly of the system was that the distribution of seats was still unfair, with many small towns having the same representation – two MPs – as large industrial cities (see Section 8.5(a)). Chamberlain carried the majority of the cabinet with him and a Reform (or Franchise) Bill passed the Commons comfortably (June 1884).

(ii) *There was strong opposition from Conservatives in the Lords* who demanded that a Redistribution Bill should be passed first. They hoped that this would cause so many local difficulties that both bills would be delayed indefinitely. Chamberlain retaliated with a series of violent speeches warning the Lords of dire consequences if they continued to block Liberal legislation; his rallying cry was 'the Peers *v*. the People'. The Queen, worried about a constitutional crisis, suggested that Gladstone and Salisbury should meet for tea and have talks. After secret negotiations between Liberal and Conservative leaders, an acceptable compromise was worked out:

(iii) *The Reform (Franchise) Act* gave the vote to all householders in the counties, adding over two million voters to the list. Altogether 5.7 million people now had the vote. The same system was extended to Ireland.

(iv) *The Redistribution Act* took away both MPs from boroughs with less than 15 000 inhabitants, while those with less than 50 000 lost one MP. This released 142 seats which were redistributed among more densely populated areas. The system was reorganised so that 647 out of 670 constituencies were represented by one MP each (single-member constituencies). The exceptions were large cities well in excess of 50 000, the Scottish Universities, and Oxford and Cambridge Universities.

(v) These Acts did not quite complete the transition to full democracy: it remained to give the vote to women and to abolish plural voting (the right of a man to vote in every constituency where he owned property).

(vi) *There were two other important results*: the disappearance of most of the two-member constituencies put a stop to the Liberal practice of running one Whig and one Radical candidate in each constituency. This meant that fewer Whigs could gain acceptance as candidates: the aristocratic Whig section began to shrink and the Radicals became the dominant wing of the party. In Ireland the changes meant that Parnell's Nationalists swept the board and could always guarantee winning at least 80 seats.

These domestic reforms, though excellent in themselves, were disappointingly few for a government with a large majority, which lasted for over five years. Part of the trouble was that Irish affairs and Irish obstruction consumed far too much of the government's time; another reason was that the Liberal party was deeply divided over a number of issues, and these are examined in the next section.

16.4 WHY WERE THERE SO MANY TENSIONS WITHIN THE LIBERAL PARTY 1880-6?

(a) There were divisions between the left (Radical) and right (Whig) wings of the party. The Whigs, mostly aristocratic landowners like Lord Hartington (later Duke of Devonshire), Lord Granville, Lord Spencer and the Duke of Argyll, were much less progressive than the Radicals, whose main figures were Joseph Chamberlain, Sir Charles Dilke and John Bright. Gladstone, careful to please the Whigs, gave them all but two of the cabinet posts, and of the Radicals only Chamberlain and Bright were included. The Radicals felt slighted and the two wings did not work smoothly together.

(b) Gladstone caused problems by his methods of running the government. As well as being Prime Minister, he took on the office of Chancellor of the Exchequer (1880) so that he was overwhelmed with a mass of financial details which prevented him from giving sufficient attention to other matters (e.g. independence for the Transvaal). Although he resigned the Chancellorship in 1882, much damage had been done. He often acted on impulse without consulting the cabinet, and was generally a difficult man to work with.

(c) The Bradlaugh case was a constant embarrassment to the government. Charles Bradlaugh was elected Liberal MP for Northampton in 1880. A Radical of somewhat unorthodox views (for the time) he was an outspoken atheist and an advocate of contraceptives. The trouble started when he refused to take the normal oath of allegiance because it included the words 'So help me God'. After a Commons select committee decided that he must take the oath, Bradlaugh agreed, but a group of young Conservative MPs led by Lord Randolph Churchill (father of Winston) stirred up the Commons to vote for Bradlaugh's expulsion. He was obliged to stand for re-election, but having again won Northampton, the same procedure was repeated when he tried to take his seat. Churchill and his friends (nicknamed 'the Fourth Party') exploited the situation to divide the Liberals. Gladstone and many Radicals supported Bradlaugh, but the Nonconformist Liberals were outraged at the presence of such an avowed atheist, and Bradlaugh was again expelled. He was re-elected and expelled a further three times, but was prevented from taking his seat until the next parliament in 1885.

(d) There was disagreement over the question of social reform. Chamberlain was keen on social and local government reform, but these matters bored Gladstone, while Hartington was positively hostile. Before the 1885 election Chamberlain launched a campaign for reform – the *Unauthorised Programme*, so called because Gladstone had not approved it. Amid mass meetings and processions, Chamberlain outlined his programme: free primary education, payment of MPs, county councils to look after rural areas, and a graduated income tax to make the wealthy foot the bill. With one eye on the new county voters, he proposed that agricultural labourers should be given smallholdings, which became known as the 'three acres and a cow' policy. In one of his speeches he declared:

> I am told if I pursue this course that I shall break up the Party . . . but I care little for the party . . . except to promote the objects which I

publicly avowed when I first entered parliament. In this rich country, an honest, a decent, an industrious man should be able to earn a livelihood for himself and his family, and should be able to lay aside something for sickness and old age. Is that unreasonable? Is that impossible?

Chamberlain and his programme were largely responsible for the Liberal success in the 1885 election, yet Gladstone made no concessions to him and ignored the case for social reform.

(e) Gladstone's foreign and imperial policies - especially independence for the Transvaal and the disaster in the Sudan - made the government unpopular with the public. Yet when he scored a success with the occupation of Egypt, some of the Radicals objected and Bright resigned from the cabinet.

(f) Irish affairs were a major cause of tension. Whatever Gladstone did, he offended one section or another of the party. When he tried to make concessions to the Irish, the Whigs objected; Chamberlain's plan for Irish local self-government on a county basis was defeated in cabinet because all the Whigs (except Granville) opposed it (May 1885). Shortly afterwards when he tried to take a hard line by stepping up coercion, the Radicals objected and Chamberlain and Dilke resigned from the cabinet. Gladstone's determination to secure Home Rule at all costs during his 1886 government was disastrous for the Liberals: most of the Whigs and the main Radical leaders opposed it. Without Chamberlain, the Liberals had little to offer, and the electorate returned to the Conservatives.

16.5 WHAT CONTRIBUTION DID THE CONSERVATIVES MAKE TO DOMESTIC REFORM 1886-92?

(a) Churchill and Tory Democracy

(i) When Salisbury's government took office it had a majority of 40 over the Liberals and could usually rely on the support of the 78 Liberal Unionists; this cancelled out the Irish Nationalists who voted with the Liberals. At first there seemed a strong possibility that it would turn out to be a great reforming ministry. The Chancellor of the Exchequer was the 37-year-old Lord Randolph Churchill who had made a name for himself with his brilliant attacks on Gladstone. He was easily the most exciting and dynamic personality in the government, and he aimed to follow the Disraeli brand of Conservatism - reform and modernisation - in order to retain working class support. In his famous *Dartford Speech* (October 1886) he announced his programme of Tory Democracy: improvement of public health and housing, compulsory national insurance, smallholdings for agricultural labourers, reform of parliamentary procedure, and the provision of parks, libraries, art galleries, museums and public baths and washhouses.

(ii) However, Churchill soon left the government after a disagreement over his controversial Budget proposals; these included increases in death duties and house duties, and reductions in income tax and in tea and tobacco duties, to be paid for by cuts in defence expenditure. W. H. Smith, the War Minister, naturally objected strongly, and when Salisbury supported Smith, Churchill suddenly resigned from the Exchequer (December 1886). He apparently thought that he was indispensable and that his action would force Salisbury to bring him back and overrule Smith. But Churchill had completely miscalculated: he had shown himself to be far too radical for the right wing of the party, and Salisbury was probably relieved to be rid of such an embarrassment. He did not ask Churchill to withdraw his resignation and instead appointed Sir Edward Goschen, a Liberal Unionist, as Chancellor. With Churchill's departure, any chance of far-reaching reform disappeared. He never again held cabinet office, and he died in 1895 at the early age of 45.

(b) Salisbury's reforms were few in number for a government which lasted six years. He believed that the function of government was to preserve and extend individual freedom, with a minimum of interference by the state in social and economic matters. He was a strong advocate of self-help: 'No men ever rise to any permanent improvement in their condition of body or of mind except by relying upon their own personal efforts'. He was not a complete reactionary though, and in a speech at Exeter early in 1892 he claimed the greatest service a government could render for a poor man was 'so to shape matters that the greatest possible liberty for the exercise of his own moral and intellectual qualities should be offered to him by law'. Measures which attempted to 'shape matters' in this way were:

(i) *The Labourers' Allotment Act (1887)* which gave local authorities the power to acquire land for allotments, so that the working classes could 'elevate themselves into a position of manly independence by their industry'. The results were disappointing: since there was no compulsion involved, many local authorities ignored it.

(ii) *The Mines Regulation Act (1887)* was more successful, extending legal protection for miners while they were at work.

(iii) *The Tithe Act (1890)* made tithes payable by the owner of land and not by the occupier. This removed a long-standing cause of friction by ending the practice of seizing tenants' cattle and other possessions in lieu of cash payment.

(iv) *In education* the government was responsible for the appointment of *the Cross Commission* (see section 12.7(d)) and for *The Fee Grant Act (1891)* which abolished fees for elementary education.

(v) *The Factory Act (1891)* raised the minimum age at which children could be employed in factories to 11, and specified that the maximum working day for women was to be 12 hours with one and a half hours for meals.

(c) The Local Government Act (1888) was the major reform, the work of C. T. Ritchie (President of the Local Government Board) and Goschen. A change was necessary because the 1835 Municipal Corporations Act had only reformed the boroughs; in the counties local government was carried out by about 27 000 different boards, which dealt separately with matters such as sanitation, drainage and street-lighting. Goschen called it 'a chaos of authorities, a chaos of jurisdictions, a chaos of rates, a chaos of franchises, a chaos, worst of all, of areas'. Unlike the town corporations, these bodies were not directly elected; local Justices of the Peace, usually landowners, appointed their members. In 1884 agricultural labourers had been given the right to vote for their MPs, so it was only logical that they should be able to choose the people who governed them at local level. *The terms of the Act were*:

(i) The old boards were abolished and replaced by 62 elected county councils. They had wide compulsory powers over matters such as the maintenance of roads and bridges and the provision of police, and they took over the administrative functions of the JPs.
(ii) Over 60 towns of more than 50 000 inhabitants were made into county boroughs: they were to have elected councils with the same powers as county councils.
(iii) London was regarded as a county of its own; subdivided into 28 Metropolitan Boroughs, its overall government was to be in the hands of the London County Council.
(iv) An important feature of the franchise for these new councils and for the borough councils was that unmarried women were given the vote, though they were not allowed to be members of councils.

In 1889 the new system was extended to cover Scotland.

After a slow start the new councils gradually took over more and more functions. There was a marked improvement in the quality of local government and the powers and influence of the landowning gentry were reduced. Further refinements were added by the Local Government Act of 1894 (see Section 16.8(a)).

Although these reforms were worthy enough, they were irrelevant to the main social and economic problem of late Victorian Britain – that a large proportion of the working class were still living in conditions of extreme poverty. In February 1886 mobs smashed shop-windows in the West End of London and set fire to cabs and carriages, to frighten 'the idle rich'. Many workers were turning towards the Labour movement and the formation of unions for unskilled workers (see Section 19.4). In 1889 the London dockers came out on strike, and so great was public support of their demand for a standard wage of six pence an hour, that after four weeks the dock companies gave way. Salisbury was worried by these developments, but although he acknowledged that they arose from genuine hardship, he could see no cure for the problems, beyond self-help.

16.6 HOW DID THE CONSERVATIVES DEAL WITH THE PROBLEMS OF IRELAND 1886-92?

This period saw a mixture of firm government and mild concessions; there was also high drama with the downfall and ruin of Parnell in a divorce case.

(i) With evictions still continuing, the Irish retaliated with the *Plan of Campaign* organised by William O'Brien and John Dillon. All the tenants on an estate would offer what they considered to be a fair rent; if the landlord disagreed, they would refuse to pay any rent and put the money into a 'fighting fund'. The plan spread rapidly, but inevitably provoked mass evictions and violence.

(ii) The government responded with a new *Crimes Act (1887)* which gave police and magistrates extra powers to deal with offenders, including the right to suspend trial by jury. The new Chief Secretary for Ireland, *Arthur Balfour* (Salisbury's nephew), applied the act rigorously, jailing anyone who broke the law. An ugly incident occurred at Mitchelstown in which police shot and killed three members of a crowd demonstrating against some evictions. Balfour ignored all protests and went calmly on, earning himself the nickname 'Bloody Balfour'.

(iii) The next developments in Irish affairs concerned Parnell. *The Times newspaper*, always strongly anti-Irish, ran a series of articles to discredit Parnell by showing that he was deliberately encouraging violence in Ireland. In April 1887 it published a letter supposed to have been written by Parnell to a friend, expressing his approval of the Phoenix Park murders. Parnell protested that the letter was a 'barefaced forgery', but very few people in England believed him. In 1888, during a libel action against *The Times*, more alleged Parnell letters were produced. The government appointed a special commission of three judges to investigate the charges; the enquiry dragged on for months, but eventually it emerged that all the letters had been forged by an Irish journalist called Pigott whose motive had been to make money by selling them. Before he could be arrested for perjury, he fled to Spain and shot himself in a Madrid hotel (March 1889). Parnell was shown to be completely innocent; he was given a standing ovation when he appeared in the Commons and there was a rush of public sympathy both for him and for Home Rule. It was the climax of his career; he was the 'uncrowned king of Ireland'.

(iv) Disaster followed in 1890 when Parnell was named as co-respondent in a divorce case. For nine years Parnell had been living with Katherine O'Shea, who had separated from her husband, Captain W. H. O'Shea, before she met Parnell. The affair was conducted so discreetly that the general public knew nothing about it. O'Shea kept quiet, hoping for political advancement from Parnell and also for a share of the large fortune which his wife was expecting to inherit from a wealthy aunt. Although the aunt died in 1889, there was a legal wrangle over the will, and the fortune was not forthcoming. O'Shea grew tired of waiting, started proceedings against his wife, naming Parnell as co-respondent, and in November 1890 was granted a divorce.

(v) The news that Parnell was an adulterer came as a bombshell. The Victorian moral code held that affairs were acceptable provided they were conducted discreetly; but once they became public in the divorce courts, the guilty parties were disgraced. Overnight Parnell was shunned by many of his supporters. Nonconformist Liberals refused to co-operate with the Nationalists unless they changed their leader; the Irish Roman Catholic Church turned against him, and 44 of the 70 Nationalist MPs deserted him. Yet he refused to resign the leadership and damaged his health trying to re-establish his authority. He died in October 1891 aged only 45, leaving the Nationalist party hopelessly split.

(vi) Parnell's disgrace and the chaos in the Nationalist party turned English opinion against Home Rule, and the government seized the opportunity to introduce some improvements. A *Land Purchase Act (1891)* extended the earlier Ashbourne Act, enabling many Irish peasants to buy land with government help. *The Congested Districts Board* was started (1891) to help over-populated areas. Using government money it introduced a variety of improvements such as draining and fencing of land, better farming methods, training schemes, railways and harbours. Living conditions gradually improved and since Irish leaders were preoccupied attacking each other rather than organising protest campaigns against the English, Ireland became comparatively calm.

16.7 FOREIGN AND IMPERIAL AFFAIRS UNDER THE CONSERVATIVES

Salisbury's main interest was in foreign affairs; for most of the time he acted as Foreign Minister as well as Prime Minister, and often remarked that he would willingly step down from the premiership so that he could concentrate on diplomatic affairs.

(a) Salisbury's aims in foreign policy:

(i) He would do his utmost to maintain peace and regarded war as 'the final and supreme evil'.

(ii) He wanted to protect British interests and 'to uphold England's honour steadily and fearlessly and always to be prone to let action go along with words rather than to let it lag behind them'.

(iii) He expected the main threats to British interests to come from France and Russia, and he hoped to use diplomatic means to counter these threats. However, he shrank from the idea of binding alliances, because these might involve Britain in war. This attitude has sometimes been described as a policy of *'splendid isolation'*, but this is a misleading phrase. Salisbury was quite happy to sign agreements with other countries, as he did with Germany, Italy and Portugal, provided they did not commit Britain to military action. Robert Taylor calls it a policy of 'limited liability' – seeking to influence events, without commitment, rather than initiating new policy.

(iv) He recognised the value of Britain's colonies but, unlike Joseph Chamberlain, he was not anxious to expand the Empire further, and was unhappy about the British occupation of Egypt which he regarded as 'a disastrous inheritance'. 'However strong you may be, there is a point beyond which your strength will not go: . . . it is madness and ruin if you allow yourself to pass it.'

The main events were:

(b) The Balkans crisis and the Mediterranean agreements

(i) Almost immediately Salisbury was faced with a serious international crisis. In 1885 Eastern Roumelia had declared itself united with Bulgaria, a clear breach of the 1878 Berlin Settlement (see Section 14.4(f)). Now that Bulgaria had turned out to be hostile to Russia, the Russians wanted Eastern Roumelia returned to Turkey; they even went to the lengths of organising the kidnapping of the Bulgarian king Alexander, in an attempt to control the country, but this misfired when the Bulgarians, with Austrian and Italian support, chose as their new king the anti-Russian Ferdinand of Saxe-Coburg.

(ii) At the same time relations between France and Germany were strained. General Boulanger, the French War Minister, was calling for revenge and the recovery of Alsace-Lorraine taken by the Germans at the end of the Franco-Prussian War (1871). Bismarck, the German Chancellor, had formed the Triple Alliance of Germany, Austria-Hungary and Italy, and was hoping for a breach between Britain and France, so that France would be completely isolated. The prospects for peace were not good. Salisbury had to try and influence the Triple Alliance powers to curb Russian designs in the Balkans, while at the same time avoid involving Britain so closely that she was drawn into a war against France. Events worked out quite successfully for Britain, although at no stage did Salisbury take the initiative:

(iii) He supported Germany and Austria in their decision to oppose Russian demands for the return of Eastern Roumelia to Turkey and for the removal of King Ferdinand from the Bulgarian throne. The Russians had to accept this check to their Balkan ambitions.

(iv) Responding to a suggestion from the Italian government, Salisbury signed the *Mediterranean Agreement* with Italy (1887). Britain would help Italy to maintain the *status quo* in the Aegean, Adriatic and Black Sea areas. Italy would support British interests in Egypt and the British navy would protect the Italian coast though only in the event of an *unprovoked* French attack on Italy. Six weeks later Austria-

Hungary also signed the Mediterranean Agreement. Bismarck was pleased that the British were moving towards the Triple Alliance, and promised Salisbury unofficially that Germany would support British interests in Egypt.

(v) Bismarck proposed a formal alliance with Britain (1889), intending it to have a strong anti-French flavour. Salisbury wanted it to include a promise of German assistance in case of Russian aggression, but Bismarck, hoping to remain on good terms with Russia, would not commit himself. Salisbury therefore declined the offer. Nevertheless relations between Britain and the Triple Alliance remained excellent right up to the resignation of Bismarck (March 1890) and while his successor Caprivi was in power (1890-4).

(c) Salisbury and the 'Scramble for Africa'

(i) The 'Scramble for Africa', lasting roughly from 1881-1900, was the operation in which the European powers established control over most of the parts of Africa which had not already been claimed. *Their motives were mixed*: sometimes governments were forced to act to protect trading companies against local rulers or against rival companies; it was hoped that there would be economic advantages - cheap raw materials and large markets; sometimes (as in the case of Egypt) European investments needed protection. Some people genuinely believed that it was the duty (the 'white man's burden') of Europeans to Christianise and civilise the African natives. There was the question of national prestige and the need to protect areas already taken by extending control into an adjacent area (the British decided to subdue the Sudan in order to consolidate their hold on Egypt).

(ii) The operation was well under way when Salisbury came to power; the French (who already owned Gabon and Algeria) started the Scramble in 1881 by declaring a protectorate over Tunisia. Britain (who already owned Cape Colony, Natal, Gambia, Sierra Leone and the Gold Coast) occupied Egypt (1882) and added Somaliland (1884) and Bechuanaland (1885) as protectorates. The Germans took South West Africa and the Cameroons (1884) followed by Tanganyika (1885), while the Italians acquired Eritrea (1885). In an attempt to avoid friction, *the Berlin Conference (1884-5)* had laid down rules of procedure which powers should follow. Each government was to inform the others which areas it was planning to settle and develop towards colonisation.

(iii) *Nevertheless disputes did occur* and Salisbury was worried in case these led to war. *The French* were highly indignant at the British occupation of Egypt where French interests were involved with the Suez Canal. *The Italians* were aggrieved at the French occupation of Tunisia, which they had been hoping to control. Salisbury was unwilling to get involved: as Taylor puts it, 'his aim was not to splash Africa with the red of the British Empire'. But he was driven to intervene by the need to protect British interests in Egypt and along the Nile,

Map 16.1 *The Scramble for Africa*

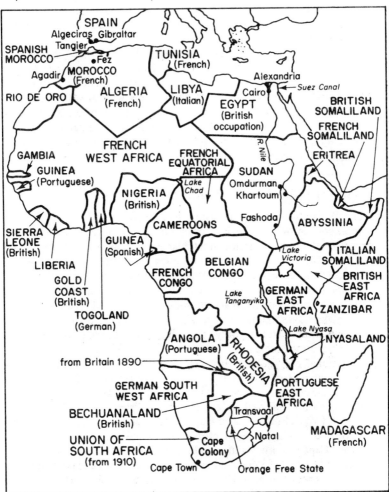

and to protect the trading companies in other parts of Africa – the Royal Niger Company clashed with the French who were trying to control the same area; the British East Africa Company was having problems with both Germans and French rivals, while Cecil Rhodes's South Africa Company was extending its operations northwards into what became known as Rhodesia, causing friction with the Transvaal Boers and the Portuguese.

(iv) *In 1890 Salisbury signed a series of remarkable agreements* which did much to reduce friction:

- The frontier between Portuguese East Africa (Mozambique) and the British areas was fixed, leaving Britain in control of Nyasaland and Rhodesia.
- The French accepted British control of Zanzibar in return for French control of Madagascar, and the northern frontier between Nigeria and French West Africa was agreed.
- The Germans recognised British control of Zanzibar, Uganda and Kenya (British East Africa); in return Britain accepted German control of German East Africa (Tanganyika), the Cameroons and South West Africa; Britain also gave Germany the North Sea island of Heligoland, which she had taken from Denmark in 1807.
- The Italians and British agreed on the frontier between Eritrea and the Sudan.

(d) A new and potentially dangerous problem appeared during the last year of Salisbury's government; Russia and France, the two powers most hostile to Britain, began to draw together in the friendship which was to lead to a full treaty of alliance in 1894. Salisbury was anxious to improve Britain's relations with France, but before he could do much about it, the Conservatives were thrown out of office.

16.8 THE LAST OF GLADSTONE (1892-4)

In the election of July 1892 the Conservatives lost 48 seats, but this was not enough to give the Liberals a decisive majority. There were 273 Liberals to 268 Conservatives; the 47 Liberal Unionists would vote with the Conservatives, and consequently Gladstone was only able to form a government with the support of the 81 Irish Nationalists. The Liberals were disappointed by the smallness of their majority, since they had been hoping to attract massive support with their *Newcastle Programme*, which included Home Rule for Ireland, a general election every three years, allotments for workers, district and parish councils, further limits on working hours, employers to be held liable for accidents to workers, and payment for MPs. However, Magnus calls the programme 'a hotch-potch which had been hastily compiled with the object of attracting as many votes from as many different sources as possible'. The Conservative defeat was probably due as much to the electorate's boredom with their record over the previous six years as it was to the Newcastle Programme.

(a) The Local Government Act (Parish Councils Act) of 1894 was the major achievement of Gladstone's Fourth Ministry.

(i) Most of the county councils set up by the 1888 Act were finding it difficult to cope with the mass of detail involved since the counties were so large. This Act subdivided the counties into urban districts and rural districts, each with its own elected council. Rural districts were further divided so that each village had its own parish council.

(ii) Married as well as single women were allowed to vote in elections for these councils and also to stand as candidates, an important new step.

(iii) The district councils gradually developed into efficient units looking after public health, roads and education. But the parish councils were never very important because the Lords insisted that their powers should be kept to a minimum. This framework of county and district councils remained the basis of local government until a new system was introduced in 1974 (see Section 31.2(e)).

(b) The Second Irish Home Rule Bill was Gladstone's final attempt to solve the Irish problem. Introduced in February 1893, it was similar to the 1886 Bill, except that Irish MPs were to be allowed to sit at Westminster. There was a tremendous struggle to get the Bill through the Commons. Chamberlain led the attack on it, and Gladstone himself, 'alert and tireless, hardly ever left the House; he gloried in every episode of the battle, and his performance, at the age of 83, must be ranked among the supreme achievements of his life' (Magnus). Once fighting broke out on the floor of the House, and it was not until September that the Bill finally passed (by 309 votes to 267). However, it was rejected overwhelmingly by the Lords (419 votes to 41). Gladstone wanted the government to resign and force a general election so that he could appeal to the country on the grounds that the undemocratic Lords were thwarting the wishes of the democractically elected Commons. The rest of the cabinet refused, and after further disagreements about naval spending. Gladstone resigned (March 1894) and retired from politics. He died in May 1898.

(c) Verdict on Gladstone. Although his first ministry (1868-74) was impressive, looking at his achievements after that, it is sometimes difficult to see what all the fuss is about. Was he a great statesman or just a self-righteous bigot? He certainly had his faults - he was self-opinionated and his reluctance to discuss policies fully with colleagues made him difficult to work with. His religious convictions led him into the irritating habit of claiming that he was at all times trying to carry out the will of God. More serious, in the words of R. T. Shannon, was that 'he had no real awareness of what the masses thought and did not care very much what they wanted ... he was moving not from right to left in the conventional manner, but rather into a lofty station of his own, remote from the main political course'. But he also had qualities which made him the outstanding figure of Victorian politics: he was prepared to fight on behalf of fair play and freedom of the individual against traditional attitudes and restrictions; this led to the great reforms of the first ministry. Above all there was his determination to stick to a course of action if he thought it was morally right and necessary, hence his obsession with Ireland and Home Rule, where his attitude was far ahead of his time. This was unfortunately his greatest failure, and the tragedy was that if the Lords had accepted the

Second Home Rule Bill in 1893, all the problems and calamities of Ireland since that date might have been avoided.

16.9 THE LIBERALS IN DECLINE: ROSEBERY'S MINISTRY (1894-5)

(a) Rosebery's government was an anti-climax after the brilliance of Gladstone. Very little was achieved because:

(i) Rosebery, though able and popular with the public, had never sat in the Commons and lacked experience of leadership and party management. The fact that he was a wealthy aristocrat who owned racehorses made him unpopular with Radicals and especially with Nonconformists (he owned the winner of the Derby in 1894 and 1895, while he was Prime Minister).

(ii) The Lords rejected almost all the government's measures, with the excuse that the Liberal majority in the Commons was too small for them to claim that they had a mandate from the electorate.

Their only achievement was *the introduction of death duties* on all forms of estate. This was designed to raise an extra four million pounds a year, mainly to pay for increased naval building. The Conservatives were highly critical of the new duties which penalised the rich, but the Lords did not reject them because they were included in Sir William Harcourt's 1894 Budget, and it was the tradition that the Lords never interfered with finance bills.

In June 1895 Rosebery resigned, hoping that public disapproval of the Lords' actions would produce a big Liberal victory in the following general election. Instead they suffered a crushing defeat: they slumped to 177 seats against 340 Conservatives and 71 Liberal Unionists. There were the usual 82 Irish Nationalists, but even so, Salisbury could count on an overall majority of around 150.

(b) Why did the Liberals lose so decisively?

(i) The Liberal party was still suffering from the split over Home Rule; there was a widespread feeling that the government should have resigned after the failure of the Second Home Rule Bill, so that instead of sympathy for their treatment at the hands of the Lords, there was only impatience.

(ii) The election coincided with a surge of public enthusiasm for imperialism which the Conservatives and Unionists seemed to stand for.

QUESTIONS

1. Irish Home Rule
Study Sources A to H and then answer the questions which follow.

Source A: cartoon by Sir John Tenniel which appeared in *Punch* at the time of Gladstone's Second Irish Land Act in 1881. The figures represent, from left to right: Parnell's Land League, Ireland, and Gladstone.

(Tenniel, 1881, reproduced by permission of the Proprietors of 'Punch'.)

THE RIVALS.

Source: *Punch*, 1881.

Source B: speech by Charles Stuart Parnell in Cork, 21 January 1885.

We shall never gain anything from England unless we tread on her toes; we will never gain a single sixpennyworth from her by conciliation . . . In 1880 I pledged myself that I should form one of an independent Irish party to act in opposition to every English government which refused to concede the just rights of Ireland (applause) . . . Every Irish politician must be forcibly driven back to the question of national self-government for Ireland (hear, hear). I do not know how this great question will be eventually settled . . . but we cannot ask for less than the restitution of the parliament which was stolen from us at the end of the last century (loud cheers).

Source: quoted in L. Evans and P. J. Pledger (eds), *Contemporary Sources and Opinions in Modern British History, vol. 2*, Warne, 1967 (adapted extracts).

Source C: speech by Gladstone in the House of Commons during the debate on the First Irish Home Rule Bill, 8 April, 1886.

Our ineffective coercion is morally worn out . . . Something must be done, something is demanded from us to restore to Ireland the first conditions of civilised life – the free course of law, the liberty of every individual in the exercise of every legal right, the confidence of the people in the law . . . The principle I am laying down is not just for Ireland . . . 51 years ago England tried to pass good laws for the Colonies; but the Colonies said – 'We do not want your good laws; we want our own.' We admitted the reasonableness of that principle. We have to consider whether it is applicable to Ireland. We stand face to face with what is termed Irish nationality, which demands complete self-government in Irish affairs. Is this an evil in itself? Is this a thing that we should view with horror? Sir, I believe that it is not.

Source: Hansard, *Parliamentary Debates*, 8 April, 1886.

Source D: extract from a book by an opponent of Home Rule.

Englishmen will find to their disappointment that they have not achieved the object which from an English point of view was the principal inducement to grant Home Rule to the Irish people, that is, freedom from the difficulty of governing Ireland. Home Rule is not Separation and nothing short of Irish independence would greatly lessen English responsibility . . . Britain remains responsible for the maintenance of peace and order. Home Rule cannot remove the causes of Irish discontent. It cannot tempt capital towards Ireland, but it may easily drive capital away. It cannot diminish poverty; it cannot soften religious bigotry; it cannot of itself remove agrarian discontent.

Source: A. V. Dicey, *England's Case against Home Rule*, John Murray, 1886.

Source E: extract from a book written in 1887.

In relation to Ireland, Mr. Gladstone has proved an evil-doer. The predicted friendship between England and Ireland is pure moonshine. Give her Mr. Gladstone's Home Rule and disloyal Ireland will hit befooled England with redoubled strength and bitterness. She will work for complete separation, and will win it. The hatred which has been nursed so long has only been intensified by untimely concession . . . On the other hand an empire still manned by Britons will not die without a fight . . . Mr. Gladstone is a calamity to Britain. What has converted him into a traitor to his country? Mainly of course, the unsteadiness of his own character.

Source: J. Tyndall, *Perverted Politics*, William Blackwood, 1887 (adapted extracts).

Source F: a comment from a modern historian.

It is impossible not to lean to the conclusion that the deciding factor in Chamberlain's career, the wrecking of Home Rule and the Liberal Party, was the belief that the summit of his political ambition was now within his grasp, were he but bold enough.

Source: P. S. O'Hegarty, *Ireland Under the Union*, Methuen, 1962.

Source G: extract from a pamphlet written in 1886.

The painful scene in the House of Commons between Mr. Gladstone and Mr. Chamberlain revealed a state of things that every true Liberal must deplore. It was evident that the 'grand old man' had been pushed too far; that Mr. Gladstone had concocted his Home Rule scheme without proper consultation with his colleagues, and that Mr. Chamberlain in particular had been treated very cavalierly. Mr. Chamberlain had rendered great service to the Liberal party and Mr. Gladstone had no right to treat him as a teacher treats a schoolboy. He deserved consideration when Mr. Gladstone was devising how to meet the claims of Ireland.

Source: G. W. Foote, *Gladstone's Irish Stew*, 1886; quoted in F. E. Huggett, *What They've Said about Nineteenth Century Statesman*, Oxford, 1972.

Source H: note from Sir William Harcourt, a member of the Cabinet, to Gladstone, March, 1886.

I do not think Chamberlain is really hostile, but you have never really discussed the [Home Rule] question with him. A great deal in the future depends on how he is personally handled.

Source: quoted in E. J. Feuchtwanger, *Gladstone*, Allen Lane, 1975.

(a) **(i)** What message is the cartoonist in Source **A** trying to put across? **4(a)**

    (ii) Using the evidence of the cartoon, explain how sympathetic you think the cartoonist is to each of the three figures shown and the people they represent. **4(a, b)**

(b) **(i)** Using the evidence of Source **B** and your own knowledge, explain why Gladstone's Second Irish Land Act did not solve the problems of Ireland. **1, 2, 4(a)**

    (ii) Explain in your own words what Parnell was asking for in Source **B**. **4(a)**

    (iii) What evidence is there in Source **B** of Parnell's popularity with the Irish people? **4(a, b)**

(c) **(i)** According to Source **C**, why had Gladstone decided in favour of Home Rule for Ireland? **4(a)**

    (ii) Using your own words, make a list of objections to Home Rule mentioned in Sources **D** and **E**. **4(a, c)**

    (iii) From the evidence of Source **E**, what is the writer's attitude towards

        A. the Irish;
        B. Gladstone.
        Explain your answers fully. **4(a, b)**

(d) **(i)** According to Source **F**, why did Chamberlain decide to oppose Home Rule for Ireland? **4(a)**

    (ii) In what ways do Sources **G** and **H** seem to differ from Source **F**? **4(a, c)**

    (iii) Why do you think the scene in the Commons between Gladstone and Chamberlain mentioned in Source **G** was one that 'every true Liberal must deplore'? **1, 2, 4(a)**

    (iv) What other reasons, not mentioned in Sources **F**, **G** and **H** did Chamberlain have for opposing Home Rule? Source **E** should give you a clue. **1, 2, 4(a, c)**

(e) In June 1886, Gladstone's First Irish Home Rule Bill was defeated in the Commons. What effect did this have over the next ten years on:

    (i) the Liberal Party;
    (ii) Ireland? **1, 2**

(f) **(i)** What are the advantages and disadvantages of each of these Sources **A** to **H** for the historian? **4(a, b)**

    (ii) Do you think the evidence provided by these Sources alone is enough to explain why Gladstone's First Irish Home Rule Bill was defeated? Explain your answer fully. **4(a, b, c)**

2. Egypt and the Sudan

Study Sources **A** to **C** and then answer the questions which follow.

Source A: report by Stephen Cave, a British official sent to make a survey of Egypt's finances, March 1876.

> The critical state of the finances of Egypt is due to the combination of two causes. She suffers from the ignorance, dishonesty, waste and extravagance of the East which have brought her to the verge of ruin; and at the same time from the vast expense caused by hasty and inconsiderate attempts to adopt the civilisation of the West . . . The expenditure, though heavy, would not of itself have produced *the present crisis* which may be attributed entirely to the ruinous conditions of loans raised for schemes such as the construction of railways . . . The resources of Egypt are sufficient if properly managed, to meet her liabilities . . . a European official should be brought in, like our Indian officials, who have done so much to raise the tone of the native races.

> Source: quoted in M. E. Chamberlain, *The Scramble for Africa*, Longman, 1974.

Source B: telegram from Gordon in Khartoum to Sir Evelyn Baring, British Consul-General of Egypt, in Cairo, March 1885.

> If Egypt is to be kept quiet the *Mahdi* must be smashed up. He is most unpopular and with care and time could be smashed. Remember that once Khartoum belongs to Mahdi, the task will be far more difficult . . . I repeat that evacuation is possible, but you will feel the effect in Egypt and will be forced to enter into a far more serious affair in order to guard Egypt.

> Source: quoted in A. Moorehead, *The White Nile*, Penguin, 1963.

Source C: extract from Sir Evelyn Baring's memoirs, published in 1908.

> Gordon was extremely pugnacious. He was hot-headed, impulsive and swayed by his emotions. He formed rapid opinions without deliberation and rarely held to one opinion for long. His imagination ran riot, and he arrived at conclusions which were grotesque, as for instance, when he insinuated that the British government hoped that he and his companions would be killed by the Mahdi. In fact, except personal courage, great fertility in military ideas, a lively repugnance to injustice, oppression and meanness, and a considerable power to influence those with whom he was brought into personal contact, General Gordon does not appear to have possessed any of the qualities which would have fitted him to undertake the difficult task he had in hand. But, when all this has been said, how grandly the character of the man comes out . . . No Christian

martyr ever faced death with more unconcern than General Gordon. His faith was sublime.

Source: as for Source **B.**

(a) **(i)** According to Source **A**, what was 'the present crisis' in Egypt?
                                                                              4(a)

   (ii) What does Stephen Cave think were the causes of the crisis?
                                                                              4(a)

   (iii) What solution does he suggest?   **4(a)**

   (iv) How would you describe Stephen Cave's attitude towards the Egyptians, in Source **A**?   **4(a, b)**

(b) **(i)** From your own knowledge of the subject, explain why Egypt was thought to be so important to Britain at this time.   **1, 2**

   (ii) What actions did British governments take in the period 1879 until September 1882 (Battle of Tel-el-Kebir) to deal with the situation in Egypt?   **1, 2**

   (iii) What was the reaction of public opinion in Britain to Gladstone's Egyptian policy?   **1, 2**

(c) **(i)** Who was the 'Mahdi' referred to in Source **B**?   **1, 2, 4(a)**
   (ii) Why did the Sudanese resent being ruled by Egypt?   **1, 2**
   (iii) From the evidence of Source **B**, why did Gordon think it was important to smash the Mahdi?   **4(a)**
   (iv) Using your own knowledge, describe the circumstances which led Gladstone to send General Gordon to Khartoum.   **1, 2**

(d) **(i)** According to Baring in Source **C**, what were Gordon's good qualities?   **4(a)**
   (ii) After a careful study of the evidence in Source **C**, would you say that Baring admired Gordon or not? Explain your answer fully.   **4(a, b)**

(e) **(i)** Describe briefly what happened in the Sudan between February 1884 (Gordon's arrival at Khartoum) and January 1885 (Gordon's death).   **1, 2**
   (ii) From the evidence of Sources **B** and **C** and your own knowledge, how far do you think Gladstone was to blame for the death of Gordon?   **1, 2, 4(a, c)**
   (iii) What hesitations might a historian have about accepting Sources **B** and **C** without question?   **4(a, b)**

3. Lord Salisbury and the Conservative Government of 1886–92
Using among other things the material suggested in brackets, show how the Conservatives tried to deal with the following:

   (a) social problems (Labourers' Allotment Act, 1887; Factory Act, 1891);

   (b) local government (Local Government Act, 1888);

   (c) the situation in Ireland (the work of Arthur Balfour);

(d)   foreign affairs (the Mediterranean Agreement, 1887);

(e)   the problems of empire (agreements with France, Germany and Italy).   **1, 2**

4   Explain the attitude and reaction of each of the following to the defeat of Gladstone's First Irish Home Rule Bill in the Commons in June 1886:

(a)   a Liberal supporter of Gladstone;

(b)   a Liberal–Unionist supporter of Chamberlain;

(c)   an Irish supporter of Parnell and Home Rule.   **1, 2, 3**

CHAPTER 17

TEN YEARS OF

CONSERVATIVE RULE

1895–1905

SUMMARY OF EVENTS

Lord Salisbury was Prime Minister from 1895 until 1902 and also acted as Foreign Minister until 1900 when Lord Lansdowne took over the Foreign Office. When Salisbury retired in July 1902 his nephew Arthur James Balfour became Prime Minister. The Liberal Unionists were now almost indistinguishable from the Conservatives, and two of their leaders, the Duke of Devonshire (formerly Lord Hartington) and Joseph Chamberlain were members of Salisbury's cabinet. In fact the Conservatives and their Liberal allies were often referred to simply as *Unionists* to denote their commitment to maintain the full union between Ireland and the rest of the United Kingdom.

Chamberlain, Colonial Secretary until his resignation in September 1903, was an outstanding figure in the government, often seeming to eclipse the Prime Minister himself. He chose to be Colonial Secretary because of his belief that it was important to build up the British Empire as a great political and economic unit; this period is therefore regarded as the heyday of *imperialism*. British influence was extended in China, and the Sudan was successfully reconquered (1898). In southern Africa Britain became involved in the *Boer War (1899–1902)* against the Transvaal and the Orange Free State; though the war eventually ended successfully, the British victory did not come easily and they were made painfully aware that they lacked friends. The so-called policy of *splendid isolation* was therefore transformed into a search for allies. Two important agreements were signed, one with Japan (1902) and the other – the famous Entente Cordiale – with France (1904). The subsequent Liberal government completed the transformation by signing an agreement with Russia (1907) (see Section 20.7(b)). As Britain's relations with France and Russia improved, those with Germany deteriorated because of economic and naval rivalry.

Queen Victoria, who had always exercised a restraining influence on her grandson, the German Kaiser Wilhelm II, died in January 1901. She had reigned since 1837 and had lived long enough to celebrate both her Golden and Diamond Jubilees (1887 and 1897). She was succeeded by her son, the 59-year-old *Edward VII*.

Ireland remained comparatively quiet and during Balfour's government, important concessions were made including *Wyndham's Land Act (1903)*. In home affairs social reforms were very few, though *Balfour's Education Act (1902)* was an important measure. In spite of the investigations of *Charles Booth* and *Seebohm Rowntree* which revealed serious poverty among the working classes, nothing was done to help, and many began to be attracted to the newly formed *Labour Party* (see Section 19.7).

Yet at the half-way stage of the period the Conservatives still retained their popularity; in the *general election of October 1900* they won an overall majority of 131, probably thanks to a great surge of *jingoism* (aggressive or excessive patriotism) during the Boer War. It was during Balfour's premiership that public opinion began to grow tired of the Conservatives. In the *election of January 1906* the Liberals won an astonishing victory with 399 seats against the Conservatives' 157. One reason for the Conservative defeat was Chamberlain's controversial campaign in favour of *tariff reform*, which fatally divided the party. It was to be 1922 before the Conservatives were able to form another government.

17.1 JOSEPH CHAMBERLAIN AND IMPERIALISM

Born in 1836, the son of a prosperous London boot and shoe manufacturer, Chamberlain went to Birmingham at the age of 18 to become a partner in a screw-making factory owned by his uncle, J. S. Nettlefold. With his acute business sense, he quickly became the driving force behind the enterprise and developed it into a highly profitable firm. In 1876 he was able to retire and live on his personal fortune, devoting most of his time to politics. The appalling conditions in Birmingham led him to stand for the town council in 1869; he spent the rest of his life deeply involved in local and national politics, though after a severe stroke in 1906 he remained an invalid. He died in July 1914. His career ran as follows:

1869–76	member of Birmingham council; Mayor, 1873-6
1876–86	Liberal MP for Birmingham; President of the Board of Trade, 1880–6
1886–95	Liberal Unionist MP for Birmingham
1895–1914	Conservative/Unionist MP for Birmingham; Colonial Secretary, 1895–1903

(a) In Birmingham Chamberlain achieved a great deal. In the mid-1860s the people of Birmingham were suffering all the evils of a new industrial city: child labour, long working hours in dangerous conditions, overcrowded slums, and no proper disposal of sewage and refuse. The town council, reluctant to spend money, had ignored opportunities for improvement. Chamberlain was determined on action: 'The town', he declared, 'shall not, with God's help, know itself!'

(i) Using his business skills and methods, he organised the Birmingham Liberal Association which enabled him and some of his friends to win seats on the council. By 1873 the Liberals were in a majority.

(ii) He gave £1000 to the Birmingham (later the National) Education League, and soon became its chairman. The League campaigned for free, compulsory and undenominational education for all. Chamberlain felt that after the 1867 Reform Act, it was essential to educate the new working class borough voters. The League played a part in the passing of Forster's Education Act in 1870 (see Section 12.7(c)), though it far from satisfied them.

(iii) The council bought up the town's two gas companies and its water-works, which were then modernised and expanded. A Medical Officer of Health was appointed and a new hospital built. A Drainage Board was set up to deal with the proper disposal of sewage and refuse. Street paving and lighting were extended and six public parks opened. Chamberlain even organised a national conference in Birmingham to encourage other authorities to follow Birmingham's example.

(iv) His most remarkable achievement was *the Improvement Scheme* made possible by the 1875 Artisans Dwellings Act (see Action 12.5(a)). About 90 acres of slums in the town centre were demolished and replaced by a fine new shopping area – Corporation Street – and by high standard housing for workers.

(v) New libraries, museums and art galleries were opened and in 1900 Chamberlain founded the University of Birmingham. Thanks to Chamberlin Birmingham was recognised as a city in 1889 and was widely regarded as a model of progressive local government.

(b) As a Liberal MP he was full of self-confidence and an excellent speaker; he soon established a reputation as 'Radical Joe', the champion of the working classes, and was not afraid to criticise anyone or anything which stood in the way of social reform, whether it was the monarchy, the House of Lords, or other members of the Liberal party. He believed that the party could only survive if it dropped its Whig elements, and he was impatient with Gladstone for his lack of interest in social questions and his obsession with Ireland. He wanted the government to 'intervene on behalf of the weak against the strong, in the interests of labour against capital, of want and suffering against luxury and ease'. Gladstone never understood or liked Chamberlain and it was with the greatest reluctance that he made him President of the Board of Trade in 1880. Working closely with his friend Sir Charles Dilke, another Radical, Chamberlain made a valuable contribution:

(i) In 1877 he formed *the National Liberal Federation* with the aim of helping Liberal candidates fight elections. Using the same techniques as his local party 'caucus' in Birmingham, the Federation provided efficient organisation in many constituencies – producing pamphlets and posters, collecting subscriptions, attracting new members and holding public meetings and social events. This was partly responsible for the Liberal victory in the 1880 general election.

(ii) Pressure from Chamberlain and the Radicals resulted in the introduction of the *Third Parliamentary Reform Bill* in 1884 (see Section 16.3(d)).

(iii) Before the 1885 election Chamberlain produced his *Unauthorised Programme* of social reform (see Section 16.4(d)). Lloyd George later paid him a handsome compliment: 'I am convinced that our victory [in the 1885 election] is all due to Chamberlain's speeches. Gladstone had no programme that would draw at all'.

(iv) He was concerned at the growing unemployment and he urged the Poor Law Guardians to use their powers to provide work for the unemployed (1886).

Chamberlain was obviously the most dynamic of the leading Liberals and was viewed in many quarters as a likely party leader when Gladstone eventually retired. However, this was not to be: serious trouble began when Chamberlain, a passionate imperialist, opposed Gladstone's decision to give Home Rule to Ireland (see Section 16.1(e)), thereby splitting the Liberal party.

(c) Colonial Secretary. When Chamberlain joined Salisbury's government in 1895 there was an hysterical chorus of criticism from Liberals; he was inconsistent, a turncoat, a traitor, a Judas. 'It seems to me', remarked Gladstone, 'that Chamberlain is the greatest blackguard I have ever come across.' Chamberlain believed that he was being perfectly consistent; he was convinced that the best way of curing the trade depression was by developing and expanding the British Empire – the larger the Empire, the more profitable British commerce would become; this would reduce unemployment and help the workers. He also believed in Britain's 'national mission' to take the benefits of civilisation to backward people. Since the Conservatives were more committed to imperialism than the Liberals, it was only logical that Chamberlain should eventually join them. So strongly did he feel about imperialism that he chose to be Colonial Secretary rather than Chancellor of the Exchequer.

Nor had he abandoned his radicalism: he hoped to push the Conservatives towards social reform, and was responsible for the *Workmen's Compensation Act (1897)* which enabled workers to claim compensation for injuries suffered at work. The Act had its weaknesses – seamen, domestic servants and agricultural labourers were not included; but at least the government had accepted the principle that employers must bear the responsibility for accidents, and eventually, by 1908, all categories of worker were included. Chamberlain also urged Salisbury to introduce *Old Age Pensions*, but nothing came of it, because the expenses of the Boer War used up all the available funds. Chamberlain's main energies though were expended on his imperial policies:

(i) In 1896 Chamberlain negotiated a successful conclusion to a dispute with Venezuela about her frontier with British Guiana. The American

President Cleveland resurrected the Monroe Doctrine (see Section 3.3(b)), threatening war if Britain tried to seize any Venezuelan territory. Tension was high but Salisbury allowed Chamberlain to visit the USA where he persuaded the Americans to submit the case to international arbitration. The verdict awarded Britain almost the entire territory she had claimed.

(ii) An expedition under Wolseley was sent to the Gold Coast to deal with the Ashanti tribesmen who were constantly raiding areas claimed as British. Early in 1896 the Ashantis were defeated and British control secured.

(iii) In 1897 a dispute arose with France about the frontier between the French colony of Dahomey and Nigeria. French troops occupied two small towns, Busa and Nikki, claimed by the British. Chamberlain retaliated by organising the West African Frontier Force commanded by Sir Henry Lugard. This firm action resulted in a compromise (June 1898) by which France kept Nikki but gave Busa to Britain.

(iv) The Sudan was reconquered (1898) and the Fashoda incident, another dispute with the French, was successfully concluded (see Section 17.3(v)-(vi)).

(v) Britain leased the Chinese port of Wei-hai-wei (1898) in response to the German seizure of Kaio-chau and the Russian occupation of Port Arthur.

(vi) As a result of the Boer War (see next section) the Transvaal and the Orange Free State were brought under British control and in 1910 they became part of the new Union of South Africa.

It was not simply a case of acquiring as much territory as possible; Chamberlain tried to improve the British possessions. 'We are landlords of a great estate', he remarked; 'it is the duty of a landlord to develop his estate'.

(vii) He encouraged the formation of Joint Stock Companies, which, in return for a monopoly of trade in an area, undertook to develop it by providing amenities such as harbours and railways.

(viii) Government money was sometimes given directly to finance projects; e.g. a railway in Uganda. *The Colonial Loans Act (1899)* provided £3 million which was spent on a variety of projects - railways in Sierra Leone, Lagos and the Gold Coast, irrigation and railway systems in Cyprus, harbours and railways in Jamaica.

(ix) Chamberlain's initiative led to the founding of two Schools of Tropical Medicine, one in London, the other in Liverpool to investigate the causes of the diseases which were holding up progress.

(x) He was responsible for organising the *Colonial Conference of 1897* where he explained his ideas for an empire customs union. He wanted the colonies to remove the duties by which they protected their industries against imported British goods, but they would only agree if Britain promised to give preference to their goods on the British market. This would require Britain to place tariffs on goods imported from countries outside the Empire, but since Britain was a free trade country, this was not possible. At the 1902 Colonial Conference, attended by representatives from Canada, Australia, New Zealand, Newfoundland, Cape Colony and Natal, the result was the same, and Chamberlain also failed to persuade them to join in an imperial federation.

Although his imperial policies had a great deal of success, Chamberlain was deeply disappointed at his failure to organise the Empire into a great customs union. Consequently he took the disastrous decision to campaign for a return to tariffs, which would enable a system of imperial preference to be introduced. He resigned from the cabinet so that he could devote himself fully to the campaign. This was to be his greatest failure, splitting the Conservatives and contributing to their crushing defeat in 1906. Peel had also split the Conservatives, and Lloyd George was to do the same to the Liberals during the First World War; but Chamberlain is the only politician to have split two major parties.

17.2 THE BOER WAR 1899–1902

(a) **What caused the war?** Since the First Boer War of 1881 after which the Transvaal was granted independence (see Section 16.2(b)), her relation-

Map 17.1 *Southern Africa during the Boer War*

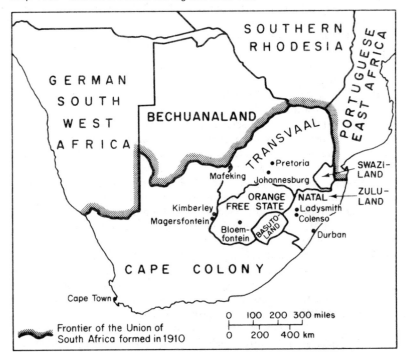

ship with Britain was not a comfortable one, although the Orange Free State remained friendly towards Britain. Relations gradually deteriorated; by 1897 the Orange Free State had joined the Transvaal and events escalated into war. The reasons were:

(i) *President Paul Kruger* of the Transvaal wanted to extend his country's boundaries, but was continually frustrated by the British who occupied Bechuanaland on the Transvaal's western frontier in 1885. *Cecil Rhodes*, head of the British South Africa Company was granted a charter which enabled him to develop Rhodesia (1888-91), hemming the Transvaal in to the north.

(ii) *Cecil Rhodes* was the central figure in British South Africa. Sent out to his brother in Natal on a health cure (for TB) in 1870 when he was only 17, Rhodes became involved in the diamond mining recently opened up at Kimberley. By 1881 he had secured control of virtually all the Kimberley mines for his company, the de Beers Corporation, and he was immensely rich. His burning ambition was to use his wealth to extend the Empire until Britain controlled the whole of southern Africa, and he had grandiose plans to build a railway linking the Cape with British-controlled Cairo in the north. A confrontation between Rhodes and Kruger was inevitable: if Rhodes had his way, the Transvaal must become part of the British Empire.

(iii) *The discovery of gold in the Transvaal* in 1886 complicated the situation. From being a poor agricultural country, the Transvaal was suddenly transformed into one of the wealthiest areas in Africa. By 1894 it seemed to Rhodes that it was becoming richer than Cape Colony; it was also becoming less dependent on the Cape, since the Boers could now export and import goods along a new railway to Delagoa Bay in Portuguese East Africa, and there was no need to pass through British territory at all. Kruger began to buy armaments from Germany and there were rumours that he was planning to take over the whole of South Africa. This was not so unlikely as it might seem: there were thousands of Boers living in the Cape, and if they co-operated with Kruger, such a plan would have been perfectly feasible. More than ever it seemed essential to Rhodes that some action must be taken against 'Krugerism'.

(iv) Rhodes, who had become Prime Minister of Cape Colony in 1890, decided on direct intervention. Thousands of settlers, many of them Cape British, had moved into the Transvaal to work in the gold mines. By 1895 these *uitlanders* (outsiders) as the Boers called them, outnumbered the Boers themselves; Kruger, afraid of being swamped and anxious to preserve the character of his country, refused them all political rights and taxed them heavily. Rhodes decided to stir up uitlander unrest into revolution which, with some outside help, might overthrow Kruger. The result of his efforts was . . .

(v) *The Jameson Raid (December 1895)*. Dr Leander Starr Jameson, an associate of Rhodes, was to lead an invasion of the Transvaal from Bechuanaland to coincide with an uprising of uitlanders in Johannesburg. However, uitlander unrest, genuine though it was, was too disorganised to produce revolution, and when Jameson rode into the Transvaal at the head of only 500 troops, he was easily defeated by the Boers. Chamberlain, the Colonial Secretary, claimed that he knew nothing about the raid, but Elizabeth Longford shows that he was deeply implicated and suggests that the probable understanding was that if the exploit failed, Rhodes should take the responsibility, which he did by resigning as Cape Prime Minister. *The results of the affair were disastrous*: to the rest of the world it seemed that Britain had authorised the unprovoked invasion of a foreign state, and the German Kaiser Wilhelm II sent a telegram to Kruger congratulating him on successfully defending his country. The raid offended the Orange Free State and Cape Boers; it confirmed all Kruger's fears about British intentions and he continued to arm heavily. War was not inevitable at this stage though, provided the British abandoned their designs on the Transvaal.

(vi) *Sir Alfred Milner*, appointed High Commissioner for South Africa in 1897, must bear much of the responsibility for the outbreak of war. A passionate imperialist, Milner suspected that Kruger might attempt to expand the Transvaal southwards, with backing from the Germans and the Cape Boers. In order to destroy Kruger, he deliberately set about provoking a crisis which could be turned into war. Given Kruger's belligerent attitude this was not too difficult, though in fact the old man was prepared to make some concessions. The uitlanders sent a telegram to Queen Victoria protesting about their 'frightful' treatment at the hands of the Boers. This prompted the British government to demand that some improvement be made in the uitlanders' position. Kruger agreed to meet Milner at Bloemfontein, capital of the Orange Free State, in June 1899; he offered to give the uitlanders the vote after the residential qualification of seven years, and there seemed a good chance of a peaceful compromise. However, Milner rejected this and demanded a five-year qualification which Kruger would not hear of; the meeting broke up without progress. Chamberlain, genuinely hoping to avoid war, attempted to reopen negotiations but without satisfactory response. British troops now began to move up to the Transvaal frontiers.

(vii) The Boers, also moving troops, responded by sending an ultimatum to the British government suggesting independent arbitration, but demanding the withdrawal of British troops from Boer frontiers and the return home of all British forces which had recently arrived in South Africa. When this was rejected the Transvaal and Orange Free State Boers immediately attacked Natal and the Cape. Kruger had therefore played into Milner's hands, and as Salisbury put it, he had 'liberated us from the necessity of explaining to the people of England why we are at war'.

(b) Events in the war

(i) The Boer armies moved swiftly and besieged Ladysmith in Natal, Mafeking and Kimberley (where Rhodes himself was trapped) in the west. *Sir Redvers Buller*, British Commander-in-Chief, split his troops into three divisions in an attempt to relieve all three towns. But in the same week in December – Black Week as it became known to the British public – each army was defeated: Buller himself advancing to relieve Ladysmith was checked by Louis Botha's troops at Colenso; the division moving along the road to Kimberley was heavily defeated by Cronje's forces at Magersfontein, while the third division was driven back at Stormberg. In January 1900 Buller again tried to relieve Ladysmith, but failed more disastrously than before, losing 1700 men at Spion Kop.

(ii) The British failures were not difficult to explain. The Boer forces outnumbered the British by two to one, they were all mounted and they were excellent marksmen, who knew the country well; they had superior German Krupps artillery and rifles. The War Office had not studied the situation properly and sent too many unmounted troops who had to operate at a great disadvantage in unfamiliar territory where the local population was hostile. Most historians have blamed the incompetence of the generals, particularly Buller, but recently Thomas Pakenham has defended Buller, claiming that he was learning fast under the most difficult circumstances, and would eventually have been just as effective as Roberts and Kitchener, the men sent out to supersede him. What was needed was large numbers of extra troops.

(iii) As vast reinforcements poured in, Lord Roberts with Kitchener as his Chief of Staff, outmanoeuvred Cronje and relieved Kimberley (February); soon afterwards Cronje was forced to surrender at Paardeberg. After that things happened quickly: Buller relieved Ladysmith (February), Roberts captured Bloemfontein (March), Mafeking was relieved (May) after a siege lasting 217 days, and finally Johannesburg and Pretoria (capital of the Transvaal) were captured (June). Kruger escaped to Europe and the Boer republics were annexed to Britain. It seemed as if the war was over and Roberts returned to Britain. British successes at this stage were a result partly of the fact that they now had many more troops at their disposal, including some from Canada, Australia and New Zealand, and partly because the Boers made the mistake of keeping too many of their troops tied up in the sieges of Ladysmith, Kimberley and Mafeking.

(iv) The Boers, however, refused to surrender or negotiate, and continued to fight in small guerrilla groups, constantly harassing the British forces. Helped and sheltered by the friendly local populations, they raided Natal and Cape Colony, destroying crops and attacking railways. Kitchener found these tactics difficult to deal with and eventually he resorted to a drastic policy of 'scorched earth': farms and crops were destroyed to deny the guerrillas food; forts or blockhouses were built to protect railways; the civilian population including women and children were rounded up into concentration camps to prevent their helping the guerrillas. Kitchener's methods were effective: the Boer leaders agreed to negotiate and a peace treaty was signed at Vereeniging in 1902.

(v) British tactics aroused world-wide criticism, since the concentration camps were overcrowded and badly mismanaged; epidemics broke out which killed over 20 000 people during 1901. Sir Henry Campbell-Bannerman, the Liberal leader, denounced government policy as 'methods of barbarism'.

(c) Results of the war

(i) *The Treaty of Vereeniging* was reasonable and generous in its terms: although the two Boer republics were annexed, they were promised eventual self-government; English was to be the official language but Afrikaans (the language of the Boers) was to be allowed in schools and law-courts. Three million pounds was given by the British government to help the Boers repair damage and re-stock farms. On the whole this settlement was satisfactory to both sides, though some Boer leaders demanded more money and doubted whether the promise of self-government would ever be kept. In fact, Campbell-Bannerman's Liberal government did carry it out in 1906, and as relations between British and Boers steadily improved, the Transvaal and the Orange Free State agreed to join the Union of South Africa, along with Cape Colony and Natal, in 1910 (see Section 20.1).

(ii) The war revealed Britain's isolated position in the world: the other major European powers – Germany and Austria-Hungary, France and Russia – all sympathised with the Boers. Consequently the British made determined efforts to find new allies.

(iii) As the war dragged on through 1901 and into 1902, the public tended to grow disenchanted with it. It had cost at least £200 million and over 20 000 British lives, and people began to question whether it had all been worth it. The effect was to turn a large section of public opinion against the Conservatives and against imperialism, which became discredited.

17.3 FOREIGN AFFAIRS 1895–1905

For the sake of simplicity it is usual to divide the period into two phases:

1895 to 1900 when Britain continued the so-called policy of *splendid isolation*;
1900 to 1905 when Britain looked for, and found, allies – Japan (1902) and France (1904).

(a) Splendid isolation. Salisbury had started the 'splendid isolation' policy during his previous government of 1886-92. His aims in foreign policy are set out in Section 16.7(a). But in fact it is a misleading term: it was not that Britain deliberately refused to have anything to do with the rest of the world – Salisbury signed the Mediterranean Agreements and negotiated boundary settlements in Africa. But Britain *was* isolated in the sense that Salisbury kept her aloof from binding alliances in case they committed her to military action.

By the time Salisbury came to power again in 1895, an important change had taken place: the two countries he most feared, *France and Russia, had signed an alliance with each other in 1894*. Germany, Austria-Hungary and Italy were already bound together in the Triple Alliance, so that Britain was the only major European country not associated with an alliance bloc. Nor was Salisbury anxious to commit Britain to one of them. He preferred to try and revive the old Concert of Europe in which *all* the powers would co-operate together in times of crisis, but he had little success. He was getting old – he was 66 in 1895 – and his health was deteriorating; he came under increasing pressure from some of his cabinet, particularly Chamberlain, Goschen and Lansdowne, for a more positive policy. Chamberlain was full of enthusiasm for an alliance with Germany, but Salisbury did all he could to avoid it. The main events illustrate the different strands:

(i) *The Venezuela dispute (1895-6)* was settled in Britain's favour (see Section 17.1(c)), but not before it had demonstrated the lack of support for Britain.

(ii) *New problems in Turkey* occurred in 1896 when the Turks, breaking their promise made at Berlin (1878), began wholesale massacres of Christian Armenians. Salisbury tried to persuade the European powers to take joint action to restrain the Turks, but the Germans who were cultivating the Sultan as an ally, would not co-operate and the attempt failed.

(iii) *British intervention in the war between Greece and Turkey (1897-8)* was one of Salisbury's successes. The Greeks tried to capture the Turkish island of Crete in the Mediterranean, but the Turks were too strong for them and retaliated by occupying a large part of Thessaly in mainland Greece. Salisbury managed to get the Concert of Europe to bring about a Turkish withdrawal from Thessaly, but Germany and Austria-Hungary would take no action in Crete itself. This time, however, the British fleet could be brought into play and Salisbury used it to expel Turkish troops from the island, after which Prince George of Greece was appointed governor.

(iv) *Britain's position in China and the Far East* was being threatened both by Russia and Germany. In 1894 the Japanese had surprised Europe by sending troops into the Chinese territory of Korea, ostensibly to help put down revolution, and then by defeating Chinese forces which tried to prevent them. China was forced to agree to the *Treaty of Shimonoseki (1895)* which gave Japan the Liaotung Peninsula, including the first-class harbour of Port Arthur.

This was too much for the Russians who themselves had designs on Port Arthur which was ice-free; with the support of France and Germany, they forced Japan to hand back Liaotung. The following year the Russians signed a treaty with the Chinese promising to defend China and receiving in return the right to build a railway across the Chinese province of Manchuria, bordering Russia. Then suddenly in 1897 the Germans seized the Chinese port of Kiao-chow; ignoring Salisbury's attempts to dissuade them the Russians followed by forcing the Chinese to grant them a 25-year lease on Port Arthur; it seemed as though China was about to be carved up, much against the wishes of Salisbury who preferred an 'open-door' policy – to keep China open for trade but politically independent. The best Britain could do was fall in with the trend and lease the port of Wei-hai-weh.

(v) *The reconquest of the Sudan* was achieved by an army under the command of *Sir Herbert Kitchener*. Salisbury agreed to the campaign for several reasons. Since Gordon's death (1885) the Sudan had been controlled by the Dervishes. Although the Mahdi died soon after Gordon, his successor, known as the Khalifa, was a constant threat to Egypt itself; in 1889 his forces had invaded Egypt and Kitchener had played an important part in repelling the attack. The Dervishes were also threatening the Italian colony of Eritrea, and the Italian government, with German support, urged Britain to destroy the Khalifa. Salisbury was suspicious of French ambitions in southern Sudan: in June 1896 the French Captain Marchand had set out from French West Africa with a small force, heading for Fashoda on the Nile above Khartoum; thus it was important to assert British control of the Sudan before the French became established. Setting out in 1896, Kitchener's expedition advanced slowly up the Nile, building a railway as they went and fighting off repeated Dervish attacks. Other hazards included cholera outbreaks and torrential rain which washed away a section of the newly constructed railway. The climax came in September 1898 when the Khalifa's army was heavily defeated at *Omdurman* just outside Khartoum. Dervish power was destroyed and British control of the Sudan was assured, though the French still had hopes in the area.

(vi) *The Fashoda incident (1898)* seemed likely to bring war between Britain and France. Only a few days after Omdurman, news was brought to Kitchener that Marchand had arrived at Fashoda, claim-ing the Upper Nile for France. Kitchener moved southwards to Fashoda and invited Marchand to withdraw, pointing out with perfect courtesy that if it came to a showdown, his force was much larger than Marchand's. The two governments negotiated and although the press in both countries adopted warlike attitudes, good sense prevailed. The French government ordered Marchand to with-draw from Fashoda. They had decided not to risk war because they could not compete with the British fleet which was cruising in the

Eastern Mediterranean, their Russian ally was unable to help, and they were afraid that the Germans might profit in some way from French preoccupation in a war with Britain. This was viewed as a personal triumph for Salisbury, though he hated confrontations of this nature and immediately began to look for ways of improving relations with the humiliated French.

(vii) *The Boer War* (1899-1902) was the climax of the Salisbury period in foreign affairs (see previous section).

(viii) *Britain and Germany*

While Bismarck and his successor Caprivi were in power, Britain's relations with Germany were generally good. But after Caprivi's resignation in 1894 the Kaiser Wilhelm II began to play a leading role in the conduct of German foreign affairs. He wanted to build Germany up into a great colonial and world power. His attitude towards Britain was difficult to understand. Envious of her naval power and at the same time full of grudging admiration, he was sometimes belligerent and arrogant, sometimes co-operative. Some historians think that he really wanted an alliance with Britain and was hoping to frighten her into joining the Triple Alliance by a show of strength:

- In January 1896 Wilhelm sent his famous telegram to Kruger congratulating him on defeating the Jameson Raid (see Section 17.2(a)). Whether the Germans intended to take any action is doubtful, though three German cruisers were in Delagoa Bay off Portuguese East Africa. In case they were, Salisbury despatched a small fleet described as a 'flying squadron', and Wilhelm realised he had gone too far. The incident had important effects: coming so soon after the Franco-Russian alliance, it shocked the British to find the Germans so hostile. On the German side it justified an expansion of the German navy, so that any future British flying squadrons could be dealt with. Britain had 33 battleships and 130 cruisers whereas Germany had only six and four respectively. Tirpitz, the Minister of Marine, was responsible for the 1897 Navy Laws which provided for the building of seven battleships and nine cruisers; in 1900 it was proposed to build three new battleships a year for the next 20 years.
- Twice, in 1898 and 1899, Chamberlain proposed an alliance with Germany, but the Germans refused on the grounds that Britain wanted to use the Germans to check Russian expansion in the Far East.
- During the Boer War Wilhelm behaved correctly and refrained from interfering; when Kruger arrived in Germany the Kaiser refused to meet him.
- *The Boxer Rising in China (1900)* brought Britain and Germany together in close co-operation. The Boxers, a Chinese nationalist group, besieged the foreign legations in Peking in protest against

the increasing outside intervention in their country. Britain played an important role in organising an international expedition to relieve the legations. At the suggestion of the British, a German officer was placed in overall command; the besieged foreigners were rescued and order restored.

- At the Kaiser's suggestion, an Anglo-German convention was signed (October 1900), sometimes known as *the Yangtze Agreement*. Both promised to maintain the 'open door' in China to the trade of all nations and to check foreign aggression.

(b) Explain why and with what results Britain sought allies after 1900

The reasons why Britain began to search for allies with more urgency after 1900 (most of them already mentioned) can be summarised briefly:

(i) All the other major European powers had allies, whereas British isolation had been clearly demonstrated by the Jameson Raid, the Venezuela incident and the Boer War. It had been difficult enough to defeat the Boers; what would happen if Britain was attacked by a great power?

(ii) France was still hostile, smarting over diplomatic defeats in Nigeria and at Fashoda, and resenting the British presence in Egypt and the Sudan.

(iii) Russia was viewed as a likely enemy, with designs on India and northern China.

(iv) Though Germany was seen as the most probable ally, the Kaiser himself was unpredictable and the Navy Law of June 1900 suggested that the Germans were setting out to match Britain's naval power. Naval rivalry was later to become the main cause of Anglo-German friction.

(v) In October 1900 Salisbury at last gave up the Foreign Office and Lord Lansdowne took his place. Lansdowne, like Chamberlain, had long been in favour of a more positive approach to finding Britain an ally.

(vi) The matter became urgent with the growth of Russian power in northern China. Towards the end of 1900 Russian troops occupied the northern part of Manchuria, and in January 1901 the details of a Russo-Chinese agreement became known which meant that in practice, Manchuria was now part of Russia. Lansdowne was determined to form some sort of alliance to check Russian ambitions.

The search for allies:

(i) Lansdowne first tried to arrange a joint Anglo-German action under the Yangtze Agreement, but the Germans refused to co-operate, arguing that this applied only to the Yangtze valley and not to Manchuria. The real reason was that they were happy for the Russians to be occupied in Manchuria, since that kept them out of the Balkans, where they might clash with Germany's ally, Austria-Hungary. Yet another attempt at a formal agreement with Germany had failed; the Germans were convinced that Britain would be unable to find allies elsewhere.

(ii) *The Anglo-Japanese Alliance* was signed in January 1902. Lansdowne realised that the power which had the closest interest in checking the growth of Russian power in the Far East was Japan. The Russians were already turning their attentions towards Korea, and the Japanese were determined not to allow Russia to control Korea as well as Manchuria. *The terms were*:

- Japan recognised Britain's interests in China and the Pacific and Britain recognised Japan's rights in Korea.
- If Japan was involved in a war with Russia, Britain would remain neutral, but if another power (presumably France) joined Russia, Britain would help Japan.

The alliance had important results: the position of both powers in the Far East was greatly strengthened; if Russia continued to press her ambitions, there was now a much greater chance that Japan would resist by force. This in fact is what happened – war between Russia and Japan followed in 1904–05. The alliance also played a part in gaining Britain her second ally:

(iii) *The Anglo-French Entente Cordiale* (friendly understanding) was signed in April 1904. On the face of it, it was a highly unlikely development: for years relations had been strained over colonial matters and during the Boer War the French press had been violently anti-British and extremely rude about Queen Victoria and Edward VII. But pressures for an understanding had built up on both sides: though the French resented British colonial power, they did not want a war with Britain, and still viewed Germany as their main enemy. They were alarmed at the Anglo-Japanese alliance and the growing danger of war between Japan and their ally, Russia. The Russians would expect help from France, but this might also provoke British help for Japan, and the French would find themselves involved in war with Britain. Delcassé, the French Foreign Minister, worked hard to improve relations. On the British side it was Chamberlain who made the first move; his motive was a desire to sort out the colonial squabble; Lansdowne was probably thinking in terms of a counter move against the build-up of German naval strength, though the government denied that it was an anti-German agreement. Edward VII helped the process of reconciliation by paying an official visit to Paris (May 1903) during which he went to great lengths to show Britain's readiness to co-operate. The outbreak of the Russo-Japanese War (February 1904) made an agreement urgent and speeded up the final negotiations. *The terms were*:

- France would give Britain a free hand in Egypt and the Sudan while Britain recognised French interests in Morocco.

- France gave up her claim to the Newfoundland coast in exchange for land in Gambia (West Africa). Agreement was reached in disputes over Siam, Madagascar and the New Hebrides.

Results of the Entente: It had the desired effect of limiting the Russo-Japanese War; there was one tense incident in October 1904 when the Russian Baltic fleet fired on some British trawlers near the Dogger Bank, apparently mistaking them for Japanese torpedo boats; the French mediated and the Russians apologised and agreed to pay compensation. The Entente was just a settling of differences, not a military alliance. However, the Kaiser soon began to view it as an anti-German move and announced that Germany too had interests in Morocco. This was clearly a challenge to the new Entente; over the next few years the German attitude pushed Britain towards closer commitment to France and away from the German camp. The next move was to be a similar agreement with France's ally Russia in 1907 (see Section 20.7(b)).

17.4 IRELAND UNDER THE CONSERVATIVES

Although the situation in Ireland was comparatively calm, the basic problem was still there – the majority of the Irish were still landless, poverty-stricken peasants. George Wyndham, who became Chief Secretary for Ireland in 1900, believed that the best solution was to enable as many tenants as possible to buy land; the more content they were, the more likely they would be to forget their desire for Home Rule. *Wyndham's Land Purchase Act (1903)* lent money to tenants who wanted to buy farms of their own in cases where a reasonable price could be agreed with the landlord. The loans were at a low rate of interest – only $3\frac{1}{4}$ per cent – and the repayments were spread over 68 years. All parties involved approved and by 1910 some 250 000 tenants had taken advantage of the measure. Earlier the administration of the country had been improved by the introduction of elected county councils on the same lines as those in Britain (1898).

17.5 WHAT WERE THE ACHIEVEMENTS OF BALFOUR'S GOVERNMENT (1902–05) AND WHY HAD IT BECOME SO UNPOPULAR BY 1905?

Arthur James Balfour had had a distinguished career – a successful Chief Secretary for Ireland, 1887–91 (see Section 16.6) and First Lord of the Treasury, 1895–1902. As Salisbury's health deteriorated, Balfour took on more and more of the burden of government. He was able, cultured and witty, though he often seemed to lack a strong commitment in any particular direction, and Lloyd George dismissed him contemptuously as 'just like the scent on a pocket handkerchief'. He remained leader of the Conservative party until 1911, but his reputation is tarnished by the fact that he led the Conservatives into the crushing electoral defeat of

1906 and then lost two further general elections in 1910. No party leader could survive that record. Yet during his short period as Prime Minister, there were some important achievements.

(a) Balfour's achievements

(i) *The Education Act of 1902* was probably his greatest achievement (see Section 12.7(e)).

(ii) *Wyndham's Land Purchase Act of 1903* (see previous Section).

(iii) *The Licensing Act of 1904* dealt with the problem of whether brewers should be compensated when a public house was closed down by having its licence withdrawn. The brewers naturally felt they were entitled to compensation in cases where licences were withdrawn because there was an excess of public houses, but in 1891 the Lords had decided that liquor licences were to last only for one year and that there should be no compensation for licences not renewed. The situation became urgent in 1902 when magistrates in certain areas launched what seemed to be a determined effort to reduce the number of public houses – in Birmingham alone over 50 had their licences withdrawn. Balfour felt that his Act achieved a masterly compromise:

- If a public house was closed because there were too many in the area and not because of any misconduct, the brewer should receive compensation.
- However, the compensation would come, not from public money, but from a fund paid into by the brewers themselves.

Opposition was therefore aroused on both sides: the antidrink movement objected to the payment of any compensation, no matter where it came from, while the brewers were not happy at having, in effect, to compensate themselves.

(iv) *Measures to improve defence.* Balfour, like other politicians, had been profoundly disturbed by Britain's poor military showing in the early stages of the Boer War. There was also the realisation that the navy, though more efficient than the army, might well have to face a challenge from Germany within a few years.

- The Prime Minister became chairman of the Committee of Imperial Defence and a thorough investigation was started into the Empire's military requirements. This had made little progress when the government fell, but at least a beginning had been made for Lord Haldane, the subsequent Liberal War Minister, to build on (see Section 20.7(a)).
- Sir John Fisher was appointed First Sea Lord and Lord Cawdor First Lord of the Admiralty. They took two crucial decisions: they created a third fleet – the Atlantic Fleet based at Gibraltar – in addition to the existing Channel and Mediterranean Fleets; and they authorised the building of a revolutionary new battleship, the *Dreadnought* launched in February 1906. Weighing 17 900

tons, equipped with eight 12-inch guns, driven by steam turbines and capable of reaching a speed of 21 knots, the *Dreadnoughts* made all other battleships obsolete. The plan was to build four *Dreadnoughts* every year.

(v) *The Anglo-French Entente* of 1904 (see Section 17.3(b)).

(b) Reasons for the government's unpopularity. Balfour was unfortunate: though some of his own policies aroused criticism, he and the Conservative party paid the price for the shortcomings and mistakes of Salisbury's governments:

(i) *There had been an almost complete absence of major social reform* from the Conservatives for the previous 20 years. This was because both Salisbury and Balfour, unlike Disraeli, had very little conception of the problems and needs of the working classes; strong believers in self-help, they were not prepared for the state to take on the responsibility for the problems of old age, sickness and unemployment. And yet there was an example to follow – in Germany the Conservative Bismarck had introduced successful schemes for sickness insurance (1883) and old age pensions (1889).

(ii) *The trade union movement was hostile to the Conservatives* because of the famous Taff Vale case, in which the House of Lords acting as the final Court of Appeal had ordered the railway union to pay heavy damages following a strike (1900). This made it impossible for any union to hold a strike without at the same time risking bankruptcy (see Section 19.5(b)). This decision and the failure of Balfour's government to take any action to reverse it, caused a surge of support for the Labour party.

(iii) *There was a reaction after the Boer War*, against the shortcomings of the government and the military, against the 'methods of barbarism' in Kitchener's concentration camps, and against imperialism itself.

(iv) *Balfour's Education Act* (1902) and the *Licensing Act* (1904) were vote losers.

(v) *The 'Chinese slavery' affair* caused a political storm. Balfour made a serious mistake by allowing the import of thousands of Chinese labourers into the Transvaal to work in the gold mines. They were not treated as free people, and were confined in barrack-like compounds even in non-working hours. There were around 50 000 of them by the end of 1905, working for very low wages. There were protests from Canada, Australia and New Zealand and the trade union movement was outraged at this inhuman treatment of fellow labourers. The Liberal opposition made the most of it, but again Balfour showed his lack of awareness and tact, merely claiming that the situation had been exaggerated.

(vi) *The tariff reform controversy* split the Conservative party. It was clear that Britain's period of industrial and commercial predominance was rapidly coming to an end. Most other countries had introduced tariffs, but since Britain persisted in remaining a free trade country, British manufacturers and farmers were suffering intense competition from abroad; German and American manufactured goods were doing most of the damage to British industry. Joseph Chamberlain was convinced that the time had come to abandon free trade and return to a policy of tariffs. This would have two advantages:

- It would protect British industry and help maintain full employment.
- It would make possible the introduction of a system of imperial preferences; this would encourage a closer union of the Empire by having low tariffs or perhaps no tariffs at all on imports from the Empire, and comparatively high tariffs on imports from foreign countries outside the Empire.

Chamberlain announced his policy in May 1903, and although there was a lot of support for him in the party, most of the cabinet was against his ideas. He therefore resigned and launched a propaganda campaign backed by the *Tariff Reform League*. Balfour tried to produce a compromise but this only annoyed both sides. The row in the Conservative party enabled the Liberals to forget their differences and spring to the defence of free trade. Their argument was that free trade guaranteed 'cheap food' whereas tariffs would put up the cost of living for the workers.

(c) The Conservative defeat

(i) Early in December 1905 Balfour suddenly resigned, but did not ask for parliament to be dissolved. This was a gamble on Balfour's part. If he asked for a dissolution there would have to be an immediate general election in which Conservative prospects could not be too bright. However, if the Liberals formed a minority government there was a chance that disagreements in the Liberal party between imperialists and anti-imperialists might suggest that they were still unfit for government.

(ii) Sir Henry Campbell-Bannerman formed a Liberal government, not without some difficulty, but it soon became clear that Balfour had miscalculated. The leading Liberals were far too shrewd to waste such a golden opportunity; they patched up their differences and began to campaign for a general election in mid-January 1906.

(iii) The election result was a massive Liberal victory; the figures were: Liberals 399, Conservatives and Unionists 157, Irish Nationalists 83 and Labour 29. No doubt all the issues mentioned above played a part in the Conservative defeat, but possibly the question of tariff reform was the crucial one. Liberal election posters showed a large loaf representing the cheap food provided by free trade and a small loaf representing the more expensive food which would result from tariffs. Even Balfour lost his seat at Manchester which he had held

illus 17.1 *Chamberlain in Birmingham speaking for tariff reform, trying
to answer the 'little loaf' argument*

for 20 years, though Chamberlain's popularity in Birmingham was such that he held his seat with an increased majority.

QUESTIONS

1. The Outbreak of the Boer War, October 1899
Study Sources A to F and then answer the questions which follow.

Source A: speech by Joseph Chamberlain in the House of Commons, 19 October 1899.

From the first day I came into office I hoped for peace, I strove for peace and I have believed in peace . . . After that extraordinary *ultimatum* which was addressed to the government, it is impossible for us to do any other than fight with all energy the war which has been thrust upon us . . . We are going to war in defence of the principles upon which this Empire has been founded. The first principle is that if we are to maintain our position in regard to other nations, if we are to maintain our existence as a great power in South Africa, we are bound to show that we are able to protect British subjects everywhere when they are made to suffer from oppression and injustice . . . The second principle is that in the interests of South Africa and the British Empire, Britain must remain the paramount power in South Africa. We are now at war because Kruger and the government of the Transvaal has placed British subjects in the Transvaal in a position of distinct inferiority.

Source: quoted in L. Evans and P. J. Pledger, *Contemporary Sources and Opinions in Modern British History, vol. 2*, Warne, 1967 (adapted extracts).

Source B: speech by Sir Henry Campbell-Bannerman (Liberal leader) in the House of Commons, 5 February 1904.

It was on June 20, 1899. The right hon. gentleman [Chamberlain] came to my room. He told me that he wished to submit to me certain proposals that the government were contemplating. The first was to send out 10,000 men to the Cape . . . he went on to say, 'You need not be alarmed. There will be no fighting. We know that those fellows' – that was the Boers – 'won't fight . . . We are playing a game of bluff.' I think I ventured to express frankly to the right hon. gentleman my opinion that such a policy was unworthy of the country. I said it was a rash and dangerous policy to begin a course of bluff when you did not know what it might lead to.

Source: quoted in J. Wilson, *CB: A Life of Sir Henry Campbell-Bannerman*, Constable, 1973 (adapted extracts).

Source C: letter from Lord Selborne, one of Chamberlain's Colonial Office Ministers, to Lord Milner, British High Commissioner in South Africa.

DOWNING STREET, 22/3/98 (Confidential) . . . Our object is the future combination of South Africa under the Union Jack . . . Our first object is to avoid war if it can be done safely, but if it is to come, what are the conditions under which we must manoeuvre for it to come? It must command the practically unanimous consent of the British in South Africa, and the approval of as large a proportion as possible of our own Dutch in South Africa, and the action must have the unanimous consent of public opinion at home.

Source: as for Source **A** (adapted extracts).

Source D: remark by Milner to Mr J. T. Molteno, a member of the Cape Parliament, 3 October 1899, reported to the *Daily Chronicle* by Mr Molteno.

Well, Mr. Molteno, it is no use; I am determined to break the dominion of Afrikanerdom.

Source: as for Source **B**.

Source E: speech by Lloyd George at Carmarthen, 27 November 1899.

I do not mean to say that there are no circumstances which would compel us to fight, but I would say that the case must be an overwhelming one indeed before we do so. In this particular instance war could have been avoided. We were negotiating, and the Boers had conceded our demands, which we then withdrew. In the meantime we sent tens of thousands of soldiers to South Africa with artillery and munitions for war . . . We are fighting for a franchise in the Transvaal which we do not give our own subjects at home . . . *I do not believe the war has any connection with the franchise. It is a question of 45 per cent dividends.*

Source: quoted in P. Rowland, *Lloyd George*, Barrie and Jenkins, 1975 (adapted extracts).

Source F: comments by a modern historian.

Milner could not imagine the Afrikaners of the Cape being loyal to the Empire while there remained an independent nation of their 'race' to the north to divert their loyalites, and he could not see the Transvaal forfeiting her independence without war. In any case she should be pushed to the limit, mainly on the issue of the *Uitlander* franchise – because it was a genuine grievance, and because if Kruger did give satisfaction on it, Britain's position in South Africa would be automatically secured: Uitlanders outnumbered Boers, most of them were British, and it was assumed that if Britons were given the vote, they would use it imperially. Consequently from the beginning of 1898 Milner devoted his energies to bringing on a crisis which could be exploited to this end . . . He did all he could to prevent a reconciliation with the Boers, and his constant fear was that Kruger would make reasonable concessions which he would have to accept, which would take from him the excuse for grabbing all he wanted. At a conference with Kruger at Bloemfontein in June 1899 he had to work hard to avoid a peaceful settlement. But he succeeded and the war he desired at last broke out . . . In the event, the fact that it was the Boers who issued the *ultimatum* and not the British, made it easier (the British had one prepared in case the Boers failed to) . . . Though it was Milner who forced the pace, the government's aims were no different from his. All ministers agreed on the importance of bringing the Transvaal to heel in order to uphold British supremacy. Where Milner and his political masters disagreed was over tactics – Milner wanted to rush in, but the ministers had to be sensitive to the reactions of public opinion; Salisbury was concerned to get the boards clear of other troubles first.

Source: B. Porter, *The Lion's Share*, Longman, 1975 (adapted extracts).

(a) (i) What is meant by the word 'ultimatum' used in Sources **A** and **F**? 1, 4(a)

(ii) According to Source **A**, why had Chamberlain's efforts to preserve peace failed? 4(a)

(iii) What criticism does Chamberlain make of Kruger in Source **A**? 4(a)

(iv) According to Chamberlain in Source **A**, what were the two principles which Britain was fighting to defend? 4(a)

(v) Using the evidence of Sources **A** and **F** and your own knowledge, explain why British subjects in the Transvaal were in need of support. 1, 2, 4(a, c)

(b) (i) Do you think the evidence in Sources **B**, **C** and **D** supports Chamberlain's claim in Source **A** (that he had worked hard for peace) or not? Explain your answer fully. 4(a, c)

(ii) What evidence is there in Source **C** that Selborne's letter represents the opinion of the British government? 4(a, b)

(c) (i) In what ways does Lloyd George in Source **E** contradict Chamberlain (Source **A**) in his explanations of the reasons for the war? 4(a, c)

(ii) Explain in your own words what Lloyd George means by the words in italics at the end of Source **E**. 1, 2, 4(a)

(d) (i) What is meant in Source **F** by the word 'Uitlander'? 1, 4(a)

(ii) According to Source **F**, why did Milner want the Uitlanders to be given the vote? 4(a)

(iii) What was Milner's 'constant fear' about Kruger? 4(a)

(e)   What are the strengths and weaknesses of each of the Sources A to E for the historian?   **4(a, b)**

(f)   Using the evidence of all the Sources and your own knowledge, explain how far you think each of the following was to blame for the Boer War:
    (i)   Milner,
    (ii)   Chamberlain and the British government,
    (iii) Kruger and the Boers.   **1, 2, 4(a, c)**

2. The Anglo-Japanese Alliance, 1902

Study Sources A to C and then answer the questions which follow.

Source A: information from a modern historian.

The issue which overshadowed all others [in 1900] was the Far East. *China had taken the place of Turkey as the pre-eminent Sick Man*; and between 1897 and 1905 the future of China determined the relations of the Great Powers. The British seemed in a hopeless position. No one would help them against Russia. The French were unfriendly because of Fashoda, the Germans were determined not to commit themselves. The Americans pretended to be satisfied and after October 1899 British forces were locked up in South Africa.

Source: A. J. P. Taylor, *The Struggle for Mastery in Europe, 1848–1918*, Oxford, 1954 (adapted extract).

Source B: the balance of naval power in the Far East in 1901.

	France	*Russia*	*Britain*	*Japan*
Battleships	1	5	4	6
Cruisers	2 (old)	6	3 (2 old)	7 (6 new)

Source: J. Telford, *British Foreign Policy, 1870–1914*, Blackie, 1978.

Source C: a Russian cartoon of 1902 showing the Russian view of British and American attitudes to the quarrel between Russia and Japan. The figures represent, from left to right, Russia, Japan, Britain and the USA.

Source: British Museum.

(a) (i) Explain in your own words what Taylor means by the words in italics in Source **A**.   **1, 2, 4(a)**

    (ii) Why were the great powers so interested in China at this time?   **1, 2**

(b) (i) From the evidence of Source **B**, which country had most battleships in the Far East in 1901?   **4(a)**

    (ii) If Britain was the world's strongest naval power, how do you explain the fact that, according to Source **B**, she had fewer ships in the Far East than Russia?   **1, 2, 4(a)**

    (iii) Using the evidence of Sources **A** and **B** and your own knowledge, explain why Britain 'seemed in a hopeless position' with regard to China.   **1, 2, 4(a, c)**

(c) Using the evidence of Sources **B** and **C** and your own knowledge, explain why

    (i) Britain wanted an alliance with Japan;

    (ii) Japan wanted an alliance with Britain.   **1, 2, 4(a, c)**

(d) What were the main points of the agreement signed between Britain and Japan in 1902?   **1, 2**

(e) (i) What point is the cartoonist trying to put over in Source **C**?   **4(a)**

    (ii) How does the cartoonist try to show what his feelings are towards the three figures on the right?   **4(a, b)**

(f)   Explain how, over the next few years, the Anglo-Japanese agreement was important with regard to

    (i)   the Russo–Japanese War of 1904–5;

    (ii)   the Anglo–French Entente of 1904.   1, 2

3.   Arthur James Balfour was Conservative Prime Minister from 1902 to 1905.

(a)   Describe the main achievements of his government.

(b)   Describe how Joseph Chamberlain's tariff reform campaign caused a major problem for the Conservative party.

(c)   Explain why, in spite of their achievements, the Conservatives lost the general election of 1906 to the Liberals.   1, 2

4.   The Anglo–French Entente Cordiale was signed in April 1904. *The Times* called it 'an event of high historic importance'. Explain the feelings and reactions of *each* of the following on hearing the news:

           (a) a Briton; (b) a Frenchman; (c) a German; (d) a Russian.
                                                     1, 2, 3

THE DOMINIONS:

CANADA, AUSTRALIA AND

NEW ZEALAND BEFORE 1914

SUMMARY OF EVENTS

At the 1907 Colonial Conference it was decided to use the word *'dominion'* instead of 'colony' to describe all the parts of the British Empire which were self-governing – Canada, Australia, Newfoundland, New Zealand and South Africa (from 1909). In the early days of overseas settlement, the theory was that colonies existed simply for the benefit of the mother country. After Britain lost her American colonies in the American War of Independence (1775-83), the idea gradually became accepted that colonies with predominantly European and British populations would eventually be allowed to rule themselves. *Lord Durham's Report on the Affairs of British North America (1839)* played a vitally important part in persuading the British government that this was the only way to hold the Empire together.

Canada, Australia and New Zealand passed through roughly similar stages of development:

(i) Direct rule by a Governor with a council chosen by himself.
(ii) Representative government – an elected council which could advise the Governor but had no real power itself.
(iii) Responsible government – an elected assembly which had the power to appoint and dismiss ministers and control internal affairs.
(iv) Federal government – the separate colonies or provinces united in a federation, keeping their own separate parliaments, but also joining in a central, federal parliament.

Canada achieved independent federal dominion status in 1867 and Australia in 1901. New Zealand became a federal self-governing state in 1856, then in 1876 decided to abandon the federal system in favour of a single parliament at Wellington. South Africa had a rather different and more troubled history, which eventually resulted in the Union of South Africa in 1910 (see Sections 17.2 and 20.1(b)).

Dominion status was rather a vague term since it had never been precisely stated how much control the British government had over the dominion

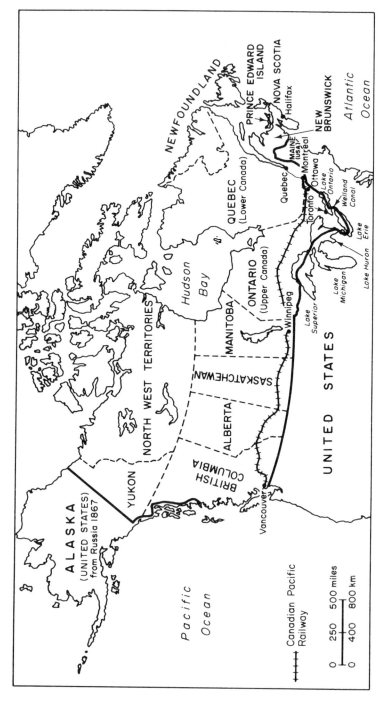

Map 18.1 Canada

governments in the last resort. In 1926 a definition was produced which seemed to satisfy all concerned: in effect the dominions were completely free from British control, but they retained a link with Britain through the monarchy.

18.1 CANADA

(a) The early settlement of Canada was carried out by rival French and British trading companies. The French were defeated in the Seven Years' War (1756-63) and by the Treaty of Paris (1763) Canada with its considerable French population became British.

(i) *The Quebec Act (1774)* was designed in part to placate the French settlers. Canada (still called Quebec at this point) was to be ruled by a British governor who could choose a council of up to 23 members to advise him. There was no elected parliament. French civil law was recognised, but English criminal law was introduced. The French Roman Catholics were given freedom of worship. At this time, the Maritime Provinces of modern Canada - Nova Scotia, Prince Edward Island, Newfoundland and New Brunswick (founded 1784) were treated as separate colonies.

(ii) *Pitt's Canada Act (1791)* arose from the changing situation brought about by the American War of Independence (1775-83). Many Americans, wanting to remain loyal to Britain, left the USA and moved into Canada. Known as *United Empire Loyalists*, some stayed on the coast in New Brunswick while others travelled inland and settled along the northern shores of Lake Ontario. At the same time immigrants were flocking in from Britain, especially from Scotland. With the influx of English-speaking settlers, Quebec began to split into a French-speaking east and an English-speaking west. Pitt's Act therefore recognised this by dividing Quebec into two provinces: *Upper Canada* (Ontario) for the British and *Lower Canada* (Quebec) which was overwhelmingly French. Each had its own Lieutenant-Governor with an elected assembly which could advise the Lieutenant-Governor and his nominated council, but had no legislative powers and could not dismiss the Lieutenant-Governor. There was also a joint governor for both provinces together. Canada had secured representative government, but there was over half a century to wait before responsible government was achieved.

(b) Unrest and the rebellions of 1837. During the Napoleonic Wars the USA fought against Britain (1812-14). American forces attacked Canada and burnt down the Upper Canada Assembly building at York (later called Toronto). The Canadians and British retaliated by setting fire to the American presidential residence in Washington. Gradually, however, both Upper and Lower Canada became impatient with British rule for a variety of reasons:

(i) In British Upper Canada there was a feeling that the Lieutenant-Governor and his advisory council gave preferential treatment in matters such as allocation of land and in civil service and political appointments, to United Empire Loyalists and their families. Another grievance was that large areas of land – known as clergy reserves – were controlled by the Church of England.

(ii) In French Lower Canada the elected assembly was naturally predominantly French, but the Lieutenant-Governor and his advisory council who had the final say in politics, were British. The French became more suspicious of British motives in 1833 when a new company calling itself the British American Land Company began to sell land to British non-Catholic immigrants.

(iii) There was a demand in some quarters, particularly among commercial interests, for a union of the two provinces, since it was felt that the existence of two separate customs systems was hampering the smooth flow of trade along the St Lawrence River.

(iv) During the 1830s the major issue in both provinces was the demand for responsible government so that the elected assemblies could enforce their will over the Lieutenant-Governors. In 1834 Lord Grey's Whig government sent out a commission of enquiry, but when it became clear that it was not prepared to recommend any major concessions, extremists in both provinces could restrain themselves no longer.

In 1837 there were two separate rebellions – the one in Lower Canada was led by Louis Papineau, a French-Canadian member of the assembly; the one in Upper Canada was organised by a Scottish-Canadian journalist, William Lyon Mackenzie. Both were easily suppressed, but they acted as a warning to the British government that they must treat Canadian grievances seriously.

(c) Lord Durham and the Canada Act (1840)

(i) Melbourne decided to send out Lord Durham, the leading Radical Whig, to investigate and report on the situation. Durham, who took with him as adviser his imperialist friend Edward Gibbon Wakefield, had vague ideas about a federation of *all* the Canadian colonies, but was disappointed to find that the maritime colonies were very cool towards the idea. He was only in Canada from May until November 1838, when he was recalled because his dictatorial attitude made him unpopular; but it was long enough for him to size up the situation.

(ii) *His Report*, published in 1839, was an important document, often regarded as setting the guidelines not just for Canada, but for the whole of the Commonwealth. He believed that representative government was not enough to keep the colonists happy and loyal; they would have to be given responsible government otherwise there was likely to be a Canadian War of Independence. He suggested that the two Canadas should be reunited, in the mistaken hope that the French

Canadians would become absorbed in language and culture into the British population, so making a completely united people. There should be one Governor with his advisory councils, and an elected assembly which would control internal affairs, defence and foreign policy. This last proposal was too radical for Lord Melbourne, but most of Durham's other suggestions were carried out in:

(iii) *The Canada Act (1840).* Upper and Lower Canada were united under a Governor-General, who had an advisory council of members nominated for life and an elected House of Assembly containing equal numbers of members from each province. This was a disappointment for the supporters of responsible government since the Assembly still had very little power. However *Lord Elgin*, who became Governor-General in 1847, was a liberal Scotsman, and Durham's son-in-law. He came to an agreement with the parties in the Assembly, that provided they maintained the connection with Britain, he would accept laws proposed by them. In effect, Canada had responsible government. At about the same time Nova Scotia, New Brunswick and Newfoundland were also given responsible government.

(d) Relations with the USA. Since the birth of the hostile USA, Canadians had been worried about the threat to their largely undefended frontiers. The events of 1812-14 had shown that their fears were justified and it seemed that the Americans were trying to outdo the Canadians at every opportunity. The Canadians retaliated effectively:

(i) In 1825 the Americans opened the Erie Canal joining Lake Erie to the Hudson River, and threatening to take trade away from the St Lawrence. The Canadians retaliated by building the Welland Canal joining Lakes Erie and Ontario. This proved a great success, but commercial rivalry continued.

(ii) A dispute about the frontier between Canada and Maine was settled by the *Ashburton Treaty (1842).* Called after the British negotiator who worked it out with the Americans, the treaty was unpopular with Canadians who felt it had given too much away.

(iii) More popular was the *Oregon Treaty (1846)* which solved a dispute about possession of the Pacific Coast. The Americans claimed the whole of the coastline right up to Alaska (owned by Russia) which would shut Canada out completely from the Pacific. There was considerable tension between Britain and the USA, whose extremists wanted war. President Polk gave way and the treaty fixed the boundary to Canada's advantage along the 49th parallel, with a detour so that the whole of Vancouver Island could be included in Canada.

(e) The move towards federation and the Dominion of Canada (1867). In the early 1850s the idea of a federation of all the Canadian colonies began to be widely discussed. There were different motives:

(i) Time showed that Lord Durham had been wrong in thinking that the

French Canadians would be assimilated into their British surroundings. In fact they became more determined to preserve their French customs and language and more worried as English-speaking immigrants continued to flood in. When gold was discovered in the Fraser River canyon in 1858 in the far west, there was the prospect of thousands more flocking into the west, tipping the balance even more heavily against the French. In 1830 the English-speaking population of Upper Canada were only half the population of French Lower Canada; by 1861, because of massive immigration, there had been a dramatic turnaround – there were 1.4 million people in Upper Canada and 1.1 million in Lower Canada. The Upper Canadians were protesting that they ought to have more MPs than the Lower Canadians. The French Canadians decided that a federal system might be the best way of saving themselves from becoming submerged: Upper and Lower Canada could be separated again and they would at least have their own assembly for internal affairs.

(ii) All the colonies realised the need for a railway to link Halifax (Nova Scotia) with Quebec. This intercolonial scheme received very little support from London and the separate colonies seemed unable to agree on a joint policy. The idea grew that only if British North America became united would the railway be built.

(iii) The colonies had economic problems. As Britain moved towards complete free trade, Canada lost its preferential rates for timber exported to Britain. The American Civil War (1861-5) adversely affected Canada's trade. The Canadians realised that the only way to survive was by closer co-operation between the provinces.

(iv) The American Civil War gave a decisive impetus to federation in another way. The Northern States and Britain were close to war and British troops shipped out to Halifax had to travel by sleigh through New Brunswick to Quebec. This convinced the British government that a united defence and an intercolonial railway were needed.

The Canadians began discussions at the Quebec Conference (1864). This broke up without agreement, but the matter became urgent in 1866 when the Fenians attacked from the USA and captured Fort Erie in Upper Canada. British troops were able to drive them back, but the constant threat from the USA convinced all the colonies that unity was essential. Talks were resumed and the Canadians produced their own plan which the British government accepted in the *British North America Act of 1867*.

Upper and Lower Canada were separated again and became the provinces of Ontario and Quebec; they joined New Brunswick and Nova Scotia to form the Dominion of Canada. It was understood that other provinces would join later as they became more populated and developed; Manitoba joined in 1870, British Columbia in 1871, Prince Edward Island in 1873, and Alberta and Saskatchewan in 1905. The last to join was Newfoundland (1949) which had been a dominion in its own right. Each province had its own parliament (which pleased the French in Quebec) which had certain specific powers over local affairs. There was a federal parliament containing representatives from all the provinces, to sit at Ottawa, the new Canadian capital; this controlled matters such as defence, taxation and overseas trade. The Act also included provision for the long needed railway to link all the provinces. The word *dominion* was chosen to solve the problem of what title to give the new confederation. 'Kingdom' of Canada offended many people, so Samuel Tilley of New Brunswick suggested a text from Psalm 72: 'He shall have dominion also from sea to sea'. Thus the Dominion of Canada came into existence.

(f) Progress since 1867

(i) The first Prime Minister of Canada was *Sir John A. Macdonald* who had played a leading part in drawing up the details of the 1867 Act. He went on to point the new state towards successful development, the first step in which was the completion of the Intercolonial Railway from the St Lawrence to Halifax in 1876.

(ii) After initial problems Macdonald was able to promote the building of the Canadian Pacific Railway linking Montreal with Vancouver on the Pacific coast. When this was completed in 1885, it enabled more and more pioneer farmers to move out west and made possible the vast expansion of wheat farming.

(iii) There was one unpleasant episode in 1885. The Federal Government had in 1869 bought up the territory of the Hudson's Bay Company which had been trading in furs for the past 200 years. These huge Northern Territories came under Federal control but the government had been surprised when *Louis Riel*, a French Indian, led a rebellion of half-breed buffalo hunters who farmed along the banks of the Red River. Macdonald agreed that their settlements should become the province of Manitoba, and calm was restored. However in 1885 Riel appeared again leading a rebellion along the Saskatchewan River. This was quickly suppressed by troops rushed from the east along the new railway. Macdonald made himself unpopular by having Riel hanged, which reawakened much of the resentment between French and British, and helped to keep alive Quebec nationalism which has survived until the present day.

(iv) Macdonald encouraged the development of Canadian industries by introducing high protective tariffs against American goods, though British goods were given preference.

(v) The link with Britain remained strong. During the Boer War Canada unhesitatingly sent troops to help the British, while during the First World War no fewer than 650 000 Canadian troops played an important role in the eventual defeat of the Central Powers.

illus 18.1   The last spike being driven into the Canadian Pacific Railway, 7 November 1885, by Lord Strathcona

18.2 AUSTRALIA

(a) New South Wales was the first Australian colony to be established.

(i) The first settlers, 750 convicts, arrived at Botany Bay in 1788, under the command of Captain Arthur Phillip. The first settlement was at Port Jackson and soon afterwards Sydney was founded. The first free settlers arrived in 1793, but the early years were violent ones: the convicts had to be kept in order by troops, and floggings and executions were common. Under pressure from the free settlers, the British government stopped the transportation of convicts to New South Wales in 1840, though the penal settlements remained open until 1866 when the last convicts finished their sentences. Convicts continued to be sent to Western Australia until 1868.

(ii) *Sheep farming* was the vital factor in the early prosperity of New South Wales and of the other colonies as well. The Spanish merino sheep had been introduced from South Africa in 1796 by Captain John Macarthur. At first sheep farmers stayed in the coastal area, but in 1813 an expedition led by William Lawson, Gregory Blaxland and W. C. Wentworth crossed the Blue Mountains and discovered the rich pastureland of the Bathurst plains. A rapid expansion of sheep farming followed and by 1850, Australia, producing high quality wool, was the world's largest wool exporter. The British woollen industry came to rely heavily on supplies from Australia.

(iii) *Gold* became the other mainstay of Australian prosperity. It was first discovered at Bathhurst in New South Wales in 1851, and soon afterwards at Ballarat and Bendigo in Victoria, which had separated from New South Wales the previous year. It was in Victoria that the largest deposits were found.

(b) The other Australian colonies. Explorers began to move into the interior and around the coasts. Midshipman Samuel Flinders and Surgeon George Bass sailed round Van Diemen's Land (later called Tasmania) in 1798 and by 1803 Flinders had sailed all the way round Australia, mapping the entire coastline.

(i) *Tasmania* was the second colony to be founded, taken by the British in 1803 to prevent the French claiming it. Hobart was the capital, but in the early days it was used as a penal settlement for the worst type of convicts. The free settlers distinguished themselves by their brutal treatment of the native aborigines who were eventually placed on Flinders Island in the Bass Straits. By 1869 all the aborigines of Tasmania had died.

(ii) *Victoria* began as a sheep-rearing settlement around the village founded in 1835 and known as Melbourne after the British Prime Minister. Development was rapid: by 1850 there were 77 000 settlers and five million sheep in Victoria, and in that year it was recognised as a

Map 18.2 *Australia and New Zealand*

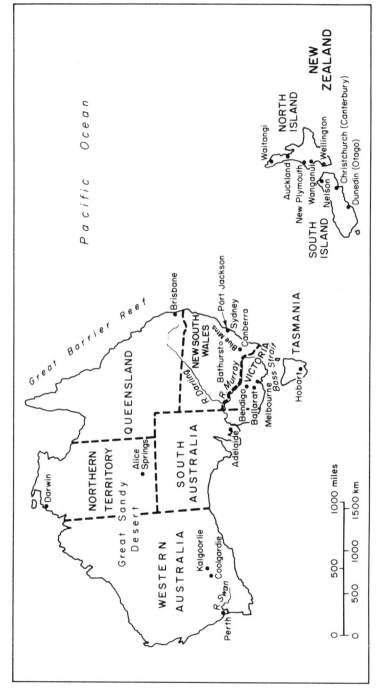

separate colony. When gold was discovered in the following year, there was a frantic rush of immigrants both from the other colonies and from Britain. 19 000 people arrived in Melbourne in one month – September 1852, while the total for the year was around 84 000. There were enormous problems of administration and law and order, but eventually the industry settled down and the mining was taken in hand by large companies.

(iii) *South Australia* was the other important colony (see below). Queensland was first used in 1824 as another dumping-ground for convicts and became a separate colony in 1859 though its population was only 25 000. The first settlers arrived at Perth in *Western Australia* in 1829, but development was slow and difficult because of the way the land was distributed. The government sold it at less than a shilling (5p) an acre, so colonists bought far more than they needed and lacked sufficient labour to work the land. They even petitioned the government to send them convicts who could work as labourers. The government gratefully obliged, sending 10 000 between 1850 and 1868. Another boost to the colony's development was the discovery of gold at Coolgardie (1892) and Kalgoorlie (1894).

(c) Wakefield and South Australia

(i) Edward Gibbon Wakefield came from a Quaker and Radical background, his father having been a close friend of Bentham and Place. The young Wakefield was wild and undisciplined. He eloped with one rich heiress and later kidnapped another who happened to be under age; this earned him three years in Newgate Prison, London. Here he had plenty of time to ponder about the plight of criminals and convicts and particularly those in Australian penal settlements. He developed a theory about how overseas colonisation should be organised; this was explained in his *Letter from Sydney* written in 1829 while he was still in prison.

(ii) The idea was that if emigration was properly organised by the government, it could be the perfect solution for unemployment and poverty in Britain. As things were at present in Australia he believed it was too easy to get land and too difficult to find labourers to cultivate it. The government should therefore sell land at a 'sufficient price', which would be high enough to ensure that only responsible people acquired it and acquired only a workable area. The money raised would be used to pay the passages of more immigrants who would have to work as labourers until they had saved enough to buy farms for themselves. The purchase money could then be used to bring out more immigrants, so that the balance between the demand for and supply of labour would always be kept. Convicts would no longer be needed.

(iii) In 1830, as soon as he emerged from prison, Wakefield started a *Colonial Society*, and almost immediately many of his ideas were adopted in the existing colonies. Between 1832 and 1842, 7000 free settlers arrived in New South Wales; since land was priced at five shillings (25p) an acre, and by 1842 at £1 an acre, most of the new arrivals had to do their stint as labourers to begin with. Transportation of convicts to New South Wales was duly stopped in 1840. This was in marked contrast to what happened in Western Australia where land was sold too cheaply (see above).

(iv) Wakefield, wanting to found a colony of his own, started the *South Australia Association (1834)* and persuaded the government to agree to the setting up of *South Australia.* The first settlers arrived in 1836 and work began on the capital, Adelaide (named after William IV's Queen). Land was offered at 12 shillings (60p) an acre. Soon, however, the problems of starting a new colony from scratch under Wakefield's system became apparent. The government allowed no cash; this was expected to materialise from land sales and loans. 12 shillings an acre proved to be too expensive to attract enough buyers, but not enough to raise sufficient cash. And a great deal was needed since there was a complete lack of facilities and not even a reasonable harbour. Wakefield quarrelled violently with the other members of the governing body – he wanted to raise the price of land to 72 shillings an acre, but they rightly felt this was unrealistic. He withdrew from the whole project and started a New Zealand Association instead.

(v) South Australia was saved from disaster when G. F. Angas floated a Company which raised £320 000, enough to provide most of the vital facilities. Progress was slow even then, but by 1850 the colony was well and truly launched. It had a population of 63 000 with around a million sheep and 60 000 cattle. The land proved to be fertile enough for wheat growing, so that the new colony developed into the granary of Australia. The discovery of copper in 1846 brought an added boost to the economy and in 1850 total exports were valued at £570 000. The success of South Australia had little to do with Wakefield, but at least his was the inspiration that founded it.

(d) Political developments: the move towards a united Australia (1901).
The colonies moved towards responsible government without the agitations and disturbances which characterised Canada. New South Wales became a Crown colony in 1826 under a Governor-General who nominated his own advisory council. In 1842 it was allowed that two-thirds of the members of the council could be elected. The other colonies followed a similar pattern until in 1855 responsible elected assemblies – with the power to decide policies – were granted in New South Wales, Victoria, Tasmania and South Australia. Responsible government came to Queensland in 1859 and to Western Australia in 1890.

For many years there was little interest in federation. The six colonies had developed separately and communications between them were so poor that any sort of union seemed impractical, at least until after 1870. It was only after 1890 that federation began to be discussed seriously. The reasons were:

(i) *External threats* began to worry many Australians. Both Germany and Japan had ambitions in the Pacific. After 1890 the Germans began to follow an aggressive policy of expansion wherever possible, and the Japanese showed their potential by defeating the Chinese decisively in 1894. A strong and united defence was essential to dissuade any foreign ambitions of expansion into Australia.

(ii) The early 1890s were a time of *economic difficulty* culminating in the crisis of 1893. In fact, South Australia had been in difficulties since around 1880 because of drought and plagues of rabbits which ruined the wheat harvests. In 1886 a sudden fall in world wool prices threw many farmers into debt in all the colonies. Though Australia had experienced an industrial revolution after 1850, much of the new industry was inefficient and in 1890 a depression set in, bringing widespread unemployment. In 1893 the crisis worked its way through to the banks as people rushed to withdraw deposits. Panic followed, and of the 32 major banks in Australia as a whole, 22 had to suspend payments. Although prosperity gradually returned the crisis had been a profound shock for the Australians and was probably the main stimulus to the federation movement. Union would remove the troublesome customs barriers between the states; the increased confidence would enable Australians to borrow from abroad. Improved communications made the idea feasible: Melbourne and Sydney were linked by rail in 1883, Melbourne and Adelaide in 1887 and Sydney and Brisbane (Queensland) in 1889.

The Commonwealth of Australia Act passed the British parliament in 1900 and came into operation on 1 January 1901. The Federal parliament was to control defence, foreign policy and treaties, trade and customs duties, postal services, marriage and divorce, banking and currency and immigration. Everything not specifically mentioned in the list, was left to the state parliaments which had more power than their counterparts in Canada, controlling social services, health, education, labour and industry, agriculture, mines, police, rivers and railways. To avoid inter-state jealousies, a new federal capital was to be built at Canberra, between Sydney and Melbourne.

(e) The Dominion or Commonwealth of Australia did not become a prosperous state overnight, but by 1914 the policies of the new federal government had stabilised the economy and the depression had disappeared. Important measures of the Federal parliament were:

(i) *The Immigration Restriction Act (1901)* in effect allowed only whites to enter the country. This was because Australians were afraid that Asian and Pacific labourers would work for very low wages, forcing down wages paid to white Australians. There was also the fear that the whites would be swamped if unrestricted immigration was allowed from countries such as Japan and India.

(ii) *An Arbitration Court* was introduced (1904) to fix 'fair and reasonable' wages and to mediate in industrial disputes; the novelty of this was that the court's decisions were binding on all parties.

(iii) Old age pensions (1908), invalid pensions (1910) and maternity allowances (1912) were introduced.

(iv) In defence matters, conscription was introduced (1911) and the first ships of the Australian navy launched in 1913. Australia played an important part in the First World War, sending over 300 000 troops to Europe.

18.3 NEW ZEALAND

(a) Early colonisation

(i) When the first Europeans arrived, New Zealand was already inhabited by the *Maoris*, a Polynesian race with light brown skins. Captain Cook had mapped both the North and South Islands in 1769, and had claimed them for Britain. The British government had ignored their existence and there was no large-scale attempt to colonise New Zealand until well into the nineteenth century. The only European settlers were escaped convicts, whalers, and missionaries trying to convert the Maoris.

(ii) *Edward Gibbon Wakefield* was responsible for the first organised settlement. After he had washed his hands of the South Australia project, he formed the *New Zealand Association (1837)* which the following year was allowed by the British government to become a chartered company. The first expedition of 1200 people arrived and four settlements started – Wellington, Wanganui and New Plymouth on North Island and Nelson on South Island. The British government announced that it had annexed the colony, just in time to forestall the French colonising party which was off the coast.

(iii) The first Governor, William Hobson, signed *The Treaty of Waitangi (1840)* with the Maoris of North Island. They agreed to regard Victoria as their queen and in return the British guaranteed the Maoris in the possession of their land. The British government would buy any Maori land that was being offered for sale, provided the whole tribe agreed. This was designed to prevent settlers from acquiring land cheaply from individual Maoris. Unfortunately, many of the settlers and officials of the company broke the treaty and simply evicted Maoris from their lands. The Maori tribes retaliated and there was some spasmodic fighting sometimes referred to as the *First Maori War (1842-6)*.

(iv) By 1845 the new colony was not a success: the Maoris were hostile, the settlements were not expanding and exports were non-existent.

(b) The New Zealand Federation 1852

(i) *Sir George Grey* became Governor of New Zealand in 1845, and immediately matters took a turn for the better. Aged only 33, he had already made a reputation as a successful governor of South Australia. He quickly subdued the Maoris, mainly by a show of military strength, but then showed great sympathy and understanding and made a study of Maori language and literature. He stopped the private sale of land and negotiated the purchase of almost the whole of South Island, where there were only about 2000 Maoris. He developed a close friendship with many of the chiefs and spent money on schools, hospitals, law-courts and agricultural advice. The farmers began to prosper as exports of foodstuffs and livestock to Australia increased in the early 1850s because of the rush to the Australian goldfields.

(ii) As the numbers of settlers increased, they began to campaign for self-government, though Grey wanted to postpone it until the land and Maori problems had been settled completely. The first major step was taken in 1852, while Grey was still Governor. *The New Zealand federation* was established by an Act of the British parliament. The six main settlements – Auckland, New Plymouth (later called Taranaki), and Wellington in North Island, and Nelson, Canterbury and Otago in South Island – were given their own elected councils, and there was a central federal assembly. Although this was representative government, it was not yet responsible government, since in the last resort the Governor was still in charge. Grey ended his first period as Governor in 1853, and the British parliament agreed that the New Zealanders could have full responsible self-government in 1856.

(c) **Relations with the Maoris** deteriorated again after Grey's departure.

(i) There was a great influx of new settlers after self-government was achieved. In 1856 there were still no more than 60 000 Europeans in New Zealand, but the numbers soared to 350 000 in 1878. There was tremendous pressure for land, causing settlements to spread from the coastal towns into the interior of North Island where the Maoris had previously been left undisturbed. Now they gathered themselves for the final desperate defence of their lands and the *Second Maori War (1860–71)* broke out.

(ii) The Maoris fought bravely, but against the superior military strength of the Europeans there was no chance of a Maori victory. Grey was recalled for a second term as Governor (1861-8), and though he did his best to bring peace, he had very little power since the introduction of self-government. However, he managed some concessions: the Maoris were allowed to have at least four representatives in the federal assembly (1867) and an agreement was reached which allowed them to live undisturbed in an area amounting to about one-third the size of North Island. Fighting gradually fizzled out, but the fact remained that the Maoris had been deprived of much of their most fertile lands, sometimes by purchase, but more often by straightforward confiscation.

(d) The United New Zealand 1876

(i) In the early 1870s a group of leading politicians, including Julius Vogel of Otago, became convinced that the provincial assemblies were largely inefficient and lacking in vision and that government could be carried on more effectively without them. An Act to abolish them passed the federal legislature and came into operation in 1876. There was to be a single parliament at Wellington.

(ii) Economically New Zealand went through a difficult period until the mid-1890s. Then prices for foodstuffs and wool began to recover and farmers enjoyed a period of great prosperity, lasting right through the First World War. The development of refrigerator ships enabled them to export lamb to Britain.

(iii) The Liberal governments of *Richard John Seddon* (1893-1906) introduced some remarkable reforms: votes for women (1893), old age pensions, cheap loans to farmers, improved working conditions and a system of compulsory arbitration of industrial disputes (the first country in the world to have such a system). Sydney and Beatrice Webb were much impressed by working-class living standards, and by the absence of serious industrial strife.

(iv) During the First World War a remarkably high proportion of New Zealand's population served in the armed forces. About 100 000 men served overseas, and many distinguished themselves, and lost their lives, in the Gallipoli Campaign of 1915 (see Section 21.1(d)).

QUESTIONS

1. Lord Durham and the Development of Canada
Read Sources **A** to **F** and then answer the questions which follow.

Source A: from a magazine, the *Edinburgh Review*, 1825.

Any man of sense knows that Canada must, at no distant period, be merged in the American republic.

Source: quoted in B. Porter, *The Lion's Share*, Longman, 1975.

Source B: petition from the House of Assembly of Lower Canada to William IV, 1836.

We solemnly repeat that the principal of the political reforms which this House and the people have for a great number of years used every effort to obtain, is to extend the elective principle to the Legislative Council, and to render the Executive Council directly responsible to the representatives of the people; to place under the control of this House the whole public revenue; to obtain the repeal of certain Acts of the

Imperial Parliament, in which the people of the province were not represented, with regard to internal affairs of the province; and to obtain for the provincial legislature with regard to internal affairs, that essential control . . .

We rejoice that we have in our just claims, the support of our brethren of Upper Canada. This support will show your Majesty that the two Canadian provinces do indeed require a responsible and popular government . . . We have frequently regretted that the destinies of the inhabitants of this portion of the British Empire should depend almost solely on a Colonial Minister acting on the other side of the ocean, and for the most part on incorrect data.

Source: W. P. M. Kennedy, *Documents of the Canadian Constitution 1791–1915*, Toronto: Oxford University Press, 1918 (adapted extracts).

Source C: remark by Lord Melbourne, British Prime Minister, to Lord Durham, 1838.

The final separation of those colonies [Canada] might possibly not be of material detriment to the interest of the Mother Country, but it is clear that it would be a serious blow to the honour of Great Britain.

Source: quoted in A. Briggs, *The Age of Improvement*, Longman, 1959.

Source D: some information from a modern historian.

The call for reform in Canada found little echo in British society at large. Nor at government level did there seem any cause for concern until rebellion broke out in 1837 led by William Lyon Mackenzie in Upper Canada and by Papineau in Lower Canada. Neither movement really amounted to a 'rebellion', but Melbourne decided to send a man capable of defining the crisis and indicating its solution. The man was Lord Durham . . . He quickly recognised that he was not merely dealing with unrest caused by the absence of truly representative government, but that the issue was complicated by a conflict of nationalities. Immigrants into Canada tended to be absorbed into the English-speaking community, while the French Canadians felt themselves more and more an 'island' in danger of being submerged by the Anglo-Saxons. They genuinely feared for their distinct identity . . . In his Report Durham advised the union of Upper and Lower Canada under one legislature with an executive ministry responsible to it . . .

Source: H. W. Koch, *Durham and the Empire*, in *History of the English Speaking Peoples*, Purnell/BPC Publishing, 1971 (adapted extracts).

358

Source E: Lord Durham's Report, 1839.

Throughout the whole of the North American Provinces there prevails among the British population an affection for the Mother Country which a wise policy on the part of the Imperial government may make the foundation of a safe and enduring connexion. But I must warn that a blind reliance on the all-enduring loyalty of our countrymen may be carried too far. It is not wise to waste and cramp their resources and to allow the backwardness of the British provinces to present a melancholy contrast to the progress and prosperity of the United States . . . The influence of the USA surrounds him on every side and is for ever present. It stamps, on all the habits and opinions of the surrounding countries, the thoughts, feelings and customs of the American people . . . The system which I propose would place the internal government of the colony in the hands of the colonists themselves. I know of no respect in which it is desirable that we should interfere with their internal legislation in matters which do not affect their relations with the Mother Country. The matters which concern us are very few – regulation of foreign relations, trade with the Mother Country, other British colonies and foreign nations . . . are the only points on which the Mother Country requires a control.

Source: quoted in D. Holman (ed.), *Portraits and Documents – Earlier Nineteenth Century 1783-1867*, Hutchinson, 1965 (adapted extracts).

Source F: letter from Lord Grey (Secretary for War and Colonies) to Lord Elgin (Governor-General of Canada), 22 February, 1848.

I can have no doubt that you must accept such a council as the newly elected Parliament will support, and their measures must be acquiesced in until it shall clearly appear that public opinion will support a resistance to them. If we over-rule the Local Legislature we must be prepared to support our authority by force, and in the present state of the world and of Canada, he must be in my opinion an insane politician who would think of doing so. I cannot see any ground for despairing of your getting on reasonably well with the new council, even if it should of necessity include Papineau himself.

Source: quoted in Earl Grey, *The Colonial Policy of Lord John Russell's Administration*, Richard Bentley, 1853 (adapted extracts).

(a) (i)   Which two parts of Canada are mentioned in Source **B**?   **4(a)**
     (ii)   In which of these two parts did the British settlers live?   **1**
     (iii) According to Source **B**, what were the main complaints of the Canadians?   **4(a)**
     (iv) What evidence is there in Source **B** that the Canadians were becoming impatient with the situation?   **4(a)**

(b) (i)   From the evidence of Sources **C** and **D**, how would you sum up the British attitude towards Canada and its problems?

                                                                                           4(a, b, c)

      (ii)   According to Source **D**, why did Melbourne send Lord Durham to Canada?   **4(a)**

   (iii)   What additional problem not mentioned in the petition (Source **B**) did Durham discover when he arrived in Canada (Source **D**)?   **4(a, c)**

   (iv)   According to Source **D**, why were the French Canadians worried?   **4(a)**

(c) (i)   What evidence can you find in Durham's Report (Source **E**) which might seem to give support to the opinion expressed in Source **A**?   **4(a, c)**

      (ii)   According to Sources **D** and **E**, what solutions did Durham suggest for the problems of Canada?   **4(a, c)**

   (iii)   To what extent were Durham's recommendations carried out in the Canada Act of 1840?   **1, 2, 4(a)**

(d) (i)   Explain in your own words the advice given by Grey to Elgin in Source **F**.   **4(a)**

      (ii)   Who was Papineau referred to in Source **F**?   **1, 4(a, c)**

   (iii)   What evidence is there in Source **F** to suggest what Grey's feelings were about Papineau?   **4(a, b)**

(e)   Using the evidence of the Sources and your own knowledge, explain why, by 1867, the possible development mentioned in Source **A** had not taken place.   **1, 2, 4(a, c)**

2. New Zealand

Read this extract from the Treaty of Waitangi, 1840, and then answer the questions which follow.

Her Majesty Queen Victoria, regarding with her Royal favour the native chiefs and tribes of New Zealand, and anxious to protect their rights and property, has deemed it necessary, in consequence of the great number of Her Majesty's subjects who have already settled in New Zealand, to appoint an official authorised to treat with the aborigines. Her Majesty has been graciously pleased to authorise and empower me, William Hobson, Captain in Her Majesty's Royal Navy, as Consul and Lieutenant-Governor, to invite the chiefs to concur in the following articles:

(i) Her Majesty confirms to the chiefs the full and undisturbed possession of their lands and estates so long as it is their wish to retain the same.

(ii) The chiefs cede to Her Majesty all rights and powers of sovereignty.

Source: quoted in T. D. Tremlett, *British History 1815-1914*, Edward Arnold, 1971.

(a) (i) According to the extract, why did the British government think it necessary to negotiate with the Maori chiefs? **4(a)**

(ii) What positions was William Hobson appointed to? **4(a)**

(iii) Explain in your own words the main points of the agreement. **4(a)**

(iv) How far was the treaty kept to over the next few years? **1, 2**

(b) Sir George Grey was Governor of New Zealand from 1845 to 1853. Describe his work with regard to:

(i) the Maoris;

(ii) the establishment of the New Zealand federation (1852). **1, 2**

(c) (i) Why did the Second Maori War (1860-71) break out?

(ii) What were the results of the war for the Maoris? **1, 2**

(d) Explain why and how New Zealand became united in 1876. **1, 2**

3. New South Wales was the first Australian colony to be founded, in 1788; it was followed by Tasmania (1803), Western Australia (1829), South Australia (1836), Victoria (1850) and Queensland (1859).

(a) (i) Show how sheep-farming and gold-mining were important in the early development of the colonies.

(ii) Describe the work and influence of Edward Gibbon Wakefield in the development of Australia.

(iii) Explain how problems of land distribution slowed down the development of Western Australia. How was this problem avoided in New South Wales?

(b) Explain why, during the 1890s, the six colonies began to think about joining together.

(c) Describe the arrangements made by the Commonwealth of Australia Act of 1900. **1, 2**

4. The year is 1867 and Sir John A. Macdonald has just become Prime Minister of the new Commonwealth of Canada. You are of British origin and live in Upper Canada (Ontario). Having been a life-long Canadian nationalist, you are now planning your memoirs. Give some extracts from these memoirs, describing and explaining, among other things:

(a) your impatience with the British government during the early 1830s;

(b) your reaction to Lord Durham's Report (1839);

(c)   your mixed feelings about the Canada Act (1840);

(d)   your attitude towards the USA;

(e)   your reasons for wanting a federation of all the Canadian colonies.   1, 2, 3

CHAPTER 19

THE GROWTH OF THE TRADE UNIONS AND THE LABOUR PARTY TO 1914

SUMMARY OF EVENTS

Between 1799 and 1824 the *Anti-Combination Laws* made trade unions (and employers' associations) illegal. Although they were given legal recognition in 1824 (see Section 2.6(b)) their powers were more or less non-existent. Between 1829 and 1834 various attempts were made to form national unions, culminating in *Robert Owen's Grand National Consolidated Trades Union of 1834*. All the attempts failed, and it was to be the last quarter of the century before there were any serious efforts to form unions for the lowest paid workers.

In the 1850s associations known as *'New Model' trade unions* were successfully founded for skilled workers; the first was *the Amalgamated Society of Engineers (1851)*. After a long campaign, the Trade Union Act of 1871 granted legal protection for union funds and in 1875 peaceful picketing was allowed.

As Britain moved into depression during the late 1870s, the low paid workers were driven to form trade unions. These so-called *'New Unions'*, unlike the Model Unions, contained some socialists. The first major triumph of the New Unionism was the successful *dockers' strike of 1889*. From 1900 to 1913 the unions were involved in legal wrangles – *The Taff Vale case (1900)* and *the Osborne Judgement (1909)* – with the courts and the House of Lords. Both were eventually resolved in a way satisfactory to the unions, but for a number of reasons there was considerable bitterness in labour relations, resulting in a wave of strikes in the years 1910 to 1913.

During the 1890s the Labour Party began to develop; in 1900 representatives of several socialist groups and of some trade unions, came together to form *the Labour Representation Committee*, which is usually taken as the beginning of the parliamentary Labour Party. Working closely with the trade unions, Labour won 29 seats in the general election of 1906, and 42 seats in 1910.

19.1 EARLY TRADE UNION DEVELOPMENTS AND FAILURES

(a) There had been unions of labourers and workmen for centuries in the form of local trade associations. Towards the end of the eighteenth century, the industrial revolution caused skilled tradesmen to combine together to protect their interests. It was unfortunate that these early combinations happened to coincide with the French Revolution, so that in the eyes of the ruling classes, unions were dangerous and revolutionary.

(i) *The Combination Acts* introduced by Pitt's government in 1799 and 1800 made it illegal to form Combinations 'for obtaining an Advance of Wages ... or for lessening ... their Hours of working'. These remained in operation through the wars with France and the period of unrest which followed after 1815.

(ii) A campaign for the repeal of the Acts, led by Francis Place and Joseph Hume, was eventually successful in 1824 (see Section 2.6(b)), but so great was the resulting crop of new unions and strikes that the government immediately introduced an *Amending Act (1825)*: trade unions could exist to negotiate about wages and hours of work, but were forbidden to obstruct or intimidate. Although some progress had been made it was still almost impossible to hold a strike without breaking the law.

(b) The attempt to form nationwide unions, 1829-33. 1825 saw the beginning of a trade depression which made it difficult for trade unions to have any impact. There were many attempts at local strikes, usually in protest at wage reductions, but employers broke them by bringing workers (blacklegs) in from nearby areas. The idea therefore grew that, instead of having separate local unions, it was essential to form nationwide unions of all the workers in a particular trade. Only in this way could the interests of the workers in that trade be protected. Beyond that, some leaders were already thinking in terms of uniting these national unions into a single national trades union.

(i) *The National Union of Cotton Spinners (1829)* was the first effective national union in a single trade. Founded by John Doherty in Manchester, it soon gained massive support, encouraging Doherty to go one step further and set up a *National Association for the Protection of Labour (1830)*. This attracted the support of 150 trade unions throughout the North and Midlands, but both unions had died out by 1832 because of cash shortages, a failure to co-ordinate their activities, and an improvement in trade.

(ii) An *Operative Builders' Union* was founded in Manchester (1832), bringing together all the various crafts in the building trade. Headed by a Grand Lodge and publishing its own journal, the new union seemed stronger than Doherty's creations, but it too had faded out by the end of 1834.

(iii) The climax of this phase of trade unionism was the formation of Robert Owen's Grand National Consolidated Trades Union in 1834.

19.2 ROBERT OWEN AND THE GRAND NATIONAL CONSOLIDATED TRADES UNION (GNCTU)

Born in Newtown, Montgomery, in 1771, Robert Owen became one of the most remarkable industrialists and reformers of the nineteenth century. From a modest background – his father was a postmaster – he was apprenticed to a draper at Stamford, and after a spell in London, he became a draper's assistance in Manchester. At the age of 18 he went into partnership with a mechanic to produce the recently introduced spinning machines and soon became manager of a large spinning mill of 500 workers. In 1794 he set up his own factory in Manchester where he introduced the spinning of American Sea Island cotton, the first British manufacturer to do so.

(a) His career as an enlightened manufacturer really began in 1800 when he moved to Scotland and became a partner in the New Lanark cotton mills. Before long he had factories of his own where he put into practice his advanced theories, so that the New Lanark mills and community facilities became a showpiece. His ideas were later published in a pamphlet – 'A New View of Society' (1813).

 (i) He believed that people's characters were a product of their environment; if miserable living and working conditions and grinding poverty drove people to crime, it was wrong to blame them. It was the duty of men with power and influence to improve the environment.
(ii) He turned New Lanark into a vast experiment to prove his theories. He enlarged the factories, making them lighter and more airy, and reduced working hours. All this was in marked constrast to the usual practices. He built new cottages for the workers and a school for the local children where there was an emphasis on outdoor activities – rambling and botany. He had parks and gardens laid out for the workers and introduced a scheme enabling them to buy goods at cost price.
(iii) He believed that capitalists should take only limited profits and that surplus profits should be used on services and facilities for workers – a theory which he certainly put into practice. He astonished his fellow manufacturers by continuing to pay wages when trade was slack and when cotton supplies were cut off during the war with the USA (1812–14). He was a strong supporter of the movement to limit children's working hours and played an important part, along with Sir Robert Peel, senior, in securing the 1819 Factory Act, though he was bitterly disappointed with its terms (see Section 12.3(b)). Although this Act was not a success, the effects of Owen's methods at New Lanark were vitally important: he had demonstrated that a manufacturer could still make a reasonable profit, while at the same

time reducing working hours and caring for his employees instead of exploiting them.

(b) The Co-operative movement was the next phase of Owen's career.

(i) Although his ideas were arousing a great deal of interest and attracting disciples, Owen was disappointed at the lack of response from government and from other industrialists. Consequently he carried his logic a step further, influenced by a theory of *David Ricardo*, a leading economist of the time. Ricardo argued that the value of a manufactured article depended entirely on the amount of labour put into it, and that workers were therefore not receiving a just reward for their labours. If Ricardo was right, then capitalists were not necessary; society should be reorganised to rid it of landowners and capitalists. *Co-operative communities* of workmen, jointly owning the means of production, would produce the goods, and fix prices according to the relative quantity of labour in each product. Sometimes they might exchange their products for the goods they wanted. He produced a scheme for co-operative villages laid out in quadrangles, some producing food, others manufacturing goods. Oddly enough Owen did not see this scheme as an attack on the rich, and he disapproved of strikes and violence to achieve it. Like the later Fabians (see Section 19.7(a)), he tried to appeal to the employers' better nature; he hoped that, as they realised the attraction of this new 'socialism', they would voluntarily give up their property and join in the experiment.

(ii) As a preliminary experiment, a 'Labour Exchange' was set up in Gray's Inn Road, London, for the exchange of goods. Workers brought their products and received certificates stating how much each article was worth in hours' work. The certificates entitled them to other goods of equivalent value. This was not a success mainly because there proved to be too much of some items and not enough of others – particularly food; the experiment was abandoned in 1834.

(iii) He started the London Co-operative Society (1824) which opened several co-operative shops. These had only limited success but the idea was taken up with spectacular results by the Rochdale pioneers in 1844 (see Section 19.2(d)).

(iv) Owen himself went to the USA in 1824 to set up an experimental co-operative village at New Harmony in Indiana, but this collapsed in 1828 and he returned to Britain.

(c) Owen and the trade unions. When he arrived back in Britain, Owen found that his co-operative ideas had great appeal among workers, and some trade union leaders were attempting to put them into practice. In 1833 the Derby silk-throwers declared that the factories which they worked were now co-operatives, but the employers, not sharing Owen's enthusiasm, announced that they would not employ any labourer who was a member of a trade union, and proceeded to lock out their workers.

Trade union leaders looked to Owen for guidance; his response was to set up *the Grand National Consolidated Trades Union* towards the end of 1833. All existing trade unions were invited to join, and within a few weeks it had attracted over half a million members. On paper it had an impressive organisation; in every district there was to be a branch of each separate trade together with a joint branch linking the different trades; in central control was a Grand Council meeting twice a year. Members were to pay a shilling a year, and co-operative workshops were to be set up; schools, recreational facilities and other services would be provided on the New Lanark model. When these were established the next step, as Owen himself explained, would be 'the union of master traders and manufacturers with the operatives and manual producers'; finally 'the Government will not only feel the necessity of uniting with them, but it will also discover the advantages to the whole empire of this national bond of union'. What Owen was aiming for was a complete reorganisation of society in which workers' control replaced private ownership and in which ultimately, the GNCTU would control the government. He hoped it could be achieved voluntarily and without violence. If not, there would have to be a general strike or 'sacred month' as it was called. However, the problems were enormous, and by August 1834 the GNCTU had more or less collapsed. *Reasons for its failure:*

(i) Four of the most important unions – builders, potters, spinners and clothiers – decided not to join, apparently afraid to lose their separate identities. In fact skilled workers tended to remain aloof.

(ii) There were problems of communication between one district and another; it was impossible to make sure that all branches knew what action they were supposed to be taking and to discipline branches which failed to co-operate.

(iii) There were disagreements between different trades and branches, some wanting immediate strikes, others wanting to wait until a nationwide general strike could be organised. Some leaders merely wanted to improve conditions, others wanted a revolution.

(iv) Employers everywhere reacted with hostility. The Derby silk-throwers were soon defeated and so were the London tailors and the Leeds clothiers. Some employers insisted on their workers signing a statement known as 'The Document', swearing that they were not members of the GNCTU. Anybody refusing to sign it was sacked.

(v) Probably most important was that the Whig government, alarmed at the wave of rick-burning and machine-breaking in the southern counties, decided to support local magistrates who dealt harshly with trade unionists. The most famous example occurred at the village of Tolpuddle in Dorset, where there was a branch of the Friendly Union of Agricultural Workers. Although there had been no violence or even strike action, the union leader, George Loveless, who was also a Methodist preacher, was arrested and convicted, along with five other men, on a charge of 'administering illegal oaths'. For this, these

illus 19.1 *Trade Union rally in 1834 to protest against the deportation of the Tolpuddle Martyrs*

Tolpuddle Martyrs were sentenced to seven years transportation to Tasmania (1834). Lord Melbourne, the Home Secretary, upheld the sentence. In the face of such harsh measures by government and employers, trade unionists became discouraged, and although many individual unions survived, the GNCTU collapsed.

Owen himself and his group of supporters continued to publicise his ideas. Calling themselves socialists – i.e. people who believe that capital and land should not be held in private hands – they founded the co-operative settlement of Queenwood (East Tytherly) in Hampshire (1839) which survived until the mid-1840s. Although none of Owen's ideas had much success outside New Lanark, he was important because he was the first person to publicise socialism.

The immediate results of the failure of the GNCTU were to turn workers towards Chartism and the Anti-Corn Law League. One of Owen's ideas that *was* taken up seriously later was the co-operative shops experiment:

(d) The Rochdale Pioneers and the Co-operative movement. In 1844 two Rochdale weavers, G. J. Holyoake and Charles Howarth, persuaded five fellow-weavers to join them in setting up a co-operative store. It was partly an act of self-help and a defence against the ineffectiveness of the 1820 Truck Act (see Section 2.4(c)). They pooled their savings, bought their goods in the usual markets like any other shopkeeper, and sold them at normal retail prices. The difference was that the profits, instead of remaining in the hands of a single shopkeeper, were shared out among the people who had bought at their shop, in proportion to their purchases. By the end of 1844 the Pioneers, as they became known, had attracted 28 members who shopped regularly at their store. The following year the store became well established and other co-operative societies began to spring up, so that by 1850 there were over a hundred. In 1863 all the stores joined together to form the *Co-operative Wholesale Society* which bought goods in bulk for sale in the local shops. In 1873 the Society began to open its own factories and by 1900 when there were over two million members, it had even bought its own tea plantation in Ceylon.

19.3 SHOW HOW THE 'NEW MODEL' UNIONS WERE ESTABLISHED IN THE 1850S AND HOW THEY GAINED LEGAL RECOGNITION

After the collapse of the GNCTU, the unions went through a difficult period lasting until 1842; there was a serious trade depression, unemployment and wage reductions. Yet many unions of skilled workers survived, and as the country moved into the prosperity of the 1850s there were new and more successful attempts to form large national unions, mainly by *skilled workers*.

(a) The 'New Model' unions

(i) In 1851 William Allan and William Newton formed the *Amalgamated Society of Engineers*. Its aim was not to change society, but simply to improve the position of its members within the capitalist system, by securing better wages and better working conditions. They were prepared to negotiate and to co-operate with employers; they were desperately keen to be respectable and looked on strike action only as a last resort. With 11 000 members each paying the high membership fee of a shilling (5p) a week, it had an income of over £500 a week, and was rich enough to provide unemployment and sickness benefits for its members. It had its own headquarters and paid officals.

(ii) Other national unions soon followed, deliberately modelling themselves on the ASE, hence the phrase 'New Model' unionism. In 1860 appeared the *Amalgamated Society of Carpenters*, which really became a national organisation in 1862 when *Robert Applegarth* was appointed general secretary at a salary of £1.10s. (£1.50) a week. Much smaller than the ASE to begin with, Applegarth built it up into an effective craft union; in 1870 it had over 10 000 members and 230 branches, and was financially sound. Other Amalgamated Societies were the Shoemakers and Tailors, while in the North, the National Union of Miners was revived and the Union of Lancashire Cotton Operatives was formed to deal with the problem of fixing piece rates.

(iii) The secretaries of these unions became powerful men; some of them - Allan, Applegarth, George Odger (Shoemakers) and Daniel Guile (Iron Founders) - used to meet regularly for consultations, and were nicknamed the *Junta*, by critics who resented their influence. The Junta went to great lengths to convince society that their Model Unions were moderate and respectable, and in no way revolutionary, and the 1867 Royal Commission Report (see below) was a great help in this respect. Applegarth was particularly successful, winning respect from politicians and the press. The Junta was also responsible for the first *Trades Union Congress (TUC)* which met in 1868; this turned into an annual meeting and soon became a permanent organisation, guiding and advising individual member unions.

(b) The unions run into difficulties, 1866-7

(i) Although it was now accepted that unions had the right to negotiate with employers, there were two areas of trade union activity which had never been specifically settled: one was whether striking and picketing were to be legalised or not, and the other was the question of the legality of a trade union's funds. Although the Junta disapproved of strikes on the whole, every union had its firebrands who were eager for strikes; many employers were waiting for an excuse to mount an attack on the unions, whether the leaders were moderate or not.

(ii) The so-called *Sheffield outrages* gave the unions' opponents their opportunity. Union extremists sometimes used crude intimidation to force workers to join or make members pay their dues, and a number of unsavoury incidents occurred in Sheffield. Workers' tools and equipment were smashed, a small workshop was blown up, and in 1866 a can of gunpowder exploded in a house belonging to a workman who had just withdrawn from the local Saw Grinders' Union. The culprit, the union treasurer, was arrested, and it emerged that he had been responsible for a whole string of similar outrages in several other towns. The employers demanded a Royal Commission to enquire into the conduct of trade unions, and the government obliged.

(iii) A further crisis for the unions arose in 1867 when the Boilermakers' Society sued the treasurer of its Bradford branch who had pocketed £24 of union funds. It was thought that union funds were protected by the 1855 Friendly Society Act, but when the case (known as *Hornby* v *Close*) came before the Court of Queen's Bench, it was ruled that a trade union was not a Friendly Society, it was an organisation 'in restraint of trade', and therefore its funds were not protected.

(iv) *The Royal Commission*, to the disgust of the employers, came out in grudging support of the unions (1868-9). Applegarth had presented a skilful defence of their activities, emphasising their disapproval of strikes, and pointing out the financial and social benefits gained by members. The Commission decided that outrages were on the decline and that union funds should be protected by law. This was a major triumph, preparing the way for the complete legalisation of trade union activities which came during the 1870s.

(c) Legal recognition for the unions (1871-6). Two considerations probably influenced the governments' thinking: following the Royal Commission Report, unions were widely considered to be 'respectable'. Also, many of their members had received the vote, thanks to the 1867 Reform Act, and both parties were anxious to win this new working-class vote:

(i) *Gladstone's Trade Union Act (1871)* recognised unions as legal bodies with the right to strike and to protect their funds at law; however, his *Criminal Law Amendment Act (1871)* made picketing illegal (see Section 13.2(d)), so that strikes were impossible to enforce.

(ii) *Disraeli's Conspiracy and Protection of Property Act (1875)* made peaceful picketing legal while the *Employers and Workmen Act (1876)* put both employer and worker on an equal footing in cases of breach of contract (see Section 14.2(c) for full details).

19.4 THE 'NEW UNIONISM' FOR UNSKILLED WORKERS

(a) Though trade unions had achieved full legal recognition by 1876, most of them represented skilled workers; the vast majority of unskilled workers were still unorganised and unprotected. During the 1880s an increasing number of semi-skilled and unskilled labourers began to show an interest in forming their own unions. The main reason was the depression of the last quarter of the century: during the serious slumps of 1879 and 1886, it was always the unskilled labourers who were laid off first and who seemed to be exploited most. The spread of education meant that intelligent labourers were literate and they were perfectly well aware of the advantages that members of the 'Model' unions enjoyed. It was only logical that they should try to follow their example. The spread of the factory system meant that there were greater concentrations of unskilled labour than ever before, which tended to encourage working-class solidarity. *Joseph Arch* had already formed the *National Agricultural Labourers' Union (1872)* which soon attracted 100 000 members. But when it asked for a wage increase from 13s. to 14s. for a 54-hour week, the farmers in Suffolk reacted decisively, locking out 10 000 labourers. The union went almost bankrupt paying out over £20 000 strike pay, and the agricultural depression soon killed it off completely.

(b) Eventually there were some successes:

(i) In 1888 there was a strike of 700 girls working in the Bryant and May match factory in London. Encouraged by the Fabian socialist *Annie Besant*, they were protesting about having to work in an atmosphere full of choking, poisonous phosphorous fumes. Amid great public sympathy, they won their case.

(ii) In 1889, *Will Thorne*, a stoker at Becton gasworks, East Ham, formed a *Gasworkers' Union*. When the union demanded an eight-hour day, the owners granted it without argument.

(iii) Most spectacular was *the London Dockers' Strike* of 1889. Encouraged by the Gasworkers' success, Ben Tillett, Tom Mann and John Burns formed a *General Labourers' Union* and asked for a minimum wage of 6d. an hour (the dockers' tanner). The dock owners refused to negotiate, so the entire dock labour force came out on strike. The dispute lasted almost five weeks, the employers trying to break the strike by bringing in blackleg labour; but quite suddenly they gave way and allowed the men their tanner. *A number of reasons contributed to the dockers' victory*: They received solid support from skilled stevedores and watermen who had their own unions, and were thus able to paralyse the entire dock system. The strike was conducted in a peaceful way with huge processions and mass meetings to publicise the justice of their claim. These won over public opinion and brought a rush of donations from sympathisers. This was vitally important since the union had no funds of its own for strike pay. Just when it seemed that the cash would run out, the dockers received an unexpected gift of £30 000 from the Australian trade unions which enabled them to continue. Finally Cardinal Manning, head of the Roman Catholic Church in Britain, supported the dockers, and together with the Lord Mayor of London, he persuaded the employers that the men's demands were reasonable.

(iv) The dockers' strike was a vital turning point in trade union development. It showed that even the lowest paid and most despised labourers could take on their employers and beat them, provided their demands were reasonable and provided they conducted their strikes in an orderly fashion. 'New Unionism' received an enormous impetus, as all types of unskilled workers formed new unions or rushed to join existing unions which had been struggling to find their feet. There was also an increase in membership of the older 'Model' unions.

(c) Differences between 'Model' and 'New' Unionism. Some historians, including Henry Pelling, argue that there was not really all that much difference in attitude and method between the two types of union. But in the 1880s and 1890s at least, there were some fairly obvious differences:

(i) The 'New' unions were much poorer, since their membership fees – usually about $1d$. a week – had to be lower than those for the skilled unions. Nor did they undertake Friendly Society benefits and pensions, believing that the state ought to provide them.
(ii) They tended to be more militant than the 'Model' unions, which seemed reluctant to face up to the problems of unemployment. According to Mann and Tillett writing in 1890: 'A kind of deadly stupor covered them and they really appeared to be dying of inanition' (lack of nourishment).
(iii) Many of the leaders of the 'New' unions were socialists who wanted political action as well as industrial action. They believed that it was the duty of the state to provide a decent standard of living for everybody by the introduction of social benefits. In the early years of the twentieth century these unionists threw their weight behind the Labour Party. But it would be wrong to generalise too much: until 1900 and the Taff Vale Case, many, perhaps even a majority, of trade unionists of both types still looked to the Liberal Party to introduce reforms, and there was nothing inevitable about their support for the Labour Party.

19.5 WHAT LEGAL PROBLEMS FACED THE TRADE UNIONS IN THE EARLY YEARS OF THE TWENTIETH CENTURY AND HOW WERE THEY OVERCOME?

Most manufacturers and men of property were genuinely afraid of trade unionism and some were determined to smash the movement. The Federation of Engineering Employers for example, refused to discuss a workers' demand for an eight-hour day. The men were locked out from July 1897 until January 1898, while the management moved blackleg labour in. The employers won, and although the unions survived, there was great bitterness. Even more serious for the unions was that the law courts seemed biased against them; several adverse judgements had serious implications for both skilled and unskilled unions:

SETTING UP THE
EARLY LABOUR
PARTY

(a) **In the Lyons v Wilkins case (1899)** the Appeal Court decided to limit the right of a union to picket. It was a vague judgement, but it could be interpreted as reversing the 1876 Trade Union Act. This prompted the TUC to vote (with a small majority) for a meeting with the various socialist societies, which set up *the Labour Representation Committee* (February 1900). Its purpose was to run independent Labour candidates for parliament. If strikes were failing and the law was against them, the only option left was to work through parliament. However, at this stage there was only lukewarm support - only ten unions affiliated to the Labour Party.

(b) **The Taff Vale case (1900-01)**

(i) This arose from a strike by the workers of the Taff Vale Railway Co. (South Wales). They wanted better working conditions and the right to join the Amalgamated Society of Railway Servants, which recognised the strike as official. The company refused to negotiate and broke the strike by bringing in blackleg labour; after two months the men had to return to work on the old terms (August 1900). Not content with this victory, the company sued the ASRS for damages suffered through loss of profits during the strike. After months of argument the House of Lords judged in favour of the company and ordered the ASRS to pay £23 000 damages, plus costs, making a grand total of £42 000. This was a disastrous decision for the trade unions, since it meant that no union could call a strike without risking bankruptcy; strike action was virtually impossible.

(ii) The only way to defeat the Taff Vale decision was for the government to pass an Act changing the law in the unions' favour. The unions had therefore to concentrate on political means to restore their powers. The Conservatives declined to co-operate, so many union leaders advised their members to support the Labour Party. By the end of 1903 a further 168 unions had affiliated to Labour, which won 29 seats in the 1906 general election. Twenty-four trade unionists were elected as Liberal MPs and one of the first measures of the new Liberal government was *the Trade Disputes Act (1906)* which said that the union could not be sued for damages and accepted that peaceful picketing was legal. This Act, possibly the most important in trade union history, left the unions more powerful than ever before and made possible the strike wave of 1910-14.

(c) **The Osborne Judgement (1909)** was another decision which displeased the unions, though in fact it was the Labour Party which suffered directly because of it.

(i) The situation was that the unions charged their members what was called the *political levy* - a small weekly payment on top of their normal union subscription, which was mostly used to provide financial help for Labour members of parliament, since at that time MPs received no salary. Not all union members were supporters of the

Labour Party and *W. V. Osborne*, a Liberal, and secretary of the Walthamstow branch of the Amalgamated Society of Railway Servants, challenged the right of his union to demand the political levy. The House of Lords ruled that it was illegal for unions to demand such a payment for the purpose of helping a political party. This was a serious blow for the Labour Party which was chronically short of funds, and it drove many trade unionists towards syndicalism (see next section).

(ii) Again, only by parliamentary means could the Osborne Judgement be defeated, and the unions and Labour launched a campaign to pressurise the Liberal government into action. This was slow to materialise since the government was beset with many other serious problems (see Section 20.3-5), but eventually satisfaction was achieved:

- In 1911 an annual salary of £400 was introduced for MPs. This fulfilled one of the Chartists' demands and eased the difficulties caused by the Osborne Judgement. But union pressure continued, resulting in:
- *The Trade Union Act (1913)*. This, in effect, reversed the Osborne Judgement: the political levy was legal, but any individual who objected to contributing to the Labour Party could 'contract out'. Since this required some personal effort, the vast majority of trade union members did not bother to 'contract out', and Labour Party funds accordingly received a life-saving boost.

On the eve of the First World War therefore, trade unions had overcome all legal obstacles; they had the power to strike and to play in important role in politics.

19.6 SYNDICALISM AND UNION MILITANCY

In the years 1910-14 many of the 'New' trade unions became much more militant and violent, influenced by French and American syndicalism or revolutionary trade unionism (*syndicat* is the French word for a trade union).

(a) Syndicalist ideas

(i) The trade union, not the state, was destined to be the main democratic organisation of the future, owning industries and land and controlling the country's economic and social policies.

(ii) This could be achieved not by political action through parliament but by direct action outside parliament. Syndicalists introduced the idea of the 'sympathetic' strike - if a union was conducting a strike, other unions in different industries would strike in sympathy, so that maximum pressure could be brought on government and employers. Ultimately they hoped to disrupt the country by a general strike so that the capitalist system would be overthrown and the trade union movement would take charge. There is some similarity to Robert Owen's ideas, though he was never as violent as the syndicalists.

(b) Why did Syndicalism develop in Britain? There was serious labour unrest because of unemployment and the fact that while prices were rising, wages were actually falling in real terms. As usual it was the unskilled, low-paid workers who suffered most. The results achieved by the skilled unions and the Labour Party in parliament were disappointing. The Osborne Judgement seemed deliberately designed to cripple the Labour Party; if parliamentary action was impossible, there remained only direct action outside parliament.

(c) The strike-wave began in July 1910 with action by railway workers, soon followed by Lancashire cotton workers, boilermakers and Welsh miners. 1911 saw a successful dock strike which affected all ports, and in Liverpool there was a transport strike during which troops were moved in and two men were killed. There seemed to be a lull during 1913, though in Dublin there was a major syndicalist strike lasting over six months.

In fact the unskilled workers were gathering themselves together for another onslaught. Several small railway unions united to form the National Union of Railwaymen and in 1914 the powerful *Triple Alliance* was formed consisting of the new NUR, the Transport Workers' Federation and the Miners' Federation. The outbreak of the First World War probably prevented a massive Triple Alliance strike in 1914, but the Alliance survived and moved into action later during the general strike of 1926.

19.7 EXAMINE THE CAUSES WHICH LED TO THE RISE OF THE LABOUR PARTY AND TRACE THE MAIN STAGES IN ITS DEVELOPMENT TO 1914

It is an oversimplification to talk about the rise of Labour Party as if it were a single homogeneous body. In fact it was an amalgamation of three different socialist groups – the Social Democrat Federation, the Fabians, and the Independent Labour Party – with some trade unions. Although these groups were all described as socialist, their aims and methods were not always the same; the word 'socialist' meant different things to different people.

(a) It was in the early 1880s that a number of factors began to converge

  (i) Basically the origin of the party lay in the poor social conditions and the poverty of the last quarter of the nineteenth century. At least 30 per cent of the working class were living close to starvation level, the agricultural and industrial depressions had worsened the situation, bringing unemployment and irregular employment. Often wages were so poor that families were living in dire poverty even when the breadwinner was in full-time employment. Many people were becoming disturbed at the striking contrast between this poverty and the comfortable existence enjoyed by the upper and middle classes.

(ii) *Progress and Poverty*, a book by an American economist, Henry George (published in Britain in 1881) focused attention on the tremendous contrasts of wealth and poverty. George blamed the problems on the greed of the landowners, and advocated a massive land tax as the cure for all ills. In a time of severe agricultural depression, the book was bound to have an impact both on middle-class intellectuals and on the working classes. Thanks to the spread of education following Forster's Education Act (1870), working people could read George's book and other socialist propaganda, such as Robert Blatchford's influential newspaper, *The Clarion*.

(iii) There was growing impatience among Radicals with Gladstone's Second Ministry (1880-5) which virtually ignored their suggestions for social reform. This was, to say the least, ill-advised, since many workers had received the vote thanks to the 1867 Reform Act, and Gladstone himself had extended the franchise to many more in 1884. more in 1884.

(iv) In 1884 two important socialist groups were formed:

- *The Social Democratic Federation* was set up by an old-Etonian, H. M. Hyndman, and also included John Burns and Tom Mann. Advocating violent revolution to overthrow the capitalist system, they achieved publicity by organising protest marches and demonstrations. The most famous one, held in Trafalgar Square in 1887, was broken up by police and is remembered as *Bloody Sunday* because of the violence on both sides.

- *The Fabian Society* was a group of middle-class intellectuals which included Sydney and Beatrice Webb and George Bernard Shaw. They believed that land and industrial capital should be owned by the community, but unlike the SDF they did not believe in violence. They took their name from Fabius, the Roman general who defeated Hannibal by waiting patiently and avoiding battle, knowing that time was on his side. The Fabians believed that society would gradually change from capitalism to socialism and their function was to persuade the political parties to accept socialism. At first they preferred this policy of 'gradual permeation' to creating a separate Labour party, but they changed their minds when it became clear that Liberals and Conservatives were not impressed by their ideas.

(v) In 1888 *James Keir Hardie*, secretary of the Scottish Miners' Federation, formed *the Scottish Labour Party*, because he was disgusted with the complacency and ineffectiveness of the Liberal Party. He became the first Labour MP in 1892 (for West Ham South) and soon played a crucial role in the formation of the Labour Party. He was convinced that the needs of working people could only be attended to by a Labour group completely independent of other parties.

(vi) A slump in the Yorkshire woollen industry in the early 1890s gave Hardie and his associate John Burgess, who ran a newspaper called *The Workman's Times*, a chance to form a new party. The whole woollen area, racked by unemployment and wage reductions, was bristling with Labour clubs – 23 of them in Bradford alone (the old Chartist tradition still lingered on). Hardie organised a conference in Bradford (1893) which resulted in the formation of the *Independent Labour Party (ILP)*. Its ultimate aim was the collective ownership of the means of production, but its priorities were vital social reforms. The ILP was a working class and very much a northern organisation; Hardie wanted the Labour Party to be a national body with middle-class support, and the final step came in 1900 . . .

(vii) The trade unions gradually moved towards the idea of a Labour Party, following incidents such as the great engineering lock-out of 1897-8 and the Lyons *v* Wilkins case of 1899 (see Section 19.5(a)). The TUC proposed a meeting with the socialist groups; representatives of some unions, SDF, Fabians and ILP attended the meeting at *the Memorial Hall, Farringdon Street, London* (February 1900) and decided to form a distinct Labour group in parliament. *The Labour Representation Committee (LRC)* was appointed to organise their election campaign, and *James Ramsay MacDonald*, later to become the First Labour Prime Minister, was its unpaid secretary. This is usually taken as the beginning of the Labour Party. Its aim was simply to represent working class interests in parliament; about socialism it was very vague.

There has been some argument about what part *Marxism* played in the formation of the Labour Party. Karl Marx (1818-83) was a German Jew who spent most of his life after 1848 in Britain. His economic and political ideas were explained in *The Communist Manifesto (1848)* and *Das Kapital (1867)*. He believed that economic factors are the real cause of historical change and that workers (proletariat) are everywhere exploited by capitalists; this must inevitably lead to the class struggle, to revolution and to the setting up of a classless society. His ideas certainly appealed to syndicalists and became the basic doctrine of communism. However, it is easy to exaggerate his influence on politics in Britain. *Das Kapital* only appeared in English translation in 1887; Hyndman had read it in a French translation in 1880-1 and the SDF was the most Marxist of the socialist groups. The ILP, which was more important than the SDF in the emergence of the Labour Party, arose out of the practical problems of the working class, though Marx's theories may have had an indirect influence.

(b) Stages in Labour Party development, 1900-14. The major priority after the formation of the LRC was to get Labour MPs elected. Already in 1892 Hardie and two other Labour MPs had been successful, but all three lost their seats in 1895.

(i) In the election of October 1900 the LRC ran 15 candidates, but only two, one of which was Hardie, were successful. It was unfortunate for the new party that the election came so soon after its formation; it was suffering from a severe cash shortage and very few trade unions supported it.

(ii) *The Taff Vale case (1900–01)* (see Section 19.5(b)) changed the situation dramatically. Ramsay MacDonald wrote to all trade unions stressing the need for a large Labour representation in parliament, and this produced a surge of trade union support and an improvement in the financial situation, thanks to the political levy.

(iii) In 1903 MacDonald came to an arrangement with the Liberals, who agreed that at the next election, they would not run candidates in certain constituencies, thus giving Labour a straight fight against the Conservatives. The Liberal motive was not to help the Labour Party but to avoid three-cornered contests in constituencies where the Conservatives were not thought to have much chance of winning. If both Labour and Liberal candidates ran, this would split the anti-Conservative vote, and allow the Conservatives to win. It was this electoral pact which allowed Labour to make the first breakthrough; in the 1906 election, Labour ran 50 candidates, 30 of whom were not opposed by Liberals. 29 were successful, and when they took their seats in parliament they decided to call themselves simply the Labour Party.

(iv) At first Labour had some success in parliament. *The Trade Disputes Act (1906)* which dealt with the Taff Vale decision, was based on the Labour Party's own bill, and they were able to add small improvements to the Workmen's Compensation Act and to the School Meals and Medical Inspections Act (see Section 20.2(b) and (c)). However, after 1907 they had very little influence on the government; they seemed to have run out of ideas and simply accepted the Liberal reforms.

(v) *The Osborne Judgement of 1909* (see Section 19.5(c)) damaged the party financially and their funds were further strained by the fact that there were two general elections in 1910. In January Labour won 40 seats which increased to 42 in December. However, only two of these had defeated Liberal candidates; the other 40 were successful because of the continuing electoral pact.

(vi) By 1914 the Labour Party, though making progress in local council elections, had failed to break away from its dependence on the Liberals; convinced socialists were disappointed with Labour's showing, particularly when MacDonald claimed in 1911 that the party was 'not socialist', but was a federation organised for 'immediate political work'. It was to be the First World War and the disintegration of the Liberals that gave Labour its chance to develop as a major party.

QUESTIONS

1. 'New' Unionism and the London Dock Strike of 1889
Study Sources **A** to **G** and then answer the questions which follow.

Source A: Ben Tillett's account of the beginning of the strike.

Trade Unionism among the general workers was an absolute
weakling, regarded as an illegitimate offspring, and treated like
one by the well-established and respectable unions of the skilled crafts and trades. To set our union on its feet and win the
respect of the craft unions, we had to demonstrate the sound-
ness of our strategy and the skill of our generalship in actual
warfare. The Dock Strike was a test, not only of intelligence
and will, but of the ability to seize opportunities as they arose,
to make use of public sympathy, and to transform militant
enthusiasm and excitement into Trade Union loyalty and
sober realism . . . Two members of the branch came to me with
a demand that the Union should declare a strike at the South
West India Dock. I could hardly believe my ears. Had the
worm indeed turned? Was it possible to strike with men who
shivered with hunger and cold, bullied and intimidated . . .
I was required to present to the Companies, in writing, a
series of demands – wages were to be raised to sixpence an
hour – the dockers' tanner. Overtime was to be paid at the rate
of eightpence an hour; employment was to be given to no man
for less than four hours at a stretch.

Source: Ben Tillett, *Memories and Reflections*, John Long,
1931.

Source B: another contemporary account.

The weather, like everything else, seemed to have been pressed
into the dockers' cause, and the sun shone down brilliantly
from a cloudless August sky . . . Thousands of dockers are
there, though nothing to the huge numbers reached in the later
stages of the strike. There are in all forty banners of trade and
friendly societies; and fish-heads, onions and tiny loaves are
carried on pikes as an object-lesson in dockers' fare to the
magnates of the city.

Source: H. L. Smith and V. Nash, *The Story of the Dockers'
Strike*, Fisher Unwin, 1889.

Source C: information from a modern work.

The demands of the dockers were meagre enough; the dock
companies refused even to discuss them, being confident that
creatures so degraded as the labourers had no staying power
and would rapidly be defeated.
A fortnight passed and the end seemed to be near. Finances
were running short and on August 29th a notice was posted

that no further relief could be paid . . . Then subscriptions began to arrive in London from Australia, first in single amounts, and then in a growing shower, like a hailstorm, until they reached the fantastic sum of £30,000. The whole aspect of the battle was changed. The companies for the first time became nervous. They issued a furious attack on the police. They had been hoping for a struggle between the police and the strikers in which batons would break down the labourers' enthusiasm. And they were foolish enough to let their disappointment be seen. But Burns had wisely kept carefully on the right side of the Metropolitan Police, and had organised his processions in obedience to their advice. Superintendent Forster's helmet next to Burns's white straw hat at the head of the marchers was an infuriating spectacle to the company directors.

On September 5th, under pressure from the Lord Mayor and Cardinal Manning, they began at last to yield and . . . the next night official terms granted practically all the dockers' demands.

Source: G. D. H. Cole and R. W. Postgate, *The Common People 1746-1938*, Methuen, 1938 (adapted extracts).

Source D: some comments from another modern writer.

John Burns cultivated the reporters. He fed them with news and by doing so got sympathetic statements of the dockers' case in all the important papers. He made the struggle of the dockers into a dramatic battle that caught the imagination of the nation and stirred the social consciences of men and women everywhere . . . The mobilisation of public opinion as an ally in the struggle of the workers had once again, as in the match girls' strike, proved of decisive consequence.

Source: F. Williams, *Fifty Years' March: The Rise of the Labour Party*, Odhams, 1950.

Source E: Tom Mann and Ben Tillett write about the 'New' unionism.

We repeat that the real difference between the 'new' and the 'old', is that those who belong to the latter, and delight in being distinct from the policy endorsed by the 'new', do so because they do not recognise, as we do, that it is the work of the trade unionist to stamp out poverty from the land. They do not believe, as we do, that existing unions should exert themselves to extend organisations where they as yet do not exist. Real grit exists in the new unions, which is evident from the substantial way in which they have contributed to the support of other trades, such as the bargebuilders, whose strike balance-sheet shows that the 'new' unions were much more prompt in rendering monetary aid than the 'old' ones . . . We are prepared to work unceasingly for the economic emancipation of the workers. Our ideal is a Co-operative Commonwealth.

Source: T. Mann and B. Tillett, *The 'New' Trades Unionism*, 1890 (adapted extracts).

Source F: from the Report of the Royal Commission on Labour, 1894, signed by a majority of the Commissioners.

With regard to those industries which are carried on on a large scale and require the co-operation of great bodies of workmen, the evidence points to the conclusion that, on the whole, the increased strength of organisation may lead to the maintenance of harmonious relations between employers and employed . . .
   The level of wage rates has risen considerably during the last fifty years, both in respect of their nominal value and their power of purchasing commodities. At the same time it appears that the daily hours of labour have in most cases been shortened, and the sanitary conditions of work have improved.

Source: L. Evans and P. J. Pledger, *Contemporary Sources and Opinions in Modern British History, vol. 2*, Warne, 1967 (adapted extracts).

Source G: from the Report of the Royal Commission on Labour, 1894, signed only by a minority of the Commissioners, including Tom Mann.

We are unable to join in the Report of the majority of the Commissioners. The fundamental cause of the disputes between employers and employed is to be found in the unsatisfactory position occupied by the wage-earning classes . . . In spite of the great increase in national wealth, whole sections of the population, at least five millions, are unable to obtain a subsistence compatible with health or efficiency. Probably two millions are driven every year to accept Poor Relief in one form or another . . . While many industrious artisans can find no work to do, thousands of others are kept to labour for unnecessarily long periods . . . Many thousands of workers still toil under circumstances which make disease and accident an inevitable accompaniment of their lives.

Source: as for Source F (adapted extracts).

(a) (i) Who was Ben Tillett, the writer of Source A?   **1, 4(a)**
   (ii) According to Tillett, what was needed to put the union on its feet?   **4(a)**
   (iii) In what way did Tillett see the Dock Strike as a test?   **4(a)**
   (iv) What were the dockers' demands?   **4(a)**

(b) (i) According to Source B, how did the dockers demonstrate their poverty?   **4(a)**
   (ii) According to Source C, why did the dock companies refuse to discuss the dockers' demands?   **4(a)**
   (iii) From the evidence of Source C, how important was the financial help from Australia?   **4(a)**

(c)   (i)   From the evidence of Sources **C** and **D**, what were the main reasons for the dockers' success?   **4(a, c)**

      (ii)   What evidence is there in Source **D** that the dockers' success was not the first victory of the 'new' unionism?   **4(a)**

      (iii)   What impression do you get from Sources **C** and **D** of the part played by John Burns in the struggle?   **4(a, c)**

      (iv)   How do the writers of Sources **A, B, C** and **D** show their sympathy with the dockers?   **4(a, b, c)**

(d)   (i)   What evidence of ill-feeling and differences between the 'old' and 'new' unions can you find in Sources **A** and **E**?   **4(a, c)**

      (ii)   From your own knowledge, what other differences were there between the two?   **1, 2**

      (iii)   Explain in your own words what the writers of Source **E** were hoping to achieve.   **4(a)**

(e)   (i)   Do you think that the Majority Report of the Royal Commission (Source **F**) approves of trade unions or not? Explain your answer.   **4(a)**

      (ii)   What evidence does Source **G** provide that workers' conditions were still far from perfect?   **4(a)**

      (iii)   In what ways does the Minority Report (Source **G**) disagree with the Majority Report (Source **F**) about conditions of employment?   **4(a, c)**

      (iv)   What reasons can you suggest for this disagreement?   **4(b)**

(f)   What are the strengths and weaknesses of each of these Sources for the historian?   **4(b)**

2. The Early Years of the Labour Party

Read the extract from Philip Snowden's account of the formation of the Labour Representation Committee, and then answer the questions which follow.

> The conference met at the Memorial Hall, London, on 27 February 1900. The three Socialist societies – the I.L.P., the Fabians and the Social Democratic Federation were represented. The Trade Unions had 500,000 members represented . . . An attempt was made by the Social Democrats to commit the conference to a declaration that the new party should be based on the recognition of the class war. This was an illustration of the tactlessness of the Social Democrats, which explained the reason for the failure of their propaganda to make any impression on public opinion. At this stage to commit the Trade Unions to an extreme Socialist programme would have made the co-operation of the bodies represented at the conference most unlikely. Keir Hardie, with a true appreciation of the situation, moved on behalf of the I.L.P., an amendment that the conference 'approve the formation of a distinct Labour group in parliament, whose policy must embrace a readiness to co-operate with any party engaged in promoting legislation in the direct interests of Labour'. This was passed unanimously.

The new organisation was to be called the Labour Representation Committee, and an executive of twelve was appointed, seven representing the Trade Unions, two the I.L.P., two the Social Democrats, and one the Fabian Society.

Source: Philip Snowden, *An Autobiography*, Nicholson & Watson, 1934 (adapted extracts).

(a) (i) What were the three societies represented at the conference?
4(a)

   (ii) Which one did Snowden belong to? 1, 4(a)

   (iii) Which other organisations were represented at the conference?
4(a)

(b) (i) Who was Keir Hardie, referred to in the extract? 1, 4(a)

   (ii) Explain in your own words the meaning of Hardie's amendment, which was passed by the conference. 4(a)

   (iii) From the evidence of the extract, how would you describe Snowden's attitude towards the Social Democrats? Explain your answer fully. 4(a, b)

   (iv) Which seemed to be the dominant group at the conference from the evidence of the extract? 4(a)

   (v) Using your own knowledge and the evidence of the extract, explain why this conference was so important in the history of the Labour Party. 1, 2, 4(a)

(c) Explain how each of the following helped to cause the formation of the Labour Party:

   (i) poor social conditions;

   (ii) the industrial slump of the early 1890s;

   (iii) the work of Keir Hardie;

   (iv) the Lyons v. Wilkins case (1899). 1, 2

(d) How successful was the newly formed Labour Party up to 1914 in

   (i) getting MPs elected to parliament;

   (ii) getting important reforms carried out. 1, 2

3. Robert Owen was one of the most remarkable industrialists and reformers of the nineteenth century.

(a) Describe his career as a progressive manufacturer at New Lanark.

(b) Explain his ideas about co-operative communities. How successful was he in carrying these ideas into practice?

(c) What were Owen's plans for the development of the Grand National Consolidated Trade Union (1833)?

(d) Explain why the GNCTU had collapsed by August 1834.

(e)   'Robert Owen, though full of good ideas, had very little success in putting them into practice.' Do you agree or disagree with this statement? Explain your answer fully.   1, 2

4.   As a socialist and trade union member, describe and explain your feelings and reactions at:

(a)   the dockers' strike (1889)

(b)   the formation of the Labour Representation Committee (1900);

(c)   the Taff Vale Case (1900–1);

(d)   the Trade Disputes Act (1906);

(e)   the Osborne Judgement (1909);

(f)   the Trade Union Act (1913).   1, 2, 3

CHAPTER 20

THE LIBERALS IN POWER 1905–14

SUMMARY OF EVENTS

The Liberal government which took office in December 1905 and won a landslide victory in January 1906 (see Section 17.5(b)(c) for statistics and reasons) in many ways marked the beginning of a new era. For the first time Britain had a government which was not dominated by wealthy landowners and aristocrats. The Radical wing of the Liberal Party had come to the forefront, and though there were some aristocrats in the cabinet (Sir Edward Grey, the Foreign Secretary) most of the senior posts were filled by lawyers (Asquith, Lloyd George and Haldane) with a sprinkling of writers and journalists. As President of the Local Government Board there was John Burns, who had worked as an engineer, helped organise the 1889 dock strike and had for a time been a member of the SDF before joining the Liberals. Also from the working class were the 29 Labour MPs and the 24 Liberals sponsored by the miners' unions, who usually sat with the Labour men.

This new Radical predominance has led some historians to describe these years as the era of *'New' Liberalism*: whereas old-fashioned Gladstonian Liberals had concentrated on *laissez-faire* and cheap and efficient administration, going in for some minor tinkering to promote equality of opportunity, the 'New' Liberalism acknowledged the need, if the party was to survive, for the state to play a new and decisive role in bringing about social reform. 'New' Liberalism had very little time to prove itself; although nobody realised it at the time, this was destined to be Britain's last Liberal government.

The Prime Minister, the 69-year-old *Sir Henry Campbell-Bannerman*, was a successful Scottish businessman who had been Liberal leader in the Commons since 1898. Generally regarded as a Radical and known affectionately in the party as C-B, he was level-headed, kindly and sympathetic, but he was also tough and determined. Though he was not a brilliant speaker and not in robust health, he turned out to be an expert at managing his cabinet, which was full of brilliant men. *H. H. Asquith* was Chancellor of the Exchequer and *David Lloyd George*, a fiery young

Welshman from a modest background, was President of the Board of Trade.

Campbell-Bannerman died in April 1908, his greatest achievement having been *the settlement of the South African problem*. Asquith became Prime Minister and a cabinet reshuffle made Lloyd George Chancellor of the Exchequer and brought *Winston Churchill* in as President of the Board of Trade.

The government had an enormous majority, so that carrying its policies into effect should have been plain sailing. However, it was a period full of tensions and crises. The House of Lords decided to use its built-in Conservative majority to block much of the Liberals' legislation, which inevitably led to *a bitter confrontation between the two houses of parliament*. The *suffragettes* mounted a determined and violent campaign to secure the vote for women; from 1910 there was *serious labour unrest* and a wave of strikes; and on top of all that there was *new trouble in Ireland* where civil war was averted only by the outbreak of the First World War in August 1914. In spite of all these distractions, the Liberals found time to introduce important *reforms to help trade unions and working people*, and though in some ways their social reforms were disappointing, it is usual to regard them as *the beginning of the welfare state*. Foreign affairs were characterised by Britain's growing friendship with France, and in spite of Grey's efforts, the deterioration of relations with Germany, which was to bring Britain into war.

The period from 1901 to 1914 is known as *the Edwardian era*, though Edward VII died in 1910, to be succeeded by his son George V who reigned until 1936.

20.1 THE LIBERALS AND SOUTH AFRICA

(a) **The problem of Chinese slavery** (see Section 17.5(b)(v)) was settled immediately, the government simply forbidding the importing of any more Chinese into the Transvaal. The existing workers had to serve out their contracts, but by 1910 the problem had disappeared.

(b) **The Transvaal and the Orange Free State**, after their defeat in the Boer War, had been promised eventual self-government in the Treaty of Vereeniging (see Section 17.2(c)). Campbell-Bannerman saw no sense in delaying it any longer: complete self-government was granted to the Transvaal (1906) where the former Boer General Botha became Prime Minister and the following year to the Orange Free State. The Boer leaders were much impressed by the government's speed and had retained an enormous respect for Campbell-Bannerman ever since he had described Kitchener's concentration camps as 'methods of barbarism'. For these reasons they decided to join Cape Colony and Natal to form *the Union of South Africa* which came into existence officially in 1910. Although this took place after C-B's death, the creation of the new dominion and the reconciliation of the Afrikaners and the British were very much his achievement. South Africa supported Britain in both world wars and stayed in the Commonwealth until 1961. There was one major criticism: no provision was made to safeguard the rights of non-whites and no guarantee was given that they would eventually be allowed to vote. However, if the government had insisted on such guarantees being written into the new constitution, the Boers would not have agreed to join the Union. The Liberals hoped that in time the more progressive attitudes of the English-speaking South Africans would prevail and ensure that non-whites received equal treatment. Unfortunately this did not happen and the policy of *apartheid* was later introduced by the Boer dominated South African government (see Section 30.6(c)); but it is surely unfair to blame Campbell-Bannerman and Asquith for this.

20.2 WHY DID THE LIBERALS INTRODUCE REFORMS TO HELP THE WORKING CLASSES? WHAT WERE THE REFORMS AND HOW SUCCESSFUL WERE THEY?

The need for reform in Edwardian Britain had been publicised by the investigations of *Charles Booth* and *Seebohm Rowntree*. In surveys carried out between 1889 and 1903, Booth showed that over 30 per cent of the population of London was living in serious poverty. Rowntree, a member of the famous chocolate-manufacturing family, discovered that in York in 1901 the percentage was almost as high; 'we are faced', he wrote, 'with the startling possibility that from 25 to 30 per cent of the town populations of the United Kingdom are living in poverty'. Both men helped to explode the Victorian myth that poverty was the result of a character defect; Booth emphasised that in a time of depression a worker might be unable, through no fault of his own, to find a job; Rowntree showed something even worse – in York wages were so low that even men in full-time employment were forced to live close to starvation level; he recommended that a minimum wage of 21s. 8d. (£1.08p) a week was needed to keep a couple with three children in 'Spartan physical efficiency'. The seriousness of the problem was also highlighted by recruitment for the Boer War when almost half the volunteers were found to be medically unfit for the army.

Liberal motives for introducing the reforms were mixed. There was an element of compassion: some Liberals felt that social justice ought to be done, that it was simply not right for a third of the population to be living in such misery. However, if this had been the only consideration it is doubtful whether much would have been done; in fact the government had no bills prepared and no programme of social reform drawn up. Probably more significant was the need for a healthy working-class for military and economic purposes. If Britain were to be involved in a major war, an efficient army would be necessary to defend the Empire. The Birmingham Chamber of Commerce called for health insurance and old age pensions on the grounds that a healthy workforce would be more efficient and more profitable. Some reform was necessary therefore for national survival. The Liberals were under pressure from the Labour Party and from the trade unions, and there was the added incentive that a limited amount of social reform would attract voters away from socialism and so defeat the challenge from the infant Labour Party. There was the need to show that Liberals had policies which clearly distinguished them from the Conservatives, so that the working class vote would not drift away in that direction. Finally there were the political ambitions of Lloyd George and Churchill, both of whom were anxious to enhance their reputations. Each reform was a response to a particular problem or situation; there was no master plan to set up a 'welfare state'.

(a) Trade union legislation

(i) *The Trade Disputes Act (1906)*. Since 1901 the trade unions had been agitating for some action to reverse *the Taff Vale decision* (see Section 19.5(b)) which made it almost impossible for a union to conduct a strike without risking bankruptcy. The cabinet agreed that something ought to be done to protect trade union funds and thus keep the support of organised labour, but it got into a tangle trying to draw up a bill which gave trade unions only limited powers. The Labour Party had its own bill prepared, so Campbell-Bannerman decided to accept it as it stood, to save time. The resulting Act was therefore more drastic than many Liberals intended: unions could not be sued for damages, and peaceful picketing was allowed. Critics felt that this gave far too much power to the unions, which were now more or less immune from the law.

(ii) *The Trade Union Act (1913)* remedied the situation caused by *the Osborne Judgement (1909)* (see Section 19.5(c) for full details). It was prompted by the desire to soothe trade union militancy. and, given the Liberals' much weaker position following the 1910 general elections (see next section), by the need to keep the support of the Labour MPs, now 42 in number.

(b) Measures to help children

(i) Local education authorities were given the power to provide free school meals for needy children (1906). This developed from a Labour bill, and its immediate effects were not as great as had been hoped, since it was *not compulsory*. By 1914 less than half the education authorities in England and Wales were providing meals, so in that year the government made it compulsory.

(ii) There were to be compulsory medical inspections at schools, and education authorities could provide free medical treatment (1907). Again this was a hesitant measure since many authorities ignored the second part of the Act. However, in 1912 government grants were made available to provide treatment and school clinics began to be set up.

(iii) Child offenders were to be tried, not in ordinary law-courts, but in special juvenile courts, and were to be sent to corrective schools (borstals) instead of to ordinary prisons. Probation officers were to be appointed for after-care. There were to be stiff penalties for those ill-treating children or selling them cigarettes and tobacco, or alcohol in unsealed bottles or jugs (1908).

(iv) On the academic side of education the Liberals introduced the 'free place' system. Secondary schools were required to reserve a quarter of their places, free of charge, for children from elementary schools (1907).

In spite of its weaknesses, this *Children's Charter*, as it became known, was important because it was the first time that any government had intervened so directly in the lives of ordinary people; it was providing help not as charity as the Poor Law did but as a right and a service to which all were entitled.

(c) Old Age Pensions were introduced at the rate of five shillings (25p) a week for people at the age of 70. No contributions had to be paid, though no one could receive the pension if his income from other sources exceeded £21 a year. Again, there was criticism; five shillings was a very small amount, and the Labour Party wanted the pension at 65, arguing that many old people would not survive until 70 to enjoy it. The government's motive for this rather belated introduction of an old age pension was not simply social concern; they had been losing by-elections, and as Lloyd George remarked: 'it is time we did something that appealed straight to the people – it will I think help to stop this electoral rot and that is most necessary'. Nevertheless the pension was enormously popular and Lloyd George gained all the credit for it, though the bill had been prepared by Asquith, and Lloyd George only handled the final stages after taking over as Chancellor of the Exchequer on Campbell-Bannerman's death.

(d) Measures to help working people

(i) *A Workmen's Compensation Act (1906)* extended the previous Act of 1897 (see Section 17.1(c)) to include all categories of worker and also allowed compensation for injury to health caused by industrial conditions as well as for injury caused by accidents.

(ii) *The Merchant Shipping Act (1906)* introduced stringent regulations covering standards of food and accommodation for crews on British registered ships. This was the work of Lloyd George who was already showing considerable drive at the Board of Trade, where he was also responsible for a *Patents Act* which gave investors more protection and for the creation of *the Port of London Authority* which took under its control the many different companies which operated London's docks.

(iii) *The Coal Mines Act (1908)* introduced a maximum eight-hour working day for miners, a remarkable milestone, since it was the first time the British government had intervened to regulate the working hours of adult males. In 1912 came the *Minimum Wage Act* which set up local boards to fix minimum wages in each district in order to help miners working in different seams. This sounds impressive, but the Act was an emergency measure forced through to end the damaging coal strike which had lasted from February to April. Nor did it fully satisfy the miners who had been campaigning for a *national minimum wage* of five shillings a day for a man and two shillings for a boy.

(iv) *Labour Exchanges* were set up (1909) by Churchill and William Beveridge at the Board of Trade. This was a simple idea pressed on the government by the Fabian, Beatrice Webb. With unemployment rising steeply in 1908–09 – in some trades it was double the figure for 1907 – Churchill decided to act. Employers with vacancies were to inform the Labour Exchanges so that unemployed workers could easily find out what jobs were available. By 1913 there were 430 exchanges in Britain and the system was working well, though it was still only voluntary.

(v) *The Trade Boards Act (1909)* was another Churchill achievement; it dealt with the problem of low-paid and depressed workers in what were called the 'sweated' industries. These usually employed female and child labour often working excessively long hours in their own homes for outrageously low wages. Described by Charles Booth as 'a body of reckless, starving competitors for work', their plight had been publicised by the National Anti-Sweating League, since the nature of their work made trade union organisation impossible. Churchill's Act set up boards to fix minimum wages in four occupations: tailoring, box-making, lace-making and chain-making. In 1913 this was extended to cover six more 'sweated' trades, so that now almost 400 000 workers were protected and were ensured a reasonable wage. This certainly broke new ground, showing that the state was prepared to make some moves towards establishing a minimum wage, but it was a pity that such a small fraction of the total workforce was affected.

(vi) *The Shops Act (1911)* gave shop assistants a statutory half-day holiday each week, but did not limit hours of work, so that assistants were often required to make up for the half day off by working later at other times during the week.

(vii) *Payment for MPs* at the rate of £400 a year was included in Lloyd George's budget of 1911. This was to placate the Labour Party which was having difficulty financing its MPs because of the Osborne Judgement (see Section 19.5(c)). Working men would now be able to afford to enter parliament, but the Conservatives were bitterly critical, arguing that salaries would attract people into parliament for personal gain rather than a wish to serve the public.

(viii) *The National Insurance Act (1911)* was Lloyd George's greatest achievement before 1914. It was a compulsory scheme in two parts: one provided some *health insurance*, the other *unemployment insurance*. The reason for the introduction of health insurance was very much the drive for greater national efficiency, though Lloyd George was genuinely concerned at the large numbers of deaths from tuberculosis – estimated at 75 000 a year. Unemployment insurance was a response to Labour party and trade union pressure. Both were certainly an attempt by the Liberals to head off socialism.

- *Health insurance* was provided by a fund into which the worker paid fourpence, the employer threepence and the state twopence. When he was off work ill, the worker would receive ten shillings a week sick pay, and was entitled to free medical attention and medicines, a maternity grant of 30 shillings and a sanatoria allowance if he developed tuberculosis. Benefits (apart from the maternity grant) did not apply to the worker's wife and children, nor to those earning more than £160 a year. It caused bitter controversy and the Conservatives succeeded in turning many workers against it by arguing that the government had no right to force workers to pay into the scheme directly out of their wages. There was also opposition from doctors who feared they would lose their independence, and there were complex problems of how to administer the scheme. It was here that Lloyd George showed his brilliance at reconciling conflicting interests and his gift for getting things done.

- *Unemployment insurance* applied only to workers in certain trades where the demand for labour fluctuated most; these were building, shipbuilding, mechanical engineering, iron-founding, vehicle construction and sawmilling. Worker and employer both paid $2\frac{1}{2}d$ into the fund and the state twopence. The unemployment benefit was seven shillings a week up to a maximum of 15 weeks in any 12-month period. Soon 2.25 million men were protected by this scheme, though its obvious drawback was that it only covered a small handful of trades. There was also the question of what would happen after 15 weeks if the worker was still unemployed.

To be fair to the Liberals, Lloyd George intended both parts of the Act to be an experimental beginning, to be extended as soon as possible, but the war got in the way. Nevertheless it was an important extension of state aid and it established the principle that health and unemployment benefit schemes should be contributory – i.e. the workers themselves should pay part of the cost. Although Labour Party moderates accepted this principle, convinced socialists like Keir Hardie denounced it bitterly. They wanted a non-contributory scheme financed by high taxes on the wealthy.

(e) How successful were the reforms? Although as we have seen, individual reforms had varying degrees of success, taken together they must have done something to alleviate the worst effects of poverty. However, in 1914 there were still some areas which had not been touched by government action. For example, the Royal Commission set up by the Conservatives to investigate the workings of the Poor Law, produced two reports in 1909 – one agreed by a majority of the commission, the other by the minority. But most of the suggestions, including the complete abolition of the Poor Law system with its workhouses and its stigma of charity, were ignored, apparently because of the ineptitude of John Burns, the Minister in charge of the Local Government Board. The result was a strange dual system in which the new state aid was being provided alongside the Poor Law system, which continued until 1929. Nothing had been done for agricultural labourers who remained the worst paid of all workers. Between 1900 and 1914 real wages rose very little, if at all, and the trade unions were not in the least impressed by the Liberal social reforms, as they showed by their increasing militancy between 1910-14. Another disturbing fact was that in 1914 the percentage of army volunteers rejected as physically unfit was almost as high as it had been in 1900. Of course, this was only to be expected; there was bound to be a time-lag before the benefits of the new state aid made themselves felt. The vitally important fact was that the Liberals had laid foundations which men like Lloyd George and Churchill fully intended to build on later.

Did the Liberals lay the foundation of the welfare state? Opinions differ sharply; Jo Grimond (Liberal leader 1956-67) not unnaturally claims that the Liberals actually created the welfare state, but Arthur Marwick believes that the welfare state was 'created' by the Labour government after the Second World War. Perhaps the best conclusion is that offered by Donald Read; he suggests that what the Liberals had achieved – and it *was* a new departure – was the beginnings of a 'social service state' rather than a 'welfare state'. The difference is this: a *social service state* is one where certain minimum standards are ensured by the government; a *welfare state* is one where the government provides the best possible services for everybody.

20.3 THE LIBERALS AND THE DISPUTE WITH THE HOUSE OF LORDS

(a) **What were the causes of the dispute?** The basic cause of the dispute was that the House of Lords with its large Conservative majority, was continually rejecting Liberal bills, although during the previous ten years of Conservative rule, it had not once interfered with a Conservative bill (see Chapter 4 summary for stages in passing a bill through parliament). The Liberal government, therefore, in spite of having been elected with a huge majority, was being prevented from carrying out its policies, by a House of Lords which was not elected; democracy was being slowly defeated. If the Lords persisted, a constitutional crisis was inevitable.

The confrontation built up gradually.

(i) Gladstone's Second Irish Home Bill had been rejected by the Lords in 1893 (see Section 16.8(b)) and this was followed by the defeat of most of Lord Rosebery's attempted measures (1894-5). The Lords' justification was that the Liberals had only a tiny majority.

(ii) In 1906 the Lords defeated two of Campbell-Bannerman's important bills, an Education Bill and a Plural Voting Bill (which would have removed the right of people owning business premises to vote more than once). The following year two more important bills were rejected and a further two were changed so drastically by the Lords that they turned out to be almost worthless. This time there could be no excuse of a flimsy Liberal majority. The Conservative leaders, Balfour and Lord Lansdowne, had decided on a blatant use of the Lords to protect the interests of their own party and class. Campbell-Bannerman warned them that if this continued, an attempt would be made to restrict their powers. The warning was ignored.

(iii) In 1908 the Lords rejected the Licensing Bill designed to reduce the number of public houses, though Edward VII advised them to pass it. The Lords were also preparing to oppose old age pensions but Asquith thwarted them by using an important loophole: it was the tradition that *the Lords never interfered with a finance bill* (usually the annual budget); Asquith shrewdly designated the pensions bill as a finance bill and it passed without controversy.

(iv) The climax came in 1909 when the Lords broke the constitutional tradition by *rejecting Lloyd George's entire budget for that year.* It was Lloyd George's first budget and it was designed to raise about £15 million of extra cash to pay for pensions, labour exchanges, and above all for Dreadnought battleships, and the wealthy were to foot the bill. *The details were:* income tax up from a shilling to 1s. 2d. in the pound on incomes over £3000; supertax of 6d. in the pound on incomes over £5000; higher taxes on tobacco and spirits (a bottle of whisky went up from 3s. 6d. to 4s.); higher charges for liquor licences; taxes on petrol and cars; taxes on mining royalties; and, most controversial of all, a 20 per cent tax on the increased value of land when it was resold.

(v) The budget was debated in the Commons from April until November - much longer than usual. The Conservatives assaulted it viciously both in the Commons and outside, forming a Budget Protest League. They complained that it was a deliberate attack on the wealthy, especially on landowners and that it was the beginnings of socialism: the new land tax would require all land to be valued, and this, they feared, could be the preliminary to the nationalisation of land. The Duke of Beaufort said he would like to see Lloyd George and Churchill 'in the middle of twenty couple of foxhounds'; Lloyd George struck back in his famous Limehouse speech, accusing landlords of being selfish creatures whose sole function was 'the stately consumption of wealth produced by others'. In November 1909 the budget passed the Commons with a huge majority (379–149), but later the same month the Lords rejected it, even though Edward VII was anxious for it to pass. Lord Lansdowne, Conservative leader in the Lords, justified this on the grounds that such a revolutionary measure ought to be put before the public, in a general election. Balfour said that the Lords were merely carrying out their proper function as the 'watchdog of the constitution', i.e. making sure that no irresponsible laws were passed. Lloyd George retorted that the Lords were acting as if they were 'Mr. Balfour's poodle'.

It has been suggested that Lloyd George deliberately produced a controversial budget to trap the Lords into rejecting it so that the Liberals would have a cast-iron case for restricting their powers. But there is little evidence of this; the government needed the money and were determined to make the wealthy pay a fair share. On the other hand the budget was cleverly framed to embarrass the Conservatives: if they did not oppose the tax increases, their landowning supporters would be furious; if they did oppose them, they would lay themselves open to charges of selfishness for refusing to contribute towards defence and help for the poor. Very few Liberals could have expected the Lords to break a 250-year-old tradition by rejecting the entire budget.

(b) The constitutional crisis and the two elections of 1910. The rejection of the budget immediately caused a constitutional crisis. If the Lords were allowed to get away with it, the basic principle of democracy which had developed in Britain would be overturned: the hereditary House of Lords, and not the elected House of Commons would control government policy. Asquith and the Liberals prepared for battle, declaring that the Lords' action was a breach of the constitution:

(i) Parliament was dissolved and a general election held (January 1910) on the issue of 'Peers *v* People'. The results were disappointing for the Liberals who lost heavily; the figures were: Liberals 275, Conservative and Unionists 273, Labour 40, Irish Nationalists 82. Liberal losses can probably be explained by the fact that some traditional Conservative seats which had fallen to the Liberals in the landslide of 1906, now returned to the Tories; many people who had voted Liberal in 1906 may have been frightened off by the government's radical policies.

(ii) Asquith was now in the unfortunate position of having to depend on Irish Nationalist support. The Irish leader, *John Redmond*, agreed to vote for Lloyd George's budget (which now had to pass the Commons again) in return for an Irish Home Rule Bill and also a restriction of the Lords' power so that the Upper House would not be able to prevent Home Rule again as it had in 1893.

(iii) April 1910 was therefore a busy month: a Parliament Bill designed to reduce the Lords' power passed the Commons, closely followed by

Lloyd George's budget. The following day the Lords approved the budget without a division, perhaps hoping to escape the Parliament Bill.

(iv) The next step was somehow to manoeuvre the Lords into passing the Parliament Bill. Asquith tried to persuade Edward VII to create about 250 new Liberal peers, enough to defeat the Conservatives in the Lords. The king would only agree if the Liberals could win another election on the issue, but Asquith dare not risk another one so soon. Edward died suddenly in May, and the new king, George V, suggested a conference which discussed the situation for the next six months. A compromise solution was almost reached, but the conference broke down over the problem of Ireland. The Conservatives wanted special loopholes in any new bill, which would enable them to block Home Rule, but Asquith would not agree.

(v) In November 1910 Asquith set the battle in motion again by sending the Parliament Bill up to the Lords; when they refused to pass it, he met the king and secretly secured a promise that if the Liberals won another election, George would create the required peers. Armed with this promise Asquith went into the general election of December 1910 which had a remarkably similar result to the previous one: Liberals 272, Conservatives 272, Labour 42, Irish Nationalists 84. The Liberals and their allies had maintained their support, and the Parliament Bill again passed the Commons with a comfortable majority (May 1911).

(vi) In July 1911 Asquith announced in the Commons that the king had promised to create as many as 500 Liberal Peers if necessary, to get the bill through the Lords. The furious Conservatives led by Lord Hugh Cecil (Salisbury's son) howled Asquith down with shouts of 'Traitor!' and he was unable to complete his speech. However, the more moderate Conservative Peers decided that it would be better to accept a reduction of their powers, rather than find themselves permanently swamped by Liberals. But it was a close thing: when the vote was taken in August, the bill passed by 131 votes to 114. The Parliament Act became law and the constitutional crisis was over.

(c) Terms of the Parliament Act (1911) and its results

(i) The Lords were not allowed to amend or reject a finance bill and the Speaker of the House of Commons was to decide which were finance bills.

(ii) The Lords could still amend and reject other bills, but if a bill passed the Commons in three successive sessions of parliament and was rejected three times by the Lords, the bill would automatically become law on its third rejection by the Lords.

(iii) There was to be a general election at least every five years instead of every seven.

The Act was of major importance in the development of the constitution. Democracy had been safeguarded – the Lords had no control over the country's finances; they could delay other legislation for two years, but could not prevent it becoming law eventually, provided the government remained in power long enough. On the other hand the Lords still had the power, if they felt like using it, to paralyse a government for the last two years of its five-year term. As for immediate results, the Lords were so incensed at the Liberals, that they used to the full the powers they had left, rejecting the Irish Home Rule Bill, a Welsh Disestablishment Bill and another Plural Voting Bill; not one of these perfectly reasonable bills had passed into law when war broke out in 1914. The Liberal Party itself therefore gained very little from the Parliament Act. Although they had emerged from the crisis 'flushed with one of the greatest victories of all time', as Dangerfield puts it, 'from that victory they never recovered'.

20.4 WOMEN'S RIGHTS AND THE SUFFRAGETTE MOVEMENT

(a) Towards the end of the eighteenth century in Britain, women were treated as second-class citizens in a variety of ways. When a woman married, all her money and possessions became the property of her husband; if the marriage broke down, the husband was legally entitled to keep the children, even if he was responsible for the breakdown. Women were not expected to take up careers, were not allowed in the universities, and were barred from professions such as medicine, law and accountancy. Nor could they become magistrates, sit on juries, vote, or become MPs.

Mary Wollstonecraft (1759-97) was one of the first to campaign for an improvement in the status of women. In her book *A Vindication of the Rights of Women* she claimed that girls should receive the same education as boys and advocated free state education for everybody. As the nineteenth century progressed a number of outstanding women began to make the breakthrough: Mary Somerville became an outstanding mathematician, Elizabeth Fry played an important part in prison reform, Florence Nightingale elevated nursing as a recognised career for women. In the 1870s the first women doctors began practising, while school-teaching and office work became common occupations for women.

(i) The legal status of women was improved by *the Married Women's Property Act (1882)* which allowed a woman to continue as the separate owner of her property when she married and by *the Guardianship of Children Act (1886)* which allowed a mother to claim custody of her children if her marriage broke up.

(ii) Women's political rights were being advanced: in 1888 unmarried women were allowed to vote for the new county and borough councils. In 1894 both married and unmarried women were allowed to vote for the new urban and rural district councils and could stand for election to these councils.

(b) **The suffragette movement**, basically middle class but with strong working class support particularly in the North, demanded that women should have the right to vote for MPs. This was nothing new – there had been women's suffrage societies since about 1870, but they attracted very little attention until the Edwardian period, when interest began to revive *for several reasons*: women had just been given the vote in New Zealand; the new ILP, particularly Keir Hardie, were encouraging, and given that women could now vote for the rural and district councils, it was logical to expect that they would soon have the right to choose their MPs.

(i) In 1903 *Mrs Emmeline Pankhurst* founded the *Women's Social and Political Union*, helped by her daughters Christabel and Sylvia. She was the widow of a Manchester barrister and she believed that only when women had the vote would sufficient pressure be brought on governments to improve social conditions. The suffragettes, as the *Daily Mail* called them, had high hopes of the new Liberal government since it was well-known that Campbell-Bannerman, Lloyd George and Grey were sympathetic. Their hopes were further raised by the *Qualification of Women Act (1907)* which allowed women to become members of county and borough councils and to act as mayors.

(ii) When a private member's bill to give women the vote was heavily defeated (1907) it became clear that however logical the women's case was, the Liberal government was not sufficiently impressed by it. One of their excuses for the lack of action was the problem of whether to give the vote to all women or just to unmarried women and widows, since married women were not considered to be householders. The real reason was that Asquith, the Prime Minister, was against it.

(iii) Faced with the government's stubbornness, the suffragettes gradually became more militant. Since 1905 they had been disrupting meetings addressed by Liberal politicians; Christabel Pankhurst and Annie Kenney, a Lancashire cotton worker, spent a week in gaol after being ejected from the Manchester Free Trade Hall where they had heckled Sir Edward Grey. Now the WSPU members turned to smashing windows, chaining themselves to the railings of Buckingham Palace and Downing Street, kicking and scratching policemen who tried to move them on, and holding massive demonstrations and processions.

(iv) By 1912 Asquith and the cabinet had accepted the principle of female suffrage and to save time made a late addition to the Plural Voting Bill which was already under discussion. The amendments gave the vote to certain categories of women. However, in January 1913 the Speaker ruled that the additions could not be allowed, since they changed the nature of the bill.

(v) This decision drove the suffragettes to desperate measures – they resorted to setting fire to churches and railway stations, and physically attacking cabinet ministers, particularly Asquith. Some extremists tried to tear his clothes off on the golf-course at Lossiemouth; later he was beaten over the head with dog-whips. Lloyd George's

illus. 20.1 *Mrs Emmeline Pankhurst being arrested outside Buckingham Palace, May 1914*

new house, which he had fortunately not moved into, was badly damaged by a bomb explosion, for which Mrs Pankhurst received three years' gaol sentence. The most horrifying incident occurred at the 1913 Derby, when Emily Davidson was killed as she threw herself in front of the king's horse. Though the government admittedly had been slow and had handled the affair ineptly, this suffragette extremism was to say the least, ill-advised. Since the Liberals had accepted the principle of votes for women in the amendments to the Plural Voting Bill, it is more than likely that they would have tried again later in 1913 and that the Commons would have approved it by 1914. But their violence discredited the suffragettes and the whole women's rights movement for the time being and disgusted the other more peaceful organisations such as the National Union of Women's Suffrage Societies which had remained non-militant. Even within the WSPU itself the Pankhursts were losing support because of their dictatorial approach.

(vi) As the suffragettes became more militant, the government response became more unpleasant and insensitive. When suffragettes went on hunger-strike in prison, the government authorised them to be forcibly fed. When this provoked criticism the government responded with the farcical *'Cat and Mouse Act'* of 1913; this permitted the release from prison of women who were in a weak physical state because of hunger strike, and allowed them to be re-arrested when they had recovered their health.

(vii) As soon as war broke out in August 1914 the suffragettes called off their campaign, having failed to achieve their objective. Over the next four years women made such a vital contribution to the war effort that it appeared even more ludicrous that they were denied full political rights. In 1918 the Lloyd George government's *Representation of the People Act* gave the vote to all men at the age of 21 and to women at the age of 30. Women were also allowed to sit in the Commons. The situation was not righted fully until 1928 when Baldwin's Conservative government gave the vote to women at 21.

20.5 WHY DID THE LIBERALS' ATTEMPTS TO SETTLE THE IRISH QUESTION FAIL BEFORE 1914?

Since the rejection of Gladstone's Second Home Rule Bill by the House of Lords in 1893, the question had been pushed into the background, and there was no prospect of Irish Home Rule during the ten years of Conservative government from 1895-1905. However, it was still very much part of the Liberal programme, and the Irish Nationalists led by John Redmond, expected satisfaction from Campbell-Bannerman and the Liberals, especially when he was so quick to give the Boers self-government. The matter came to the forefront after the election of January 1910 when Asquith found that to make certain of Irish support for Lloyd George's budget, he had to promise a measure to reduce the powers of the Lords. When the resulting Parliament Act passed (August 1911), the way was open for the *Third Irish Home Rule Bill* which passed the Commons in 1912, but was immediately rejected by the Lords. The same happened in 1913, but under the terms of the Parliament Act, the bill had only to pass the Commons a third time to become law at some point during 1914. Unfortunately this was not to be; in August 1914 a solution to the Irish problem was as far away as ever, and Ireland was on the verge of civil war.

The reasons were complex:

(a) The Irish Nationalist Party was being eclipsed by a more extreme group known as Sinn Fein (ourselves alone). Tired of waiting for the British to allow Home Rule, they wanted to go ahead and set up their own parliament in Dublin which would gradually take over the function of governing the whole of Ireland. At first they were not committed to a complete break with Britain, but eventually they moved to the position of demanding an independent republic. This was not necessarily fatal for chances of a solution, but it meant that at the very time when Home Rule was imminent (thanks to the Parliament Act), a large section of the Irish wanted something much more drastic.

(b) The problem of Ulster was more serious than before. At the time of the First Home Rule Bill (1886), Lord Randolph Churchill had tried to stir up the Ulster Protestants against the Bill with warnings that they would be swamped by the Catholics of Southern Ireland. At the time this was perhaps not a dominant issue, but by 1912 the situation had changed. Ulster had developed industrially, particularly the shipbuilding at Belfast, while the rest of Ireland remained agricultural and backward. The Protestant Ulstermen felt themselves to be a separate community both economically and in religious matters. Four counties – Antrim, Armagh, Derry and Down – were overwhelmingly Protestant and they emphatically did not want to be part of an independent Ireland in which they would be dominated and perhaps discriminated against by the Catholic South. Even before the Home Rule Bill was introduced into the Commons, the Ulster Unionists began to organise themselves to resist Home Rule. Appointing *Sir Edward Carson*, a prominent barrister and Unionist MP as their leader, they held massive demonstrations and threatened to set up a provisional government if the bill passed. Hundreds of thousands of Ulstermen signed a Covenant swearing to fight any government which tried to thrust Home Rule on them.

(c) The Conservatives (Unionists) intensified the crisis by encouraging the Ulster Unionists. They were still smarting from the Parliament Act and the loss of three consecutive general elections; in the words of Roy Jenkins, 'they were sick with office hunger'. The Ulster situation was the perfect weapon with which to embarrass Asquith and perhaps bring the government down. When Carson openly organised a military force, the Ulster

Volunteers, and held drills and parades, Andrew Bonar Law, the new Conservative leader, actually went over to Ireland to take the salute at a review. He told a Conservative Party rally at Blenheim Palace in July 1912: 'I can imagine no length of resistance to which Ulster will go, which I shall not be ready to support' In other words, the leader of the British Conservative Party was encouraging armed rebellion against a law about to be passed by the legally elected British government.

(d) Asquith was partly to blame for the stalemate. Probably because he realised that the Conservatives were only using the Irish situation as a lever to get the government out, he decided to let events take their course, or as he put it, 'wait and see'. He could have eased the situation from the beginning by discussing the possibility of a partition, allowing at least the four Protestant counties of Ulster to remain under British rule. There would have been opposition from the Nationalists, but it was not out of the question for them to accept such a compromise and it would have avoided the formation of the Ulster Volunteers. Not until early in 1914 did Asquith show that he was prepared to exclude Ulster. By this time the Nationalists had already organised their private army, the Nationalist Volunteers. Here was another fatal omission by Asquith: he should have taken prompt action to ban all private armies and the import of arms. Nothing was done, and both the Ulster Volunteers and the Nationalist Volunteers openly imported arms and built up their troops. Only in March 1914 did Asquith decide to send troops into Ulster to guard strategic points and arms depots.

(e) The so-called Curragh Mutiny seemed to undermine the government's position, though in fact no actual mutiny took place. When the government's intention to send troops to Ulster became known, about 60 army officers stationed at the Curragh in Dublin, threatened to resign if they were ordered to coerce the Ulstermen into accepting Home Rule. The Secretary for War, J. E. B. Seely, assured them in an astonishing statement, that the army would not be used to force Home Rule on Ulster. At this, Asquith insisted on Seely's resignation and took over the War Office himself. However, the impression remained that in the event of fighting breaking out, the government might not be able to rely on the loyalty of the army; this could only encourage the Ulster Volunteers into bolder action.

(f) The Larne gun-running incident (April 1914) inflamed the situation further. The Ulster Volunteers were allowed to smuggle in 30 000 rifles without interference from the police, though by this time there was supposed to be a ban on arms imports.

(g) The Home Rule Bill passed the Commons for the third time (May 1914), but it still contained no provision for a separate Ulster. Frantic negotiations followed culminating in an all-party conference (July). At one point a solution seemed near, with Redmond, faced with civil war, apparently agreeing to the exclusion of the four Protestant counties from Home Rule. But the Unionists stepped up their demands and insisted that Ulster should include Fermanagh and Tyrone, whose population was at least 50 per cent Roman Catholic. Redmond could not agree to this and the conference broke up. On 26 July occurred *the Howth incident* which showed the precariousness of peace in Ireland. The Nationalist Volunteers brought in 1500 rifles, in spite of the efforts of troops sent to prevent them. A hostile crowd gathered, angry that the Nationalists should be treated differently from the Ulster Volunteers. Stones were thrown at the troops who opened fire, killing three people and wounding 38. Tension was high and Ireland seemed to be on the brink of civil war. Only a few days later the First World War broke out, and the government suspended the Home Rule Bill until the war was over. No solution had been found, but it was generally hoped that the Irish would remain quiet and support the war effort. Many did, but the convinced republicans had other ideas, as they showed at Easter 1916 (see Section 25.2(a)).

20.6 WHY WAS THERE SO MUCH POLITICAL AND INDUSTRIAL UNREST BETWEEN 1909 AND 1914 AND HOW DID ASQUITH'S GOVERNMENT DEAL WITH IT?

Most of the information to answer the question has appeared earlier in the chapter, but it will be helpful to summarise the points briefly:

(a) **The Commons v Lords conflict**, brought to a climax by Lloyd George's 1909 budget; skilfully handled by Asquith, probably his greatest achievement.

(b) **The suffragette agitation**; not particularly well handled by the government, which ought to have introduced a women's suffrage bill before the situation got out of hand; Asquith, however, opposed votes for women.

(c) **The Irish situation**; worsened by the attitude of the Conservatives, but again, ineptly dealt with by Asquith and his 'wait and see' approach.

(d) **The Osborne Judgement** contributed towards trade union unrest; this was put right, though only after a delay of four years, by the Trade Union Act (1913).

(e) **Industrial unrest** was caused sometimes by unemployment, especially in 1908-09, but more often by the fact that wage increases were not keeping pace with rising prices. In 1908, 1909 and 1910, average real wages were lower than in 1900. Syndicalism also played a part in causing the strike wave (see Section 19.6). The government tried to handle the strikes by a mixture of conciliation and firmness. Churchill as Home Secretary allowed troops to be used in a mining dispute at Tonypandy in South Wales. Asquith's attitude was that essential services must be maintained at all costs, and he authorised the use of troops during the 1911 railway strike, resulting in the deaths of two men at Llanelly. This sort of approach was an over-reaction and did nothing to calm the situation. Eventually Asquith handed the railway strike over to Lloyd George, who had developed considerable skill as a conciliator. Somehow or other he soothed tempers and within four days he had found a compromise. The 1912 coal strike was settled when the government manoeuvred both sides into accepting the Minimum Wage Act (see Section 20.2(e)).

Historians have argued about *how serious the threats to law and order were*, given the amount of violence and unrest. George Dangerfield in his vividly written *The Strange Death of Liberal England* argued that in 1914 Britain stood on the verge of anarchy and perhaps revolution. He believes that there would have been a massive general strike led by the Triple Alliance, probably in October, 'an appalling national struggle over the question of the living wage'. Coinciding with civil war in Ireland, this would have placed an enormous strain on the government's resources. Could the Liberals possibly have maintained law and order? Only the outbreak of the First World War saved Britain from an internal social catastrophe. On the other hand, many writers feel that this is exaggerated. T. O. Lloyd points out that there were the beginnings of a trade depression early in 1914 which would have made a strike less likely. Although people were uneasy about what might happen, 'England in 1914 was not on the verge of plunging into disorder and chaos'.

20.7 LIBERAL DEFENCE AND FOREIGN POLICIES (1905-14)

Britain's foreign policy was conducted largely by *Sir Edward Grey*, the Foreign Secretary. It was a period full of international tensions and there were a number of incidents – the Morocco Crisis (1905-06), the Bosnia Crisis (1908), the Agadir Crisis (1911) and two Balkan Wars (1912 and 1913) which seemed likely to cause a major European conflict. When Grey took over at the Foreign Office, Britain had already moved a long way from her isolation of Salisbury's time, having recently signed an alliance with Japan (1902) and the Entente with France (1904) (see Section 17.3(b)). *Grey's aims* were to build on these alliances while at the same time working for good relations with the Germans, who, as we saw earlier, viewed Britain's understanding with France as a hostile gesture against them. Grey's task was difficult; the British were bound to see the build-up of the German fleet (which started with the 1897 Navy Laws) as a challenge to their naval supremacy. Although Britain was well ahead of Germany in numbers of ships, the problem was that whereas the British fleet was strung out across the world defending the Empire, the German fleet would be concentrated in the North Sea, where it might on occasion outnumber the available British ships. There was a need therefore for Britain to press ahead with her Dreadnought programme, and also to make some improvements in her army which was pitifully small by European standards. Yet the more Britian increased her military strength and the closer she drew in friendship towards France, the more difficult it would be to improve relations with Germany. On the whole Grey performed with great skill and steered Britain successfully through the crises. But the general trend of events was for Britain to find herself supporting France against Germany, and consequently Grey failed to reconcile Britain and Germany.

(a) Britain's defences improved

(i) *In the army* very little had changed since the days of Cardwell's reforms during Gladstone's First Ministry (1868-74). Some reorganisation was needed as the army's performance in the Boer War had shown. The Liberal Secretary for War, *R. B. Haldane*, had spent some time being educated in Germany at Göttingen and Dresden and was an expert on German affairs. He used his experiences to good effect in bringing the British army up to date. Beginning in 1907, he introduced a *General Staff* to give an efficient and co-ordinated direction to army leadership. An *Expeditionary Force* was organised consisting of six infantry divisions and a cavalry division, 160 000 troops in all, together with the necessary accessories - artillery, transport, medical units and reserves. All the various volunteer and part-time soldiers were organised into the *Territorials* - around 300 000 men who were to be fully equipped and trained so that they could compare in efficiency with the regulars. To improve the supply of officers, Haldane brought the Officers' Training Corps at the public schools under the control of the War Office. This was a fine achievement by Haldane; when he left the War Office in 1912 to become Lord Chancellor, the only drawback was that the army was not large enough.

(ii) *The navy* was Britain's great strength, but it was also expensive to maintain. Campbell-Bannerman decided to reduce the *Cawdor-Fisher plan* (see Section 17.5(a)); instead of building four *Dreadnoughts* a year, only three were built in 1906 and two in 1907. C-B hoped this would induce the Germans to slow down their naval programme and prepare the way for disarmament, but it had the opposite effect - Tirpitz saw it as a chance to catch up, and the Germans built three ships in 1906 and four each year from 1907 to 1909. This caused a public outcry in Britain, and when the government announced a plan to build six *Dreadnoughts* in 1909, the First Sea Lord, still the forceful and determined Fisher, urged the press into mounting a campaign for eight; 'we want eight and we won't wait' ran the slogan. The public got their eight *Dreadnoughts*, though the expense was alarming, and led to Lloyd George's controversial budget. A further five were built in 1910 and five more in 1911. Fisher and the government had already in 1906 created the Home Fleet based on the Nore (London). When he retired in 1912, Fisher left Britain with a marked superiority in numbers of ships and in gunpower, though it was discovered during the war that individual German ships were better equipped than their British counterparts.

(b) Events leading up to the outbreak of war

(i) *The Morocco Crisis (1905–06)* was already under way when Grey came to power. It began as a German attempt to test the new Anglo-French Entente, with its implication that France would soon add Morocco to her overseas empire. The Germans announced that they regarded Morocco as independent and would assist its ruler to maintain that independence; they demanded an international conference to discuss Morocco's future. A conference was duly held at *Algeciras* in Spain (January 1906). Grey believed that if the Germans had their way it would be tantamount to acknowledging German diplomatic control of Europe and North Africa as well. At the conference he came out strongly in support of the French demand to control the Moroccan bank and police. Russia, Spain and Italy also supported France, and the Germans suffered a serious diplomatic defeat. This was an impressive start for Grey; he had shown that the Anglo-French Entente meant something, and he had helped to preserve the balance of power. The French were most grateful and Anglo-French 'military conversations' were started.

(ii) *The British agreement with Russia (1907) was another blow to Germany*. Britain's motive was not to build up an anti-German bloc, it was more a desire to settle differences with the Russians. For years the British had viewed Russia as a major threat to her interests in the Far East and India, but recent events had changed all that. Russia's defeat by the Japanese had weakened her and she no longer seemed much of a danger. The remaining area of dispute was Persia, and it seemed desirable to both sides, particularly the Russians who were anxious to attract British investment, to eliminate rivalry. Such an agreement was only logical, since Russia had reached an alliance with France, Britain's Entente partner, as far back as 1894. Persia was divided into 'spheres of influence'. The north was to be Russian, the south (bordering Afghanistan and India) British, and the central area to remain neutral.

(iii) *The Bosnia Crisis (1908)* caused high tension. The Austrians, taking advantage of a revolution in Turkey, annexed Bosnia, (still technically Turkish territory) as a deliberate blow against Serbia which also hoped to acquire Bosnia. The Serbs appealed for help to their fellow Slavs, the Russians, who called for a European conference, expecting French and British support. When it became clear that Germany would support Austria in the event of war, the French drew back, not wanting to become involved in a war in the Balkans, and Grey, anxious to avoid a breach with Germany, contented himself with a formal protest to Austria. Austria kept Bosnia; it was a triumph for the Austro-German alliance, but *it had unfortunate consequences*: Serbia was bitterly hostile towards Austria, and it was this quarrel which developed into the First World War; the humiliation stimulated Russia into a massive military build-up; and Grey and Asquith were now convinced that Germany was out to dominate Europe, an impression confirmed when Tirpitz seemed to be speeding up the naval building programme. The outcome was the hysterical 'we want eight' campaign and an intensification of the naval arms race.

(iv) *The Agadir Crisis (1911)* arose when French troops occupied Fez, the Moroccan capital, to put down a rebellion against the Sultan. A French annexation of Morocco seemed imminent; the Germans sent a gunboat, the *Panther*, to the Moroccan port of Agadir, hoping to browbeat the French into giving them some compensation, perhaps the French Congo. Grey was concerned in case the 'compensation' turned out to be German acquisition of Agadir, a vital naval base which could be used to threaten Britain's trade routes. With the intention of strengthening French resolve, Lloyd George (with Grey's permission) made a famous speech at the Lord Mayor's banquet (at the Mansion House) warning the Germans that Britain would not stand by and be taken advantage of 'where her interests were vitally affected'. Eventually the gunboat was removed, and the Germans agreed to recognise the French protectorate over Morocco in return for two strips of territory in the French Congo. This was seen as a further triumph for the Anglo-French Entente, but in Germany, public opinion became intensely anti-British. Inevitably the French and British were driven into closer co-operation; a *joint naval strategy* was discussed and to ease the burden on both, it was agreed (1912) that the British fleet would patrol the Atlantic and the Channel while the French would concentrate on the Mediterranean. The French pressed for a definite written alliance with Britain, but Grey was unable to agree for fear of committing Britain irrevocably against Germany.

(v) *The Balkan Wars. The First Balkan War (1912)* broke out when Serbia, Greece, Montenegro and Bulgaria (calling themselves the Balkan League) attacked Turkey and captured most of her remaining European territory. All the great powers felt their interests threatened: the Russians were afraid of the Bulgarians taking Constantinople, the Austrians feared that Serbia would become too powerful, the Germans thought that their hopes of controlling Turkey via the railway to Baghdad, would be disappointed if the Balkan states became too powerful and the Turkish Empire collapsed. Grey siezed the opportunity to show that Britain and Germany could still work together; *a peace conference met in London*, where it was decided which territories the Balkan states should take from Turkey. The Serbs were not pleased with the outcome, since they wanted Albania to give them an outlet to the sea; but the Austrians with German and British support, insisted that Albania should

Map 20.1 *The Balkans in 1913 showing changes of territory from the Balkan Wars (1912–13)*

become an independent state. This was yet another attempt by Austria to prevent Serbia from becoming too strong. The Bulgarians were also dissatisfied: they were hoping for Macedonia but most of it was given to Serbia. Bulgaria therefore attacked Serbia starting *the Second Balkan War (1913)*, but her plan misfired when Greece, Romania and Turkey rallied to support Serbia. The Bulgarians were defeated, and by *the Treaty of Bucharest*, lost most of their gains from the first war. Grey was pleased with the outcome, feeling that joint British and German influence had prevented an escalation of the wars by restraining the Austrians who were itching to attack Serbia. Unfortunately Grey did not realise at the time *the seriousness of the consequences*: Serbia had been strengthened and was now determined to stir up the Serbs and Croats inside the Austrian Empire; war between Austria and Serbia was only a matter of time. Turkey was now so weak that she fell more and more under German influence. The Germans took Grey's willingness to co-operate as a sign that Britain was ready to be detached from France and Russia.

(vi) *The naval race* meanwhile was continuing. From time to time the British proposed a joint slow-down in the *Dreadnought* programme. In 1911, shortly after Agadir, Haldane went to Berlin, but although the Kaiser expressed an interest, he wanted Britain to promise not to intervene again in disputes between Germany and another state. This, of course, Haldane could not accept. The British tried again in 1912 and 1913, hoping that their joint action during the Balkan Wars would encourage the Germans to co-operate. Churchill proposed that there should be a 'naval holiday' during which all building of warships should stop; the Germans declined. However, right through 1913 Anglo-German relations were good. According to A. J. P. Taylor, the naval rivalry had lost its bitterness: 'the British had come to tolerate the German navy and were outstripping it without undue financial strain'. In June an Anglo-German agreement was reached over a possible partition of the Portuguese colonies of Mozambique and Angola which were being badly misgoverned by the mother country.

(vii) *The assassination of the Austrian Archduke Franz Ferdinand at Sarajevo (28 June 1914)* was the event which sparked off the war. The Archduke was the nephew and heir to the Habsburg emperor Franz Josef. Against all advice he paid an official visit to Sarajevo, the Bosnian capital. He and his wife were shot dead by a member of the Black Hand Gang, a secret Serbian terrorist society. For the Austrians, this was a heaven-sent excuse for war. They chose to blame the Serbian government and sent them a stiff ten-point ultimatum which the Serbs accepted, apart from the final point – a demand for Austrian troops to be allowed to police Serbia. However, this was enough for the Austrians: already assured of German support, they declared war on Serbia (28 July). The Russians, determined not to let the Serbs down this time, ordered a general mobilisation, whereupon Germany declared war on Russia (1 August) and on France (3 August). When German troops entered Belgium on their way to invade France, Britain, who had promised (in 1839) to defend Belgian neutrality, demanded their withdrawal. When the Germans ignored this, Britain entered the war (4 August).

(c) What caused the war? It is clear that the Austrian quarrel with Serbia precipitated the outbreak of war. Austria was genuinely afraid that if Serbia acquired Bosnia (which contained about three million Serbs), all the other Serbs and Croats living inside the Habsburg Empire would want to join Serbia; other national groups – Czechs, Poles and Italians would be encouraged to demand independence, and the result would be the collapse of the Habsburg Empire. For the Austrians, it was an essential 'preventive' war. It is more difficult to explain why this should have escalated into a major war, and historians have still not managed to agree. Some blame Russia, the first country to order a general mobilisation, some blame Germany for making Austria more aggressive with her promises of support, and some blame Britain for not making it clear that she would undoubtedly support France; this, it is argued, might have dissuaded the Germans from declaring war on France. Many other reasons have been suggested, and rejected:

(i) The existence of the two opposing alliance systems or armed camps – The Triple Alliance (Germany, Austria-Hungary and Italy) and the Triple Entente (Britain, France and Russia) is said to have made war inevitable. But these had not proved binding earlier – Britain and France had not supported Russia during the Bosnia Crisis, and Austria kept aloof from Germany during the Agadir Crisis.

(ii) Colonial rivalry. This had caused friction in the past, but in 1914 there were no specific quarrels; Britain and Germany had reached agreement about the Portuguese colonies.

(iii) Anglo-German naval rivalry. This was probably no longer a major cause of friction, since Britain's lead was unassailable.

More plausible causes are:

(i) The Russians were deeply worried about the Balkans where both Bulgaria and Turkey were under close German influence. Russia's existence depended on the free passage of merchant ships through the Dardanelles and this now seemed threatened. Once Austria declared war on Serbia, the Russians felt they must mobilise – it was a struggle for survival.

(ii) German backing for Austria was vitally important; in 1913 Germany had restrained Austria from attacking Serbia, yet in 1914 the Kaiser egged them on, and promised German help without conditions. This could mean that the Germans now felt ready for war and wanted to get on with it – either because they were set on world domination (as the German historian Fritz Fischer believed) or because they felt encircled and threatened by British naval power and by the massive Russian military build-up. In this case a preventive war, a war for survival, was necessary before the end of 1914, before the Russians became too strong.

(iii) Taylor believes that there is very little evidence to show that the Germans deliberately timed the war for August 1914, and suggests that all the countries involved became victims of their own mobilisation plans and timetables, and also of the belief that the opening battles would be the decisive ones – as had been the case in the Balkan Wars. The German *Schlieffen Plan* assumed that in the event of war, France would automatically join Russia; therefore the bulk of German forces were to be sent through Belgium to knock France out in six weeks, after which they would be rushed across Europe by train to face Russia. Once Moltke, the German Commander-in-Chief, knew that Russia had ordered a general mobilisation, he demanded immediate German mobilisation, which, under the Schlieffen Plan, required German troops to enter Belgium. The Kaiser suggested a partial mobilisation against Russia, hoping that Britain would stay neutral if Germany refrained from attacking France. But Moltke insisted on the full Schlieffen Plan, and Belgian territory was violated, bringing Britain into the war.

Whatever the truth, it is clear that Germany must take much of the responsibility for the war. For years the Kaiser's aggressive attitude had alarmed Britain, France and Russia, and given the impression that Germany wanted to dominate Europe. Her encouragement of Austria and the invasion of Belgium were vital factors.

(d) Why did Britain enter the war?

(i) The immediate British instinct on the outbreak of war was to remain neutral. The public knew little about Serbia and Britain did not seem directly threatened. Grey tried to organise a conference to discuss Serbia, but the Germans refused, and events moved so quickly after 28 July, that there was no time for negotiation. Grey warned the Germans not to count on British neutrality and warned the French and Russians not to count on British help. However, when German troops entered Belgium, Grey immediately sent an ultimatum to Germany warning them to withdraw. Britain had promised, in the 1839 *Treaty of London*, along with France and Prussia, to guarantee the neutrality of Belgium. When the ultimatum was ignored, Britain declared war on Germany.

(ii) Although defence of Belgium was the official reason given for Britain's entry, there was more to it than that. There was the moral obligation to the French; having given them solid diplomatic support since 1904, to desert them in their hour of greatest need would have damaged Britain's international prestige. Probably more important, a German victory would endanger Britain's trading interests and ruin the balance of power in Europe. The real reason for Britain's entry was therefore the need to resist German domination of Europe. The attack on Belgium was convenient because it enabled Grey to unite the Liberals in favour of war and so bring Britain in as early as possible.

(iii) Grey has often been accused of being too indecisive, of not making it clear that Britain would support France. But this is unfair. It was hardly possible for him to act differently, because the cabinet was not united in favour of intervention until the last minute, and even then two leading members resigned. In any case, given the attitude of the German generals and the Schlieffen Plan, it is difficult to imagine anything that Grey could have done to prevent the war spreading. All that remained for him, as he looked out of the Foreign Office window late on the evening of 4 August, was to make his most memorable remark: 'The lamps are going out all over Europe; we shall not see them lit again in our lifetime'.

QUESTIONS

1. The Commons v. Lords Crisis and the 1909 Budget
Study Sources **A** to **F** and then answer the questions which follow.

Source A: a cartoonist's view of the crisis – Lord Lansdowne was the Conservative leader in the House of Lords.

Standing for his Trade Photograph (Christmas and New Year Season, 1908-9).
(Lord Lnsd-wne.)

Source: *Punch*, 1909.

Source B: speech by A. J. Balfour, the Conservative leader, at Manchester, November 1909.

> The object of a second chamber is not, and never has been, to prevent the people, the electorate, determining what policy they should pursue; it exists for the purpose of seeing that on great issues the policy which is pursued is not the policy of a temporary majority elected for a different purpose, but carries

the conviction of the people for the few years in which it carries their *mandate* . . . The object is to see that what concerns the people should be referred to the people, and that the people shall not be betrayed by hasty legislation, having perhaps some vindictive policy to carry out.

Source: quoted in K. Benning, *Edwardian Britain – Society in Transition*, Blackie, 1980 (adapted extracts).

Source C: speech by Lord Morley, a senior Liberal peer, during the budget debate in the Lords, November, 1909.

If you tell the House of Commons that they are liable to have a conclusion of their own submitted to other people – whether they be members of this House or the people in the country – you weaken their own personal individual and collective responsibility. My view is that when an elector goes to the poll, he is voting for the House of Commons to make laws, to support a Minister or a party for a certain number of years in Parliament.

Source: quoted in R. D. H. Seaman, *The Reform of the Lords*, Edward Arnold, 1971 (adapted extracts).

Source D: speech by Lloyd George at the 'Edinburgh Castle' public house, Limehouse, July 1909.

This budget is introduced for the purpose of raising fertile taxes that will bring forth fruit – the security of the country, provision for the aged and deserving poor. It is rather a shame for a rich country like ours – probably the richest country the world has ever seen – that it should allow those who have toiled all their days to end in poverty and possible starvation (Hear, hear) . . . There are many in this country blessed with great wealth, and if there are amongst them men who grudge out of their riches a fair contribution towards the less fortunate of their fellow-countrymen, they are shabby rich men. (Cheers). We are raising money to provide against the evils and sufferings that follow from unemployment. (Cheers) . . . But the Tories say, 'We protest against the Budget in the name of democracy (loud laughter), liberty and justice . . . It is not so much the *Dreadnoughts* we object to, it is the pensions' . . . Where does the democracy come in this system of land-ownership? We claim that the tax we impose on land is fair, just and moderate. (Cheers) . . . No country, however rich, can permanently afford to have quartered upon it a class which refuses to do the duty which it was called on to perform . . . I am one of the children of the people. (Loud and prolonged cheering). I was brought up among them. I know their trials; I made up my mind in framing this Budget, that at any rate no cupboard should be bared.

Source: quoted in J. H. Bettey (ed.), *English Historical Documents, 1906–1939*, Routledge & Kegan Paul, 1967 (adapted extracts).

Source E: speech by Lord Lansdowne during the budget debate in the Lords, November, 1909.

This budget seems to me to go out of its way to deprive the Lords of their legitimate chances of dealing with the subject-matter of the bill. I may remind your Lordships that in 1907 a Land Valuation Bill dealing with Scotland came before this House, and that your Lordships declined to pass it into law. Again in 1908 your Lordships rejected a Licensing Bill. You have included in this Budget another Licensing Bill every bit as crushing in its severity as the bill of 1908, but you are told that you cannot deal with it because it is bound up in the cover of a Finance Bill . . . In all seriousness, we have a right to ask where this kind of thing is going to stop. If you can graft Licensing Bills and Land Valuation Bills on the Finance Bill, what is to prevent you grafting on it, let us say, a Home Rule Bill. You have no right to give your consent until you have been assured by the people of the country that they desire it to pass into law.

Source: as for Source **D** (adapted extracts).

Source F: comments from a modern historian, Lord Blake, a Conservative peer since 1971.

The consequences of the insane decision to reject the budget of 1909 in the Lords added new discords to the party. Balfour cannot be acquitted of blame here. There is nothing to suggest that he doubted its wisdom or tried to restrain the backwoodsmen. The resulting struggle over the Parliament Act was to unseat Balfour himself and produce a major convulsion in the party . . .

Why did such a balanced man as Balfour see nothing objectionable in this use of the House of Lords? Deep in the subconscious mind of the party was a sense of prescriptive right to rule, inculcated by twenty years of domination after 1886. This was an error that neither Disraeli nor Derby would have committed. The most revealing remark of all was made by Balfour just after his personal defeat in Manchester in 1906. It is the duty of everyone, he said, to ensure that 'the great Unionist [Conservative] party should still control, whether in power or in opposition, the destinies of this great Empire'. If this proposition is taken literally, it is a denial of parliamentary democracy. Indeed many Conservatives behaved as if the verdict of 1906 was some freak mistake on the part of the electorate, and that it was the Conservatives' duty, through the House of Lords, to preserve the public from the consequences of its own folly till it came to its senses.

Source: R. Blake, *The Conservative Party from Peel to Thatcher*, Collins/Fontana, 1985 (adapted extracts).

(a) (i) From the evidence of the cartoon (Source **A**) which bills had Lord Lansdowne and the Lords butchered?   4(a)

(ii)   Which of these bills did Lansdowne later refer to in his speech (Source E)?   **4(a, c)**

(iii)   Explain the main points which the cartoonist is trying to get over.   **4(a)**

(iv)   Do you think the cartoonist sympathises with Lansdowne and the Conservatives or not? Explain your answer fully.   **4(a, b)**

(b)   (i)   According to Source **B**, what did Balfour see as the purpose of the House of Lords?   **4(a)**

    (ii)   What does Balfour mean by the word 'mandate' in Source **B**?   **1, 4(a)**

    (iii)   In what ways does Lord Morley in Source **C** disagree with Balfour?   **4(a, c)**

(c)   (i)   What were 'Dreadnoughts' mentioned by Lloyd George in Source **D**?   **1, 4(a)**

    (ii)   According to Source **D**, why was Lloyd George introducing his budget?   **4(a)**

    (iii)   What evidence does Source **D** provide of Lloyd George's skill as a speaker?   **4(a, b)**

    (iv)   What evidence does the speech contain of Lloyd George's attitude towards the wealthy?   **4(a, b)**

(d)   (i)   According to Source **E**, why did Lansdowne think Lloyd George's budget was a bad bill?   **4(a)**

    (ii)   From the evidence of Sources **D** and **E** and your own knowledge, which part of the budget annoyed the Conservatives most?   **1, 2, 4(a, c)**

(e)   (i)   Do you think Balfour's statement, quoted in Source **F**, contradicts what he said later in Source **B**, or not? Explain your answer.   **4(a, c)**

    (ii)   How does Blake (Source **F**) show his lack of sympathy with the Conservatives' rejection of the budget?   **4(a, b)**

    (iii)   Which of the Sources **B**, **C** and **E** is closest to the views expressed by Blake in Source **F**? Explain your answer fully.   **4(a, c)**

(f)   (i)   What are the strengths and weaknesses of each of the Sources **A** to **F** for the historian?   **4(a, b)**

    (ii)   Which one of these Sources could be taken by a historian as the most reliable? Give reasons for your answer.   **4(a, b, c)**

(g)   Using all the Sources and your knowledge, explain whether or not you agree with the opinion that the rejection of the budget was not a wise move by the Conservatives.   **1, 2, 4(a, b, c)**

2. Liberal Social Reforms
Read the extract and then answer the questions which follow.

Article from *The Times* on the introduction of free school meals for poor children.

We have already made a serious inroad upon personal responsibility and personal independence by relieving parents of the duty of educating their children. This is now used as an argument for relieving them of the duty of feeding their children. When we have done that, the argument will be stronger than ever for relieving them of the duty of clothing their children. It will be said that we pay vast sums for teaching and feeding, but that the money is wasted if the children are not properly clad. From that, it is an easy step to paying for their proper housing; for what, it will be asked, is the use of feeding, clothing and teaching children if they come to school from close and insanitary bedrooms? The proposed measure would go far to sap the remaining independence of the parents . . . The habit of looking to the State for their maintenance would become ingrained in them.

Source: *The Times*, 2 January 1905.

(a) **(i)** Do you think the writer of the *Times* article is in favour of free school meals for poor children or not?

(ii) What arguments does he use to support his opinion?   **4(a, b)**

(b) **(i)** Make a list of the other important social reforms, apart from free school meals, which were introduced by the Liberal governments of 1906-14.   **1**

(ii) What were the Liberals' motives for introducing these reforms?   **1, 2**

(c) Choose any two of the reforms on your list in **(b)** above, and for each one explain:

(i) why the reform was needed;
(ii) the details of the changes introduced;
(iii) whether or not the changes were successful.   **1, 2**

(d) 'The Liberal Party was responsible for setting up a wonderful new institution – the Welfare State.' Explain fully whether you agree or disagree with this statement.   **1, 2**

3. Britain and Germany

Study Sources **A** and **B** and then answer the questions which follow.

Source A: letter from Sir Arthur Wilson, First Sea Lord, 1 August 1912.

Thanks to Fisher, we are in the satisfactory position of having twice as many Dreadnoughts in commission as Germany, and a number greater by one unit than the whole of the rest of the world put together. I don't think there is the very faintest fear of war.

Source: quoted in J. Telford, *British Foreign Policy 1870-1914*, Blackie, 1978.

Source B: speech by Lloyd George in the Commons, 23 July 1914.

Our relations [with Germany] are very much better than they were a few years ago. The two great Empires begin to realise that they can co-operate for common ends, and that the points of co-operation are greater and more numerous and more important than the points of possible controversy.

Source: As for Source **A**.

(a) (i) Who was Fisher mentioned in Source **A**? **1, 4(a)**
   (ii) Why does the writer of Source **A** think there was little chance of war? **4(a)**
   (iii) Describe briefly Fisher's work from 1905–1912 in building up the British navy. **1, 2**

(b) (i) Why does Lloyd George in Source **B** think relations between Britain and Germany have improved? **4(a)**
   (ii) Describe and explain *two* 'points of co-operation', i.e. occasions on which Britain and Germany had co-operated in the period 1912–14. **1, 2**

(c) (i) Make a list of the 'points of controversy' which had existed between Britain and Germany 'a few years ago', i.e. from 1905 to 1911. **1, 2**
   (ii) Choose *two* of these controversies from your list and describe and explain what happened in each case. **1, 2**

(d) (i) In what way do Sources **A** and **B** differ in their reasons for thinking war between Britain and Germany was unlikely?
   4(a, c)
   (ii) Explain why Britain went to war with Germany only a few days after Lloyd George's statement. **1, 2**

4. The Liberal Irish Home Rule Bill passed the House of Commons for the third time in May 1914, but it contained no provision for a separate Ulster, and so explosive was the situation in Ireland that the government postponed the operation of the bill. Following the Howth incident (July) when British troops fired on a hostile crowd, killing three people, Ireland seemed on the verge of civil war.

Describe and explain the feelings about, and attitudes towards this situation of *each* of the following:

(a) an Irish Protestant supporter of Carson and the Ulster Unionists;

(b) an Irish Nationalist supporter of John Redmond;

(b) a supporter of Asquith's Liberal government;

(c) a supporter of Bonar Law and the Conservative opposition.
   1, 2, 3

CHAPTER 21

BRITAIN, THE FIRST WORLD WAR AND ITS AFTERMATH

SUMMARY OF EVENTS

The combatants in the war were:

The Central Powers	*The Allies*
Germany	Britain and the Empire
Austria-Hungary	France
Turkey (entered November 1914)	Russia (left December 1917)
Bulgaria (entered October 1915)	Italy (entered May 1915)
	Romania (entered August 1916)
	USA (entered April 1917)

Most people, and certainly the Germans, thought the war would only last a matter of weeks. In Britain there was a general feeling that it would 'all be over by Christmas'. But *Lord Kitchener*, the newly appointed Secretary for War, was not so sure; he dismayed the cabinet by telling them that it would last nearer three years than three months. And Kitchener was right – the German Schlieffen Plan failed to achieve the rapid defeat of France. Although the Germans penetrated deeply, Paris did not fall, and stalemate quickly developed on *the western front*, with all hope of a short war gone. Both sides dug themselves in and spent the next four years attacking and defending lines of trenches which were difficult to capture because the increased fire-power provided by magazine rifles and machine-guns made frontal attacks suicidal and rendered cavalry useless. The British, desperately looking for a way to break the stalemate, opened up a new front by attacking Turkey at *the Dardanelles* (1915); but everything went wrong and the troops were withdrawn.

In eastern Europe there was more movement with Russian successes against the Austrians, who constantly had to be helped out by the Germans, causing friction between the two allies. But by December 1917, the Germans had captured Poland (Russian territory) and forced the defeated Russians out of the war. Britain, suffering heavy losses of merchant ships through submarine attacks, and France, whose armies were paralysed by mutiny, seemed on the verge of defeat. Gradually the tide turned; the

Allies, helped by the entry of the USA in April 1917, wore down the Germans, whose last despairing attempt at a decisive breakthrough in France failed in the spring of 1918. The success of the British navy in blockading German ports and defeating the submarine threat by defending merchant convoys, was also telling on the Germans. By the late summer of 1918 they were nearing exhaustion. An armistice was signed on 11 November 1918 although Germany itself had scarcely been invaded; a controversial peace settlement was signed at Versailles the following year.

21.1 MONS TO THE SOMME 1914-16

(a) The British Expeditionary Force (BEF) was quickly mobilised under the command of *Sir John French* and sent to join the French army at Maubeuge. It was extremely small – only four divisions, compared with 70 French and 72 German, but it made an important contribution to slowing down the German push towards Paris. The Schlieffen Plan had already been held up by unexpectedly strong Belgian resistance, and it took the Germans over two weeks to capture Brussels. This was a vital delay, giving the French time to make full preparations, and leaving the Channel ports free for the BEF to land. Instead of sweeping around in a wide arc, capturing the Channel ports and approaching Paris from the west, the Germans found themselves making straight for Paris just east of the city. They penetrated to within twenty miles of the capital and the French government withdrew to Bordeaux; but the nearer they got to Paris, the more the German impetus slowed up; there were problems in keeping the armies supplied with food and ammunition, and the troops became exhausted by long marches in the August heat.

(i) The first British engagement occurred at *Mons* (23 August) where the BEF suddenly found itself in the path of the advancing German 1st Army under von Kluck. The British distinguished themselves by fighting back the Germans who had been surprised to encounter any British troops. However, when the French army retreated to the Marne, the British had no alternative but to move with them.

(ii) *At the Battle of the Marne* (September) the French under Joffre attacked the wilting Germans and drove them back to the River Aisne where they were able to dig trenches. The British played a valuable supporting role and suffered only a few casualties. The battle was vitally important; some historians have called it one of the most decisive in modern history. It ruined the Schlieffen Plan once and for all: France would not be knocked out in six weeks; hopes of a short war were dashed and the Germans would have to face full-scale war on two fronts. The war of movement was over; the trench lines eventually stretched from the Alps to the Channel coast and there was time for the British navy to bring to bear its crippling blockade of German ports.

(iii) The BEF was moved suddenly northwards into Flanders to protect

Map 21.1 *The Western Front*

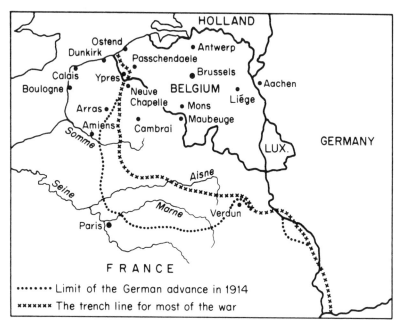

Ypres from the German advance following their capture of Antwerp. In the bloody *First Battle of Ypres* (October–November) the British hung on to the city, though it proved to be a vulnerable point right through the war. This is usually taken to mark the end of the BEF. Casualties were extremely high, especially at Ypres; over half the force was wounded and about one-tenth killed. For its size it had made a remarkable contribution to the early stages of the war; von Kluck paid it the highest compliment, claiming that it was British resistance which had prevented him from taking Paris.

(b) Kitchener's most important contribution to the war was to raise a new army

(i) He decided that Britain needed an army of 70 divisions, and since Asquith refused to introduce conscription (compulsory military service), Kitchener mounted a propaganda campaign, to encourage volunteers. Soon Britain was bristling with huge posters of Kitchener pointing his finger, and the words: 'Your Country needs You'. The response was amazing: 100 000 men volunteered within a few days, and by mid-September the total was 500 000. By the end of February 1915 a further 500 000 had been recruited. The dominions sprang to the call – Canada and Australia sent 30 000 men each and New Zealand 8500.

(ii) Having arrived at the front, the new troops found that they could make no headway against the German trench line. The stalemate on the western front continued throughout 1915, though several attempts were made to break through. The British tried at *Neuve Chapelle* (March) and at *Loos* (Septmber) where they suffered heavy casualties. The Germans attacked again in Flanders at the *Second Battle of Ypres* (April–May), but all attempts failed. *The reasons for these continued failures*, right through until 1918, were always the same: there was no chance of a surprise attack because a massive artillery bombardment always preceded the infantry attack to clear the barbed wire from no man's land between the two lines of trenches, and generally to soften up the enemy; reconnaisance aircraft and observation balloons could spot troop concentrations on the roads leading up to the trenches. Even when the trench line was breached, advance was difficult because the ground had been churned up by the artillery barrage and there was deadly machine-gun fire to contend with. Any ground won was difficult to defend since it usually formed *a salient* or bulge in the trench line; the flanks of a salient were always vulnerable. At Ypres the Germans used poison gas but when the wind changed direction it was blown back towards their own lines and they suffered more casualties than the Allies, especially when the Allies released some gas of their own. Nevertheless, when all possible allowances have been made, it is clear that Sir John French was not an outstanding commander. He was therefore replaced by *Sir Douglas Haig*. But French was not the only one to find himself at a loss in these new conditions: Kitchener commented to Grey: 'I don't know what is to be done. This isn't war'.

(c) **On the eastern front** the Russians, having mobilised more quickly than the Germans expected, made the mistake of invading both Austria and East Prussia at the same time. Though they were successful against Austria, occupying the province of Galicia, the Germans called Hindenburg out of retirement and twice defeated the Russians at *Tannenberg* (August 1914) and *the Masurian Lakes* (September), driving them out of Germany. Worse was to come: in 1915 the Germans occupied Poland and the Turks began to blockade the Dardanelles, severing supply lines to the Russians who were already running short of arms and ammunition.

(d) **The Gallipoli (Dardanelles) Campaign (1915)** was launched by the British to open up the vital supply lines to Russia. It was an idea strongly pressed by Winston Churchill (First Lord of the Admiralty) to escape the deadlock in the west by eliminating the Turks, thought to be the weakest of the Central Powers because of their unstable government. Success against Turkey would enable help to be sent to Russia and might also bring Bulgaria, Greece and Romania into the war on the Allied side; it would then be possible to attack Austria from the south. The campaign was a total failure; the first attempt in March, an Anglo-French naval attack through the Straits to capture Constantinople, failed because of mines. This ruined the surprise element, so that when the British attempted landings at the tip of the Gallipoli peninsula, the Turks had strengthened their defences and no advance could be made (April). Further landings by Australian and New Zealand troops (Anzacs) in April and British in August were equally useless and positions could be held only with great difficulty. In December the entire force was withdrawn. *The consequences were serious*: besides being a blow to Allied morale, it turned out to be the last chance of relieving Russia via the Black Sea and probably caused Bulgaria to join the Central Powers. A Franco-British force landed at Salonika in neutral Greece to try and relieve Serbia, but it was too late. When Bulgaria entered the war in October, Serbia was quickly overrun by Bulgarians and Germans. The year 1915 therefore was not a good one for the Allies: casualties at Gallipoli had been heavy; 250 000 wounded and 43 000 British, Australians and New Zealanders dead. On the other hand, Turkish losses were heavier, and the Turkish army probably never recovered fully. It is possible to argue that Gallipoli weakened the Turks and made possible the later British victories against them in Palestine (1917). But this was very much in the future, and there were more British disasters to come before then. A British army sent to protect Anglo-Persian oil interests found itself surrounded by Turks at *Kut-el-Amara* in Mesopotamia. After a siege lasting from December 1915 until April 1916, General Townshend surrendered with 12 000 men, of whom some 8000 later died in the dismal conditions of the Turkish prison camps.

(e) The Battle of the Somme (1916) was the major operation involving the British on the western front in that year. In February the Germans, under Falkenhayn, launched a massive attack on the French fortress town of *Verdun*, but the French defended stubbornly. It was partly to relieve pressure on the French that Haig decided to attack the German lines near the River Somme; he also hoped that by keeping the Germans fully committed they would be unable to risk sending troops to the eastern front against Russia. The campaign began on 1 July with disastrous results: the preliminary artillery bombardment failed to destroy the barbed wire in no man's land; advancing British troops were caught up in the wire and came under murderous German machine-gun fire. 21 000 were killed and over 35 000 wounded on the first day, with no gains to show for it. Yet incredibly, Haig continued with these attacks until November. At the end of it all, the Allies had made only limited advances varying between a few hundred yards and seven miles along a thirty-mile front. *The real importance of the battle* was the blow to German morale as they realised that Britain (where conscription was introduced for the first time in May) was a military power to be reckoned with. Losses on both sides killed or wounded, were appalling (Germans 650 000; British 418 000; French 194 000) and Haig came under severe criticism for persisting with suicidal frontal attacks. However, they probably helped to wear down the German armies: Hindenburg himself admitted in his *Memoirs* that they could not have survived many more campaigns like Verdun and the Somme. The Somme also contributed to the fall of the Prime Minister, Asquith, who resigned in December 1916, after mounting criticism, to be replaced by Lloyd George.

21.2 LLOYD GEORGE AT THE HELM

Since the beginning of 1915, when it became clear that the war was going to be a long affair, Asquith had been facing criticism of his government's apparent lack of urgency. In May 1915 he therefore brought some leading Conservatives - Bonar Law, Lansdowne, Balfour, Carson and Lord Curzon - and the Labour Party leader Arthur Henderson, into the cabinet. This was the end of a purely Liberal government and the beginning of government by coalition. The most important move was the appointment of *Lloyd George as Minister of Munitions*. He soon emerged as the outstanding member of the cabinet, his vigour and panache contrasting sharply with Asquith's detachment and lack of energy. After Kitchener's death (he was drowned on his way to Russia when his ship, the *Hampshire*, struck a mine) Lloyd George took his place as War Minister. As news of the terrible casualties on the Somme became known, moves began to oust Asquith and replace him with Lloyd George. Asquith was manoeuvred into resigning, much against his will, and Lloyd George became Prime Minister of another coalition government.

(a) Asquith's failings as a war leader were many. He had been a competent peace-time Prime Minister as long as there were no major crises, but his 'wait and see' attitude to the Irish and suffragette problems was not a good omen for his performance during the war. Unfortunately he continued his detached approach after hostilities had started. He believed it was the generals' job to run the war and was most reluctant to interfere even when French turned out to be incompetent and when there was a serious shortage of shells in 1915. There was a complete lack of urgency in all departments, just at the time when decisive leadership was needed. As Taylor puts it, 'Asquith was as solid as a rock, but like a rock, incapable of movement'.

(b) Lloyd George as Minister of Munitions, showed again, as he had as Chancellor of the Exchequer, that he was a man who got things done instead of just talking about them. He sliced through all the official red tape in the most unconventional ways. He began by requisitioning a hotel to house his new ministry and appointed businessmen to important positions because he thought they were more decisive than politicians. He made sure that the supply of shells increased and was responsible for the widespread adoption of the machine gun. At the outbreak of war each battalion had only two machine guns, which in Haig's view was 'more than sufficient'. Kitchener thought four would be a good idea, but the British Army School of Musketry had recommended six. Lloyd George is reputed to have said: 'Take Kitchener's figure. Square it. Multiply it by two. Then double it again for good luck'. This figure was achieved. There were two further occasions on which Lloyd George superseded Kitchener. In January 1915 Wilfred Stokes demonstrated his new light mortar, but the War Office thought it was too dangerous. Lloyd George persuaded a wealthy Indian prince to finance the first thousand Stokes mortars, and it soon proved to be one of the most effective weapons of the war. Kitchener was apparently not impressed with the tank, which had been developed from an idea of Major E. D. Swinton, and first demonstrated in February 1916; Lloyd George was most enthusiastic, and the first order for 40 tanks was placed. Lloyd George was also responsible for the Munitions of War Act, giving the government power to take control of factories responsible for armaments and other war work. Strikes and lock-outs were prohibited and measures were taken to combat drunkenness so that the war effort would not be impaired. Most controversial of all, conscription was introduced (May 1916) to apply to all males aged 18 to 41.

(c) Lloyd George as Prime Minister. Even after he became Minister for War, Lloyd George was still prevented from doing all he wanted by the dithering Asquith. But as soon as he became Prime Minister, he began to run the country almost like a dictator. According to K. O. Morgan, 'Lloyd George's war premiership was without parallel in British history. No previous Prime Minister had ever exercised power in so sweeping and dominating a manner'. Almost everything he did provoked controversy and offended somebody, but so great was the crisis facing the country that he was able to get away with it.

(i) He set up a small war cabinet of five men (himself, Bonar Law, Curzon, Henderson and Milner, the former governor of Cape Colony) which took all the main decisions and he appointed men from outside parliament to head important ministries: Sir Joseph Maclay, a Glasgow shipowner, made an excellent ship-building organiser, Lord Beaverbrook, owner of the *Daily Express*, a brilliant Minister of Propaganda.

(ii) He introduced the Cabinet Secretariat under Sir Maurice Hankey to organise cabinet business. This was so successful in coordinating the different departments and advisers that it was kept after the war. Lloyd George also had his own private secretariat and advisers, including Waldorf Astor, owner of the *Observer*. This was known as the 'Garden Suburb' because it met at first in huts in the garden behind No. 10 Downing St.

(iii) More government controls were introduced than ever before. All merchant shipping was brought under government direction, to defeat the submarine threat. Farmers were ordered to cultivate extra land to meet the food shortages, factories were told what to produce (for example, army blankets and khaki for uniforms), and the coal industry was taken directly under government control. The new Ministry of National Service decided which men would be called up, depending on whether their jobs were vital or could be carried out by women. Food was rationed and prices and wages controlled.

(iv) He was able to do less on the military side of the war. However, he was mainly responsible for the adoption of the convoy system (see Section 21.3(e)) which saved Britain from starvation in 1917. He disapproved of Haig's costly and unimaginative tactics but could find nobody better to replace him; however, he did manage to have the French Marshal Foch appointed as Supreme Allied Commander on the western front, which reduced Haig's influence to some extent.

Unfortunately for Lloyd George and his future in politics, these policies and the style in which he carried them out, made him many enemies. Asquith and his supporters never really forgave him for the way in which Asquith was removed from the premiership, causing a fatal split in the Liberal Party. Lloyd George has therefore been blamed for the decline of the Liberal Party; but it has to be said in his defence that like Peel, he was never a party man. For Lloyd George the paramount aim was to win the war, not preserve the Liberal Party. Most historians would agree that if Asquith had remained Prime Minister for another year, Britain would have lost the war.

21.3 THE WAR AT SEA

The general public in Germany and Britain expected a series of naval battles of the Trafalgar type between the rival Dreadnought fleets. But both sides were cautious and dared not risk any action which might result in the loss of their main fleets. The British Admiral Jellicoe was particularly cautious; as Churchill pointed out, he 'was the only man on either side who could have lost the war in an afternoon'. Nor were the Germans anxious for a confrontation because they had only 16 of the latest Dreadnoughts against 27 British.

(a) The Allies aimed to blockade the Central Powers, preventing goods entering or leaving, and slowly starving them out. At the same time trade routes must be kept open between Britain, her empire and the rest of the world, so that the Allies themselves would not starve. A third function of the navy was to transport British troops to the continent and keep them supplied via the Channel ports. The British were successful in carrying out these aims: they went into action against German units stationed abroad.

The most important battle was at the *Falkland Islands* (December 1914). Admiral von Spee with a squadron of two cruisers and three light cruisers was about to bombard the Falklands when he was attacked by a much stronger British squadron (which included two battle-cruisers) commanded by Admiral Sturdee. The Germans were no match for the superior fire-power of the British battle-cruisers, and von Spee's entire squadron was destroyed. By the end of 1914 most of the German armed surface vessels had been sunk or badly damaged and the Falklands engagement made the Kaiser unwilling to lose any more ships. One fleet continued to blockade the Baltic in order to cut off supplies to Russia, but the main German fleet did not venture out of port until the Battle of Jutland in

1916. The Kaiser had some idea of keeping his fleet intact as a bargaining counter in peace negotiations, and the British were happy with this situation which left them in control of the surface, though not the submarines. The navy made an important contribution during 1915 to the Gallipoli campaign, though this was not one of its successes (see Section 21.1(d)).

(b) The Allied blockade caused problems: Britain was trying to prevent the Germans using the neutral Scandinavian and Dutch ports to break the blockade; this involved stopping and searching all neutral ships and confiscating any goods suspected of being intended for enemy hands. The USA objected strongly to this, being anxious to continue trading with both sides.

(c) The Germans retaliated with mines and submarine attacks, which was their only alternative since their surface vessels were either destroyed or blockaded. At first they respected neutral shipping and passenger liners, but it was soon clear that the German U-boat blockade was not effective, partly because of insufficient U-boats and partly because of problems of identification, as the British tried to fool the Germans by flying neutral flags and by using passenger liners to transport arms and ammunition. In April 1915 the British liner *Lusitania* was sunk by a torpedo attack. (It has recently been proved that the *Lusitania* was armed and carrying vast quantities of arms and ammunition, as the Germans well knew; hence their claim that the sinking was not just an act of barbarism against defenceless civilians.) *This had important consequences*: out of the thousand dead, 118 were Americans. Woodrow Wilson, the American President, found that the USA would have to take sides to protect her trade; whereas the British blockade did not interfere with the safety of passengers and crews, German tactics certainly did. For the time being, however, American protests caused the Germans to tone down the submarine campaign, rendering it even less effective.

(d) The Battle of Jutland (31 May) was the main event of 1916, the only time the main battle-fleets emerged and engaged each other; the result was indecisive. The German Admiral von Scheer tried to lure part of the British fleet out from its base so that that section could be destroyed by the numerically superior Germans. However, more British ships came out than he had anticipated, and after the two fleets had shelled each other on and off for several hours, the Germans decided to retire to base, firing torpedoes as they went. On balance the Germans could claim that they had won the battle since they lost only 11 ships to Britain's 14, but *the real importance of the battle* lay in the fact that the Germans had failed to destroy British sea power; the German High Seas Fleet stayed in Kiel for the rest of the war leaving Britain's control of the surface complete. In desperation at the food shortages caused by the British blockade, the Germans embarked, with fatal results, on:

(e) 'Unrestricted' submarine warfare (January 1917). As they had been concentrating on the production of U-boats since the Battle of Jutland this campaign was extremely effective. They attempted to sink all enemy and neutral merchant ships in the Atlantic and although they knew that this was bound to bring the USA into the war, they hoped that Britain and France would be starved into surrender before the Americans could make any vital contribution. They almost did it: the peak of German success came in April 1917 when 430 ships were lost; Britain was down to about six weeks' corn supply and although the USA came into the war in April, it was bound to be several months before their help became effective. However, the situation was saved by Lloyd George who insisted that the Admiralty adopt the convoy system in which a large number of merchant ships sailed together protected by escorting warships. This drastically reduced losses and the German gamble had failed.

In an attempt to finish off the U-boat threat completely, the navy carried out daring raids on the captured Belgian ports of *Ostend* and *Zeebrugge*, which the Germans were using as submarine bases. On the night of 22 April 1918, under cover of smoke-screens. ships loaded with cement were brought in and sunk to block the exits from the ports. The operation at Zeebrugge was the more successful one, and although not as much damage was inflicted as had been hoped, Zeebrugge was rendered almost useless as a German base. This, together with extra defences at the Straits of Dover made it almost impossible for the Germans to attack the Straits, and increasingly difficult for submarines to slip through.

The German 'unrestricted' submarine campaign was extremely important because it brought the USA into the war. By mid-1918 the British navy, helped by the Americans and the Japanese, had achieved their three aims mentioned under (a) and played a vitally important role in the defeat of the Central Powers.

21.4 VIMY RIDGE TO THE ARMISTICE 1917-18

(a) There were some limited allied successes on the western front during 1917. In April the Canadians captured *Vimy Ridge*, north of Arras. This was an impressive achievement, though at the time it was not followed up; in March 1918 allied possession of the ridge turned out to be a serious obstacle in the way of the German spring offensives. The allied campaign at Vimy was accompanied by a massive French offensive under their new commander, Nivelle, on the Aisne; it achieved absolutely nothing and provoked the French army to mutiny. Nivelle was replaced by Pétain who successfully calmed the situation. From June to November the British fought *the Third Battle of Ypres*, usually remembered as *Passchendaele*, in appallingly muddy conditions; British casualties were enormous - 324 000 compared with 200 000 Germans for a four-mile advance. More significant was *the Battle of Cambrai* which demonstrated that tanks, properly used, might break the deadlock of trench warfare. 381 massed British tanks made a wide breach in the German line, but lack of reserves prevented the success from being followed up.

However, the lesson had been observed: Haig realised that the best tactic was to stop the advance once a breach had been made in the German line and to start another attack at a different point. The technique was therefore a series of short, sharp jabs instead of a prolonged push at one point. This avoided creating an awkward salient and would force the enemy to fall back at several points, eventually withdrawing the whole line. This was the technique successfully adopted by Haig after the German spring offensives of 1918.

Meanwhile the Italians were heavily defeated by Germans and Austrians at *Caporetto* (October 1917) and retreated in disorder. This rather unexpectedly proved to be an important turning point. Italian morale revived perhaps because they were faced with having to defend their homeland against the hated Austrians. The defeat also led to the setting up of an Allied Supreme War Council. The new French premier Clemenceau, a great war leader in the Lloyd George mould, rallied the wilting French.

(b) On the eastern front disaster struck the Allies when Russia withdrew from the war. Continuous defeat by the Germans, lack of arms and supplies and utterly incompetent leadership caused two revolutions (March and November 1917) and the Bolsheviks, who took over in November, were willing to make peace. Thus in 1918 the entire weight of German forces could be thrown against the west; without the USA the Allies would have been hard pressed.

On the other hand, encouragement was provided by British victories against the Turks. More troops and supplies were sent out, and Kut was taken at the end of February 1917. The capture of Baghdad (March) encouraged the Arabs of Syria and Palestine to revolt against Turkish rule, which was an important reason for the Turkish defeat. The British supplied the Arabs with arms and *T. E. Lawrence* (Lawrence of Arabia), an archaeologist working with the Arab Bureau, helped to organise an Arab campaign which captured the port of Aqaba and ruined Turkish communications by constantly blowing up railway lines. Allenby captured Jerusalem (December 1917) and after a delay during the first half of 1918 when some of his forces were rushed to the western front to help stem the German spring offensives, he entered Damascus (October 1918). The way was clear to Constantinople, and the Turks signed an armistice with Britain on 30 October.

(c) The entry of the USA into the war (April 1917) was provoked partly by the German U-boat campaign, and also by the discovery that Germany was trying to persuade Mexico to declare war on the USA, promising her Texas, New Mexico and Arizona in return. The Americans had hesitated about siding with the autocratic Russian government, but the overthrow of the tsar in the March revolution removed this obstacle. The USA made an important contribution to the Allied victory: they supplied Britain and

France with food, merchant ships and credit; actual military help came slowly. By the end of 1917 only one American division had been in action, but by mid-1918 over half a million men were fighting. Most important was the psychological boost which the American potential in resources of men and materials gave the Allies and the corresponding blow it gave to German morale.

(d) The German spring offensive (1918) was launched by Ludendorff in a last desperate attempt to win the war before too many US troops arrived and before discontent in Germany led to revolution. It almost came off: throwing in all the extra troops released from the east, the Germans broke through on the Somme (March) and by the end of May were only 40 miles from Paris; the Allies seemed to be disintegrating. However, under the overall command of the French Marshal Foch they managed to hold on as the German advance lost momentum and created an awkward bulge. Lloyd George, helped by Sir Joseph Maclay, organised the recall and transportation to the front of 88 000 British troops who were at home on leave, and others were brought from Palestine.

(e) An allied counter-offensive began (8 August) near Amiens. With Haig using his new tactics, hundreds of tanks attacked in short, sharp jabs at many different points and forced the Germans to withdraw their entire line. Slowly but surely the Germans were forced back until by the end of September the Allies were through the Hindenburg Line. Though Germany itself had not yet been invaded, Ludendorff was convinced that they would be defeated in the spring of 1919. He insisted that the German government ask President Wilson for an armistice (3 October) hoping to get less severe terms based on Wilson's 14 points (see Section 21.6(a)). By asking for peace in 1918 he would save Germany from invasion and preserve the army's reputation. Fighting continued for another five weeks, but eventually an armistice was signed on 11 November.

(f) Why did Britain and her Allies win the war? The reasons can be briefly summarised:

(i) Once the Schlieffen Plan had failed, removing all hope of a quick German victory, it was bound to be a strain for them, facing war on two fronts.
(ii) Allied sea power was decisive, enforcing the crippling blockade which caused desperate food shortages, while keeping Allied armies fully supplied.
(iii) The German submarine campaign failed in the face of convoys protected by British, American and Japanese destroyers; the campaign itself was a mistake because it brought the USA into the war.
(iv) The entry of the USA brought vast resources both of men and materials to the Allies.

(v) Allied political leaders at the critical time – Lloyd George and Clemenceau – were probably more competent than those of the Central Powers; the unity of command under Foch in 1918 probably helped, while Haig learned lessons from the 1917 experiences about the effective use of tanks and the avoidance of salients.

(vi) The continuous strain of heavy losses was telling on the Germans – they lost their best troops in the 1918 offensive and the new troops were young and inexperienced; an epidemic of deadly Spanish flu did not help the situation, and morale was low as they retreated.

(vii) Germany was badly let down by her allies and was constantly having to help out the Austrians and Bulgarians. The defeat of Bulgaria by the British (from Salonika) and Serbs (29 September) was the final straw for many German soldiers, who could see no chance of victory then. When Austria was defeated by Italy at Vittorio-Veneto and Turkey surrendered (both in October), the end was near.

The combination of military defeat and dire food shortages produced a great war weariness leading to mutiny in the navy, destruction of morale in the army and revolution at home.

21.5 EFFECTS OF THE WAR ON THE HOME FRONT

(a) As more and more men joined the army, women began to fill the vacancies in a wide variety of jobs that had previously been done by men. Girls worked in munitions factories, on farms and on the buses, railways and docks. Even more remarkably, women were to be found as police, window cleaners, blacksmiths and quarry workers and even did very heavy work in gasworks and foundries, carrying sacks of coal and coke and stoking furnaces. 'Many is the time,' recalled one lady, 'the girls would be affected by the gas, the remedy being to walk them up and down in the fresh air and then drink a bottle of Guinness.' Middle class women went into banking and took clerical jobs in administration, commerce and education.

Many became nurses, and worked both at home and in Europe, like Vera Brittain who wrote a moving account of her experiences in *Testament of Youth*. Women had made such a vital contribution to the war effort that their whole position in society was changed. Many men were amazed at what women had proved themselves capable of, and the war was an important step forward in the emancipation of women and their acceptance as the complete equals of men. It was therefore only logical that they deserved to be given the vote. Many of the men fighting in the trenches were not entitled to vote either. Lloyd George put this right with:

(b) The Representation of the People Act (June 1918). This gave the vote to women at the age of 31 and to all males at the age of 21. Voting at general elections was to take place on the same day instead of being spread over several weeks. The idea of the 'deposit' was introduced: in order to exclude the lunatic fringe, every candidate had to pay a deposit of £150; if he failed to win one eighth of the total votes cast, he forfeited his deposit.

(c) As we saw earlier (Section 21.2(c)) there was much greater government control of industry and labour than had ever been known in Britain, and ordinary people found their lives interfered with by the government as never before.

(i) From May 1916 conscription meant that most men aged 18 to 41 were compelled to join the armed forces; this was later extended to 51. Consequently the majority of wives were left struggling on inadequate army pay, while children often missed their father's discipline and there was an increase in child crime.

(ii) Early in the war trade unions were not happy about the regulations which prevented workers from leaving jobs in munitions factories and other vital industries. However, Lloyd George won them over by guaranteeing reasonable minimum wages and by favouring firms which used union labour. This encouraged more workers to join trade unions, which generally enhanced their reputation with their responsible attitude throughout the war. However, the unions did not have things off their own way; although strikes were illegal under the Munitions of War Act, there were several strikes, mostly about wage rates. In July 1918 during a strike of munitions workers in Coventry, Churchill, by this time Minister of Munitions, gave them a choice - either return to work or be called up for military service; they returned to work. An important feature of the war-time industrial unrest, particularly in engineering and shipbuilding, was the emergence of a new type of union leadership - the shop-steward, who organised workers in individual factories and workshops.

(iii) The food situation caused problems. At first there were no actual shortages, but prices increased substantially; in June 1916 food prices on average were 59 per cent above the level of July 1914. Towards the end of 1916, supplies of imported goods began to dwindle and long queues formed outside shops. In some areas local rationing schemes were started and worked extremely well. The government adopted the idea nationally in 1918, rationing meat (to one pound per head a week), sugar (half a pound), bacon, ham and jam. This eased the situation and the queues disappeared. One highly unpopular government policy was its interference with drinking habits. It was felt that much absenteeism from work was caused by drunkenness; in 1915 therefore, opening hours of public houses were restricted (normally from midday to 2.30 p.m. and from 6.30 p.m. to 9.30 p.m.), and beer was made weaker and more expensive.

(d) The Education Act of 1918 was a product of the war. Lloyd George's Minister of Education, the historian *H. A. L. Fisher*, believed that the war had created an 'increased feeling of social solidarity'; if the performance of the working classes during the war required them to be given the vote, it also entitled them to a better education, in order to avoid 'intellectual wastage'. Fisher's Act raised the school-leaving age to 14, and made teachers' salaries uniform throughout the country; more free places were provided at secondary schools for bright children from poor backgrounds.

(e) The war speeded up the decline of the Liberal Party. It had not enhanced its reputation with its fumbling conduct of the first year of the war, but the split between the Lloyd George and Asquith factions, which continued after the war was over, kept the party fatally divided and allowed the Labour Party to become the viable alternative opposition to the Conservatives. The war had another important effect on the development of the Labour Party; while he was a member of the War Cabinet, Arthur Henderson had more than once been offended by Lloyd George's high-handed attitude. He decided it was time for Labour to break away from its dependence on the Liberals and establish its identity as a separate party. Sidney Webb, the Fabian, was given the job of producing the new and attractive manifesto, *Labour and the New Social Order*, while Henderson himself was responsible for encouraging the formation of party organisations at constituency level.

(f) There were repercussions in Ireland, where at Easter, 1916, the Irish Republican Brotherhood decided to turn Britain's preoccupation with the war to their own advantage (see Section 25.2(a)).

(g) The war had serious economic effects. Britain had lost some 40 per cent of her merchant shipping and had run up enormous war debts, mainly to the USA, which would have to be repaid with interest. House building had been held up and it was calculated that at least half a million new houses were needed. Most serious of all, though this did not become apparent until after the war, Britain never regained many of the export markets which had been closed to her during the war.

21.6 BRITAIN AND THE PEACE SETTLEMENT

A peace conference met at Versailles in January 1919 to decide what should be done with the defeated powers. The three most important people at the conference turned out to be Lloyd George, Clemenceau (representing France) and the American President Woodrow Wilson. It quickly emerged that they depending on their war aims, had rather different ideas about how to treat the Central Powers, and Germany in particular.

(a) **Britain's war aims** had been vague at the outset. The public was told that the intention was to defend Belgium. In January 1918, probably to encourage the troops by presenting them with some clear objectives to fight for, Lloyd George spelled out Britain's war aims in more detail; they included the defence of democracy and the righting of the injustice done to France in 1871 (the Germans had taken Alsace and Lorraine from France), the restoration of Belgium and Serbia, an independent Poland, democratic self-government for the nationalities of Austria-Hungary, self-determination for the German colonies and an international organisation to prevent war.

In an off-the-cuff speech made in December, which he later regretted, Lloyd George said that Germany should be made to pay the whole cost of the war. Sir Eric Geddes, a recent member of the war cabinet, suggested that Germany should be 'squeezed until you can hear the pips squeak'. These were popular slogans in preparation for the election which the Lloyd George coalition won with an overwhelming majority in December 1918 (see Section 22.1(a)). Once the election was safely over, Lloyd George toned down his language and at the conference argued that a lenient approach to Germany was essential so that she would not become embittered and so that international trade could settle down to normal again. On the other hand he now felt that Britain ought to be given Germany's African colonies and should be allowed to keep the Turkish territories in the Near East with their valuable oil supplies. Clemenceau and the French wanted the harshest possible treatment of Germany in revenge for France's defeat in the Franco-Prussian war of 1870–1 and in payment for all the damage inflicted by the Germans over the previous four years; Germany must be completely crippled so that she could never again invade the sacred soil of France. Woodrow Wilson's peace aims were set out in his 14 Points, also issued in January 1918. They were similar to Lloyd George's aims but emphasised the idea of national self-determination – peoples should have democratic governments of their own nationality. It was difficult to reconcile these conflicting aims, but eventually a settlement was hammered out.

(b) **The Treaty of Versailles dealt with Germany.** She had to lose territory in Europe; Alsace-Lorraine to France; Eupen, Moresnet and Malmédy to Belgium; North Schleswig to Denmark (after a plebiscite), West Prussia and Posen to Poland, though Danzig, the main port of West Prussia, was to be a free city under League of Nations administration, because its population was wholly German. Memel was given to Lithuania; the Saar was to be administered by the League of Nations for 15 years, when a plebiscite would decide whether it should belong to France or Germany. In the meantime France was to have the use of its coalmines. Germany's African colonies were taken away and became 'mandates' under League supervision. This meant that various member states of the League 'looked after' them. In particular it meant that Britain acquired Tanganyika, and Britain and France divided Togoland and the Cameroons between them. German

Map 21.2 *European Frontiers after the First World War and the Peace Treaties*

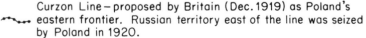

Territory lost by Germany

Former territory of tsarist Russia

Austria-Hungary until 1918

Curzon Line – proposed by Britain (Dec. 1919) as Poland's eastern frontier. Russian territory east of the line was seized by Poland in 1920.

armaments were strictly limited: a maximum of 100 000 troops and no conscription (compulsory military service); no tanks, armoured cars, military aircraft or submarines, and only six battleships. The Rhineland was to be permanently demilitarised (German troops were not allowed in the area). The War Guilt clause fixed the blame for the outbreak of the war solely on Germany and her allies. Germany was to pay reparations for damage done to the Allies; the actual amount was not decided at Versailles, but announced later (1921) after much argument and haggling as £6 600 million. A League of Nations was set up, its aims and organisation being set out in the League Covenant; its main aim was to settle international disputes by discussion, and so prevent war.

(c) Germany's defeated allies were dealt with by separate treaties. When Austria was on the verge of defeat, the Habsburg empire disintegrated as the various nationalities declared themselves independent. Austria and Hungary separated and declared themselves republics, but both lost huge areas which went to make up the new states of Czechoslovakia and Yugoslavia, to enlarge Romania and to make up the newly reconstituted state of Poland. By the Treaty of Sèvres (1920) Turkey was allowed to keep Constantinople but was forced to hand the rest of her European territory and the area around Smyrna in Asia Minor to Greece. Her Arab territories were taken away; Iraq, Palestine and Transjordan became mandated territories supervised by Britain, and Syria became a French mandate.

(d) Lloyd George was reasonably satisfied with the terms and was given a hero's welcome on his return from Paris. However, it gradually emerged that there were many faults with the settlement. The most common charges are that it was too hard on the Germans and that some of the terms - reparations payments and German disarmament - were impossible to carry out. There was much controversy about the size of the reparations bill. J. M. Keynes, a British economic adviser at the conference, argued that £2000 million was a realistic figure which the Germans could afford to pay without bankruptcy. On the other hand, some of the British and French extremists were demanding £24 000 million, so the final figure was kinder to the Germans than it might have been. The settlement had the unfortunate effect of dividing Europe into the states which wanted to revise it (Germany being the main one), and those which wanted to preserve it, and on the whole even they turned out to be lukewarm in their support. The USA failed to ratify the settlement, to the disgust of Woodrow Wilson, and never joined the League of Nations; this in turn left France completely disenchanted with the whole business because the Anglo-American guarantee of her frontiers could not now apply. Italy felt cheated because she had not received the full territory promised her in 1915, and Russia was ignored. All this tended to sabotage the settlement from the beginning, and it became increasingly difficult to apply the terms fully. Worst of all, it *did* embitter the Germans, yet did not weaken them sufficiently to prevent further aggression. Only 20 years were to pass before Hitler's armies invaded Poland, beginning the Second World War.

QUESTIONS

1. The Battle of the Somme, 1916
Study Sources **A** to **G** and then answer the questions which follow.

Source A: map of the battle.

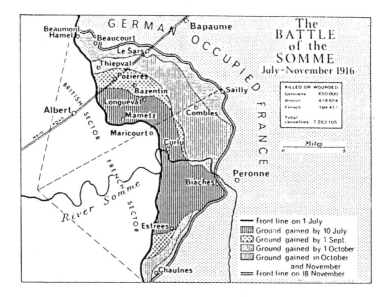

Source: M. Gilbert, *Recent History Atlas 1860 to 1960*, Weidenfeld & Nicolson, 1966.

Source B: Lloyd George's War Memoirs, published 1933–36.

The casualties on both sides were well over a million. It was not responsible for the failure of the German effort to capture Verdun. It was only an element in slackening a German offensive which had already slowed down. The French Commander in Chief said in May that the Germans had already been beaten at Verdun . . . The Somme campaign certainly did not save Russia . . . the battle prevented us from perceiving the approaching catastrophe in Russia, and therefore we did not take measures to avert it . . . It is claimed that the battle of the Somme destroyed the old German Army by killing off its best officers and men. It killed off far more of our best and of the French best. The official history of the war says: 'For this disastrous loss of the finest manhood, there was only a small gain of ground to show' . . . Nor did it prevent the Germans from detaching several divisions and sending them from France to help the Austrians and Bulgarians and to begin an attack on Roumania . . . The whole mind of the western strategists was concentrated on one or other of the hamlets along the Somme. They were only waiting for the final break of the German barrier. This is no exaggeration of their illusions . . .

Source: D. Lloyd George, *War Memoirs*, Nicholson & Watson, 1938 edition (adapted extracts).

Source C: from Sir Douglas Haig's Journal, 3 August 1916.

The 'Powers that be' are beginning to get a little uneasy in regard to the situation – whether a loss of say 300,000 men will lead to really great results, because if not, we ought to be content with something less than what we are now doing. I replied (to the Chief of the Imperial General Staff) in a despatch dated August 1st:

(a) Pressure on Verdun relieved. Not less than six enemy divisions besides heavy guns have been withdrawn.

(b) Successes achieved by Russia last month would certainly have been prevented had enemy been free to transfer troops from here to the Eastern Theatre.

(c) Proof given to world that Allies are capable of making and maintaining a vigorous offensive and of driving enemy's best troops from strongest positions.

(d) We have inflicted very heavy losses on the enemy. In another 6 weeks, the enemy should be hard put to it to find men.

(e) The maintenance of a steady offensive pressure will result eventually in his complete overthrow.

Source: quoted in R. Blake (ed.), *The Private Papers of Douglas Haig*, Eyre & Spottiswoode, 1952 (adapted extracts).

Source D: letter from Lloyd George to Haig, written 21 September 1916, after his visit to the Somme front.

I can say, on behalf of my colleagues in the Cabinet as well as for myself, that the heartening news of the last few days has confirmed our anticipations and hopes that the tide has now definitely turned in our favour. I congratulate you most warmly on the skill with which your plans were laid . . . I hope you will let me come over to visit the scenes of your fresh triumphs.

Source: as for Source C (adapted extracts).

Source E: Haig's despatch of 23 December 1916.

The enemy's position to be attacked was of a very formidable character. During nearly two years' preparation the enemy had spared no pains to render these defences impregnable. The front of the trenches in each system was protected by wire entanglements, many of them in two belts forty yards broad, built of iron stakes interlaced with barbed wire almost as thick as a man's finger . . . The enemy's power has not yet been broken, nor is it yet possible to form an estimate of the time the war may last before the objects for which the Allies are fighting have been attained. The German army, despite all the advantages of the defensive, suffered defeat on the Somme this year.

Source: J. H. Boraston (ed.), *Sir Douglas Haig's Despatches*, J. M. Dent, 1919.

Source F: the memoirs of the German General Ludendorff.

The situation on the Western Front gave cause for greater anxiety than I had anticipated, but at the time I did not realise its full significance. It was just as well. Otherwise I should never have had the courage to take the important decision to transfer still more divisions from the heavily engaged Western Front to the Eastern, in order to recover the initiative there and deal Roumania a decisive blow . . . As a result of the Somme fighting we were completely exhausted on the Western Front. If the war lasted, our defeat seemed inevitable. I cannot see as I look back, how the German High Command could have mastered the situation if the Allies had continued their blows as they did in 1916.

Source: Joint Matriculation Board question.

Source G: the view of a modern historian.

Haig did not hesitate. He had become convinced that a powerful offensive, even on the Somme would win the war. On 1 July thirteen British divisions *went 'over the top'* in regular waves. The attack was a total failure. The barrage did not obliterate the Germans. Their machine guns knocked the British over in rows: 19,000 killed, 57,000 casualties sustained – the greatest loss in a single day ever sustained by a British army. Haig had talked beforehand of breaking off the offensive if it were not at once successful. Now he set his teeth and kept doggedly on – or rather the men kept on for him. The slaughter was prolonged for weeks, then for months, when it foundered in the mud. No strategical gain had been made.

Source: A. J. P. Taylor, *English History 1914-45*, Oxford, 1965.

(a)   (i)   What information does the map in Source **A** give you about how the French and British troops were positioned in the Somme area?   **4(a)**

    (ii)   Who had advanced furthest by 10 July, the British or the French?   **4(a)**

(iii) Which two villages were captured by the British between 10 July and 1 September?   **4(a)**

(iv) Which village was captured by the French in September?   **4(a)**

(v) By 18 November, approximately how far had allied troops advanced at the point of deepest penetration?   **4(a)**

(b) (i) What evidence is there in Sources **B** and **C** to suggest why the Somme attack was launched?   **4(a, c)**

(ii) Do you think the evidence in Source **A** supports the statement in Source **B** that 'there was only a small gain of ground to show' for the battle of the Somme?   **4(a, c)**

(iii) What important criticism does Lloyd George (Source **B**) make of the strategy of the British generals?   **4(a)**

(c) (i) Who was Sir Douglas Haig (Sources **C, D, E** and **G**)?   **1, 4(a)**

(ii) How does Haig (Source **C**) differ from Lloyd George (Source **B**) about the success of the battle of the Somme?   **4(a, c)**

(iii) What reasons can you suggest for this difference of opinion?   **4(a, b)**

(d) (i) What differences and contradictions can you find between Lloyd George's War Memoirs (Source **B**) and Lloyd George's letter to Haig (Source **D**)?   **4(a, c)**

(ii) From the evidence of Source **A**, what do you think 'the heartening news of the last few days' (Source **D**) might have been?   **4(a, c)**

(iii) What reasons can you suggest for the differences between Sources **B** and **C**, both written by Lloyd George?   **4(a, b)**

(e) (i) What evidence is there in Sources **E** and **G** to explain why the battle was not as successful as the allies had hoped?   **4(a, c)**

(ii) What signs are there in Source **E** that Haig was perhaps less confident of final victory than he had been in Source **C**?   **4(a, c)**

(f) (i) What does A. J. P. Taylor mean in Source **G** by the phrase 'went "over the top" '?   **1, 4(a)**

(ii) Why do you think Taylor included the word 'even' in the second sentence of Source **G**?   **4(a, c)**

(iii) What sort of opinion does Taylor seem to have of Haig? Give reasons for your answer.   **4(a, b)**

(g) (i) What are the advantages and disadvantages of each of Sources **B, C, D, E** and **F** for the historian?   **4(a, b)**

(ii) Using the evidence of all the Sources, explain whether you agree or disagree with the statement that, from the British point of view, the battle of the Somme was a total failure.   **4(a, b, c)**

2. The Convoy System and the British Navy

Read the extract below and then answer the questions which follow.

Unrestricted submarine warfare began; British shipping losses rose from 1.1m. tons in 1915 and 1.5m. tons in 1916 to about 2.5m. tons in the first half of 1917. Despite efforts to economize on shipping, and a few steps towards the rationing of food, it was estimated that England would have to ask for peace. The Admiralty wrung its hands and said everything possible was being done but that with 2,500 ships a week coming into English ports, it was impossible to protect them all . . .

Lloyd George made his inquiries, consulting junior officers secretly and in defiance of custom. He learnt that, out of the 2,500 ships, 2,400 were in the coasting trade; only 100 ships a week had to be protected against attacks on the high seas. The Admiralty had insisted that merchant seamen were incapable of the precise navigation needed for sailing in convoy. At the end of April the War Cabinet made it known that the convoy system was going to be imposed on the Admiralty; on 30 April Lloyd George took over the Admiralty for the day and saw to it that convoys would be organised. It is not formally correct to say that Lloyd George changed naval policy during his visit, because the admirals had been given two or three days' notice that they would have to submit, but this was one of the decisive interventions of the war. And it was one that made Lloyd George even less respectful about expert opinion than before.

Source: T. O. Lloyd, *Empire to Welfare State – English History 1906-1985*, Oxford, 1986 edn.

(a) (i) Why did the Germans begin 'unrestricted submarine warfare'?

1, 2

(ii) Describe what happened during this campaign. 1, 2

(iii) What effects did the campaign have on Britain and the USA?

1, 2, 4(a)

(b) (i) According to the extract, how and why did Lloyd George and the Admiralty disagree about introducing the convoy system?

4(a)

(ii) What vital mistake had the Admiralty made in its calculations?

4(a)

(iii) How did Lloyd George finally get his own way, according to the extract? 4(a)

(c) (i) What impression of the Admiralty does the writer of the extract give? 4(a, b)

(ii) What evidence does the extract provide about how Lloyd George ran the government? 4(a)

(d) Explain how important the convoy system was in helping Britain to survive. 1, 2

(e) (i)   What were the main aims of the British navy throughout the war? 1, 2

(ii)   Describe how these aims were achieved. 1, 2

(iii)   How important do you think the British navy was in helping to defeat Germany and her allies? 1, 2

3.   Study the following list of important events which happened during the First World War.

(a)   September 1914: the Battle of the Marne.

(b)   March–December 1915: the Gallipoli (Dardanelles) Campaign.

(c)   July–November 1916: the Battle of the Somme.

(d)   December 1916: Lloyd George becomes Prime Minister.

(e)   April 1917: the USA enters the war.

Show how and why each one of these events was important in the course of the First World War. 1, 2

4.   You are a mother with two young children aged eight and six. Your husband has been away in the Army since the introduction of conscription, and you are receiving only 21s. a week Army allowance to keep yourself and your children.

Explain your feelings and describe your reactions at the following developments:

(a)   the introduction of conscription, May 1916;

(b)   food shortages and rising prices towards the end of 1916 and during 1917;

(c)   the introduction of food rationing, 1918;

(d)   the Representation of the People Act, June 1918;

(e)   the announcement of the armistice, 11 November 1918. 1, 2, 3

CHAPTER 22

POLITICS IN CONFUSION
1918–24

SUMMARY OF EVENTS

At the end of the war politics did not return immediately to the normal two-party system. Lloyd George was still Prime Minister of the wartime coalition, supported by his own section of the Liberal party and most of the Conservatives. The coalition won an overwhelming victory in the election of December 1918 and stayed in government for the next four years. The problems of peace-time Britain proved to be as awkward to deal with as the problems of war and Lloyd George was unable to find permanent solutions for the post-war depression and for the chronic difficulties encountered by the coal-mining industry. His popularity gradually ebbed away, and when his Conservative supporters decided to withdraw from the coalition to fight the next election on normal party lines, Lloyd George was left with less than half a party to lead, as the Liberal split continued. This enabled the Labour Party to make a major breakthrough, coming in second place to the Conservatives in the election of November 1922. Although the Conservatives seemed set to rule for the next five years, the revival of the old tariff problem caused another general election only a year later, in which the Labour Party won enough seats to form a government, with James Ramsay MacDonald as the first Labour Prime Minister (January 1924). Lacking a majority, this government proved to be only a short-lived experiment, and yet another election followed (October 1924) which was won decisively by Stanley Baldwin and the Conservatives who remained in office for the next five years. The Liberals slumped badly at that election, confirming that Labour was now the alternative party of government to the Conservatives.

22.1 THE LLOYD GEORGE COALITION 1918–22

(a) The election of December 1918 was the first since December 1910; it is remembered as the *'coupon election'* because Lloyd George and Bonar Law issued 'coupons' (signed letters) to their supporters to show the electorate which were genuine coalition candidates. The result of the election was difficult to predict because of the large number of extra voters – six million women and two million men – enfranchised by the recent Representation of the People Act (see Section 21.5(b)). In the event the coalition won easily mainly because of Lloyd George's great

illus 22.1 *A woman voting at Lloyd George's 'coupon election' – the first general election in which women were able to vote*

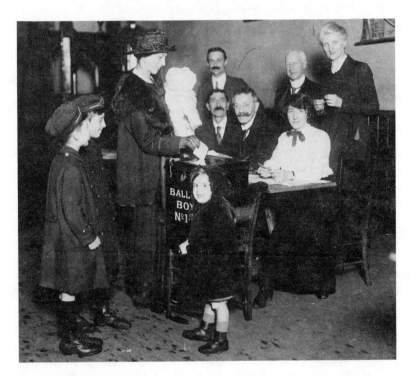

popularity as the man who had led Britain to victory, and his promises to create a 'fit country for heroes to live in' and to make Germany pay 'the whole cost of the war'. The coalition won 484 seats, made up of 338 Conservatives, 136 Lloyd George Liberals, and 10 Labour and other supporters. The main opposition consisted of 59 Labour members, 26 Asquith Liberals and 48 Conservatives who refused to support the coalition. There were also 73 Sinn Feiners, but they refused to take their seats at Westminster and set up their own parliament in Dublin. The result was a disaster for the Liberals whose representation in parliament was almost halved; even Asquith lost his seat. Though it seemed to be a triumph for Lloyd George, he was left dependent on the Conservatives, who had enough seats to form a government of their own.

(b) What problems faced Lloyd George and how successful was he in dealing with them? The situation in the aftermath of the war was chaotic and needed all Lloyd George's brilliance:

(i) Difficulties arose with demobilisation when the government began to release holders of key civilian jobs first, leaving the ordinary rank-and-file troops until last. Some alarming protest demonstrations broke out and the government smartly changed its tactics, adopting a 'first in, first out' policy. This worked well, and by the autumn of 1919 over four million troops had been successfully 'demobbed'. Most of them found jobs, thanks to the post-war boom – an encouraging beginning.

(ii) There was a sudden period of inflation at the end of the war partly caused by the removal of government wartime controls on prices, profits and guaranteed wage levels. Prices and profits rose but wages lagged behind. Trade unions were determined to protect their members, and during 1919 and 1920 there were over 2000 strikes. However, it was not simply a desire for higher wages; there were other reasons for labour unrest: there was a terrible disillusionment among the working class caused by their experiences in the trenches; this seemed to emphasise the gulf between workers on the one hand and on the other capitalists and profiteers who had done well out of the war. The Russian Revolution (1917) gave tremendous publicity to nationalisation and worker control, and some of the strikes in 1919 threw the government into a panic in case they developed into a revolution. In February and March 1919 a strike of Clydeside engineers and shipbuilders demanding a 40-hour week seemed ominously like the start of a revolution: huge demonstrations, rioting and a red flag hoisted in George Square, Glasgow, caused the government to move in troops and tanks. Order was quickly restored and two of the leaders, Willy Gallacher and Emmanuel Shinwell, were sent to jail. The Miners' Federation threatened a national strike if their demands for a six-hour day, a 30 per cent wage increase and continued government control of mines through nationalisation were not accepted. This time Lloyd George avoided a confrontation and played for time: he offered a seven-hour day, continued government control for the time being, and a Royal Commission (the Sankey Commission) to investigate the problem; the miners accepted his offer.

(iii) There was a slump beginning early in 1921 which threw about two million people out of work by the end of the year. The unemployment figure never fell below a million again until the Second World War. The slump had a variety of causes; in a sense it was a continuation of the slow decline of the British economy which had begun in the 1870s. The requirements of the war economy had stimulated the steel, coal and textile industries, but as soon as peace returned, this extra demand disappeared. Many foreign buyers who had been unable to obtain British goods during the war had found alternative sources of supply or had developed their own manufacturing industries; thus demand for traditional British exports - ships, textiles, coal, iron and steel - never revived to its pre-war level. Already in 1920 the government had extended the 1911 National Insurance Act so that unemployment payments were made, for not more than 15 weeks in any one year, to all workers earning less than £250 a year (except agricultural labourers, domestic servants and civil servants). At that point boom conditions still applied and mass unemployment was not expected. When it came in 1921 the new scheme could not cope: payments to the unemployed far outweighed contributions. However, having once conceded the principle of state benefit for the unemployed, the government could hardly do a U-turn simply because unemployment increased. During 1921 therefore, benefit was extended to two 16-week periods in the year with a gap between. Much of this was financed by straight 'gifts' from the treasury and these became known as the 'dole'. Extra payments were introduced for wives and children. The government aid probably eased the situation and may even have prevented revolution; nevertheless it was criticised by Labour because it only treated the symptoms and did nothing to remove unemployment. Labour MPs claimed that the benefits were too low and were 'mocking the poor', while Conservatives condemned them on the grounds that they would demoralise the workers.

(iv) The trouble in the coal industry over whether it should remain under government control or be returned to private ownership had been simmering since the appointment of the Sankey Commission. Matters came to a head on 1 April 1921 when the entire industry came out on strike. This was because the Sankey Commission had been unable to agree on a solution to the problems. Some members recommended nationalisation and others the return of the mines to private ownership. This bitterly disappointed the miners who wanted nationalisation, and it gave Lloyd George the opportunity to avoid permanent nationalisation. The government announced that mines and railways would be handed back to private control on 1 April. Mine-owners informed the men that wages would be reduced because of the slump in exports. For a time the miners' strike threatened to develop into a general strike, but on 15 April the miners' allies in the Triple Alliance, the railwaymen and transport workers, decided to abandon the idea; this the miners regarded as a betrayal, and the day was remembered as the 'Black Friday' of the trade union movement. The miners continued alone and their strike lasted three months; but without support their position was hopeless and they had to give way on all points. Soon afterwards workers in other trades (engineering, shipbuilding, docks, building, textiles, printing and railways) had to accept wage reductions.

Lloyd George had solved this problem in the sense that the strike had failed and a general strike had been averted, but he was fast losing his popularity with the workers.

(v) There was a reduction in government revenue (money flowing into the Treasury from taxation). This was caused partly by the general falling-off of business during the slump and partly by the enormous expense of unemployment benefits. A committee under Sir Eric Geddes recommended retrenchment (drastic cuts in expenditure); the government took the advice, saving itself £64 million. The policy became known as *the Geddes Axe* and involved greatly reduced expenditure on the army, navy, education, health services, and council house building. The economy measures were successful, but highly unpopular with the Labour Party who criticised the government for 'making the children pay while the ladies of Mayfair spend extravagantly on dresses and the rich betake themselves to St Moritz'.

(vi) Trouble flared up in Ireland immediately after the election when the 73 Sinn Fein MPs (who wanted Ireland to be independent from Britain) set up their own parliament (Dail) in Dublin and proclaimed the Republic of Ireland. The IRA began a campaign of terrorism against the police and the government retaliated by using the Black and Tans. Although Lloyd George found a temporary settlement by partitioning Ireland (see Section 25.2(a) for full details), he had made enemies in doing so: many Liberals resented his use of the Black and Tans, whereas the Conservatives were furious at the way in which the union between Britain and Ireland had been destroyed. This was serious for Lloyd George because the survival of his coalition depended on continued Conservative support.

(vii) There were numerous problems in foreign affairs which took up a large proportion of the Prime Minister's time throughout the four years. Sometimes, at the Paris Peace Conference for example (see Section 21.6) he was successful; but there were also failures, and the overall impact of his foreign policies was to damage his reputation.

- Under strong pressure from his Conservative supporters, Lloyd George sent British troops to help the anti-Bolshevik forces in the Russian civil war. By the end of 1919 the Bolsheviks were victorious and the British troops were withdrawn, having achieved nothing. The Russian Communists and many among the British working class who admired them, resented Lloyd George's intervention. In fact he was anxious for a reconciliation and consequently an Anglo-Russian trade treaty was signed (March 1921).
- *The Genoa Conference (1922)* took place on Lloyd George's initiative. There was growing tension between Germany and France over reparations, since the Germans were already complaining that they would not be able to afford the next instalment. Lloyd George hoped to calm the situation by persuading the French to reduce their demands. Other problems to be discussed were the need to resume diplomatic relations with

Russia and Europe's war debts to the USA. The conference was a dismal failure: the French refused all compromise and insisted on full reparations payments; the Americans refused to attend; and the Russians were affronted at the suggestion that they should honour all debts owed by the Tsarist government. The Germans and Russians withdrew and signed a separate agreement at nearby Rapallo, whereby Germany recognised the Soviet government and both countries wiped off their mutual debts. The other nations were alarmed at this reconciliation between two 'suspect' states and blamed Lloyd George. To be fair though, the fault was more that of the French premier, the bitterly anti-German Poincaré, for his refusal to compromise.

- *The Chanak incident (1922)*, though successfully concluded by Lloyd George, brought about his downfall. The Turks threatened to break the Versailles settlement by moving troops into a neutral zone, thereby clashing with the British occupying force based at Chanak on the Dardanelles. Lloyd George took a strong line, warning the Turks that if the neutral zone was violated, they would face war with the British Empire. Eventually a compromise was reached by the Treaty of Lausanne (1923), allowing Turkey to keep Eastern Thrace and Smyrna. The crisis passed, war was averted, and it seemed that Lloyd George had triumphed. Unfortunately he had made the mistake of not consulting the Commonwealth Prime Ministers before committing them to action against the Turks. Many of his Conservative supporters were outraged at what they saw as his unforgivable rashness, and his days in power were numbered.

(c) The coalition found time for some improvements in domestic affairs:

(i) *The Sex Disqualification Removal Act (1919)* allowed women to stand for Parliament; the first woman to take her seat was Nancy Astor, the American-born wife of Viscount Waldorf Astor.

(ii) *The Addison Housing Act (1919)*, the work of Christopher Addison, the Minister of Health, provided subsidies for local authorities to organise the building of 'homes fit for heroes'; 213 000 council houses were built in England and Wales by the end of 1922. Though this was not enough to solve the housing shortage, and the scheme suffered from the Geddes Axe, the principle had been established that housing was a social service and later on local authorities continued Addison's work.

(iii) The extension of unemployment insurance already mentioned meant that an extra nine million workers had at least some cover against unemployment and though the amounts paid were often inadequate, again an important principle had been accepted: it was the state's responsibility to protect workers from the effects of industrial variations.

(iv) *The Rent Act (1920)* protected working-class tenants against exorbitant rent increases.

(d) The fall of the Lloyd George coalition (October 1922). Unfortunately for Lloyd George his achievements were not enough to save the coalition. He had been losing working-class support steadily and it was significant that Labour won 13 by-elections between 1918 and 1922. Much depended on whether the Conservative MPs would continue to support him at the next general election which he intended to hold fairly soon. A meeting of Conservative MPs was held at the *Carlton Club* (29 October) and the vote was 187 to 87 in favour of ending their support of Lloyd George. The main anti-Lloyd George speech which swayed the meeting was made by Stanley Baldwin. Lloyd George immediately resigned and Andrew Bonar Law became Prime Minister of a Conservative government.

The Conservatives decided to abandon him because he had outlived his usefulness. They resented his solution of the Irish problem and his handling of the Chanak incident, and they criticised him because he allowed the sale of knighthoods and other honours to unsuitable candidates. More than that, they were afraid that if the coalition continued much longer, Lloyd George would split the Conservative Party (between coalition supporters and anti-coalitionists) as he had split the Liberal Party. This was the point made forcibly by Baldwin when he said that although Lloyd George was a dynamic force, such a force was a 'very terrible thing'.

He was still only 59, but he was never again to hold an important political office, though he remained an MP until the end of 1944 when he became Earl Lloyd George of Dwyfor. He died in March 1945. A. J. P. Taylor calls him 'the most inspired and creative British statesman of the twentieth century'. If this is so, then it must be seen as a national tragedy that Lloyd George had to sit on the side-lines during the problems of the 1920s and 1930s, while, in the words of C. L. Mowat 'the pygmies, the second-class brains, frittered away Britain's power in the world'.

22.2 THE CONSERVATIVES AND TARIFF REFORM AGAIN

(a) The Conservatives won a clear victory at the general election held in November 1922 with 347 seats, a majority of 88 over all other parties combined. It was a disaster for the Liberals, who fought the election in two separate groups: Asquith Liberals won 60 seats, Lloyd George Liberals 57. The combined Liberal total of 117 seats was well behind Labour's 142 and it was clear that Labour had emerged as the main opposition party to the Conservatives.

However, the new Conservative government did not last long. After Bonar Law's resignation through ill health in May 1923, Stanley Baldwin became Prime Minister. After only a few months in office he decided that another general election was necessary, though the Conservatives still had their comfortable overall majority.

(b) Tariff reform, Joseph Chamberlain's cure for all ills (see Section 17.5(b)(vi)), was the question at issue. Baldwin had decided that tariffs must be re-introduced; but since Bonar Law had earlier pledged that this was exactly what the Conservatives would not do, Baldwin felt it only fair for the electorate to decide for or against protection. Tariffs would make foreign goods more expensive in Britain and thus give a much-needed boost to British industry; the growing unemployment problems would thus be solved. The two sections of the Liberal party reunited under Asquith's leadership and campaigned for free trade, traditional Liberal policy. Together with Labour they argued that continued free trade and foreign imports would keep down the cost of living for the workers. The results were: Conservatives 258, Labour 191 and Liberals 158, a clear defeat for protection and a further confirmation that Labour had replaced the Liberals as the alternative party to the Conservatives. The Conservatives could not remain in government, because although they were still the largest single party they had lost their overall majority, and both Liberals and Labour were against their policy of protection. Labour, the second largest party, therefore formed a government, with a promise of Liberal support in the Commons. In January 1924 the first Labour government took office. with James Ramsay MacDonald as Prime Minister.

22.3 THE FIRST LABOUR GOVERNMENT (JANUARY-OCTOBER 1924)

It was an exceptional achievement for MacDonald to become Prime Minister; born at Lossiemouth, the illegitimate son of poor parents, his only formal education was at the local board school and then as a pupil teacher. He went to London where he worked as a clerk and as a political journalist, and after joining the ILP (1893) he became secretary of the Labour Representation Committee (1900) and Labour MP for Leicester in 1906. After opposing Britain's entry into the war, he was forced to resign the leadership, and lost his seat in 1918. Re-elected to parliament in 1922, his prestige had recovered sufficiently for him to become leader of the party again.

There was near panic in some quarters when the election results became known. Some people thought that everybody's savings would be confiscated by a Labour government, which would usher in a period of profound social revolution. Some Conservatives felt that they should patch up their differences with the Liberals over tariffs, and form a government of national unity to keep Labour out. However, nothing spectacular happened: MacDonald's cabinet, with only two exceptions, consisted of moderates – Philip Snowden as Chancellor of the Exchequer, Henderson, J. H. Thomas and Sydney Webb. He even brought in three former Liberals including Haldane as Lord Chancellor. In fact this Labour government, and the one which followed in 1929-31, were disappointing to their socialist supporters.

(a) Why were they not more successful?

(i) Both were minority governments lacking an overall majority, and dependent on Liberal votes to stay in office. They had therefore to pursue moderate policies, and it was out of the question to introduce nationalisation and disarmament even if MacDonald had wanted to. This meant that their policies were very little different from those of Liberal governments.

(ii) Labour had difficulty in projecting itself as a truly national party, since from the beginning it had claimed to be the party of the industrial workers and was closely tied to the trade unions. It was distrusted by people of property who feared nationalisation and the link with militant trade unionism.

(iii) Labour could not break its ties with the trade unions because they provided the majority of its funds. In return the unions expected to be able to control the party which caused serious friction because union leaders were preoccupied with furthering the interests of their members. They gave very little support to the 1924 Labour government and made no allowances for its dependence on Liberal support. criticising it for its 'half-measures'. Almost immediately there was a dockers' strike in support of a demand for an extra two shillings a day. This was organised by *Ernest Bevin*, general secretary of the Transport and General Workers' Union. Following the success of this strike London Transport workers also came out, and the situation became serious enough for MacDonald to proclaim a state of emergency, enabling the government to use armed lorries for moving essential supplies. In the end this was not necessary because the employers gave way and made an acceptable wage offer, but it was embarrassing for the government and left its relationship with the unions strained.

(iv) It proved impossible to work out a joint plan of action between the parliamentary Labour party and the trade unions. When some Labour intellectuals suggested that the two should cooperate to avoid a repetition of the 1924 fiasco, Bevin dismissed the idea; according to him such theorists did not understand the working class.

(v) Both governments were unfortunate enough to have to deal with serious economic problems: a million unemployed in 1924 and the world economic crisis in 1930-1. Labour had no answer beyond nationalisation, and since that was out of the question they were helpless.

(vi) The divisions between left and right within the party were shown up by MacDonald's attitude. He immediately offended the left by not giving them a fair representation in the cabinet, and affronted them by calmly accepting the limitations of a minority government. The Scottish Clydeside MPs and the ILP wanted him to bring in genuine socialist measures, which would be defeated in the Commons, giving Labour a chance to appeal to the electorate. MacDonald had no intention of attempting such heroics; he wanted moderate policies to gain the confidence of the country, and condemned strikes for wage increases as 'not socialism'. It was not long before the left decided that MacDonald himself was really no socialist.

(b) Domestic achievements of the first Labour government. The 1924 government could point to a few achievements in spite of the disappointments:

(i) *Wheatley's Housing Act* provided grants of £9 million a year to local authorities for the building of council houses. By 1933 when the subsidy was abolished, 521 700 houses had been built which did much to relieve the housing shortage.

(ii) Old age pensions and unemployment benefit were increased and the gap between the two 16-week benefit periods was removed.

(iii) The number of free places in grammar schools was increased and state scholarships to universities brought back.

(iv) *Sir Henry Hadow* was appointed to work out the needs of education. Although his report did not appear until 1926, the Labour Minister of Education, C. P. Trevelyan, must take the credit for the initiative. The Hadow Report was an important milestone in English education, introducing the break between primary and secondary education at 11, and recognising the principle that the whole population was entitled to some secondary education.

(c) Achievements in foreign affairs. MacDonald acted as Foreign Secretary as well as Prime Minister, and had clear ideas about what he hoped to achieve. Like Lloyd George he felt it was essential to improve relations between Germany and France which had deteriorated sharply during 1923; following the German refusal to pay their reparations instalment, the French sent troops to occupy the Ruhr (the important German industrial area which includes the cities of Essen and Dusseldorf), in an attempt to force the Germans to pay. MacDonald was also anxious to resume normal diplomatic relations with Russia, to promote disarmament and to support the new League of Nations as the best hope for the maintenance of peace. His policy produced quick and impressive results.

(i) He was largely responsible for the *Dawes Plan (1924)* which solved the problem of Franco-German relations for the time being. By the end of 1923 the French occupation of the Ruhr had succeeded only in producing galloping inflation and the collapse of the German mark. MacDonald invited Herriot, the new French premier, and Stresemann, the new German Foreign Minister, to a conference in London and persuaded the Americans to participate as well. The conference was chaired for part of the time by the American representative, General Dawes. No reduction was made in the total amount Germany was expected to pay, but it was agreed that she should pay annually only what she could reasonably afford until she became more prosperous; a foreign loan of 800 million gold marks, mainly from the USA was to be made to Germany; France, now assured of at least some reparations from Germany, agreed to withdraw her troops from the Ruhr. The plan was successful: the German economy began to recover on the basis of the American loans and international tensions gradually relaxed. MacDonald was fortunate that the formidable Poincaré had fallen from office and his successor Herriot was anxious for reconciliation; nevertheless he made excellent use of the situation and showed that a Labour government could conduct a successful foreign policy.

(ii) MacDonald gave full diplomatic recognition to the Soviet regime in Russia, signed a trade treaty and opened discussions about a British loan to Russia. This was a realistic policy, but the Conservatives and Liberals strongly disapproved.

(iii) MacDonald made a serious effort to make the League of Nations work; he attended its meetings in Geneva and tried to strengthen it by introducing the Geneva Protocol, a proposal which would have made arbitration of international disputes compulsory. Unfortunately the Labour government fell before the Protocol was accepted and the Conservative government which followed felt unable to ratify it.

(d) The fall of the first Labour government (October 1924). The end of the government came rather suddenly over *the Campbell Case.* J. R. Campbell, editor of the Communist *Workers' Weekly*, was arrested and charged with incitement to mutiny (he had written an article urging soldiers not to fire on their fellow workers in the event of a strike). However, the Labour Attorney-General withdrew the prosecution, and both Conservatives and Liberals, already alarmed by MacDonald's opening of relations with Russia, accused the government of being sympathetic towards Communists. The Liberal demand for an inquiry into the matter was carried by 364 votes to 198; MacDonald took this as a vote of no confidence and resigned. The following election was complicated by the affair of *the Zinoviev Letter.* This appeared in the *Daily Mail* four days before polling and claimed to be from the Russian Communist leader Zinoviev to the British Communist Party. It was marked 'very secret' and contained instructions on how to organise a revolution. The fact that the Foreign Office protested to the Russians about this interference in British affairs made the letter appear genuine, though it seems fairly certain that it was a forgery. But it caused a sensation at the time and was taken to show that Labour sympathy towards Russia was encouraging the British Communists. Labour dropped to 151 seats, Liberals lost disastrously winning only 42 seats, while the Conservatives emerged triumphant with 419 seats.

Labour blamed their defeat on the Zinoviev Letter, but historians seem to agree that the Conservatives would have won anyway. Although short, the first Labour government was not without significance: it proved that a Labour government could work, and it won respect both at home and abroad for its handling of foreign affairs.

22.4 WHY DID THE LIBERAL PARTY CONTINUE TO DECLINE?

At the time of the great Liberal victory of 1906 very few people could have foreseen that within less than 20 years the Liberals would be on the way out and Labour would be forming a government. Suggested explanations are:

(a) Even before 1914 there were signs of a split in the party between the left (which favoured state action to bring about social reform) and the right (which favoured old-fashioned Gladstonian *laissez-faire*). However, though this may eventually have let the Labour Party in, all the signs in 1914 suggest that there was plenty of life remaining in the Liberal Party; Labour seemed to be running out of steam and was not winning many seats in its own right.

(b) The First World War started the rot, according to some historians. Trevor Wilson compares the war to a 'rampant omnibus' which first knocked down and then ran over the Liberal Party. First its prestige was ruined by the incompetent way in which it ran the war and then Lloyd George split the party by the way in which he manoeuvred Asquith into resigning in 1916. Asquith's supporters never forgave Lloyd George for this 'betrayal' and the party remained divided until the election of November 1923, just as Labour was presenting a strong challenge.

(c) Other historians place more emphasis on long-term developments – increasing urbanisation, the greater concentration of industry, and the steadily rising cost of living – which slowly turned some sections of the working class towards the Labour Party. It was always possible as more of the working class got the vote (as they did in 1884, 1918 and 1928) that Labour projecting itself as the party of the working people, might entice them away from the Liberals. Towards the end of the war, local Labour Party organisations were set up in every constituency, and Sydney Webb of the Fabian Society wrote a new programme – *'Labour and the New Social Order'* – which included the nationalisation of coal, land, railways, and electricity, plus a levy on capital. Thus in the elections of 1918 and 1922 Labour seemed better organised than the Liberals; in 1922 for the first time Labour won more seats than both groups of Liberals combined (142 to 117). It may be that the 1918 Representation of the People Act was a crucial factor in the Labour breakthrough. By trebling the electorate, it brought the industrial working classes into a majority for the first time; it was this new mass electorate which the Liberals had to attract if they were to survive as a major party.

(d) By 1922 both Liberal leaders were something of a liability: Asquith did not provide inspiring leadership and was out of touch with the working classes while Lloyd George had lost his popularity, being tainted in working class eyes by his co-operation with the Conservatives. Asquith did not retire from the leadership until 1926 when it was too late for the party to recover.

(e) The Liberals were beginning to lose right-wing support, as many wealthy businessmen switched to the Conservatives as the surest way of keeping Labour out. This was serious because it removed much of the Liberals' financial support; three elections between 1918 and 1923 left the party short of funds; Labour was able to rely on trade union cash.

(f) Once Labour had formed a government in 1924 without the expected social revolution, Liberal election prospects faded; anti-Conservatives began to vote Labour as the only way to keep the Tories out.

(g) The Liberals were at a disadvantage because of the electoral system. With three parties contesting many seats, a high proportion of MPs were returned on a minority vote; many Liberals came second and their votes were not reflected in the Commons. In 1922 Liberals polled slightly more votes than Labour, yet won only 117 seats to Labour's 142. (Hence the Liberal agitation ever since for some sort of proportional representation.)

(h) The 1929 election is usually regarded as the Liberals' last chance; Lloyd George led a united party with an attractive programme, but they managed only 59 seats to Labour's 288. There was a lack of confidence in Lloyd George and a feeling that Baldwin and MacDonald, though less spectacular, were more solid and reliable.

Perhaps the neatest conclusion is that given the circumstances in the years after the First World War, with the Conservatives firmly established as the party of the propertied classes and the ratepayers, and Labour in alliance with the trade unions as the party of the workers, there was no remaining interest group large enough to keep the Liberals going as a serious contender for power.

QUESTIONS

1. The decline of the Liberal Party
Study Sources **A** to **H** and then answer the questions which follow.

Source A: General Election Results and Statistics.

Year	Conservatives MPs	Conservatives % of vote	Liberals MPs	Liberals % of vote	Labour MPs	Labour % of vote	Total votes cast
1910 (Jan)	273	46.9	275	43.2	40	7.6	6.6m
1918 (Dec)	338	36.0	162	25.6	59	23.7	10.7m
			131 coalition	12.6			
			26 independent	13.0			
1922 (Nov)	397	38.5	117	28.3	142	28.2	14.4m
			60 Asquith	18.9			
			57 Lloyd George	9.4			
1923 (Dec)	258	38.0	158	29.7	191	30.7	14.5m
1924 (Oct)	419	48.3	40	17.6	151	33.0	16.5m

Source: quoted in C. Cook, *The Age of Alignment 1922–29*, Macmillan (1975).

Source B: memorandum by Herbert Gladstone, director of Liberal Headquarters, written in November 1924.

The results of the 1918 election broke the party, not only in the House of Commons, but in the country. Local associations perished, or maintained an existence in name only. Masses of our best men passed away to Labour. Others drifted to Conservatism or independence. Over and over again our remnants in the constituencies declined even to hold meetings. In the election of 1922, many constituencies actually refused to fight, even though candidates and funds were available.

Source: quoted in C. Cook, *The Age of Alignment 1922–29*, Macmillan, 1975 (adapted extracts).

Source C: diary of C. P. Scott, the Liberal editor of the *Manchester Guardian*, 1921.

What struck me most about Asquith was his immobility. He had not moved – did not really know about things. He could see no good in Lloyd George or anything he did. All the time he (Asquith) laid down the law with great positiveness. Altogether a somewhat grumbling and very old old man . . .

Sir Donald Maclean [an Asquith Liberal MP] told me, 'I have done with Lloyd George. I could never work with him or under him'. Of Asquith himself, though entirely loyal, Maclean said that he was not gaining but losing ground in the country. He had missed a great and unique opportunity by his failure to make any impact in Parliament since his return, mainly because of laziness.

Source: T. Wilson (ed.), *The Political Diaries of C. P. Scott 1911-28*, Collins, 1970 (adapted extracts).

Source D: a letter written by Sir Charles Hobhouse, a Liberal journalist and former MP, to C. P. Scott, 7 November 1924.

I doubt if the Liberal party any longer stands for anything distinctive. My reasons are on the one side that moderate Labour – Labour in office – has represented essential Liberalism better than the organised party since Campbell-Bannerman's death. The Liberal Party never seems agreed within on essentials. Part leans to the Tories, part to Labour, part has nothing distinctive. Tradition and class distinctions kept many good Liberals outside Labour. Now Labour has grown so much that it tends to absorb them and to leave only the 'bad' Liberals who lean towards the Tories.

Source: quoted in C. Cook, *The Age of Alignment 1922-29*, Macmillan, 1975 (adapted extract).

Source E: Annual Report of Home Counties Liberal Federation, May 1924.

All through our areas the revival of Liberalism continues . . . Political activity is greater than at any time since the outbreak of the Great War . . . Liberalism has never been more active in this area except in the years preceding the landslide of 1906.

Source: as for Source D (adapted extract).

Source F: statement by the Secretary of the Midland Liberal Federation, 5 September 1925.

It has become a very difficult thing since the war to secure candidates, because in dark times like these when there are so few decent chances to offer a candidate, it has become exceedingly difficult to find men and women who are prepared to face a contest and provide all the money.

Source: as for Source D (adapted extract).

Source G: information from a modern work.

There was a lack of consultation between Asquith and Lloyd George. No Liberal leader really thought about the possibility that the party, though supporting Labour in Parliament [during the first Labour government, 1924] might find itself constantly under attack in the constituencies . . . The Liberals voted Labour into offiee without any understandings or conditions, and without having considered how they would fare if Labour refused to co-operate . . . Either the Liberals would have to support Labour measures or vote against them. To vote against meant an election which, for financial reasons, the Liberals did not want.

Source: C. Cook, *The Age of Alignment 1922–29*, Macmillan, 1975 (adapted extracts).

Source H: comments from a modern historian.

The problems stemmed, not from the split of Asquith and Lloyd George, but from fundamental and long-term weaknesses in the structure, social composition and outlook of the party in the industrial areas . . . It was a middle-class party which failed to accommodate working-class candidates or to produce a relevant industrial policy. Perhaps the war accelerated these factors, but fhey were quite clearly at work before 1914 . . . After the war, a succession of body-blows coming on top of the changing social structure reduced the party from supremacy to powerlessness . . . [The final body-blow was] *the folly of the Liberal course of action in the months of 1924* . . . By 1923, despite the collapse of so much constituency organisation, the process of decline had not reached the stage when recovery was impossible. A year later [November 1924] it was difficult to deny that the Liberal decline had passed the point of no return.

Source: as for Source G (adapted extract).

(a) (i) From the evidence of the statistics in Source **A**, in which election did the Liberals lose most seats?   **4(a)**

(ii) In which election did the Liberals' share of the vote fall most?
          4(a)

(iii) In which elections did the Liberals increase their share of the vote?   **4(a)**

(iv) Which elections did the Liberals fight as a divided party?   **4(a)**

(v) Why do you think so many more people voted in 1918 than in 1910?   **1, 2**

(b) (i) Source **B** states that 'the result of the 1918 election broke the party'. Using the statistics in Source **A**, show how the 1918 election was a serious blow to the Liberals in the Commons.
          4(a, c)

(ii) Why does Gladstone think the result 'broke the party . . . in the country'?   **4(a)**

(c) (i) What evidence do Sources **C** and **D** provide to explain the decline of the Liberal party?   **4(a, c)**

(ii) According to Source **D**, what was it that used to keep many Liberals from joining Labour?   **4(a)**

(iii)   Why do you think Hobhouse (Source **D**) calls Liberals who were drifting towards the Tories 'bad' Liberals?   **4(a, b)**

(d) **(i)**   How do Sources **E** and **F** seem to contradict each other about the fortunes of the Liberal party?   **4(a, c)**

(ii)   Using evidence from the other Sources, especially **A** and **G**, try and explain this difference of opinion.   **4(a, c)**

(iii)   What further cause of Liberal difficulty does Source **F** suggest which is not mentioned in the other Sources (apart from **H**)?   **4(a, c)**

(e) **(i)**   Source **H** suggests that the Liberal leaders acted foolishly in 1924. What evidence can you find in Source **G** which supports this view?   **4(a, c)**

(ii)   When does the writer of Source **H** think the Liberal party began to decline?   **4(a)**

(iii)   According to Source **H**, which was the vital period during which a Liberal recovery became impossible?   **4(a)**

(f) **(i)**   Sources **B**, **C**, **D**, **E** and **F** were all written by Liberals. What do you think are the advantages and disadvantages of each of these Sources for the historian?   **4(a, b)**

(ii)   Do you think these five Liberal Sources give enough evidence for a full explanation of the Liberal decline? Give reasons for your answer.   **4(a, b, c)**

(g)   The historian Trevor Wilson in his book, *The Downfall of the Liberal Party*, argues that the First World War was mainly responsible for the decline of the Liberals, because of the way in which it split the party between Asquith and Lloyd George supporters. Using the evidence from all the Sources and your own knowledge, explain whether you agree or disagree with Trevor Wilson.   **1, 2, 4(a, b, c)**

2. The First Labour Government, 1924

Study Sources **A** to **C** and then answer the questions which follow.

Source A: article by Clifford Sharp, editor of the *New Statesman*, a left-wing magazine, 7 August 1924.

> The obvious answer to the question 'Can Labour Govern?' is 'No' . . . The actual achievements of the Labour Government have not been substantial. It has not attempted to carry out, or even to introduce, any single one of those items in its programme which distinguished it from other parties, and its left wing is seriously disgruntled.

> **Source:** quoted in C. Cook, *The Age of Alignment 1922–29*, Macmillan, 1975.

Source B: from the diary of Beatrice Webb, a Fabian socialist, for 1924.

MacDonald wants 8 million voters behind him and means to get them even if it involves shedding the I.L.P., the revolutionary section who pushed him into power. I do not accuse him of treachery: for he was never a Socialist. Where he has lacked integrity is in posing as a Socialist, and occasionally using revolutionary jargon . . . Yet as a political performer he is showing himself a supreme artist. We had never realised that he had genius in this direction.

Source: M. Cole (ed.), *Beatrice Webb's Diaries, 1924-32*, Longman, 1956 (adapted extracts).

Source C: the view of a modern historian.

Given all the restraints of inexperience, lack of time and MacDonald's insistence on moderate measures, the government was able to enact some useful, if in the main unexciting, legislation, and to record some impressive achievements in foreign affairs . . . Even though its legislative achievement was so limited, the first Labour government had justified MacDonald's strategy. It had proved, to his party and to the people, that Labour could and would govern. Even more important, MacDonald's strategy in capturing the middle ground of politics from the Liberals was succeeding.

Source: C. Cook, *The Age of Alignment 1922-29*, Macmillan, 1975 (adapted extracts).

(a) **(i)** What criticisms does the writer of Source **A** make of the Labour government? **4(a)**

    (ii) Mention two items which the writer of Source **A** probably had in mind as ones which 'distinguished [the party] from other parties'. **1, 2, 4(a)**

(b) **(i)** What are Beatrice Webb's criticisms of MacDonald in Source **B**? **4(a)**

    (ii) What was the I.L.P. referred to in Source **B**? **1, 2, 4(a)**

    (iii) From the evidence of Source **A**, would you say that Beatrice Webb was an admirer of MacDonald or not? **4(a, b)**

(c) **(i)** According to Source **C**, in what ways were MacDonald and the first Labour government successful? **4(a)**

    (ii) Do you think Source **C** contradicts Source **A** completely, or not? Explain your answer. **4(a, c)**

    (iii) What reasons can you suggest for the disagreements between the writers of Sources **A** and **C**? **4(a, b, c)**

(d) **(i)** Describe the 'useful . . . legislation' mentioned in Source **C**. **1, 2, 4(a)**

    (ii) Describe and explain the 'impressive achievements in foreign affairs' mentioned in Source **C**. **1, 2, 4(a)**

(e) **(i)** Why did the Labour government end in October 1924? **1, 2**

(ii) From the evidence of Source **A** in Question 1 (election statistics), do you think MacDonald and Labour had succeeded in 'capturing the middle ground . . . from the Liberals', as Source **C** puts it, by November 1924? **4(a, c)**

3. The Lloyd George Coalition, 1918–22

(a) Show how, and with how much success, Lloyd George dealt with the following problems:

(i) unemployment;
(ii) relations between workers and employers;
(iii) the housing shortage;
(iv) the shortage of government revenue;
(v) the situation in Ireland.

(b) Explain why Lloyd George fell from power in October 1922.
1, 2

4. As a Conservative, explain your feelings and reactions towards events during the chaotic period in British politics from December 1918 until October 1924. You can refer, among other things, to:

(a) the Lloyd George Coalition and its collapse;

(b) the short Conservative government of 1922–23 and its defeat over tariff reform;

(c) the first Labour government (1924) and its downfall;

(d) the Conservative election victory of October 1924. **1, 2, 3**

CHAPTER 23

BALDWIN, THE CONSERVATIVES AND THE GENERAL STRIKE (1924–9)

SUMMARY OF EVENTS

With a massive overall majority in excess of 200, the Conservative government was in a powerful position. The rebel wing of the party, including Austen Chamberlain (Joseph's son) and Lord Birkenhead, which had favoured continuing support of the Lloyd George coalition, was now safely back in the fold. Chamberlain was Foreign Secretary and Winston Churchill, who had drifted back to the Conservatives after 20 years as a Liberal, became Chancellor of the Exchequer. Neville Chamberlain, another of Joseph's sons, was one of the most successful members of the government; as Minister of Health, he was responsible for steering no fewer than 21 bills through parliament. The government lasted for almost its full term of five years, introducing a mass of solid, if unspectacular legislation. The only dramatic incident was the General Strike of 1926 which aroused considerable emotion, fears and excitement, though it lasted less than two weeks. Throughout the period, with his image of a plain and honest man puffing contentedly at his pipe, Stanley Baldwin presided over the country's fortunes.

23.1 CONSERVATIVE ACHIEVEMENTS

(a) **Stanley Baldwin** was the son of a wealthy iron and steel manufacturer. After leaving Cambridge, he worked in the family business and was over 40 when he first became an MP (1908). He was President of the Board of Trade in Lloyd George's coalition (1921-2), but grew to dislike Lloyd George's methods; it was his speech at the Carlton Club (October 1922) attacking Lloyd George which established him as one of the leading Conservatives, and Bonar Law made him Chancellor of the Exchequer when the Conservatives took office at the end of 1922. When Law resigned in 1923 Baldwin was the surprise choice as next Prime Minister; the obvious candidate, Lord Curzon, was unpopular with the party because he was pompous and arrogant. When told of the choice, Curzon is reported to have described Baldwin as 'a person of the utmost insignificance'. In fact he was an extremely able politician and a much better manager of people than Lloyd George who offended many of his colleagues. He gave the impression of being honest and lacking in deviousness, unlike Lloyd George whom Baldwin regarded as 'a corrupter of public life'. Baldwin wanted a return to 'clean government' and donated to the Exchequer a large slice of the profits he had made from the manufacture of armaments during the war. He was essentially a moderate – treating his own work-force with sympathy and understanding, he applied the same methods to national labour relations (though at the time of the General Strike the more extreme members of the cabinet gained the upper hand) and was highly respected by Labour MPs. Probably his greatest achievement was in helping to re-unite the Conservative Party and holding it together until his retirement in 1937. On the other hand, he was blamed for neglecting Britain's defences in face of the threat from Nazi Germany, especially when he was Prime Minister of the National Government (1935-7). His main failing, apart from his lack of originality, was his reluctance to take the initiative. Neville Chamberlain was the real driving force behind most of the domestic achievements of this government.

(b) What were the domestic achievements of the Conservatives?

(i) *The Widows, Orphans and Old Age Contributory Pensions Act (1925)* provided a pension of 10s. a week for widows with extra for children, and 10s. a week for insured workers and their wives at 65. Both workers and employers contributed to the scheme which was compulsory (the non-contributory pension at 70 still continued).

(ii) The vote was extended to women at the age of 21. Labour objected strongly because the plural vote was not abolished.

(iii) *The Unemployment Insurance Act (1927)* increased contributions and reduced benefits, but had the great advantage that benefits would be paid for an indefinite period, provided an unemployed person had been genuinely seeking work.

(iv) *The Local Government Act of 1929* was Chamberlain's greatest achievement, providing a complete overhaul of local government organisation, rates and provision for the poor: Poor Law Unions and their boards of guardians who had provided relief for the poor since 1834 were abolished, and their function taken over by county and county borough councils. Agricultural land and farm buildings were to be exempt from payment of rates, and industrial property and railways were to pay only one-quarter of the previous rate. This was designed to encourage farmers and industrialists to expand operations and provide more jobs. Local councils would receive a block grant from the government to cover the costs of services to the poor and of other functions such as public health, slum clearance, roads, and town and country planning. This was a much fairer system because expenses were being shared by the whole body of taxpayers in the country, instead of poor areas with high unemployment having to foot the bill from rates collected locally. However, the Labour party protested bitterly that it was an attack on the independence of local councils, since the government could now cut off grants to councils which did not follow their wishes.

(v) *The Central Electricity Board* appointed by the Minister of Transport was made responsible for the distribution of electricity. The National Grid was started with its thousands of pylons connecting the generating stations; it was completed by 1933.

(vi) *The British Broadcasting Company* became a public corporation, to be controlled by governors appointed by the Postmaster-General. John Reith, the first governor-general of the BBC, was determined that it should provide more than just light entertainment. He built the BBC up into an important educational and cultural influence, with its own symphony orchestra. There were regular news bulletins and educational programmes, and leading politicians were invited to broadcast. Baldwin and Philip Snowden soon developed an excellent radio technique but Lloyd George and MacDonald, used to addressing huge live audiences, never mastered the new medium.

(vii) Depending on one's viewpoint, it is possible to argue that the government's handling of the General Strike was an achievement. The strike lasted less than two weeks, and has never been repeated. The 1927 Trade Disputes Act reduced the powers of the trade unions (see next section).

(c) Overseas affairs were in the hands of Austen Chamberlain, the Foreign Secretary.

(i) He made an important contribution to the signing of the *Locarno Treaties (1925)*, a number of different agreements involving Germany, France, Britain, Italy, Belgium, Poland and Czechoslovakia. The most important one was that Germany, France and Belgium promised to respect their joint frontiers; if one of the three broke this agreement, Britain and Italy would assist the state which was being attacked. Germany signed agreements with Poland and Czechoslovakia providing for arbitration over possible disputes. The agreements were greeted with wild enthusiasm all over Europe, and the reconciliation between Germany and France was referred to as the 'Locarno honeymoon'. Later, historians were not so enthusiastic about Locarno: there was one notable omission from the agreements – no guarantees were given about Germany's eastern frontiers with Poland and Czechoslovakia. By ignoring this problem, the signatories at Locarno were also ignoring the fact that by signing the League of Nations Covenant they had undertaken to guarantee all members against aggression. Locarno gave the impression that no action need necessarily be taken if Germany attacked Poland and Czechoslovakia and that Britain had perhaps turned her back on eastern Europe. Indeed Chamberlain talked of Poland's frontier with Germany as something 'for which no British government ever will or ever can risk the bones of a British grenadier'. The Conservatives continued to be cool towards the League of Nations; Chamberlain had already rejected MacDonald's Geneva Protocol; this latest slight made the League even less realistic than before, and can be interpreted as the beginning of appeasement (see Section 26.1). For the time being though, as the world enjoyed a period of great economic prosperity, any uneasy thoughts were pushed into the background; Germany was admitted to the League in 1926 and Stresemann and Briand (French Foreign Minister from 1925 to 1932) met regularly and had friendly discussions; often Austen Chamberlain joined them. This 'Locarno spirit' culminated in:

(ii) *The Kellogg-Briand Pact (1928)*. This originated in an idea of Briand who proposed that France and the USA should sign a pact renouncing war. Frank B. Kellogg, the American Secretary of State, suggested that the whole world should be involved; eventually 65 states, including Britain, signed the pact, agreeing to renounce war as an instrument of national policy. This sounded impressive, but was completely useless because no mention was made of sanctions against any state which broke its pledge. Japan for example signed the pact, but was not prevented from waging war against China only three years later.

(iii) No attempt was made to develop the new relationship with Soviet Russia, started by the Labour government; in fact relations deteriorated sharply. The Conservatives had no love for the Communists. Chamberlain immediately told the Russians that Britain would not keep to the treaties which the Labour government had signed with them. The British attitude stiffened when evidence appeared suggesting that Russian propaganda was partly responsible for the unrest in India (see Section 25.3). Police raided the British Communist Party headquarters in London (1925) and the premises of Arcos, a Soviet trading organisation based in London (1927), and claimed to have found evidence of Russian plotting with British Communists to overthrow the capitalist system. The government expelled the mission and broke off diplomatic relations with the Russians, who replied by arresting some British residents in Moscow. It has been argued that conciliation would have been a more rational approach, which might have persuaded the Russians to emerge from their isolation.

(iv) The way was prepared for *The Statute of Westminster* (eventually signed in 1931) which defined the relationship between Britain and the rest of the Commonwealth (see Section 25.1(b)). Baldwin also set up *the Simon Commission (1927)* to report on the situation in India (see Section 25.3(b)(ii)).

23.2 WHAT CAUSED THE GENERAL STRIKE OF 1926?

(a) In the background was the post-war economic depression, bringing falling exports and mass unemployment.

(b) On the whole, industrialists failed to promote greater efficiency and more mechanisation which would have enabled them to compete better with other countries. They tended to blame declining profits on higher wages, and their attempts to reduce wages caused strained relations with their workforces.

(c) The problems of the coal industry were important because it was here that the strike began. Coal sales were probably worse hit than those of any other industry, partly because more gas, electricity and oil were being used, and because there was stiff competition from Germany and Poland which had modern mechanised pits. In 1925 only 20 per cent of British output was by coal-cutting machines, the rest was by hand-picks.

(d) The government had refused to nationalise the mines, though it was widely believed that only government control could bring about the essential modernisation that would enable the industry to survive. Mine-owners were unwilling to take any initiative.

(e) The return to the gold standard in April 1925 worsened the export position of all British industries, not just coal. According to the economist J. M. Keynes, the Chancellor of the Exchequer, Churchill, had over-valued the pound by 10 per cent, making British exports that much more expensive.

(f) The situation worsened in June 1925 when there was a sudden drop in coal exports, following a brief revival while the German mines in the Ruhr were closed during the French occupation. The owners announced that they would have to lower wages and increase hours. The miners protested but Baldwin saved the situation for the time being by providing a subsidy for nine months to keep wages at the existing levels, and by appointing a Royal Commission under Sir Herbert Samuel to try and find a solution.

(g) Meanwhile the TUC made it clear that they would support the miners because if their wages were reduced it was likely that those of other workers would soon follow. This stiffened the attitude of the miners.

(h) Everything hinged on whether the *Samuel Report* could find a solution. It appeared in March 1926 and was an eminently sensible document. It recommended that mine-owners should press ahead with reorganisation and modernisation, should not insist on longer hours (which would lead to over-production) and should not reduce wages (which would enable them to avoid reorganisation). The government should not continue the subsidy. For the time being until the crisis passed, miners must accept some wage reductions. Neither the owners nor the miners would accept the report, though the TUC welcomed it and tried to keep negotiations going because they were not prepared for a general strike. The government made no attempt to force its acceptance even though one moderate mine-owner, Sir Alfred Mond, urged Baldwin to do so.

(i) The mine-owners brought a showdown one step nearer by announcing that wages would be reduced on 30 April to which the miners replied that they would strike on 1 May. The owners got in first and staged a lockout on Friday 30 April. The coal strike had begun. Ernest Bevin announced that a general strike would begin on 3 May if a settlement was not reached.

(j) The TUC was still trying to find a solution but was thwarted by circumstances. Negotiations between cabinet and TUC were hampered all through 2 May because the miners' leaders had gone home, leaving the TUC to handle the talks. Baldwin heard that the *Daily Mail* compositors had refused to print an article which claimed that a general strike would be a revolutionary action. He described this as an 'overt act', a sign that the general strike had begun, whereas in fact it was an unofficial action. Baldwin called off the negotiations and although TUC representatives went to Downing Street in the early hours of 3 May to protest about the abrupt ending to the talks, they found that the cabinet had dispersed and Baldwin had gone to bed. No solution had been found and so the General Strike began.

Who was to blame? Left-wing historians have no hesitation in blaming Baldwin; they argue that he should have followed Mond's advice and insisted on all parties accepting the Samuel Report; nor should he have broken off the negotiations so abruptly when the TUC was prepared to go on talking. On the other hand, the miners were completely inflexible, their favourite slogan being 'not a minute on the day, not a penny off the pay'. The mine-owners (with a few exceptions) were equally inflexible, insisting on district wage agreements (instead of a national wage rate), longer hours and lower wages. Even Lord Birkenhead, no friend of the miners, remarked that he had thought the miners' leaders were the stupidest men in the country until he had the misfortune to meet the owners.

23.3 THE STRIKE AND ITS RESULTS

(a) The strike itself was an impressive show of working-class solidarity. In the industries called out (road, rail, docks, printing, gas and electricity, building, iron, steel and chemicals), the response was almost 100 per cent, which seemed to show how alienated the workers had become from employers and government. However, by 11 May there was no sign that the government would give way. When Sir Herbert Samuel offered to act as mediator, the TUC accepted. He produced the *Samuel Memorandum* suggesting a short-term renewal of the subsidy to maintain wage levels, no wage reductions until reorganisation was assured, and a National Wages Board.

On 12 May the TUC called off the General Strike, hoping that the memorandum would be accepted, though it was strictly unofficial and

Baldwin had given no guarantees. The strike lasted unofficially until 14 May, but the miners refused to go back. Since the mine-owners refused to compromise, the coal strike dragged on until Demember, but in the end the miners had to give way and go back to longer hours and lower wages. There was much bitterness about the TUC 'betrayal'.

(b) Why did the TUC call off the General Strike so soon? They were dismayed when at the end of the first week there was no sign of a softening in the government's attitude; in fact the cabinet extremists were talking of 'unconditional surrender'. The TUC, completely unprepared for a general strike anyway, was anxious to end it before provocative government actions caused events to take a more violent turn (see below). There were doubts about the legal position – Sir John Simon (a Liberal lawyer) said in the Commons that the strike was 'an illegal proceeding', not an industrial dispute, and that the leaders were liable to be sued for damages and gaoled. The Labour party's attitude was unhelpful and the strike was proving expensive – the TUC had already used £4 million out of their total strike fund of £12.5 million.

(c) How well did Baldwin handle the strike? This question has evoked sharply contradictory views:

(i) The left-wing view is that Baldwin acted in his usual indolent way, scarcely 'handling' the strike at all. Worse still, he allowed the right-wing 'fire-eaters' in his cabinet (Churchill and Sir William Joynson-Hicks, the Home Secretary) to take aggressive actions which might have provoked the strikers into violence. There is plenty of evidence to support this view. Baldwin put Churchill in charge of the *British Gazette*, the government emergency newspaper, which printed uncompromising passages and fighting exhortations to the police and special constables, though the TUC had given strict orders that all violence was to be avoided. These passages became so blatant that King George V, who showed himself in a very favourable light throughout the strike, protested to Baldwin, and the *Gazette* became more restrained. It was Churchill's idea to use armoured cars to protect food convoys; 'we are at war', he said, 'we must go through with it; the strike must be crushed'. In fact, the specials had been protecting the food convoys perfectly adequately.

(ii) The sympathetic view is that Baldwin played a skilful waiting game, knowing that the TUC had no stomach for a prolonged strike. He took the view that the strike was an attack on the constitution and not an ordinary industrial dispute; therefore no negotiations could begin until the strike was called off. He concentrated on operating emergency plans prepared months earlier, and these worked efficiently. Volunteers kept food supplies moving, unloaded ships and drove trains and buses. Food convoys were organised and protected by special constables (later by Churchill's armoured cars) while the navy manned power stations. At the same time he was usually conciliatory in tone – in a broadcast on 8 May he told the country that he was a man of peace and appealed to the strikers to trust him to secure a fair deal for everybody.

Whichever view one accepts, the fact remains that the General Strike failed and the government claimed the credit.

(d) What were the results of the strike?

(i) There was a good deal of working-class disillusionment with the TUC for its 'betrayal' of the miners. Membership dropped from over eight million to well under five million the following year.

(ii) The TUC turned against the idea of a general strike, convinced that one could never succeed.

(iii) There was no solution to the coal industry problems and no modernisation; the industry continued in slow decline with exports falling steadily. 73 million tons had been exported in 1913; by 1929 the figure had fallen to 60 million tons, and even more disastrously to 39 million tons in 1932.

(iv) The government introduced the *Trade Disputes Act (1927)* designed to make another general strike impossible. Sympathetic strikes and intimidation were illegal. Trade union members were not required to contribute to the union's political fund (the political levy paid to the Labour party) unless they chose to do so and gave written notice of their intention. This was known as 'contracting-in' which now replaced 'contracting-out' introduced by the 1913 Trade Union Act. The new act placed the onus on the member; many did not bother to contract in, hence a fall of over 25 per cent in the Labour party's income.

The Act seems to have been largely unnecessary since the TUC had had enough of general strikes, and it was bitterly resented by the unions. It was not repealed until 1946.

(v) The working class realised that only by parliamentary action could their aims be achieved and this, plus bitterness at the Trade Disputes Act and unemployment standing at over a million, caused an increase in Labour party support and was partly responsible for the Labour victory in the 1929 general election.

(vi) The strike was not without some beneficial results for the workers. It acted as a warning to other employers who, on the whole, were more reasonable than the mine-owners and avoided drastic wage reductions. Some employers made genuine efforts to improve labour relations; for example, Sir Alfred Mond, founder of Imperial Chemical Industries (ICI), began a series of talks with Ernest Bevin of the Transport and General Workers' Union, and with other leading trade unionists.

23.4 THE GENERAL ELECTION OF 1929

(a) This election was a strangely quiet affair with no dramatic issues under debate. The main Conservative slogan was 'Safety First', while the Labour programme played down full socialism and concentrated on immediate reforms. Much the most interesting was the new Liberal programme, *We Can Conquer Unemployment*. United under Lloyd George's leadership,

illus 23.1 *No single issue dominated the election of 1929. This Conservative poster shows the nation enjoying every conceivable benefit under Stanley Baldwin*

the party proposed a series of far-reaching reforms for agriculture, town-planning, housing, road-building and railway modernisation. The Conservatives lost over 140 seats and slumped to 260. Labour came top of the poll with 288 seats, while the Liberals, though managing to win an extra 17 seats, were bitterly disappointed to reach a total of only 59.

(b) Why did the Conservatives lose? The government had done nothing to solve unemployment, which, though lower than when they took office, still stood at over a million. The coal-mining industry continued to decline and the balance of payments was unhealthy (this means that the value of goods imported was greater than the value of goods exported, causing a drain on gold and foreign currency reserves to make up the difference). The government – Chamberlain excepted – seemed dull and lacking in inspiration and energy. Probably the main reason for the swing to Labour was the aftermath of the General Strike (see previous section). In a sense, though, it was an indecisive result: Labour still lacked an overall majority and more people had voted Conservative (8.6 million) than Labour (8.4 million). The Liberal vote of 5.3 million was not fairly reflected in their 59 seats. Over 60 per cent of the electorate did not want a Labour government, but there was no possibility of a coalition between Conservatives and Liberals because of Baldwin's detestation of Lloyd George.

QUESTIONS

1. The General Strike, 3–12 May 1926, and its Aftermath
Study Sources **A** to **H** and then answer the questions which follow.

Source A: the memoirs of J. C. C. Davidson, a friend of Baldwin, a Conservative MP and, from 1926, Conservative Party Chairman.

It has got to be made absolutely clear, in everything which is written about Baldwin and the General Strike, that his vision and his judgement were *clear and decisive*, and that he didn't waffle. The idea was always put about that he was under pressure. But there was no question of pressure; he saw the thing as clear as crystal. The decision he took was that *there should be no parley*. The Constitution would not be safe until we had won the victory, and victory depended on the surrender of the TUC.

Source: R. R. James (ed.), *Memoirs of a Conservative*, Weidenfeld & Nicolson, 1969.

Source B: the diary of Tom Jones, one of Baldwin's senior advisers, May 1926.

The chief asset in keeping the country steadfast during the negotiations was the Prime Minister's *reputation for fair deal-*

ing enhanced later by his sincere plea against malice and vindictiveness. His seeming weakness had been his strength. Had he yielded to the *Diehard influences*, he would have prolonged the strike by rallying the whole of Labour in defence of Trade Unionism.

Source: K. Middlemass (ed.), *Whitehall Diary 1916-1930, 3 vols*, Oxford, 1969–71.

Source C: letter from Lord Beaverbrook to a friend, 24 May 1926. Beaverbrook was the owner of the *Daily Express*, a Conservative and a friend of Lloyd George.

The praises which are being poured upon Baldwin are pure hysteria. I have worked with him intermittently at one time for ten years at a stretch, and he is a man absolutely without a mind or a capacity to make one up.

Source: quoted in A. J. P. Taylor, *Beaverbrook*, Penguin, 1974.

Source D: information from a modern historian.

On the evening of 8 May Baldwin broadcast to the nation:
I am a man of peace, I am longing and working and praying for peace, but I will not surrender the safety and the security of the British Constitution. You placed me in power eighteen months ago by the largest majority given to any party for many years. Have I done anything to forfeit that confidence? Cannot you trust me to ensure a square deal and to secure even justice between man and man? . . .
On the same day that the General Strike was called off, Baldwin again broadcast to the nation. 'Our business is not to triumph over those who have failed in a mistaken attempt', he said, and he went on to assure his large audience that he would lose no time in resuming negotiations with the miners and owners. He offered to operate the Samuel Report if the two sides would accept it first. However, the miners refused and the stoppage dragged on for the remainder of the year. The miners were eventually forced back to the pits by cold and starvation, being forced to accept longer hours and lower wages.

Source: H. M. Hyde: *Baldwin – the Unexpected Prime Minister*, Hart-Davis, MacGibbon, 1973 (adapted extracts).

Source E: information from another modern historian.

Baldwin issued proposals two days after the end of the strike, but they were rejected. Neither side would budge. In July Baldwin gave way to the owners and introduced an Eight Hours Act (increasing the miners' working day from seven hours to eight), hoping that the owners would offer concessions in return. But the owners had no such intention. Their tactics were to wait until there was a split in the miners' unity. At the end of November the miners were forced to give in. It was a total defeat.

Source: M. Morris, *The General Strike*, Penguin, 1976 (adapted extracts).

Source F: the opinion of Jim Griffiths, a South Wales miners' leader and later a Labour MP.

Looking back, I think it would have been better if we'd all gone back together. Maybe the miners would have got better terms than they did in the end. Perhaps if we'd had a better negotiator we might have managed it, but Herbert Smith was determined to stay out. He was a very stubborn man, a strong leader, but no negotiator. Neither was Cook. It left such bitterness behind.

Source: quoted in M. Morris, *The General Strike*, Penguin, 1976.

Source G: the opinion of Bill Ballantyne, a member of the I.L.P. and a committee member of the Carstairs branch of the National Union of Railwaymen.

The failure of the general strike was a tremendous setback to the trade union and Labour Movement: it knocked the bottom out of many men and women who had given their lives to the movement. It began a process of an enforced reduction in all standards of life.

Source: as for Source F.

Source H: the opinion of Walter Citrine, a leader of the Electrical Trades Union, member of the TUC General Council in 1926 and later TUC General Secretary and a life peer.

I do not regard the General Strike as a failure. It is true that it was ill-prepared and that it was called off without any consultation with those who took part in it . . . But it demonstrated the potential power of the trade unions. It served as a warning to the government and the employers. It was publicly stated that the trade of the country had lost £400 million and the government about £80 million. Would any government gleefully contemplate a repetition in an effort to teach Labour its proper place . . . and we had a Labour government in 1929; I'm sure that was a result of it.

Source: Lord Citrine, *Men and Work*, Hutchinson, 1964 (adapted extracts).

(a) (i) According to Source A, what did victory for the government depend on? 4(a)

(ii) What does the writer of Source A mean by the words 'there should be no parley'? 4(a)

(iii) What do you think the pressure was that Baldwin was said to be under in Source **A**? Source **B** will give you a clue.   4(a, c)

(b) (i) What do you think the writer of Source **B** means by the words 'Diehard influences'?   1, 4(a)

(ii) How might Source **B** be said to disagree with Source **A** on the point about pressure being put on Baldwin?   4(a, c)

(iii) What evidence is there in Source **D** to support the statement in Source **A** that Baldwin was 'clear and decisive . . . he didn't waffle'?   4(a, c)

(iv) What evidence is there in Source **D** to support the claim in Source **B** that Baldwin had a 'reputation for fair dealing'?   4(a, c)

(c) (i) In what ways does Source **C** disagree with Sources **A**, **B** and **D** about Baldwin and the strike?   4(a, c)

(ii) From the evidence of these extracts and your own knowledge, can you suggest any reasons why the writer of Source **C** should disagree with the other three?   1, 2, 4(a, b, c)

(iii) From the evidence of Sources **A**, **B**, **C** and **D**, how well did Baldwin handle the General Strike?   4(a, c)

(d) (i) According to Source **D**, how did Baldwin try to settle the coal strike after the General Strike was called off?   4(a)

(ii) From the evidence of Source **D**, why did his attempt fail?   4(a)

(iii) How does Source **E** differ from Source **D** in its explanation of why Baldwin failed to end the coal strike?   4(a, c)

(iv) Which explanation – Source **D** or **E** – does Source **F** support?   4(a, c)

(e) (i) Why do the writers of Sources **F** and **G** think the failure of the General Strike was a setback for the trade union and Labour movement?   4(a, c)

(ii) What reasons does the writer of Source **H** give for not regarding the General Strike as a failure?   4(a)

(iii) What reasons can you suggest as to why the writer of Source **H** should disagree with the writers of Sources **F** and **G**?   4(a, b, c)

(f) What are the strengths and weaknesses of each of the Sources **A**, **B**, **C**, **F**, **G** and **H** for the historian trying to understand the General Strike and its aftermath?   4(a, b)

(g) Using the evidence of the Sources and your own knowledge, explain whether you agree or disagree with the opening statement in Source **H** – 'I do not regard the General Strike as a failure'.   1, 2, 4(a, c)

2. Conservative Achievements

Study Sources **A** to **C** and then answer the questions which follow.

Source A: speech by Neville Chamberlain, Minister of Health, 1925.

> The very title of this bill [Widows, Orphans and Old Age Contributory Pensions Bill] conjures up at once scenes of tragedy and of pathos; everyone of us can recall the longing we had to relieve sufferings that were so acute and so unnecessary . . . Our policy is to use the great resources of the State, not for the distribution of indiscriminate free gifts, but to help those who have the will and desire to raise themselves to higher and better things.
>
> Source: quoted in K. Feiling, *The Life of Neville Chamberlain*, Macmillan, 1947 (adapted extracts).

Source B: information from a modern historian.

> The [Conservative] government's achievements were many and decisive. It restored the gold standard and de-rated industry, destroyed *Poplarism*, and broke the general strike. Its Local Government Act was the greatest administrative reform since Gladstone's day, and it vastly extended social insurance. At the Imperial Conference of 1926 it laid down a new doctrine for the Empire; . . . the peace of Locarno and the Kellogg Pact all encouraged men to hope that peace would be preserved . . . In this struggling for a better world, *Neville Chamberlain's achievement stands out massive and unquestioned.*
>
> Source: K. Feiling, *The Life of Neville Chamberlain*, Macmillan, 1947 (adapted extracts).

Source C: another modern view.

> Neville Chamberlain left a lasting mark on British life as Minister of Health. He had long experience of local government. Lloyd George described him, not unfairly, as a 'good mayor of Birmingham in an off-year'. He had efficiency, clarity, resolution, spoiled only by his unsympathetic manner. He sounded mean even when he was conferring benefits. It was typical of him that he announced twenty-five bills to the cabinet when he took office; typical also that he carried through twenty-one. His first target was 'Poplarism' – the defiant way in which councils with Labour majorities paid higher wages and rates of relief than those approved by the Ministry of Health, often with borrowed money. In July 1926 an act gave the Minister of Health power to over-rule such councils . . . Labour was deeply stirred and Chamberlain was branded as the enemy of the poor.
>
> Source: A. J. P. Taylor, *English History 1914-45*, Oxford, 1965 (adapted extracts).

(a) (i) Why does Chamberlain (Source **A**) think the title of the bill 'conjures up . . . scenes of tragedy and pathos'?   **1, 3, 4(a)**

    (ii) Explain in your own words the main idea which Chamberlain is putting forward in this speech.   **4(a)**

(b) (i) Using the information in Source **C**, explain what is meant by the word 'Poplarism' referred to in Source **B**.   **4(a, c)**

    (ii) Explain why, according to Source **C**, 'Poplarism' was seen to be a problem.   **4(a)**

   (iii) According to Source **C**, how did Neville Chamberlain deal with 'Poplarism'?   **4(a)**

   (iv) From the evidence of the Sources, why did Labour think Chamberlain was an 'enemy of the poor'?   **4(a, c)**

    (v) What evidence is there in the Sources to suggest that this view of Chamberlain was unfair?   **4(a, c)**

(c) (i) In what ways do Sources **B** and **C** seem to differ in their opinion of Chamberlain's achievements?   **4(a, c)**

    (ii) From the evidence of Source **C**, would you say that the writer admires Chamberlain or not? Explain your answer fully.   **4(a, b)**

   (iii) What evidence can you find in Source **B** to suggest that the writer might have Conservative sympathies?   **4(a, b)**

(d) (i) Make a list of the main changes introduced by the Local Government Act mentioned in Source **B**.   **1, 2**

    (ii) Explain why the Labour Party objected to some of these changes.   **1, 2**

(e) (i) In what ways did the Conservative government 'vastly [extend] social insurance', as Source **B** puts it?   **1, 2**

    (ii) What was the 'new doctrine for the Empire' laid down in 1926?   **1, 2**

(f) (i) What were the main points of the Locarno agreement and the Kellogg Pact?   **1, 2**

    (ii) To what extent were these two agreements successful?   **1, 2**

(g) Using the evidence of the Sources and your own knowledge, explain whether you agree or disagree with the statement at the end of Source **B**, that 'Neville Chamberlain's achievement stands out massive and unquestioned'.   **1, 2, 4(c)**

3. The following were important during the Conservative government of 1924–29:

Locarno Treaties, 1925; Samuel Report, 1926; Trade Disputes Act, 1927; Local Government Act, 1929.

(a) For each one explain:

    (i) the main points agreed, suggested or introduced;

   (ii) what important results came from it.

(b) Explain why, in spite of its achievements, the Conservative Party lost the General Election of 1929. 1, 2

4. The following headline appeared in the *Daily Chronicle* on 13 May 1926:

THE GENERAL STRIKE CANCELLED

"VICTORY · FOR COMMON SENSE."

National Rejoicing Over the Dramatic Decision.

Describe and explain the feelings and reactions of each of the following on hearing the news:

(a) a supporter of Stanley Baldwin and the Conservative government;

(b) a member of the TUC;

(c) a miner. 1, 2, 3

CHAPTER 24

THE SECOND LABOUR GOVERNMENT (1929–31), THE WORLD ECONOMIC CRISIS AND ITS AFTERMATH

SUMMARY OF EVENTS

Again Labour was in a minority, though this time the government was slightly stronger since Labour was the largest single party. MacDonald did not attempt to combine the premiership with the Foreign Office, which went to Arthur Henderson. The cabinet was again solidly moderate, with a fair sprinkling of ex-Liberals; it contained one left-winger, George Lansbury, in a minor post, and, for the first time ever in Britain, a woman, Margaret Bondfield, who became Minister of Labour.

The government's main achievements were in foreign affairs, but its promise was blighted by the *World Economic Crisis (the Great Depression)* which began with the *Wall Street Crash*, a dramatic fall in share prices on the New York Stock Exchange (October 1929). By May 1931 the unemployment figure in Britain had risen to 2.5 million and there was a financial crisis. The Labour cabinet could not agree on what measures to adopt, and consequently MacDonald handed in the government's resignation (August). However, he himself stayed on as Prime Minister of a coalition government of Labour, Conservative and Liberal MPs, to the intense fury of the majority of the Labour movement, which accused MacDonald of betraying the party. The new *National Government* as it was called, introduced emergency measures and then won an overwhelming victory in a general election held in October 1931. After more emergency measures, the country began to recover gradually from the worst effects of the depression, though unemployment remained a serious problem in certain areas.

MacDonald remained Prime Minister until his retirement in June 1935, when Baldwin took over. The following November the National Government won another election, which proved to be the last one until July 1945. Baldwin retired in May 1937, and Neville Chamberlain was Prime Minister until May 1940 when he was replaced by Winston Churchill. The main issues of these last years were the question of rearmament in face of the worsening international situation (see Section 26.2 and 3) and the abdication crisis of 1936.

24.1 LABOUR POLICIES AT HOME AND ABROAD

(a) **Domestic achievements** included *the Housing Act of 1930*, the work of Arthur Greenwood, the Minister of Health; this renewed the government subsidy for council house building and organised the speeding up of slum clearance. The Act was suspended during the financial crises of 1931-4, but then the National Government began to apply it later in 1934 and by 1939 vast slum areas had been cleared. *The Coal Mines Act (1930)* reduced the miners' working day from eight hours to seven and a half. But there was little else to show: an attempt to repeal parts of the 1927 *Trade Disputes Act* (see Section 23.3(d)) was defeated by the Liberals and an Education Bill to raise the school-leaving age to 15 was rejected by the House of Lords, showing its remaining teeth again after slumbering for five years.

(b) Overseas affairs

(i) Henderson was anxious to continue Britain's conciliatory attitude towards Germany and was involved in *the Young Plan* (1929). This aimed to settle the remaining problem of reparations – the Dawes Plan had left uncertain the total amount payable. The French were willing to compromise, and a committee chaired by an American banker, Owen Young, decided to reduce reparations from £6600 million to £2000 million, to be paid on a graded scale over the next 59 years. This was the figure that Keynes had urged at Versailles, and its acceptance ten years later was an admission of error by the Allies. The plan was welcomed in Germany, as was the withdrawal of Allied troops from the Rhineland five years ahead of schedule, at Henderson's suggestion. Unfortunately there was hardly time to put the Young Plan into operation before a series of events following in rapid succession destroyed the fragile harmony of Locarno: the death of Stresemann (October 1929) removed one of the outstanding 'men of Locarno'; the Wall Street Crash in the same month soon developed into the Great Depression, bringing mass unemployment in Germany. Hopes of peace and tranquillity were kept alive by the Lausanne Conference (1932) at which Britain and France released Germany from most of her remaining reparations payments. However, in January 1933 Hitler became German Chancellor and after that, international tension mounted.

(ii) Relations with Russia improved again when the Labour government, encouraged by the new pro-western Foreign Minister, Maxim Litvinov, resumed diplomatic relations in 1929 and signed another trade agreement the following year; but the improvement was only short-lived since the Conservative-dominated National government cancelled the trade agreement in 1932.

(iii) Henderson was an enthusiastic supporter of the League of Nations and was greatly respected by foreign governments. He worked unceasingly for disarmament and was rewarded by being chosen as president of the World Disarmament Conference which was planned to open at Geneva in 1932. Bitter disappointment was to follow though: by the time the conference met, Henderson was out of office, and the proceedings ended in failure when the Germans walked out (October 1933).

(iv) MacDonald scored a personal triumph with his visit to the USA (1929) which did much to heal the rift caused by disagreements over Britain's war debts to the USA. MacDonald followed this up by organising a conference in London (1930) attended also by the Japanese, at which the three states reaffirmed the 5 : 5 : 3 ratio of cruisers, destroyers and submarines agreed at an earlier conference in Washington (1921-2). This was successful in re-establishing friendship between USA and Britain, although the Japanese soon exceeded their limits.

Less successful were the Labour government's attempts to deal with the problems in India (see Section 25.3), Palestine (see Section 25.4) and Egypt. Most serious of all were the economic problems which led to the downfall of the government.

24.2 SHOW HOW THE ECONOMIC CRISIS BROUGHT DOWN THE LABOUR GOVERNMENT IN 1931

It was the financial crisis resulting from the Great Depression which caused the government's resignation.

(a) Why was there an economic crisis?

(i) The root of the problem was that American industrialists, encouraged by high profits and helped by increased mechanisation, were producing too many goods for the home market to absorb, at a time when foreign countries were increasingly reluctant to buy American goods. This was partly because the Americans had introduced tariffs to keep foreign goods out, which prevented European states from making the profits they needed, both to buy American goods and to pay their war debts to the USA. The result was a general stagnation of trade which began to show itself during 1929 and which caused some of the better informed investors to sell their shares. Confidence in the future was shaken, and in a panic, thousands more investors rushed to sell their shares; with confidence shaken, very few people were prepared to buy them, and share prices tumbled on the New York Stock

Exchange in Wall Street. One particularly bad day was 24 October 1929 – Black Thursday – when nearly 13 million shares were 'dumped' on the stock market at depressingly low prices. This was the so-called *Wall Street Crash* which ruined millions of investors and almost half the country's banks. As the demand for goods of all types fell away, men were laid off and factories closed. By 1933 almost 14 million Americans were out of work.

(ii) The crisis in the USA affected most European countries. Europe's prosperity since 1924 (particularly in Germany) had much to do with American loans under the Dawes Plan, which enabled Germany to revive her industries and pay reparations to Britain, France, Belgium and Italy. This in turn enabled these countries to pay their war debts to the USA and thus Europe and America were closely linked in a circle of loans and repayments. Disaster in one part of the circle inevitably had repercussions elsewhere. The USA ceased to import goods from Europe, stopped all further loans to Germany and called in the short-term loans already made. The effects were most serious in Germany, where in 1931 unemployment was approaching four million, but the effects in Britain were dramatic enough.

(b) Unemployment in Britain, already standing at over a million, shot up to 2.5 million by December 1930 and the government took no action to reduce it. There was no shortage of advice: economic radicals among both Labour and Liberal supporters proposed that the government should create jobs by spending money. *Sir Oswald Mosley* (Labour's Chancellor of the Duchy of Lancaster) produced a memorandum, after consultations with *J. M. Keynes*, suggesting import restrictions, subsidies for farmers (to reduce food imports), bulk purchase from the Dominions, government control of banks to ensure that industry was allowed more credit (to enable new industries to expand), old age pensions at 60 and the school leaving age at 15 (instead of 14); the last two measures would be expensive, but would make an immediate impact on unemployment. *Lloyd George urged the Liberal programme* of public works – town-planning and road-building. But MacDonald and Snowden were far too cautious; they ignored all advice, and cut expenditure as much as possible, hoping that trade would revive. The government's minority position was no excuse for its inaction, since the Liberals would have voted for a big programme of government investment to create jobs. There was much support within the Labour Party for Mosley, but when the leaders rejected his proposals, he left Labour and launched the New Party. This had no success and Mosley later founded the British Fascist Party.

(c) Payment of unemployment benefit was placing a severe strain on the government's finances, with nothing to show for it. A committee was appointed under *Sir George May* to investigate national expenditure; its report published in July 1931 was an extremely gloomy document. It forecast that by April 1932 there would be a government deficit of

£120 million. To stave off the crisis it proposed a general reduction of salaries in public sector jobs – i.e. members of the armed forces, civil servants, judges and police. Teachers were singled out for the largest cut of all – 20 per cent, and the report recommended that unemployment benefit should be cut by the same amount. This caused foreign investors to conclude that Britain must be on the verge of bankruptcy and they rushed to withdraw gold, plunging the country into a deeper financial crisis. The Bank of England informed the government that immediate economies were needed to restore foreign confidence, while French and American bankers demanded economies before further loans could be made. MacDonald and Snowden were prepared to implement the May Report's recommendations though with only a 10 per cent reduction in unemployment benefit. However, even this was too much for some of their colleagues, and after a fierce argument in cabinet, 10 out of the 21 members would not agree to any cut in benefit.

MacDonald claimed that there was nothing else for it but to resign; he handed in the government's resignation, but to the amazement of almost the whole of the Labour party he stayed on as Prime Minister of what was called a National government with a cabinet consisting of Conservatives, Liberals and just three other Labour men (24 August 1931).

(d) Did MacDonald betray his party? The majority of the party was furious with MacDonald and condemned him as a traitor to the Labour movement. They accused him of being vain, ambitious and out of touch with the grass-roots of the party, which was true, and claimed that he had been planning to ditch the party for some time, so that he could remain in power. There is no solid evidence to support this view; David Marquand believes that George V and Baldwin persuaded MacDonald to stay on as Prime Minister of an all-party government as the best way of restoring confidence and avoiding a general election. Robert Skidelsky suggests that MacDonald's real betrayal of the party occurred not in August 1931, but in the earlier part of his government, when he ignored advice and failed to take actions which might have avoided the crisis of 1931.

24.3 THE NATIONAL GOVERNMENT AND ITS ATTEMPTS TO PROMOTE RECOVERY

The new government had a small cabinet of only 10 – four Labour (MacDonald, Snowden, Thomas and Lord Sankey), four Conservatives (Baldwin, Neville Chamberlain, Sir Samuel Hoare and Sir Philip Cunliffe-Lister) and two Liberals (Sir Herbert Samuel and Lord Reading).

(a) Emergency measures were introduced in Snowden's budget which implemented much of the May Report to try and restore confidence. These included raising income tax from 4*s*. 6*d*. to 5*s*. in the pound, and reducing salaries of public employees and unemployment benefits by 10 per cent. These did not produce the desired effect and foreigners continued to withdraw funds from Britain. Nor was the situation helped by the *Invergordon Mutiny* (September 1931) when naval crews protested against proposed salary cuts, though this soon petered out when the government assured them that cuts would not exceed 10 per cent. In the end the government went off the gold standard, so that the value of the pound fell by about one-quarter on the foreign exchanges. Though this might have been expected to help British trade by making exports cheaper, there was no immediate revival; unemployment continued to rise, reaching a peak in January 1933 at 2.98 million. Soon after Snowden's budget, MacDonald appealed to the country for 'a doctor's mandate' to do whatever was necessary for recovery, including the introduction of tariffs. In the election of October 1931 the National Government won a landslide victory with 521 MPs; Labour was reduced to 52, probably because the voters blamed it for the depression, and because Snowden, in a vindictive broadcast, described its programme as 'Bolshevism run mad'. For the Liberals the election was a total disaster: they were now split into three groups – 35 MPs led by Sir John Simon supported the National Government, 33 led by Sir Herbert Samuel remained independent, and the four Lloyd George Liberals were pro-Labour. Although MacDonald was Prime Minister, it was in effect a thinly disguised Conservative government, since 473 of his supporters were Conservatives, and Neville Chamberlain became Chancellor of the Exchequer in place of Snowden who retired to the Lords.

(b) Further government action. Free trade was abandoned by Neville Chamberlain's *Import Duties Act of 1932*, placing a 10 per cent duty on most imports, except those from the empire. This, as well as increasing sales of British goods at home, brought in extra revenue, so that Chamberlain was able to avoid raising the income tax again. However, an attempt at the Ottawa Conference to develop Empire trade met with little success (see Section 25.1(c)). Defence expenditure and interest on war loans were reduced. Some attempt was made to reorganise iron and steel, shipbuilding, textiles and coal, and to persuade new industry to move into areas of high unemployment, though without much success (see next Section 24.4(e)). Remaining off the gold standard made British goods cheaper abroad and led to an increase in exports. Bank rate was reduced from 6 per cent to 2 per cent mainly to reduce debt charges; however, many local authorities took advantage of low interest rates to borrow money for house building. This provided extra jobs not only for builders but for all the allied trades, including gas and electricity.

These measures helped to stabilise the financial situation and to increase sales at home and abroad, though it can be argued that foreign manufacturers, deprived of markets in Britain by the new import duties, became competitors in export markets. It has to be emphasised too that *the recovery was probably due more to favourable circumstances than to the efforts of the National Government.*

(c) **Favourable circumstances.** These would probably have occurred whatever action the government had chosen to take:

(i) As prices of all products (both British and imported) fell during the depression, the cost of living also fell and, even with wage reductions, there was an increase in real wages (what one could actually buy with the cash available).

(ii) This enabled people to spend their extra cash on British consumer goods and even on luxuries such as radios and holidays, which stimulated the creation of jobs.

Unemployment fell gradually to two million in 1935 which encouraged Baldwin to hold an election in November of that year. This brought another convincing victory for the National Government with 427 seats; Labour recovered to 154 but the independent Liberals slumped to only 20.

(d) **Signs of prosperity.** As the recovery continued after 1935, the majority of the population began to enjoy a higher standard of living than ever before. New council houses were available and the sales of consumer goods increased rapidly – radios, electric cookers, refrigerators, modern furniture and telephones. Some workers were able to afford an Austin or Morris car – the number of private cars registered doubled between 1930 and 1939. Cinemas and dancehalls were packed and the annual holiday at the seaside became a national institution; the first Butlin's holiday camp was opened at Skegness in 1937. Higher real wages also meant an improvement in diet – more fresh fruit, vegetables and dairy produce were eaten, helping to improve the health of the nation.

One disturbing fact that emerged was that though Britain seemed to have recovered from the depression by 1938, unemployment would not go away completely. This was a problem quite separate from the World Economic Crisis, and it needs to be examined separately.

24.4 UNEMPLOYMENT IN THE 1930s

(a) Unemployment was not a general phenomenon during the 1930s; it was confined to certain trades and certain areas. The total unemployed in Britain were (in millions):

1927 = 1.1	1931 = 2.7	1935 = 2.0
1928 = 1.3	1932 = 2.8	1936 = 1.7
1929 = 1.2	1933 = 2.5	1937 = 1.4
1930 = 1.9	1934 = 2.1	1938 = 1.9

The main industries affected were shipbuilding (30.6 per cent of workers in that industry were unemployed in 1936), steel, coal-mining (25 per cent), shipping (22.3 per cent) and textiles (13.2 per cent). The areas where these industries were situated were greatly depressed; they included the whole of Scotland, the Tyne-Tees area, Cumberland, Lancashire, and also Northern Ireland and South Wales. In some towns the individual figures were startling: Jarrow had 68 per cent of its total workforce unemployed in 1934; in Merthyr Tydfil the figure was 62 per cent, while in St Albans at the same time it was only 3.9 per cent. The Midlands and the South were much better off because they had new industries such as motor cars, aircraft and chemicals.

(b) The effects of long-term unemployment could be devastating. In areas of high unemployment, shops and other businesses were forced to close down, and places like Jarrow and Merthyr became like ghost towns. Rowntree carried out another survey in York, discovering that 31.1 per cent of working-class families were living in serious poverty. In Stockton-on-Tees the average income of families where the wage-earner was unemployed was less than £1.50 a week, and clearly unemployment benefit was insufficient. Men had to resort to casual labour which brought very poor reward; families fell into debt and many were evicted for non-payment of rent. Diet suffered and health deteriorated. This was reflected in the infant mortality rate which in 1935 in the South was 42 per 1000 live births, while in South Wales it was 63 and in Durham and Northumberland it was 76. In Jarrow it was as high as 114. There was an increase in diseases such as rickets and anaemia, and prolonged unemployment could cause nervous depression and mental disorders.

(c) Why was unemployment so persistent in the depressed areas?

(i) They contained the older export industries - coal, textiles, shipbuilding, and iron and steel - which had flourished until the 1880s but had then begun to decline. Their decline was accelerated after the First World War because many countries which found alternative sources of supply during the war did not resume buying British after 1918. They suffered fierce competition from more highly mechanised and more efficient foreign industries and cheaper foreign goods, such as Japanese and east European textiles; India, the main British market for textiles before the war, was rapidly developing her own industry. Coal exports were badly hit by cheap coal from Germany, Poland, Holland, Spain and the Far East. In any case the world demand for coal was decreasing as oil, gas and electricity came into wider use. By 1939 over half the world's merchant ships used oil instead of coal. More efficient rival shipyards had opened in the USA, Japan, Holland and Scandinavia. Britain's competitiveness was further reduced when foreign countries began to raise tariff barriers to protect their home industries; some governments began to subsidise their industries - particularly shipbuilding - to enable them to compete more successfully. Yet in Britain very little attempt was made to modernise these ailing industries. There were far too many small coal-mines which were expensive to operate and therefore uncompetitive; the cotton industry was slow to adopt automatic looms and electric power, and

illus 24.1   *A hunger march to London in 1932*

unfortunately the more profits fell, the less cash was available for re-investment in new techniques and equipment. Worse still was that foreign rivals were gaining a foothold in the British market; there were textiles from India, as well as foreign ships and iron and steel. These factors caused a steady growth of unemployment - known as *structural unemployment* - throughout the 1920s, before the impact of the Great Depression.

(ii) The World Economic Crisis worsened the situation in the depressed areas and caused unemployment in other areas. This is known as *cyclical unemployment*, since it was caused by the operation of the *trade cycle* - trade flows in a fairly regular cycle of a boom followed by a slump which gradually develops into another boom.

(iii) It is also argued, as we saw earlier, that Chamberlain's import duties worsened the export position of the old industries still further.

(iv) The depressed areas had concentrated exclusively on the old industries so that there was no alternative employment to be had, and since the majority of unemployed could not afford to move elsewhere, they had to stay put.

(d) Suggested remedies for unemployment

(i) *J. M. Keynes* (the Liberal economist) suggested that the government should spend its way out of the depression by investing in order to stimulate new industries, while at the same time organising the contraction of the declining industries. The government should also give financial aid to enable people to move out of depressed areas.

(ii) *'Peace and Reconstruction'*, a document produced in 1935 by a group of young Conservative MPs led by *Harold Macmillan* (MP for Stockton-on-Tees) set out detailed schemes such as road-building, electrification, housing and national parks which could be organised by government and local authority expenditure, using cash which would have been spent on unemployment benefit.

(iii) *Labour's solution* was explained in a pamphlet called *'The Theory and Practice of Socialism'* (1936) written by *John Strachey*. He argued that boom, overproduction and slump were inevitable in an uncontrolled capitalist economy. What was needed was the *controlled economy* which nationalisation would provide. Under state control, production could be limited to need, and unemployment could be eliminated.

(e) Government action to deal with unemployment.
Like the Labour government before it, the National government ignored most of the advice offered. Its response was unimaginative and its measures failed to get to the root of the problem.

(i) *The Unemployment Act (1934)* set up the National Unemployment Assistance Board whose branches in every part of the country would pay out benefit after an unemployed man ran out of the normal period of insurance benefit. The way in which this act was applied

caused great bitterness among the unemployed since it was based on the *'means test'* introduced in 1931. This took into account the total family income and savings of an unemployed man when assessing the amount of relief he should receive, and caused demoralisation when
. it appeared that the careful and thrifty were being penalised.

(ii) *The Special Areas Act (1934)* appointed two unpaid commissioners and provided them with £2 million to try and revive Scotland, west Cumberland, Tyneside and South Wales. This had little effect because employers could not be compelled to move into the depressed areas. Later the government offered rates, rent and income tax remission to encourage firms to move in, which resulted in the setting up of trading estates such as the ones at Treforest (South Wales), North Hillington and Larkhall (near Glasgow); but these provided only a few thousand jobs, many of them for women.

(iii) The Bank Rate reduction mentioned in the previous section helped the housing boom and encouraged local authorities to embark on road-building. But the government partially defeated its own ends by continually warning local authorities to economise, revealing that it only imperfectly understood the workings of economics.

(iv) An attempt was made to revive the steel industry by imposing a tariff on foreign steel and setting up the British Iron and Steel Federation. Government pressure resulted in the building of two new steel works at Ebbw Vale and Corby, but the federation was bitterly criticised for refusing to allow one to be built at Jarrow. However, the steel industry was showing signs of revival.

(v) Loans were provided to encourage shipbuilding, including the completion of the *Queen Mary*.

(vi) From 1936 onwards the rearmament programme helped in the creation of extra jobs.

Although by the end of 1937 total unemployment had fallen to 1.4 million, there had been little improvement in the depressed areas where most of the 1.4 million were concentrated. In spite of plenty of available advice the government had failed to produce any positive strategy for curing long-term unemployment in these areas, largely because it refused to accept that the problem could be solved.

24.5 BALDWIN AND THE ABDICATION CRISIS, 1936

(a) George V died in January 1936 and was succeeded by his 41-year-old unmarried son, Edward VIII. The new king was popular and unconventional and seemed genuinely to care about the problems and hardships of his people. In November he paid a visit to some of the South Wales mining valleys where unemployment was still high. Appalled by the poverty, he is reported to have said, 'terrible, terrible, something will be done about this'.

(b) Edward had fallen in love with Wallis Simpson, an American lady who had been divorced from her first husband and was now married to a London stockbroker. In October 1936 Mrs Simpson was granted a divorce from her second husband, and Edward intended to marry her; however, the story was not mentioned in the British press, and the general public knew nothing about it.

(c) Baldwin decided, for once, that decisive action was needed. He pointed out to Edward that his marriage to a twice divorced American lady would not be popular with the government or the British people, and tried to dissuade him from going ahead. There was the prospect of a serious constitutional crisis if Edward acted against his cabinet's wishes, since presumably Baldwin would resign and no other party leader would serve as Prime Minister under Edward. It was an agonising dilemma for the king, particularly when the whole affair was reported in the papers on 3 December. There was some support for him in the country; many people, including Churchill and Mosley, and the powerful newspaper owners, Beaverbrook and Rothermere, believed that he ought to be allowed to marry whoever he wanted. But the majority opinion supported Baldwin and the government; the Archbishop of Canterbury, Dr Lang, was against the marriage on the grounds that the king, as Head of the Church of England, ought not to marry a divorcee. *The Times* announced self-righteously that the monarchy would be fatally weakened if 'private inclination were to come into open conflict with public duty and be allowed to prevail'.

(d) Edward hoped that an arrangement could be made allowing Mrs Simpson to marry him and remain a private citizen, without becoming Queen (a morganatic marriage). When the cabinet refused to agree to this, Edward decided that he must abdicate the throne. This he did on 11 December, and was succeeded by his brother George VI. He took the title Duke of Windsor and married Mrs Simpson the following year. The Windsors spent most of their married life in exile from Britain.

(e) It was generally agreed that Baldwin had handled the situation well, and his popularity, which had waned considerably earlier in 1936 at the time of his limp conduct of foreign affairs (see Section 26.2(d) and (e)) was suddenly restored. He had avoided an awkward constitutional crisis, saved the monarchy from a damaging controversy and secured the smooth succession of George VI and his wife, Queen Elizabeth, both of whom became popular with the public. Baldwin retired to the House of Lords soon after the coronation in May 1938. Before long, however, his reputation lay in ruins: when the Second World War started (September 1939), Baldwin was blamed for having left Britain with inadequate defences.

QUESTIONS

1. Formation of the National Government, August 1931
Study Sources **A** to **F** and then answer the questions which follow.

Source A: from *The Times*, Tuesday 25 August 1931.

> The Prime Minister yesterday handed in the resignation of the Government to the King who entrusted Mr. MacDonald with the task of forming a National Government for the sole purpose of meeting the present financial emergency . . . All concerned are to be warmly congratulated on this result, so fully in accord with the patriotic spirit which has inspired a week's most anxious negotiations . . . A General Election has been averted. That in itself is a great thing gained, for a General Election now would have been disastrous, whatever its result. The country would have been for weeks without an effective government at a time when it never needed to be more governed. And for this the public has no-one to thank more sincerely than the King himself.

> Source: *The Times*, 25 August 1931 (adapted extracts).

Source B: the account by Philip Snowden, Chancellor of the Exchequer in the Labour Government of 1929–31.

> Mr. MacDonald at the palace meeting on the Monday morning agreed to the formation of a National Government, with himself as Prime Minister, without a word of previous consultation with any of his Labour colleagues . . . When the Labour Cabinet as a whole refused to agree to a reduction of Unemployment pay, Mr. Macdonald assumed too readily that this involved the resignation of his government. He neither showed nor expressed any grief at this regrettable development. On the contrary, he set about the formation of the National Government with an enthusiasm which showed that the adventure was highly agreeable to him . . . A meeting of the Parliamentary Labour Party was held on August 28th. Mr. MacDonald did not attend it, nor did he send any message or appeal. This was naturally taken as an indication that he had finally separated himself from the Party and did not want its support . . . Taking all these things together, I think they give ground for the suspicion that *Mr. MacDonald deliberately planned the scheme of a National Government*, which would at the same time enable him to retain the position of Prime Minister and to associate with political colleagues with whom he was more in sympathy than he had ever been with his Labour colleagues.

Source: P. Snowden, *Autobiography*, Nicolson & Watson, 1934 (adapted extracts).

Source C: memoirs of Emmanuel Shinwell, a junior minister in the 1929–31 Labour government.

I prefer to take a tolerant view of MacDonald's activities at this time. On the personal plane it must be remembered that MacDonald was 65 and appeared much older . . . What I am bound to say is that MacDonald believed he was right. He felt he was doing his duty on behalf of the nation; this conviction was the motive rather than any personal ambition to hold on to office. What hurt him was that through his actions he had been misunderstood and had lost the support and friendship of people like myself who had previously stood by him . . .

To dismiss MacDonald as a traitor is nonsense. His contribution in the early years was of enormous value. There has probably never been an orator with such natural magnetism in the party's history.

Source: E. Shinwell, *I've Lived Through it All*, Gollancz, 1973 and *Conflict without Malice*, Odhams, 1955 (adapted extracts).

Source D: memoirs of Clement Attlee, another junior minister in the 1929–31 Labour government.

In the old days I had looked up to him [MacDonald] as a great leader. He had a fine presence and great oratorical power. The unpopular line which he took during the First World War seemed to mark him as a man of character. I had not appreciated his defects until he took office a second time. I then realised his reluctance to take positive action and noted with dismay his increasing vanity and snobbery. His habit of telling me, a junior Minister, the poor opinion he had of all his Cabinet colleagues, made an unpleasant impression. I had not, however, expected that he would carry out *the greatest betrayal in the political history of this country*.

Source: Earl Attlee, *As It Happened*, Heinemann, 1954 (adapted extracts).

Source E: information from a modern historian.

There can be no doubt that MacDonald truly intended to resign. For the past two days he had been saying so to all who would listen. He telephoned his son Malcolm with the message on both Saturday and Sunday. At Buckingham Palace on Sunday morning he declared that he had no other course, and afterwards wrote in his diary: 'I commit political suicide to save the crisis!' *Something made him change his mind*; whatever else persuaded MacDonald to head a National Government, it was not premeditated ambition.

Source: K. Rose, *King George V*, Weidenfeld & Nicolson, 1983 (adapted extracts).

Source F: the opinion of another modern historian.

Three times the King urged MacDonald to stay on as Prime Minister, the third time in language that suggested that resignation would be tantamount to desertion. It is clear from his diary that MacDonald attached great value to the King's good opinion. Most people need someone to talk to in moments of crisis . . . MacDonald had no wife and no close friend either . . . the king's gruff exhortations had a special importance . . . they were expressed in terms to which MacDonald was specially likely to respond – patriotism, duty, self-respect and the implied suggestion that he would be running away from a post of danger if he resigned . . .

Source: D. Marquand, *Ramsay MacDonald*, Jonathan Cape, 1977 (adapted extracts).

(a) (i) Who was the Prime Minister referred to at the beginning of Source **A**, who handed his government's resignation to the King? **4(a)**

(ii) Which party – Conservative, Liberal or Labour – did this government consist of? **4(a)**

(iii) On what date did this government resign? **4(a)**

(iv) Which king was the resignation handed to? **4(a)**

(b) (i) What evidence in Source **A** tells you that *The Times* approved of the formation of the National Government? **4(a)**

(ii) Why did *The Times* reporter think it was a good idea? **4(a)**

(c) (i) According to Source **B**, what convinced MacDonald that his government must resign? **4(a)**

(ii) What reasons does Snowden give (Source **B**) for thinking that MacDonald 'deliberately planned the scheme of a National Government'? **4(a)**

(iii) What does he think were MacDonald's motives for this action? **4(a)**

(d) (i) In what ways do Shinwell (Source **C**) and Snowden (Source **B**) differ in their opinions of MacDonald's motives for forming the National Government? **4(a, c)**

(ii) In Source **D**, what does Attlee mean by the words 'the greatest betrayal in the political history of this country'? **1, 2, 4(a)**

(iii) Do you think Attlee (Source **D**) agrees with Shinwell (Source **C**) or Snowden (Source **B**) about MacDonald's motives? Explain your answer fully. **4(a, b, c)**

(iv) In what ways do Shinwell (Source **C**) and Attlee (Source **D**) agree in their attitudes towards MacDonald? **4(a, b, c)**

(v) In what ways do they disagree in their attitudes towards MacDonald? **4(a, b, c)**

(vi) *The Times* (Source **A**) thinks the formation of the National Government was a good idea while Attlee (Source **D**) calls it a 'betrayal'. What reasons can you suggest for this difference of opinion? **4(a, b, c)**

(e) (i)   What evidence does Source **E** provide to back up the claim made in the first sentence (in italics)?   **4(a)**

    (ii)   According to Source **E**, 'Something made him change his mind'. From the evidence of Source **F**, explain in your own words what that 'Something' was.   **4(a, c)**

(f)   From the evidence of all the extracts and your own knowledge, which of the three Sources written by Labour politicians (**B, C** and **D**) is the most reliable? Explain your answer fully.

                                                        4(a, b, c)

2. Unemployment in the 1930s
Read the extract and then answer the questions which follow.

Report of the Royal Commission on Unemployment Insurance, June 1931.

The causes of the depression in the industries of exceptional unemployment are easy to understand. These industries fall into three broad classes which, to some extent, overlap. There is first, the class of industry which is still suffering from a war-time expansion in excess of normal peace-time requirements . . . In this class fall iron and steel, shipbuilding, and to some extent coalmining. Second, the class of industry that before the war was dependent to a great extent on exports, and that has suffered since the war a loss of part of its overseas markets, coupled in some cases with an invasion by imports of its home market . . . This accounts for the exceptional unemployment in the textile and coalmining industries. Third, a class of industries which has been expanding rather than contracting, and in which employment is almost as much a matter of internal organisation as of bad trade. To this class belong building, docks and road transport . . . The indications are that unemployment will not fall during the next few months and may reach 2,500,000. At this rate the unemployed will be drawing out of the Unemployment Fund more than two and a half times the amount paid in contributions by employers and workers We recommend:

(1) A limit upon the period for which benefit may be paid of 26 weeks within a period of 12 months.
(2) An increase in the weekly rates of contributions by worker, employer and Exchequer.

Source: quoted in J. H. Bettey (ed.), *English Historical Documents 1906-39*, Routledge & Kegan Paul, 1967 (adapted extracts).

(a) (i)   From the evidence of the extract, how many people might soon be unemployed?   **4(a)**

    (ii)   Was the Report correct in its prediction of this figure?   **1, 2**

    (iii)   According to the extract, why was unemployment high in the coalmining and textile industries?   **4(a)**

- (iv) Why was unemployment high among dockers and building workers? **4(a)**
- (v) What other causes, apart from those mentioned in the extract, contributed to unemployment in the 1930s? **1, 2, 4(a)**

(b) **(i)** Using the evidence in the extract, explain why the high level of unemployment was causing a financial problem for the government. **4(a)**

   (ii) The Commission was accused of being unsympathetic towards the unemployed. What evidence can you find in the extract to support this accusation? **4(a, b)**

(c) What remedies were suggested for unemployment by:

- (i) J. M. Keynes and the Liberals;
- (ii) Harold Macmillan and some Conservatives;
- (iii) John Strachey and some socialists. **1, 2**

(d) What were the social effects of long-term unemployment? **1, 2**

(e) What action did the National Governments take to deal with unemployment? **1, 2**

(f) How successful had this action been by 1938? **1, 2**

3. The National Government

(a) Explain briefly why a National Government was formed in 1931 with Ramsay MacDonald as Prime Minister.

(b) What emergency measures did the National Government take during August to October, to deal with the crisis?

(c) How successful were these measures?

(d) The economic situation gradually improved after 1932. Explain the part played in this recovery by:

- (i) government action such as the Import Duties Act of 1932;
- (ii) favourable circumstances. **1, 2**

4. It is October 1931 and you are standing as an Independent Labour candidate (i.e. not a supporter of MacDonald and the National Government) in the approaching General Election. Write a draft of your election address to be sent to all voters in your constituency. Among the points you can make are the following:

(a) Labour can govern successfully – mention achievements of 1929–30;

(b) Labour was unfortunate – world economic crisis was beyond its control;

(c)   your opinion about the row in the Labour cabinet over reducing unemployment benefit (August 1931);

(d)   why you think MacDonald acted wrongly in forming the National Government;

(e)   your criticisms of the National Government's emergency measures (August to October 1931) and Labour's alternative policies.   1, 2, 3

CHAPTER 25

BRITAIN AND THE

PROBLEMS OF EMPIRE

BETWEEN THE WARS

SUMMARY OF EVENTS

Britain had the largest Empire in the world; it included vast areas of Africa, Malaya, India, Burma, the West Indies, and the Arab territories of Iraq, Transjordan and Palestine, which had been acquired from Turkey as mandates at the end of the First World War. There was a special feature which no other Empire could boast - the white dominions - Canada, Australia, New Zealand and South Africa. After the First World War Britain was troubled in several parts of the Empire - India, Egypt and the Arab mandates - with the development of nationalist movements aiming at independence. The Irish did not wait for the end of the war - republicans staged the Easter Rising in 1916. Even the white dominions were unhappy about exactly what the term 'dominion status' meant, and pressed for a clear definition.

The attitude of British governments was that territories would be allowed to proceed to independence in gradual stages. Southern Ireland was granted dominion status in 1922, Egypt took steps towards independence in 1922 and 1936; and Iraq gained full independence in 1932. The Statute of Westminster (1931) satisfied the dominions about their relationship with Britain and saw the formation of the British Commonwealth; however, progress in India was far too gradual for the nationalists' liking, and their relationship with Britain was uneasy. It was only in 1947 that India was granted its independence.

25.1 BRITAIN AND HER RELATIONS WITH THE COMMONWEALTH

(a) Britain's white dominions, Canada, Australia and New Zealand, as well as South Africa, and the Irish Free State (since 1922), were already self-governing as far as internal affairs were concerned, but traditionally acted along with Britain for foreign policy, which was one of the reasons why they all fought on Britain's side in the First World War. By the end of the war a desire to run their own foreign affairs had developed, partly because the war had made them more aware of their importance as separate nations (together they had put over a million men in the field); in addition they were encouraged by Woodrow Wilson's support for the principle of national independence, and they were worried in case Britain should drag them into another war. Consequently Canada and South Africa refused to help Britain during the Chanak incident (see Section 22.1(b)(vii)) and they all refused to sign the treaties of Lausanne (1923) and Locarno (1925) (see Section 23.1(c)). South Africa in particular became increasingly hostile to Britain and seemed determined to leave the Empire. Clearly some initiative was needed, and happily for the future of the Commonwealth, as it was beginning to be called, this was taken at:

(b) The Imperial Conference of 1926. Under the chairmanship of Balfour, the former Conservative Prime Minister, the conference showed that Britain was prepared to conciliate the dominions. Balfour produced a famous formula which defined the dominions as free countries, equal to each other and to Britain, and in complete control of their own internal and foreign affairs; they were to be 'freely associated as members of the British Commonwealth of Nations'. This satisfied the dominions (even South Africa for the time being) and was passed through the British parliament as *The Statute of Westminster (1931)*. The Commonwealth was a unique experiment in international organisation but because of the degree of independence enjoyed by the dominions, the achievements of the new 'white man's club', as it was described, were often something of a disappointment. There was no Commonwealth parliament or other set machinery for co-operation to take place, though from time to time conferences were held.

(c) An Imperial Economic Conference was held at Ottawa, July–August 1932. It met during the depression, soon after Britain had introduced tariffs; Baldwin and Chamberlain hoped that they could increase trade within the Empire by offering preferential rates for Commonwealth goods in return for concessions by the dominions for British manufactured goods. The conference was not a success. The dominions were as badly hit by the depression as Britain and were desperate to protect their own industries against British goods. The discussions were often heated and more than once the conference almost broke up. Eventually 12 agreements were signed: Britain agreed to give preference to foodstuffs and certain other commodities from the Empire; the dominions on the whole would not agree to lower tariffs on British goods, but they did raise tariffs on foreign goods. It was a kind of preference, but not quite what the British had hoped for, since the tariffs against British goods were already too high.

(d) The Imperial Conference of May 1937 took place while the dominions Prime Ministers were in London for the coronation of George VI. It was unremarkable except that they all expressed support for Britain's policy of appeasing Hitler (see Section 26.1-2). This was predictable since they had no wish to find themselves involved in another war.

25.2 **BRITAIN AND IRELAND 1916–39**

In the summer of 1914 the operation of the Third Irish Home Rule Bill, which would have given self-government to Ireland, was postponed until the end of the war. Thus the future of Ireland and the dilemma of whether to include the Ulster Protestants in Home Rule (see Section 20.5) was put on ice. The British government hoped that Ireland would remain quiet for the duration of the war, but their hopes were dashed when violence broke out again at Easter 1916.

(a) What were the problems in Ireland between 1916 and 1923, and how did British governments try to solve them?

 (i) Though the majority of the Irish seemed prepared to wait until the war was over for Home Rule (thousands actually volunteered to fight for Britain against the Germans), a minority hoped to seize independence while Britain was preoccupied with the war. In 1916 they launched *the Easter Rebellion* proclaiming a republic and seizing several strong-points in Dublin, including the General Post Office, in the hope that the rest of the country would rise in sympathy and force the British to withdraw. However, no sympathetic rising took place and British troops soon put an end to the rebellion which was militarily a total failure.

 (ii) Though the rebellion was over within a few days, British treatment of the rebels caused a wave of disgust throughout Ireland and the USA which had a large Irish population. Fifteen of the leaders were shot; one of them, James Connolly, was already dying of gunshot wounds and, being unable to stand, was shot sitting in a chair. This caused many more people to want not just Home Rule, but complete independence from Britain, and there was a rush of support for *Sinn Fein*, which, now committed to republicanism, set about organising the powerful IRA (Irish Republican Army).

(iii) There was still a chance that the Irish might be pacified if Home Rule could be introduced immediately. Lloyd George got the Ulstermen to agree to a Home Rule scheme, thus detaching the Home Rulers from *Sinn Fein*. Unfortunately the British Conservatives (Unionists) who were against Home Rule and wanted the Irish to be repressed, refused to accept the scheme; consequently what was probably the last chance of settling the Irish problem peacefully was lost.

(iv) The problem developed a stage further when in the British general election of December 1918 *Sinn Fein* won 73 out of the 105 Irish seats, but instead of going to the British parliament at Westminster, they proclaimed an independent Irish republic with their own parliament (*Dail Eireann* – Assembly of Ireland) in Dublin, and elected Eamonn de Valera as leader. He was one of the few surviving leaders of the Easter Rising and became the symbol of Irish republicanism. Together with Michael Collins and Arthur Griffith, he organised an effective government which ignored the British and ran the country in its own way, collecting taxes and setting up law courts. The British Prime Minister, Lloyd George, hoped that the Government of Ireland Act (February 1920) would win moderate support back to the British. This was a revised version of the original Home Rule Bill of 1912, delayed by the Lords and then by the war; this time Ireland was partitioned, with one parliament for the South at Dublin and another for the six counties of Ulster at Belfast. The Belfast parliament was for the benefit of the Ulster Protestants, who still refused to be ruled by a Dublin-based Roman Catholic government. Although Ulster reluctantly accepted their parliament, Sinn Fein rejected the entire act, because it gave them control only of certain domestic matters, whereas they were determined on a complete break with Britain; also they wanted control of Ulster.

(v) Violence continued as the IRA pursued a campaign of terrorism against the police (Royal Irish Constabulary). Lloyd George retaliated by letting loose the notorious Black and Tans (recently demobilised British soliders) against the IRA, and both sides committed terrible atrocities. By the summer of 1921 Lloyd George realised that such a situation could not continue; under pressure from Labour, from many Liberals and from King George V, who hated the British campaign of violence and pleaded for peace and common sense, Lloyd George decided to try negotiations. The IRA, close to exhaustion, responded, and Lloyd George managed to persuade both *Sinn Fein* and the British Conservatives to sign a treaty (December 1921). Southern Ireland became independent with the same status as the dominions, and accepted membership of the Commonwealth; the British navy was to be allowed to use three ports.

(vi) The troubles were still not over: a section of *Sinn Fein*, led by de Valera, refused to accept the settlement because of the partition and the remaining connection with Britain, and civil war broke out between the two *Sinn Fein* factions. This ended in April 1923 with a victory for supporters of the treaty. The Irish Free State came into existence officially in December 1922.

(b) The relationship between Britain and the Irish Free State after 1923 continued to change gradually. De Valera formed a new party, *Fianna Fail* (Soldiers of Destiny) which won the election of 1932, mainly because the slump and unemployment had made the government of William Cosgrave highly unpopular. De Valera, Prime Minister for the next 16 years, set about destroying the links with Britain, though without taking the final step of declaring a republic. The oath of allegiance to the British monarch was ignored and in 1937 the Irish seized the chance offered by the recent abdication of Edward VIII to introduce a new constitution, making Eire completely independent in practice. Neville Chamberlain, the British Prime Minister, made concessions in the hope of winning Eire's friendship. Debts amounting to £100 million still owing by Eire were written off, and the three naval bases handed back. However, Eire remained unco-operative: de Valera would never be satisfied until he controlled Ulster. Consequently Eire took no part in the Commonwealth, remained neutral during the Second World War, and in 1949 finally declared itself an independent republic.

25.3 THE INDIAN STRUGGLE FOR INDEPENDENCE

(a) **Indian nationalism** began in he late nineteenth century when many middle-class Indians, having received a British-style education, often at Oxford or Cambridge, felt frustrated that their country continued to be run by the British while they were allowed no say in government and only a very minor role in local affairs. They founded a party called *the Indian National Congress* (1885) to press for greater participation by Indians in government, in response to which the British introduced the 1909 *Morley-Minto reforms* (Morley was the Secretary of State for India, Lord Minto the Viceroy, who ruled India on behalf of the King). Indians were allowed to sit on the executive councils which advised the provincial governors, and for the time being the Indians seemed satisfied. After 1914 nationalist feeling intensified, probably encouraged by the important contribution made by Indians to the war effort, and perhaps by the successful revolutions in Russia and by Woodrow Wilson's talk of self-determination for subject peoples.

(b) **How did British governments deal with the demands for Indian independence?** The British were slowly coming round to the idea that India would have to be given a measure of self-government; in 1917 the Indians were promised 'the gradual development of self-governing institutions with a view to the progressive realisation of responsible government in India as an integral part of the British Empire'. However, many Conservatives, including Winston Churchill and Lord Birkenhead (Secretary of State for India from 1924 to 1928) were utterly opposed to the idea. Not surprisingly, the pace was far too slow for the impatient nationalists, whose leaders, the *Mahatma Gandhi* and *Jawaharlal Nehru*, both lawyers educated in London, organised the anti-British campaign. The stages in the gradual move towards independence were:

(i) In 1918 Montagu (Secretary of State for India) and Lord Chelmsford (Viceroy), put forward plans which eventually became *the Government of India Act* (1919). There was to be a national parliament with two houses; about five million of the wealthiest Indians were given the vote; in the provincial governments the ministers of education, health and public works could now be Indians; a commission would be held ten years later to decide whether India was ready for further concessions. Congress was bitterly disappointed because the British kept complete control of the central government and of the key provincial ministries such as law and order and taxation. Moreover the Indians were enraged at the slowness with which the British put even these limited advances into operation. Rioting broke out and at *Amritsar* in the Punjab, after five Europeans had been murdered, General Dyer dispersed an excited crowd of over 5000 Indians with machine-gun fire, killing 379. Order was soon restored, but the Amritsar massacre was an important turning point: it provoked so much fury that Congress was transformed from a middle-class party into a mass movement. 'After Amritsar,' writes Martin Gilbert, 'no matter what compromises and concessions the British might suggest, British rule would ultimately be swept away.' By this time Gandhi was the leading figure of Congress. He believed in non-violent protest and the equality of all classes. Always dressed as a simple peasant, he somehow managed by sheer force of personality to persuade Indians to refuse to work, stage sit-down strikes, fast, stop paying taxes and boycott elections. Unfortunately he was unable to control his more extreme supporters and violence often developed; in 1922 he called off his first non-co-operation campaign.

(ii) The next British move, apart from putting Gandhi in gaol, was that Baldwin, acting a year early, appointed *the Simon Commission* (1928), as the 1919 Act had recommended. In 1930 this proposed self-government for the provinces but was treated with contempt by the Indians, who were not even represented on the commission and who were demanding immediate dominion status. As soon as he was out of gaol Gandhi began his second civil disobedience campaign by breaking the law that only the government could manufacture salt. After a symbolic 250-mile march to the sea, he produced salt from seawater; but again violent incidents developed and again Gandhi was arrested.

(iii) *Lord Irwin* (Viceroy 1926-31) was a humane and enlightened politician, sympathetic to the Indians; before the Simon Report appeared in 1930 he had expressed the view that dominion status must come, so that the Indians felt even more let down when the report made no mention of it. Irwin was convinced that negotiations must take place and he was fully supported in this view by Ramsay MacDonald who had just become Prime Minister. Consequently two *Round Table Conferences* (1930 and 1931) were held in London. The first was unsatisfactory because, although the Indian princes were represented and accepted the idea of an Indian federation, no Congress representatives were there: most of them were in prison. Irwin had them released and prevailed upon Gandhi to travel to London to attend the second conference, much to the horror of Churchill who described Gandhi as 'this malignant and subversive fanatic'. Again little progress was made, this time because of disagreements about Muslim representation in an independent Indian parliament.

(iv) A major step towards independence was *the Government of India Act of 1935*, introduced as a result of co-operation between MacDonald and Baldwin, and in spite of bitter opposition from Churchill. The elected Indian assembly was to have a say in everything except defence and foreign affairs; the eleven provincial assemblies were to have more or less full control over local affairs. The nationalists were still not satisfied: the act fell short of dominion status (the white dominions controlled their own defence and foreign policies), and the princes who still ruled certain areas of India refused to co-operate; thus their areas remained outside the system. Another failure of the act was that it ignored the religious rivalry between Hindus and Muslims. Roughly two-thirds of the Indians were Hindus, and the next largest group, the Muslims (who believed in the Islamic religion) were afraid that in a democratic India they would be dominated and unfairly treated by the Hindus. When Nehru's Congress party, which was overwhelmingly Hindu, won control of eight out of the eleven provinces in the 1937 elections, the Muslim League under its leader J. A. Jinnah demanded a separate state of their own called Pakistan, while Congress and Gandhi were determined to preserve a united India. No further developments took place before the Second World War, but mounting Hindu/Muslim hostility boded ill for the future, and provided some justification for the British reluctance to grant full self-government. (For the events leading to independence in 1947 see Section 30.2.)

25.4 BRITAIN AND THE MIDDLE EAST MANDATES

In 1916 the Arabs in the Turkish empire rose in revolt, and helped by the British Colonel T. E. Lawrence (Lawrence of Arabia) and later by British troops under Allenby, they played an important part in liberating the Arab territories from Turkish control. As a bribe to win Arab support against Turkey, the British had made vague promises that when the war was over, the Arabs would be allowed to set up independent states; but about the same time (1916), doubtless under the pressure of war, the British had also made the contradictory *Sykes–Picot agreement* with France, whereby Turkey's Arab lands would be divided between the two of them. In 1919 therefore, to their intense disappointment, the Arabs found their territories handed over as mandates (to be 'looked after' and prepared for self-government) to Britain (Iraq, Transjordan and Palestine) and France (Syria and Lebanon). Again Britain was reluctant to sever all connections with her mandates because of the Middle East oil resources, particularly in Iraq, and wanted to be allowed to station troops there to guarantee a sure source of oil. On the other hand, the British dared not offend the Arabs too deeply or oil supplies might equally be threatened. Consequently steady progress towards independence was made in Iraq and Transjordan, though with strings attached; however, the situation in Palestine was complicated by the Jewish/Arab problem.

(a) In Iraq, after some initial nationalist rioting, the British set up an Iraqi national government in which each minister had a British adviser. The *Amir Feisal* (who had just been driven out of Syria by the French) was accepted as king. Although extreme nationalists did not approve, this set-up was agreed by the Anglo-Iraqi Treaty of 1922 and worked well. An elected parliament was introduced in 1924 and Feisal, a man of great personal charm and political ability, proved to be an excellent ruler. With British help, industry and agriculture were organised and an efficient administrative system introduced; the British won Iraqi support by successfully opposing Turkish claims to the province of Mosul with its vast oil resources. In 1932 Iraq became fully independent, though Britain was allowed to keep two air bases; according to one Arab nationalist, George Antonius, 'the modern state of Iraq owes its existence largely to the efforts and devotion of its British officials.'

(b) In Transjordan the British set up Feisal's brother Abdullah as king, and allowed him to run the country's internal affairs, which he did competently. However, Transjordan was a poor state, lacking in resources and with no oil, and was therefore dependent on Britain for subsidies and for defence. In 1946 it was given complete independence, though Abdullah kept on the British officers who led his army.

(c) Palestine proved to be the most troublesome mandate because of the growing hostility between Jews and Arabs. The problem originated about two thousand years earlier in AD 71 when most of the Jews were driven out of Palestine, their homeland, by the Romans. In fact small communities of Jews remained behind in Palestine and over the following seventeen hundred years there was a gradual trickle of Jews returning from exile, though until the end of the nineteenth century there were never enough to cause the Palestinian Arabs to feel threatened. However, in 1897 some European Jews founded *the World Zionist Organisation* at Basle in Switzerland, an event which was to be of profound importance for the Middle East. Greatly disturbed by the recent persecution of Jews in Russia, Germany and France, the Zionists demanded a Jewish national home in Palestine. Even before they received the mandate over Palestine, the British had become involved in the controversy and must take much of the blame for the chaos that followed, especially after 1945.

How did Britain become involved and how did the situation develop up to 1939?

(i) During the First World War the British had made three contradictory promises, which were bound to lead to frustration and hostility. There were the two already mentioned: independent states for the Arabs and the partition of the Arab territories between Britain and France; the third was *the Balfour Declaration* (November 1917) in which the British Foreign Minister pledged British support for a Jewish 'national home' in Palestine. The British motive, apart from genuine sympathy with the Zionists, was a belief that the Jews would help to safeguard the Suez Canal and provide a buffer between the canal zone and the French in Syria.

(ii) Faced with bitter Arab protests both against the British failure to grant independence and against the arrival of increasing numbers of Jews, the British government stated (1922) that there was no intention that the Jews should occupy the whole of Palestine and that there would be no interference with the rights of the Arabs in Palestine. The British hoped to persuade Jews and Arabs to live together peacefully in the same state and they failed to understand the deep religious gulf between the two.

(iii) Jews continued to arrive complete with Zionist money, bought land from Arabs who were at first willing to sell, started industries and reclaimed land. It was soon clear that they intended to develop not just a national home but a Jewish national state; by 1928 there were 150 000 of them. The Arabs rioted and began murdering Jews and consequently in 1930 the British Labour government decided that Jewish immigration must cease for the time being. Now it was the turn of the Zionists to rage against the British to such an extent that MacDonald felt obliged to allow immigration to continue.

(iv) The situation took a turn for the worse after Hitler came to power in Germany (1933): Nazi persecution caused a flood of refugees until by 1935 about a quarter of the total population of Palestine was Jewish. Arabs again began to attack Jews while British troops struggled to keep order.

(v) In 1937 the British Peel Commission suggested dividing Palestine into two separate states, one Jewish, one Arab, but the Arabs rejected the idea.

(vi) As war loomed in 1939 the British felt the need to win Arab support, and in a White Paper they agreed to limit Jewish immigration to 10 000 a year and promised to set up an independent Arab state in ten years, thus guaranteeing an Arab majority in the new state. At this point, with nothing resolved, the British hoped to shelve the problem until after the war (see Section 30.3 for later developments).

QUESTIONS

1. India and the Amritsar Massacre 1919
Study Sources A to E and then answer the questions which follow.

Source A: information from a modern historian.

The First World War made it less likely that the promise of reforms to India, when it did come, would be enough to stem the nationalist tide. Indian nationalism was fired enormously by the war, its grievances increased, its support expanded, its organisation greatly improved and its expectations increased

. . . In April 1919 there was a rash of rebellions in the Punjab serious enough to convince at least one British general that the Indian Mutiny was about to be repeated; this persuaded him to open fire on a crowd of unarmed Indians in a public square in Amritsar, and to continue firing into their backs until his ammunition ran out, killing at least 380 and wounding 1,200 . . . General Dyer was mildly censured by the army and then vigorously defended by his superiors, by the House of Lords, by much of the press, by most Conservative MPs and by a large number of ordinary people who subscribed £26,000 in a month to a fund set up on his behalf by the Morning Post. The effect of all this on Indian nationalist opinion was disastrous. Gandhi made it the occasion for his first non-co-operation campaign, and repression only undid the gains made by the earlier policies of concession.

Source: B. Porter, *The Lion's Share*, Longman, 1975 (adapted extracts).

Source B: General Dyer's official report of his action.

There was no reason to further parley with the mob; evidently they were there to defy the arm of the law. If I fired, I must fire with good effect, *a small amount of firing would be a criminal act of folly*. I had the choice of carrying out a very distasteful and horrible duty, or of neglecting to do my duty, of suppressing disorder or of becoming responsible for all future bloodshed. My duty and my military instincts told me to fire. What faced me was what on the morrow would be the Rebel Army. I fired and continued to fire until the crowd dispersed. I consider this was the least amount of firing that would produce the necessary moral and widespread effect, from the military point of view, not only on those who were present, but more specially throughout the Punjab.

Source: M. Woodruff, *The Men Who Ruled India*, Cape, 1954 (adapted extract).

Source C: Comment's from a modern writer.

Amritsar from Apil 10th to the 12th was in the hands of a mob. Dyer took great care to make public by beat of drum, orders forbidding meetings and warning the inhabitants that meetings would be fired on. On the afternoon of the 13th, a meeting was held in defiance of these orders. Dyer found himself in command of a small force – fifty men with rifles and forty with staves – all of the Indian army, confronting a crowd variously estimated at between five thousand and twenty thousand. Dyer said that he expected the mob to attack, and believed that his first duty as a soldier was to preserve the force under his command . . . He therefore dispersed the crowd . . . That evening the city was completely quiet . . . The mob was being addressed by men who were later said by the courts to be dangerous agitators. It was made up mostly of Sikhs armed with the six-foot quarterstaff and many of them with the kirpan, the short Sikh sword. Sikhs are a violent people, quick to flare into fury; it was potentially as dangerous as a mob could be . . . A British official from a neighbouring district wrote, 'I held many meetings and heard on all sides that this incident had saved the situation'. General Dyer came to think himself the saviour of India.

Source: as for Source **B** (adapted extracts).

Source D: speech by Winston Churchill in the House of Commons, July 1920.

Let me marshal the facts. The crowd was unarmed except with bludgeons. It was not attacking anybody or anything. When fire had been opened upon it to disperse it, it tried to run away. Pinned up in a narrow place considerably smaller than Trafalgar Square, with hardly any exits, and packed together so that one bullet would drive through three or four bodies, the people ran madly this way and the other. When the fire was directed upon the centre, they ran to the sides. The fire was then directed upon the sides. Many threw themselves down on the ground, and the fire was then directed on the ground. This was continued for 8 or 10 minutes, and it stopped only when the ammunition had reached the point of exhaustion . . . After 379 persons, which is about the number gathered together in this Chamber today, had been killed, and when most certainly 1,200 or more had been wounded, the troops, at whom not even a stone had been thrown, swung round and marched away.

Source: Hansard, *Parliamentary Debates*, July 1920.

Source E: information from another modern historian.

The good effects of this modest advance – the Government of India Act (1919) – were spoiled by the Amritsar massacre in April 1919, and perhaps even more spoiled by the strong support – official and unofficial – that General Dyer received in British India and Britain for his indefensible actions . . . Churchill strongly supported the dismissal of Dyer after Amritsar, and in his speech in defence of the government's action, had stated firmly that 'our reign in India or anywhere else has never stood on the basis of physical force alone'. But his acceptance of the permanence of British rule over India was complete. While prepared to support policies that would calm nationalist ambitions, he was not prepared to contemplate equality in government between British Indians and was outraged by the suggestion of any reduction of British supremacy.

Source: R. R. James, *Churchill – A Study in Failure 1900-1939*, Weidenfeld & Nicolson, 1970 (adapted extracts).

(a) (i) According to Source **A**, why was there a great increase in Indian nationalism in 1919?   **4(a)**

     (ii) How did this nationalism show itself in April 1919?   **4(a)**

     (iii) According to Source **A**, what action did General Dyer take to deal with the situation?   **4(a)**

(b) (i) Explain in your own words what, according to Source **B**, were Dyer's motives for this action.   **4(a)**

     (ii) Using evidence from Source **C**, explain what Dyer meant when he said in Source **B**, 'a small amount of firing would be a criminal act of folly'.   **4(a, c)**

(c) (i) Using evidence from Source **D**, describe in your own words what happened in the 10 minutes after the troops opened fire.   **4(a)**

     (ii) How do the descriptions of the Indian crowd differ in Sources **C** and **D**?   **4(a, c)**

(d) (i) What evidence can you find in Source **A** of the British attitude towards the Indians?   **4(a, b)**

     (ii) According to Source **E**, what did Churchill think about independence for India?   **4(a)**

(e) (i) Do you think each of the writers of Sources **C**, **D** and **E** approves of General Dyer's actions or not? Explain your answers fully.   **4(a, b)**

     (ii) Using the evidence of the other Sources, especially **E**, to help you decide, explain whether or not you think Source **D** is one that can be relied on by the historian.   **4(a, b, c)**

(f) From the evidence of Sources **A** and **E**, why was the Amritsar Massacre important in Anglo–Indian relations?   **4(a, c)**

2. Ireland

Read the extract and then answer the questions which follow.

Terms of the Act of Parliament setting up the Irish Free State, March 1922.

(1) Ireland shall have the same constitutional status in the British Empire as the Dominion of Canada, with a Parliament having the power to make laws; it shall be known as the Irish Free State.

(2) The oath to be taken by MPs of the Irish Free State shall be in the following form:
I, ..., do solemnly swear allegiance to the constitution of the Irish Free State, and that I will be faithful to H.M. King George V.

(3) The government of the Irish Free State shall allow His Majesty's Imperial forces:

(a) In time of peace such harbour and other facilities as may be agreed and . . .

(b) In time of war or of strained relations with a Foreign Power such harbour and other facilities as the British Government may require.

(4) If an address is presented to His Majesty by the Parliament of Northern Ireland to that effect, the powers of the Irish Free State shall no longer extend to Northern Ireland.

(5) Neither the Parliament of the Irish Free State nor the Parliament of Northern Ireland shall make any law to prohibit or restrict the free exercise of any religion, or impose any disability on account of religious belief.

Source: quoted in J. H. Bettey, *English Historical Documents 1906–1939*, Routledge & Kegan Paul, 1967 (adapted extracts).

(a) (i) According to the extract, what was the constitution of the new Irish Free State going to be like? **4(a)**

(ii) Which king was on the throne when this Act was passed? **4(a)**

(b) (i) Explain in your own words what the Act says about the relationship of the Irish Free State with Northern Ireland. **4(a)**

(ii) From your own knowledge, when and how had Northern Ireland come into existence? **1, 2**

(c) (i) According to the extract, how did the Act try to deal with the religious differences in Ireland? **4(a)**

(ii) According to point (3), Britain was to be allowed certain military facilities in the Irish Free State. How did these differ in peace and war? **4(a)**

(d) The agreement was passed by the Irish Parliament by a small majority, but de Valera and the republicans refused to accept it, causing a civil war.

(i) Which parts of the agreement given here do you think they would be unhappy about? Explain your answers fully. **4(a, b)**

(ii) Which side won the civil war – supporters or opponents of the agreement? **1, 2**

(e) Show how each of the following had earlier helped to increase the demand for Irish independence:
(i) the Easter Rising, 1916; (ii) the setting up of the Dail by Sinn Fein, 1918; (iii) the Government of Ireland Act, February 1920; (iv) Lloyd George's use of the Black and Tans. **1, 2**

(f) Describe how the relationship between the Irish Free State and Britain changed between 1923 and 1949. **1, 2**

3. (a) Show how the following were important in the Indian campaign for independence from Britain:
(i) the Amritsar Massacre (1919); (ii) Mahatma Gandhi's campaign of non-violence; (iii) Round Table Conferences (1930–31); (iv) the Government of India Act (1935).

(b)   Why do you think the Indians had not been given full independence by 1939?   1, 2

4.   Describe and explain the feelings and reactions of a Palestinian
Arab towards the following:

(i)   formation of the World Zionist Organisation (1897);
(ii)   Balfour Declaration (1917);
(iii)   arrival of thousands of Jews in Palestine, especially during
1933–35, following the Nazi persecution;
(iv)   Peel Commission Report (1937);
(v)   limiting of Jewish immigrants to 10,000 a year (1939).   1, 2, 3

CHAPTER 26

APPEASEMENT AND THE OUTBREAK OF THE SECOND WORLD WAR: FOREIGN AFFAIRS 1931–9

SUMMARY OF EVENTS

British foreign policy during this period was dominated by one principle – *appeasement*. Briefly this was the practice of making concessions to aggressive foreign powers – Japan, Italy and Germany – in order to avoid war. The National governments of MacDonald (1931–5) and Baldwin (1935–7) followed this policy, and Neville Chamberlain, Prime Minister from 1937 to 1940, was its main exponent, though he did abandon it belatedly in March 1939. The policy failed completely and culminated in the outbreak of the Second World War (1939–45); for this reason 'appeasement' came to be looked on as a term of abuse.

Between 1924 and 1929, following the Dawes Plan (1924) and the Locarno Treaties (1925), international relations were harmonious. But the Great Depression plunged the world's industrial powers into severe economic crisis, with dwindling markets and mass unemployment. The Locarno spirit of sweetness and goodwill disappeared suddenly and it was a case of every country for itself. Three states – Japan, Italy, and Germany, all of which had right-wing nationalist governments, tried to solve their economic problems by territorial expansion, which meant aggression against other states. The League of Nations, vainly trying to operate a policy of *collective security* (joint action to keep the peace) but lacking strong support, failed to curb the aggressors. Britain and France, instead of backing the League and collective security, preferred appeasement. Consequently all three aggressors successfully defied the League and the majority of world opinion until 1939.

Japan was the first aggressor with her successful invasion of the Chinese province of Manchuria (1931). Adolf Hitler, who became German Chancellor in January 1933, began cautiously by announcing the reintroduction of conscription (March 1935), a breach of the Versailles Treaty. Mussolini, the Italian fascist dictator, sent his troops to conquer Abyssinia (October 1935) and in 1936 German troops re-occupied the Rhineland, another breach of Versailles. During the summer of 1936 the Spanish Civil War broke out and Hitler and Mussolini sent military help to General Franco, leader of the Spanish right-wing in their revolt against the left-wing republican government. By 1939 Franco was victorious and a third fascist dictator was installed in Europe.

By this time it was clear that the League of Nations working through collective security was totally ineffective; consequently Hitler carried out his most ambitious project to date – the annexation of Austria (known as the *Anschluss* – March 1938). Next he turned his attentions to Czechoslovakia and demanded the Sudetenland, an area containing three million Germans adjoining the frontier with Germany. When the Czechs refused Hitler's demands, Chamberlain, anxious to avoid war at all costs, attended a conference at Munich (September 1938) at which it was agreed that Germany should have the Sudetenland, but no more of Czechoslovakia. War seemed to have been averted. However, the following March Hitler broke this agreement and sent German troops to occupy Prague, the Czech capital. At this Chamberlain decided that Hitler had gone too far and must be stopped. When the Poles rejected Hitler's demands for Danzig, Britain and France promised to help Poland if the Germans attacked. Hitler was not sufficiently impressed by these British and French threats and grew tired of waiting for Poland to negotiate. Having first secured a non-aggression pact with Russia (August 1939), the Germans invaded Poland on 1 September. Britain and France accordingly declared war on Germany.

Map 26.1   *Hitler's gains before the Second World War*

26.1 WHAT WAS APPEASEMENT AND WHY DID BRITAIN FOLLOW SUCH A POLICY?

(a) Appeasement was the policy followed first by the British and later by the French of avoiding war with aggressive powers such as Japan, Italy and Germany, by giving way to their demands provided these were not too unreasonable. There were two distinct phases of appeasement.

(i) From the mid-1920s until 1937 there was a vague feeling that war must be avoided at all costs, and Britain and sometimes France drifted along accepting the various *faits accomplis* (Manchuria, Abyssinia, German rearmament, Rhineland reoccupation).

(ii) When Neville Chamberlain became British Prime Minister in May 1937 he gave appeasement new drive; he believed in taking the initiative: he would find out what Hitler wanted and show him that reasonable claims could be met by negotiation rather than by force.

The origins of appeasement can be seen in British policy during the 1920s with the Dawes and Young Plans, which tried to conciliate the Germans, and also with the Locarno Treaties and their significant omission: Britain did not agree to guarantee Germany's eastern frontiers, which even Stresemann, the 'good German', said must be revised. When Austen Chamberlain, the British Foreign Minister (and Neville's half-brother), remarked at the time of Locarno that no British government would ever risk the bones of a British grenadier in defence of the Polish Corridor, it seemed to the Germans that Britain had turned her back on Eastern Europe. Appeasement reached its climax at Munich, where Britain and France were so determined to avoid war with Germany that they made Hitler a present of the Sudetenland and so set in motion the destruction of Czechoslovakia. Even with such concessions as this, appeasement failed.

(b) At the time appeasement was being pursued, however, there seemed much to commend it and the appeasers, who included MacDonald, Baldwin, Sir John Simon (Foreign Secretary 1931-5), Sir Samuel Hoare (Foreign Secretary June-December 1935) and Lord Halifax (Foreign Secretary 1938-40) as well as Chamberlain, were convinced of the rightness of their policies:

(i) It was essential to avoid war which was likely to be more devastating than ever before, as the horrors of the Spanish Civil War demonstrated. Moreover, Britain, still in the throes of the economic crisis, could not afford vast rearmament and the crippling expenses of a major war. British governments seemed to be supported by a strongly pacifist public opinion. In February 1933 the Oxford Union voted that it would not fight for King and Country, and Baldwin and the National Government won a huge victory in November 1935 shortly after he had declared: 'I give you my word of honour that there will be no great armaments'.

(ii) Many felt that Italy and Germany had genuine grievances: Italy had been cheated at Versailles, Germany treated too harshly. Therefore Britain should react with sympathy and with regard to Germany, try to revise the most hated clauses of Versailles. This would remove the need for German aggression and lead to Anglo-German friendship.

(iii) Since the League of Nations seemed to be helpless, Chamberlain believed that the only way to settle disputes was by personal contact between leaders; in this way he would be able to control and civilise Hitler, and Mussolini into the bargain, and bring them to respect international law.

(iv) Economic co-operation between Britain and Germany would be good for both; if Britain helped the German economy to recover the internal violence would die down.

(v) Fear of Communist Russia was great especially among British Conservatives, many of whom believed the Communist threat to be greater than the danger from Hitler. Many British politicians were willing to overlook the unpleasant features of Nazism in the hope that Hitler's Germany would be a guarantee against Communist expansion westwards; in fact many admired Hitler's drive and achievements.

(vi) Underlying all these feelings was the belief that Britain ought not to take any military action in case it led to a full-scale war which Britain was totally unprepared for; at the same time the USA was for isolation and France was weak and divided.

26.2 APPEASEMENT IN ACTION

(a) The Japanese invasion of Manchuria (September 1931) brought a Chinese appeal for help to the League of Nations, which condemned Japan and ordered her troops to be withdrawn. However, there was a certain amount of sympathy in Britain for the Japanese and Sir John Simon attemped to put both sides of the case at the League Assembly in Geneva. Unfortunately Simon had one serious defect which, according to A. J. P. Taylor, made him unfit to be British Foreign Secretary – he was 'too cool and rational'. He pointed out that Japan had been involved in the province since the 1890s and had been given a privileged position in south Manchuria as a result of the Russo-Japanese War. Since then the Japanese had invested millions of pounds in Manchuria in the development of industry and railways, and could not stand by and see themselves gradually squeezed out of such a valuable province with a population of 30 million, especially when they were suffering economic hardship because of the great depression.

At Simon's suggestion the League appointed an investigating commission under Lord Lytton which decided (1932) that there were faults on both sides and proposed that Manchuria be governed by the League. However, Japan rejected this and withdrew from the League (March 1933). The question of economic sanctions, let alone military ones, was not raised, because Britain and France had serious economic problems and were reluctant to apply a trade boycott of Japan in case it led to war, which they were ill-equipped to win, especially without American help. It is possible to argue that Simon's policy was the only realistic one, but it meant that Japan had successfully defied the League, a fact which was carefully noted by Mussolini and Hitler.

(b) The failure of the World Disarmament Conference (1932-4) came about when the French refused to agree that the Germans should be allowed equality of armaments with France. This gave Hitler an excuse to walk out of the conference and to take Germany out of the League, marking the end of MacDonald's great hope - to maintain peace by disarmament and collective security, working through the League. This led to the publication in March 1935 of a government White Paper called *'Statement Relating to Defence'*, which announced that since Britain could no longer rely on collective security, her own military strength must be built up. It was, in fact, the decision to rearm; this new policy was put into operation, though very gradually at first. The White Paper gave Hitler the excuse to announce that he intended to introduce conscription and build the Germany army up to 600 000 men; both actions were breaches of Versailles. In response, MacDonald, now physically almost on his last legs, met Mussolini and Laval (French Foreign Minister) at Stresa in Northern Italy; they condemned Hitler's actions and promised to resist any further unilateral breaches of treaties which might endanger the peace of Europe. This agreement was known as the *Stresa Front* (April 1935); it was significant that both the British and French carefully avoided discussion of the Abyssinian crisis which was already brewing, and Mussolini took this to mean that they would turn a blind eye to an Italian attack on Abyssinia, regarding it as a bit of old-fashioned colonial expansion.

(c) The Anglo-German Naval Agreement (June 1935) soon broke up the Stresa Front. This astonishing move occurred when Hitler, shrewdly realising how frail the Front was, offered to limit the German navy to 35 per cent of the strength of the British navy. Britain eagerly accepted this offer and even went further, allowing Germany to build up to 45 per cent of Britain's total of submarines. This agreement was reached without any consultation whatsoever with the French and Italians: it meant that Britain was condoning German rearmament, which proceeded with gathering momentum. This was Hoare's first action as Foreign Minister; his justification was that since the Germans were already breaking Versailles by building a fleet, it would be as well to have that fleet limited. However, it convinced Mussolini of Britain's cynicism and self-interest and disgusted Laval who decided there was more to be gained from co-operation with Mussolini.

(d) The Italian invasion of Abyssinia (October 1935)

(i) It had been obvious for months that Mussolini was preparing for an invasion of Abyssinia, the last major African territory not subject to European control. Abyssinia was a member of the League, and Baldwin was in the awkward position of wanting to support the League in preserving Abyssinian independence while at the same time avoiding a confrontation with Italy. The British hoped that the Stresa Front still had some meaning and wanted to use Italy as an ally against Germany, which was now perceived as the real threat to the peace of Europe. This dilemma helps to explain Britain's apparently weak and sometimes contradictory policy throughout the crisis.

(ii) *Sir Anthony Eden*, Minister for League of Nations Affairs, was sent to Rome to make an offer to Mussolini – he could take part of Abyssinia and Britain would give Abyssinia part of neighbouring British Somaliland as compensation. Mussolini rejected this, arguing that Italy ought to have a similar position in Abyssinia to that of Britain in Egypt – a difficult point for the British to answer.

(iii) *Sir Samuel Hoare* made what sounded like a fighting speech at the League Assembly in Geneva (September 1935). Hoping to warn Mussolini off, he affirmed that Britain would support the League against acts of unprovoked aggression. Mussolini ignored the warning and went ahead with the invasion of Abyssinia (3 October). The League, responding to a moving appeal from the Abyssinian Emperor Haile Selassie, immediately imposed economic sanctions on Italy; these included a refusal to buy Italian goods and a ban on exports of iron ore, rubber, tin, scrap iron and other metals to Italy. Britain seemed to be taking the lead in support of the League and collective security, and public opinion generally approved.

(iv) With collective security apparently working, Baldwin decided that this was a good time to hold a general election (November). During the campaign he told the electorate 'I give you my word that there will be no great armaments'; he wanted a mandate simply to 'remedy the deficiencies which have occurred in our defences'. This was what people wanted to hear at the time, and the National government won a convincing victory (see Section 24.3(c)); later Baldwin was accused of having deliberately misled the country by keeping quiet about the need for rearmament.

(v) By the time the election was over, it was clear that the existing sanctions were not working; Italy had not been brought to her knees. Chamberlain suggested sanctions to stop the export of oil and coal to Italy which Mussolini later admitted would have forced him to make peace within a week. The cabinet rejected this idea, fearing it would provoke Mussolini to declare war, for which Britain was unprepared. The League's prestige suffered a further blow when it emerged that Hoare had been to Paris and made a secret deal with Laval (December) to hand over a large section of Abyssinia to Italy provided military action ceased. This was more than the Italians had managed to capture at the time, and when news of the *Hoare-Laval Pact* leaked out, public opinion in Britain and France was so outraged that the plan had to be dropped. Hoare, who had made the agreement without cabinet approval, resigned in disgrace. No further action was taken and by April 1936 the Italian conquest of Abyssinia was complete. In June it was decided to discontinue the ineffective economic sanctions.

(vi) *The results were disastrous*: the League and the idea of collective security were discredited; Mussolini was annoyed by the sanctions and began to be drawn towards friendship with Hitler, who had not criticised the invasion and refused to apply sanctions; in return Mussolini dropped the objections to a German takeover of Austria; Hitler took advantage of the preoccupation with Abyssinia to send troops into the Rhineland. Baldwin's popularity slumped dramatically.

(e) German troops reoccupied the Rhineland (March 1936), committing another breach of Versailles. Though the troops had orders to withdraw at the first sign of French opposition, no resistance was offered beyond the usual protests. Hitler, well aware of the mood of pacifism among his opponents, soothed them by offering a peace treaty for 25 years. Baldwin and Eden, the new Foreign Minister, judged that British public opinion would not have supported military action, since the Rhineland *was* part of Germany. Indeed, Lord Londonderry (a Conservative and Secretary of State for Air from 1931-5) was reported to have sent Hitler a telegram congratulating him on his success, while Lord Lothian remarked that the German troops had merely entered their own 'back garden'.

(f) The Spanish Civil War (1936-9). In July 1936 an army revolt broke out against the Spanish left-wing republican government. Franco soon assumed the leadership of the revolt, and a quick victory was expected. However, the republicans controlled most of the south, including Madrid, and a bitter struggle developed in which both sides committed terrible atrocities. Most of the states of Europe, including Britain, France, Germany and Italy, signed an agreement promising not to interfere in Spanish affairs. However, Hitler and Mussolini broke the agreement and sent extensive help to Franco - 60 000 Italian troops and many planes, together with hundreds of German planes and tanks. In Britain opinion was divided; some left-wing groups - the ILP and the Communist Party wanted the government to support the republic against Spanish fascism; however, the Labour Party under its new leader Clement Attlee, did not want to become involved, and shrank back from any action which meant co-operation with Communists. Baldwin and Chamberlain were determined on non-intervention since most Conservatives disapproved of the Spanish republican government with its anarchist and Communist connections. Volunteers were allowed to go - about 2000 Britons, many of them unemployed miners, fought for the Spanish republic in the International

Brigade; but no official help was sent. British policy reached rock bottom in April 1938 when the Foreign Minister, now Lord Halifax, tried to resurrect the Stresa Front by agreeing to recognise Italian possession of Abyssinia in return for the withdrawal of Italian troops from Spain. However, Mussolini ignored his side of the bargain and the British government had been made to look weak and treacherous, condoning Mussolini's aggression and betraying the efforts of the League of Nations. By this time nobody took the League seriously. Eventually Italian and German help proved decisive in securing victory for Franco.

(g) The German occupation of Austria (March 1938), was Hitler's greatest success to date. Having first reached an understanding with Mussolini (the Rome–Berlin Axis of 1936) and signed the Anti-Comintern Pact with Japan, Hitler carried out the *Anschluss* (union), yet another breach of Versailles. Matters came to a head when the Austrian Nazis staged huge demonstrations in Vienna, Graz and Linz, which Chancellor Schuschnigg's government could not control. Realising that this could be the prelude to a German invasion, Schuschnigg announced a plebiscite about whether or not Austria should remain independent. Hitler decided to act before this took place, in case the vote went against union; German troops moved in and Austria became part of the Third Reich. It was a triumph for Germany: it revealed the weaknesses of Britain and France who again did no more than protest; it demonstrated the value of the new understanding with Italy, and it dealt a severe strategic blow at Czechoslovakia which could now be attacked from the south as well as from the west and north. All was ready for the beginning of Hitler's campaign to acquire the German-speaking Sudetenland, a campaign which ended in triumph at the Munich Conference in September 1938.

26.3 MUNICH TO THE OUTBREAK OF WAR: SEPTEMBER 1938 TO SEPTEMBER 1939

Hitler's most pressing aims in foreign affairs were to destroy the hated Versailles settlement, to recover lost territory such as the Saar (already returned to Germany by a plebiscite or referendum in 1935) and the Polish Corridor, and to bring all areas containing German people within the Reich. Much of this, culminating in the annexation of Austria, had already been achieved; the rest would require the acquisition of territory from Czechoslovakia and Poland, both of which had large German minorities.

There is some disagreement about what, if anything, Hitler intended beyond these aims. Most historians believe that the annexation of Austria and parts of Czechoslovakia and Poland was only a beginning, to be followed by the seizure of the rest of Czechoslovakia and Poland and by the conquest and permanent occupation of Russia as far east as the Ural Mountains. This would give him what the Germans called *Lebensraum* (living space) which would provide food for the German people and an area in which the excess German population could settle and colonise. An additional advantage was that Communism would be destroyed. However, not all historians agree about these further aims; A. J. P. Taylor, for example, claims that Hitler never intended a major war and was at most prepared only for a limited war against Poland.

(a) Hitler, Chamberlain and Czechoslovakia. It seems likely that Hitler had decided to destroy Czechoslovakia as part of his *Lebensraum* policy and because he hated the Czechs for their democracy as well as for the fact that their state had been set up by the Versailles Treaty. His excuse for the opening propaganda campaign was that 3.5 million Sudeten Germans under their leader Konrad Henlein were being discriminated against by the Czech government, though in fact they were not being seriously inconvenienced. The Nazis organised huge protest demonstrations in the Sudetenland and clashes occurred between Czechs and Germans. The Czech President, Benes, feared that Hitler was fomenting the disturbances so that German troops could march in 'to restore order'. Chamberlain and Daladier, the French Prime Minister, both feared that war between Germany and Czechoslovakia was imminent.

It was now that Chamberlain took the initiative. He was determined to play a leading role in international affairs, and felt it his duty to go to almost any lengths to prevent war. His aim was to prevail upon the Czech government to offer concessions to Hitler which would make a German invasion unnecessary. Under pressure, Benes agreed that the Sudeten Germans might be detached from Czechoslovakia. Chamberlain flew to Germany and had talks with Hitler at Berchtesgaden (15 September) explaining the offer. Hitler seemed to accept, but at a second meeting at Godesberg (22 September) he stepped up his demands: he wanted more of Czechoslovakia and the immediate entry of German troops to the Sudetenland. This Benes would not agree to and he immediately ordered mobilisation of the Czech army.

When it seemed that war was inevitable, Hitler invited Chamberlain and Daladier to a four-power conference which met at Munich (29 September). Here a plan produced by Mussolini (but drafted by the German Foreign Office) was accepted. The Sudetenland was to be handed over to Germany immediately, but Germany along with the other three powers guaranteed the remainder of Czechoslovakia. Neither the Czechs nor the Russians were invited to the conference; the Czechs were told that if they resisted the Munich decision they would receive no help from Britain or France, even though the latter had guaranteed the Czech frontiers at Locarno. When Chamberlain arrived back in Britain he received a rapturous welcome from the public which thought war had been averted. Chamberlain himself remarked: 'I believe it is peace for our time'. However, not everybody was so enthusiastic: Churchill called Munich 'a total and unmitigated defeat', and Alfred Duff-Cooper, the First Lord of the Admiralty, resigned from the cabinet saying that Hitler could not be trusted to keep the agreement. Chamberlain, arrogant, narrow and lacking imagination, persisted in treating Hitler as a responsible statesman and ignored his ill-treatment of the Jews and the mass of evidence (for example the way in which he increased his demands at Godesberg when he realised how committed Chamberlain was to maintaining peace at all costs) suggesting that Hitler was not reliable. Chamberlain totally misunderstood Hitler: on his return from Godesberg, he told the cabinet that he had established some influence over Hitler, a man who would be 'rather better than his word'.

Duff Cooper and Churchill were right; Czechoslovakia was crippled by the loss of 70 per cent of her heavy industry and almost all her fortifications to Germany. Slovakia began to demand semi-independence and when it looked as though the country was about to fall apart, Hitler pressurised President Hacha into requesting German help 'to restore order'. Consequently in March 1939 German troops occupied the rest of Czechoslovakia. Britain and France protested but took no action: according to Chamberlain, the guarantee of Czech frontiers did not apply because technically Czechoslovakia had not been invaded: German troops had entered by invitation. However, the German action caused a great rush of criticism: for the first time the appeasers were unable to justify what Hitler had done; he had broken his promise and seized non-German territory. Even Chamberlain felt that this was going too far and his attitude hardened.

(b) Hitler, Chamberlain and Poland. After taking over the Lithuanian port of Memel (which was admittedly peopled largely by Germans), Hitler turned his attentions to Poland. The Germans resented the loss of Danzig and the Polish Corridor at Versailles, and now that Czechoslovakia was safely out of the way, Polish neutrality was no longer necessary. At the end of March 1939, Chamberlain, still outraged at the German occupation of Prague, wrote to the Polish government promising that if their independence were threatened, Britain and France 'would at once lend them all the support in their power'. In April Hitler demanded the return of Danzig and a road and railway across the corridor. This demand was, in fact, not unreasonable since Danzig was largely German-speaking; but coming so soon after the seizure of Czechoslovakia, the Poles were convinced, probably rightly, that the German demands were only a prelude to invasion. Already fortified by the British promise of help, the Foreign Minister, Colonel Beck, rejected the German demands and refused to attend a conference, no doubt afraid of another Munich. Chamberlain now began to have second thoughts as the threat of war increased again. Britain urged the Poles to surrender Danzig, but Beck stood firm.

Meanwhile there was pressure from certain quarters in Britain for some sort of alliance with the USSR. The Labour Party, Lloyd George and Churchill all pointed out that the promise of British help to Poland was meaningless unless there was military help from the Russians, threatening Germany's eastern frontier. Stalin was anxious for an understanding with Britain and negotiations opened in April. However, Chamberlain and Halifax both detested Communism and were sceptical of Russia's military strength. An added difficulty was that the Poles were as nervous of the Russians as they were of the Germans, and would not agree to Russian troops crossing Poland to take up positions on the frontier with Germany. The negotiations dragged on without any result, and in the end the Russians grew tired of British stalling and signed a non-aggression pact with Hitler (24 August).

Also agreed was a partition of Poland between Germany and the USSR. Hitler was convinced that with Russia neutral, Britain and France would not risk intervention; when the British ratified their guarantee to Poland, Hitler took it as a bluff. When the Poles still refused to negotiate, a full-scale German invasion began early on 1 September. Chamberlain had not completely thrown off appeasement and still shrank from committing Britain to war. He suggested that if German troops were withdrawn, a conference could be held – there was no response from the Germans. Only when pressure mounted in parliament and in the country did Chamberlain send an ultimatum to Germany. When this expired at 11 a.m. on 3 September, Britain was at war with Germany. Soon afterwards, France also declared war.

(c) **Britain's defences**. Britain had never begun actively to disarm, though in the years before Hitler came to power, the government had been spending progressively less each year on armaments. For example the Conservatives had spent £116 million in 1926-7, Labour £110 million in 1930-1, and the National Government £102 million in 1932-3. As soon as Hitler became German Chancellor (January 1933), Churchill pressed the government to build up Britain's armaments, and especially her air defences. He warned that if war broke out, Britain would be subjected to heavy bombing: 'the crash of bombs exploding in London, and cataracts of masonry and fire and smoke will warn us of any inadequacy in our aerial defences'. The government responded, though slowly. In July 1934 it was announced that over the next five years an extra 820 planes would be built, bringing the strength of the RAF up to 1304 front-line planes. Churchill thought this inadequate; in May 1935 Hitler told Simon that his airforce was already larger than Britain's. This was an exaggeration, but it helped to speed up British rearmament, especially after German troops entered the Rhineland (March 1936).

Until Munich, German rearmament was much more rapid that Britain's; in 1938 Britain spent £350 million, whereas Germany spent £1600 million. At the end of that year Germany had 2800 front-line planes, Britain still fewer than 1000. After Munich Chamberlain was responsible for a dramatic surge in arms production, though it was only in the spring of 1940 that British aircraft production overtook Germany's, and Germany was still in the lead at that point. There was also a fourfold increase in the number of anti-aircraft guns; perhaps most vital of all in the air-defence system was the building up of a chain of 20 radar stations to track enemy planes.

However, there are still doubts about how committed Chamberlain really was. Cabinet papers and Chamberlain's letters show that he hoped

Munich would turn out to be a permanent understanding with Germany, so that rearmament would be unnecessary. With unemployment approaching two million on the eve of war, the government was certainly not rearming to full capacity.

26.4 WHO OR WHAT WAS TO BLAME FOR THE WAR?

The debate is still going on about who or what was responsible for the Second World War. The Versailles treaties have been blamed for filling the Germans with bitterness and the desire for revenge; the League of Nations and the idea of collective security have been criticised because they failed to secure general disarmament and to control potential aggressors; the world economic crisis has been mentioned, since without it Hitler would probably never have come to power. While these factors no doubt helped to create the sort of tensions which might well lead to war, something more was needed. It is worth remembering also that by the end of 1938 many of the German grievances had been removed: reparations were largely cancelled, the disarmament clauses had been ignored, the Rhineland was remilitarised, Austria and Germany were united, and 3.5 million Germans had been recovered from Czechoslovakia. Britain had even offered some compensation for lost German colonies. Germany was, in fact, a great power again. What went wrong?

(a) During and immediately after the war **there was general agreement outside Germany that Hitler was to blame.** By attacking Poland on all fronts instead of merely occupying Danzig and the corridor, Hitler showed that he intended not just to recover the territory the Germans lost at Versailles, but to destroy Poland. Martin Gilbert argues that his motive was to remove the stigma of defeat in the First World War; 'for the only antidote to defeat in one war is victory in the next'. Hugh Trevor-Roper and many other historians believe that Hitler intended a major war right from the beginning; they argue that he hated Communism and wanted to conquer Russia and control it permanently, and this could be achieved only by a major war; the destruction of Poland was an essential preliminary to the invasion of Russia; the non-aggression pact with Russia was simply a way of lulling Russian suspicions and keeping her neutral until Poland had been dealt with. Their evidence for this theory is taken from statements in Hitler's book *Mein Kampf* (My Struggle) and from the Hossbach Memorandum, a summary made by Hitler's adjutant, Colonel Hossbach, of a meeting held in November 1937, at which Hitler explained his plans to his generals. If this theory is correct, appeasement can be discounted as a cause of war; war was inevitable anyway sooner or later.

(b) **Other historians claim that appeasement was equally to blame**; their theory is that Hitler was prepared to get what he wanted either by war or by diplomatic means. Britain and France ought to have taken a firm line with Hitler before Germany became too strong. An Anglo-French attack on western Germany at the time of the Rhineland occupation would have taught Hitler a lesson and might even have toppled him from power. But with each success, Hitler's position became progressively stronger and he became increasingly contemptuous of the western powers. After the surrender at Munich, nothing could stop the German attack on Poland. As W. R. Rock points out: 'What a different policy could have done was to force the dictators to pursue their aggressive intentions in circumstances much less favourable to their military success, thus significantly altering the appeal of any war which they might consider.' Chamberlain has also been criticised for choosing the wrong issue over which to make a stand against Hitler. It is argued that German claims for Danzig and routes across the corridor were more reasonable than her demands for the Sudetenland (which contained about a million non-Germans); Poland was difficult for Britain and France to defend and was militarily much weaker than Czechoslovakia. Chamberlain ought therefore to have made his stand at Munich and backed the Czechs. Chamberlain's defenders claim that his main motive at Munich was to give Britain time to rearm for an eventual fight against Hitler, but his critics argue that if Chamberlain had genuinely intended to curb Hitler, it would have been better to have fought alongside Czechoslovakia, which was militarily and industrially strong and had excellent fortifications.

(c) A. J. P. Taylor has produced the most controversial theory about the outbreak of the war. He believes that Hitler did not intend to cause a major war, and expected at the most a short war with Poland. According to Taylor, Hitler's aims were similar to those of previous German rulers – Wilhelm II and Stresemann; only his methods were more ruthless. Hitler was a brilliant opportunist taking advantage of the mistakes of the appeasers and of events such as the crisis in Czechoslovakia in February 1939, the German occupation of which was not the result of a sinister long-term plan; 'it was the unforeseen by-product of events in Slovakia' (the Slovak demand for more independence from the Prague government). Whereas Chamberlain miscalculated when he thought he could make Hitler respectable, Hitler misread the minds of Chamberlain and the British; how could he be expected to foresee that the British and French would be so inconsistent as to support Poland (where his more reasonable claim lay) after appeasing him over Czechoslovakia (where his case was much less valid)? Thus for Taylor, Hitler was lured into the war almost by accident, after the Poles had called his bluff.

(d) The USSR has been accused of making war inevitable by signing the non-aggression pact with Germany. It is argued that she ought to have allied with the west and with Poland, thereby frightening Hitler into keeping the peace. On the other hand, the British were most reluctant to ally with the Russians; Chamberlain distrusted them, as did the Poles, and believed them militarily weak. Russian historians justify the pact on the grounds that it gave the USSR time to prepare their defences against a possible German attack.

What is the unfortunate student to believe if historians cannot agree? It has to be said that the majority view is that Hitler was largely responsible. Perhaps it is appropriate to allow the German historian, Joachim Fest, the final word: 'There can be no question about whose was the guilt . . . Hitler's urge to bring things to a head so shaped events that any wish to compromise on the part of the western powers was bound to come to nothing. His entire career was oriented towards war'.

QUESTIONS

1. Britain and Russia, 1938–39

Study Sources A to G and then answer the questions which follow.

Source A: Neville Chamberlain's diary, 26 March 1939.

> I must confess to the most profound distrust of Russia. I have no belief whatever in her ability to maintain an effective offensive, even if she wanted to. And I distrust her motives, which seem to me to have little connection with our ideas of liberty, and to be concerned only with *getting everyone else by the ears.* Moreover, she is both hated and suspected by many of the smaller States, notably by Poland, Roumania, and Finland. I suspect that they [the Russians] are concerned to see the 'capitalist' powers tear themselves to pieces whilst they stay out themselves.

> **Source:** quoted in K. Feiling, *The Life of Neville Chamberlain,* Macmillan, 1947.

Source B: speech by Lloyd George in the House of Commons, May 1939.

> The Polish army is a brave one, but in no way comparable to Germany's. If we are going in without the help of Russia, we are walking into a trap. It is the only country whose armies can get there. If Russia is not being brought into this matter because the Poles feel that they do not want them there, it is for us to declare the conditions, and unless the Poles are prepared to accept the only conditions with which we can successfully help them, the responsibility must be theirs . . . Without Russia, these three guarantees of help to Poland, Roumania and Greece, are the most reckless commitments that any country has ever entered into. It is madness . . . Did the General Staff advise the government before they entered into these commitments that there was the slightest chance of achieving victory? If they did they ought to be removed from the War Office and confined to a lunatic asylum. They are entirely impossible without Russia. I see no sign that the government has worked out this problem. What force can they

put into the field? How can they get them there? What would happen if the Straits of Gibraltar were blocked?

Source: quoted in P. Rowland, *Lloyd George*, Barrie & Jenkins, 1975 (adapted extracts).

Source C: comments by Iain Macleod, a Conservative politician.

Chamberlain was not attracted to the idea of an alliance with Soviet Russia. He agreed with Beck, the Polish Foreign Minister, that 'such an alliance might lead Hitler to make an attack which he hoped it might still be possible to avoid'. He also feared that it would make any subsequent negotiation with Germany and Italy difficult if not impossible . . . But the great obstacle to an agreement with Russia, as Churchill has pointed out, was 'the terror of Poland and Roumania of receiving Russian help in the shape of Soviet armies marching through their territories to defend them from the Germans, and incidentally incorporating them in the Soviet-Communist system, of which they were the most determined opponents'. Chamberlain shared this deep and justifiable emotion. He had as little taste for what he called 'the Bolshies' as he had for the Nazis.

Source: I. Macleod, *Neville Chamberlain*, Muller, 1961 (adapted extracts).

Source D: the opinion of Winston Churchill, who succeeded Chamberlain as Prime Minister in 1940.

There can be no doubt even in the after light that Britain and France should have accepted *the Russian offer*, proclaimed the Triple Alliance, and left the method by which it could be made effective in case of war to be adjusted between allies engaged against a common foe . . . The Alliance of Britain, France and Russia would have struck deep alarm into the heart of Germany in 1939, and no-one can prove that war might not even then have been averted. The initiative would have been regained by our diplomacy.

Source: W. Churchill, *The Gathering Storm*, Cassell, 1947.

Source E: comments by Francis Williams, a left-wing journalist and writer.

Maisky, the Soviet ambassador, called at the Foreign office with a message offering to assist in the defence of Roumania. Three days later the Russians proposed a Triple Alliance of Britain, France and Russia to resist aggression in Europe against any one of them, to be followed by a military agreement and joint guarantees of all the smaller states from the Baltic to the Black Sea . . . To such a step Chamberlain could not bring himself. He sat on the Russian offer for twenty-two days. At the end of this time he ignored the offer of a Triple Alliance and asked Russia to agree to join in the defence of the states on her border, without, however, any specific Anglo-French promises in return to assist her if she should be involved in a war as a result of her own obligations to any European state.

Source: F. Williams, *A Pattern of Rulers*, Longman, 1965 (adapted extracts).

Source F: information from a modern historian.

British and French military missions were appointed, and proceeded leisurely to Leningrad by sea. The military talks from 12 to 21 August were the final stage. The British representatives had been instructed to 'go very slowly'. The British government acted as though they had all the time in the world. They were mainly concerned to conciliate public opinion. As well, they hoped to give Hitler a vague fright. They did not at any time seek Soviet military aid in practical terms. Not only did they fear the consequences of Soviet victory and German defeat. They were hoping all along to strike a bargain with Hitler when the prospect of resistance had made him more moderate.

Source: A. J. P. Taylor, *English History 1914–1945*, Oxford, 1965 (adapted extracts).

Source G: the opinion of Chamberlain's biographer.

As the weakness of Poland and Roumania, left to themselves, became clear, the majority of the Cabinet swung hard towards the Russian alliance. The French already feared that failure to achieve this would result in a Russo–German Pact . . . Chamberlain was driven from his first tactic, which had been simply to persuade Russia to guarantee Poland and Roumania, towards a triple alliance between Russia, Britain and France. This basis was accepted in May, and by late July our sincerity was proved by the dispatch of a military mission to Russia.

Source: K. Feiling, *The Life of Neville Chamberlain*, Macmillan, 1947 (adapted extracts).

(a) **(i)** According to Source **A**, which countries did not like Russia?
    4(a)

   (ii) What did Chamberlain think about Russia's military strength?
    4(a)

   (iii) What do you think Chamberlain meant in Source **A** by the words 'getting everyone else by the ears'? **4(a)**

(b) **(i)** According to Source **B**, which countries had Britain promised to help? **4(a)**

   (ii) What difficulties did Lloyd George (Source **B**) think stood in the way of Britain helping these countries? **4(a)**

   (iii) How does Lloyd George (Source **B**) differ from Chamberlain (Source **A**) in his opinion of Russia's military strength? **4(a, c)**

(c) (i) According to Source **C**, what was the main obstacle to an agreement with Russia? **4(a)**

(ii) How does Lloyd George (Source **B**) think this obstacle should be overcome? **4(a, c)**

(iii) What opinion does Lloyd George (Source **B**) seem to have of the government's policy and of the Army General Staff?

4(a, b)

(iv) What evidence is there in Source **C** that the writer, Iain Macleod, like Chamberlain, does not trust the Russians? **4(a, b)**

(d) (i) Source **D** mentions 'the Russian offer'. Using the evidence in Source **E**, explain in your own words what this offer consisted of. **4(a, c)**

(ii) From the evidence of Source **E**, how did the Russian offer to Britain differ from what Chamberlain offered to the Russians?

4(a)

(iii) From the evidence of Sources **C** and **D**, how did Chamberlain and Churchill differ in what they thought would be the results of an agreement between Britain and Russia? **4(a, c)**

(e) (i) According to Source **F**, how did the British and French negotiators get to Russia? **4(a)**

(ii) How long did the final phase of the talks last? **4(a)**

(f) (i) What are the advantages and disadvantages of each of the Sources for the historian? **4(b)**

(ii) What evidence is there in these Sources that Chamberlain did not have a high opinion of the Russians? **4(a, b, c)**

(iii) From the evidence of Sources **E**, **F** and **G**, explain whether you agree or disagree with the opinion that Chamberlain and the Cabinet, in spite of their distrust, genuinely wanted an alliance with Russia. **4(a, b, c)**

2. Munich and Appeasement

Study Sources **A** to **C** and then answer the questions which follow.

Source A: the memoirs of Hugh Dalton, a Labour MP in 1939 and a supporter of rearmament.

There has been much propaganda on behalf of Chamberlain that '*he gained a precious year*', that Britain was much stronger in September 1939 than in September 1938. I have little doubt that we lost a precious year ... First we lost the Czechs, who had a million and a half men behind the strongest fortress line in Europe, and equipped by a highly organised and powerful industrial machine. They also had a formidable Air Force. An attack on Czechoslovakia would have absorbed a large part of the German Army and Air Force, in addition to which, considerable German forces would have been needed on the French and Polish frontiers ... At that time the Germans were not well equipped with tanks and other armour. All that came later, much of it taken from the Czech Army and some produced in Czech arsenals . . . The machines with which the Germans overran Poland and France were captured or constructed in the year 'gained' by Chamberlain at Munich or in the eight months of *the 'Phoney War'* . . . Though the weakness of the British Air Force compared with the German was a terrible fact, yet the Germans were farther away in 1938 than in 1940 when they overran Holland and France. Their bombers attacking Britain would have had much farther to fly in 1938, and without fighter escort.

Source: H. Dalton, *The Fateful Years*, Muller, 1957 (adapted extracts).

Source B: the memoirs of Lord Halifax, the Foreign Secretary 1938-40.

Once *the Austrian Anschluss* had taken place, it was no longer possible to defend Czechoslovakia . . . When all has been said, one fact remains unchallengeable. When war did come a year after Munich, it found a country and Commonwealth wholly united and prepared, and convinced that every conceivable effort had been made to avoid war. And that was the big thing that Chamberlain did.

Source: Lord Halifax, *Fulness of Days*, Collins, 1967 (adapted extracts).

Source C: a letter from Neville Chamberlain to Stanley Baldwin, 17 October 1940.

Never for one single instant have I doubted the rightness of what I did at Munich. Nor can I believe that it was possible for me to do more than I did to prepare the country for war after Munich. I still further increased the programme for a larger Air Force and I began all the Air Raid Precaution measures which have developed since. I also introduced *Conscription*. In Sept. '38 we only had 60 fire pumps in London, which would have been burned out in a week. Some day these things will be known. My critics differed from me because they were ignorant, it is only fair to add, deliberately ignorant in many cases. So I regret nothing in the past.

Source: quoted in K. Feiling, *The Life of Neville Chamberlain*, Macmillan, 1947 (adapted extracts).

(a) (i) In Source **B** explain what is meant by 'the Austrian Anschluss'.
   1, 2, 4(a)

   (ii) From the evidence of Source **B** and your own knowledge, explain why Halifax thought that it was no longer possible to defend Czechoslovakia. **1, 2, 4(a)**

(b) (i) Explain the meaning of the word 'Conscription' in Source **C**.
   1, 4(a)

   (ii) From your own knowledge, explain what happened at Munich in September 1938 and what part Chamberlain played. **1, 2**

(iii)   What evidence is there in Sources **B** and **C** to support the statement at the beginning of Source **A** that Chamberlain 'gained a precious year' at Munich?   **4(a, c)**

(iv)   From the evidence of Source **C**, what was Chamberlain's opinion of his critics?   **4(a, b)**

(v)   How would you describe Chamberlain's mood or state of mind as shown in this letter?   **4(a, b)**

(c) (i)   What does Dalton (Source **A**) think about the British Air Force?   **4(a)**

(ii)   What does he mean by the phrase, the 'Phoney War'?   **1, 2, 4(a)**

(iii)   In what ways does Dalton disagree with Sources **B** and **C** about the importance of the year following Munich?   **4(a, c)**

(d)   What doubts might a historian have about accepting the evidence in these Sources?   **4(b)**

(e)   The Munich Conference is said to be the climax of the British policy of appeasement.

(i)   Explain what is meant by the word 'appeasement'.   **1, 2**

(ii)   What other acts of appeasement had Britain carried out since 1935?   **1, 2**

(iii)   Explain why the British government followed this policy of appeasement.   **1, 2**

(iv)   To what extent do you think appeasement helped to cause the Second World War?   **1, 2**

3 Describe and explain Britain's reactions and policies during the 1930s towards:

(a)   the Japanese invasion of Manchuria (1931);

(b)   the Italian invasion of Abyssinia (1935);

(c)   the Spanish Civil War (1936–39);

(d)   Hitler's demands on Czechoslovakia (1938).   **1, 2**

4. (a)   As a supporter of appeasement, describe and explain your feelings and reactions at the following:

(i)   the Anglo–German Naval Agreement (1935);

(ii)   the German occupation of the Rhineland (1936) and the Anschluss with Austria (1938);

(iii)   the Munich Conference (1938);

(iv)   the German occupation of Prague (1939);

(v)   Hitler's demands on Poland in 1939.

(b)   As a critic of appeasement, describe your feelings and reactions at each of the above.   **1, 2, 3**

CHAPTER 27

BRITAIN AND THE

SECOND WORLD WAR

1939–45

SUMMARY OF EVENTS

Though Britain had declared war on Germany ostensibly to help Poland, there was very little that Britain herself could do; her army was minute in comparison with those of Germany and France. As in 1914 it would be possible to send only a token force to the western front, until a realistic army had been assembled. Until then it would be a question of defending Britain against whatever Hitler decided to throw against her; most people expected immediate bombing raids as Churchill had prophesied in 1934. However, there was a long delay, and it was July 1940 before the expected onslaught arrived. There were other surprises too: unlike the 1914-18 war, the Second World War was a war of rapid movement and was altogether a more complex affair. Major campaigns took place in western and central Europe, in the heart of Russia, in Burma and the Far East and in the Pacific and Atlantic Oceans. It will be helpful to divide the war into four phases:

(i) *Opening moves: September 1939 to December 1940*. By the end of September the Germans and Russians had defeated and occupied Poland. After a five-month pause (known as the 'phoney war'), the Germans took over Denmark and Norway (April 1940); a British attempt to dislodge them failed and caused Chamberlain to be replaced as Prime Minister by Winston Churchill, who proved to be as outstanding a war leader as Lloyd George in the First World War. In May attacks were made on Holland, Belgium and France, who were soon defeated, leaving Britain alone to face the dictators (Mussolini had declared war in June, just before the fall of France). Hitler's attempt to bomb Britain into submission was thwarted in the Battle of Britain (July to September), but Mussolini's armies invaded Egypt and Greece.

(ii) *The Axis offensive widens: 1941 to the summer of 1942*. The war now began to develop into a world-wide conflict. First Hitler, confident of victory over Britain, launched an invasion of Russia (June 1941), breaking the non-aggression pact signed less than two years

Map 27.1 *Main German thrusts in 1940*

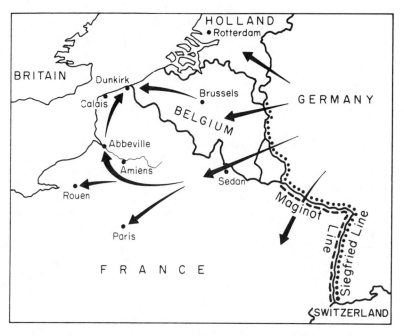

previously; then the Japanese forced the USA into the war by attacking the American naval base at Pearl Harbor (December 1941) and proceeded to occupy the British territories of Malaya, Singapore and Burma, as well as the Philippine Islands. At this stage of the war there seemed to be no way of stopping the Germans and Japanese, though the Italians were less successful.

(iii) *The offensives held in check: summer 1942 to summer 1943*. This phase of the war saw three important battles in which Axis forces were defeated. In June 1942 the Americans drove off a Japanese attack on Midway Island, inflicting heavy losses. In October the Germans advancing into Egypt, were halted by the British at El Alamein and later driven out of North Africa. The third battle was in Russia where, by September 1942, the Germans had penetrated as far as Stalingrad. Here the Russians put up such a fierce resistance that the following February the German army was surrounded and compelled to surrender. Meanwhile the war in the air continued with both sides bombing enemy cities, and at sea, where, as in the First World War, the British and Americans gradually got the better of the German submarine menace.

(iv) *The Axis powers defeated: July 1943 to August 1945*. The enormous power and resources of the USA and the USSR combined with an all-out effort from Britain and her empire slowly but surely wore the

Axis powers down. Italy was eliminated first and this was followed by an Anglo-American invasion of Normandy (June 1944) which liberated France, Belgium and Holland and crossed the Rhine to capture Cologne. In the east the Russians drove the Germans out and advanced on Berlin via Poland. Germany surrendered in May 1945 and Japan in August after the Americans had dropped atomic bombs on Hiroshima and Nagasaki.

27.1 EARLY SETBACKS: NORWAY AND DUNKIRK

(a) **The Poles** were defeated swiftly by the German *Blitzkrieg* (lightning war); this consisted of rapid thrusts by motorised divisions and tanks (*Panzers*) with air support: the *Luftwaffe* (the German air force) put the Polish railway system out of action and destroyed the Polish air force. This was the first demonstration of the vital role which air support was destined to play in the war. Polish resistance was heroic but pathetic; they had no motorised divisions and attempted to stem the German advance by massed cavalry charges. Britain and France did little to help their ally directly because French mobilisation procedure was slow and it was difficult to transport sufficient troops to Poland to be effective. The main British actions were to begin a blockade of German ports, as in the First World War, in the hope that Hitler would soon lose heart, and to send troops across to France. Chamberlain brought Churchill into his War Cabinet as First Lord of the Admiralty and there were several successful naval actions, including the defeat of the German pocket-battleship *Graf Spee* by three British cruisers. It was soon clear though that the submarine was to be as much of a menace as in the previous war: in October a U-boat slipped through the defences at the Scapa Flow naval base in the Orkneys, and sank the battleship *Royal Oak*. However, throughout the winter of 1939–40 there was no large-scale military action; this led American journalists to call it the 'phoney war'.

(b) **Norway (April 1940).** On 4 April 1940, Chamberlain said that Hitler had 'missed the bus', but his complacency was rudely shattered a few days later when Hitler's troops occupied Denmark and landed at the main Norwegian ports. Control of Norway was important for the Germans because Narvik was the main outlet of Swedish iron ore to Germany, which was vital for her armaments industry. The British were interfering with this trade by mining Norwegian coastal waters, and the Germans were afraid that they might occupy some of Norway's ports, as they were indeed planning to do. Admiral Raeder, the German navy chief, realised that the fjords would be excellent naval bases from which to attack Britain's trans-Atlantic supply lines. When a British destroyer chased the German vessel *Altmark* into a Norwegian fjord and rescued 300 British prisoners, Hitler decided it was time to act. On 9 April the Germans landed at Oslo, Kristiansand, Stavanger, Bergen and Trondheim, and although British and French troops arrived a few days later, they were unable to dislodge the Germans who were already well-established. After a temporary success at Narvik, all Allied troops were withdrawn by early June because of the growing threat to France itself.

The Germans were successful because the Norwegian forces were not even mobilised, and local Nazis under their leader Vidkun Quisling gave the invaders every assistance. In addition the British had no air support, whereas the German air force constantly harassed the Allies. *This Norwegian campaign had important results*: Germany was assured of her bases and her iron ore supplies, but had lost three cruisers and ten destroyers, which rendered the navy less effective at Dunkirk than it might have been. It showed up the incompetence of Chamberlain's government, which in the words of Churchill, had been 'forestalled, surprised and outwitted'. In the Commons debate on the campaign, it became clear that a large section of the Conservatives was turning against Chamberlain and wanted a more decisive leader. Leo Amery, quoting Oliver Cromwell's remarks to the Long Parliament, told Chamberlain: 'You have sat too long here for any good you have been doing. Depart, I say, and let us have done with you. In the name of God, go'. In the division, Chamberlain's majority dropped to 81 instead of the usual 240, and he resigned soon afterwards expecting Lord Halifax to succeed him. Halifax did not seem anxious for the job, and it was Churchill who formed a new government, on the same day (10 April) that Hitler's forces attacked Holland, France and Belgium.

(c) Churchill as war leader. Aged 65 when he became Prime Minister, Churchill was generally regarded as something of a failure in his parliamentary career so far. He was blamed for using troops at Tonypandy (1910), for the failure of the Gallipoli Campaign (1915), for his mistaken revaluation of the pound (1925), for his aggressiveness during the General Strike (1926), for his opposition to the India Act (1935) and for his support of Edward VIII (1936). All these suggested that his judgement was questionable. He had changed parties – Conservative to Liberal and back to Conservative again, so that many regarded him as unreliable and inconsistent. However, two things he had always been consistent about were the need to rearm and the need to stand up to Hitler; his aggressiveness which had so often seemed inappropriate in peace-time, was exactly the quality needed for an effective war leader. As A. J. P. Taylor suggests, 'it was as if all his life had been an unconscious preparation for this hour'.

Churchill set up a War Cabinet of five: himself as Prime Minister and Minister of Defence, Neville Chamberlain (who died in November 1940), Halifax, and from the Labour Party, Attlee and Greenwood. Later he brought in Beaverbrook as Minister of Aircraft Production and Ernest Bevin as Minister of Labour. Other Labour men included were Herbert Morrison and Hugh Dalton, while the Liberal leader, Sir Archibald Sinclair, became Air Minister. It was a genuinely national government which turned out to be extremely effective; according to L. C. B. Seaman, 'it was the ablest administration to conduct the nation's affairs since 1908'. He goes on to sum up its achievements:

> It gave the lift to national morale without which the trials of 1940-1 might not have been surmounted, and then piloted it with zest and skill, through the worst of the strategic and diplomatic hazards of a world-wide war; it so organised and sustained the civilian population that the stresses imposed by total war were endured with unexpected equanimity; and it provided the blueprints and in some cases the administrative framework, of most of the social reforms implemented after its dissolution in 1945.

The Emergency Powers Act (May 1940) which was rushed through parliament in one day, gave the government almost unrestricted power over all British citizens and their property; whatever action was thought necessary could be taken. Churchill dealt with general strategy and diplomacy; his mind was brimming with original ideas, some of which were impractical and even dangerous. The Chief of the Imperial General Staff, Sir Alan Brooke (from the end of 1941), spent much of his energy persuading Churchill to drop some of his wilder suggestions. Even so, mistakes were made: Churchill was at least partly responsible for the defeats in Libya and for the loss of Singapore. However, the great advantage of Churchill's methods was that they kept all the military leaders constantly on the alert, so that failures became fewer as the war went on. On the whole Churchill left the details of home front planning to Attlee (who acted as Deputy Prime Minister), Bevin, Beaverbrook, Morrison and the others.

Churchill's greatest contribution to the war effort was the sheer impact of his larger-than-life personality and his will to win. He provided an all-important psychological boost to a country which, within a few days of his taking office, seemed on the verge of defeat. For a 65-year-old, he had enormous physical vitality and mental energy; he was full of bulldog pugnacity, and everybody soon realised that with Churchill in command, decisive action would be taken. He actually seemed to be enjoying himself and this came over in his broadcasts. He had a brilliant command of words, and his speeches in the Commons, and particularly over the radio were highly effective. He spoke in language ordinary people could understand, rallying the nation in one supreme co-operative effort – the Dunkirk spirit. He left people in no doubt about what to expect: three days after becoming premier he told them: 'I have nothing to offer you but blood, toil, tears and sweat'. Britain's war aim was simple: 'Victory – victory at all costs, victory in spite of all terror, victory, however long and hard the road may be; come then, let us go forward together with our united strength'. With a man like this in charge, the majority of people did not think about defeat.

(d) Dunkirk and the fall of France (May–June 1940). German troops attacked Holland, Belgium and France simultaneously on 10 May and again *Blitzkrieg* methods brought swift victories. The Dutch, shaken by the bombing of Rotterdam which killed almost a thousand people, surrendered after only four days. Belgium held out longer but her surrender at the end of May left the British and French troops in Belgium trapped in a pincer movement as German motorised divisions swept across northern France; only Dunkirk remained in Allied hands. The British navy played the vital role in evacuating over 338 000 troops, two-thirds of them British, from Dunkirk between 27 May and 4 June. Dunkirk was a remarkable achievement in the face of constant *Luftwaffe* attacks on the beaches; it would perhaps have been impossible if Hitler had not ordered the advance towards Dunkirk to halt (24 May) probably because the marshy terrain and numerous canals were unsuitable for tanks.

The events at Dunkirk were important: a third of a million troops were rescued to fight again and Churchill used it for propaganda purposes to boost British morale with the 'Dunkirk spirit'. In fact it was a serious blow for the Allies: the armies at Dunkirk had lost all their arms and equipment so that it became impossible for Britain to help France. Churchill flew to France several times to try and rally the government and even offered them an Act of Union to turn Britain and France into one nation. But the situation was hopeless. The Germans now swept southwards; Paris was captured on 14 June and France surrendered on the 22nd. At Hitler's insistence the armistice was signed at Compiègne in the same railway coach which had been used for the 1918 armistice. The Germans occupied northern France and the Atlantic coast, giving them valuable submarine bases, and the French army was demobilised. Unoccupied France was allowed its own government under Marshal Pétain at Vichy, but it had no real independence and collaborated with the Germans. The fall of France was the high-water mark of Hitler's achievements. Britain and her empire stood completely alone against the dictators, and Hitler immediately began to prepare for Operation Sealion – the invasion of Britain.

27.2 THE BATTLE OF BRITAIN (AUGUST–SEPTEMBER 1940)

(a) In July Hitler began to assemble an invasion fleet of barges to carry the first wave of 260 000 troops which would be landed between Brighton and Folkestone. But he had his problems: he had neglected the German navy, not really expecting a full-scale war with Britain; it was therefore up to the *Luftwaffe* to clear the British Navy out of the Channel and destroy the RAF so that the invasion could go ahead unhindered. In one of his most stirring broadcasts Churchill warned of what to expect:

Hitler knows that he will have to break us in this island or lose the war. If we can stand up to him, all Europe may be free and the life of the world may move forward into broad, sunlit uplands. But if we fail, then the whole world, all that we have known and cared for, will sink into the abyss of a new Dark Age ... Let us therefore brace ourselves to our duties, and so bear ourselves that, if the British Empire and its Commonwealth last for a thousand years, men will still say, 'This was their finest hour'.

Already in July the *Luftwaffe* was attacking convoys in the Channel, though without much success; the Germans lost twice as many aircraft as the RAF lost fighters. In August the *Luftwaffe* switched to bombing RAF aerodromes and communication systems; 8 August saw the fiercest battles so far: the RAF shot down 31 German planes, and lost 20 themselves. On 12 August the radar station at Ventnor (Isle of Wight) was put out of action, but shortly afterwards Goering, head of the *Luftwaffe*, called off these attacks, under-estimating the importance of radar. The Germans made their greatest effort on 15 August, believing that the British must soon run out of fighters; but again their losses were heavy - 75 to 34 British.

(b) The crucial period of the battle was the fortnight from 24 August to 6 September. The RAF began to lose heavily - on 6 September alone they lost 161 planes against 190 German planes shot down. Many of the British fighters were bombed on the ground, and the aircraft factories could not keep up with losses of this magnitude. Also serious was the loss of pilots - during that fortnight 103 were killed and 128 wounded; again it was impossible to make up these losses with experienced pilots. Six out of seven major airfields in the south-east were badly damaged. Then, probably not realising how close they were to victory, Goering switched to bombing London and the other large cities, in retaliation for a British raid on Berlin. He was hoping to destroy civilian morale and reduce industrial production, but although enormous damage was caused and thousands of civilians killed, the German bombers suffered heavy casualties in daytime raids and were forced to change to night bombing. After the shock of the first raids in the 'blitz' (over a thousand people were killed in the first three days in London) morale rallied well as the civilian population soon learned how to cope with the resulting chaos and disruption. On 15 September the Germans lost 60 aircraft to Britain's 26. The Germans had failed to gain air superiority, and two days later Hitler called off the invasion of Britain. Bombing raids continued until May 1941 when Hitler was almost ready to launch his attack on Russia. The Battle of Britain is usually taken as finishing at the end of September, when it was clear that Britain had been saved from a German invasion. Altogther in the battle the Germans are thought to have lost 1389 planes against 792 lost by the British.

(c) **Reasons for the British victory**. Vitally important was the chain of 51 radar stations which gave plenty of warning of German attacks; this worked right through the battle and the Germans failed to realise the importance of disrupting the system. German bombers were poorly armed and German

Messerschmitt fighters, though not significantly inferior to the British Spitfires and Hurricanes, were hampered by limited range; they carried enough fuel for 90 minutes' flight, which gave them only a few minutes fighting time over Britain before they had to head for home. The switch to bombing London was a major error, because although it caused great damage and loss of life, it relieved pressure on British airfields and fighters at the critical moment. British aircraft production was highly effective; monthly output of fighters had been running at 250 early in the war, but this increased to 325 in May 1940 and reached a peak of 496 in July; even in September at the height of the blitz, 467 were produced. The Germans could not match this, and Britain always had more reserves than the *Luftwaffe*. Finally there was the skill and spirit of the fighter pilots and the careful strategy of Air Marshals Dowding and Park. As Churchill remarked when he paid them tribute: 'Never in the field of human conflict was so much owed by so many to so few'.

(d) The Battle of Britain was important because it showed that the Germans were not completely invincible. To the general surprise of the rest of the world, Britain was able to remain in the struggle and her prestige stood high. It meant that Hitler, who was poised to begin his invasion of Russia, would be faced with war on two fronts, a situation which had proved fatal to Germany in the First World War.

27.3 THE AXIS OFFENSIVE WIDENS

As the war developed into a world-wide conflict during 1941, Britain, having survived the immediate danger of invasion, now had to counter the threat to her empire – in Egypt and the Far East.

(a) Greece and Crete. Mussolini, who had already captured Albania, wanted a large Balkan empire. His forces invaded Greece (September 1940) but were soon driven back into Albania. Mussolini was clearly going to be an embarrassment to Hitler who began 1941 by helping out his faltering ally. Churchill decided to support Greece as a matter of prestige, to encourage other countries such as the USA and Turkey, to enter the struggle. 60 000 British, Australian and New Zealand troops arrived in Greece, only to be driven out immediately by a massive German invasion which soon overran the Greek mainland (April). The allies withdrew to the Greek island of Crete which had been under British occupation for six months. However, they had failed to fortify the island adequately, and it was captured by the Germans in a spectacular parachute attack, which forced the allies to withdraw again, with heavy losses (June). They had no air protection, and lost some 36 000 men with their equipment. The government was criticised for intervening in Greece, but the Germans also suffered, losing a third of their troops and 220 aircraft; they did not attempt another operation of this sort again. It has also been argued that

Hitler's involvement in Greece and Crete delayed his attack on Russia by about five weeks. If this was so, it may well have saved Moscow.

(b) North Africa. Fighting in this area was, in the end, much more successful from Britain's point of view, and helped to keep hopes of ultimate victory alive.

(i) *Mussolini had opened hostilities* by invading Egypt from the Italian colony of Libya (September 1940). A mixed army of British, Indian, Australian, New Zealand, French and Polish troops commanded by Wavell, pushed the Italians out of Egypt back into Libya and defeated them at Bedafomm, capturing 130 000 prisoners and 400 tanks. Tobruk and Benghazi were captured, but in February 1941 the British advance was stopped on Churchill's orders, so that many of Wavell's troops and planes could be used in the Greek campaign. This was unfortunate since only a few days later Hitler sent Rommel, one of his best generals, to Tripoli with a large German army, to stiffen Italian resistance. By April Rommel had driven the British out of Libya, though they managed to hold on to Tobruk behind the German

Map 27.2 *North Africa and the Mediterranean*

Allied advances and offensives 1942–4

lines. The unfortunate Wavell was replaced by Auchinleck, who succeeded in relieving Tobruk (December) but made no further headway.

(ii) *British forces in North Africa were labouring under enormous difficulties.* The main problem was that the further westwards the British advanced the more their lines of communication and supply with Egypt became strained. The other source of supply was from the sea across the Mediterranean. There was a constant battle for control of the Mediterranean where Britain's vital naval base was Malta; this was subject to the most intensive German and Italian bombing and was in danger of being starved into surrender. Between January and July 1941, very few ships managed to get through to Malta, though the situation eased after Hitler withdrew most of the *Luftwaffe* for the attack on Russia. Even so the loss of the aircraft carrier *Ark Royal* was a serious blow, and for much of 1941 and 1942, British troops in Egypt had to be supplied by ships sailing round the Cape of Good Hope and up through the Suez Canal. Additional problems were the extreme heat of the desert and the sandstorms, which made the job of the mechanics more difficult than usual. Moreover it seemed that the British position in Egypt was not secure; there was a large anti-British party which demanded the withdrawal of British troops and stores from Cairo and Alexandria. The British moved swiftly to deal with this problem: in February 1942 tanks surrounded the royal palace and the Egyptian king was forced to accept a pro-British government. The crisis was reached in June 1942 when Rommel's forces suddenly struck, capturing Tobruk and penetrating deep into Egypt until they were only 70 miles from Alexandria.

(iii) *The Battle of El Alamein (October 1942)* was the real turning point in North Africa when Rommel's *Afrika Korps* was driven back by Montgomery's Eighth Army. This great battle was the culmination of several engagements fought in the El Alamein area: first the Axis advance was temporarily checked (July); when Rommel tried to break through he was halted again at Alam Halfa (September); finally, seven weeks later in the October battle, he was chased out of Egypt and almost out of Libya too by the British and New Zealanders. Tripoli was captured in January 1943. The Allies were successful partly because during the seven-week pause, massive reinforcements had arrived so that the Germans and Italians were heavily outnumbered (80 000 men and 540 tanks against 230 000 troops and 1440 tanks); in addition Allied air power was vital, constantly attacking the Axis forces and sinking their supply ships crossing the Mediterranean, so that by October there were serious shortages of food, fuel oil and ammunition; at the same time the air force was strong enough to protect the Eighth Army's own supply routes. Montgomery's skilful preparations probably clinched the issue, though he has been criticised for being over-cautious and for allowing Rommel and half his forces to escape into Libya. However, there is no doubt that *the El*

Alamein victory was one of the three major turning points in the war (the other two were the Japanese defeat by the Americans at Midway Island (June 1942) and the German defeat at Stalingrad which ended in surrender in February 1943). El Alamein prevented Egypt and the Suez Canal from falling into German hands and ended the possibility of a link-up between the Axis forces in the Middle East and those in the Ukraine. More than that, it led on to the complete expulsion of Axis forces from North Africa; it encouraged landings of American and British troops in the French territories of Morocco and Algeria to threaten the Germans and Italians from the west while the Eighth Army closed in on them from Libya. Trapped in Tunisia, 275 000 Germans and Italians were forced to surrender (May 1943) and the Allies were well-placed for an invasion of Italy. The desert war had been a serious drain on German resources which could have been used in Russia where they were badly needed.

Map 27.3 *The War in the Pacific*

(c) The Far East: Malaya, Singapore and Burma. Here there was nothing but disaster for Britain. The Japanese, after their successful attack on Pearl Harbor (7 December 1941), went on to invade British territories in the Far East, all of which were inadequately defended. Hong Kong was taken and Japanese troops landed on the coast of northern Malaya, capturing all the airfields. This deprived the British of air protection and Japanese planes sank the *Repulse* and the *Prince of Wales* (10 December) with the loss of 600 lives. These were the two main capital ships meant to maintain control of the area. Meanwhile Japanese troops advanced down the Malay peninsula until by the end of January 1942 only Singapore remained in British hands. The Australians now seemed on the verge of panic, thinking that they were next in line for a Japanese attack; it was mainly to satisfy them that Churchill sent more troops to Singapore. But it was too late: it was primarily a naval base and was not equipped to withstand an assault from the land. On 15 February, with the supply of fresh water cut off, the British commander surrendered with 60 000 troops. Though it was not the knockout blow that Hitler hoped, it was a serious blow to Britain's prestige as an imperial power. For the first time the British had suffered a major defeat at the hands of an Asian power. This encouraged opposition to British rule in India, and it meant that after the war the Indians would be content with nothing less than full independence. Australia began to look towards the USA as her main defence against Japan. The loss of Singapore led to the Japanese occupation of Burma (March), and the fall of India seemed imminent. However, although the British did not realise it at the time, they need not have worried: the Japanese were mainly concerned with the Pacific and had no immediate plans to conquer India. This came much later – in March 1944 (see Section 27.6(d)).

27.4 THE WAR AT SEA

As in the First World War, the British navy had a vital role to play. This included protecting merchant ships bringing food supplies, sinking German submarines and surface raiders, blockading Germany, and transporting and supplying the Allied troops fighting in North Africa and later in Italy. At first success was mixed, mainly because the British failed to understand the importance of air support in naval operations and had few aircraft carriers. Thus they suffered defeats in Norway and Crete where the Germans had strong air superiority. In addition the Germans had numerous naval bases in Norway, Denmark, France and Italy. British weakness in the Far East led to the fall of Hong Kong, Malaya, Singapore and Burma. However, there were some successes:

(a) Aircraft from the carrier *Illustrious* sank half the Italian fleet at Taranto (November 1940); the following March five more warships were destroyed off Cape Matapan.

(b) The threat from surface raiders was removed by the sinking of the *Bismarck*, Germany's only battleship at the time (May 1941).

(c) The navy destroyed the German invasion transports on their way to Crete (May 1941), though they could not prevent the landing of parachute troops.

(d) They provided escorts for convoys carrying supplies to help the Russians; these sailed via the Arctic to Murmansk in the far north of Russia. Beginning in September 1941 the first twelve convoys arrived without incident, but then the Germans began to attack them, until convoy 17 lost 23 ships out of 36 (June 1942). After this disaster Arctic convoys were not fully resumed until November 1943, when stronger escorts could be spared. Altogether 40 convoys sailed: 720 out of a total of 811 merchant ships arrived safely, with valuable cargo for the Russians including 5000 tanks and 7000 aircraft as well as thousands of tons of canned meat.

(e) Their most important contribution was their victory in *the Battle of the Atlantic*. This was the struggle against German U-boats attempting to deprive Britain of food and raw materials. At the beginning of 1942 the Germans had 90 U-boats in operation and 250 being built; in the first six months of that year the Allies lost over 4 million tons of merchant shipping and destroyed only 21 U-boats; losses reached a peak of 108 ships in March 1943, almost two-thirds of which were in convoy. However, after that the number of sinkings began to fall, while U-boat losses increased; by July 1943 the Allies could produce ships at a faster rate than the U-boats could sink them, and the situation was under control. *The reasons for the Allied success* were that more air protection was provided for convoys by long-range Liberators, both escorts and aircraft protection improved with experience, and the British introduced the new centimetric radar sets which were small enough to be fitted into aircraft, so that submarines could be detected in poor visibility and at night. The victory was just as important as Midway, El Alamein and Stalingrad: Britain could not have remained in the war for long if she had continued to sustain the losses of March 1943.

27.5 THE WAR IN THE AIR

(a) The first significant achievement from the British point of view was the Battle of Britain (1940) when the RAF beat off the *Luftwaffe* attacks, causing Hitler to abandon his invasion plans (see Section 27.2).

(b) In conjunction with the British navy, aircraft played a varied role: the successful attacks on the Italian fleet at Taranto and Cape Matapan, the sinking of the German battleship *Tirpitz* by heavy bombers in Norway (November 1943), the protection of convoys in the Atlantic, and anti-submarine operations. In fact, in May 1943 Admiral Doenitz, the German navy chief, complained to Hitler that since the introduction of the new radar devices, more U-boats were being destroyed by aircraft than by naval vessels.

(c) The American air force together with the navy played a vital part in winning the Pacific War against the Japanese. Dive-bombers operating from aircraft carriers won the Battle of Midway Island in June 1942. Later, in the 'island-hopping' campaign, attacks by heavy bombers prepared the way for landings by marines, for example at the Mariana Islands (1944) and the Philippines (1945). American and RAF transport plans kept up the vital flow of supplies to the Allies during the campaign to recapture Burma.

(d) The RAF took part in specific campaigns which would have been hope-less without them; for example, during the desert war, operating from bases in Egypt and Palestine, they constantly bombed Rommel's supply ships in the Mediterranean and his armies on land.

(e) British and Americans later flew in parachute troops to aid the landings in Sicily (July 1943) and Normandy (June 1944) and provided air protection for the invading armies. (However, a similar operation at Arnhem in September 1944 was a failure.)

(f) The most controversial aspect was the Allied bombing of German and later Japanese cities. The Germans themselves had bombed London and other important cities and ports during 1940 and 1941, but these raids dwindled after the German attack on Russia which required all the *Luftwaffe*'s strength. The British and Americans retaliated with a 'strategic air offensive' – massive attacks on military and industrial targets in order to hamper the German war effort. The Ruhr, Cologne, Hamburg and Berlin all suffered badly. Sometimes raids seem to have been carried out purely to undermine civilian morale, as when about 40 000 people were killed during a single night raid on Dresden (February 1945). Early in 1945 the Americans launched a series of devastating raids on Japan from bases in the Mariana Islands. In a single raid on Tokyo (March) 80 000 people were killed and a quarter of the city destroyed. The Americans dropped the atomic bombs which brought about the Japanese surrender (August).

There has been some argument about how important the bombing campaigns were in bringing about the defeat of the Axis powers. The conclusion now seems to be that the campaign against Germany was not effective until the autumn of 1944. Industrial production continued to increase until as late as July 1944. After that, thanks to the increasing accuracy of the raids, synthetic oil production fell rapidly, causing acute fuel shortages; in October the vital Krupp armaments factories at Essen were put out of action permanently, and the war effort ground to a halt in 1945. By June 1945 the Japanese had been reduced to the same state. In the end, therefore, after much wasted effort early on, the Allied strategic air offensive was one of the decisive reasons for the Axis defeat; besides slowly strangling fuel and armaments production and destroying railway communications, it caused the diversion of many aircraft from the eastern front, thereby helping the Russian advance into Germany.

27.6 THE DEFEAT OF THE AXIS POWERS

(a) The fall of Italy was the first stage in the Axis collapse. British and American troops landed in Sicily from sea and air (10 July 1943) and quickly captured the whole island. This caused the downfall of Mussolini who was dismissed by the king. Allied troops crossed to Salerno, Reggio and Taranto on the mainland and captured Naples (October 1943) by which time Marshal Badoglio, Mussolini's successor, had signed an armistice and brought Italy into the war on the Allied side. However the Germans, determined to hold on to Italy, rushed troops through the Brenner Pass to occupy Rome and the north. The Allies landed a force at Anzio, 30 miles south of Rome (January 1944) but bitter fighting followed before Monte Cassino (May) and Rome (June) were captured; Milan in the north was not taken until April 1945. The campaign could have been finished much earlier if the Allies had been less cautious in the early stages and if the Americans had not insisted on keeping many divisions back for the invasion of France. Nevertheless the elimination of Italy did contribute towards the final victory: it provided air bases for the bombing of the Germans in central Europe and the Balkans and kept German troops occupied when they were needed to resist the Russians.

(b) The invasion of France (known as the Second Front) began on 'D-Day', 6 June 1944. It was felt that the time was ripe now that Italy had been eliminated, the U-boats controlled and Allied air superiority achieved; the Russians had been urging the Allies to start this second front ever since 1941 to relieve pressure on them. The landings took place from sea and air on a 60-mile stretch of Normandy beaches between Cherbourg and Le Havre. There was strong German resistance, but at the end of the first week, aided by prefabricated 'Mulberry' harbours and by PLUTO (pipeline under the ocean) carrying motor fuel, 326 000 men with tanks and heavy lorries had landed safely; eventually over three million Allied troops were landed. Within a few weeks most of northern France was liberated (Paris on 25 August), putting out of action the sites from which the German V1 and V2 rocket missiles had been launched with devastating effects on south-eastern Britain. Brussels and Antwerp were captured in Septmber.

(c) The assault on Germany itself followed, but the end was delayed by desperate German resistance and disagreements between the Americans and British. Montgomery wanted a rapid thrust to reach Berlin before the

Map 27.4 *The Western Front 1944–5*

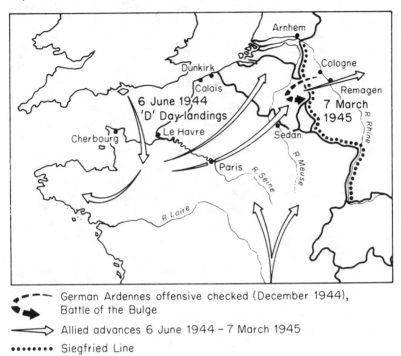

Arnhem
Dunkirk
Cologne
Calais
6 June 1944
'D' Day landings
Remagen
7 March
1945
Le Havre
Cherbourg
Sedan
R. Rhine
Paris
R. Seine
R. Meuse
R. Loire

‒ ‒ ‒ ‒ German Ardennes offensive checked (December 1944),
Battle of the Bulge

⟶ Allied advances 6 June 1944 – 7 March 1945

•••••••• Siegfried Line

Russians, but the American General Eisenhower favoured a cautious advance along a broad front. The British failure at Arnhem in Holland (September 1944) seemed to support Eisenhower's view, though in fact the Arnhem operation (an attempt by parachute troops to cross the Rhine and outflank the German Siegfried Line) might have worked if the troops had landed nearer the two Rhine bridges.

Consequently, Eisenhower had his way and Allied troops were dispersed over a 600-mile front, with unfortunate results: Hitler was able to launch a last offensive through the weakly defended Ardennes towards Antwerp; the Germans broke through the American lines and advanced 60 miles causing a huge bulge in the front line (December 1944). Determined British and American action stemmed the advance and pushed the Germans back to their original position. But the *Battle of the Bulge* as it became known, was important because Hitler had risked everything on the attack and had lost 250 000 men and 600 tanks, which at this stage could not be replaced. Early in 1945 Germany was being invaded on both fronts; the British still wanted to push ahead and take Berlin before the Russians, but supreme commander Eisenhower refused to be hurried, and Berlin fell to Stalin's forces in April. Hitler committed suicide and Germany surrendered.

(d) The defeat of Japan took longer. Since the Battle of Midway (June 1942) the Japanese had never recovered from their losses of aircraft carriers and strike planes. The Americans always maintained their lead. Under the command of General MacArthur, they began to recover the Pacific islands, beginning in August 1942 with landings in the Solomon Islands. It was a long and bitter struggle which continued through 1943 and 1944 by a process known as 'island hopping'. The British contributed to the Japanese defeat by prising them out of Burma. The prelude to this operation came in March 1944 when the Japanese advanced into Assam and besieged the town of Imphal. They were resisted by a joint army of British and Indians under Mountbatten; both sides had to endure appalling jungle conditions – intense heat, snakes and disease, mainly malaria. The Japanese were amazed at the ferocity of the resistance – since the fall of Singapore they had been contemptuous of British fighting powers. After eight weeks they were forced to abandon the siege and withdraw into Burma. It turned into a humiliating defeat for the Japanese, who lost 53 000 of the 85 000 troops who had started the campaign. The main reason for the British and Indian victory was that the RAF was able to fly constant supplies of food and ammunition into Imphal. The Japanese air force, under heavy pressure in the Pacific, was unable to supply the besieging armies who were short of food, ammunition and medical supplies. The Japanese in Burma now found themselves pressed by the British and Indians from the north-west, and from landings on the south-west coast and by the Chinese from the north. When the Japanese-trained Burmese army joined the British, the fate of the Japanese was sealed. Rangoon, the capital, was captured in April 1945, and soon afterwards the Japanese withdrew into Malaya.

(e) The end came for Japan in August 1945. On 6 August the Americans dropped an atomic bomb on Hiroshima, killing 84 000 people, and one on Nagasaki three days later which killed another 40 000, after which the Japanese government surrendered. The dropping of these bombs was perhaps the most controversial action of the whole war: President Truman's justification was that he was saving American lives, since the war might otherwise have dragged on for another year. Many historians believe that this bombing was not necessary since, in fact, the Japanese had already put out peace feelers in July via Russia. Liddell-Hart suggests that the real reason was to end the fighting swiftly before the Russians (who had promised to enter the war against Japan) gained too much territory which would entitle them to share the occupation of Japan.

(f) Why did the Axis powers lose the war? The basic reason was that they simply took on too much; by attacking Russia before Britain had been eliminated, Hitler was facing two powerful enemies. The allies learned how to check *Blitzkrieg* attacks and began to appreciate the importance of air support and aircraft carriers. Italian incompetence was a constant drain on German resources, and the longer the war went on, the more the strain began to tell. Italy and Japan suffered from a shortage of raw materials and even Germany was short of rubber, cotton, nickel and, after mid-1944, oil. On the other hand, the combined resources of the USA, the USSR and the British Empire were potentially overwhelming.

(g) East–West relations at the end of the war. Towards the end of the war the harmony which had existed between Britain, the USA and the USSR began to show signs of strain, as the old mutual suspicions revived. The deterioration could be seen in two conferences, at Yalta and Potsdam.

(i) *The Yalta Conference* (February 1945) held in the Crimea, was attended by Stalin, Roosevelt and Churchill. At the time it was generally thought to be a success, agreement being reached on several points: the United Nations Organisation should be set up; Germany was to be divided into zones – Russian, American and British (a French zone was included later) – while Berlin (which would be in the Russian zone) would be split into corresponding zones; similar arrangements were to be made for Austria; free elections would be allowed in the states of eastern Europe; Stalin promised to join the war against Japan on condition that Russia received the whole of Sakhalin Island and some territory in Manchuria. However, there were ominous signs over Poland: when the Russians swept through Poland, pushing the Germans back, they had set up a Communist government in Lublin, even though there was a Polish government-in-exile in London. It was agreed at Yalta that some members (non-Communists) of the London-based government should be allowed to join the Lublin government, while in return Russia would be allowed to keep the strip of eastern Poland which she had occupied in 1939; but Roosevelt and Churchill refused to agree to Stalin's demands that Poland should be given all German territory east of the Rivers Oder and Neisse.

(ii) *The Potsdam Conference* (July 1945) held in Berlin revealed a distinct cooling-off in relations. The main representatives were Stalin, Truman (replacing Roosevelt who had died in April) and Churchill (replaced by Clement Attlee who became British Prime Minister after Labour's election victory). The war with Germany was over but no agreement was reached about her long-term future beyond what had been decided at Yalta (it was understood that she should be disarmed, the Nazi party disbanded and its leaders tried as 'war criminals'). Moreover Truman and Churchill were annoyed because Germany east of the Oder–Neisse Line had been occupied by Russian troops and was being run by the pro-Communist Polish government which expelled some five million Germans living there; this had not been agreed to at Yalta! Truman did not inform Stalin about the nature of the atomic bomb, though Churchill was told about it during the conference. A few days after the conference closed the two atomic bombs were dropped on Japan and the war ended quickly on 10 August without the need for Russian aid (though the Russians declared war on Japan

Map 27.5 *Europe after 1945*

Land taken by Poland from Germany: territory east of the *Oder–Neisse* Line and part of East Prussia

Land acquired by the USSR during the war

Occupation zones in Germany and Austria:
1 Russian   3 French
2 British   4 American

on 8 August and invaded Manchuria). Though they annexed south Sakhalin as agreed at Yalta they were allowed no part in the occupation of Japan.

27.7 WHAT WERE THE EFFECTS OF THE WAR ON BRITAIN?

(a) The civilian population was more directly involved in this conflict than in the First World War. It was a 'total war' summed up perfectly by Churchill in one of his speeches:

> The whole of the warring nations are not only soldiers but the entire population, men, women and children. The fronts are everywhere. The trenches are dug in the towns and streets. Every village is fortified, every road is barred. The workmen are soldiers with different weapons but the same courage.

Immediate measures included the mass evacuation of children from cities and large towns to escape the expected bombings, the frantic digging of air-raid shelters and piling up of sand-bags and the issue of gas masks to civilians, in case of poison gas attacks. A complete blackout was imposed so that no chinks of light would remain to guide the German bombers; this had the unfortunate effect of doubling road accidents, and before the end of 1939, partial or 'glimmer' lighting of streets was allowed. Cinemas and theatres were closed and football matches banned, in case of bombing, but regulations were relaxed before Christmas and never reimposed.

In 1940, with the German invasion imminent, the government began to take more drastic action. The Emergency Powers Act (May 1940) gave the authorities full power to do whatever they pleased. Signposts, place-names and station name-boards were removed to confuse the Germans (if they arrived). Rationing of bacon, butter, cheese and meat was introduced and during 1941, as the German submarine campaign reached its peak, regulations were further tightened. The weekly rations per person were austere to say the least: eight ounces of meat, one ounce of cheese, four ounces of bacon or ham, eight ounces of sugar, two ounces of tea, two ounces of butter and two ounces of jam or marmalade. A 'points' system was introduced for other foods: each person was allowed 16 points for four weeks, so that the wealthy were prevented from buying up all the supplies. Goods available on the points system included tinned foods, rice, sago and tapioca, peas and tomatoes, breakfast cereals and condensed milk, and syrup, treacle and biscuits. Bread, beer and tobacco were never rationed, but beer was watered until it had no more than two-thirds its original alcohol content. Later, clothing and fuel were rationed. There were chronic shortages of all household goods as the war effort drew in most of the available raw materials. On the whole, people accepted the rationing without too much complaint because it seemed to be fair.

Conscription was immediately put into operation and applied to women as well as men, if they were required. The government also called for local volunteers, aged 40 to 65 to act as a Home Guard in the event of an invasion; by mid-1940 over a million men had joined. Though their potential value as a fighting force has been questioned, they fulfilled a useful function in guarding the British coast, so that the professional army was free to undergo intensive training.

German bombing was the worst trial. Starting in early September 1940, London was bombed for 76 consecutive nights and the attacks continued into May 1941. Other cities also suffered - Coventry, Liverpool, Manchester, Plymouth, Hull, Glasgow, Belfast, and many more took a battering. About 60 000 people were killed, half of them in London, and perhaps 100 000 seriously injured. Hundreds of thousands of people were made homeless and had to be housed in emergency centres - cinemas, theatres, schools, or whatever was convenient. In London, thousands took refuge in the tube stations, since government preparations for civil defence were largely inadequate. This caused a great deal of resentment, particularly in London's East End, but on the whole, morale stayed remarkably high, and American journalists were amazed at the calmness with which ordinary people tried to continue business as usual among the damage and disruption.

The war economy produced full employment for the first time since 1918, and the poorer working class groups probably benefited from this. The government tried to keep prices under control to avoid inflation, and although it did not succeed completely, wages rose faster than prices. At the beginning of the war, average weekly earnings were around 53*s*., while at the end they were 96*s*. Bevin had the power to direct workers where they were needed, and he did his job with such tact and sensitivity that with very few exceptions, the workers were reasonably happy.

(b) **Long-term social effects of the war** are more difficult to be sure about. Some historians believe that the war caused a social revolution, while others, such as Angus Calder think this is an exaggeration and that, at most, it hastened British society 'in its progress along the old grooves'. Certainly the war caused a great deal of heart-searching about the social problems. Many of the middle class were appalled at the deprivation of the evacuee children who came to stay with them. Yet, as Calder points out, in a total war 'the nation's rulers, whether they liked it or not, depended on the willing co-operation of the ruled, including even scorned and under-privileged sections of society, manual workers and women'. It was widely felt that the poor, by their co-operation and all-out efforts, had earned concessions - better education, a higher standard of living and better welfare services. There was the added incentive that if the workers were not given what they wanted, they might try and take it by revolution. The two most striking results of this thinking were:

(i) *The Beveridge Report (1942).* The government appointed a committee under Sir William Beveridge, a Liberal, to investigate the problems of social insurance. His report claimed that the great evils to be overcome were want, disease, ignorance, squalor and idleness, and suggested that the government should fight them with insurance schemes, child allowances, a national health service and a policy of full employment. However, this was strong stuff for the Conservatives and Churchill did not approve of the Report. Only one of its recommendations was introduced before the end of the war – payment of child allowances at the rate of 5s. a week for each child after the first. It was left to the Labour governments of 1945–51 to introduce a Welfare State (see Section 28.3).

(ii) *The Butler Education Act* (1944). The work of R. A. Butler, the Conservative President of the Board of Education in the coalition government, this act made secondary education available to all, free and without restriction, and raised the school-leaving age to 15 (to take effect in 1947). It also laid down that secondary schools were to be of three types – grammar, technical and modern.

(c) The main political effect of the war was to cause the election of a Labour government with a huge majority in July 1945. In normal circumstances a general election would have been due in 1940, and looking at the trends during the 1930s, it seems most unlikely that Labour would have won. Even if they had, they would have lacked the programme and the experience to act in the way they did after 1945. The war provided them with both.

(d) Economically, the cost of the war was ruinous for Britain. In 1939 her gold reserves stood at £864 million, but by March 1941 they had plunged to £3 million. At that point the US Congress passed the *Lend-Lease Act* which enabled the British to obtain crucial supplies from America, to be paid for later. American help kept Britain going during the war, but it was not given free – by the autumn of 1945 Britain's overseas debts (not all to the USA) stood at well over £3000 million. On the defeat of Japan, Truman, the new American president, abruptly ended Lend-Lease, leaving Britain with much of her foreign investments sold off and her capacity to export sadly reduced. The only solution seemed to be to request another loan from the USA, which was granted on unfavourable terms to Britain. Britain was therefore reduced to a close and uncomfortable dependence on the USA.

(e) Britain's world position was changed. Her empire had survived intact, but as we saw earlier, British defeats had stirred up nationalist feelings, especially in India and the Far East. Within 20 years most of Britain's empire had become independent, though within the Commonwealth. The war revealed the USA and the USSR as the world's most powerful states, while Britain, though victorious, was now only a second-rate power.

(f) There was no all-inclusive peace settlement of the type reached at Versailles at the end of the First World War; this was mainly because the suspicion and distrust, which had re-emerged between Russia and the west in the final months of the war, made a comprehensive settlement impossible. The results of a number of separate treaties can be summarised briefly: Italy lost her African colonies and renounced her claims to Albania and Abyssinia (Ethiopia); Russia took the eastern tip of Czechoslovakia, the Petsamo district and the area round Lake Ladoga from Finland and held on to Estonia, Latvia, Lithuania and eastern Poland which had been occupied in 1939. Russia also took Bessarabia and northern Bukovina from Romania, who recovered northern Transylvania which the Hungarians had occupied during the war. Trieste, claimed by both Italy and Yugoslavia, was declared free territory protected by the United Nations. Later in San Francisco (1951) Japan agreed to surrender all territory acquired during the previous 90 years, which included a complete withdrawal from China. The Russians refused to agree to any settlement over Germany and Austria beyond that they should be occupied by Allied troops and that East Prussia should be divided between Russia and Poland.

QUESTIONS

1. Churchill as a War Leader
Study Sources **A** to **F** and then answer the questions which follow.

Source A. the memoirs of Lord Halifax.

At the Foreign Office and in the War Cabinet I shared responsibility under the Prime Minister [Churchill] until the end of 1940, through the days which preceded, witnessed, and followed the collapse of France and Belgium, and the miracle of Dunkirk. The main burden of all this fell upon Churchill, and inspired him to give leadership to the British people, matchless and unforgettable . . . I asked him one day if he could ever imagine circumstances in which he might think it right to recommend the King and Government to move to Canada. He thought for a moment, and then said with great emphasis that he could imagine no such circumstances; every man ought to fight to the death on his own soil, and 'if they come to London, I shall take a rifle and put myself in the pillbox at the bottom of Downing Street and shoot till I've no more ammunition, and then they can damned well shoot me' . . . [in his speeches] the Prime Minister was expressing with complete accuracy the mind of the nation, as each successive misfortune made sharper the contrast between what looked to be inevitable defeat, and on the other hand what every British citizen, with indomitable refusal to accept the verdict, believed the result would somehow be.

Source: Lord Halifax, *Fulness of Days*, Collins, 1957 (adapted extracts).

Source B: a historian's opinion.

From first to last, his part in winning the war was greater than any man's – British, American or Russian. He was fertile in resource, inexhaustible in argument, and a spur and stimulus to bold action of any kind. As Prime Minister, Churchill oversaw every department of the country's life and moulded it into an instrument for total war. This gigantic man fired the whole nation with his passionate indignation, pugnacity, impatience and refusal to admit defeat. Even his faults, when tempered by advice, contributed as much to victory as his virtues. Without him there would have been no triumph . . . When in 1940 Churchill took on the offices of both Prime Minister and Minister of Defence, the three Service Chiefs became responsible to him alone. This close and direct contact between PM and Service Chiefs ensured the correlation of political and military authority and prevented the dangerous division of responsibility, so nearly fatal in the First World War, between politicians ignorant of military matters, and military advisers who had no means of making their advice effective . . . Without the public realising it, this silent revolution of the Prime Minister's ended the separation of military and political control. After 1940 almost every major question affecting Britain's war effort – fleets, armies, air-forces, manpower, shipping, industry and agriculture – was referred to Churchill and the Chief of Staff Committee.

Source: A. Bryant, *Triumph in the West 1943–1946*, Collins, 1959 (adapted extracts).

Source C: the diary of Field Marshal Lord Alanbrooke, Chief of the Imperial General Staff and Chairman of the Chiefs of Staff Committee, 1941–46.

October 6th, 1943. Found PM in a great flutter owing to German attack and capture of Cos. Meeting taken up discussing situation created by German capture of island, PM's anxiety to recapture it, and effect of its loss on the proposed operations to capture Rhodes. It is quite clear in my mind that with the commitments we have in Italy we should not undertake serious operations in the Aegean . . . By 3.25 PM determined to go for Rhodes without looking at the effects on Italy. I had a heated argument with him.

October 7th. Another one-and-a-half hours' battle with PM to hold on to what I think is right. The same arguments brought up again and again.

October 8th. I can now control him no more. He has worked himself into a frenzy of excitement about the Rhodes attack, has magnified its importance so that he can no longer see anything else. He has set his heart on capturing this one island even at the expense of the Italian campaign.

January 19th, 1944. PM starting off in his usual style. We had a meeting with him at 5.30pm for two hours and another from 10.30pm for another two hours. And we accomplished nothing. In all his plans he lives from hand to mouth; he can never grasp a whole plan – selects individual pieces of the vast jigsaw puzzle and concentrates on it at the expense of all others.

March 29th, 1945. I feel that I can't stick another moment with him and would give almost anything never to see him again.

July 25th, 1945. I shall always look back on the years that I worked with him [Churchill] as some of the most difficult and trying of my life. For all that, I thank God that I was given an opportunity of working alongside such a man, and of having my eyes opened to the fact that occasionally such supermen exist on this earth.

Source: quoted in A. Bryant, *Triumph in the West 1943–1946*, Collins, 1959.

Source D: broadcast by Hitler to the German people, 29 September 1942.

If someone describes even Dunkirk as the biggest victory in history, obviously we cannot even begin to compare our own modest successes with that . . . So if Mr. Churchill now says 'We want to leave the Germans to fret and ponder on where and when we will open the Second Front', then I can only say, 'Mr. Churchill, you never gave me cause to worry yet'. But that we must ponder – you've got a point there, because if my enemy was a man of stature I could deduce fairly accurately where he would strike; but if one is confronted by military nincompoops, obviously one hasn't the faintest idea, for it might be the most lunatic undertaking imaginable. With paralytics and drunkards you can never tell what they'll be up to next.

Source: quoted in D. Irving, *Hitler's War 1939–1942*, Macmillan, 1983.

Source E: the opinions of a military historian.

Then came the catastrophes of May and June 1940 when France collapsed and Italy entered the war. In that appalling crisis, the first need was to build up the defence of Britain, and the second to provide for the defence of the Mediterranean area. Those two needs were difficult to meet simultaneously. Churchill's boldest and greatest action was seen in the risks he took to strengthen the defence of Egypt before Britain itself was secure against invasion . . . In March 1941 Churchill declared that the new government of Yugoslavia would receive 'all possible aid and succour from Britain'. Hitler could not tolerate such an insult and at once decided to invade Yugoslavia as well as Greece. Yugoslavia was overrun within a week and

Greece in just over three weeks, and the British force was hustled back into its ships. The outcome reflected on Churchill's judgement and on those who had told him military intervention was feasible . . . The effects of the loss of Malaya and Singapore were disastrous. It is clear that the responsibility for the failure to reinforce Malaya's inadequate defences rests principally with Churchill himself – and was due to his insistence on launching a premature offensive in North Africa.

Source: B. H. Liddell Hart, *History of the Second World War*, Cassell, 1970 (adapted extracts).

Source F: a letter from Churchill to Sir John Dill, Brooke's predecessor as Chief of the Imperial General Staff, May 1941.

I gather you would be prepared to face the loss of Egypt rather than lose Singapore. I do not take that view, nor do I think the alternative is likely to happen . . . Should Japan enter the war, the US will in all probability come in on our side, and in any case Japan would not be likely to attack Singapore as this would be a dangerous operation for her.

Source: quoted in B. H. Liddell Hart, *History of the Second World War*, Cassell, 1970.

(a)   (i)   According to Source **A**, which two countries suffered defeat in 1940?   **4(a)**

    (ii)   What position did Halifax hold in the government until the end of 1940?   **4(a)**

    (iii)   In Source **A**, why does Halifax describe Dunkirk as a 'miracle'?   **1, 2, 4(a)**

    (iv)   According to Source **A**, why did Churchill not like the idea of moving the King and Government to Canada?   **4(a)**

(b)   (i)   According to Source **B**, how did Churchill control the military side of the war?   **4(a)**

    (ii)   In what ways was this an improvement on the methods used during the First World War?   **4(a)**

    (iii)   What evidence is there in Source **A** of the way in which, as Source **B** puts it, Churchill 'fired the whole nation'?   **4(a, c)**

(c)   (i)   According to Source **C**, which Greek island had been captured by the Germans?   **4(a)**

    (ii)   According to Source **C**, why did Brooke not want an attack on Rhodes?   **4(a)**

    (iii)   What evidence is there in Source **C** of Churchill's methods of running the war?   **4(a)**

    (iv)   From the evidence of Sources **A** and **C**, would you say that Halifax and Brooke admired Churchill or not? Explain your answer fully.   **4(a, b)**

(d) **(i)** In Source **D**, what criticisms does Hitler make of Churchill?
$\qquad$ **4(a)**

$\quad$ **(ii)** How would you describe Hitler's attitude towards Churchill in this speech (Source **D**)? $\qquad$ **4(a, b)**

(e) **(i)** According to Source **E**, what was Churchill's 'boldest and greatest action'? $\qquad$ **4(a)**

$\quad$ **(ii)** What two mistakes did Churchill make, according to Liddell Hart? $\qquad$ **4(a)**

(f) **(i)** Do you think the evidence of Churchill's letter (Source **F**) supports or refutes the accusation made in Source **E**? Explain your answer fully. $\qquad$ **4(a, c)**

$\quad$ **(ii)** What do you think are the strengths and weaknesses of Sources **A, C, D** and **F** as reliable historical sources? $\qquad$ **4(b)**

(g) Using the evidence of the Sources and your own knowledge, explain whether or not you agree with the opinion that without Churchill, Britain would not have won the war. $\qquad$ **1, 2, 4(a, c)**

2. The War and the Home Front
Read the extract and then answer the questions which follow.

The attack on Coventry – 14 November 1940

$\qquad$ The Germans poured hundreds of tons of bombs into Coventry in an attack which lasted for ten hours. The city centre was destroyed, one third of its houses made uninhabitable, 554 people were killed and 865 seriously wounded. There were signs of hysteria and panic as darkness approached . . . A hundred thousand loaves were rushed from neighbouring cities in a single day. The Women's Voluntary Service brought in mobile canteens and cooked stew in the ruined streets . . . Much damage had been done to production. 21 important factories, 12 of them directly concerned with aircraft manufacture had been severely affected by fire or by direct hits. But the limitations of terror bombing were exposed. The buildings were destroyed but not the machines inside them. Most of the roof had been blasted off the Morris Motor Engines works. But the workers went on with their jobs under the open sky. Within six weeks production was back to normal . . . The Germans, foolishly, did not repeat the attack.

$\qquad$ **Source:** A. Calder, *The People's War: Britain 1939–1945*, Granada, 1971 (adapted extracts).

(a) **(i)** What were the total casualties in Coventry on 14 November 1940? $\qquad$ **4(a)**

$\quad$ **(ii)** According to the extract, how did people react to the disaster? $\qquad$ **4(a)**

$\quad$ **(iii)** How serious was the effect of the bombing on production? $\qquad$ **4(a)**

(iv) Why do you think the author of the extract describes the German failure to repeat the attack as foolish? **4(a)**

(b) **(i)** Describe the actions taken in Britain's cities to cope with the German bombing raids.

(ii) Describe how the rationing system was applied and how success-fully it worked. **1, 2**

(c) Two long-term social effects of the war were the Beveridge Report (1942) and the Butler Education Act (1944).

(i) Explain why they can be seen as results of the war.
(ii) What were the main recommendations of the Beveridge Report?
(iii) How far had these recommendations been carried out by the end of the war?
(iv) Explain why the Butler Education Act was considered to be so important.

(d) Explain how the war affected the British economy. **1, 2**

3. From the British point of view the following battles were vitally important to the final outcome of the Second World War:

(a) Battle of Britain (1940);

(b) Battle of El Alamein (1942);

(c) Battle of the Atlantic (1942–43).

For each one:

(i) Describe briefly what happened during the battle.
(ii) Explain why the British were successful.
(iii) Explain why the battle made an important contribution to the final British victory. **1, 2**

4. On 6 June 1944, 'D' Day, allied troops landed on the beaches of Normandy. The 'Second Front' had begun.

Describe and explain the feelings and reactions of each of the following on hearing the news:

(a) an ordinary British civilian;

(b) a British soldier waiting to take part in the next phase of the invasion;

(c) a German soldier serving in Normandy;

(d) a French person living in German-occupied Paris.

CHAPTER 28

LABOUR IN POWER:
THE ATTLEE GOVERNMENTS
1945–51

SUMMARY OF EVENTS

As soon as Germany was defeated (7 May 1945), the Labour Party was anxious to withdraw from the wartime coalition and fight a general election, since the parliament was ten years old. Churchill would have liked to fight an election as leader of a national government, as Lloyd George had in 1918, but Labour's attitude made this impossible. Voting day was 5 July, though the results were not declared until three weeks later, to allow the armed forces to vote.

Labour gained a massive victory, winning 393 seats to the Conservatives' 213, while the Liberals could muster only 12. There was general amazement at this result; most people expected that after Churchill's splendid leadership during the war, the Conservatives would win comfortably. However, Churchill himself had doubts: 'I am worried about this damned election', he remarked in June; 'I have no message for them now'. *The basic reason for their defeat* was that, although Churchill was still popular, the Conservatives were not. Now that the war was almost over (Japan surrendered on 10 August) many people remembered the depression and held the Conservatives responsible for getting Britain into the war. The Conservatives had shown no enthusiasm for the Beveridge Report whereas Labour promised to carry out its proposals. Leading Labour politicians had gained ministerial experience during the wartime coalition, and there were no doubts about their competence.

This was the first Labour government to enjoy an overall majority, and it would now be able to achieve its most cherished objectives – a Welfare State, nationalisation, work for everybody, and an open foreign policy based on genuine co-operation – without too much opposition, except perhaps from the House of Lords, which held up some of the nationalisation programme. Unfortunately *the government was hampered by the most appalling economic problems*, in the aftermath of the war; the USA had immediately stopped Lend-Lease (see Section 27.7(d)), two-thirds of Britain's export trade had disappeared, much of her merchant fleet had been lost in the war, and without American aid she lacked the capital to

illus 28.1 *A Labour Party general election poster of 1945*

bring the economy back to normal peacetime production, so that she could begin to recover overseas markets. There were problems of international relations and the Cold War (see Section 30.1) and there was the dilemma of what to do about India (see Section 30.2).

The new Prime Minister, *Clement Attlee*, came from a middle-class background; educated at public school and Oxford, he had intended to become a barrister, but instead became interested in social work in the poverty stricken East End of London. He became MP for Limehouse in 1922 and leader of the Labour Party in 1935. In appearance he was mild and inoffensive, which led many people to underestimate him. Churchill described him as 'a sheep in sheep's clothing' and later as 'a modest little man with plenty to be modest about'. But this was far from the truth; Attlee was shrewd and determined, and like Lord Liverpool, was an excellent manager of the cabinet, which contained several strong-minded and potentially awkward people. The Foreign Secretary was *Ernest Bevin*; the son of a Somerset farm labourer, he had started work at the age of 11 as a farm boy; later he became a drayman and then leader of the Transport and General Workers' Union. After the 1926 General Strike he had turned against industrial action and was an outstanding success as Churchill's wartime Minister of Labour. The other leading members of the government were *Hugh Dalton* as Chancellor of the Exchequer (replaced by *Sir Stafford Cripps* in 1947), *Herbert Morrison*, leader of the House of Commons and *Aneurin Bevan*, Minister of Health. All, apart from Bevan, had served in Churchill's coalition, and formed a capable and experienced group.

The government was responsible for a remarkable though controversial set of achievements - a large dose of nationalisation, social reforms, financial measures, economic recovery and independence for India. Inevitably, aspects of their policies aroused opposition and in the general election of February 1950, Labour's position weakened as their overall majority fell to only five. The government struggled on until October 1951 when another election gave the Conservatives a slim overall majority of 17. Churchill became Prime Minister for the second time.

28.1 WHY AND HOW DID LABOUR INTRODUCE A POLICY OF NATIONALISATION?

(a) **The reasoning behind nationalisation** was that it would give the government control of the country's most important industries. This would permit more efficient planning and co-operation between industries and would ensure fair treatment and better conditions for the workers. The coalmining industry was a prime example of inefficiency and bad labour relations which could only be improved, it was felt, by government control. Under the general direction of Morrison, the programme was carried through. First came the nationalisation of the Bank of England (1946) followed in the same year by civil aviation. In 1947 it was the turn of coalmining (to be controlled by *the National Coal Board*), cables and wireless. Public transport (1948) was to be controlled by *the British Transport Commission* which was divided into six boards: Docks and Inland Waterways, Railways, London Transport, Road Haulage and Road Passenger Transport. The generation and supply of electricity were also nationalised in 1948, and gas followed in 1949. The only delay in the programme was with iron and steel nationalisation which met with opposition in the House of Lords; their argument was that since the iron and steel industries were reasonably efficient they did not need to be helped out by nationalisation.

To overcome this opposition the government passed *the Parliament Act (1949)* which reduced the powers of the House of Lords: instead of being able to delay bills for three sessions of parliament (i.e., two years), the delay could now be only two sessions (one year in actual time). At the same time plural voting was abolished and the Universities lost their representation in parliament. However, with all the delays, it was only after the 1950 election that the nationalisation took effect, and if Labour had lost the election, the bill would have been scrapped.

(b) Nationalisation aroused considerable criticism from the Conservatives who disapproved of any interference with private enterprise in peacetime, but also from some socialists who were disappointed by the actual form that nationalisation took. *Their criticisms were:*

(i) The newly nationalised industries were in practice public corporations like the Central Electricity Board and the BBC, set up by the Conservatives in the 1920s (see Section 23.1(b)). Workers had no control, no say in decision-making, and no share of the profits. It was felt that the previous owners had been compensated excessively; the mine owners received £164 million, and it seemed to the miners that many years' profits would be needed to pay off such a sum. What the government had actually done was to buy out the former owners while keeping the same management.

(ii) Only about 20 per cent of the nation's industries had been nationalised and most of those taken over were either unprofitable, or in need of investment for development, or both. Profitable industries remained largely in the hands of private enterprise. Yet the government felt unable to afford sufficient investment and consequently the nationalised industries, particularly coal and transport, continued to provide an inefficient service and ran up large deficits. This convinced the public that nationalisation automatically implied inefficiency and waste, and Labour failed to point out that the problems were of long-standing and that compensation was accounting for most of the profits.

28.2 HOW DID LABOUR ATTEMPT TO RESTORE TRADE AND PROSPERITY?

The immediate need was to revive the main industries so that Britain could once again begin to export at something like her pre-war level. Only then could *the balance of payments deficit* be removed (this is the deficit which results when the value of goods imported is greater than the value of goods exported, causing the difference to be made up from gold and foreign currency reserves). With her enormous debts and the stoppage of American aid, insufficient funds were available; desperate measures were needed:

(a) J. M. Keynes, the famous economist, was sent to Washington to negotiate an interest-free loan of 6000 million dollars. The Americans were unsympathetic and drove a hard bargain - they would lend only 3750 million dollars at 2 per cent interest, and repayments were to start in 1951; in 1947 Britain would be required to make the pound sterling freely convertible (exchangeable) for dollars. The loan was made available in July 1946, but within a year it had almost been used up. Industry was recovering and exports had actually reached 17 per cent above the 1939 level; but this was not enough - the balance of payments deficit stood at £438 million. However, help was on the way: the American Secretary of State, George Marshall, worried about the poor prospects for American exports and about the possible spread of communism in Europe, launched his *European Recovery Programme*, offering grants to any country in Europe which cared to accept them. In 1948 Britain gratefully took the lead, accepting what amounted to a gift of £1263 million (known as Marshall Aid). This enabled the recovery to be completed, and by 1950 British exports stood at 75 per cent above the 1938 level. There were several other reasons for the recovery:

(b) The government kept a close control on all aspects of the economy, particularly after *Sir Stafford Cripps* replaced Dalton as Chancellor of the Exchequer in October 1947. Descended from an aristocratic family, educated at public school, and with a successful career as a barrister behind him, Cripps was 40 when he was converted to socialism. He was a devout Anglican, moral and upright (many thought him sanctimonious) and had a highly developed sense of duty and service to his fellow men. He was a teetaller and a vegetarian and seemed to believe that *austerity* was the way to conquer Britain's economic problems. He left the country in no doubt about his priorities: 'First are exports, second is capital investment in industry, and last are the needs, comforts and amenities of the family'. The public must 'submerge all thought of personal gain and personal ambition'. No wonder an observer listening to a Cripps speech once remarked: 'you can just see the home-made lemonade boiling in his veins'.

(i) Since there was a world shortage of food, wartime rationing was continued. Bread rationing was in operation from 1946 to 1948, and potato rationing was introduced in December 1947; in almost all cases the allowances were lower than the wartime average. As the situation improved, certain commodities were de-rationed, but even in 1951, meat, bacon, butter, tea and sugar were still rationed. However, the government provided subsidies to keep food prices down, and gave help to farmers (price guarantees, subsidies for modernisation, and the National Agricultural Advisory Service to provide the expertise). This helped to bring about a 20 per cent increase in agricultural output between 1947 and 1952, and made Britain's farming industry one of the most mechanised and efficient in the world.

(ii) During the disastrously cold winter of 1946-7, demand for coal and electricity was so enormous that all fuels were severely rationed. For several weeks it was illegal to use electricity in the home between

9 a.m. and midday and between 2 p.m. and 4 p.m. Many factories had to close through lack of coal, and in March 1947 two million people were out of work.

(iii) Building materials were rationed and licences had to be obtained for all new buildings; this was to make sure that resources went into building factories, schools and council houses instead of into frivolous projects like dance-halls and cinemas.

(iv) Rents, profits and interest rates were controlled and a tight rein kept on foreign currency so that holidays abroad were out of the question for most people.

(v) Imports were controlled in the struggle to achieve a favourable balance of payments. The government bought supplies of raw materials for industry and allocated them to those industries which would contribute towards the export drive: cars, motorcycles, tractors, ships, engineering products, aircraft and chemicals. Cripps's exhortations to businessmen to export at all costs certainly worked, but it left a chronic shortage of consumer goods for the home market.

(vi) Cripps persuaded the trade unions to accept a policy of wage restraint between 1948 and 1950; at a time of rising prices this was a considerable achievement.

(vii) In August 1949, in response to a recession in the USA and a drain of Britain's gold reserves, Cripps devalued the pound so that it was worth $2.80 instead of $4.03. Many people felt that Cripps had over-reacted, but the devaluation made imports more expensive and British exports cheaper, so that for a time exports were boosted.

Exhausted by the strains of office, Cripps resigned in October 1950; he died in 1952 at the age of 63. Thanks to a combination of Marshall Aid and government direction, Britain was well on the way to recovery in 1950. Inflation was under control, there was full employment and exports were increasing. In the final year of its life - 1951 - the Labour government suffered an economic setback with the Korean War (see Section 30.1(e)). As the USA frantically rearmed, prices of raw materials were forced up on the world market so that goods imported by Britain rose sharply in price; when Britain also decided to increase her rearmament programme this caused more economies and shortages. When the new Chancellor, Hugh Gaitskell, tried to save money by the introduction of charges for spectacles and dental treatment, Bevan (the architect of the health service) resigned, along with Harold Wilson, the President of the Board of Trade, causing a serious split in the party. As Seaman says, 'the gains so painfully achieved between 1945 and 1950 were almost entirely eclipsed in the public mind, and the Conservatives were returned to power in 1951'.

28.3 WHAT MEASURES HELPED TO CREATE A WELFARE STATE?

The phrase Welfare State means one in which the government tries to provide the best possible social services for everybody; this Labour government is usually given most of the credit for setting up such a system in Britain. *The Beveridge Report (1942)* had provided plenty of ideas about what a Welfare State should aim for – the elimination of want, disease, ignorance, squalor and idleness; but the Labour Party had its own plans for social reform long before that. The party conference of 1942 which met before the Beveridge Report came out, committed a future Labour government to a comprehensive social security scheme, family allowances and a National Health Service. In spite of the country's economic difficulties Attlee was determined to undertake wide-reaching reforms, and a mass of new legislation reached the statute book. It has been described as a 'peaceful revolution', though other historians think that the reforms were not *revolutionary* at all, but merely *evolutionary* – i.e. they occurred naturally as the result of a long process of development.

(a) The National Health Service (1946) was the most spectacular of Labour's social reforms. It was the work of the Minister of Health, *Aneurin Bevan*, a former Welsh miner. Many people thought the task would be beyond him, but Bevan was an outstanding personality: he had educated himself and had read widely, he was a fluent speaker and a formidable debater – one of the few who could successfully stand up to Churchill. Within a very short time he had mastered the intricacies of the health and hospital situation, he had the vision to see exactly what he wanted and the energy and courage to make sure that he got it, in the face of some strong opposition from the medical profession. Starting in 1948, the system entitled everybody, free of charge, to medical care from general practitioners, specialists and dentists, to hospital and ophthalmic treatment, spectacles and false teeth, medicines and drugs, and midwifery, maternity and child welfare services. The scheme was financed mainly from taxation, but some of the revenue came from National Insurance contributions. To make sure that the same high standard of health care was provided in all parts of the country, Bevan decided that the hospitals should be nationalised. For health purposes England and Wales were divided into 14 areas, each under a regional hospital board; Scotland had five regional boards. Appointed by the Minister himself, these boards controlled general policy, while the day-to-day running of the hospitals was looked after by local management committees, of which there were 388 in England and Wales and 84 in Scotland.

There was considerable opposition to the scheme from family doctors who disliked the proposal that they should be paid a salary by the government. This, they argued, would reduce them to the status of Civil Servants, which, they seemed to think, was beneath their dignity. It would also, in some mysterious way, interfere with the doctor–patient relationship. In February 1948, 90 per cent of the members of the British Medical Association threatened to boycott the whole scheme. Bevan finally overcame their hostility by a clever device: instead of being paid a salary, doctors would receive fees based on the number of patients they had on their lists. This made all the difference, and when the scheme was introduced on 5 July, 90 per cent of all GPs took part.

The service was expensive, costing more than £400 million in its first year. This led Hugh Gaitskell to begin charging adults half the cost of false teeth and spectacles (1951). Bevan resigned from the government, furious that his principle of a completely free health service had been violated. It was a sad end to Bevan's ministerial career, but he will always be remembered as the architect of the National Health Service. It worked remarkably smoothly and soon brought a striking improvement in the health of the working class, while deaths from tuberculosis, pneumonia and diphtheria were greatly reduced. According to Sked and Cook, the new health service 'constituted an almost revolutionary social innovation since it improved the quality of life of most of the British people; . . . it was soon to become the social institution of which the British would feel most proud'.

(b) The National Insurance Act (1946) extended the original 1911 National Insurance Act to cover all adults. The scheme was compulsory; in return for a weekly contribution from worker, employers and government, the individual was entitled to sickness and unemployment benefit, old age pensions for women at 60 and men at 65 (26s a week and 42s for a married couple), widows' and orphans' pensions, and maternity and death grants.

(c) The National Assistance Act (1948) filled in any loopholes not covered by the National Insurance Act, which was supposed to apply to the entire population. However, people joining the insurance scheme for the first time were not entitled to full pension benefits for 10 years, and there were tens of thousands of old people whose only income was the non-contributory pension (now 10s a week, but still inadequate) introduced in 1908. The Act set up *National Assistance Boards* to which such people could apply for further assistance. This was an innovation, a decisive break with the past, since although applicants had to undergo a 'means test', the money for the extra relief was provided by the government from taxation, and thus it was a move away from the idea that poverty was a matter for local administration. As well as cash benefits the Act also provided personal services, and here the government did make use of local authorities, placing on them the duty of providing homes and other welfare services for the elderly and handicapped. Together with the National Insurance Act, this measure provided a whole new social security structure. It was generally welcomed, and unusually, the opposition chose not to vote against either bill.

(d) The National Insurance Industrial Injuries Act (1946) was a vast improvement on the old Workmen's Compensation Acts under which it had been difficult and expensive for a workman to prove that an injury or disability had been caused by his job, and since the employer had to foot the bill, it had been even more difficult to win adequate compensation. The new Act made it compulsory for both workers and employers to join the state in making weekly contributions to a fund which would provide compensation to injured workers and pensions for those who were disabled.

(e) In education the government concentrated on carrying out the *Butler Education Act of 1944* (see Section 27.7(b)), making secondary education until the age of 15 free, and providing meals, milk and medical services at schools. An examination was introduced to select which children were thought to be suitable for a grammar school education (or for a secondary technical school in the few areas where these existed) and which would go to secondary modern schools. In one sense the new system was an outstanding success: it allowed a whole new generation of able working class children to move up the educational ladder, many of them as far as university, which would have been unthinkable before the war. A successful Youth Employment Service was set up and the government embarked on an expansion of university and technical education. Many Labour supporters felt that by merely accepting the Butler Act, the government showed a disappointing lack of imagination. Within a few years *two main criticisms had emerged:*

(i) The education service provided varied in type and quality from area to area. Some counties, which could afford to provide technical schools as well as grammar schools, could boast that up to 40 per cent of their secondary places were in grammar and technical schools; but in some counties the figure was as low as 15 per cent. The 11-plus examination therefore did not indicate which children were suitable for which type of school: it simply selected the required number of children to fill the places available. In some areas children who were 'suitable' for a grammar school education, had to go to secondary modern schools, because there were insufficient grammar school places.

(ii) The system was divisive: the view rapidly developed that secondary modern schools were second-class institutions to which the 11-plus failures went; a new type of class distinction was therefore created. If primary education worked successfully without different types of school, then it ought to be possible, critics argued, for secondary education to be conducted in 'comprehensive' schools to which all children went at the age of 11, without selection. It was felt that Labour had missed a wonderful opportunity to introduce a comprehensive system free from class distinction, before the Butler system became established.

(f) Housing was a major problem. Apart from the housing shortage already existing in 1939, a further 700 000 houses had been destroyed in the war. In March 1945 Churchill's government announced that 750 000 new houses would be needed as soon as the war was over. Housing came under the control of Bevan's ministry, and although he was preoccupied with the Health Service, he still found time and energy to launch a housing drive. Economic conditions were not helpful – raw materials were in short supply and expensive; nevertheless, Bevan had considerable success. Only 55 400 new houses were completed in 1946, but this rose to 139 690 in 1947, and 284 230 (including pre-fabricated houses) in 1948. There was a slight decline after that, but in 1949–51 Labour still averaged well over 200 000 houses a year (most of which were council houses) and Bevan had provided far more new houses than Churchill had asked for. Unfortunately the figure of 750 000 turned out to be an underestimate; what nobody had foreseen was the increase in marriages and the rapid increase in the birth-rate; in spite of Bevan's undoubted achievement, given the difficult economic situation, there was still a serious housing shortage when Labour left office in 1951. Bevan protected tenants who lived in houses owned by private landlords, by introducing rent controls.

(g) The New Towns Act (1946) gave the government the power to decide where new towns should be built and to set up development corporations to carry out the projects. The aim was to create towns which were healthy and pleasant to live in as well as being geared to the needs of the towns-people, unlike the ugly monstrosities which had grown up without any planning during the nineteenth century. The first to be completed was Stevenage, followed by Crawley, Hemel Hempstead and Harlow. Altogether 14 New Towns were operational before the end of the Labour government, and these were not just in the south; successful examples elsewhere were East Kilbride, Peterlee and Glenrothes. Seaman believes that this Act was 'by far the most imaginative and revolutionary contribution which the government made to the improvement of urban living'.

(h) The Town and Country Planning Act (1947) was another Bevan measure designed to improve the environment. It gave the job of planning to the county authorities, who were all required to produce land develop-ment plans for the next 20 years. The planning authorities were given much wider powers of compulsory purchase and the right to control advertisements and preserve historic buildings. Government grants were available whenever necessary. If there was any increase in land values as a result of profitable development, the government had the power to levy a development charge on the increase.

(i) The Trade Disputes Act (1946) repealed Baldwin's 1927 Act of the same title (see Section 23.3(d)). The political levy was now legal again, and it was up to individuals to 'contract out' if they did not wish to make a financial contribution to the Labour Party.

28.4 WHY DID LABOUR LOSE THE 1951 GENERAL ELECTION?

(a) The country was becoming tired of rationing and the housing shortage, and there was a feeling that austerity had gone on too long. There was a new round of restrictions and shortages as a result of the government's decision to increase its armament programme when Britain became involved in *the Korean War* (1950-3) (see Section 30.1(e)). The period of compulsory military service (introduced in 1947) was increased from 18 months to two years in 1950, and this was an unpopular move.

(b) The government had just had to deal with *a crisis in Iran* (Persia), when the Iranian government suddenly nationalised the oil refinery at Abadan owned by the Anglo-Iranian Oil Company, in which the British government owned a majority of the shares. The Conservatives urged the government to send troops to recapture the refinery, but the Labour cabinet took no action, and thus laid itself open to the charge of weakness. The Conservatives were able to cash in with the cry that in situations like the Korean War and the Iranian Oil crisis, Churchill was the man needed to lead the country (a compromise solution was reached in 1954 allowing British Petroleum 40 per cent of the shares).

(c) The Conservatives produced an attractive programme promising to build 300 000 houses a year and to give the people 'more red meat', a tempting proposal at a time when meat was still strictly rationed.

(d) Labour campaigned on its achievements in office, which were certainly impressive. However, with the resignation of Bevan and Harold Wilson (President of the Board of Trade) over the introduction of national health charges, the party seemed to be split, and the government had a general air of exhaustion after its six frantically busy years in office.

(e) It is thought that Liberal supporters in constituencies where there was no Liberal candidate (only 109 Liberals stood) tended to vote Conservative. Even so, the Labour defeat was very narrow: Labour actually polled more votes (13.9 million) than the Conservatives (13.7 million) yet won only 295 seats to the Conservatives' 321. The main reason for this strange state of affairs was apparently that many Labour MPs in safe seats were elected with huge majorities whereas, on the whole, Conservative majorities tended to be much smaller. Only six Liberals were successful, together with three independents, giving the Conservatives an overall majority of 17.

QUESTIONS

1. The 1945 Labour Election Victory
Study Sources **A** to **I** and then answer the questions which follow.

Source A: 1945 election statistics.

Party	Votes gained	Percentage of vote	Average vote per MP	Number of MPs
Labour	11,995,152	47.8	30,522	393
Conservatives	9,988,306	39.8	46,892	213
Liberals	2,248,226	9.0	187,352	12
Communists	102,780	0.4	51,390	2
Others	751,514	3.0	–	20
	25,085,978	100.0		640

Source: D. Butler and A. Sloman, *British Political Facts, 1900–75*, Macmillan, 1976.

Source B: memoirs of Harold Macmillan, a Conservative who lost his seat at Stockton in the election.

As soon as electioneering began in earnest, I knew what the result would be . . . Many people believed that Churchill's first speech on the wireless was a turning point to our disadvantage. It was certainly unbalanced and ill-advised. He prophesied a growing control of all our lives if the Socialists won . . . the kind of political features that were associated with the Gestapo. But the use of this terrible word in connection with his opponents was a grievous error. Moreover, his implied attack on colleagues with whom he had been working in perfect harmony for the last five years could easily be laughed at as an outrage – men of moderate opinions such as Attlee, Morrison and, above all, Bevin . . . at the time it shocked as well as angered ordinary folk. I do not believe, however, that this incident was in any way decisive. The election, in my view, was lost before it started . . .

Vast crowds who had hardly seen Churchill in person since the beginning of the war and had only heard his voice through those famous broadcasts, flocked out to see and applaud him. They wanted to thank him for what he had done for them. But this did not mean that they wanted to entrust him and his Tory colleagues with the conduct of their lives in the years that were to follow . . . They had not forgotten the years before the war. Pamphlets and books attacking the '*guilty men* of Munich' were published and circulated in vast numbers. It was not Churchill who lost the 1945 election; it was the ghost of Neville Chamberlain.

Source: H. Macmillan, *Tides of Fortune 1945-1955*, Macmillan, 1969 (adapted extracts).

Source C: remark by Quintin Hogg (later Lord Hailsham), a Conservative MP.

The result of the election was not intended as a vote against Mr. Churchill . . . the decision can only be explained as the consequence of a long, pent-up and deep-seated revulsion against the principles, practice and membership of the Conservative party.

Source: quoted in A. Sked and C. Cook, *Post-War Britain*, Penguin, 1979.

Source D: speech by Clement Attlee, the Labour Prime Minister, in the Commons, 5 December 1945.

The electors did not accept the Right Hon. Gentleman [Churchill]; the alternative to Labour and a Socialist programme was the Right Hon. Gentleman. Throughout the election he had the spotlight. All those able and experienced front-benchers were mere chorus-girls; he was the star and he held the stage. The very candidates opposite [the Conservative MPs] were recommended to the electors not on their individual merits, but as the chosen supporters of the Right Hon. Gentleman.

Source: K. Harris, *Attlee*, Weidenfeld & Nicolson, 1982.

Source E: a comment by Attlee's biographer.

There were many among the Conservatives who believed that Churchill had personally lost them the election.

Source: as for source D.

Source F: the view of Michael Foot, a Labour MP.

Long before 1945, at every available by-election, the electors had shown the same deliberate demand for change. The vote in 1945 was a sober judgement on how the national energy displayed in war could be used to plan for the future. This, with the determination not to permit the disorder, misery and mass unemployment which had followed the 1918 armistice, was the central appeal Labour had made to the nation. The 1945 election was a victory for clear political principles and ideas, set out with reasonable accuracy in the party manifesto *Let Us Face the Future*, presented to the pre-election Party Conference at Blackpool.

Source: M. Foot, *Aneurin Bevan 1945-1960*, Granada, 1975 (adapted extracts).

Source G: comments by a historian.

Why did Labour win the 1945 election? The reasons are directly related to the war-time experience of the British people, since it was then that opinion swung towards Labour and gave it its decisive electoral victory. One reason for this was the happenings of 1940. The events of Dunkirk and the new spirit of national unity and social awareness, meant that public opinion turned against those held responsible for pre-war unemployment, the policy of Appeasement and the failure to rearm – Baldwin, Chamberlain and the official Conservative party . . . In the election campaign of 1945 Attlee's qualities of moderation and commonsense shone out, particularly in comparison with Churchill's over-dramatic speeches.

Source: P. Adelman, *British Politics in the 1930s and 1940s*, Cambridge, 1987 (adapted extracts).

Source H: article by George Orwell, a socialist and writer, published in 1945.

Everyone who took an interest saw that the only chance of getting the Tories out was to vote Labour and the minor parties were ignored . . . I don't think this means that Britain is on the verge of revolution. In spite of the discontent smouldering in the armed forces, the mood of the country seems to me less revolutionary, less hopeful, than it was in 1940 or 1942.

Source: G. Orwell, *Collected Essays, Journalism and Letters*, Penguin, 1970.

Source I: the view of two historians.

Churchill could not be totally divorced in people's minds from the Conservative Party record. He was regarded by nearly everybody as the perfect example of a Tory and by working people as their most irreconcilable enemy – he had suppressed the Tonypandy miners and opposed the general strike. His natural belligerence and warlike spirit now worked against him – the nation, having won the war, was seeking an enduring peace . . .
    The nation had also changed. They had accepted the need for controls and restrictions to win the war, and assumed that these would be necessary to achieve better housing and better social services after it. They knew that these benefits were more likely to be provided by Labour than by the Tories. The leaders of the Conservative Party – and Churchill in particular – totally misjudged the national desire for social change . . . Labour's manifesto promised, in addition to the nationalisation of many parts of the economy, both a comprehensive social security system and a national health service.

Source: A. Sked and C. Cook, *Post-War Britain*, Penguin, 1979 (adapted extracts).

(a) (i)   From the statistics in Source A, what was the Labour majority over the Conservatives in the Commons?   **4(a)**
     (ii) What was the Labour majority over all other parties combined?
                                                                   4(a)

(iii) If the Liberals had won 9 per cent of the seats as well as 9 per cent of the votes cast, roughly how many seats would they have had in the Commons? **4(a)**

(iv) What do the statistics in the column headed 'average vote per MP' tell you about the electoral system? Explain your answer fully. **4(a)**

(b) (i) What criticisms does Macmillan make in Source **B** about Churchill's radio speech? **4(a)**

(ii) Why do you think this speech 'shocked [and] . . . angered ordinary folk'? **4(a, b)**

(iii) According to Source **B**, why did vast crowds gather to see Churchill? **4(a)**

(iv) What reasons does Macmillan give for Labour's election victory? **4(a)**

(v) Macmillan mentions the 'guilty men'. What evidence is there in Source **G** to suggest who these men were and what they had been guilty of? **4(a, c)**

(c) (i) In what ways do Sources **D** and **E** differ from **B** and **C** in their explanations of the Labour victory? **4(a, c)**

(ii) What evidence is there in Sources **B** and **I** which would support those Conservatives mentioned in Source **E**? **4(a, c)**

(d) (i) According to Source **F**, where was the Labour election programme first presented? **4(a)**

(ii) From the evidence of Sources **F** and **I**, what did Labour's election manifesto contain? **4(a, c)**

(iii) How does Source **F** differ from Sources **B, C, D** and **E** in its explanation of Labour's victory? **4(a, c)**

(iv) What reasons can you suggest for this difference? **4(a, b)**

(e) (i) Do you think George Orwell (Source **H**) supports the explanations of the Labour victory given in Sources **B, C, D** and **E**, or the one given in Source **F**? **4(a, c)**

(ii) What evidence is there in Source **H** of Orwell's sympathy for Socialism? **4(a, b)**

(f) How reliable do you think Sources **B, C, D, F** and **H** are for the historian? Explain your answer fully. **4(b)**

(g) Using the evidence of all the Sources, explain whether you agree or disagree with the opinion that Labour won the 1945 election not because people especially wanted a Labour government, but simply because they were tired of Churchill and the Conservatives. **4(a, b, c)**

2. Read this extract from a conversation between Attlee and a journalist, Francis Williams, and then answer the questions which follow.

Williams: Had you a complete working pattern of policy already in mind when you became Prime Minister?

Attlee: Certainly. I was definitely determined to go ahead with plans of *nationalisation*. There was no difficulty with the Bank of England, Cable and Wireless, gas and electricity and there wasn't much with the mines. Transport was much more difficult and iron and steel had not been worked out . . . There were a lot of problems to clear up but I felt we must push ahead. Nationalisation had to go ahead because it fell in with the essential planning of the country. It wasn't just nationalisation for nationalisation's sake, but the policy in which we believed: that fundamental things – central banking, transport, fuel and power – must be taken over by the nation as an essential part of a planned economy – a basis on which the rest of re-organisation of the country would depend. There was the making of *the health service*, the co-ordination of all the various social services and *the advance in education*. All this could not be delayed. And there were practical things – building houses and many new factories . . .

Source: F. Williams, *A Prime Minister Remembers*, Heinemann, 1961 (adapted extracts).

(a)   (i)   Explain the meaning of the word 'nationalisation'.   1, 2, 4(a)

     (ii)   Make a list, in your own words, of all the things Attlee hoped the Labour government would be able to do.   4(a)

    (iii)   From the evidence of the extract, how well prepared was Labour for carrying out its policies?   4(a)

    (iv)   According to Attlee, why was nationalisation so important to the Labour government?   4(a)

     (v)   Which part of Labour's programme proved most difficult to carry out?   4(a)

    (vi)   Can you suggest any doubts which an historian might have about the reliability of this extract?   4(b)

(b)   (i)   From your own knowledge, explain why there was a delay before iron and steel could be nationalised.

     (ii)   Explain how the iron and steel nationalisation was eventually achieved.

    (iii)   What criticisms were made of Labour's nationalisation policy?

                                       1, 2

(c)   Attlee mentions the health service, which was introduced in 1946.

     (i)   Describe briefly the main features of Labour's new health service.

     (ii)   Why was there some opposition to the introduction of the national health service?

    (iii)   Explain how Aneurin Bevan, the Health Minister, overcame this opposition.   1, 2

(d)   Attlee also refers to 'the advance in education'.

   (i)   Describe the Labour government's policy towards education.
   (ii) What criticisms were made of Labour's approach to education?
                                                                1, 2

(e)   How successful were the policies mentioned by Attlee in this
            extract?   1, 2, 4(a)

3.   'Britain was well on the way to economic recovery in 1950.
            Inflation was under control, there was full employment, and
            exports were increasing.'

(a)   Explain how each of the following contributed towards Britain's
            economic recovery:

   (i)   American loans and Marshall Aid;
   (ii) Sir Stafford Cripps and his policy of austerity.

(b)   Explain why, in spite of its achievements, the Labour Party
            lost the general election of 1951.   1, 2

4.   Write the scripts for two radio broadcasts to be made as part
            of the election campaign of October 1951, by:

(a)   a Labour MP who reviews what he sees as his party's achieve-
            ments in government over the last six years and explains why
            people should continue to vote Labour.

(b)   a Conservative MP who reviews what he sees as Labour's
            disastrous policies and tries to persuade people that the time
            has come for a return to Conservative government.   1, 2, 3

CHAPTER 29

'NEVER HAD IT SO GOOD': CONSERVATIVE RULE 1951–64

SUMMARY OF EVENTS

After the Conservative election victory in October 1951, *Churchill* became Prime Minister until his retirement in 1955. At the age of 77, he was no longer the dynamic leader of the early 1940s, and left much of the heavy work to his acknowledged successor, Anthony Eden. Eden became Prime Minister on Churchill's retirement (April 1955) and immediately held a general election in which the Conservatives increased their slim lead to a comfortable overall majority of 60. Reasons for their victory were the country's growing prosperity and rising living standards, together with the fact that Labour was seriously split over defence policy. While the official Labour line was to go along with the government's rearmament programme, Bevan and his supporters – Harold Wilson, Richard Crossman, Barbara Castle and others – criticised it bitterly; Bevan was on the verge of being expelled from the party after his attacks on Attlee.

Eden's premiership (1955–7) was a disappointment. Much was expected of him: his reputation as an international statesman stood high, he had a social conscience, and since he was charming and handsome, he even looked the part of the successful Prime Minister. Within a few months, however, he was giving the impression of not being in full control of his cabinet, and even the Conservative press mounted a campaign against him, claiming that what was needed was a 'smack of firm government'. His disastrous handling of the Suez Crisis in 1956 (see Section 30.4) and his deteriorating health caused him to resign (January 1957).

Harold Macmillan was chosen as Conservative leader in preference to R. A. Butler, and was Prime Minister from January 1957 until October 1963. Macmillan was a member of the famous publishing family, and had aristocratic connections, having married the daughter of the Duke of Devonshire. According to Sked and Cook, he was 'a fascinating personality, a strange mixture of the hard-headed professional politician and the amateurish country gentleman, indulging a somewhat theatrical, Edwardian style of political presentation'. During the 1930s he had acquired a reputation as a progressive Conservative, with the publication of his plans for dealing with unemployment (see Section 24.4(d)). He still believed that the Tories should follow Disraeli's example, as Quintin Hogg (another Tory reformer) put it, 'to lead and dominate revolution by superior statesmanship instead of to oppose it, to by-pass the progressives by stepping in front of current controversy instead of engaging in it'. As Housing Minister, Macmillan had recently demonstrated his social awareness by building more houses per year than the previous Labour government. He soon revealed himself as a natural leader, commanding the respect of his cabinet and establishing a rapport with the public through his television appearances. By the time the next election took place (October 1959) the country seemed to have forgotten Suez, and the Conservatives coasted to an easy victory under 'Super-Mac''s leadership. Their overall majority increased to 100 seats; it was the third consecutive election victory for the Conservatives and a personal triumph for Macmillan.

The Macmillan years were a crucial period in British history; despite the Prime Minister's many gifts, even he was unable to disguise permanently the fact that Britain was no longer a great power. Most of her Empire gained independence without Britain's obtaining any compensatory influence in Europe. When she missed an opportunity to join the Common Market (1957) and was refused entry in 1963, Macmillan's foreign policy had largely failed (see Section 30.7). In home affairs Britain enjoyed a period of prosperity and rising living standards; as Macmillan himself told the electorate: 'You've never had it so good'. But in the early 1960s, the economy seemed to be stagnating and by January 1963, almost 900 000 people were out of work. Later that year, Macmillan, approaching 70 and in poor health, decided to resign and *Sir Alec Douglas-Home* became Prime Minister, until a general election was held the following October 1964. Labour won a tiny overall majority of four seats, and Harold Wilson became Prime Minister.

During the years of Conservative government there was no dramatic change from the policies of the Labour government. The term *Butskellism* was coined from the surnames of R. A. Butler (Churchill's Chancellor of the Exchequer) and Hugh Gaitskell (leader of the Labour party from 1955 until his death in 1963), to show that this was a time of *consensus politics*, i.e. there was very little to choose between the policies of the two main parties. There were differences in emphasis, of course, but certainly the Tories accepted most of Labour's nationalisation (only iron and steel and road transport were de-nationalised), the Welfare State and full employment.

Assessments of these 13 years vary widely. Some historians, pointing to the increasing prosperity and the *affluent society*, as economists called it, claimed that they were successful years. The Conservatives themselves emphasised this as their main achievement, as their slogans for the 1959 election proclaimed: 'Life is better with the Conservatives'; 'Don't let Labour ruin it'. However, critics concentrate on the rather confused 'stop-go' economic policies of the Conservatives and their failure to enter the

EEC; they see the period as one full of missed opportunities - 13 wasted years.

29.1 WHAT DID THE CONSERVATIVE GOVERNMENTS ACHIEVE?

(a) The improvement in living standards was the most striking feature of these 13 years.

(i) The first sign was the government's decision to move away from 'austerity' by reducing as many of Labour's controls as possible. During Churchill's government, restrictions of all sorts were swept away: all types of rationing and restrictions on building were ended, income-tax was reduced and restrictions on hire-purchase sales and even on the right to strike were removed.

(ii) Between 1951 and 1963 wages rose on average by 72 per cent while prices rose by only 45 per cent; this meant that people could afford more consumer goods than ever before. For example, the number of cars rose from under three million to well over seven million, while licensed televisions rose from 340 000 to almost 13 million. In 1961 the working week was reduced from 48 to 42 hours.

(iii) There was an increase in house building, thanks to the efforts of Macmillan at the new Ministry of Housing. He was determined to outdo the previous Labour government's record - their best year had been 1947 when 284 230 new houses had appeared. Macmillan threw all his energies into the 'national housing crusade', as he later described it. Unlike Labour, he encouraged local authorities to allow private contractors to build more houses and abolished Labour's tax on land development. Churchill told him he must produce 300 000 new houses a year, but Macmillan did even better - 327 000 in 1953 and 354 000 in 1954. The worst of the housing shortage was clearly over.

(b) There were some important extensions of the Welfare State: benefits were raised, and the Mental Health Act (1959) laid down that mental illness was to be regarded no differently from physical illness. However, the introduction of a 2s prescription charge roused the Labour opposition to fury. There was also criticism that very few new hospitals were built during the 1950s. In 1962 the government announced that 90 new hospitals would be built over the next 10 years, but the Conservatives were out of office before the programme got under way.

(c) Help was provided for agriculture in the form of grants for all types of improvements, so that efficiency was further increased and production continued to rise.

(d) There was an education expansion. About 6000 new schools were built and 11 new universities, while the existing universities were encouraged to expand. Realising the importance of technological education, the government introduced Colleges of Advanced Technology. The great debate in education during the 1950s was about the relative merits of comprehensive and grammar schools. By the time of the 1959 election, Labour was committed to supporting comprehensive education on the grounds that it would reduce class distinctions and because the 11-plus examination was not thought to be a reliable method of predicting future academic development and achievement. For most of their 13 years the Conservatives supported the grammar schools and prevented county councils from introducing comprehensive systems. By 1963 they were just beginning to recognise the possible advantages of comprehensive education and their support for the grammar schools was weakening.

Critics of the government pointed out that the list of achievements did not seem particularly impressive compared with what Labour achieved in a much shorter period. It has also been suggested that the affluent society, the most striking of the Conservative 'achievements', developed from the improvement in world trade, which had really very little to do with government policies. Some economists go further and argue that the government's 'stop-go' policies hindered the country's economy so that Britain's prosperity under the Conservatives might have been even more marked than it was.

29.2 ON WHAT GROUNDS CAN CONSERVATIVE POLICIES BE CRITICISED?

(a) The Conservatives did not find a permanent solution to the interconnected problems of economic growth, inflation and the balance of payments. Successive Chancellors of the Exchequer tried different methods, sometimes trying to limit spending, sometimes allowing more freedom; this approach came to be called 'stop-go'.

(i) *R. A. Butler*, Churchill's Chancellor, inherited an unhealthy economic situation from Labour. The Korean War (1950-3) caused a rise in world raw material prices, so that the cost of Britain's imports increased appreciably; Butler found that the balance of payments deficit was approaching £700 million. He decided that he must bring about a reduction in demand; a number of restrictions was introduced, including controls on credit (the bank rate was raised from 2 per cent to 4 per cent to discourage people from borrowing money) and strict limits on imports. This was the first of the Conservative 'stop' phases; it seemed to work: by the end of 1952 the deficit had been converted into a surplus of £300 million. It was generally thought that Butler's 'stop' had been responsible for the improvement but it is now clear to economists that the main reason was that the increase in import prices caused by the Korean War lasted only a short time. During 1952 import prices fell to the old levels, whereas Britain's exports continued to sell at roughly the same prices. It seems therefore that the deficit would have righted itself without any interference from Butler, whose measures had the unfortunate effect of reducing investment in industry at a time when industrialists ought to have been aiming for rapid growth. The disturbing fact was that although there was a surplus at the end of 1952, British exports were actually falling. The significance of this did not seem to be appreciated at the time: the Tories seem to have drawn the conclusion that whenever an unfavourable balance of payments seemed likely, a quick 'stop' was all that was needed to work the economic miracle. The fact that these stops hindered economic growth was ignored.

(ii) During 1953 and 1954 Butler instituted a 'go' phase, cutting the bank rate, encouraging investment and producing some industrial expansion. There was full employment, exports increased and the economy moved into a period of boom. The situation seemed so promising that shortly before the 1955 election Butler took sixpence off income tax. Now a different problem developed: full employment brought rising wages, and the demand for goods at home increased, causing rising prices - *inflation*. The increased demand had to be met partly by increasing imports. At the same time exports were adversely affected by large numbers of strikes, and therefore 1955 saw another unfavourable balance of payments. Butler tried to reduce home demand by raising purchase tax and hire purchase deposits. This change of tack so soon after the income tax reduction gave the impression that Butler's judgement was at fault, and he was soon replaced as Chancellor by Macmillan.

(iii) *Macmillan* continued Butler's 'stop' policy, raising the bank rate to 5.5 per cent, so that it was more expensive to borrow cash. This is known as a *credit squeeze:* an attempt to reduce spending in order to check inflation and reduce imports, thereby improving the balance of payments. This was successful in that it produced a favourable trade balance for 1956.

(iv) This is what led *Thorneycroft* (Chancellor 1957-8) to relax the squeeze and risk a 'go': taxes and credit restrictions were reduced and an export boom followed; but at the same time more cash was available to spend at home, causing an increase in demand and a consequent rise in prices and imports. Price rises led to wage demands and strikes, so that exports were soon affected and the balance of payments was threatened again. The next Chancellor, *Heathcoat Amory*, tried to hold down wage increases and began a further credit squeeze in 1960, but this was not enough and his successor, *Selwyn Lloyd*, took tougher measures: he raised interest rates, put 10 per cent on purchase tax and raised import duties. He also tried a new idea - a pay pause which managed to hold wages of government employees down for almost a year, but was repeatedly breached after that; this was the first attempt at a definite pay policy: it failed. By the early 1960s the repeated 'stops' were holding back industrial expansion and Britain was lagging behind her competitors in Europe.

(v) The Conservatives realised that a new approach was needed: first, in 1961, they applied for membership of the EEC, but the application was turned down by France: later the same year they set up the

National Economic Development Council (Neddy) followed by a National Incomes Commission (1962) to try and plan the economy centrally.

(b) The Conservatives can be criticised for failing to join the EEC at the outset in 1957, with unfortunate consequences for British production and exports (see Section 30.7(d) and (e)).

(c) Not enough cash was directed into important industries; this was partly because the 'stops' discouraged industrialists from risking long-term investment and because too much of the available money was invested abroad. Many argued that the government was spending far too much on defence, manufacturing the H-bomb in a vain attempt to keep up with the USA and the USSR. Thus certain industries declined, particularly textiles (hampered by competition from Portugal, Japan and India), and shipbuilding (competition from Japan); although other industries were expanding (aircraft, cars and chemicals), production costs were high which often made British goods expensive; in the face of some strong foreign competition, exports did not boom as much as they might; consequently there was a constant struggle to keep costs down. Unemployment became more of a problem in the 1960s especially in the North of England and in Scotland; early in 1963 there were almost 900 000 out of work. A combination of failure to enter the EEC, economic stagnation and a final 'go' period which caused a sudden surge in imports, resulted in a record balance of payments deficit of £748 million for 1964.

In addition to its economic problems the government's reputation was tarnished by scandal. First in October 1962, William Vassall, a clerk at the Admiralty, was found guilty of spying for the Russians; he had been blackmailed because he was a homosexual, and it was suspected that two government ministers had attempted a cover-up. Though the two ministers, T. Galbraith and Lord Carrington were cleared by an enquiry, the affair left an uncomfortable atmosphere. The next scandal was much more damaging to the government, since it directly involved the Minister for War, John Profumo. In June 1963 it emerged that he had been having an affair with a certain Christine Keeler, who at the same time happened to be associating with a Russian diplomat. Apart from the moral question involved, there was also the security risk. Profumo, who had earlier denied in the Commons that there was anything improper in his relationship with Miss Keeler, was forced to resign. The new Labour leader, Harold Wilson, seized the opportunity to make a scathing attack on Macmillan for not treating the affair seriously enough at the outset.

Finally, after Macmillan's retirement, there was a rather unseemly squabble to choose his successor. There were three main candidates: Lord Hailsham (Quintin Hogg) who resigned his peerage so that he could become a member of the Commons, Butler and Reginald Maudling. However, after 'consultations' and 'soundings', Lord Home (Foreign Secretary since 1960) emerged as the new leader. He also had to resign his peerage and became

Prime Minister as Sir Alec Douglas-Home. Although he was amiable and popular within the party, and was much more shrewd than the opposition gave him credit for, there was some resentment among Conservatives about the way he had been chosen, which compared unfavourably with Wilson's straightforward election as Labour leader. Labour claimed that Home's aristocratic background, his lack of experience in the Commons and his remoteness from ordinary people made him totally unsuitable for the leadership of the country.

All these Conservative failures and tribulations contributed to the Labour victory in October 1964. Another important factor was that Wilson had revitalised the Labour party, presenting an attractive programme of improved welfare services, modernisation and planning of the economy; Wilson also stressed the need for the government to sponsor scientific and technological development so that Britain could catch up with the USA and Japan in these areas. Even so the Labour victory was a narrow one – 317 seats against 303 Conservatives and nine Liberals – but it was enough to bring an end to the 13 years of Conservative rule.

QUESTIONS

1. Conservative Economic Policies

Study Sources **A** to **F** and then answer the questions which follow.

Source A: information from an historian.

By 1959 the economy stood on the edge of *a great leap forward*. Macmillan said in July 1957 that the people 'have never had it so good'. At the time he said it, it may not have been accurate; production figures in 1958 were no higher than in 1955. But between September 1958 and December 1959 there was *a sudden explosive expansion*, and Macmillan's slogan dominated politics and everyday life. Partly because the expansion was started by making credit easier to come by, and partly because of a change in people's wants, a great deal of the expansion was devoted to buying 'consumer durables'. A majority of families had a washing-machine, about one family in three had a refrigerator, and in the south the proportion was higher; about one family in three owned a car. In 1955 40 per cent of homes owned a television set; by 1959 the figure had risen to 70 per cent.

Source: T. O. Lloyd, *Empire to Welfare State – English History 1906–1985*, Oxford, 1986 edn.

Source B: an economist's opinion in 1961.

The object of every economic system is to increase the supply and range of consumer goods and services available to its people, in other words to increase the standard of living as fast as possible. In the long run, this can only be done by expanding production . . . When Mr. R. A. Butler was Chancellor of Exchequer [April 1955] the cost of living was deliberately pushed up by raising purchase tax on a wide range of goods, and at the same time a number of measures were taken to discourage capital investment. Mr. Butler's policies were followed by his two successors . . . it was only reversed at the onset of the recession in 1958. What did this policy achieve? It did eventually succeed in slowing down the pace of wage increases which was one of the main factors behind the 1955 inflation. But it took nearly three years to do so, at the cost of a virtually complete industrial standstill and a number of financial crises and industrial disputes . . . It is too early to assess the long-term damage to the British economy from this period of enforced standstill, but it certainly left us with a lot of leeway to catch up.

Source: M. Shanks, *The Stagnant Society, 1961*; Penguin edn 1971.

Source C: Nigel Fisher, a Conservative MP since 1950, writes about Conservative economic policies.

The summer months [of 1961] showed no improvement in the economy. The June trade figures were again bad, with a deficit of £80 million, and money continued to flow out of the reserves. The pattern was familiar: rising personal demand was not being matched by any compensating improvement in productivity. In 1960–1 wages and salaries had increased by 8 per cent, and production by only 3 per cent, and so Britain was becoming increasingly uncompetitive, and it was essential to reduce government expenditure and restrain wage demands . . . The Chancellor, Selwyn Lloyd, raised the bank rate, curbed government spending and increased indirect taxation. Most controversial was the introduction of the 'pay pause', which was felt to be unfair to nurses, teachers, civil servants and other public sector employees, whose wages the government could directly control. Although unpopular, the pause was justified, and the public reaction to it need not have been so hostile if it had been better presented; the art of public relations was not Selwyn Lloyd's long suit . . .

Macmillan was an instinctive expansionist and by the end of 1961 strong political considerations were reinforcing his economic thinking. Labour was moving ahead in the opinion polls, because the rising prosperity had been checked at the very time when a more affluent society was becoming more expectant of a continuous improvement in its standard of living. The public wanted expansion and were being given restraint. The pay pause was plainly unfair . . .

Macmillan was dismayed at the lack of imaginative ideas coming from the Chancellor, who gave no real lead to the Cabinet. Macmillan regarded Selwyn Lloyd's approach as politically unacceptable and far too cautious. Macmillan would have to face a General Election within a year or two. He needed a boom to coincide with an appeal to the country; he had stage-managed this successfully in 1959 and was anxious to repeat the performance. He tried hard to persuade Lloyd to expand the economy but failed – so the Chancellor, who had become a political liability, had to go.

Source: N. Fisher, *Harold Macmillan*, Weidenfeld & Nicolson, 1982 (adapted extracts).

Source D: the opinion of Lord Blake, Conservative peer and historian.

Selwyn Lloyd had done nothing other than loyally carry out the policy endorsed by the Cabinet, but he was bad at public relations and he had none of the politician's gift of dressing up unpopular policies ... Lloyd was replaced by Reginald Maudling whose expansionist views on the economy were far closer to Macmillan's. His period at the Treasury was to be more helpful to the party than Lloyd would have been; his budgets produced a pre-election boom which nearly carried Macmillan's successor to victory. Whether it worked in the long-term interests of the country is more questionable. Lloyd was the second case of a Chancellor being jettisoned by Macmillan for trying to restrain public expenditure . . . The raging inflation of the 1970s lay ahead.

Source: R. Blake, *The Conservative Party from Peel to Thatcher*, Collins/Fontana, 1985 edn (adapted extracts).

Source E: the view of two historians.

Superficially, the thirteen years of Conservative rule appear to have been fairly successful ones. After years of austerity the people of Britain could afford to relax . . . they had surely earned the right to take things easy for a while and take advantage of Macmillan's hire-purchase society? Everyone from the middle-aged mum with her domestic appliances to teenagers with their transistor radios agreed on that . . . but as far as economic policy was concerned, the Tories did very little in their years of power . . . they manipulated budgets but gave little impression of knowing how the economy really worked. Little attention was paid to Britain's sluggish economic growth or the long-term challenge posed by Germany and Japan . . . for most of the time their energy was devoted to maintaining Britain as a world power, whatever the cost to the economy . . .

Moreover, Tory economic complacency ensured that the necessary economic growth would never be generated. Not enough money was channelled into key industries; stop-go policies undermined the confidence of industry to invest in the long term; too much money was allowed to be exported abroad; and too much money was spent on defence.

Source: A. Sked and C. Cook, *Post-War Britain*, Penguin, 1979 (adapted extracts).

Source F: Nigel Fisher sums up the Macmillan years.

It must be remembered that the period of his Premiership was one of prosperity, during which inflation and unemployment were low and the standard of living high for a large majority of the British people. History will assess whether it was a time of real achievement or of missed opportunities, disguised by Macmillan's own inimitable style. The conclusion may be that it was a combination of the two: that genuine gains were made but that the chance to modernise the industrial structure of Britain was not fully taken.

Source: N. Fisher, *Harold Macmillan*, Weidenfeld & Nicolson, 1982.

(a) **(i)** According to Source **A**, roughly what percentage of the population owned a refrigerator? **4(a)**

  (ii) Which three Chancellors of the Exchequer are mentioned in these Sources? **4(a, c)**

  (iii) What evidence does the author of Source **A** provide to show that there was 'a sudden explosive expansion' of the economy from September 1958? **4(a)**

  (iv) What evidence is there in Source **A** that prosperity was greater in the south than in the north? **4(a)**

  (v) What explanations of the sudden expansion can you find in Sources **A** and **B**? **4(a, c)**

(b) **(i)** Explain in your own words what, according to Source **B**, is the aim of every economic system. **4(a)**

  (ii) What evidence is there in Source **B** to explain the production for 1958 mentioned in Source **A**? **4(a, c)**

  (iii) According to Source **B**, what did Mr Butler's policies achieve? **4(a)**

  (iv) What criticisms does the writer of Source **B** make about Mr Butler's policies? **4(a)**

  (v) Why does the writer of Source **B** feel unable to assess the long-term effects of Mr Butler's policies? **4(a)**

(c) **(i)** From the evidence of Source **C**, why was the 'great leap forward' mentioned in Source **A** not achieved? **4(a, c)**

  (ii) What action did Selwyn Lloyd, the Chancellor of the Exchequer, take to deal with the economic crisis of 1961? **4(a)**

  (iii) According to Source **C**, how did Macmillan and Lloyd differ in their ideas about the economy? **4(a)**

  (iv) How would you sum up Fisher's attitude to Lloyd in Source **C**? **4(a, b)**

  (v) Do you think that Blake in Source **D** supports Fisher's view of Lloyd or not? **4(a, b, c)**

(d) **(i)** What evidence can you find in Sources **C** and **D** that Macmillan was perhaps more concerned with winning the next election rather than with simply getting the economy right? **4(a, c)**

(ii)   What doubts might an historian have about accepting the evidence of Sources **C**, **D** and **F** as reliable? In each case, explain whether you think these doubts are justified.   **4(b)**

(e)   **(i)**   In what ways do Sources **A** and **E** agree with each other about Conservative economic policies?   **4(a, c)**

        (ii)   In what ways do Sources **A** and **E** differ in their comments on Conservative economic policies?   **4(a, c)**

        (iii)   How do Sources **C** and **E** differ in their explanations of the causes of Britain's economic problems?   **4(a, c)**

(f)   The British people 'never had it so good'.

        'Thirteen wasted years.'

        These are two conflicting views of the years of Conservative rule from 1951 to 1964. Using the evidence of the Sources and your own knowledge, explain which of these views you think is more accurate.   **1, 2, 4(a, b, c)**

2.   Read this extract from a history of the Conservative Party by the Conservative peer, Lord Blake, and then answer the following questions.

        Home was the first peer to be Prime Minister since Lord Salisbury in 1902. He at once resigned his peerage . . . Sir Alec entered office under many disabilities: he was not a public figure; he had left the House of Commons, where he had never been a notable performer, as long ago as 1951; he did not come over well on television; he was an Old Etonian fourteenth earl when the 'spirit of the times' was anti-aristocratic and anti-traditional; he seemed hardly the man to modernise Britain; he knew little of economics which he could only understand, he said, by using matchsticks. Moreover, *the circumstances of his appointment were unhelpful* . . . Butler would have been better at dealing with Harold Wilson who had succeeded to the Labour leadership and soon proved himself to be a masterly leader of the Opposition . . . And yet Sir Alec was generally respected for his honesty. He was one of the least devious politicians and one of the nicest and least conceited or pompous men to become Prime Minister. Despite *Vassall and Profumo*, the party almost pulled off a fourth victory . . . Wilson had only a majority of 4 overall.

        Source: R. Blake, *The Conservative Party from Peel to Thatcher*, Oxford, 1985 edn (adapted extracts).

(a)   **(i)**   Why did Sir Alec Douglas Home resign his peerage soon after becoming Prime Minister?   **1, 2**

        (ii)   What evidence does this extract contain which might help to explain why the Conservatives lost the 1964 election?   **4(a)**

    (iii)   Do you think Blake is sympathetic towards Home or not? Explain your answer.   **4(a, b)**

    (iv)   What evidence is there in this extract of Blake's attitude towards Wilson?   **4(a, b)**

    (v)   How reliable do you think Blake's assessment of the two politicians is likely to be?   **4(b)**

(b)   According to the extract 'the circumstances of his appointment were unhelpful':

    (i)   Using your own knowledge, describe the circumstances of Home's appointment as party leader.   **1, 2**

    (ii)   Explain why these circumstances were 'unhelpful'.   **1, 2**

(c) (i)   Describe what happened in the Vassall and Profumo affairs mentioned in the extract.   **1, 2**

    (ii)   Why were they damaging to the Conservative government?   **1, 2**

(d)   What other factors not mentioned in this extract help to explain the Conservative defeat in the 1964 general election?   **1, 2, 4(a)**

3. (a)   In what ways did the standard of living of the British people improve between 1951 and 1964?

(b)   The Conservative governments of 1951–64 were criticised for their 'stop-go' policies. Explain:

    what is meant by a 'stop–go' policy. Illustrate your answer with examples of the policies of Conservative Chancellors of the Exchequer (e.g. R. A. Butler, Harold Macmillan, Selwyn Lloyd);

    (ii)   why the Conservative Chancellors followed these policies;

    (iii)   why these policies aroused criticism.   **1, 2**

(c)   Explain why:

    (i)   Eden and the Conservatives won the general election of 1955;

    (ii)   Macmillan and the Conservatives won the general election of 1959;

    (iii)   Home and the Conservatives lost the general election of 1964.   **1, 2**

4.   It is October 1963 and Harold Macmillan has just announced his resignation as Conservative leader and Prime Minister. Write two contrasting newspaper articles assessing his career as a leading Conservative in office since 1951:

(a)   for a newspaper with Conservative sympathies such as *The Times*;

(b)   for a journal with left-wing sympathies such as the *New Statesman*.

CHAPTER 30

BRITAIN AND HER
PLACE IN THE
WORLD AFTER 1945

SUMMARY OF EVENTS

The twenty years after the end of the war saw Britain declining from her pre-war position as one of the world's leading powers, to become just an ordinary European state among the rest. However, British governments, both Labour and Conservative, were unwilling to accept what was happening and tried to act as though Britain was still on an equal footing with the USA and the USSR. In 1946 her empire was still intact and she had troops in Germany, Greece, Iran, India, Egypt, Palestine, Malaya and Singapore. This was extremely expensive to maintain for a country whose resources had been strained to the limit by the war effort. There was some disagreement in the Labour cabinet about how long Britain might go on maintaining her world-wide military presence; Hugh Dalton, the Chancellor of the Exchequer, was anxious to economise, and felt that at least British troops could be withdrawn from Germany. However, *Ernest Bevin*, the Foreign Secretary, was a dominating figure who enjoyed the full support of Attlee, the Prime Minister. Between them they were determined that Britain should play a world role for as long as possible, even to the extent of producing her own nuclear weapons.

The problems facing Bevin were complex: the need for a settlement of Germany, Britain's role in the Cold War, the Korean War, the Indian demand for independence and the Jewish/Arab violence in Palestine. Bevin negotiated these problems with great skill, though he failed to resolve the Arab/Israeli situation which in desperation he handed over to the United Nations Organisation.

After the Conservatives came to power in 1951, foreign affairs were dominated by *Anthony Eden*, first as Foreign Secretary (1951-5) and then as Prime Minister (1955-7). He seemed to be handling affairs well until *the Suez War (1956)* ended in humiliation for Britain and caused his downfall. To many people, this seemed conclusive proof that Britain, incapable of conducting an independent foreign policy without American approval, was no longer a world power. However, while *Harold Macmillan* was Conservative Prime Minister (1957–63), he somehow managed to keep up the illusion for a little longer.

It was under Macmillan's premiership that Britain gave up most of her empire, though the vast majority of the newly independent states chose to remain within the Commonwealth. India (1947), and Ceylon and Burma (1948) had already been granted independence; they were soon followed by Malaysia and Gold Coast (1957), Nigeria and Cyprus (1960), Tanganyika and Zanzibar (together forming Tanzania, 1961), Uganda (1962), Kenya (1963), and Nyasaland, Northern Rhodesia, Guiana and Malta (1964). Later Bechuanaland (1966) and Aden (1967) became independent.

At the same time as she was withdrawing from her empire, Britain missed an opportunity to join the other states of Western Europe, when she decided not to become a member of the European Economic Community on its formation in 1957. When Macmillan eventually decided that it would be advantageous for Britain to join after all, her entry was blocked by the French (January 1963). Britain was thus left largely isolated from the rest of Europe and at the same time had offended the Commonwealth by applying to join the EEC. Britain seemed to be floundering and it was to be another 10 years before the EEC opened its ranks to admit her. Dean Acheson, a former American Secretary of State (who was reasonably pro-British), summed the situation up well when he remarked (December 1962) that Britain 'has lost an Empire but has not yet found a role'.

30.1 BRITAIN AND THE COLD WAR

(a) **What was the Cold War and what caused it?** Towards the end of the war the harmony that had existed between the USSR, the USA and the British Empire began to evaporate and all the old suspicions came to the fore again. Relations between Soviet Russia and the West soon became so difficult that although no actual armed conflict took place directly between the two opposing camps, the decade after 1945 saw the first phase of *the Cold War* which continued, in spite of several 'thaws', into the 1980s. This means that instead of allowing their mutual hostility to express itself in open fighting, the rival powers confined themselves to attacking each other with propaganda and economic measures and with a general policy of non-co-operation. Both super-powers gathered allies about them: between 1945 and 1948 the USSR drew into its orbit most of the states of Eastern Europe. A Communist government was established in North Korea (1948) and the Communist bloc seemed to be further strengthened in 1949 when Mao Tse-tung was at last victorious in the long-drawn-out civil war in China. On the other hand, the USA hastened the recovery of Japan and fostered her as an ally and worked closely with Britain and 14 other European countries as well as with Turkey, providing them with vast economic aid in order to build up an anti-Communist bloc. Whatever one bloc suggested or did was viewed by the other as having only ulterior and aggressive motives; thus, for example, there was a long wrangle over where the frontier between Poland and Germany should be, and no permanent settlement for Germany and Austria could be agreed on. Then in the mid-1950s after the death of Stalin (1953), the new Russian leaders began to talk about 'peaceful co-existence' and the icy atmosphere between the two blocs began to thaw. It was agreed to remove all occupying troops from Austria (1955); however, relations did not warm sufficiently to allow agreement on Germany.

The basic cause lay in the differences of principle between the Communist states and the capitalist or democratic states; this had existed ever since the Communists set up a government in Russia in 1917. Only the need for self-preservation had caused them to ignore their differences, and as soon as it became clear that the defeat of Germany was only a matter of time, both sides, Stalin in particular, began to plan for the post-war period. His aim was to take advantage of the military situation to strengthen Russian influence in Europe; this involved occupying as much of Germany as possible as the Nazi armies collapsed and acquiring as much territory as he could get away with from other states such as Finland, Poland and Romania. When Stalin extended Russian control over most of Eastern Europe, the West became more and more alarmed at what seemed to be Russian aggression and this caused the onset of the Cold War.

In the final phase of the war with Germany, President Roosevelt had been inclined to trust Stalin, but Churchill thought differently. He wanted British and American troops to make a dash for Berlin before the Russians took it, but he was overruled by the Americans. However, the new American President, Truman, was much more suspicious of the Russians, and his misgivings were confirmed at the *Potsdam Conference* in July 1945, when Stalin refused to come to any agreement about Germany's future (see Section 27.6(g)). However, it was 1947 before Truman abandoned completely his belief in Stalin's good faith.

Bevin's attitude in this situation was similar to Churchill's. He had no love for Communists and thought that Britain must stand up to the Russians in order to maintain a balance of power in Europe. The best way to achieve this was by co-operation with the Americans, and he hoped for a concerted Anglo-American effort to prevent the expansion of Russian power and of Communism in Eastern Europe. But the Americans, even Truman, were reluctant to interfere in the affairs of Eastern Europe, believing that, even if Poland and Hungary fell under Russian influence, Stalin would allow them to have democratic governments if they wished. The Americans soon received an unpleasant shock: by the end of 1947, Communist governments had been established, under Russian influence, in Poland, Hungary, Romania, Bulgaria and Albania. In addition, Stalin treated the Russian zone of Germany as if it belonged to Russia, banning all political parties except the Communists, and draining it of vital resources.

(b) The Truman Doctrine and the Marshall Plan. The situation in Greece led to a closer American involvement in European affairs.

(i) British troops had helped liberate Greece from the Germans in 1944 and had restored the monarchy. They were now feeling the strain of supporting the king against Communist guerrillas who were receiving help from Albania, Bulgaria and Yugoslavia. If Greece fell to the Communists, there was every chance that Turkey and Iran would follow. In Bevin's view, only Britain stood between Russian control of the Eastern Mediterranean, the Dardanelles and the Middle East.

(ii) Churchill (although he was no longer in the government) tried to shake the Americans into an awareness of what was happening. In a speech at *Fulton*, Missouri (March 1946), he declared: 'From Stettin in the Baltic to Trieste in the Adriatic an iron curtain has descended across the continent'; the Russians were bent on 'indefinite expansion of their power and doctrines'. He called for a western alliance to stand firm against the Communist threat, 'since our difficulties and dangers will not be removed by merely waiting to see what happens'.

(iii) An added difficulty was that Anglo-American relations were strained by the abrupt ending of Lend-Lease and by the unfavourable terms insisted on for the American loan in 1945 (see Section 28.2(a)). Many Americans were hostile to Britain's Empire and continued to view Britain as a serious trade rival. This was one reason for the lack of enthusiasm for Britain's anti-Communist stand in Greece.

(iv) At last (February 1947) Bevin told the Americans clearly that Britain's economic position made it impossible for her to continue the struggle in Greece. If America wanted Greece and Turkey saving from Russia, she would have to do it herself. Truman responded with what became known as the *'Truman Doctrine'*: the USA would 'support free peoples who are resisting subjugation by armed minorities or by outside pressures'. Greece immediately received massive amounts of arms and other supplies and by 1949 the Communists were defeated. Turkey, which also seemed under threat, received aid worth about 60 million dollars.

(v) *The Marshall Plan* (announced June 1947) was an economic extension of the 'Truman Doctrine'. American Secretary of State George Marshall produced his European Recovery Programme (ERP) which offered economic and financial help wherever it was needed. 'Our policy', he declared, 'is directed not against any country or doctrine but against hunger, poverty, desperation and chaos'. Its aim was to promote the economic recovery of Europe, thus ensuring markets for American exports; in addtion, Communism was less likely to gain control in a prosperous Western Europe. The only proviso was that the European nations themselves must co-operate with each other to produce a plan for the best use of American aid. Bevin eagerly took the lead, and together with the French Foreign Minister, called an international conference in Paris. By September 16 nations (Britain, France, Italy, Belgium, Luxembourg, Netherlands, Portugal, Austria, Switzerland, Greece, Turkey, Iceland, Norway, Sweden, Denmark, and the three western zones of Germany) had drawn up a joint plan for using

American aid; during the next four years over 13 000 million dollars of Marshall Aid flowed into Western Europe, fostering the recovery of agriculture and industry which in many countries were in chaos as a result of war devastation. The Russians were invited to the conference, but declined to attend. They were well aware that there was more to Marshall Aid than pure benevolence. Although aid was in theory available to Eastern Europe, Molotov, the Russian Foreign Minister, denounced the whole idea as 'dollar imperialism', seeing it as a blatant American device for gaining control of Western Europe, and worse still, for interfering in Eastern Europe, which Stalin considered to be in the Russian 'sphere of influence'. Russia rejected the offer, and neither her satellite states nor Czechoslovakia, which was showing interest, was allowed to take advantage of it. By now the 'iron curtain' seemed a reality and the Cold War was well under way (for further examples of co-operation between Britain and Europe, see Section 30.7).

(c) The Berlin blockade and airlift (June 1948 - May 1949) brought the Cold War to its first climax. The crisis arose out of disagreements over the treatment of Germany:

(i) At the end of the war, as agreed at Yalta and Potsdam, Germany and Berlin were each divided into four zones. While the three western powers set about organising the economic and political recovery of their zones, Stalin, determined to make the Germans pay for the damage inflicted on Russia, continued to treat his zone as a satellite, draining its resources away to Russia.

(ii) Early in 1948 the three Western zones were merged to form a single economic unit whose prosperity, thanks to Marshall Aid, was in marked contrast to the poverty of the Russian zone. At the same time, outraged at the Russian-backed coup in Czechoslovakia (February 1948), the Western powers began to prepare a constitution for a self-governing West Germany, since the Russians had no intention of allowing complete German reunification. However, the Russians were alarmed at the prospect of a strong independent West Germany which would be part of the American bloc.

(iii) When in June 1948 the West introduced a new currency and ended price controls and rationing in their zone and in West Berlin, the Russians decided that the situation in Berlin had become impossible. Already irritated by the island of capitalism deep in the Communist zone, they felt it impossible to have two different currencies in the same city and were embarrassed by the contrast between the prosperity of West Berlin and the poverty of the surrounding area.

The Russian response was immediate: all road, rail and canal links between West Berlin and West Germany were closed; their aim was to force the West to withdraw from West Berlin by reducing it to starvation point.

The Western powers, convinced that a retreat would be the prelude to a Russian attack on West Germany, were determined to hold on; they decided to fly supplies in, rightly judging that the Russians would not risk shooting down the transport planes. Over the next 10 months the Americans and British airlifted 2 million tons of supplies to the blockaded city in a remarkable operation which kept the 2.5 million West Berliners fed and warmed right through the winter. In May 1949 the Russians admitted failure by lifting the blockade. *The affair had important results:* the outcome provided a great psychological boost for the Western powers, though it brought relations with Russia to their worst ever; it caused the Western powers to co-ordinate their defences by the formation of NATO. In addition it meant that since no compromise seemed possible, Germany was doomed to be permanently divided. The German Federal Republic (*West Germany*) came into existence in August 1949; the Russians followed, setting up their zone as the German Democratic Republic (*East Germany*) in October 1949.

(d) The formation of NATO (North Atlantic Treaty Organisation) took place in April 1949. The Berlin blockade demonstrated the West's military unreadiness and frightened them into making definite preparations. Already Bevin had made the first moves to bring about close co-operation in Western Europe: in March 1948 Britain, France, Belgium, Holland and Luxembourg had signed the *Brussels Defence Treaty* promising military collaboration in case of war. Now they were joined by the USA, Canada, Portugal, Denmark, Ireland, Italy and Norway. All signed the *North Atlantic Treaty*, agreeing to regard an attack on any one of them as an attack on them all, and placing their defence forces under a joint NATO Command Organisation which would co-ordinate the defence of the West. This was a highly significant development: the Americans had abandoned their traditional policy of 'no entangling alliances' and for the first time had pledged themselves in advance to military action.

Justifiably Bevin was exultant, seeing NATO as *the crowning achievement of his career:* he had contributed to the formulation of the Truman Doctrine, taken the lead in planning for Marshall Aid, played an important part in preparations for the Brussels Treaty, and supported Truman in the Berlin airlift. The climax of the process was NATO.

(e) The War in Korea (1950-3). The origins of the war lay in the fact that the country had been divided into two zones in 1945 at the end of the Second World War. It was divided at the 38th parallel by agreement between the USA and the USSR for purely military reasons – so that they could organise the surrender of the occupying Japanese forces; it was not intended to be permanent political division. However, the unification of Communist North Korea with the non-Communist South soon became part of the Cold War rivalry and no agreement could be reached. In 1949 Russian and American troops were withdrawn, leaving a potentially dangerous situation: most Koreans bitterly resented the artificial division forced on their country by outsiders. Without warning, North Korean troops invaded South Korea in June 1950.

The Communists had just gained control of China under the leadership of Mao Tse-tung and Chou En-lai. President Truman was convinced that the attack on South Korea, coming so soon after Cold War events in Europe, was part of a vast Russian plan to advance Communism wherever possible in the world, and believed it essential for the West to take a stand by supporting South Korea. American troops in Japan were ordered to South Korea before the UN had decided what action to take. The UN Security Council called on North Korea to withdraw her troops, and when this was ignored, asked member states to send assistance to South Korea. This decision was reached in the absence of the Russian delegation, who were boycotting meetings in protest against the UN refusal to allow Mao's new Chinese regime to be represented, and who would certainly have vetoed such a decision. In the event, the USA and 14 other countries (Australia, Britain, Canada, New Zealand, Nationalist China (Formosa or Taiwan, under Chiang Kai-shek), France, Netherlands, Belgium, Colombia, Greece, Turkey, Panama, Philippines and Thailand) sent troops, though the vast majority were Americans. All forces were under the command of US General MacArthur.

Their arrival was none too soon: by September Communist troops had overrun the whole of South Korea except the south-east, around the port of Pusan. Then followed a complete reversal of fortune: Communist forces were soon chased out of the South and by the end of October UN troops had occupied two-thirds of North Korea, and reached the Yalu River, the frontier between North Korea and China.

The Chinese government was seriously alarmed: in November they launched a massive counter-offensive with over 300 000 troops described as 'volunteers'; by mid-January 1951 they had driven the UN troops out of North Korea and crossed the 38th parallel; Seoul was captured again. MacArthur was shocked at the strength of the Chinese forces and argued that the best way to beat them and stop the spread of Communism was to attack Manchuria, with atomic bombs if necessary.

At this point Attlee paid a surprise visit to Washington to urge Truman not to use atomic bombs on China. Possibly influenced by Attlee, Truman decided that this would be too risky and might cause a large-scale war which the USA did not want. He decided to settle for merely 'containing' Communism; MacArthur was removed from his command. In June UN troops cleared the Communists out of South Korea again and fortified the frontier; peace talks at Panmunjom lasted for two years, ending in July 1953 with an agreement that the frontier should be roughly along the 38th parallel.

Although Britain sent the second largest contingent of troops, suffering over 4000 casualties (almost 700 killed), this was small compared with the American commitment (they lost over 33 000 killed). The main importance of the war for Britain was the way in which it set back her economic recovery (see Section 28.2(b)) and caused a split in the Labour Party (over how to meet the expense) which contributed to its defeat in the election of 1951 (see Section 28.4).

(f) Britain and her defences

(i) Attlee and Bevin had authorised the manufacture of an atomic bomb, though this was generally unknown, even to Parliament. The bomb was successfully tested in 1952, and it was thought that this put Britain back on a level with the USA and the USSR. However, development of atomic weapons moved fast; before long Britain had to decide whether to produce a hydrogen bomb. In 1954 Churchill announced that Britain would go ahead with its manufacture and by 1957 the first British H-bomb had been successfully exploded.

(ii) The nuclear arms race soon became far too fast and too expensive for Britain. The next development was the inter-continental ballistic missile – a nuclear warhead carried by a rocket. When Britain tried to develop her own rocket system – *Blue Streak* – the expense became impossible and in 1960 Blue Streak was abandoned.

(iii) At about the same time the *Campaign for Nuclear Disarmament (CND)* was started. Its supporters argued, on moral grounds, that Britain should withdraw from the nuclear arms race and disarm unilaterally. Their case was strengthened when evidence began to build up showing that nuclear tests carried out in the atmosphere caused a highly dangerous radio-active fall-out.

(iv) *Harold Macmillan* quickly built up an impressive reputation as an international statesman. He was convinced of the value of summit conferences between world leaders and worked hard to organise one. He visited Moscow in February 1959 and established good relations with Khrushchev, the Russian leader. Macmillan was at least partly responsible for Khrushchev's decision not to press for a Western withdrawal from West Berlin. Soon afterwards Macmillan went to Paris, Bonn and Washington, and as the Cold War tensions eased, he was able to persuade the Western leaders that a summit with the Russians might be fruitful. Unfortunately, when the conference eventually met in May 1960, it was unsuccessful. An American U-2 spy plane had just been shot down over a thousand miles inside Russia. The Russians demanded an apology, and when the American President, Eisenhower refused, Khrushchev walked out.

(v) By 1963 it was clear that Britain had ceased to be a world power. She simply lacked the economic strength and the resources to remain on a level with the two super-powers, and had been forced to abandon the idea of manufacturing her own nuclear weapons. The best that Macmillan could manage was to persuade the new American President, John F. Kennedy, to supply Britain with American nuclear *Polaris missiles* which could be fired from British nuclear submarines. Britain had been humiliated at Suez in 1956 (see Section 30.4) and during the Cuban missile crisis (1962) she was unable to play any useful role. The crisis occurred when Kennedy demanded the removal of Russian missiles from Cuba, less than 100 miles from the American coast. The two powers seemed on the brink of nuclear war, but common sense prevailed and Khrushchev agreed to remove the missiles. Soon afterwards Britain was refused entry to the EEC (January 1963) and at the same time had almost lost her Empire.

(vi) Macmillan had one final achievement before his retirement: he played an important part in the signing of a *Nuclear Test Ban Treaty* by the USA, the USSR and Britain (July 1963). It was agreed that in order to avoid polluting the atmosphere, nuclear tests would only be carried out underground. Kennedy paid Macmillan a handsome tribute, claiming that the British Prime Minister's role in bringing about the limitation of nuclear testing had been indispensable.

30.2 WHY AND HOW DID THE BRITISH LEAVE INDIA IN 1947?

By 1945 Indian independence could not be delayed much longer after the nationalist campaign (see Section 25.3). The British had promised to allow dominion status once the war was over, and the Labour government, wanting to show that it disapproved of 'exploiting' the Indians, was anxious to go ahead. Bevin had earlier toyed with the idea that independence might be delayed for a few years to enable the British government to finance a development programme for India. This idea was abandoned because the Indians would be intensely suspicious of any delay, and probably more important, because Britain could not afford the expense, given her own economic difficulties. Attlee and Bevin therefore decided to grant India full independence, allowing the Indians to work out the details for themselves. This seemed the best way to solve India's internal problems and at the same time to make sure that India stayed within the Commonwealth. Unfortunately this was by no means a simple matter: the problems were so complex that India had to be divided into two states – India and Pakistan.

(a) Why was the partition of India necessary?

(i) The problem sprang from religious hostilities between Hindus who made up about two-thirds of the population and the rest who were mostly Muslims. After their victories in the elections of 1937 (see Section 25.3(b)), the Hindu Congress party unwisely called on the Muslim League to merge with Congress; this alarmed the League who were now convinced that an independent India would be dominated by Hindus. Jinnah, the Muslim leader, demanded a separate Muslim state of Pakistan.

(ii) Attempts to draw up a compromise constitution acceptable to Hindu leaders (Nehru and Gandhi) and to Jinnah, failed. The British proposed a federal scheme in which the central government would have only limited powers while those of the provincial governments would be extensive; thus provinces with a Muslim majority would be able to control their own affairs, and there would be no need of a separate state. Both sides accepted the principle but could not agree on details.

(iii) Violence broke out in August 1946 when the Governor-General, Lord

Wavell, invited Nehru to form an interim government, still hoping that details could be worked out later. Nehru formed a cabinet which included two Muslims, but Jinnah, convinced that the Hindus could not be trusted, called for 'direct action' to achieve Pakistan. Fierce rioting followed in Calcutta, where 5000 people were killed, and spread to Bengal where Muslims set about slaughtering Hindus. As Hindus retaliated the country seemed on the verge of civil war.

(iv) To try and force the Indians into a more responsible attitude, Attlee announced early in 1947 that the British would leave no later than June 1948. The new Viceroy, *Lord Mountbatten*, turned out to be an inspired choice by Attlee. He quickly decided that partition was the only way to avoid civil war. He realised that there would probably be bloodshed anyway, but felt that partition would probably produce less than if Britain tried to insist on the Muslims remaining inside India. Within six weeks of arriving, in spite of all the complexities, Mountbatten had produced a plan by which the country could be divided and power transferred from the British. This was accepted by Nehru and Jinnah (though not by Gandhi). Afraid that delay would cause more violence, Mountbatten advanced the date for British withdrawal to August 1947.

(b) How was partition carried out? The Indian Independence Act was rushed through the British Parliament (August 1947) separating the Muslim majority area (the north-west and north-east of India) from the rest of India as the independent state of Pakistan, which was in two sections, over a thousand miles apart. But it was not easy to operate the act:

(i) It had been necessary to split the provinces of the Punjab and Bengal which had mixed Hindu/Muslim populations and inevitably millions of people found themselves on the wrong side of the new frontiers.

(ii) Fearing persecution, millions made for the frontier, Muslims trying to get into Pakistan and Hindus into India. Clashes occurred developing into near-hysterical mob violence, especially in the Punjab, in which about 250 000 people were murdered. Violence was not quite so widespread in Bengal where Gandhi, still preaching non-violence and toleration, managed to calm the situation.

(iii) Violence began to die down before the end of 1947, but in January 1948, Gandhi was shot dead by a Hindu fanatic who detested his tolerance towards Muslims. It was a tragic end to a disastrous set of circumstances, but the shock seemed to bring people to their senses, so that India and Pakistan could begin to think about their other problems. From the British point of view, the government could claim that, although the deaths were regrettable, the granting of independence to India and Pakistan was an act of far-sighted statesmanship. Attlee insisted, probably rightly, that Britain could not be blamed for the violence which followed independence; this was due, he said 'to the failure of the Indians to agree among themselves'. V. P. Menon, a distinguished Indian political observer, believed that Britain's decision to quit India 'not only touched the hearts and stirred the emotions of India; . . . it earned for Britain universal respect and goodwill'. Certainly both India and Pakistan were happy to remain within the Commonwealth (though Pakistan withdrew in 1972).

30.3 BRITAIN WITHDRAWS FROM PALESTINE

In 1945 Britain was still heavily committed in the Middle East: Palestine had been a British mandate since 1919, British troops were still stationed in the Suez Canal zone of Egypt, and Britain owned a controlling interest in the Anglo-Iranian Oil Company. Serious problems arose in all three areas, but it was in Palestine that the first crisis occurred.

Map 30.1 *The Middle East*

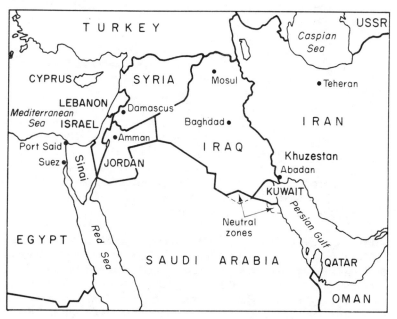

(a) What caused the crisis?

(i) The problem originated soon after the First World War when large numbers of Jews began to settle in Palestine, hoping to set up a Jewish 'national home' (see Section 25.4(c)). The Arabs in Palestine were implacably hostile to the idea of a separate Jewish state in what they considered to be their homeland. In order to retain Arab friendship and their own oil supplies the British limited Jewish immigration to 10 000 a year (1939).

(ii) The Second World War intensified the problem with hundreds of thousands of Jewish refugees from Hitler's Europe looking for somewhere to go. In 1945 the USA pressed Britain to admit 100 000 of them into Palestine; this demand was echoed by David Ben Gurion, one of the Jewish leaders, but the British refused, not wanting to offend the Arabs. The British were particularly exasperated by Truman's attitude: he criticised the British government for not admitting the refugees, yet would give no help and refused to allow any more Jews into the USA.

(iii) The Jews, after all that their race had suffered at the hands of the Nazis, were determined to fight for their 'national home'. They began a terrorist campaign against both Arabs and British, the most spectacular incident of which was the blowing up of the King David Hotel, the British headquarters in Jerusalem, with the loss of 91 lives (1946). The British responded by arresting Jewish leaders and by turning back ships such as the *Exodus* crammed with intending immigrants.

(iv) Bevin hoped to be able to find some sort of compromise to satisfy both Jews and Arabs and one which would preserve British influence. He met the leaders of both sides, but no compromise was possible: the Jews wanted their own state, the Arabs refused all concessions, and neither side would budge. By February 1947 therefore, Bevin invited the United Nations to deal with the problem, and in November the UN voted to partition Palestine, creating an independent state of Israel for the Jews. The UN also suggested that Britain should put the plan into operation. Bevin was against partition, even though the UN announced that the existing Arab population would be able to continue living in Israel; his argument was: why should the Palestinian Arabs become a minority in a Jewish state when the Jews were refusing to become a minority in an Arab state? Consequently the British refused to operate the partition and in May 1948 they withdrew altogether from Palestine, thus ending the mandate.

(b) Why did the British decide to withdraw? There were several motives. British public opinion had gradually turned against the Jews because of their terrorist outrages; the peace-keeping operation had already proved expensive, and the prospect of enforcing the partition (which they did not approve of and which would be even more costly, at a time when Britain was in economic difficulties) to the advantage of the Jews, appalled Bevin. Nor did Bevin see why the British should have the sole obligation of acting as international policemen in the Middle East; there was a distinct feeling that since the Americans had taken up a pro-Jewish stance, then they ought to be allowed to get on with carrying out the partition. Finally there was the possibility that British troops might be needed in Europe, in view of the growing tension over Berlin.

When the British withdrew, fighting had already broken out between Jews and Palestinians, who bitterly resented the loss of half of Palestine. Ben Gurion declared the new state of Israel independent and it was immediately attacked by Egypt, Syria, Jordan, Iraq and Lebanon. However, amid general surprise, the Israelis defeated their enemies and their new state soon became established; they have defended it successfully ever since.

The most tragic result of the war was the plight of the Palestinian Arabs who found themselves inside the new state of Israel. After Jewish terrorists had slaughtered the entire population of an Arab village, nearly a million Arabs fled into Egypt, Lebanon, Jordan and Syria where they lived in miserable refugee camps.

Many of the parties involved blamed Britain for the chaos which followed her withdrawal. However, Bevin always maintained that the fault was not his. He had striven to find a compromise solution which would accommodate both Jews and Arabs in their own autonomous provinces within a state of Palestine. But given the intransigence of both sides, especially the Jews, and Britain's inability to force a solution, it is difficult to see what else he could have done.

30.4 BRITAIN AND THE SUEZ CRISIS 1956

(a) The causes of the crisis were quite complex: it was partly a continuation of the Arab–Israeli conflict; it was partly a struggle between Arab nationalism, in the person of the Egyptian leader *Nasser*, and the British (and French) in the person of *Anthony Eden*, who wanted to prolong British influence in the Middle East; it was also an episode in the Cold War between the USA and the USSR.

(i) Colonel Gamal Abdel Nasser, the new ruler of Egypt (who came to power in 1954 soon after the overthrow of the unpopular King Farouk), was aggressively in favour of Arab unity and independence including the liberation of Palestine from the Jews.

(ii) He organised guerrilla bands (*fedayeen:* self-sacrificers) to sabotage and murder inside Israel and blockaded the Gulf of Aqaba leading to the Israeli port of Eilat.

(iii) He insisted that Britain evacuate her base at Suez (the agreement signed in 1936 allowing her to keep the base expired in 1956), sent aid to the Algerian Arabs in their struggle against France, prodded the other Arab states into opposing the British-sponsored Baghdad Pact and forced King Hussein of Jordan to dismiss his British chief of staff.

(iv) In September 1955 Nasser signed an arms deal with Czechoslovakia for Russian fighters, bombers and tanks, and Soviet experts went to train the Egyptian army.

(v) The Americans saw this as a Russian attempt to 'move into' the Middle East and cancelled a promised grant of 56 million dollars towards the building of a dam at Aswan (July 1956); the intention was to force Nasser to abandon his new links with the Communists.

(vi) Nasser immediately retaliated by nationalising the Suez Canal, intending to use its revenues to finance the dam; share-owners, a majority of whom were British and French, were promised compensation. However, British Prime Minister Anthony Eden believed that Nasser was on the way to forming a united Arabia under Egyptian control and Communist influence, which could cut off Europe's oil supplies at will. He viewed Nasser as another Hitler or Mussolini and according to Hugh Thomas, 'saw Egypt through a forest of Flanders poppies and gleaming jackboots'. He was not alone in this: Churchill remarked: 'We can't have this malicious swine sitting across our communications', and the new Labour leader, Hugh Gaitskell, agreed that Nasser was extremely dangerous. Eden was sure of one thing: Nasser must not be appeased in the way that Hitler and Mussolini had been appeased in the 1930s.

(vii) Secret negotiations took place between the British, French and Israelis; it was decided that Israel should attack Egypt across the Sinai peninsula, whereupon British and French troops would occupy the canal zone on the pretext that they were protecting it from damage in the fighting. Anglo-French control of the canal would be restored and the defeat, it was hoped, would topple Nasser from power.

(b) **Hostilities began** with the planned Israeli invasion of Egypt (29 October), which within a week had captured the entire Sinai peninsula. Meanwhile the British and French bombed Egyptian air-fields and landed troops at Port Said at the northern end of the Suez Canal. The attacks caused an outcry from the rest of the world, and the Americans, who were afraid of alienating the Arabs and forcing them into closer ties with the USSR, refused to support Britain although they had earlier hinted that support would be forthcoming. At the United Nations, Americans and Russians joined in demanding a cease-fire; with the pressure of world opinion against them, Britain, France and Israel agreed to withdraw, while UN troops moved in to police the frontier between Egypt and Israel.

(c) **The war was a diplomatic disaster**. It was a total humiliation for Britain and France. Nasser was still in power, and his prestige as the leader of Arab nationalism against European influence was greatly enhanced. The Egyptians blocked the canal, the Arabs reduced oil exports to Western Europe, where petrol rationing had to be introduced for a time, and Russian aid replaced that from the USA. King Feisal of Iraq and his premier, Nuri-es-Said, who were pro-British, were seriously embarrassed by Britain's actions, and came under increasing attack from other Arab governments. Both were murdered in 1958, so that Britain had lost a valuable Middle East ally. Even more serious, the Anglo-American alliance was weakened at a time when it needed to present a strong front against the Russians who were in the process of crushing the Hungarian uprising. Britain was seen to be incapable of conducting a foreign policy independently of the USA.

(d) The war was a personal disaster for Eden. In some quarters he was criticised for having sent troops into Suez in the first place, without any real moral case (everybody seemed to overlook the fact that Nasser had offered compensation). Others thought that having gone in, British troops ought to have ignored the UN and captured the whole canal zone, which would have been possible within a few days. What would have happened then is not certain, and it seems that Eden had not thought the consequences through clearly enough. Always highly strung, he was exhausted by the strain of the crisis, and on his doctor's orders, he resigned in January 1957.

30.5 BRITAIN, MALAYA AND CYPRUS

Malaya was liberated from the Japanese occupation in 1945 but there were two different problems to be faced before the British could think of withdrawing:

(a) How could such a complex area be organised? It consisted of nine states each ruled by a sultan, two British settlements, Malacca and Penang, and Singapore, a small island less than a mile from the mainland. The population was multi-racial: mostly Malays and Chinese but with Indians and Europeans as well. It was decided to group the states and the settlements into the *Federation of Malaya* (1948) while Singapore remained a separate colony. Each state had its own legislature for local affairs; the sultans retained some power, but the central government had firm overall control. Since everybody had the vote, the Malays, the largest group, usually dominated affairs.

(b) Chinese Communist guerrillas who had led the resistance to the Japanese, now began to stir up strikes and violence against the British, and the situation was serious enough for a state of emergency to be declared in 1948. The British dealt with the problem successfully, though it took time: all Chinese suspected of helping the guerrillas were re-settled into specially guarded villages; it was made clear that independence would follow as soon as the country was ready for it; this ensured that the Malays remained firmly pro-British and gave little help to the Communists, who were Chinese. Even so the emergency remained in force until 1960.

The move towards independence was accelerated when the Malay party under their able leader, Tunku Abdul Rahman, joined forces with the main Chinese and Indian groups to form the *Alliance Party*, which won 51 out of 52 seats in the 1955 elections. This seemed to suggest stability and the British were persuaded to grant full independence in 1957 when Malaya was admitted to the Commonwealth.

(c) The Federation of Malaysia was founded in 1963. Malaya soon settled down under the leadership of Tunku Abdul Rahman, and its economy, based on exports of rubber and tin, was the most prosperous in South East Asia. Thus in 1961 when Abdul Rahman proposed that Singapore and the three British colonies of North Borneo (Sabah), Brunei and Sarawak should join Malaya to form the Federation of Malaysia, Britain agreed. Abdul Rahman had something of an ulterior motive: the island of Singapore with its prosperous port would be a valuable acquisition, but since three-quarters of its population were Chinese, the Malays would be outnumbered if union took place just between Malaya and Singapore; if the other three colonies with their predominantly Malay population also joined the federation, the Malay majority would be preserved. Singapore, Sabah and Sarawak were in favour but objections came from two quarters:

(i) In Brunei groups of people opposed to joining the federation started a revolt (December 1962). Although this was quickly suppressed by British troops flown in from Singapore, the Sultan decided not to join. This was a disappointment for Abdul Rahman since Brunei had rich oil resources.

(ii) President Sukarno of Indonesia protested because he hoped that Sabah and Sarawak would become part of Indonesia once the British left.

After a United Nations investigation team reported that a large majority of the populations concerned was in favour of the union, the Federation of Malaysia was officially proclaimed (September 1963).

Malaysia survived an attempt by neighbouring Indonesia to bring about its disintegration (1963-6). Britain, Australia and New Zealand supplied vital military assistance so that the Malaysians could control the situation. However, in 1965, Singapore chose to leave the Federation, becoming an independent republic. Brunei ceased to be a British colony and became an independent state in 1984.

(d) Cyprus presented more serious problems, which were not very well handled by Eden.

The problems were:

(i) The population was mixed – about 80 per cent were Greek-speaking Christians of the Orthodox Church, while the rest were Muslims of Turkish origin. The Greek Cypriots wanted union with Greece (*enosis*); the Turks strongly opposed this, but there was no serious trouble until 1954, when:

(ii) Churchill's government produced a new constitution which allowed Cypriots far less power than the previous Labour government had envisaged. There were hostile demonstrations, which had to be dispersed by British troops.

(iii) Eden, Churchill's successor, thought Britain needed Cyprus as a military base to protect her interests in the Middle East, and announced that Cyprus must remain permanently British, though the Greek government promised that they could retain their military bases even if *enosis* took place.

(iv) The Greek Cypriots led by Archbishop Makarios, pressed their demands while a guerrilla organisation called *Eoka*, led by General Grivas, waged a terrorist campaign against the British who declared a state of emergency (1955) and deployed about 35 000 troops to try and keep order. British policy also involved deporting Makarios and executing terrorists.

(e) Macmillan, Eden's successor, adopted a conciliatory approach and appointed the sympathetic and tactful Hugh Foot as governor. He persuaded Makarios to agree to a compromise: the Archbishop dropped *enosis* and in return Cyprus was granted full independence; Turkish interests were safeguarded, Britain retained two military bases and, along with Greece and Turkey, guaranteed the independence of Cyprus; Makarios became first president (1960). It seemed a masterly solution, but unfortunately it lasted only until 1963 when civil war broke out between Greeks and Turks. Since 1974 the island has been divided, the Turks in the northern part, the Greeks in the south. United Nations forces police the frontier and keep the peace.

30.6 BRITAIN WITHDRAWS FROM AFRICA

African nationalism spread rapidly after 1945; this was because more and more Africans were being educated, many of them in Britain and the USA where they were made aware of racial discrimination. Colonialism was seen as the humiliation and exploitation of blacks by whites, and working-class Africans in the new towns were particularly receptive to nationalist ideas. They were greatly encouraged by Indian independence (1947) and by the sympathetic attitude of Attlee and the Labour government (1945-51).

(a) West Africa presented comparatively few problems, since the British in that area tended to be administrators rather than permanent settlers with estates to defend.

In the *Gold Coast* Kwame Nkrumah, educated in London and America and since 1949 leader of the Convention People's Party (CPP), organised the campaign for independence. There were demonstrations, some of which got out of hand, and Nkrumah was twice imprisoned. However, the British soon agreed to allow a new constitution which included the vote for all adults, an elected assembly and an eleven-man Executive Council of which eight were chosen by the assembly. In the 1951 elections, the first under the new constitution, the CPP won 34 seats out of 38; Nkrumah was released from prison and became Prime Minister in 1952. For the next five years the African politicians gained experience of government under British supervision until in 1957 Ghana, as it was now known, became independent.

In Nigeria, the leading nationalist was Nnamdi Azikiwe; popularly known as 'Zik', he had been educated in the USA, and after his return to Nigeria in 1937 soon gained enormous prestige. Nigeria was a more difficult proposition than Ghana because of its great size and its regional differences

602

Map 30.2 *Africa becomes independent*

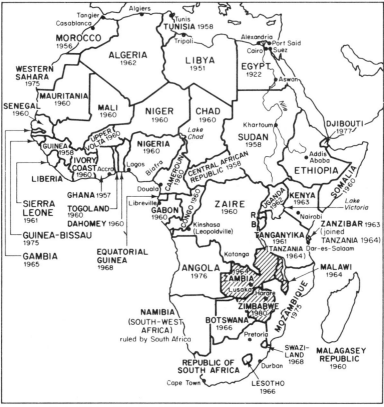

The Central African Federation 1953-63
Northern Rhodesia (Zambia), Southern Rhodesia (Zimbabwe) and
Nyasaland (Malawi)

R Ruanda 1962
B Burundi 1962

between the huge Muslim north, the western region (dominated by the
Yoruba tribe) and the eastern region (the Ibo tribe). However, after
Azikiwe had organised an impressive general strike in 1945, the British
gradually began to prepare Nigeria for independence. It was decided that a
federal system was most suitable; in 1954 a new constitution introduced
local assemblies for the three regions with a central (federal) government
in Lagos, the capital; the regions assumed self-government first and the
country as a whole became independent in 1960. Unfortunately tribal
differences caused civil war to break out in 1967; the Ibos declared the
eastern region the independent state of Biafra. Only after long and bloody
fighting was Biafra defeated (1970) and Nigerian unity preserved.

(b) East Africa included Tanganyika, Uganda and Kenya, and here the problems of independence were complicated by the presence of European and Asian settlers who were afraid for their future under black African government. The Tanganyika African National Union (TANU) led by Dr Julius Nyerere, who had been educated at Edinburgh University, insisted that the government must be African, and Macmillan's government (1957-63), impressed by Nyerere's ability and sincerity, accepted this view and granted independence (1961).

This marked an important change in British policy: they had begun in 1945 by thinking that independence was not as necessary in East Africa as in the west, and that when it came it would be under multi-racial governments. By 1960 Macmillan talked of 'the wind of change' in Africa; it was inevitable that Ghana's example would be followed in both East and Central Africa, and Macmillan dropped the idea of multi-racial governments in favour of black majority rule. Independence for *Uganda* was delayed by tribal squabbles; the ruler of the Buganda area (known as the *Kabaka*) objected to the introduction of democracy. Eventually a solution was found in a federal constitution which allowed the *Kabaka* to retain some powers in Buganda. Uganda itself became independent in 1962 with Dr Milton Obote as Prime Minister. *Kenya* was the most troublesome area. Here Jomo Kenyatta and his Kenya African Union led the struggle for independence and at first made little progress, the only British concession being to allow six Africans on the Legislative Council of 54 members. African impatience burst out in a campaign of terrorist attacks on European farms and African workers, organised by the *Mau Mau* secret society. A state of emergency was declared in 1952, and Kenyatta and other nationalists were arrested; thousands of British troops were used to flush out the terrorists and by 1960 the emergency was over. By this time, no doubt encouraged by the strength of African feeling, and by the expense of the anti-terrorist operations, the British change of heart had taken place. Kenya became independent under a black African government with Kenyatta as Prime Minister (1963); this was in spite of bitter resistance from the European settlers, many of whom left the country.

(c) Central Africa (Nyasaland, Northern and Southern Rhodesia) was the most difficult area to deal with because this was where the white settlers were most strongly entrenched, particularly in Southern Rhodesia. Alarmed at the spread of African nationalism to the north, the whites, with the approval of Churchill's government, set up the *Central African Federation* (1953), a union of the three states. Their aim was to preserve the supremacy of the white minority (about 300 000 Europeans out of a total population of 8.5 million), and the federal parliament at Salisbury (in Southern Rhodesia) was heavily weighted to favour the whites, who hoped the Federation would soon gain full independence from Britain with dominion status. The Africans watched with growing distrust, and as outstanding nationalist leaders emerged, such as Dr Hastings Banda (Nyasaland), Kenneth Kaunda (Northern Rhodesia) and Joshua Nkomo (Southern

Rhodesia), they became more militant. As violence spread, a state of emergency was declared in Nyasaland and Southern Rhodesia with mass arrests of Africans (1959).

However, there was much support for the Africans in Britain, especially in the Labour Party, and the Conservative Colonial Secretary, Iain Macleod, was sympathetic. *The Monckton Commission* (1960) recommended votes for Africans, an end to racial discrimination and the right of territories to leave the Federation. The British introduced new constitutions in Nyasaland and Northern Rhodesia which in effect allowed the Africans their own parliaments (1961-2); both wanted to leave the Federation, which was terminated in December 1963. The following year Nyasaland and Northern Rhodesia became fully independent as Malawi and Zambia.

There still remained *the problem of Southern Rhodesia*, or Rhodesia as it was now known. Here the ruling whites, more numerous than in the other two areas, opposed any change in the constitution which would increase African rights; they demanded independence, but Harold Wilson, the new British Labour Prime Minister, refused this unless the whites showed a willingness to move towards black majority rule. No compromise could be reached and in 1965 Rhodesia declared itself independent against the wishes of Britain (a unilateral declaration of independence or UDI).

Under its Prime Minister, Ian Smith, Rhodesia continued its illegal independence. All the African Nationalist parties were banned and black citizens had their rights severely curtailed. Wilson twice met Smith (aboard HMS *Tiger* in 1966 and HMS *Fearless* in 1968), but no compromise could be reached. Towards the end of 1976, as Zimbabwean guerrilla activities became more difficult to control and South Africa showed itself less willing to support Rhodesia, Smith admitted that black majority rule would have to come within a few years. He was determined to try every trick he knew to delay it as long as possible. Though a conference to consider possible solutions met at Geneva, it was impossible to pin Smith down to a definite commitment. He was able to present the divisions between the Zimbabwean nationalist leaders as his excuse for the lack of progress. This was a genuine problem: ZAPU (Zimbabwe African People's Union), the party of the veteran nationalist Joshua Nkomo, and ZANU (Zimbabwe African National Union), the party of the Rev. Ndabaningi Sithole, seemed to be bitter enemies; in addition there was Bishop Abel Muzorewa's United African National Council (UANC), as well as the supporters of Robert Mugabe, leader of the guerrilla wing of ZANU.

(d) The end of white rule in Rhodesia. Smith at last began concessions which were soon to lead to the transference of power to the blacks. This happened in two stages:

(i) Smith introduced his own scheme which allowed blacks to vote on equal terms. A general election was held in April 1979 for a new parliament in which 72 of the 100 MPs were to be black. Bishop Muzorewa's party won 51 seats, and Smith stepped down for Muzorewa to become

Prime Minister. However, this was not a success: ZAPU decided not to fight the election and both Britain and the USA felt that any viable settlement must include Nkomo and Mugabe; Sithole, whose party had won only 12 seats, claimed that the whites had rigged the elections so that the more amenable Muzorewa would win. Both the UN and the Organisation of African Unity (OAU) condemned the elections as invalid. The guerrilla war continued and by November 1979 the Patriotic Front (the two main guerrilla groups led by Nkomo and Mugabe) had 15 000 troops in Rhodesia fighting against the Muzorewa government. Smith was forced to concede that his scheme had failed.

(ii) *The Lancaster House Conference* (September–December 1979) convened by Britain and held in London, involved representatives from all parties including the Patriotic Front. After skilful manoeuvring by Lord Carrington, the British Foreign Secretary, the conference agreed on a constitution for the new republic of Zimbabwe, arrangements for elections and an end to the guerrilla war. Muzorewa agreed to step down as Prime Minister and Lord Soames was to be governor during the transitional period until elections were held. These were contested by all parties and Mugabe's ZANU won a sweeping victory taking 57 out of the 80 seats reserved for Africans in the 100-seat parliament. Nkomo's ZAPU won 27 while Muzorewa's UANC was reduced to 3 seats. With a comfortable overall majority Mugabe, a self-proclaimed Marxist, became Prime Minister and Zimbabwe became officially an independent republic (April 1980). The transference to black majority rule was welcomed by all African and Commonwealth leaders as a triumph for common sense and moderation, though some British Conservatives accused the British government of betraying Muzorewa and allowing Zimbabwe to fall to Marxism. During the early years of independence, the main danger was that the long tribal hatred between ZANU and ZAPU, shelved temporarily during the fight against Smith, might flare up into civil war.

(e) South Africa. The situation in the Union of South Africa was different from that in the other British parts of Africa. South Africa had enjoyed dominion status since 1909 (see Section 20.1) and therefore had more say over its own affairs than the other areas, which were colonies. The majority of the white population was of Boer origin and therefore did not have the same close affiliations with Britain as the whites in the British colonies. While the colonies gained independence under black majority rule and stayed within the Commonwealth, South Africa preserved white minority rule and left the Commonwealth in 1961.

The whites form less than 20 per cent of the population. In 1974 there were almost 18 million black Africans, known as Bantus, 2.3 million coloureds, 700 000 Asians and 4.2 million whites. Roughly two-thirds of the whites were of Dutch (Boer) origin and known as Afrikaaners; the rest were of British origin. With the granting of independence to India and Pakistan in 1947, white South Africans became alarmed at the growing racial equality within the Commonwealth and were determined to preserve their supremacy. Most of the whites were against racial equality but the most extreme were the Afrikaaner Nationalists led by Dr Malan, who claimed that the whites were a master race and that non-whites were inferior beings. The Dutch Reformed Church (the official state church) supported this view, though the Christian Church in general believes in racial equality. The Nationalists won the 1948 elections with promises to rescue the whites from the 'black menace'; Malan's policy was *apartheid*.

This involved complete separation or segregation of the different races in order to preserve the racial purity of the whites and thus their supremacy. There had been some segregation before 1948; for example, Africans were forbidden to buy land outside special reserve areas. But Malan's apartheid was much more systematic. Africans have to live in special reserves and townships with separate and inferior facilities. Marriages and sexual relations between whites and non-whites are forbidden. Africans have no political rights and are not represented in parliament.

There was mounting criticism of apartheid from all over the world. Most of the Commonwealth members were strongly opposed to it, and early in 1960, Britain's Prime Minister, Harold Macmillan, had the courage to speak out against it in the South African parliament in Cape Town. In a speech which soon became famous, he told the South African government: 'the wind of change is blowing through the continent. Whether we like it or not, this growth of national consciousness is a political fact ... our national policies must take account of it'. His warnings were ignored and shortly afterwards the world was horrified by the Sharpville massacre when 67 Africans were killed in clashes with the police.

At the 1961 Commonwealth Conference, criticism of South Africa was intense and many thought she should be expelled. In the end the Prime Minister, Verwoerd, withdrew South Africa's application for continued membership (in 1960 she had decided to become a republic instead of a dominion, thereby severing the connection with the British crown; because of this she had to apply for readmission to the Commonwealth) and she ceased to be a member of the Commonwealth.

30.7 BRITAIN, EUROPEAN UNITY AND THE COMMON MARKET

(a) In every country in western Europe there were people from all parts of the political spectrum who believed in closer co-operation between the states, while some thought in terms of a united federal Europe on the same lines as the United States of America. Their reasoning was simple: only by a co-operative effort and a pooling of resources could Europe recover from the ravages of war; the countries were too small to be economically and militarily viable separately, in a world dominated by the super-powers, the USA and the USSR; there would be less likelihood of war between the countries; the threat from Russia could be met only by joint action. West Germany especially supported the idea because it would gain her early acceptance as a responsible nation, and *Winston Churchill* was one of its most eloquent advocates: in March 1943 he spoke of the need for a Council of Europe, and in a speech at Zurich in 1946 he argued that only as a United States of Europe could the countries count for anything in the world.

(b) Although federalists have been bitterly disappointed by their failure to achieve complete integration, some progress was made. *The Organisation for European Co-operation (OEEC)* was the first move towards unity; it was set up in 1947 in response to the offer of Marshall Aid. Britain and 15 other European nations joined, and it was extremely successful in apportioning American aid, and in encouraging trade among its members by reducing restrictions. *NATO* was another example of European co-operation (see Section 30.1(d)), though France withdrew from it in 1966. *The Council of Europe (1949)* was an attempt at political unity. By 1971 all the states of Western Europe (except Spain and Portugal) had joined and Turkey was included (making 16 members in all). Based at Strassbourg, it consists of the foreign ministers of the member states and an Assembly of representatives chosen by the parliaments of the states. It has no powers, however, since several states, particularly Britain, refused to join any organisation which threatened their own sovereignty. It can make recommendations and has achieved useful work sponsoring human rights agreements, but it has been a grave disappointment to the federalists. The organisation which has made the most direct impact on the ordinary people of Europe, and certainly the one which is best known in Britain, is the EEC.

(c) The European Economic Community (EEC) known in Britain as the Common Market, was established by the *Treaty of Rome* in 1957. However, Britain refused to join at this stage and the EEC consisted of only six countries: Belgium, Netherlands, Luxembourg, France, West Germany and Italy. The stages in its evolution were:

  (i) In 1944 the exiled governments of Belgium, Netherlands and Luxembourg formed *the Benelux Union*, a customs and trading association which came into operation in 1947.
 (ii) By *the Treaty of Brussels* (1948) Britain and France joined the three Benelux countries in pledging 'military, economic, social and cultural collaboration'. While the military collaboration eventually resulted in NATO, the next step in economic co-operation was:
(iii) *The European Coal and Steel Community (ECSC)* (1951). It was the brainchild of Robert Schuman, the French Foreign Minister, who hoped by involving West Germany to improve Franco-German relations as well as to make European industry more efficient. Six countries joined: France, West Germany, Italy, Belgium, Netherlands and Luxembourg. All duties and restrictions on trade in coal, iron and steel between the Six were removed, and a High Authority created to administer the community and organise a joint programme of expan-

sion. The only disappointment for the federalists was that *Britain declined the invitation to join* because she disliked surrendering control of her industries to a supra-national authority. The Labour government was in the throes of nationalising iron and steel, which would be a pointless exercise if they were to be handed over to the High Authority immediately afterwards. Attlee therefore announced that although Britain sympathised with any activities which improved Franco-German relations, Britain could not undertake to join the scheme immediately.

The ECSC went ahead without Britain and was such an outstanding success, with steel production rising by almost 50 per cent during the first five years, that the Six decided to extend it to include all production. Consequently the full EEC came into operation on 1 January 1958.

The six countries would gradually remove all customs duties and quotas so that there would be free competition and a common market. Tariffs would be kept against non-members, though even these were reduced. The treaty also spoke of improving living and working conditions, expanding industry, encouraging the development of the world's backward areas, safeguarding peace and liberty, and working for a closer union of European peoples: obviously something much wider than just a common market was in the minds of the statesmen of the six countries. By 1967 the machinery to run the EEC had been refined to include the Commission (which manages the EEC), the Council of Ministers, an Assembly or Parliament (containing representatives since 1979 directly elected by voters in all member states), a Secretariat and a Court of Justice. Associated with the EEC was EURATOM, an organisation in which the Six pooled their efforts towards the development of atomic energy. Like the ECSC, the EEC was soon off to a flying start; within five years it was the world's biggest exporter and buyer of raw materials and was second only to the USA in steel production.

(d) Why did Britain refuse membership of the EEC? It was ironic that though Churchill (who retired as Prime Minister in 1955) was one of the strongest supporters of a united Europe, both Labour and Conservative governments drew back from committing themselves too far. Eden and Macmillan were very cool towards the negotiations which preceded the signing of the Treaty of Rome. Their main objection was that Britain would no longer be in complete control of her own economy which would be at the mercy of a supra-national authority – the EEC Commission in Brussels. There was also the fear that Britain's relationship with the Commonwealth might be ruined if she were no longer able to give preference to Commonwealth goods such as New Zealand lamb and butter; the Commonwealth with its population of over 800 million seemed a more promising market than the EEC with 165 million. Nor did Britain want to risk upsetting her special relationship with the USA by becoming too deeply involved in economic integration with Europe, which many Europeans wanted to see extended into political integration.

Britain and other countries outside the EEC were worried about being excluded from trade with the Six by their high external tariffs. Consequently Britain took the lead in organising *the European Free Trade Area (EFTA)* in 1959. Britain, Denmark, Norway, Sweden, Switzerland, Austria and Portugal agreed gradually to abolish tariffs between each other, but there was no mention of common economic policies. By 1961, however, the British had had a complete change of mind, and Macmillan announced that they wished to join the EEC.

(e) Why did the British attitude to the EEC change? In the first place it was clear that by 1961 the EEC was an outstanding success - without Britain. Since 1953 French production had risen by 75 per cent while German production had increased by almost 90 per cent; Britain's, however, was only 30 per cent up. EFTA had been successful in increasing the trade of its members, but to nothing like the same extent as the EEC. In fact, the British economy seemed to be stagnating in comparison with that of the Six. The Commonwealth, in spite of its size, could not compare with the purchasing power of the EEC, and Macmillan pointed out that there was no clash of interest between Britain's membership of the EEC and trade with the Commonwealth: there were signs that the EEC was willing to make special arrangements for the Commonwealth countries to become associate members and to allow Britain's EFTA partners to join as well. Another argument was that once Britain was in, competition from the other EEC members would stimulate British industry to greater effort and efficiency. Macmillan also made the point that Britain could not afford to be left out if the EEC developed into a political union. He seems to have had some idea that Britain could take over the leadership and build the Community up into a strong defensive unit against the USSR, and in partnership with the USA. This may well have been Macmillan's primary motive, though naturally he could hardly give it much publicity. The Labour party was hostile to British entry: Harold Wilson said it would mean 'selling our friends and kinsmen down the river . . . for a marginal advantage in selling washing machines in Düsseldorf'.

Negotiations for British entry opened in October 1961, and though there were some difficulties, it came as a shock when in January 1963 the French President, de Gaulle, broke off the talks and announced that Britain was not ready for membership.

(f) Why did the French oppose British entry to the EEC? At the time de Gaulle claimed that Britain had too many economic problems and would therefore weaken the EEC. Though the French colonies were associate members, he objected to any concessions being made for the Commonwealth since this would be a drain on Europe's resources. It was suggested in Britain that de Gaulle wanted to continue dominating Europe; if Britain came in she would be a serious rival, while her close ties with the

USA would bring unwelcome American influence producing, as he himself said, 'a colossal Atlantic grouping under American dependence and control'. He was perhaps annoyed that Britain had just agreed to receive American Polaris missiles without first consulting France, while he was determined to prove that France was a great power and in no need of American assistance. Finally there was the problem of French agriculture: the EEC protected its farmers with high tariffs so that prices were much higher than in Britain whose agriculture was highly efficient and subsidised to keep prices relatively low. If this continued after Britain's entry, French farmers, with their small and inefficient farms, would be exposed to competition from Britain and perhaps from the Commonwealth.

(g) Britain's entry into the Common Market eventually took place on 1 January 1973. It was made possible by two factors: after de Gaulle's resignation in 1969, his successor Pompidou was more amenable to Britain, while the new British Conservative Prime Minister, Edward Heath, a committed European, negotiated with obstinate determination for British admission. Eire and Denmark also joined. In 1975 a referendum was held in Britain in which 67 per cent of those who voted expressed approval of British membership.

(h) What have been the EEC's main problems? The EEC has faced several crises and problems. During the 1960s de Gaulle caused tensions first by his high-handed attitude towards British entry and later by his hostility to the Commission which was becoming too powerful for his liking. In 1965 he threatened to withdraw from the EEC if the Commission's powers were not reduced. He got his own way but held up progress for almost a decade. There was, and still is, the problem of producing a common agricultural policy acceptable to all members. France objected to imports of cheap wine from Italy and lamb from Britain, and on occasion refused them entry, though this was a breach of the community rules. A major crisis blew up in 1980 when Britain protested about her budget contribution for that year which seemed unreasonably high at £1209 million compared with £699 million from Germany and only £13 million from France. The difference was so marked because the contribution was calculated partly as a levy on each country's duties received from imports from outside the EEC. Since Britain imported much more from the outside world than the other members, her contribution soared. Fortunately, after some ruthless bargaining by the British Prime Minister, Margaret Thatcher, a compromise was reached whereby Britain's contribution was reduced to a total of £1346 million over the next three years. Similar wrangling took place in the summer of 1983 before a compromise satisfactory to Britain could be arrived at. The Labour party remained hostile to the Community and made British withdrawal one of the main points in its manifesto for the general election of June 1983. But this, like the rest of Labour's programme, failed to make much of an impact. The Conservative victory seemed to indicate that the general public, while not feeling wildly enthusiastic about it, was at least reconciled to permanent British membership of the Community. The main British complaint was that far too much of the EEC budget went on paying inflated prices to farmers who continually produced more than could be sold. The dispute was particularly bitter in 1984 when Britain, West Germany and the Netherlands pressed for a top limit to be placed on farm subsidies. Britain blamed France for the failure to find a long-term solution, while the French press savaged Mrs Thatcher for her intransigence and her unwillingness to take 'one small step' towards her EEC partners.

A further complication arose with the admission of three new members - Greece (1981) and Spain and Portugal (1986), bringing the total membership to 12 and the community population to over 320 million. Their arrival increased the influence of the southern, less industrialised countries, and the pressure to improve the economic balance between wealthy and poor regions.

An encouraging development occurred early in 1986 when all 12 members working closely together, negotiated a *reform package* which included a move to a complete common internal market by 1992; more control over health, safety and environmental and consumer protection; encouragement of scientific research and technology; greater powers for the European Parliament so that measures could be passed with less delay; measures to help backward regions.

Nevertheless, in 1987 the Community was facing a massive *budget crisis* - £3 billion in the red and with debts of £10 billion. The cause was the same old problem - the *Common Agricultural Policy* (CAP), which was using up two-thirds of the EEC's total spending every year to subsidise farm prices. In spite of strict production quotas introduced for the first time in 1984, Europe's farmers still produced vast surpluses of milk and butter which could not be sold. By 1987 the 'butter mountain' had reached ludicrous proportions - 1½ million tonnes - enough to supply the entire EEC for a year. There was enough milk powder to last five years and storage fees alone were costing a million pounds a day. Efforts to get rid of the surplus involved selling it off cheaply to the USSR, India, Bangladesh and Pakistan, distributing it free of charge to the poor within the Community, using it to make animal feed, and burning the oldest butter in boilers.

As 1987 progressed, the community made a real attempt to solve the problem by introducing a harsh programme of production curbs and a price freeze to put a general squeeze on Europe's farmers. By the end of 1988 it seemed that the programme was having some success and the surpluses were steadily shrinking. By this time, the member states were concentrating on preparing for *1992*, when the introduction of *a single European market* would see the removal of all internal barriers and much greater monetary integration. However, Mrs Thatcher upset some of the other European leaders when, during a tour of some of the member states (September 1988), she spoke out against any movement towards a politically united Europe: 'a centralised federal government in Europe would be a nightmare; co-operation with other European countries must not be at the expense of individuality, the national customs and traditions which made Europe great in the past'.

QUESTIONS

1. The Suez War 1956
Study Sources **A** to **G** and then answer the questions which follow.

Source A: (i) Sir Anthony Eden's speech to the Cabinet, 27 July 1956.

The nationalisation [of the Suez Canal] is not just a legal matter, it is one of the widest international importance . . . *Colonel Nasser's action* has presented us with an opportunity to find a lasting settlement of this problem, and we should not hesitate to take advantage of it . . . Our essential interests in this area must, if necessary, be safeguarded by military action and the necessary preparations to this end must be made . . . Even if we have to act alone, we cannot stop short of using force to protect our position if all other means of protecting it prove unsuccessful . . . Any failure on the part of the Western Powers to take the necessary steps to regain control over the Canal would have disastrous consequences for the economic life of the Western Powers and for their influence in the Middle East.

(ii) Eden's telegram to President Eisenhower of the USA, 4 November 1956.

As we see it, we are unlikely to attain our objectives by economic pressures alone . . . my colleagues and I are convinced that we must be ready in the last resort to use force to bring Nasser to his senses . . . If we had allowed everything to drift, everything would have gone from bad to worse. Nasser would have become a kind of Moslem Mussolini taking the tricks all around the Middle East. I am sure that this is the moment to curb Nasser's ambitions. By this means, we shall have taken the first step towards re-establishing our authority in this area for our generation.

Source: quoted in R. Lamb, *The Failure of the Eden Government* Sidgwick & Jackson, 1987 (adapted extracts).

Source B: information from Anthony Nutting, Minister of State at the Foreign Office, who resigned on 6 November in protest at Eden's policy.

Challe [Deputy Chief of Staff for the French Air Force] outlined a possible plan of action for Britain and France to gain control of the Suez Canal . . . Israel would be invited to attack Egypt, and then France and Britain, having given Israeli forces time to get through Sinai close to the Canal, should order 'both sides' to withdraw their forces from the Suez Canal and permit an Anglo–French force to intervene and occupy the Canal with the excuse that they were saving it from damage by fighting . . . This would restore the running of the Canal to Anglo–French management and enable us to supervise all shipping movements through the Canal and so break the Egyptian blockade of Israel . . .

I knew that no matter what contrary advice he might receive over the next 48 hours, Eden had already made up his mind to go along with the French plan . . . designed to topple Nasser and seize the Suez Canal . . . Relations would be poisoned between Britain and Egypt and the Arab world for generations to come. To make matters even worse, Britain had obviously acted in *collusion* with Israel; proof of this was plain in the ultimatum which demanded that both sides withdraw to a distance of ten miles from the Canal at a moment when the Egyptian army was still trying to halt the Israelis 125 miles to the east of the Canal. This meant that Britain and France, who were pretending to put a stop to the fighting, were ordering the victim of aggression to withdraw 134 miles, while the aggressor was being allowed to advance up to 115 miles!

Note: *collusion* = a secret agreement made in order to trick somebody.

Source: A. Nutting, *No End of a Lesson*, Constable, 1967 (adapted extracts).

Source C: speech by Selwyn Lloyd, the Foreign Secretary, in the Commons, 31 October 1956.

The Right Hon. Gentleman asked whether there had been collusion with regard to this matter . . . It is quite wrong to state that Israel was incited to this action by her Majesty's government. There was no prior agreement between us about it. It is of course true that the Israeli mobilisation gave some advance warning, and we urged restraint upon the Israeli Government and in particular drew attention to the serious consequences of any attack on Jordan.

Source: *Hansard*, October 1956.

Source D: plan agreed at Sèvres (France) by British, French and Israeli representatives, 24 October 1956.

On the afternoon of 29 October 1956 Israeli forces will launch a large scale attack on the Egyptian forces, with the object of reaching the Canal Zone on the following day. Having been informed of the event, the Governments of Britain and France will, on 30 October, address the following appeals:

To the Egyptian Government:

– Absolute cease fire.
– Withdrawal of all forces to 15 kilometres from the Canal.

– Acceptance of the occupation by Anglo–French forces of key positions on the Canal . . .

To the Israeli Government:

– Absolute cease fire.
– Withdrawal of forces to 15 kilometres from the Canal . . .

Israel will not attack Jordan while the operation against Egypt is proceeding.

Source: quoted in R. Lamb, *The Failure of the Eden Government*, Sidgwick & Jackson, 1987.

Source E: comments from Richard Lamb, the most recent historian to write about Suez.

The Cabinet agreed that they were on weak ground over the question of the illegality [of Nasser's nationalisation of the Canal], since Nasser was offering to pay compensation to shareholders in the Suez Canal Company . . . The French refused to hand over their copies [of the Sèvres agreement] on the grounds that the Israelis had taken their copy back to Tel Aviv. Without doubt Eden destroyed all English copies of the document. They are not in the Public Record Office . . . he intended to keep the collusion plan secret indefinitely. It was an amazing error of judgement for a statesman with Eden's experience to imagine this would be possible. It is hard to avoid the conclusion that his health and the remedies prescribed by his doctors had affected his judgement . . . it was bound to be leaked by the French and Israelis. The plan was not even disclosed to the Cabinet, which was downright dishonesty. But Eden's hands were tied because by the Sèvres agreement Britain had promised the French and Israelis that collusion would stay a close secret . . .

At 5 p.m. on Monday, 29 October, Israeli forces began their assault through Sinai, as agreed with the British and French at Sèvres, and soon posed a threat to the Canal . . . On 30 October the ultimatum was delivered . . . On the night of 31 October the British dropped bombs on thirteen targets . . . On 5 November British seaborne landings were made at Port Said which surrendered . . . On the 30 November *the decision was taken to withdraw British troops* . . . Clearance of the Canal was now [4 December] in the hands of the U.N. Nasser was triumphant. His propaganda was that his army had defeated the British, French and Israeli forces so that they had been obliged to withdraw ignominiously. His popularity in Egypt and the Arab world soared.

Source: R. Lamb, *The Failure of the Eden Government*, Sidgwick & Jackson, 1987 (adapted extracts).

Source F: an Australian cartoon of early November 1956 showing Eden making a speech about the Suez War.

Source: *Sydney Morning Herald*.

Source G: the opinion of Michael Foot, a Labour MP at the time of Suez.

> The great upsurge of British radical opinion was one reason why the Egyptian war was brought to a sudden halt; Eden's temperament and perhaps his health was another; a third was threats of retaliatory action from the Soviet Union; a fourth the strong objections of the Commonwealth; a fifth, the instructions from the United Nations; and sixth and most powerful of all, the direct pressure from the US Government and the threat to the pound ... Instead of opening the Canal, it was blocked; instead of saving British lives and property, they had been put at Nasser's mercy; instead of toppling Nasser, he was enthroned; instead of keeping the oil flowing, it was soon to be rationed; instead of winning friends, we had lost them ... the expedition had achieved the exact opposite of the Government's declared intention. But there were counter-arguments: a war had been stopped and the com-batants had been kept separate.

Source: M. Foot, *Aneurin Bevan 1945-1960*, Granada, 1975.

(a)   (i)   What was Colonel Nasser's action referred to in Source **A(i)**?   **4(a)**

    (ii)   According to Source **A(i)** why was Eden worried about the situation in the Middle East?   **4(a)**

    (iii)   According to Source **A(ii)**, what two types of action was Eden thinking about to deal with Nasser?   **4(a)**

    (iv)   From the evidence of the other Sources, which of the two did Eden choose?   **4(a, c)**

(v)   From the evidence of Source **A**, what was Eden's attitude towards Nasser? **4(a, b)**

(vi)   From the evidence of Sources **A** and **B**, what was Eden hoping to achieve by his action in the Middle East? **4(a, c)**

(b) (i)   According to Source **B**, why did Anthony Nutting not approve of the plan of action? **4(a)**

(ii)   Using the information in Source **B** and the map on p. 595, explain in your own words why, according to Nutting, the ultimatum proved that there was collusion between Britain and Israel. **4(a, c)**

(c) (i)   In what ways does the statement by Selwyn Lloyd in Source **C** contradict Nutting's claims in Source **B**? **4(a, c)**

(ii)   What possible Israeli action is mentioned by Lloyd (Source **C**) but not by Nutting (Source **B**)? **4(a, c)**

(d) (i)   According to Source **D**, how soon was the Israeli action to begin after the signing of this agreement? **4(a)**

(ii)   Does the evidence in Source **D** support Nutting (Source **B**) or Lloyd (Source **C**)? Explain your answer fully. **4(a, c)**

(e) (i)   According to Source **E**, why was the Cabinet on weak ground when it claimed that Nasser's nationalisation of the Suez Canal was illegal? **4(a)**

(ii)   Why do you think Eden wanted to keep the collusion plan secret? **4(a)**

(iii)   Why did it prove impossible to keep the plan secret? **4(a)**

(iv)   What is the attitude of the author of Source **E** to Eden's behaviour over the secret plan? **4(b)**

(f) (i)   What message is the cartoonist trying to get across in Source **F**? **4(a)**

(ii)   Why do you think Eden is shown smoking an outsize cigar? **4(a, b)**

(iii)   Do you think the cartoonist approves or disapproves of the British attack on Egypt? Explain your answer fully. **4(b)**

(g) (i)   According to Source **G**, what external pressures led to the British decision underlined in Source **E**? **4(a, c)**

(ii)   Do you think the cartoon (Source **F**) proves or disproves the claim in Source **G** that the Commonwealth did not like Eden's policy? Explain your answer. **4(a, b, c)**

(iii)   What does Michael Foot see as the main achievement of Britain's action in Egypt? **4(a)**

(iv)   How do Sources **B** and **D** show that Foot was wrong to claim this as an achievement? **4(a, c)**

(v)   Can you suggest any reasons why Foot made a mistake on this point? **4(b)**

(h) (i) Explain how Sources **B**, **C** and **G** – i.e. writings by people involved in some way with the events they are describing –
present problems for the historian.   4(b)

(ii) 'From Britain's point of view the Suez War was a disaster'.
Make a list of evidence from the Sources which supports this
statement.   4(a, c)

2. Britain and Palestine

Study Sources **A** and **B** and then answer the questions which follow.

Source A: memoirs of Hugh Dalton, Chancellor of the Exchequer 1945–
November 1947.

On 17 January 1947 I recorded: 'On Palestine a number of us
have been shouting for Partition. The present state of things
cannot be allowed to drag on. There must be a Jewish state –
it is no good boggling at this – and even if it is small, at least
they will control their own immigration, so that they can let in
lots of Jews, which is what they madly and murderously want'.
Already armed attacks and other outrages by Jews against
British troops were losing them [the Jews] sympathy . . . They
used a pretty girl to decoy two young British sergeants and
then hanged them in an olive grove . . . After that I went
absolutely cold towards the Jews in Palestine . . .

24 February: 'Bevin has now wasted more than a year and
created intolerable conditions for British troops by waiting
until now to send this wretched problem to the UN. He goes
round and round with Arabs and Jews and nothing ever
happens except more outrages'.

The miserable affair dragged on until May 14th, 1948, when
the *Mandate* legally ended and the new State of Israel was
born.

Source: H. Dalton, *High Tide and After: Memoirs of Hugh
Dalton 1945–1960*, Frederick Muller, 1962 (adapted extracts).

Source B: recent comments from a historian.

Without question Bevin's conduct of the Palestine question did
his reputation immense harm. On the other hand it is difficult
to see any other possible policy which the Labour government
could have adopted. They were left with rival promises dating
from the twenties to both Arabs and Jews, which were impossible to reconcile . . . In Bevin's defence it may be said that his
insistence that any solution must be acceptable to the Arabs,
and that an imposed solution would lead to decades of bitterness and instability in the Middle East, has been borne out by
later events. The decision to leave Palestine was undoubtedly
popular in Britain.

Source: K. O. Morgan, *Labour in Power 1945–1951*, Oxford,
1984 (adapted extracts).

(a) (i) When, according to Source **A**, did the new state of Israel come into existence? **4(a)**

   (ii) What was the author's solution to the problems of Palestine? **4(a)**

   (iii) What did he mean by the word 'Mandate'? **1, 4(a)**

   (iv) From the evidence of Source **A**, how would you sum up Dalton's attitude towards the Jews? **4(a, b)**

   (v) What seems to be Dalton's opinion of Bevin, the Foreign Secretary? **4(a)**

(b) (i) Do you think that Source **B** supports Dalton's opinion of Bevin or not? **4(a, b, c)**

   (ii) How reliable do you think Source **A** is for the historian? **4(b)**

(c) Using the evidence in Source **B** and your own knowledge, explain how the problem between Jews and Arabs in Palestine had arisen. **1, 2, 4(a)**

(d) Explain why the British decided to leave Palestine. **1, 2**

(e) What were the results of the British decision? **1, 2**

3. Britain and the Common Market

(a) Explain why Britain failed to join the Common Market at its beginning in 1957.

(b) Why did the British change their minds and apply to join in 1961?

(c) Explain why Britain was refused membership in 1963 and was then allowed to join in 1973.

(d) What problems did Mrs Thatcher's governments have with the Common Market during the 1980s? **1, 2**

4. Rhodesia Becomes Zimbabwe

Describe and explain the feelings and reactions of each of the following towards the events which changed Rhodesia into Zimbabwe.

(a) a supporter of Robert Mugabe and member of ZANU;

(b) a supporter of Joshua Nkomo and member of ZAPU;

(c) a white Rhodesian supporter of Ian Smith;

(d) a British Conservative.
The main events were:

   (i) the election of April 1979 won by Archbishop Muzorewa;

   (ii) the Lancaster House Conference, September–December 1979;

   (iii) the ZANU election victory of 1980. **1, 2, 3**

CHAPTER 31

BRITAIN SINCE 1964

SUMMARY OF EVENTS

With its tiny overall majority of four when it took office in October 1964, Wilson's new government was precarious. After an encouraging by-election victory at Hull North in January, 1966, Wilson decided to risk a general election the following March, in the hope of increasing Labour's majority. He had already been Prime Minister long enough to make a good impression on the electorate; his superb television technique together with his familiar pipe and Gannex raincoat combined to project the image of the capable and reliable father-figure who had the country's fortunes well under control. At the same time the Conservatives had a new and untried leader in *Edward Heath*, and a majority of the voters saw no reason to desert Labour so soon. Wilson won the mandate he had asked for, securing 363 seats against 253 Conservatives and 12 Liberals. In spite of their large majority, Labour's path was far from smooth: there were constant economic crises, and it was not until 1969 that a favourable balance of payments was achieved.

It seemed that the Labour government had not been noticeably more successful than the Conservatives before them, and in the election of June 1970 there was a swing from Labour big enough to give the Conservatives an overall majority of 30. Edward Heath was Prime Minister until February 1974 when a confrontation between government and miners led to a narrow Conservative defeat and the return of Wilson as Prime Minister, though without an overall majority. In October 1974 Wilson went to the country again, and although Labour strengthened its position, the results fell well below Wilson's hopes. With 319 seats, Labour had a comfortable lead over Conservatives (277) and Liberals (13), but there were 26 assorted Nationalists and others, so that Labour's overall majority was tiny. In spite of this Labour remained in office until May 1979, though Wilson himself resigned in April 1975. *James Callaghan* was Prime Minister for the remainder of the Labour government.

The election of May 1979 saw a decisive result: the Conservatives won a comfortable overall majority of 43, and their new leader, *Margaret Thatcher*, became Britain's first woman Prime Minister. This was destined to be the beginning of another long period of Tory rule; in the general election of June 1983, with the Labour party in complete disarray, the Conservative lead was extended to 144 in a victory of landslide proportions. Another comfortable Conservative victory followed in June 1987.

31.1 THE WILSON GOVERNMENTS 1964-70

Wilson and his cabinet seemed to spend most of their time wrestling with insoluble economic problems and strikes, and matters were complicated by the situation in Rhodesia and by violence in Ireland.

(a) **The balance of payments deficit** inherited from the Conservatives was the most pressing problem.

(i) The Chancellor of the Exchequer, Callaghan, borrowed heavily from the International Monetary Fund to replenish Britain's rapidly dwindling gold reserves which were being used up to cover the deficit. In yet another squeeze he tried to cut spending by holding wages down and raising import duties. The government's efforts were ruined by a dockers' strike (May 1966) which brought trade almost to a standstill, causing a drastic fall in exports. Some foreign bankers feared that the unions were getting out of control and the pound was adversely affected on the foreign exchanges. Even after the strike was settled, the value of the pound continued to fall and some members of the cabinet suggested devaluation. However, Callaghan would not hear of it: 'devaluation is not the way out of Britain's difficulties', he declared in July 1967. Soon another dock strike affecting London and Liverpool reduced exports again and it was clear that there would be a massive trade deficit by the end of the year. With the drain on gold reserves increasing, the government decided that the only alternative was to devalue the pound from 2.80 to 2.40 dollars (November 1967). It was hoped that, apart from stabilising the financial situation, devaluation would cause a surge in exports, since British goods would now be cheaper abroad. However, the immediate effect was to bring about Callaghan's resignation; after his declaration against devaluation only a few months earlier, it was felt that he could hardly remain at the Treasury. His replacement was *Roy Jenkins*.

(ii) During 1968 the new Chancellor cut government spending by £750 million and raised tariffs on cigarettes, alcohol and petrol. This aroused bitter criticism from the party's left wing, but Jenkins was determined to stick by his policies, and gradually they began to show results – a balance of payments surplus of £387 million for 1969. Unfortunately the ending of the policy of pay restraint in 1970 led to steep wage increases which in turn brought rising prices.

(b) **The economy was damaged by large numbers of strikes** particularly among dockers and in the motor-car industry. Often they were unofficial and seemed irresponsible. Wilson tried to introduce a bill to reform trade unions and curb unofficial strikes, but there was such strong opposition within the Labour party and from the TUC, that the bill was dropped. Wilson's attempt to reform the unions had failed.

(c) The situation in Rhodesia (see Section 30.6(c–d)) was handled sensibly and skilfully by Wilson. Economic sanctions were placed on the Smith regime, though they were ineffective. Wilson twice met Smith, aboard HMS *Tiger* (1966) and HMS *Fearless* (1968), but no solution was reached.

(d) There was serious violence in Northern Ireland which had been comparatively calm since Lloyd George's 1922 settlement (see Section 25.2). However, the IRA (Irish Republican Army) would never rest until the north was united with Eire; this the Protestant-dominated Northern Ireland parliament would never agree to. Since the mid-1950s, there had been sporadic terrorist outrages and the situation suddenly deteriorated in 1969. The Northern Ireland Catholics (about one-third of the population) claimed that they were being deprived of full civil rights: they were being discriminated against in jobs, housing and voting. In 1968 the Catholics began to campaign for full equality, but in October, Protestant extremists and the police (Royal Ulster Constabulary) took to breaking up civil rights marches, provoking retaliation by Catholics. By mid-1969 violence had reached alarming proportions and the province seemed on the verge of civil war. In August Wilson *sent troops into Belfast and Londonderry* to restrain the two factions and particularly to protect Catholic areas from attacks by Protestants.

(e) There were some achievements among the many crises, though many of Labour's plans had to be abandoned in view of the economic situation. For example, prescription charges were abolished from February 1965 but were re-introduced early in 1968 as part of the emergency measures. Constructive achievements included the introduction of rent rebates, votes at 18, the abolition of the death penalty and the creation of the Ombudsman, to investigate complaints against inefficient administrators. The Race Relations Act (1968) made it illegal to discriminate in employment, housing, insurance, education and other areas. Many would see Labour's most lasting achievement to be in the field of education. There was a determined move towards comprehensive secondary education and the Open University was created, using radio and television to enable people to receive a university education at home. In general living standards continued to improve with a larger proportion of households than ever before having refrigerators, washing-machines and televisions.

All this was not enough to dispel the impression that Labour, apart from its last year in office, had made many of the same mistakes as the Conservatives and had not 'got the economy right'. Several key industries – coal-mining, shipbuilding, textiles and railways – continued to contract; together with increased automation in other industries, this caused unemployment to rise from around 400 000 in 1964 to just over 600 000 in

1970. Though the opinion polls predicted a narrow Labour victory, the result went the other way.

31.2 THE HEATH GOVERNMENT 1970-74

Heath believed it was possible to escape from the 'stop-go' trap by reducing controls to a minimum and taking Britain into the EEC, which would stimulate British industry. Unfortunately, almost immediately the government suffered a tragic blow with the death of Iain Macleod, the Chancellor of the Exchequer, a politician of enormous ability. The new Chancellor, Anthony Barber, lacked Macleod's experience and authority. After this, very little went right for the government.

(a) **Barber introduced decisive measures**, cutting taxes and reducing restrictions on hire purchase and credit; Britain's entry into the EEC was secured in 1972, Heath's greatest achievement (see Section 30.7(g)). However, the hoped-for investment in industry failed to materialise and inflation became serious again, causing Heath to introduce a sharp about-turn: a policy of holding wages down, and re-imposing controls; but there was no rapid improvement: 1973 showed a balance of payments deficit of over £900 million, unemployment hovering at over 850 000 and inflation still rising.

(b) **The Family Income Supplement** and rate and fuel rebates helped poor families but were criticised by many Conservatives as being too much like socialism.

(c) **The Industrial Relations Act (1971)** reformed trade union law in an attempt to cut down strikes and curb extremists. It set up a National Industrial Relations Court and introduced a 'cooling-off period' and ballots for strikes. Although in many quarters this was seen as a moderate and sensible measure, the unions opposed it bitterly, with a wave of strikes, the most serious of which was the miners' strike (1974) which led to a three-day working week to conserve fuel.

(d) **Disturbances continued in Ireland** where the British army soon found itself in the impossible situation of trying to prevent Catholics and Protestants slaughtering each other while at the same time having to endure attacks from the IRA and another group calling itself the Provisional IRA. The government decided to suspend the Northern Ireland parliament and bring the province under direct rule from Westminster. When early in 1974 a new coalition government was set up in which the Catholics had more say than ever before, Protestant extremists organised massive strikes which quickly paralysed the country; after only a few weeks parliament was again suspended. Since then no government has been able to make any progress, and a solution seems as far away as ever.

(e) The reform of local government (came into operation in 1974) which reduced the number of counties, in many cases changing names and boundaries, was not popular.

(f) The oil crisis was a serious blow to the government. The problem began in the autumn of 1973, following the Arab-Israeli War. The Arab oil-producing states decided to show their displeasure towards certain countries which, they felt, had been too friendly towards Israel. Britain found that her oil imports were cut by 15 per cent while the Arabs imposed a series of price increases which more than trebled the cost of Britain's oil imports. Not only did this cause a petrol shortage, it also ruined any faint chance that there would be a favourable balance of payments for 1973. Worse was to follow:

(g) The miners introduced an overtime ban (November 1973) in protest against Heath's attempts at wage restraint. A similar ban by electricity workers and railway drivers soon followed, adding to the general fuel shortage. Heath was determined not to allow his wages strategy to be breached and would make no increased offer to the miners. Instead, a series of drastic emergency measures was introduced to save power: from the beginning of 1974 industry was allowed to work only a three-day week, there was to be a 50 mph speed limit and the most unpopular move of all in the eyes of many - television was to close down at 10.30 p.m. The miners responded with an overwhelming vote in favour of an all-out strike which began on 9 February 1974. Heath decided on a general election, hoping to win public support for his stand against the miners' wage demands.

(h) The election of February 1974 was a bitter and dramatic affair. Heath campaigned on the need for strong government and a firm wages policy, while Labour seemed to have very little new to offer. The voters may have been swayed by the publication of two sets of statistics a few days before the election: the first showed that food prices had risen by 20 per cent during 1973; the second showed that during February the trade deficit had reached an all-time high. In addition, Enoch Powell, a leading if somewhat eccentric Conservative, announced that Heath had been wrong to fight an election on the issue of miners' pay and urged everybody to vote Labour. The result was more a vote of no confidence in the Conservatives than a positive vote for Labour. The Conservatives lost over a million votes, but Labour also polled 500 000 fewer votes than in 1970. The Liberals, who had won several sensational by-election victories over the Conservatives, saw their total shoot up to over six million, as they took votes from both major parties. However, the electoral system meant that they still won only 14 seats - the vast majority of Liberal votes were wasted in constituencies where Liberal candidates came second. The final figures were: Labour 301, Conservatives 297, Liberals 14, Nationalists and others 23.

31.3 LABOUR IN POWER AGAIN 1974-79

(a) **Wilson faced an unenviable task** in trying to 'get the economy right' as he put it. He began briskly: he settled the miners' strike by allowing their full wage claim and ended the three-day week. This was followed by a rash of other wage increases which helped to push up prices and fuel inflation. By the end of 1974 there was no sign that the government would be able to remedy the basic weakness of the economy.

(b) **What was wrong with the economy?** The simple fact was that British industry was not producing enough goods for export at the right prices; foreign competitors could produce more cheaply and secured a larger share of the market. The reasons for the inefficiency are a matter of controversy; management blamed unions for excessive wage demands and opposition to new techniques and processes; certainly the power of the unions had increased over the previous decade, and both Wilson and Heath had failed to control them. The *Financial Times* even went so far as to call them 'the robber barons of the system'. On the other hand unions blamed unimaginative management. Some economists also criticised management on the grounds that they were so greedy for profit that too little was ploughed back for development. It was also suggested that governments should have spent more on grants to develop industry and less on social services. Also there is no doubt that the government's 'stop-go' policies, which neither party had been able to escape from, slowed down industrial expansion.

(c) **Wilson's resignation** (April 1975) came as a complete surprise, though he had apparently told the Queen of his decision the previous December. He gave as his reasons that he had had enough of the strains of top-level politics and, though he was only 60, he did not want to lead the party into another general election, having already gone through four. He therefore felt it only right that his successor should be given a chance to establish himself before the next election. Wilson's unkindest critics claimed that his real motive was that he wanted to escape the humiliation of failure, since he knew that he was incapable of solving the economic problems of the country.

(d) **Callaghan's government**, after early setbacks, began to make an impact on the problems. This government's main weapon, already used under Wilson, was known as *The Social Contract*. This developed from an understanding between the Labour party and the TUC. The latter promised to try and persuade its members to agree to voluntary wage restraint in return for food subsidies, rent restrictions and the repeal of Heath's Industrial Relations Act. The idea was that annual wage increases should be negotiated in relation to price rises, so that inflation would be controlled. By the spring of 1975 it was clear that the policy was not working, since wage settlements were on average higher than price rises. *Denis Healey*, the Chancellor of the Exchequer, introduced a tough budget, reducing defence spending and raising income tax to 35p in the pound. VAT, which he had introduced the previous year at 8 per cent, was raised to 25 per cent on certain luxury items. In July the government tried more stringent controls by fixing a maximum wage increase at six pounds a week. Gradually these policies began to have an effect and by 1978, when Britain was beginning to enjoy the advantages of her own North Sea oil, the annual inflation rate, which had touched 24 per cent in 1975, had fallen below 10 per cent, and there was a modest balance of payments surplus. Other important developments were:

(i) A referendum was held (April 1975) to find out whether the British people wished to remain in *the Common Market*. The result was decisive: 67.2 per cent of those who voted favoured continued membership.

(ii) *The Devolution Act* (December 1978) provided for the establishment of regional assemblies in Scotland and Wales, on condition that 40 per cent of the electorate showed themselves to be in favour. However, in a referendum held the following March, only 12 per cent of the Welsh electorate approved, while in Scotland the figure was 33 per cent. Consequently devolution was quietly forgotten.

(iii) *The Lib-Lab Pact*. By January 1977 Labour's overall majority was down to one. To make sure that his government survived, Callaghan made a pact with *David Steel*, the Liberal leader. The Liberals would vote with Labour in Parliament and in return they would be allowed to see Labour's proposed bills before they were introduced into the Commons. They would then signify whether or not they were prepared to support Labour's proposals, so that in effect they could veto future legislation. Steel was angling for a possible deal on a reform of the electoral system – the introduction of some form of proportional representation which would give the Liberals a fairer representation in the Commons. Nothing came of Steel's hopes, but from Labour's point of view the pact was a success, helping to keep Callaghan's government in office for a further two years.

(e) The election of May 1979. Most informed observers expected that Callaghan would have an election in the autumn of 1978, to take full advantage of the improving economic situation. However, he decided to wait until the spring of 1979, and this turned out to be a fatal delay. The unions refused to accept his proposal to extend the Social Contract for a further period by limiting wage increases to 5 per cent. When the government tried to enforce the limit, a number of embarrassing strikes followed in what became known as the 'winter of discontent'. When Callaghan eventually decided on a May election, the damage had been done. There were over a million unemployed, the trade unions seemed to be a liability to Labour, and the party had run out of ideas and reforming zeal. By contrast the Conservatives were full of new purpose; the unfortunate Heath had been dropped after suffering two general election defeats in a year, and their new leader, Margaret Thatcher, was aggressive and self-confident. Already dubbed 'the Iron Lady' by the press, she made the most of the chaos of the previous winter, calling the strikes 'a reversion to barbarism'. Not only would she stand no nonsense from the unions, but also, in *monetarism*, she offered a new policy to cure the country's economics ills. The combination was irresistible and the voters gave her a mandate.

31.4 THE THATCHER GOVERNMENTS SINCE 1979

(a) **Margaret Thatcher** was the daughter of a Grantham grocer who was a local councillor and alderman. After reading Chemistry at Oxford, she married Denis Thatcher, a rich industrialist. She first stood for Parliament, unsuccessfully, in 1950 at the age of only 23, and was eventually elected as MP for Finchley in 1959. Before her election as leader, her experience of high office had been unusually limited - her only major post was as Minister of Education under Heath. She was firmly on the right wing of the party, having none of the paternalism of Macmillan or of William Whitelaw, her chief rival for the leadership. She believed in individualism and self-help and soon established her image as exactly the sort of decisive, forceful, strong-willed and self-assured leader which Britain needed. 'The mission of this government,' she announced soon after her victory, 'is much more than economic progress. It is to renew the spirit and the solidarity of the nation. At the heart of a new mood in the nation must be a recovery of our self-confidence and our self-respect.'

(b) **Monetarism**. Thatcher and her Chancellor, *Sir Geoffrey Howe*, were greatly influenced by the theories of the American economist *Milton Friedman*, who argued that socialism stifled initiative and freedom, and that a monetarist approach - a careful control of the money supply - was the best way of stimulating an economic revival. Previous governments in their 'stop' phases had controlled money supply temporarily by raising the bank rate. The Thatcher government aimed to pursue it wholeheartedly and without relaxation. The theory was that a tight hold must be kept on the money supply via the Bank of England by maintaining high rates of interest, so that firms and individuals were forced to reduce borrowing. Management must therefore keep costs down by laying off workers and streamlining operations for greater efficiency. There would be no government grants to prop up inefficient firms, so that only those which made themselves competitive would survive. Such a policy meant a high unemployment level, but its supporters claimed that it was like a major surgical operation - drastic, but effective in the long term: British industry, though much contracted, would be efficient and competitive overseas. With purchasing power reduced as unemployment rose, inflation would be controlled and wage demands moderated accordingly. An advantage of monetarism was that the control it exercised was more impersonal than Heath's wage restraint, and therefore there was less chance of a direct confrontation between government and unions. Another advantage, particularly attractive to the Conservatives, was that trade unions would be less powerful: workers, thankful to be in a job at a time of high unemployment, would be less willing to strike.

Thatcher and Howe stuck resolutely to this policy with a cripplingly high minimum lending rate of 17 per cent early in 1980, though this was reduced to 14 per cent, by the end of the year. There were also massive spending cuts affecting housing, education and transport. They confidently predicted that the annual rate of inflation, which had soared to 20 per cent again early in 1980, would be down to 10 per cent by the end of 1981. Their predictions were not far wrong, and inflation continued to fall. However, the disturbing feature was that monetarism, together with a deepening world recession, caused unemployment to soar past the three million mark by the autumn of 1981, the highest level since the great depression of the early 1930s. Many small companies went bankrupt, and in the summer of 1981 there were riots in London, Liverpool and Manchester. When some Tory left-wingers, or 'Wets' as they were known, ventured to criticise her policies, Thatcher unceremoniously removed them from the cabinet, and brought in two self-made men – *Cecil Parkinson* (as Party Chairman), a successful industrialist and son of a railwayman, and *Norman Tebbit* (Minister for Employment), a former pilot and son of a shop manager (July 1981).

By this time the government was becoming unpopular. Thatcher seemed obsessed with self-help and apparently showed little sympathy for the plight of the three million unemployed. The government lost a number of by-elections, the most spectacular defeat being at Crosby where a Conservative majority of over 19 000 was converted into a 5000 majority for Shirley Williams, the candidate of the newly formed Social Democrat Party.

(c) The Formation of the Social Democrat Party (SDP). If the Conservatives had their internal squabbles, the Labour Party was in a much worse state. The right wing of the party was becoming more and more impatient with the left because of its support for militant trade unionism, unilateral disarmament, withdrawal from the Common Market and further nationalisation. The election of veteran left-winger, *Michael Foot* as party leader (1980) convinced some of the right that they had no future in the Labour Party. Four of them, *Roy Jenkins, Dr David Owen, Shirley Williams and William Rodgers* – soon to be known as the Gang of Four – left the Labour Party and in a blaze of publicity launched the brand new SDP (March 1981). Jenkins narrowly failed to win a by-election at Warrington, but after the SDP formed an alliance with the Liberals, successes followed. A Liberal, William Pitt, won Croydon, Shirley Williams won Crosby and in March 1982, Jenkins captured Glasgow Hillhead. All three seats were taken from the Conservatives. Suddenly, soon after the Hillhead by-election, the political scene was transformed by the Falklands Crisis.

(d) The Falklands War (April–June 1982)

(i) The Argentinian claim to the British-owned Falkland Islands in the South Atlantic had been discussed on and off by the two governments for the previous 20 years. The Argentinians may well have got the impression that the British would not be averse to an eventual transfer of power; but the stumbling block was that the 1800 Falklanders were adamant that they wished to remain under British sovereignty.

(ii) Argentinian forces invaded the islands (2 April) as well as their dependency, South Georgia. The United Nations Security Council condemned their action and urged the Argentinians to withdraw, to no avail. Thatcher acted decisively and astonished the world by the speed of her response. A British task force was swiftly assembled and sent off to recapture the Falklands. It consisted of some 70 ships including the aircraft carriers *Invincible* and *Hermes* and about 6000 troops.

(iii) During the three weeks that it took the task force to sail the 8000 miles via Ascension Island to the South Atlantic, frantic attempts were made, notably by *Alexander Haig*, the American Secretary of State, to reach a negotiated solution. However, the British, refuting South American charges of colonialism, pointed out that the islanders wished to remain associated with Britain; they refused to negotiate unless Argentinian troops were withdrawn. The Argentinians, safe in possession of the islands, naturally refused to budge, and Haig's efforts came to nothing. Meanwhile *Lord Carrington*, the Foreign Secretary, had resigned, accepting responsibility for 'the humiliating affront to this country'. He was replaced by *Francis Pym.*

(iv) The task force arrived in Falklands waters during the final week of April and soon enjoyed complete success. South Georgia was recaptured (25 April) and the *General Belgrano*, an elderly Argentinian cruiser carrying troops and deadly Exocet missiles, was sunk by a British nuclear submarine (2 May). HMS *Sheffield* was badly damaged by an Exocet missile (4 May), but this did not prevent successful British landings at Port San Carlos (21 May) and later at Bluff Cove and Fitzroy near Port Stanley (early June); two British frigates were sunk during the landings. British troops won engagements at Darwin and Goose Green and finally captured Port Stanley. On 14 June the Argentinian troops surrendered and the recapture of the Falklands was complete. The British had lost 254 men killed, the Argentinians 750. The expedition cost Britain around £700 million.

(v) The effects of the crisis on the home front were little short of sensational. There was an outburst of patriotism such as had not been seen since the Second World War, and approval of the government's decisive action caused their sagging popularity to revive with a vengeance. This was reflected in the local election results in May 1982 and in two by-elections which the SDP could have expected to win, judging from their earlier performances, and which the Conservatives won comfortably. In the euphoria of the Falklands victory, the government was able to ignore long-term questions about the future of the islands, whether for example, Britain could afford to defend the Falklands indefinitely, and whether it was logical or sensible to hang on to the islands merely to meet the wishes of 1800 people.

[For Thatcher's successful negotiations over the Common Market budget see Section 30.7(h) and for Carrington's settlement of the Rhodesia problem see Section 30.6(d).]

(e) The election of June 1983. With over three million out of work, Labour ought to have had a fighting chance of victory, but several factors worked in the Conservatives' favour. They had succeeded in bringing the annual inflation rate down to around 4 per cent which they had claimed all along to be one of their main aims. Critics of the unions were pleased with the *Employment Act* (October 1982) which restricted the operation of closed shops and made trade unions more accountable for their actions; compensation was to be paid to workers who had been dismissed from their jobs for non-membership of a union. Above all, there was the continuing effect of the 'Falklands factor'. Labour's election programme with its two main planks - unilateral disarmament and withdrawal from the Common Market - failed to arouse sufficient enthusiasm. Labour's chances of victory were further diminished during the campaign when both Healey and Callaghan appeared to disagree with the party line on unilateral disarmament. Labour could hardly expect to win the confidence of the electorate if it was divided on such an important issue. The Liberal/SDP Alliance conducted an impressive campaign projecting itself as the only viable alternative government to the Conservatives; though it failed to make a breakthrough in terms of seats, it took crucial votes away from Labour. The results showed an overwhelming Conservative victory with 397 seats, against 209 for Labour, 23 for the Alliance and 21 others. It was a disaster for the Labour Party which polled its lowest vote since 1935.

The Conservatives and most of the press enthused about their landslide victory. But in fact the voting figures revealed something rather different. The Conservative vote fell from the 1979 figure (from 13.68 million to 13.01 million), suggesting not that there was a great surge of enthusiasm for Mrs Thatcher, but rather that the electors decidedly did not want a Labour government (Labour's vote fell from 11.5 million to 8.5 million). Many Labour voters and some disillusioned Tory supporters switched to the Liberal/SDP Alliance, whose 7.8 million poll was one of the most striking features of the election. This revealed more clearly than ever before the unfairness of the British electoral system. Labour's 27.6 per cent of total votes cast entitled them to 209 seats; but the Alliance, not so very far behind with 25.4 per cent, secured only 23 seats. It was the old story of the single-vote, single-member constituency system working to the disadvantage of a party which came second in a large number of constituencies. The demand for proportional representation revived but there was little prospect of its introduction, since the Conservative government, not unnaturally, was happy with the existing system.

(f) The second Thatcher government (1983–7). Fortified by its huge Commons majority, the government pushed confidently ahead with its programme against a background of continuing monetarism. Its record contained some major achievements, though all were highly controversial:

(i) *Privatisation* was strongly advocated on the grounds that it would increase efficiency, encourage more concern for the customer, and enable the general public and employees to become shareholders. Also attractive to the government were the proceeds – £2500 million in 1985–6 and about £4700 million in each of the next three years. By January 1987 no fewer than 14 major companies (including British Aerospace, British Petroleum, British Telecom, Britoil, the Trustee Savings Bank and British Gas) had been sold off to private ownership. This was bitterly attacked by the Labour Party with its belief in nationalisation, and even some Conservatives were uneasy; Lord Stockton (formerly Harold Macmillan) called it 'selling off the family silver'.

(ii) Strict maintenance of *law and order and public security*. The government took a tough line with the trade unions, banning union membership at Government Communications Headquarters (GCHQ) and refusing to compromise in a year-long mineworkers' strike (February 1984–March 1985). This was a bitter struggle which ended in total failure for the miners and seemed to exacerbate the divisions in society. The army and police were used several times to remove peace campaigners from Greenham Common and Molesworth RAF bases; they were protesting against American cruise missiles being deployed there. The BBC was continually attacked for allegedly being biased against the government; the BBC offices in Glasgow were raided and films said to threaten Britain's security were seized (February 1987). Among them was a programme about Zircon, a new spy satellite for eavesdropping on the Russians.

(iii) *Government and local authority spending* was closely controlled. Top-spending local authorities had a maximum rate placed on them (rate-capping) to force them to economise (February 1986) and the Greater London Council (GLC) and the six other Metropolitan County Councils were abolished on the grounds that they were a costly and unnecessary layer of local government.

(iv) *The Anglo-Irish Agreement* (November 1985) was a new attempt to secure peace and stability in Northern Ireland: any change in the status of the province would come about only with the consent of a majority of the people of Northern Ireland; Britain and Eire would confer regularly about the situation in Northern Ireland and about relations between the two parts of the island. This was seen by many as a statesmanlike initiative by Mrs Thatcher and Dr Garret Fitzgerald, the Irish Prime Minister, coming as it did in the wake of IRA outrages such as the bomb explosion which killed five people at the Brighton hotel where Thatcher and most of her cabinet were staying during the

Conservative Party conference (October 1984). However, amid massive demonstrations, it was immediately denounced by the two main Unionist parties as a sell-out, while Charles Haughey (then Irish opposition leader) called it 'a very severe blow to the concept of Irish unity'.

(v) A tough stance against *international terrorism*. Britain broke off diplomatic relations with Libya after a policewoman was killed by shots fired from the Libyan People's Bureau in London (April 1984). In April 1986 Thatcher supported the USA's punitive action against Libya, allowing American F1-11 bombers to fly from bases in Britain to take part in air strikes on Tripoli and Benghazi which killed over a hundred people. The US claimed that they were aiming for 'terrorist-related targets', but the raids aroused world-wide condemnation for causing the deaths of so many innocent civilians. Britain also broke off relations with Syria (October 1986) whose government was allegedly involved in an attempt to blow up a jumbo jet at Heathrow Airport.

(vi) *An agreement was signed with China* (1984) by which Britain promised to hand over Hong Kong in 1997 and the Chinese in return offered safeguards, including maintaining the existing economic and social structure for at least 50 years.

Meanwhile the government came under increasing fire from its critics. Unemployment stubbornly refused to come down below 3 million and it seemed that Britain was rapidly becoming 'two nations'. The government's own statistics revealed (1987) that 94 per cent of job losses since the Conservatives took office were in the North while the South was largely thriving and prosperous. Since 1979 there had been a 28 per cent drop in manufacturing and construction jobs, which compared badly with an 8 per cent drop in Germany, a 2 per cent drop in the USA and a 5 per cent increase in Japan. Inner cities were neglected and there was a rundown in public services, especially the health service, where in 1986-7 a chronic shortage of beds caused many patients to be turned away and lengthened waiting-lists for operations. When challenged before the 1983 election, the government had assured the public that the Health Service was safe, but now there seemed a real danger of creating a *two-tier Health Service*: for those who could afford it, a private sector which was flourishing and efficient, for those who couldn't, a public sector which was short of cash, understaffed and generally second-rate.

In addition the government suffered a number of embarrassments and scandals. A public conflict of attitude between two cabinet ministers (Heseltine and Brittan) over the future of the ailing Westland Helicopter Co., led to the resignation of both and called into question Thatcher's integrity and political judgement (January 1986). Early in 1987 there was a scandal on the Stock Exchange when it emerged that some directors of the Guinness Co. had illegally bolstered the price of their own shares during their battle to take over the Distillers' Co.

A measure of their unpopularity was the fact that the Conservatives lost four by-elections (three to the Alliance and one to Labour) between June 1984 and May 1986, reducing their overall majority from 144 to 136. However, as another election approached, the Chancellor, Nigel Lawson, suddenly announced extra spending of £7.5 billion for 1987 on education, health and social services. This seemed to be a U-turn away from monetarism, though the government did not admit it. With the inflation rate well under control at only 3 per cent and the promise of good times ahead, opinion polls showed a revival in the Conservatives' popularity.

(g) **The election of June 1987.** Although the Labour Party fought a lively campaign under its new leader, Neil Kinnock, the Conservatives won a third successive victory. They took 380 seats, Labour 229 and the Alliance 22, a Conservative overall majority of 102. The relatively prosperous South and Midlands were apparently well satisfied with Tory rule and were confident that the economic recovery would continue; Labour's defence and economic policies seemed to put many voters off. It was clearly a remarkable achievement by Mrs Thatcher to lead her party to three successive election victories and in January 1988 she broke Asquith's record as the longest serving British Prime Minister this century. There were two other striking points about the 1987 election: the Conservatives did badly in Scotland, winning only 10 out of the 72 seats, and further entrenching the North–South divide; and over the country as a whole, almost three people in five voted against the Conservatives. Under the existing electoral system, with Labour and Alliance candidates splitting the anti-Tory vote it was difficult to foresee how the Conservatives could ever lose an election.

(h) **After the 1987 election.** As the economic recovery continued, the government pressed on with privatisation, selling off its remaining holdings in BP (October 1987) and announcing plans for the privatisation of the electricity supply in England and Wales. Valued at £27,000 million, this was easily the largest slice of privatisation so far. Fifteen months into Mrs Thatcher's third government, the debate was raging about whether the Thatcherite economic miracle had really happened. Supporters of the government insisted that Conservative policies had been successful, pointing out that the economy was booming, productivity had increased, exports were up by one third and unemployment had fallen to 2.3 million. In his budget of March 1988, the Chancellor, Nigel Lawson, had kept his pre-election promise by reducing the basic rate of income tax from 27 per cent to 25 per cent. On the other hand, Wynne Godley, one of the 364 economists who in 1981 had signed a statement criticising the government's economic policies (see Question 1, Source C), still remained unconvinced in 1988. Writing in the Observer (18 September) he pointed out that although exports might well have risen by a third, imports had gone up by half, creating an unfavourable balance of trade: 'Almost every major indicator - output, unemployment, industrial investment and the balance of payments - has performed poorly over the nine Thatcher years taken as a whole. The improvement in productivity, unless accompanied by an improvement in production, merely redistributes income from those who become unemployed to those who remain in work. And now inflation is sneaking back towards the 9 per cent she inherited'.

Meanwhile important developments had been taking place in the Liberal/SDP Alliance camp. Bitterly disappointed by their poor election performance, at least in terms of seats won, the two parties began talks to try and bring about a full-scale merger. The negotiations went well and in January 1988 the new party - the Social and Liberal Democrats (SLD) - was born. After 12 gruelling years as Liberal leader, David Steel decided to stand down, and Paddy Ashdown was elected leader of the new party. It remained to be seen whether the Social and Liberal Democrats would be able to make any real contribution towards ending the period of Tory domination.

QUESTIONS

1. Mrs Thatcher and Monetarism
Study Sources A to E and then answer the questions which follow.

Source A: two journalists write about monetarism and how it works in practice.

There was an economic theory growing in fashionability during the seventies . . . in Chicago, led by Milton Friedman - *monetarism* . . . Put simply, Friedman argued that 'inflation occurs when the quantity of money rises more rapidly than output, and the more rapid the rise in the quantity of money per unit of output, the greater the rate of inflation . . . keeping the money supply under control would reduce inflation on its own . . . The main means of reducing the supply of money in the economy was to reduce the Public Sector Borrowing Requirement - the difference between the government's expenditure and revenue - by cutting public expenditure and restricting the amount that the banks could borrow. Thus there was a sound reason to reduce the state's contribution to a whole range of goods and services in which the government should, in any case, have no part. Here was a magic cure which combined two elusive goals: inflation could be beaten by withdrawing the state from people's lives, thus overcoming the creeping state socialism which had progressed steadily since the war . . .

Mrs Thatcher was determined to try out monetarism - an experiment which no major nation had attempted . . . To reduce the supply of money, interest rates were held high, thus causing a curtailment in investment, the laying off of men from employment and the bankruptcy of firms . . . Britain was plunged into recession. The speed of job loss and bankruptcies were unprecedented, and many in the Cabinet warned of civil disorder if the stern measures were continued.

Source: N. Wapshott and G. Brock, *Thatcher*, Macdonald, 1983 (adapted extracts).

Source B: information and comment from a political expert – Anthony Sampson.

As Mrs Thatcher stuck to her economic policies, the moderates in her cabinet – the *'Wets'* – became more exasperated by her obstinacy. Ian Gilmour, Jim Prior and Francis Pym . . . were worried about joblessness and the disintegrating inner cities . . . In July 1981 a sudden social crisis focused all their arguments. A succession of riots broke out in inner cities – first in Brixton, then in Liverpool, then in Manchester – with looting, violence and hatred of the police. Many Wets in the Cabinet saw the riots as revealing the ultimate danger of impersonal monetarism, a warning that the government could not turn its back on the needs of communities . . .

But in July the Prime Minister had decided she could dispense with the Wets, and that she needed a more resolute Cabinet. In September she purged her Cabinet ruthlessly and brought in new men – Cecil Parkinson, a self-made industrialist and Norman Tebbit, the hardest of the hard men: a 'semi-house-trained polecat', Michael Foot called him. But he was invaluable as the man who could beat the unions . . . After three years in power she was proud of having changed the mood of the country, diminished the power of the unions, cut back the nationalised monopolies, and compelled big business to become more efficient . . . However, her promotion of self-help and enterprise meant little to the three million unemployed or the inhabitants of desolate inner cities. Her encouragement for small businesses looked increasingly hollow as high interest rates bankrupted enterprising small companies while lazy giant corporations survived.

Source: A. Sampson, *The Changing Anatomy of Britain*, Hodder & Stoughton, 1982 (adapted extracts).

Source C: a statement signed by 364 university economists, which caused something of a sensation when it appeared in December 1981.

(a) there is no basis in economic theory and no supporting evidence for the Government's belief that by deflating demand they will bring inflation permanently under control and thereby induce an automatic recovery in output and employment.

   (b) present policies will deepen the depression, erode the industrial base of our economy and threaten its social and political stability.

   (c) the time has come to reject monetarist policies and consider urgently which alternative offers the best hope of sustained economic recovery.

P. Riddell, *The Thatcher Government*, Martin Robertson, 1983 (adapted extracts).

Source D: comments by Peter Riddell, an economist and Political Editor of the *Financial Times*.

The twelve-month rate of growth of retail prices was 10.3 per cent in May 1979. The rate rose to a peak of 21.9 per cent in May 1980 before falling back to single figures in April 1982 and declining to 3.7 per cent in May 1983, the lowest level for fifteen years . . .

By early 1983 there was the first deficit in trade in manufactured goods since the Industrial Revolution two centuries ago. Britain's share of world trade continued to decline in the 1980s and there was a further sharp increase in the share of the domestic market taken by imports . . .

The UK total of unemployed rose from 1.22 million in May 1979 to 3.05 million, equivalent to 12.8 per cent of the labour force . . .

The pronounced drop in employment during the recession contributed to a large improvement in productivity, as measured by output per person employed. For the whole economy, productivity rose by 3 per cent between 1979 and the end of 1982, at a time when total output fell by over 3 per cent . . .

At the end of four years in office the Thatcher administration still had almost everything to prove about its economic policies.

Source: as for Source C (adapted extracts).

Source E: article by Michael Jones in the *Sunday Times*, 28 August 1988.

Nigel Lawson was on holiday last week when he was told that the July trade figures would be the worst ever. Recent information from the Treasury has all told the same story about booming Britain: on course, slightly overheating, but nothing to worry about. But nobody was prepared for the figure that Lawson and Thatcher were now looking at: a record £2.15 billion – double the figure the City expected. Thatcher quickly approved a rise in interest rates to 12%. Consumer demand that was dragging in imports and pushing up prices had to be choked at all costs. Fear about recession has given way to fear about inflation . . . It all represents a dramatic turnaround from Lawson's ebullient optimism at the time he presented his tax-cutting budget five months ago. The danger of running up a higher trade deficit was no problem. John Smith, Labour's

636

shadow chancellor, protested at the time this was not so and as it turns out, he was right. He also today condemned the government's 'easy credit society' and pointed to the lowest rates of personal savings for the past four years ... Inside the Treasury the official line is that there is no need to panic, and that the economy is basically sound, though house prices have soared over the past two years to an all-time high, particularly in southeast England. Company profits are at 20-year high and unemployment is falling steadily ... Lawson must think that if only consumers would consume a little less, everything would come right once more.

Source: *Sunday Times*, 28 August 1988.

(a) **(i)** According to Source **A**, who was the leader of the monetarist economists and where was he based? **4(a)**

    (ii) From the information given in Source **A**, explain briefly in your own words the main points of the monetarist theory. **4(a)**

    (iii) According to Source **A**, what is the Public Sector Borrowing Requirement? **4(a)**

    (iv) What two reasons attracted Mrs Thatcher to monetarism? **4(a)**

    (v) From the evidence of Source **A**, in what ways did monetarism help to cause the recession of 1981? **4(a)**

(b) **(i)** According to Source **B**, who were the main Tory 'Wets' in the Cabinet? **4(a)**

    (ii) From the evidence of Source **B**, what did the term 'Wet' mean? **4(a)**

    (iii) In what ways did the riots of 1981 affect the Wets' opinions of monetarism? **4(a)**

    (iv) What evidence is there in Source **B** about the way in which Mrs Thatcher ran her government? **4(a)**

    (v) Do you get the impression that the writer of Source **B** is an admirer of Mrs Thatcher or not? Explain your answer. **4(b)**

(c) **(i)** Explain in your own words the criticisms of monetarism made in Source **C**. **4(a)**

    (ii) Why do you think the publication of this document produced something of a sensation? **4(b)**

(d) **(i)** According to Source **D**, by how much had unemployment risen between May 1979 and May 1983? **4(a)**

    (ii) By how much did total output fall between 1979 and 1983? **4(a)**

    (iii) From the evidence of Source **D**, explain how it was possible for total output to fall at a time when production per person was increasing. **4(a)**

    (iv) Do you think the evidence in Sources **B** and **D** supports or conflicts with the criticisms of monetarism made in Source **C**? **4(a, c)**

(e)   From the evidence of Source **E**, by 1988 what changes had taken place since 1983 in:

        (i) the recession; (ii) unemployment; (iii) the balance of trade; (iv) inflation.   **4(a, c)**

(f)   What evidence is there in Source **E** that Mrs Thatcher must have relaxed her monetarist policies in 1988?   **4(a)**

(g)   From the evidence of all the Sources, to what extent do you think Mrs Thatcher's 'economic miracle' had really happened:

        (i) by 1983 and (ii) by 1988?   **4(a, c)**

2. Devaluation and Financial Policy

Read the extract and then answer the questions which follow.

Harold Wilson, Labour Prime Minister 1964–70, writes about the financial crisis of 1967.

There was every reason to feel that the carrying out of devaluation had gone successfully. But the political consequences were still to follow. My first task was to broadcast on both television channels on Sunday night, 19th November. I said that devaluation was a set-back, but that this should not be allowed to detract from what we had achieved in ridding Britain of the £800 millions deficit which we [Labour] had inherited. Our task was now to re-deploy our resources away from home consumption to export. If we seized our opportunities, we could combine a faster rate of industrial expansion and full employment with a healthy balance of payments . . . I went on to say: 'It does not mean that the pound in our pockets is worth 14 per cent less to us now than it was this morning . . . However, the goods we buy from abroad will be dearer, including some of our basic foods. It's vital that price rises are limited to those cases where increased import costs make this unavoidable'.

Nothing said by any political leader has been more twisted for political purposes, by a hundred Tory speeches and a thousand press features. Mr. Heath, in a shrill broadcast, interpreted it as a misleading pledge that prices would not rise as a result of devaluation. He omitted to make any reference at all to my statements that prices would rise.

Source: H. Wilson, *The Labour Government 1964–1970*, Weidenfeld & Nicolson, 1971 (adapted extracts).

(a) (i)   From the evidence of the extract, by how much had the Labour government devalued the pound?   **4(a)**

     (ii)   According to Wilson, what was the immediate advantage brought by devaluation?   **4(a)**

    (iii)   How did Wilson feel that devaluation could be used to improve the British economy?   **4(a)**

(iv) What did Wilson mean when he said that Labour had 'inherited' a deficit? **1, 2, 4(a)**

(b) (i) In view of what he says in the rest of his broadcast quoted in this extract, do you think that Wilson is correct when he says devaluation 'does not mean that the pound in our pockets is worth 14 per cent less'? **4(a)**

(ii) Explain in your own words what criticisms Wilson is making of Mr Heath's broadcast. **4(a)**

(iii) In this extract how does Wilson show his disapproval of the Conservatives? **4(a, b)**

(c) (i) From your own knowledge, explain what effects the devaluation had up to 1970 on politics and on the economy? **1, 2**

(ii) How far do you think economic problems were responsible for Labour losing the general election of 1970? **1, 2**

(d) (i) Describe the attempts of Edward Heath and the Conservative Government of 1970–74 to solve Britain's economic problems. Why were they no more successful than Labour? **1, 2**

(ii) Explain briefly what was wrong with the British economy in the 1960s and 1970s. **1, 2**

3. (a) Explain why serious violence broke out in northern Ireland in 1969.

(b) Describe how Harold Wilson and Edward Heath and their respective governments tried to deal with the problems in Ireland from 1969 until 1974.

(c) Describe Margaret Thatcher's attempt to improve the situation by the 1985 Anglo–Irish Agreement.

(d) Why have all attempts to solve the Irish problem failed since 1969? **1, 2**

4. It is January 1988 and Margaret Thatcher has just broken Asquith's record as the longest serving British Prime Minister this century. Write an article for a major newspaper such as the *Daily Telegraph* or *The Times*, with Conservative sympathies, in which you celebrate what you see as Mrs Thatcher's achievements in office. **1, 2, 3**

FURTHER READING

'Purnell' refers to *Purnell's History of the English-Speaking Peoples* (London: BPC Publishing, 1971). The place of publication is London unless otherwise stated.

CHAPTER 2

Beales, D., *From Castlereagh to Gladstone, 1815–1855* (Nelson, 1969)

Brasher, N. H., *Arguments in History – Britain in the Nineteenth Century* (Macmillan, 1968)

Cookson, J. E., *Lord Liverpool's Administration, 1815–22* (Scottish Academic Press, 1975)

Hinde, W., *George Canning* (Collins, 1973)

Hilton, Boyd, *Corn, Cash, Commerce – The Economic Policies of the Tory Governments, 1815–30* (Oxford, 1977)

Longford, E., *Wellington, Pillar of State* (Weidenfeld & Nicolson, 1972)

Revill, P., *The Age of Lord Liverpool* (Blackie, 1979)

Thompson, E. P., *The Making of the English Working Class* (Gollancz, 1963: Penguin edition, 1968)

White, R. J., *From Waterloo to Peterloo* (Mercury, 1963)

CHAPTER 3

Crawley, C. W., *Greek Independence, 1821–33* (Cambridge, 1955)

Derry, J. W., *Castlereagh* (Allen Lane, 1976)

Dixon, P., *Canning: Politician and Statesman* (Weidenfeld & Nicolson, 1976)

Ward, D. R., *Foreign Affairs, 1815–1865* (Collins, 1972)

White, R. J., *Castlereagh* (Purnell, pp. 2780–1)

CHAPTER 4

Brock, M. G., *The Great Reform Act* (Hutchinson, 1973)

Hamburger, J., *James Mill and the Art of Revolution* (Yale University Press, 1963)

Hobsbawm, E. J., and Rudé, G., *Captain Swing* (Lawrence and Wishart, 1969)

Rudé, G., *Captain Swing* (Purnell, pp. 2922–7)

Thompson, E. P., *The Making of the English Working Class* (Gollancz, 1963: Penguin, 1968)

Wright, D. G., *Democracy and Reform 1815–1885* (Longman, 1970)

CHAPTER 5

Brundage, A., *The Making of the New Poor Law, 1832–39* (Hutchinson, 1978)

Cecil, D., *Melbourne* (Constable, 1954)

Dinnage, P., *Melbourne and Victoria* (Purnell, pp. 2938–41)

Finlayson, G. B. A. M., *England in the Eighteen Thirties* (Arnold, 1969)

Longmate, N., *The Workhouse* (Temple Smith, 1974)

Rose, M. E., *The Relief of Poverty, 1834–1914* (Macmillan, 1972)

Watson, R., *Edwin Chadwick, Poor Law and Public Health* (Longman, 1969)

CHAPTER 6

Briggs, A. (ed.) *Chartist Studies* (Macmillan, 1969)

Cole, G. D. H., *Chartist Portraits* (Macmillan, 1965)

Jones, D., *Chartism and the Chartists* (Allen Lane, 1975)

Read, D. and Glasgow, E. L., *Feargus O'Connor* (Arnold, 1961)

Ward, J. T., *Chartism* (Batsford, 1973)

CHAPTER 7

Clark, G. Kitson, *Peel* (Duckworth, 1936)

Gash, N., *Sir Robert Peel* (Longman, 1976)

Gash, N., *Peel's Achievement* (Purnell, pp. 2958–60)

Grinter, R., *Disraeli and Conservatism* (Arnold, 1968)

McCord, N., *The Anti-Corn Law League* (Allen and Unwin, 1958)

Randell, K. H., *Politics and the People 1835–1850* (Collins, 1972)

Read, D., *Cobden and Bright* (Arnold, 1967)

Woodham-Smith, C., *The Great Hunger* (Hamish Hamilton, 1962)

CHAPTER 8

Blake, R., *Disraeli* (Eyre and Spottiswoode, 1966; Methuen University paperback, 1969)

Briggs, A., *Victorian People* (Penguin edition, 1965)

Cowling, M., *1867: Disraeli, Gladstone and Revolution* (Cambridge, 1967)

Magnus, P., *Gladstone* (John Murray, 1963 edition)

Smith, F. B., *The Making of the Second Reform Bill* (Cambridge, 1966)

CHAPTER 9

Ridley, J., *Lord Palmerston* (Constable, 1970)
Southgate, D. G., *The Most English Minister: Policies and Politics of Palmerston* (Macmillan, 1966)
Taylor, A. J. P., *The Struggle for Mastery in Europe* (Oxford, 1954; paperback edition, 1971)
Ward, D. R., *Foreign Affairs, 1815–1865* (Collins, 1972)

CHAPTER 10

Anderson, M. S., *The Eastern Question* (Macmillan, 1966)
Hibbert, C., *The Destruction of Lord Raglan* (Longman, 1961: Penguin, 1963)
Taylor, A. J. P., *The Struggle for Mastery in Europe* (Oxford, paperback edition, 1971) chapters 3, 4 and 5
Thomas, D., *Charge! Hurrah! Hurrah! A Life of Cardigan of Balaclava* (Routledge, 1974; Futura paperback edition, 1976)
Woodham-Smith, C., *The Reason Why* (Constable, 1953)

CHAPTER 11

Edwardes, M., *British India* (Sidgwick and Jackson, 1967)
Farwell, B., *Queen Victoria's Little Wars* (Allen Lane, 1973)
Porter, B., *The Lion's Share: A Short History of British Imperialism 1850–1970* (Longman, 1975)
Spear, P., *A History of India* (Penguin, 1965)
Woodruff, P., *The Men who Ruled India* (Cape, 1953)

CHAPTER 12

Battiscombe, G., *Shaftesbury* (Constable, 1974)
Briggs, A., *Victorian Cities* (Penguin, 1963)
Chesney, K., *The Victorian Underworld* (Temple Smith, 1970)
Finer, S. E., *The Life and Times of Edwin Chadwick* (Methuen, 1952)
Fraser, D., *The Evolution of the British Welfare State* (Macmillan, 1973)
Longmate, N., *King Cholera* (Hamish Hamilton, 1966)
Musgrave, P. W., *Society and Education since 1800* (Methuen, 1968)
The book by Watson mentioned in ch. 5.

CHAPTER 13

Abbott, B. H., *Gladstone and Disraeli* (Collins, 1972)
Feuchtwanger, E. J., *Gladstone* (Allen Lane, 1975)
Lyons, F. S. L., *Ireland since the Famine* (Fontana, 1974)

Magnus, P., *Gladstone* (John Murray, 1963 edition)
O'Hegarty, P. S., *Ireland under the Union* (Methuen, 1962)

CHAPTER 14

Adelman, P., *Gladstone, Disraeli and Later Victorian Politics* (Longman, 1970)
Shannon, R. T., *Gladstone and the Bulgarian Agitation, 1876* (Nelson, 1963)
Smith, P., *Disraelian Conservatism* (Routledge & Kegan Paul, 1967)

The books mentioned earlier by Abbott (ch. 13), Blake (ch. 11), Farwell (ch. 10), Grinter (ch. 7) and Taylor (ch. 9).

CHAPTER 15

Aldcroft, D., *The Development of British Industry and Foreign Competition 1875-1914* (Allen & Unwin, 1968)
Hobsbawm, E., *Industry and Empire* (Pelican, 1969)
Mathias, P., *The First Industrial Nation* (Methuen, 1969)
Saul, S. B., *The Myth of the Great Depression* (Macmillan, 1969)
Thompson, F. M. L., *The Golden Age of Farming?* (Purnell, pp. 3400–05)

CHAPTER 16

Abels, J., *Tragedy of Parnell* (Bodley Head, 1966)
Chamberlain, M. E., *The Scramble for Africa* (Longman, 1974)
James, R. R., *Lord Randolph Churchill* (Weidenfeld & Nicolson, 1969)
James, R. R., *Rosebery* (Weidenfeld & Nicolson, 1963)
Marlowe, J., *Mission to Khartoum: General Gordon* (Gollancz, 1969)
Moorehead, A., *The White Nile* (Hamish Hamilton, 1960)
Morton, G., *Home Rule and the Irish Question* (Longman, 1980)
Taylor, R., *Lord Salisbury* (Allen Lane, 1975)

The books mentioned earlier by Abbott (ch. 13), Farwell (ch. 10), Feuchtwanger, Lyons and Magnus (ch. 13).

CHAPTER 17

Churchill, W. S., *Frontiers and Wars* (Penguin, 1972)
Fraser, P., *Joseph Chamberlain* (Cassell, 1966)
Jay, R., *Joseph Chamberlain: a Political Study* (Oxford, 1981)
Longford, E., *Jameson's Raid* (Weidenfeld & Nicolson, 1982 edition)
Magnus, P., *Kitchener: Portrait of an Imperialist* (John Murray, 1958)
Marlowe, J., *Cecil Rhodes* (Elek, 1972)
Pakenham, T., *The Boer War* (Weidenfeld & Nicolson, 1979)
Taylor, R., *Lord Salisbury* (Allen Lane, 1975)
Young, K., *Balfour* (Bell, 1963)

CHAPTER 18

Bloomfield, P., *Edward Gibbon Wakefield* (Longmans, 1961)
Clark, C. M. H., *A History of Australia* (Macmillan, 1982)
Metge, J., *The Maoris of New Zealand* (Routledge, revised edition, 1976)
Morton, W. L., *The Critical Years: The Union of British North America* (Toronto, 1964)
New, C. W., *Lord Durham* (Dawson, 1969)

CHAPTER 19

Adelman, P., *The Rise of the Labour Party, 1880-1945* (Longman, 1972)
Cole, G. D. H., *The Life of Robert Owen* (Cass, 1965)
Morgan, K. O., *Keir Hardie* (Oxford, 1967)
Musson, A. E., *British Trade Unions, 1800-1875* (Macmillan, 1972)
Pelling, H., *A History of British Trade Unionism* (Penguin, 1968)
Pelling, H., *The Origins of the Labour Party, 1880-1900* (Oxford, 1965)
Thompson, E. P., *The Making of the English Working Class* (Penguin edition, 1968)

CHAPTER 20

Benning, K., *Edwardian Britain – Society in Transition* (Blackie, 1980)
Cross, C., *The Liberals in Power* (Barrie and Rockliff, 1966)
Dangerfield, G., *The Strange Death of Liberal England* (Fontana edition, 1982)
Jenkins, R., *Asquith* (Collins, 1964)
Lloyd, T. O., *Empire to Welfare State* (Oxford, 1970)
Read, D., *Edwardian England* (Harrap, 1972)
Rowland, P., *Lloyd George* (Barrie & Jenkins, 1975)
Telford, J., *British Foreign Policy 1870-1914* (Blackie, 1978)
Turner, L. C. F., *Origins of the First World War* (Arnold, 1970)

CHAPTER 21

Brittain, V., *Testament of Youth* (Virago-Fontana edition, 1979)
Graves, R., *Goodbye to All That* (Penguin edition, 1969)
James, R. R., *Gallipoli* (Batsford, 1965)
Liddell-Hart, B., *History of the First World War* (Cassell, 1970)
Macdonald, L., *They Called it Passchendaele* (Michael Joseph, 1978)
Marwick, A., *The Deluge: British Society and the First World War* (Bodley Head, 1965)
Morgan, K. O., *Lloyd George* (Weidenfeld & Nicolson, 1974)
Taylor, A. J. P., *An Illustrated History of the First World War* (Penguin, Winter, D., *Death's Men* (Allen Lane, 1978)

CHAPTER 22

Adelman, P., *The Decline of the Liberal Party, 1910–1931* (Longman, 1981)
Cook, C., *A Short History of the Liberal Party, 1900–76* (Macmillan, 1976)
Kinnear, M., *The Fall of Lloyd George* (Macmillan, 1973)
Marquand, D., *Ramsay MacDonald* (Cape, 1977)
Middlemass, K. and Barnes, J., *Baldwin* (Weidenfeld, 1969)
Mowat, C. L., *Britain between the Wars, 1918–40* (Methuen, 1955)
Seaman, L. C. B., *Post-Victorian Britain* (Methuen, 1975)
Taylor, A. J. P., *English History, 1914–1945* (Penguin, 1970)
Wilson, T., *The Downfall of the Liberal Party, 1914–1935* (Collins 1966; Fontana 1968)

CHAPTER 23

Hyde, H. M., *Baldwin – The Unexpected Prime Minister* (Hart-Davis, McGibbon, 1973)
Macleod, I., *Neville Chamberlain* (Muller, 1961)
Morris, M., *The General Strike* (Penguin, 1976)

The books by Middlemass and Barnes, Mowat, Seaman and Taylor mentioned under Chapter 22.

CHAPTER 24

Adelman, P., *The Rise of the Labour Party, 1880–1945* (Longman, 1972)
Bassett, R., *Nineteen-Thirty One: Political Crisis* (Macmillan, 1958)
Constantine, S., *Unemployment in Britain between the Wars* (Longman, 1980)
Cross, C., *Philip Snowden* (Barrie and Rockliff, 1967)
Donaldson, F., *Edward VIII* (Weidenfeld and Nicolson, 1978)
Skidelsky, R., *Politicians and the Slump: the Labour Government of 1929–31* (Penguin, 1970)

The books by Marquand, Middlemass and Barnes, Mowat, Seaman and Taylor mentioned under Chapter 22.

CHAPTER 25

De Paor, L., *Divided Ulster* (Penguin, 1971)
Lyons, F. S. L., *Ireland Since the Famine* (Fontana, 1974)
Pandey, B. N., *The Break-up of British India* (Macmillan, 1969)
Porter, B., *The Lion's Share* (Longman, 1975)
Watson, J. B., *Empire to Commonwealth, 1919–1970* (Dent, 1971)

CHAPTER 26

Bullock, A., *Hitler: A Study in Tyranny* (Penguin, 1969)
Fest, J., *Hitler* (Penguin edition, 1982)

Gilbert, M. and Gott, R., *The Appeasers* (Weidenfeld & Nicolson, 1963; paperback edition, 1967)

Middlemass, K., *Diplomacy of Illusion: the British Government and Germany, 1937-39* (Weidenfeld & Nicolson, 1972)

Rock, W. R., *British Appeasement in the 1930s* (Arnold, 1977)

Taylor, A. J. P., *The Origins of the Second World War* (Penguin edition, 1964)

Thorne, C., *The Approach of War, 1938-39* (Macmillan, 1967)

CHAPTER 27

Calder, A., *The People's War: Britain, 1939-45* (Jonathan Cape, 1969)

Calvocoressi, P. and Wint, G., *Total War* (Allen Lane, 1972; Penguin edition, 1974)

Liddell-Hart, B., *History of the Second World War* (Cassell, 1970)

Pelling, H., *Britain and the Second World War* (Collins/Fontana, 1970)

Pelling, H., *Winston Churchill* (Macmillan, 1974)

Taylor, A. J. P., *The Second World War* (Hamish Hamilton, 1975)

CHAPTER 28

Calvocoressi, P., *The British Experience, 1945-74* (Penguin, 1979)

Foot, M., *Aneurin Bevan* (Paladin paperback edition, 1975)

Fraser, D., *The Evolution of the British Welfare State* (Macmillan 1973)

Harris, K., *Attlee* (Weidenfeld and Nicolson, 1982)

Morgan, K. O., *Labour in Power 1945-51* (Oxford, 1984)

Sked, A. and Cook, C., *Post-War Britain: a Political History* (Penguin, 1979)

CHAPTER 29

Fisher, N., *Harold Macmillan* (Weidenfeld and Nicolson, 1982)

Lamb, R., *The Failure of the Eden Government* (Sidgwick and Jackson, 1987)

McKie, D. and Cook, C., *The Decade of Disillusion: British Politics in the 1960s* (Macmillan, 1972)

Proudfoot, M., *British Politics and Government, 1951-1970* (Faber, 1974)

The books by Calvocoressi and Sked and Cook mentioned under ch. 28.

CHAPTER 30

Cross, C., *The Fall of the British Empire, 1918-1968* (Hodder & Stoughton, 1968)

Northedge, F. S., *The Descent from Power: British Foreign Policy 1945-73* (Allen and Unwin, 1974)

Nutting, A., *No End of a Lesson (Suez)* (Constable, 1967)

Thomas, H., *The Suez Affair* (Weidenfeld & Nicolson, 1976)

The books by Lamb (ch. 29) and Morgan (ch. 28).

CHAPTER 31

James, R. R., *Ambitions and Realities: British Politics 1964-70* (Weidenfeld & Nicolson, 1973)

Lapping, B., *The Labour Government* (Penguin, 1971)

Sampson, A., *The Changing Anatomy of Britain* (Hodder & Stoughton, 1982)

Wapshott, N. and Brock, G., *Thatcher* (MacDonald, 1983)

Wilson, H., *The Labour Government, 1964-70: A Personal Record* (Penguin, 1974)

The books by Calvocoressi and Sked and Cook mentioned under Chapter 28.

INDEX